THE CORRESPONDENCE OF GEORGE BERKELEY

George Berkeley (1685–1753), Bishop of Cloyne, was an Irish philosopher and divine who pursued a number of grand causes, contributing to the fields of economics, mathematics, political theory, and theology. He pioneered the theory of 'immaterialism', and his work ranges over many philosophical issues that remain of interest today. This volume offers a complete and accurate edition of Berkeley's extant correspondence, including letters both written by him and to him, supplemented by extensive explanatory and critical notes. Alexander Pope famously said, 'To Berkeley every virtue under heaven,' and a careful reading of the letters reveals a figure worthy of admiration, sheds new light on his personal and intellectual life, and provides insight into the broad historical and philosophical currents of his time. The volume is an invaluable resource for philosophers, modern historians and those interested in Anglo-Irish culture.

MARC A. HIGHT is Elliott Associate Professor of Philosophy at Hampden-Sydney College. He is the author of *Idea and Ontology* (2008) and the co-ordinating editor of *Berkeley Studies*.

THE CORRESPONDENCE
OF
GEORGE BERKELEY

Edited by
MARC A. HIGHT

CAMBRIDGE
UNIVERSITY PRESS

CAMBRIDGE
UNIVERSITY PRESS

University Printing House, Cambridge CB2 8BS, United Kingdom

Cambridge University Press is part of the University of Cambridge.

It furthers the University's mission by disseminating knowledge in the pursuit of
education, learning and research at the highest international levels of excellence.

www.cambridge.org
Information on this title: www.cambridge.org/9781316502389

© Marc A. Hight 2013

First published 2013
First paperback edition 2015

A catalogue record for this publication is available from the British Library

ISBN 978-1-107-00074-2 Hardback
ISBN 978-1-316-50238-9 Paperback

For all my colleagues, known and unknown, who study Berkeley

CONTENTS

ACKNOWLEDGEMENTS

I am grateful to the following individuals and institutions for their assistance and (when applicable) their permission to publish the texts of the letters.

The © British Library Board and its staff; Lucy McCann and the Bodleian Library of Commonwealth and African Studies at Rhodes House; Peter Meadows and the Cambridge University Library Department of Manuscripts; Andrew Peppitt; Chatsworth House, Bakewell; Janet McMullin and the library at Christ Church, Oxford; Susan Hamson and the staff of the rare manuscript department of the Butler Library, Columbia University; the staff at the library of the Historical Society of Pennsylvania; Susan Halpert and the Houghton Library, Harvard University; Christian Hogrefe at the Herzog August Bibliothek, Wolfenbuettel; Naomi Percival and the Lambeth Palace Library; the staff at the Marsh Library, Dublin; the staff at the National Library of Ireland, Dublin; Bert Lippencott and the Newport Historical Society; the staff at the Redwood Library and Athenaeum in Newport, Rhode Island; Dr. Raymond Refaussé and the library of the Representative Church Body, Dublin; the staff at the Rhode Island Historical Society Library; the staff at the Royal Irish Academy library, Dublin; the Southampton Civic Centre library; the staff at the library of Trinity College, Dublin; and Diane Kaplan in the Manuscripts and Archives section of the Beinecke Library at Yale University.

I am grateful to those many staff members at the institutions listed above, including many people unnamed who assisted me with my work. In addition, I owe a debt of gratitude to Bertil Belfrage and David Berman, who first put me on to this project and helped start me on my way. Tom Jones at the University of St. Andrews provided some texts early in the project and my thanks to David Raynor at the University of Ottawa, who kindly made me aware of some additional letters and also gently prodded me on my progress over the years. I am thankful to Sheila Hight, Jane Holland, and Paula Parkhurst for their kind assistance on the drafts and for their moral support during its composition. Brian Burns assisted me with cover ideas and its design. My thanks to Neil Smith, who in the summer of 2010 helped search for new letters with me at the British Library: at least one previously unpublished letter appears in this volume owing to his efforts. I also acknowledge my debts to the friends and scholars who assisted with the transcription and translation work: their names are to be found below.

Work on this project was supported by a grant from the National Endowment for the Humanities (2011), a Mednick Fellowship from the Virginia Foundation for Independent Colleges (2011), and by several Faculty Research Grants from Hampden-Sydney College (2009–11). I am grateful for their support, without which this volume would not have been completed.

GENERAL INTRODUCTION

The correspondence of Berkeley does justice to Alexander Pope's famous poetic pronouncement, "To Berkeley every virtue under heaven."[1] The character portrait that emerges from a careful reading of his letters reveals a figure worthy of admiration not only as a philosopher and a divine, but as an individual who passionately pursued a number of grand causes. He is a figure reflective of his time, and his letters provide insight into both his own thought as well as access to broader historical and philosophical currents.

It is, I think, the not so secret desire of those who compile the correspondences of philosophers and historical notables to uncover new letters that profoundly reshape how we understand them or their thought. More often than not, however, we must settle for simply providing a service to fellow scholars, researchers, and the merely curious. In this volume it is unlikely the reader will find letters that provide new philosophical insights into Berkeley's philosophical views. They *will* find, however, a much more complete collection of letters than ever previously published, including letters addressed to Berkeley. After a search of several years, this volume includes a number of previously unpublished letters written by and to him, some or all of which, I hope, will be of use to scholars.

There has been no successful prior attempt to provide a *complete* collection of Berkeley's extant correspondence. A. C. Fraser published many new letters in his *Life and Letters*, but he excluded most of the correspondence written *to* Berkeley. Benjamin Rand presented most of the correspondence between Berkeley and Percival in his now aging work *Berkeley and Percival* (published in 1914), but he missed a number of letters in the archives and was unaware of several others that have since come to light. A. A. Luce hoped to have a complete edition of Berkeley's letters (see *Life*, p. vi), but he too made the decision to not publish the vast majority of the letters addressed to Berkeley. Luce also missed letters in the archives and some new ones have since come to light, including many published here for the first time. That said, the present volume relies heavily on the excellent work done by all three of these pioneering early Berkeley scholars. The informed reader will recognize at a few points that my critical comments are drawn from these earlier works. Where something has been done accurately and properly before there is no need for

---

[1] Alexander Pope's epilogue to the *Satires*, Dialogue II, line 72.

revision. I have endeavored to check all the facts, however, and my corrections to the previous editions are present in the notes.

Despite my wish that this volume include all of the correspondence of Berkeley, it is necessarily defective on at least two accounts. First, the best it could hope to achieve is to be the complete collection of the *known* and *extant* correspondence of Berkeley. There are references to many other letters, including a presumably healthy exchange of letters with Jonathan Swift, some of which are said to have been burned and others simply lost.[2] As an additional example, we know that Berkeley corresponded with Edwin Elphin on the strength of a letter written by Elphin to Berkeley's son on 26 January 1753 (see British Library Add. ms 39311, fol. 70). The list of persons that corresponded with Berkeley where there are no surviving letters is long. Second, I have reason to believe that there are additional letters extant but held by private collectors. Finding these letters is difficult at best and even taking out advertisements in various venues produced small return. Luce and others occasionally make reference to letters "privately held" without any additional information, and in most cases those letters have been impossible to track down. It is my hope that any collectors who have letters penned by or to Berkeley and who read this introduction will seek to contact me and allow me to transcribe and preserve them.

When compiling and adding the notes to this volume, I have endeavored to use as a model a graduate student starting work on a thesis. Historians might not know details philosophers would take for granted, and philosophers might not know facts considered commonplace to early modern historians. I have thus erred on the side of caution; if some of the notes are deemed "too obvious," then I can only beg the reader's pardon and ask for indulgence. I have worked scrupulously to remove myself, and especially my philosophical predilections, from the letters as much as possible. There are no notes with philosophical comments and I have assiduously endeavored to make the texts free of any taint associated with particular readings of Berkeley, whether of a personal or a philosophical nature. The present volume is also not a diplomatic edition; after consulting with a number of colleagues in the fields of early modern history and early modern philosophy, the consensus was for an edition of the letters that is accessible and easy to use. As a result, I have standardized and modernized some of the language where it is both absolutely clear what is in the text and when doing so improves readability. My conjectures or notes about textual matters are marked by square brackets throughout the volume. To keep the text reasonably clean and uncluttered, insertions and deletions have been noted but generally moved to footnotes where possible.

---

[2] See A. A. Luce, "A New Berkeley Letter and the Endorsement," *Proceedings of the Royal Irish Academy* 51, section C (1945/46): 85. Apparently there were photographs of Berkeley–Swift letters as late as 1910, but according to Luce, by 1946 all trace of them had been lost.

TEXTUAL INTRODUCTION

DESCRIPTION OF MAIN MANUSCRIPT REPOSITORIES

Bodleian Library, Rhodes House, Oxford University. The archives of the Society for the Propagation of the Gospel in Foreign Parts (SPG), now the United Society for the Propagation of the Gospel in Foreign Parts, are held at Rhodes House in Oxford. Catalogues of SPG correspondence, letterbook copies of official correspondence, and some original autographed letters are available, although one letter unfortunately went missing when the materials were rebound. SPG catalogue, C/AM9, A24. ser. B vol. 15 (letter 191 missing), 191a, 249.

British Library, London. The Berkeley Manuscripts are bound volumes containing notes, reflections, and other materials by Berkeley and others in his family. British Library (BL) Add. MSS 39304, 39305, 39306, and 39311 include a number of letters and drafts of letters, many in Berkeley's hand. Also present at the British Library are the Egmont Papers. These records were formerly housed at the Public Records Office in London but have since been moved to the British Library. They include John Percival's records and letterbooks that contain copies (typically in a secretary's hand) of much of his correspondence with Berkeley, along with some correspondence between Percival's son (also named John) and Berkeley. The volumes in the Egmont Collection (BL Add. MSS 46964–47213) with letters include BL Add. MSS 46986, 46997, 46998, 47000, 47012B, 47013B, 47014A, 47025, 47026, 47027, 47028, 47029, 47030, 47031, 47032, and 47033. The letter to Sloane comes from the Sloane Manuscripts (BL Sloane MS 4040) and two other volumes contained letters as well: BL Add. MSS 32710 and 46688.

Beinecke Library, Yale University. MS Vault File Berkeley and the Johnson Family Papers (MS 305) both have loose autographed letters of Berkeley along with other miscellaneous Berkeleiana. Two additional letters are present in the Osborn Files "B" folders 1118 and 1184.

Butler Library, Columbia University. The Johnson Papers are held here. They contain a number of letters and copies of letters between Johnson and Berkeley. The collection includes three bound volumes and a box of loose materials. The library also has two autograph collections with one Berkeley letter each, the Edwin Seligman Special Collection and the David Eugene Smith Special Collection.

Cambridge University Library, Cambridge, UK. The letterbooks of the Society for Promoting Christian Knowledge (SPCK) are now housed at Cambridge University Library. Copies of letters to and from Berkeley (Henry Newman is the principal correspondent) are present in bound volumes: MS D4/23, MS D4/24, MS D4/28, MS D4/29, MS D4/41, and MS D4/42.

Chatsworth House, Derbyshire. The Devonshire Collection ref. 364.0 contains a single autographed letter (see Letter 366).

Christ Church Library, Oxford. This library holds most of the correspondence of Archbishop William Wake, including one autographed letter written by Berkeley (see Letter 132).

Harvard University Library, Cambridge, MA. In the Orrery Papers one bound volume has a copy of a letter (see Letter 359).

Historical Society of Pennsylvania, Philadelphia. Several autographed letter collections here contain Berkeley correspondence, specifically the Ferdinand Dreer Collection in the English and American Clergy series, and the Simon Gratz Collection in the British Authors series.

Lambeth Palace Library, London. The Fulham Papers at Lambeth hold a single letter from Berkeley to the then Bishop of London, Edmund Gibson (see Letter 210) and a second autographed letter in their manuscript collection (see Letter 333).

National Library of Ireland, Dublin. Only a few letters are held at the National Library. MS 2979 contains a single letter (see Letter 325) and MS 987 is a bound volume with a letter from Dorothea Annesley and a reply from then Bishop Berkeley (see Letters 391–92). Microfilm copies of letters held elsewhere are usefully present as well (Microfilm 2510 and 2761).

Redwood Library, Newport, RI. The Roderick Terry Jr. Autograph Collection contains a single autographed letter by Berkeley (see Letter 388).

Representative Church Body of the Church of Ireland Library, Dublin. D6/150/6: a single autographed letter by Berkeley (see Letter 250).

Rhode Island Historical Society Library, Providence, RI. MS 294 in the Gabriel Bernon papers is a "scrapbook" with two letters in French from Berkeley (see Letters 178 and 183).

Royal Irish Academy Library, Dublin. There are no letters penned by Berkeley here, but MS 3D8 contains two letters between *a* George Berkeley and Nelson in 1721. Swift Johnston effectively established that these letters are not by the relevant Berkeley and, having examined the originals, I concur. See Swift Johnston, "Supposed Autograph Letter of Bishop Berkeley in the Library of the Royal Irish Academy," *Proceedings of the Royal Irish Academy* 6.2 (January 1901): 272–78. The library does contain a complete collection of the Academy's *Proceedings* and other period pieces.

Southampton Civic Centre, Southampton. D/M1/2 contains a letterbook of Samuel Molyneux with copies of four letters from Berkeley. The letterbook also holds copies of other letters received by Molyneux.

Trinity College Library, Dublin. In addition to other Berkeleiana, including multiple drafts of his letter about the cave of Dunmore, several original letters are preserved in bound volumes: TCD MS 1186, 2167, and 4309.

University of Amsterdam Library, Amsterdam. J3b: two original letters, loose but well preserved, from Berkeley to LeClerc.

DESCRIPTION OF NON-MANUSCRIPT SOURCES

As many of the original letters are lost, often our best sources for the letters are copies preserved in other ways, frequently as copies in previously published works. The following is a list of those non-original manuscript sources (organized by title) from which letters have been drawn for this volume.

Authentic Narrative, by Thomas Prior (London: 1746).

Berkeley Studies (formerly *Berkeley Newsletter*). One letter that was auctioned in 1979 and is now in (unknown) private hands was transcribed and published in the *Berkeley Newsletter* immediately before its sale by David Berman (see Letter 173).

Correspondence of Sir Thomas Hanmer, Bart., by Sir Henry Bunbury (London: Edward Moxon, 1838). One letter to Hanmer from Berkeley appears in the text, original unknown (see Letter 314).

L'Adamo, ovvero il Mondo Creato, by Tommaso Campailla (Rome: Rossi, 1728). In the preface, Campailla reproduces two letters sent to him by Berkeley (see Letters 91 and 120).

Life and Correspondence of Samuel Johnson, by E. Edwards Beardsley (New York: Hurd & Houghton, 1874). Beardsley reproduces a number of letters to and from Johnson for which we have originals, and generally does so accurately. At least one of the originals (Letter 373), however, has been lost and this volume is our only source.

Life and Letters of George Berkeley, D.D., by A. C. Fraser (Oxford: Clarendon, 1871). Some of the letters Fraser published in this volume are no longer extant, making his book the best source that remains to us (especially several exchanges with Johnson). See Letters 246, 253, 259, 271, and 272, where Fraser's transcriptions are the only records that remain. The work is also valuable for checking the accuracy of letters lost but published elsewhere.

The Life and Times of the Rev. John Wesley, by L. Tyerman (London: Hodder & Stoughton, 1880), 5th edn. Tyerman reproduces extracts of letters from Berkeley to Lloyd concerning the preaching of John Wesley in Berkeley's bishopric (see Letters 368–69).

Literary Relics: Containing Original Letters..., by George Monck Berkeley (London: T. Kay, 1789; reprinted in a corrected 2nd edn., 1792). Many of the letters to Thomas Prior are originally preserved only in this volume. In the preface the younger Berkeley (the grandson) says he received the Berkeley letters from Mr. Archdale, but there is no hint as to where the originals might be located at the present, if they survive.

Memoirs of George Berkeley: Late Bishop of Cloyne in Ireland, by Joseph Stock (London: J. Murrary, 1784), and Stock's preface to the *Works of George Berkeley* (London, 1784). Both works contain extracts of letters penned by Berkeley, most of which fortunately overlap with other published collections (such as George Monck Berkeley's *Literary Relics* and Fraser's *Life and Letters of George Berkeley, D.D.*).

Poems by the late George Monck Berkeley (London: J. Nichols, 1797). The preface, written by Eliza Berkeley, reproduces one letter to Benson (see Letter 375).

Siris: Grundliche Historische Nachricht vom Theer-Wasser, by D. W. Linden (Amsterdam and Leipzig: Peter Mortier, 1745). In the preface to the work Linden reproduces his letter to Berkeley (see Letter 317).

Siris. Recherches sur les Vertus de l'eau de Goudron, ou l'on a Joint des Réfléxions Philosophiques sur Divers Autres Sujets (Amsterdam: Pierre Mortier, 1745). A French translation of Berkeley's *Siris*, it contains the earliest appearance I could find of Berkeley's response to D. W. Linden's letter in an appendix (see Letter 318).

Lastly, I have relied on the following journals in which letters have appeared:

Daily Gazetteer, *Dublin Journal*, *Gentleman's Magazine*, *Guardian*, *Newcastle Journal*, and *Philosophical Transactions*.

PRINCIPLES OF INCLUSION

This is an edition of letters to and from George Berkeley. I have not attempted to include letters that merely mention Berkeley. Aside from that easy exclusion, it can be difficult to ascertain what counts as a letter and what does not. Not everything with a signature is a letter, and many items without one would be of interest to scholars. I have followed two general guidelines in assembling this volume. First, if previous scholarship has treated a piece of work as a letter, I have preserved that tradition independently of any reservations I might have. Second, I have otherwise tried to include only those letters that are genuinely intended to be correspondence, as opposed to a political or polemical statement. There are a number of "letters" that were published and addressed to Berkeley but in no way constitute correspondence. For instance, an anonymous letter (from a "Gentleman in the Army") was published in the *Harleian Miscellany*, vol. III (1745) addressed to Berkeley. The letter is a long and rambling Tory rant in broad support of Berkeley's claims made in his *Discourse Addressed to Magistrates*. As the author did not expect a reply, it is not genuinely correspondence and thus is not included here. On the other hand, a few similar "letters" are included only because they have been traditionally classified as letters. Thus, following my first principle above, *A Word to the Wise*, some of the *Guardian* essays, and some presentations to academic societies are included.

Of all of his works, *Siris* arguably provoked the greatest response, but his tracts on mathematics and political economy also generated interest in literate society. Many of these responses are styled as letters but take the form of polemical pamphlets and have thus been excluded on the above-mentioned grounds. I here provide a brief representative sample of some of the responses Berkeley provoked, all available in the British Library.

"A Cure for the Epidemical Maddess of Drinking Tar Water, Lately Imported from Ireland by a certain R—t R—d Doctor, in a Letter to his L—p, the B—p of C—ne," by T. R., M.D. (London: John and Paul Knapton, 1744). The letter is dated 1 June 1744. See BL catalogue 1171.h22/7.

"The Bishop of Cloyne Defended: or, Tar-water Proved Useful," by Philanthropos (London: J. Rivington, n.d.). See BL catalogue 1171.h22/8.

"A Letter to the Right Reverend Bishop of Cloyne, Occasioned by his Lordship's Treatise on the Virtues of Tar-water, Impartially Examining how far that Medicine Deserves the Character his Lordship has Given It" (no author, presumably a physician), 2nd edn. (London: Jacob Robinson, 1744). This is a stridently negative account of tar water. See BL catalogue 1171.h22/4.

"The Minute Mathematician: or, the Free-Thinker no Just Thinker. Set forth in a Second Letter to the Author of the Analyst; Containing a Defence of Sir Isaac Newton and the British Mathematicians, Against a Late Pamphlet, Entitled, *A Defence of Free-Thinking in Mathematics*," by Philalethes Cantabrigiensis (London: T. Cooper, 1735). See BL catalogue 8532.b.33.

"A Letter to Dion, occasioned by his book called *Alciphron or the Minute Philosopher*," by the author of the *Fable of the Bees* (London: J. Roberts, 1732). See BL catalogue 702.g.4 (4).

PRINCIPLES OF TRANSCRIPTION

Whenever possible I have used originals for the transcription of the manuscripts. For many of the letters, however, this is simply not possible. Often a period copy is all that we have. In a number of cases we cannot even do that well; what remains are published versions of letters for which no original or period copy remains. In those cases we must rely on the good work of earlier scholars.

Since the content of most of the letters is fairly mundane, the likelihood that someone would intentionally fabricate a letter is quite low. Thus even where we only have a copy or a transcription from a secondary source, I have included those letters unless I have evidence to think the letter is not by or intended for Berkeley.

Before I began this project I canvassed a number of scholars, mainly early modern philosophers and historians, and asked what would be most useful to them. There was a broad consensus for a volume that made the content of the letters easily accessible. I have thus partially modernized the language and spelling (but not correcting for British English). I am fortunate that there are no cases in Berkeley's letters where such changes present any danger of altering the content or meaning of the text. For clarity I have replaced "&c" with "etc." but have left the ampersand in cases where "and" is intended. The ligatures æ and œ are presented as "ae" and "oe" respectively. Unambiguous contractions (e.g., 'tis) have been expanded. For consistency, I have adopted the American style of capitalization for the titles of works in the notes, but left mention of titles as they were written in the actual letters. I have clarified contractions and modernized the spelling, but did not otherwise change the grammar or text. Letters in a language other than English I have left as I found them in the original, providing a translation that favors a more literal reading.

I have standardized the presentation of the letters. Each letter is numbered, labeled by author and recipient, and includes the place (if available) and date of its writing. To the right I have included the provenance. Typically that is a reference to the original letter or a contemporary copy, but where no such originals exist, I cite what my work has revealed to be the earliest and/or most reliable source. Where the provenance of the letter is more complicated, I have appended a note. The dates have been standardized for clarity and ease of use. Any additional information, like a date at the end of a letter, has been left as in the original.

Berkeley's handwriting varies in terms of its legibility. He has a number of peculiarities in the formation of his letters, especially his *r*s, which are often incompletely formed and resemble other letters (notably *v*s and *n*s). His *e*s at the end of words drop off and can be hard to separate from a variety of other letters. The handwriting of his correspondents predictably varies from immaculate to difficult, but there were seldom problems transcribing them. Where the letters are damaged or illegible, I use square brackets to record transcriptions where the text is damaged but the word is clear from context. Where I have a reasonable guess about an uncertain text, I use square brackets but append a question mark. Variations in the spellings of names I mark by placing the alternate in rounded parentheses. There are relatively few complicated cases with respect to the transcription of the letters, and so in such rare cases I have used footnotes to clarify matters.

TRANSLATIONS

The letters are written mostly in English, but there are a few in Latin, French, and German. I have included those letters in their original language but appended my translations immediately after them. The translations are mine in the sense that any defects therein should be attributed to me, but to the extent that they are quality translations, I owe a considerable debt to a number of colleagues. I aimed for slightly more literal readings and consulted multiple experts to supplement my own (often insufficient) skills. For the letters in Latin, Daniella Widdows, Douglas Jesseph, and James Arieti provided invaluable service. Jesseph also provided the transcription for the letter to Sloane (Letter 2). With the French letters I had the assistance of Sébastien Charles, Renée Severin, and Salif Traoré. Dirk Johnson and Uli Wilson assisted me with the German letters, and Patrizia Johnson rendered assistance on a few clauses in Italian. I am most grateful for their time and effort on behalf of myself and this project.

REFERENCES

I have not attempted to provide a comprehensive bibliography, either of work contemporary to Berkeley or of scholarship since. In the former case the information that one might provide would be too voluminous, and in the latter any attempt to provide a comprehensive list of recent scholarship lies beyond the scope of this endeavor. Since I have consciously sought to remove any philosophical bias from the presentation of the letters and their content, I have refrained from directing the reader to recent scholarship not directly related to the publication or transcription of the letters. The bibliography thus contains works cited in the text and editorial material only.

DATES

The Old Style Julian calendar was used in England until after Berkeley's death, although the New Style Gregorian calendar was increasingly popular. The Old Style calendar was ten days behind the Gregorian and typically placed the start of the new year on 25 March. England did not change to the new system until 1752, when the Calendar Act of 1750 officially set the start of the new year as 1 January. Berkeley uses both dating styles, but like many of his contemporaries was consciously shifting to the New Style. As a result, I use the New Style as the default dating system. But as the dating of some of the letters is uncertain and depends on which style has been used, I preserve the Old Style dates as well by the use of a slash (e.g. 1724/25). Thus 20 February 1724/25 refers in modern parlance (New Style) to 20 February 1725.

For consistency and ease of use, I employ a day-month-year style for the dates throughout, although I have left alternate styles unaltered inside the letters themselves.

THE BIOGRAPHICAL AND PLACE REGISTER

At the end of this work is appended a register of names and places. Included in the register are the names of all of Berkeley's correspondents as well as many names and places that appear frequently in the text and that merit some elaboration. In order to reduce the intrusiveness of many long and repetitive footnotes, I have marked such names and places with an asterisk. These typically occur in the footnotes where references in the text are clarified. The reader should consult the register for a brief biography or discussion of the relevance of the marked name or place to Berkeley. There are exceptions. References to Berkeley himself never have an asterisk. There are ample other sources for information on Berkeley and a brief biographical sketch with a chronology is provided in this volume. References to some prominent persons are excluded, since the reader can easily obtain biographical information elsewhere. Each of the biographical entries seeks to provide the reader with only a brief outline of the individual and any relationship the person has to Berkeley. The point is to provide nothing more than an initial context for reading and studying the letters while reducing the necessity for repetitive footnotes.

BIOGRAPHICAL SKETCH OF GEORGE BERKELEY

George Berkeley was born 12 March 1685 and spent most of his youth at Dysert Castle near Thomastown in the county of Kilkenny, Ireland. Of English descent, Berkeley was the eldest son of William Berkeley, a gentleman farmer. He had five brothers and one sister.

He entered Kilkenny College on 17 July 1696 and Trinity College, Dublin, on 21 March 1700. He was graduated with a BA in 1704, having studied mathematics, philosophy, and Classics. After graduation he remained at Trinity and was elected fellow on 9 June 1707. During this time he composed his *Notebooks*. Ordained a deacon on 19 February 1709 and a priest the following year, he remained at the college, teaching and holding a variety of appointments, from tutor and librarian to junior dean and junior lecturer in Greek. During this time he was already publishing; his *Arithmetica* and *Miscellanea Mathematica* appeared in 1707, *An Essay Towards a New Theory of Vision* in 1709/10, and *A Treatise Concerning the Principles of Human Knowledge* in 1710.

In 1713 he travelled to London for the first time, primarily to publish *Three Dialogues Between Hylas and Philonous*. There he met and favorably impressed a number of London literary wits, including Jonathan Swift, Joseph Addison, Richard Steele, and Alexander Pope. Swift introduced Berkeley at court and they both contributed pieces to *The Guardian*. In October of 1713 Berkeley was appointed chaplain to the Earl of Peterborough and traveled to Italy via France. He returned to England in the summer of 1714 and was in Dublin by February 1715.

Berkeley, having been appointed by Bishop Ashe to serve as tutor to his son, St. George Ashe, embarked on a second tour of France and Italy in 1716. He returned to London in the fall of 1720, renewing his friendships and making connections with the court. He was introduced to the Duke of Grafton, who promised him preferment when he was made lord lieutenant of Ireland in 1721. Back in Dublin at Trinity College, Berkeley secured a DD and worked for the college while pursuing preferment. In 1722 the Duke of Grafton appointed him to the deanery of Dromore, but the bishop of the diocese appointed his own candidate and a legal dispute ensued.

Sometime in 1722 Berkeley conceived of a scheme to found a college (to be named St. Paul's College) in Bermuda to educate young men and help spread

Christianity amongst the natives and slaves. His efforts were aided in 1723 when Hester Van Homrigh died, surprisingly having named Berkeley coexecutor of her estate. He did not know her well, apparently, but after several years of work to settle the estate, he profited nearly £3,000. He took the bequest as a providential sign in favor of his scheme, which he pursued with greater vigor.

Appointed dean of Derry on 4 May 1724, he resigned his fellowship at Trinity College and publicly announced his plan to found St. Paul's College in Bermuda. Despite opposition, Berkeley managed to gather support for the plan both in the House of Commons and from King George I. The charter was granted in 1725 and approved by Parliament in 1726. Some £20,000 was earmarked for the college, which was to be funded by the sale of crown land on St. Christopher Island (St. Kitts). In expectation of receiving the grant, Berkeley arranged to travel to the American colonies to establish a farm intended to supply the college in Bermuda. Not long before he left he married Anne Forster in August 1728, sailing for America the following month.

Landing first in Virginia, Berkeley settled in Rhode Island while awaiting the grant. He purchased a farm of one hundred acres and built a house ("Whitehall"). Berkeley stayed there for just under two years and spent his time preaching and writing. *Alciphron* was composed there and he discussed philosophy with Samuel Johnson. Finally receiving word that the grant for the college, though technically approved, would not be paid, Berkeley returned to England in October 1731.

Back in London, Berkeley again sought preferment. He was nominated to the deanery of Down, but political opposition in Ireland precluded his appointment. Two years later, in January 1734, he was made bishop of Cloyne, being consecrated in St. Paul's Church, Dublin, on 19 May 1734. From that point onward, Berkeley spent the majority of his life in Cloyne, performing his ecclesiastical duties and continuing to write. His literary endeavors then turned more towards the welfare of Ireland and its people. He worked to reform the economy and industries of Ireland, establishing a spinning school and various charities. His last large work, *Siris* (1744), made him famous for the espousal of tar water as a curative.

In 1752 he left Cloyne for Oxford to oversee the education of his son George, who was matriculating at Christ Church. Berkeley died in Oxford on 14 January 1753 and was buried in the chapel of Christ Church.

CHRONOLOGY AND PUBLICATION OF MAJOR WORKS

1685	12 March, born at Kilkenny, County Kilkenny, Ireland.
1700	21 March, matriculated at Trinity College, Dublin.
1705	Graduated BA at Trinity College, Dublin.
1707	9 June, admitted as fellow at Trinity College, Dublin. 15 July, graduated MA at Trinity College, Dublin. *Arithmetica* with *Miscellanea Mathematica* published.
1709	19 February, ordained a deacon. *An Essay Towards a New Theory of Vision* published.
1710	May, *A Treatise Concerning the Principles of Human Knowledge* published.
1712	*Passive Obedience* published.
1713	January, first trip to London. March–August, *The Guardian* publishes essays. October, appointed chaplain to Lord Peterborough and travels to France and Italy.
1714	August, returns to England, lives in London.
1715	*Advice to the Tories* published.
1716	Appointed tutor to St. George Ashe and travels to France and Italy for a second time; stays on the Continent for about four years.
1721	*Essay Towards Preventing the Ruin of Great Britain* published. Appointed senior fellow at Trinity College, Dublin. *De Motu* published. 14 November, graduated DD from Trinity College, Dublin.
1722	February, appointed dean of Dromore, but the position is contested. Decides to found St. Paul's College in Bermuda.
1723	June, named coexecutor of the estate of Hester Van Homrigh.
1724	4 May, made dean of Derry. *A Proposal for the Better Supplying of Churches in the Plantations* published.
1728	August, marries Anne Forster. September, sails for America.

1729	23 January, arrives in Newport, Rhode Island.
	June, Henry Berkeley born.
1731	Lucia Berkeley born; dies an infant.
	30 October, leaves to return to England.
1732	January, arrives and stays in London.
	Alciphron, or, The Minute Philosopher published.
	A Sermon Preached Before the Society for the Propagation of the Gospel published.
1733	28 September, George Berkeley born.
1734	March, *Analyst* published.
	19 May, consecrated bishop of Cloyne.
1735	11 April, John Berkeley is born; dies an infant in October of the same year.
	A Defence of Free-thinking in Mathematics published.
	The Querist, Part I published
	Reasons for not Replying to Walton published.
1736	10 December, William Berkeley is born.
1737	*Queries Relating to a National Bank* published.
1738	*Discourse Addressed to Magistrates* published.
	15 October, Julia Berkeley born.
1739	Sarah Berkeley born; dies an infant in March 1740.
1744	March, *Siris: A Chain of Philosophical Reflexions and Inquiries Concerning the Virtues of Tar Water* published.
	June, *A Letter to T[homas] P[rior] Esq.* published.
1745	October, *A Letter to the Roman Catholics* published.
1747	*A Letter to Thomas Prior* published.
	Two Letters to Prior and Hale published.
1750	*Maxims Concerning Patriotism* published.
1752	August, moves to Oxford.
	September, *A Miscellany* published.
1753	14 January, dies in Oxford.

ABBREVIATIONS

Add.	additional
Beardsley	E. Edwards Beardsley, *Life and Correspondence of Samuel Johnson* (New York: Hurd & Houghton, 1874)
BL	British Library, London
CCS	Civic Centre, Southampton (city archives)
Chandler	Thomas Bradbury Chandler, *The Life of Samuel Johnson, D.D. the First President of King's College, in New York* (New York: T. & J. Swords, 1824)
CU	Butler Library, Columbia University
EP	Egmont Collection (Papers), now in the British Library (BL Add. MSS 46964 *passim* through 47213)
fils	fils (French, referring to the son)
FP	Fulham Papers (in Lambeth Palace Archives)
FRS	Fellow of the Royal Society
Hone and Rossi	J. M. Hone and M. M. Rossi, *Bishop Berkeley* (London: Faber & Faber, 1931)
HSP	Historical Society of Pennsylvania
Lambeth	Lambeth Palace Archives, London
LL	Alexander Campbell Fraser, *Life and Letters of George Berkeley, D.D.* (Oxford, 1871)
LR	George Monck Berkeley, ed., *Literary Relics: Containing Original Letters....* (London, 1792)
LRIHS	Library of the Rhode Island Historical Society, Providence, RI
MP	Member of Parliament
MS	manuscript
NLI	National Library of Ireland, Dublin
PRIA	Proceedings of the Royal Irish Academy
r	recto (front of a folio)
Rand	Benjamin Rand, *Berkeley and Percival* (Cambridge University Press, 1914)
RCB	Representative Church Body Library, Church of Ireland, Dublin

Schneider	Herbert and Carol Schneider, eds., *Samuel Johnson, President of King's College: His Career and Writings*, 4 vols. (New York: Columbia University Press, 1929)
SPCK	Society for Promoting Christian Knowledge
SPG	Society for the Propagation of the Gospel in Foreign Parts
Stock	Preface to Joseph Stock, *Works of George Berkeley*, 1784; BL catalogue 1602/196 (2 volumes)
TCD	Trinity College Library, Dublin
v	verso (back of a folio)
Works	A. A. Luce and T. E. Jessop, eds. *The Works of George Berkeley*. London: Nelson, 1948–57
Yale	Beinecke Library, Yale University

LIST OF LETTERS

LETTERS

1 BERKELEY TO AN ILLUSTRIOUS ASSEMBLY

TCD MS *888/2, fols. 244–53. Additional drafts present in TCD* MS *4309, fol. 13 and BL Add.* MS *39305.*

10 January 1705/6

by Mr. Berkeley Jan: 10, 1705/6[1]

Mr. President and Gentlemen,

There is one of the rarities of this kingdom which though I judge considerable enough to take place among the rest, yet so it is I neither find it described nor so much as mentioned by those who are curious in enquiries of this nature. I mean the cave of Dunmore.[2] Wherefore having had the curiosity to see it, in defect of a better I present you with my own account of this wonderful place so far as I shall be able to copy it from what I remember either to have seen my self or heard from others.

This rarity[3] is distant four miles from Kilkenny & two from Dunmore his Grace the Duke of Ormond's[4] country house whence it has its name. Its mouth or entrance is situated in a rising ground and affords a very dismal prospect being both wide & deep & all its sides rocky & precipitious save one which is a slope, part whereof is fashioned into a path & in some places into steps by the frequent descents of those who out of curiosity visit this stupendous cave. This as well as the rest of the sides is overrun with elder and other shrubs which add to the horrour of the place & make it a suitable habitation for ravens, screech-owls & such like feral birds that dwell in the cavities of the rocks.

At the foot of this descent by an opening which resembles a wide arched gate we entered into a vast cavern the bottom whereof is always slabby by reason of the continual distillation of rock water. Here we bad farewell to day-light plunging into a more than Cimmerian darkness that fills the hollows of this subterranean dungeon into whose more retired apartments we were admitted

---

[1] Two drafts are present in the manuscript file. The first ends abruptly as noted below. A version of these manuscripts appears from the same period on pages 292–301 in a tome entitled *A Natural History of Ireland* (with I.1.3 on the spine) to be found in the manuscripts room of the library at Trinity College, Dublin. Fraser published yet a fourth version from the Commonplace Books in 1871. Luce uses the manuscripts at TCD, as do I. The opening remark indicates the letter was received and read in Berkeley's absence at some scientific society. Luce not unreasonably speculates the society was at Trinity College on the evidence that the draft manuscript is near to rules for such a society copied into his commonplace book. See Luce, *Life of George Berkeley* (London: Nelson & Sons, 1949; reprinted London: Thoemmes, 1992), p. 35.

[2] Berkeley likely visited the cave in the summer of 1699, judging from his remark in his 26 November 1709 letter (Letter 7) to Samuel Molyneux. The account in this letter is thus from memory some six and a half years later.

[3] The Commonplace Book of Berkeley has "cave" instead of "rarity."

[4] James Butler* (1665–1745), second Duke of Ormond.

by two passages out of this first cavern; for having by candlelight spy'd out our way towards the left hand & not without some difficulty clambered over a ruinous heap of huge unwieldy stones, we saw a farther entrance into the rock but at some distance from the ground; here nature seemed to have made certain round stones jut out of the wall on purpose to facilitate our ascent.

Having gone through this narrow passage we were surprised to find our selves in a very vast and spacious hall, the floor [of] which as well as the sides & roof is rock, though in some places it be cleft into very frightful chasms yet for the most part is pretty level & coherent; the roof is adorned with a multitude of small round pipes as thick as a goose-quill and (if I misremember not) a foot long or thereabouts;[5] they are made of an almost transparent stone and are easily broken, from each of them there distills a drop of clear water which congealing at the bottom forms a round, hard, & white stone, the noise of those falling drops being somewhat augmented by the echo of the cave seems to make an agreeable harmony amidst so profound a silence; the stones (which I take to be three or four inches high they all seeming much of a bigness) standing pretty thick in the pavement make it look very oddly. Here is likewise an obelisque of a duskish, gray colour & (I think) about three or four foot high, the drop which formed it has ceased so that it receives no farther increment.

This cave in the great variety of its congelations as well as in some other respects seems not a little to resemble one I find described under the name of Les grottes d'Arcy, in a French treatise *de l'origine des fontaines* dedicated to the famous Huygenius & printed at Paris in 1678,[6] but I must own that French cave has much the advantage of ours on account of the art & regularity which nature has observed in forming its congelations; or else that author has infinitely surpassed me in strength of fancy, for after having given a long detail of several things which he says are by them represented, he concludes with these words: *enfin l'on y voit les ressemblances de tout ce qu'on peut imaginer, soit d'hommes, d'animaux, de poissons, de fruits,*[7] etc. i.e. in short, here you may see the resemblance of whatever you can possibly imagine, men, beasts, fishes, fruits etc.; now though as much be confidently reported & believed of our cave yet to speak ingenuously it is more than I could find to be true, but on the contrary am mightily tempted to think it proceeds from strength of imagination, for like as we see the clouds so far comply with the fancy of a child as to resemble trees,

---

[5] The following clause was inserted with a caret marking its place.
[6] Pierre Perault, *De l'Origine des Fontaines* (Paris, 1678).
[7] "Finally one sees the resemblances in everything that one can imagine, whether men, animals, fish, or fruit."

horses, men or whatever else he's pleased to think on, so it is no difficult matter for men of a strong imagination to shape the irregular congelations after the model of their fancy; in short they need only for their diversion conceive printed on the petrified water the impression of their own brain to see men, beasts, fishes, fruits or any thing else they can possibly imagine.

By what has been already observed it appears the congelations are not all of the same colour, for the colour of the pipes is much like that of alum, the stones formed by their drops are of a white inclining to yellow, and the obelisque I mentioned differs from both. Moreover there is a quantity of this congealed water that by reason of its very white colour and irregular figure at some distance resembles a heap of snow and such at first sight I took it to be, much wondering how it could come there. When we approached it with a light it sparkled and cast a lively lustre, and we discovered in its superficies a number of small cavities as you may see in the above cited treatise, p. 279 & 287. But the noblest ornament of this spacious hall is a huge, channeled pillar which standing in the middle reaches from top to bottom. There is in one side of it a cavity which from its figure is called the alabastre chair. The congelations which form this column are of a yellowish colour & as to their shape something like the pipes of an organ; but organs I find are no rarity in places of this nature, they being to be met with not only in the caves of Arcy and Antiparos (an isle in the archipelago) but also in one near the firth of Forth in Scotland mentioned by Sir Robert Sibbald[8] in the *Philosophical Transactions*, number 222. This I look upon to be in all respects by far the greatest pillar I ever saw, & believe its pedestal (which is of a dark colour & with a glorious sparkling reflects the light of a candle) is as much as three men can well fathom.

I am concerned that I did not take the dimensions both of this lofty pillar & of the other things I endeavoured to describe. I am sorry I cannot furnish this illustrious assembly with an exact account of the length, breadth & height of these subterranean chambers, and have reason to think I have been by this time often censured for using such undetermined expressions as wide, narrow, deep, etc. where something more accurate may be looked for; but I have this to offer in my excuse, that when I visited this place I had no thoughts of satisfying any ones curiosity besides my own, having done it purely for my diversion[9] and by consequence might well be supposed to omit several things that may be taken notice of by a curious observer & expected in an exact & accurate description

---

[8] Sir Robert Sibbald (1641–1722), Scottish physician, geographer, and antiquary.
[9] Struck out is the following: "in the company of some other schoolboys merely out of a childish humour and a parcel of young boys."

which I am far from pretending this to be. Moreover the vast horrours of this melancholy place had so far filled the capacity of my mind that I was obliged to overlook several things that demanded a particular regard.

Here it was, I desired one of the company to fire of his gun (which he brought with him to kill rabbits that we saw in great numbers about the mouth of the cave): the sound we heard for a considerable time roll through the hollows of the earth & at last it could not so properly be said to cease as to go out of our hearing. I have been told that a noise made in the cave may be heard by one walking in St. Canice's church at Kilkenny, but know no one who ever made the experiment.

Having viewed the wonders of this place & not discovering any further passage, we returned through the narrow entrance we came in by. By this time some of our company thought they had seen enough and were very impatient to get out of this dreadful dungeon; the rest of us went on through a passage opposite to the former and much of the same wideness that led us into another cave which appeared every way formidably vast being of a prodigious length and astonishing height, & though the interval of time may have rendered my ideas of several particulars I there saw dim & imperfect, yet the dismal solitude, the fearful darkness & vast silence of that stupendous cavern have left lasting impressions in my memory. The bottom is in great part strewed with huge, massive fragments which seem by the violence of an earthquake to have been torn from the rock. The roof (as far as we could discern it by reason of the height) seemed to be of a blackish rock, and was destitute of the crystal pipes above-mentioned; advancing forward we met with a great white congelation set against the side of the cave which resembles a pulpit with a canopy over it, and hard by we saw the mold newly turned up at the entrance of a rabbit hole, and I have heard others affirm that very far in this dark and dismal place they have met with fresh rabbit's dung. Now to me it seems difficult to conceive what these little animals can live on, for it passes imagination to think they can find the way in and out of the cave except their eyes be fashioned to see in consummate darkness. Having gone a little farther we were surprised with the agreeable murmur of a rivulet falling through the clefts of the rock, it skims along the side of the cave & may be (as I guess) about six foot over; its water is wonderfully cool & pleasant & so very clear yet where I thought it had scarce been an inch deep I found my self up to my knees; this excellent water runs but a little way ere the rock gapes to receive it.

But what is most surprising is that the bottom of this spring is all over spread with dead men's bones & for how deep I cannot tell. It is likewise reported & (if

I mistake not) I have discoursed w[i]th some who said they themselves had seen great heaps of dead men's bones piled up in the remote recesses of this cavern. Now what brought these bones hither there is not the least glimmering of tradition that ever I could hear of to inform us. It is true I remember to have heard one[10] tell how an old Irish man who served for a guide into the cave solved him this problem by saying that in days of yore a certain carnivorous monster dwelling there was wont furiously to lay about him & whoever were unhappy enough to come in his way hurry them for food into that his dreadful den. But this (methinks) has not the least show of probability; for in the first place Ireland seems the freest country in the world from such man-slaughtering animals, & again, allowing there was some such pernicious beast, some anamolous [sic] production of this country, then these bones being supposed the relics of devoured men, one might reasonably expect to find them scattered up & down in all parts of the cave rather than piled up in heaps or gathered together in the water. And here if I may be allowed to publish my conjectures, I think it more probable that in former times this place served the Irish for the same purpose for which the huge subterraneous vaults of Rome & Naples called catacombs were intended by the ancients, i.e. that it was a repository for their dead; but still what should move them to deposit the bones we saw in the water I cannot devine [sic]. It is likewise very hard to imagine why they should be at the pains to drag the corpses through long & narrow passages that so they may interr it farther in the obscure depths of the cave; perhaps they thought their deceased friends might enjoy a more undisturbed security in the innermost chambers of this melancholy vault.

Proceeding forward we came to a place so low that our heads almost touched the top; a little beyond this we were forced to stoop, & soon after to creep on our knees; here the roof was thick set with the crystal pipes, but (I think) they had all given over dropping; they were very brittle and as we crept along we broke them off with our hats which rubbed against the roof; on our left hand we saw a terrible hiatus that by its black & dreadful looks seemed to penetrate a great way into the bowels of the earth, and here we met with a good quantity of petrified water in which though folks may fancy they see the resemblances of a great many things, yet I profess I know not what more fitly to compare it to than the[11] blearings of a candle; these congelations standing in our way had almost stopped up the passage; so that we were obliged to return.

---

[10] Scratched out here but legible is "my father."
[11] One draft of the manuscript ends abruptly here.

I will not deny that there are other passages which by a diligent search we might have discovered or a guide acquainted with the place have directed us to; for it is generally reported[12] that no one ever went to the end of this cave; but that being sometimes forced to creep through narrow passages one comes again into great and spacious vaults. I have heard talk of several persons who are said to have taken these subterraneous journeys; particularly one, St. Leger, who having provided a box of torches and victuals for himself and his man is said to have travelled two or three days in the abstruse paths of this horrible cave, and that when his victuals were well nigh spent, and half his torches burnt out, he left his sword standing in the ground and made haste to return; also I have been informed that others having gone a great way writ their names on a dead man's skull which they set up for a monument at their journey's end. But I will not vouch for the truth of these and other stories. I have heard many whereof[13] are apparently fabulous.

I have likewise been told that people are apprehensive of damps in this place, but this[14] is a groundless fear indeed where the air impregnated with sulphureous exhalations and pent up in some close hole may get vent by the digging of the collier; it is not unlikely such things may happen, but here I do not think there is any thing which cause the like effect.[15] I am sure so far as we went the candles after all burnt very clear the air being exceeding temperate & calm.

I have known some so unreasonable as to doubt whether this cave was not the workmanship of man or giants in old times, notwithstanding that it has all the rudeness & simplicity of nature, & might easily be accounted for without having recourse to art, considering its entrance is in a hill, and the country all around it hilly and uneven, for from the origine of hills and mountains as it is delivered by Descartes and since him by our later theorists, it is plain they are hollow and enclose vast caverns which is farther confirmed from experience and observation.

This is all I have to say concerning the cave of Dunmore. I have every where endeavoured to raise in your imagination the same ideas I had myself when I saw it as far as I could call to mind at the distance of almost seven years.

log: num. 216
test: num: 257[16]

---

[12] One draft has "generally reported" struck out, replacing it with "commonly believed." The other has "generally reported" followed by the words "and thought" struck out.

[13] The words "a great many" are struck out here.

[14] "I conceive" is struck here in one draft, left in the other.

[15] In the draft this sentence is defective and illegible, but is clear in the version published in *Natural History of Ireland*.

[16] A reference to *Philosophical Transactions* 216 and 257 (1698). See A. A. Luce "Berkeley's *Description of the Cave of Dunmore*," *Hermathena* 46 (1931): 152–53.

[In the copy in the volume of the *Philosophical Commentaries* the following last paragraph is substituted for the last paragraph above:]

Soon after I finished the foregoing description of the cave, I had it revised by Mr. William Jackson, a curious and philosophical young gentleman, who was very lately there. He said the account I gave was very agreeable to what he himself had seen, and was pleased to allow it a greater share of exactness than I durst have claimed to it. He had with him an ingenious friend, who designed to have taken the plan and dimensions of the several caverns, and whatever was remarkable in them; but the uneasiness they felt from a stifling heat hindered them from staying in the cave so long as was requisite for that purpose. This may seem somewhat surprising, especially if it be observed that we on the contrary found it extremely cool and refreshing. Now, in order to account for this alteration, it is to be observed those gentlemen felt the heat about the beginning of spring before the influence of the sun was powerful enough to open the pores of the earth, which as yet were close shut by the cold of the preceding winter; so that those hot streams which are continually sent up by the central heat—for that there is a central heat all agree, though men differ as to its cause, some deriving from an incrusted star, others from the nucleus of a comet sunburnt in its perihelium—remained pent up in the cavern, not finding room to perspire through the uppermost strata of rock and earth: whereas I was there about a month after the summer solstice, when the solar heat had for a long time and in its full strength dwelt upon the face of the earth, unlocking its pores and thereby yielding a free passage to the ascending streams. Mr. Jackson informed me of another observable [fact] that I had not taken notice of, viz. that some of the bones which lay in the water were covered over with a stony crust; and Mr. Bindon[17] (so was the other gentleman called) told me he met with one that to him seemed petrified throughout.

Before I have done I must crave leave to advertise my reader that where, out of compliance with custom, I use the terms congelation, petrifaction, etc., I would not be understood to think the stones formed of the droppings were made of mere water metamorphosed by any lapidific virtue whatever; being, as to their origin and consistence, entirely of the learned Dr. Woodward's[18] opinion, as set forth in his *Natural History of the Earth*, pp. 191 and 192, where he

---

[17] Perhaps a reference to Thomas Bindon (?–1740), later dean of Limerick in 1721.

[18] Dr. John Woodward (1665–1728), geologist and professor of physic at Gresham College, London. He authored *An Essay Toward a Natural History of the Earth. With an Account of the Universal Deluge and of the Effects that it had upon the Earth* (1695), which defends a biblical account of the fossil record.

takes that kind of stone, by naturalists termed stalactites, to be only a concretion of such stony particles as are borne along with the water in its passage through the rock from whence it distils.

2 BERKELEY TO SLOANE

BL Sloane MS *8 4040, fol. 176.*

11 June 1706

Vidi nuper librum D. Mead M. D & S.R.S cui titulus de imperio Solis & Lunae in corpora humana, & in eo quidem aestum aeris utpote celeberrimi Newtoni principiis innixum prono animo amplexus sum. Verum an author ingeniosus eventuum quorundam isthuc pertinentium causas tam recte assecutus sit non adeo constat. Siquidem tribuit ille altiorem aeris circa aequinoctia tumorem figurae spheroidali terrae, differentiam insuper inter aeris intumescentiam quae a luna meridionali & illam quae a luna (ut ita dicam) antimeridionali in Sphaera oblique excitatur eidem causae acceptam refert. Ego vero neutrius effectus explicationem ab oblata sphaeroide pe-tendam duco propterea quod 1.º quamvis sententia quae globum terrae pro ista figura commu-tatum vult hunc celebratissimorum virorum Huygenii imprimmis & Newtonii suffragiis, tum rationibus tam physicis quam mathematicis comprobetur & nonnullis item phaeno-menis pulchre respondeat, non tamen apud omnes usque adeo obtinet ut nulli veteris vel etiam oppositae sententiae fautores hodie reperiantur. Et sane memini D. Chardellou S.R.S Astronomiae peritissimus mensibus abhinc plus minus quatuordecim mihi indiccasse sibi ex observationibus Astronoicis axem terrae diamietro aequatoris compertum esse longiorem adeoque, terram Sphaeroidem sed qualem vult Burnetius ad polos assurgen-tem prope aequatorem vero humiliorem. [A]ttamen quod ad me attinet mallem viri doctissimi observations in dubium vocare quam argumentis quae terram esse oblatam, demonstrant obviam ire nihilominus quoniam sententia ista non omnibus aequearridet, illam tanquam principium phaenomeno ulli declarando adhiberi nollem nisi res aliter explicari nequeat. Sed 2º tantum abest quod supra-dictorum effectum explicatio sphaeroidalem terrae figuram necessario poscat ut vix ullam inde lucis particulam mutari videatur, id quod appositis quae in hanc rem scribit vir cl. ostendere conabor. [A]ltius (inquit p. 9) solito se attollit aer circa duo aequinoctia quoniam cum aequinoctialis linea illi globi terrestris circulo adversa respondeat qui diametru habet maximam, utrumque sidus dum in illâ versatur terrae est vicius.[19] [A]t vero utrum vicinior iste luminarium situs par sit attollendo aeri in cumulum solido sensibiliter altiorem merito ambigi potest. Etenim tantilla est differentia inter axem transversum & secundum ellipseos cujus circumvolutione gignitur Sphaerois terrestris ut illa ad Spaeram quam proxime accedat. verum ut majori ἀκρίβεια rem prosequamur, designet (Fig. 1) abcd sectionem per polos massae aero-terrestris in qua sit dc axis, ab diameter aequatoris jam inito calculo deprehendi vim lunae attracticem in b vel a non esse 1/5000 sui parte fortiorem quam foret in c vel d si illa polo alterutri directe incumberet, proinde differentiunculam istam effectui ulli sensibili edendo imparem omnino esse, considerandum insuper lunam ab aequatore nunquam tertia parte arcus cb distare dictamque adeo quantulamcunque; differentiam adhuc valde minuendam esse. Porro quod de luna diximus id de Sole cum multis vicibus longius absit adhuc magis constabit. Verum quidem est D. Mead alias insuper causas aestus prope aequinoctia altioris attulisse viz. agitationem fluidi Spheroidis in majori orbe se resolventis majorem, praeterea vim centrifugam effectum habentem eo loci longe maximum. [Q]uod ad primam, etsi illa primo intuitu nonnihil posse se ferre videatur, fatendum tamen est[,] me non omnino intelligere quomodo aliquid inde ad distinctam rei propositae explicationem faciens clare colligi possit quod ad secundam, constat sane vim centrifugam prope aequatorem esse longe maximam & propterea massam aero–terrestrem figuram oblatae. Sphaeroidis induere, quid vero aliud hinc sequatur non video. verum etiamsi concedamus aerem propter causas a c. [a cl.?] viro allatas prope aquinoctia ad aequatorem altius tumefieri, non tamen inde liquet qua ratione apud nos qui tam procul ab aequatore degimus eodem tempore altius solito attallatur: quinimo contrarium sequi videtur. Sequenti pagina sic scribit D. Mead ut finem tandem faciam in iisdem paralleis ubi lunae declinatio est illum coeli polum versus qui altissimus insurgit, validissima est attractio cum illa ad ejus loci meridiamum verticem accedit, minima vero ubi pervenit ad meridiamum loci opposti quod contra contingit in parallelis his adversis. [C]ausa est in spheroide terrae aetherisque figura. Ego vero causam non esse in terra & ambientis aetheris figura propterea puto quod posita terra vel perfecte Spaearica vel etiam oblonga idem certe eveniret, uti infra patebit. Restat ut harum rerum explicationem ipse aggrediar, nimirum eo praesertim nomine suspecta mihi fuit ratio a spheroidali terrae figura deducta quod nulla illius habita ratione est tota clarissime simul ac facillime exponi posse videbatur. Newtonus operis sui physico-mathematici lib. 3. prop. 24 haec habet pendet etiam effectus utriusque

---

[19] All underlining in the letter is present in the original.

luminari ex ipsius declinatione seu distantia ab aequatore nam si luminare in polo constitueretur, traheret illud singulas aquae partes constanter absque actionis intensione & remissione adeoque nullam motus reciprocationem cieret, igitur luminario recedendo ab aequatore polum versus effectus suos gradatim amittent & propterea minores ciebunt aesttus in syzygiis solstitialibus quam in aequinoctialibus. Atqui non alia causa videtur querenda ullius phaenomeni aestus aerei quam quae simili effectui in aestu marino excitando sufficiat. Sed ut id quod a Viro celeberrimo breviter adeoque forsan subobscure traditum est uberius exponam[.] Sit (Fig. 1) acbd planum meridiani in quo ab axis terrae, Sol autem & luna in po[lo] constitui supponantur manifestum est unamquamque massae aereae partem puta c durante circumvolutione diurna eandem semper distantiam a luminaribus tueri adeoque vi ubique aequale in eorum corpora trahi proinde aer non uno tempore attolitur, alio deprimitur sed per totum diem in eadem haeret altitudine. Verum iterum; repraesentet (Fig. 1) acbd aequatorem aut parallelum quemvis, luminaria interim in plano aequinoctiali existant, quo tempore manifestum est tum ipsum aequatorem tum singulos parallelos ellipticam induere figuram, manifestum insuper est aerem qui, a, apicem axis transversi obtinet adeoque altissimus insurgit, post sex horas c extremum axis secundi ubi humillimus deprimetur occupatum in[e] maximamque adeo motus reciprocationem cieri. [Q]uod si ponantur luminaria locum aliquem inter polum & aequatorem intermedium occupare, rem perpendenti liquido constabit aestum fore majorem minoremve prout illa aequatori vel polo fuerint viciniora. Reliquum est ut ostendam differentiam inter aestuum quemvis & subsequentem sive terra ponatur oblata, sive ad amussim spherica sive etiam oblonga perinde causeri. Sit (Fig. 2) ab axis terrae, gd aequator, k locus quivis, fk loci perallalus, hl axis sphaeroidis aereae ob actionem potissimum lunae uterinque termentis. ps parallelus prior ex adverso respondens, luna autem prope l constituatur demonstrandum est (ck) altitudinem aeris luna prope loci meridianum exsistente majorem esse (cf) aeris altitudine ubi luna meridianum loci opposite transsierit, contrarim autem in parallelo huic adverso evenire. Patet arcum fh majorem esse arcu kl ergo propter ellipsin recta fs minor est recta kp & cf minor ck & cs minor cp q.e.d.

Atque haec sunt vir clarissime, quae super hanc rem actis tuis philosophicis (si modo ea non indigna putes) mandare vellem.

Sunt & alia nonnulla quae nescio an omnino ingrata habebis viz. anni ultimo elapsi mense Novembri Juvenis cujusdam Academici in horto sub noctem mingentis urina ubi in terram decidit vividissimam spargebat lucem. [I]s confestim in aedes alios qui spectaculi compotos fierent accersitum it, dum redit autem omnis extincta est lux. [P]orro juvenis quo pacto phosphorus accendi soleat in mentem revocans nonnihil sabuli urina madidum manum inter & vestem strenue fricabat, illud autem non solum pristinum recuperavit splendorem, verum etiam cuicunque rei affricaretur eundem impertivit. [N]on ignoro cum muriam tum aquam marinam pro noctilucis nonnumquam haberi; an vero de urina humana (etsi ex ea praeparetur phosphorus vulgaris) tale aliquid jam ante observatum sit prorsus nescio, nontandum insu[p]er est dictam juvenem Academicaum tunc temporis male se habuisse, nimirum frigus corpore conceptum speciem quandam febricula concitarat.

Alius quidam e nostris cum nuper conchas marinas (Ang. cockles) vesceretur disrupta cujusdam quae inter caeteras occurrebat testa, intus quasi in proplasmate lapidem quem vocant conchiten inclusum reperit. [A]tque hinc fortassis illa quae apud D. Woodward (tell. hist. natur. par. 5 cons. 5) de hujusmodi lapillorum origine extant, lucem aliquam mutuari poterint.

Ut tu interim, Vir Celeberrime, haec qualiacunque aequo animo accipere digneris, atque (quemadmodum soles) in reipublicae Philosophicae bonum vivas & valeas enixe rogat

Tui observantissimus

G. B.

e Musaeo in Trin. Coll. Dub. Junii 11. 1706

Distinguished Sir,

I recently saw the book of Mr. Mead, M.S. and F.R.S., whose title is *On the Influence of the Sun and Moon on the Human Body*,[20] and I happily accept [what he writes] in it of the tide of the atmosphere as based on the principles of the celebrated Newton.[21] But whether the ingenious author has so rightly ascertained the causes of some events pertaining to it is not so certain. Since he attributes a greater elevation of the air about the equinoctial line to the spheroidal figure of the earth, he also credits the agreed difference between the swelling of the air which is obliquely raised in the sphere from the meridianal moon and that from the antimeridianal moon (if I may use the expression) to the same cause. But I consider that the explanation of neither effect should be sought in the oblate spheroid. This is because, first, although the opinion that holds the globe of the Earth to have been changed into this figure is supported both by the opinions of the most celebrated men, chiefly Huygens[22] and

---

[20] Richard Mead, *De Imperio Solis ac Lunae in Corpora Humana, et Moribus inde Oriundis* (London, 1704).
[21] Isaac Newton (1642–1727).
[22] Christiaan Huygens (1629–95).

Newton, as well as by reasonings [arguments] both physical and mathematical, and it also agrees excellently [beautifully] with some phenomena; nevertheless, it is not accepted by everyone, including none of the ancients, and today even those who favor (promoters of) the opposite opinion can be found. And indeed I recall that Mr. Chardellou,[23] F.R.S. and a man most skilled in astronomy, told me some fourteen months ago that he had ascertained from astronomical observations that the axis of the Earth is longer than the diameter of the equator, and so the Earth is a spheroid, but one such as Burnet held it to be, rising up at the poles but lower near the equator.[24] But for my part I would rather call the observations of a most learned man into doubt than oppose the arguments that demonstrate the Earth is oblate. Nevertheless, since this opinion does not equally please everyone, I would not favour applying it as a principle in accounting for any phenomenon to be explained, unless the matter cannot be otherwise accounted for. But, secondly, the explanation of the above-mentioned effects is so far from necessarily requiring a spheroidal figure of the Earth that it seems scarcely a particle of light is gained from it, which I will attempt to show by adding what this distinguished gentleman writes on this matter. 'The air (he says, p. 9) rises above its usual level about the two equinoxes, because when the opposite equinoctial line corresponds to that circle of the terrestrial globe which has the greatest diameter, both of the heavens [heavenly bodies] are nearer the earth when they turn in that line.'[25] Yet it can well be doubted whether that nearer position of the luminous bodies is sufficient for raising the mass of air perceptibly above the usual level. For, in fact, the difference between the transverse axis and the second [axis] of the ellipse by whose circumvolution a terrestrial spheroid is generated is so small that it very nearly approaches a sphere. But in order that we may follow the matter with greater precision [ἀκρίβεια], let *abcd* (Fig. 1) designate the section through the poles of the aero-terrestrial mass, in which *dc* is the axis and *ab* the diameter of the equator. Now by computed calculation

---

[23] Jean Chardellou (*c.* 1664–1771), elected F.R.S. on 30 November 1702. He was a correspondent of Flamsteed.

[24] Thomas Burnet's *Sacred Theory of the Earth* (London, 1684) marshals arguments from natural philosophy, ancient literature, and Scripture to show that the earth is an ovoid, with the polar axis greater than the diameter at the equator. He concludes: "considering that this notion of the Mundane Egg, or that the World was Oviform, hath been the sence and Language of all Antiquity, Latins, Greeks, Persians, Egyptians, and others ... Which being prov'd by Reason, the Laws of Nature, and the motions of the Chaos; then attested by Antiquity, both as to the matter and for of it; and confirm'd by Sacred Writers, we may take it now for a well-established truth, and proceed upon this supposition" (2.8, p. 270).

[25] "[A]ltius solito se attollit *Aer* circa duo Aequinoctialis Linea illi Globi Terrestris Circulo adversa respondeat qui Diametrum habet maximam, utrumque Sidus dum in illa versatur Terrae est Vicinius" (Mead, *Imperio Solis*, p. 9).

I have discovered that the attractive force of the moon at *b* or *a* is not even a 1/5000 part stronger than it would be at *c* or *d*, if that force were directly inclined toward either pole, and therefore that this tiny difference is utterly unequal to producing any sensible effect. It is further to be considered that the moon is never distant from the equator by a third part of the arc *cb*, and the said very small difference must even be diminished a great deal more. Furthermore, what we have said of the moon will hold even more for the Sun, as it is so many times more distant. It is indeed true that Mr. Mead has also adduced other causes of the tide being higher around the equinoxes, viz. 'The greater agitation of the fluid spheroid revolving itself in a greater orb, and further the centrifugal force having a much greater effect there.'[26] As to the first, although this at first sight seems that it could be of some consequence, I must nevertheless admit that I do not at all understand how something can be gathered from it that would clearly contribute to the distinct explication of the matter proposed. As to the second, it is surely agreed that the centrifugal force is greatest by far near the equator and therefore the aero-terrestrial mass takes on the shape of an oblate spheroid; but I do not see what else should follow from this. But even if we should admit that the air swells out at the equator because of the causes adduced by the distinguished man, yet it does not follow from this why among us, who live so far from the equator, it should at the same time be raised higher than usual; instead, the contrary seems to follow. On the following page Mr. Mead writes this: 'To conclude at last, in the same parallels where the declination of the moon is toward that pole of the heavens which rises highest, the attraction is the strongest, when it [the declination] approaches the meridian of the place, but it is least, when it reaches the meridian of the opposite place; the contrary of which happens in the opposite parallels. The cause is in the spheroid shape of the earth and aether.'[27] But I think that the cause is not in the shape of the earth and the ambient aether, because, having posited that the earth is either perfectly spherical or even oblong, the same thing would certainly happen, as will be manifest below. It remains that I should undertake the explication of these things myself, of course principally on account of the fact that reasoning drawn from the spheroidal shape of the earth appeared suspect to me, because it seemed that, making no consideration of it, the whole matter can be explained at the same time very clearly and easily. Newton, in his physico-mathematical work, book 3, proposition 24, has this: 'The effect of either luminary doth

---

[26] Mead, *Imperio Solis*, p. 9.
[27] Mead, *Imperio Solis*, p. 10.

likewise depend upon its declination or distance from the equator; for if the luminary were placed at the pole, it would constantly attract all the parts of the waters without any intensification or remission of its action, and could cause no reciprocation of motion. And, therefore, as the luminaries decline from the equator towards either pole they will, by degrees, lose their force, and on this account will excite lesser tides in the solstitial than in the equinoctial syzygies.'[28] And so it seems that no other cause is to be sought of any phenomenon of the tide of the air than that which suffices to excite the similar effect in the marine tide. But in order that I might explain more fully that which has been set out very briefly and perhaps somewhat obscurely by this most famous man, let (in Figure 1) *acbd* be the plane of the meridian, in which *ab* is the axis of the earth, and let the sun and moon be supposed placed at the poles. It is manifest that each and every part of the aerial mass, for instance *c*, will always maintain the same distance from the luminaries during the diurnal circumvolution, for it is drawn everywhere by an equal force in their bodies. Thus the air is not elevated at one time and depressed at another, but maintains the same altitude through the whole day. But again [secondly], let *acbd* (Figure 1) represent the equator or any parallel, and (for the moment) let the luminaries be in the equinoctial plane, at that time it is manifest that both the equator itself as well as individual parallels will assume an elliptical shape, and it is further manifest that the air which is at *a*, the apex of the transverse axis, and thus rises highest, will after six hours occupy *c*, the extreme of the second axis, where it will be depressed to the lowest, and so is moved into the greatest engaged reciprocation of movement. Because if the luminaries are taken to occupy some intermediate place between the pole and equator, anyone considering the matter clearly will certainly agree that the tide will be greater or less according as they [the luminaries] are closer to the equator or the pole. It remains that I should show that the difference between any tide and the subsequent [following] one will arise in the same manner, whether the earth is taken to be oblate, or exactly spherical, or even oblong. Let (Fig. 2) *ab* be the axis of the earth, *gd* be the equator, *k* be any place, *fk* be the parallel of the place, *hl* be the axis of the spheroid of the air, swelling on both sides principally because of the action of the moon, *ps* be the parallel corresponding to the first on the opposite side, and let the moon be placed near *l*. It is to be demonstrated that (*ck*), the altitude of the air when the moon is near the meridian of the [one] place is greater than (*cf*), the altitude of the air

---

[28] Isaac Newton, *Philosophiae Naturalis Principia Mathematica* (London, 1687), pp. 430–31, following the Motte-Cajori translation, 2:437.

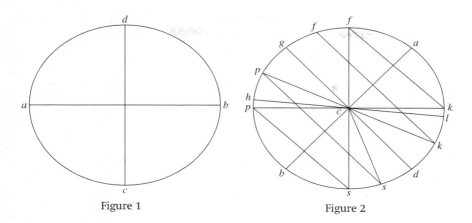

Figure 1   Figure 2

when the moon has passed through the meridian of the opposite place, but that the contrary happens in the parallel opposite to this one. It is obvious that the arc *fh* is greater than the arc *kl*, therefore because of the ellipse, the right line *fs* is less than the right line *kp*, and *cf* is less than *ck* and *cs* is less than *cp*. Q.E.D.

And these, distinguished sir, are the things concerning this matter that I would wish to be sent to your *Philosophical Transactions* (provided that you do not think them unworthy).

There are also some other things you will perhaps not find altogether unprofitable [displeasing]. For instance, at the end of the month of November of the past year, the urine of a young man of a certain college who was urinating at night in the garden cast off the most vivid light when it hit the ground. He immediately went inside to fetch others who might be made witnesses of this spectacle, but when he returned all the light was extinguished. Then the young man, recalling the manner in which phosphorus is usually ignited, vigorously rubbed some sand between his hand (which had been moistened with urine) and his clothing, and now this stuff not only regained its previous splendor, but also bestowed the same on anything it was rubbed against. I am aware that both brine and sea water are sometimes considered as noctiluminous, but in truth I do not know whether such a thing has been observed of human urine before now (although phosphorous is commonly prepared from it). Further, it should be noted that the young student afterwards was ill for a time, no doubt a chill taken in by the body had incited a kind of mild fever.

Another of us, while he was recently eating sea mussels ('cockles' in English) found held within the opened shell of one which lay among the others a stone which they call a *conchiten*, as if it were pressed from a mold. And perhaps those

17

things that appear in Mr. Woodward (*Natural History of the Earth*, part. 5, cons. 5) on the origin of small stones of this sort will be able to shed some light.[29]

That in the meanwhile you, most famous man, may think these and other such things worthy to be received with an open mind and (in the manner that is your custom) that you may live and thrive in the good of the philosophical republic, earnestly asks

Your most observant,

G. B.

From the museum at Trinity College, Dublin. 11 June, 1706

3 BERKELEY TO MOLYNEUX

CCS D/M1/2. Copy at NLI, microfilm 2680, p. 1586.

Burton, 1 August 1709

Dr. Molyneux,

Had any thing happened in this place that I could have thought worth imparting to you, you should have heard from me before now. But nothing of that moment occurred. My business here has been little else than eating drinking sleeping discoursing & variously sporting to pass away the time. My curiosity has not led me to make any diligent search after the antiquities or other observables that may possibly be here about, though I believe there are not many, so that you must not expect any thing from me, that may tend[30] to the illustration of natural history.[31] The other day Mr. Clerk[32] & I viewed the monastery of Buttefont ,[33]

---

[29] "That therefore the *Shells* served as *Plasms* or *Moulds* to this *Sand*; which, when *consolidated*, and afterwards in tract of time by this means *freed* from its *investient Shell*, is of the same *Shape* and *Size* as the *Cavity* of the *Shell*, of what kind soever that *Shell* happened to be. That is the true *Origin* of those *Stones* (consisting of *Sand*) which are called by Authors, *Conchlitae, Conchitae, Muitae, Ostracitae, Cteniae,* etc. and which are of *constant regular*, and *specific Figures*; as are the *Cochleae, Conchae,* and other *Shells* in which they were *moulded*, and from which, by reason of their so near *resemblance* of the insides of them, they borrow their several *Denominations*." John Woodward, *An Essay towards a Natural History of the Earth*, 2nd. edn. (London, 1702), Part V, section 5, p. 233.

[30] Luce mistakenly has "lead" for "tend."

[31] From the evidence of his letterbooks, Samuel Molyneux had been corresponding with an "E. S.," who was writing an account of the natural wonders he found in his travels in Ireland. Molyneux wrote on 21 May 1709 asking to participate in securing accounts of areas around Ireland, an offer E. S. more or less accepted. Molyneux apparently then wrote his friends asking for bits relevant to this project.

[32] An unknown acquaintance of Berkeley. There were many Clerkes in Ireland at the time, especially in and around Dublin.

[33] A Franciscan monastery founded in 1251 (on an even earlier foundation) by David Oge Barry (?–1278), Lord Buttefont (Buttevant).

which is reported to have been formerly a place of great note, though now I could perceive nothing remarkable in it except some remains of painting in fresco which gives me but a low idea of the skill of the ancient Irish in that art. There are also a great number of skulls & dead mens' bones pil[e]d up in a very regular manner, which for the oddness of it gave me some surprise. The building is in all respects as large and magnificent as could be expected from the Irish before they were civilized. There is likewise upon Sir John's Estate [34] a castle named Liscarol, which in the War of '41 was greatly distinguished: it has a large oblong court consisting of a high & thick wall with four regular turrets.[35] But what is most remarkable is, that at some fields distance from the castle a country man showed us the entrance into a cave which seems to be the work of nature. He told us it reached all the way to the castle, and was used as a sally port by the beseigd in '41. I had not the courage to go into it for fear of a damp. If you have any news, any objections, or thoughts relating to the *Essay of Vision* or can give me an account of what others you converse with think of it, or any thing else you will please to inform me of, I shall gladly hear from you. Remember me to all friends. I am,

  your affectionate friend & servant,

  Geor: Berkeley

Enclose your letter in a cover to – Sir John at Burton near Charleville.

4 BERKELEY TO PERCIVAL

EP, BL Add. MS *47025, fols. 133v–34.*

Trinity College, Dublin, 22 September 1709

Dear Sir,

I am sorry to hear from Dan. Dering[36] that you have lost your statues, medals, etc. that you had coming from Italy; though on second thoughts I almost doubt whether it may be reckoned a loss. Nobody purchases a cabinet of rarities to please himself with the continual light of them, nothing in it being of any farther use to the owner than as it entertains his friends; but I question if your neighbours

---

[34] John Percival* (1683–1748).

[35] Liscarol Castle, about five miles distant from the Buttefont monastery, was beseiged in the 1641 uprising of the Irish and a battle was subsequently fought there on 3 September 1642.

[36] Daniel Dering* (?–1730).

in the county of Cork would relish that sort of entertainment. To feed their eyes with the sight of rusty medals and antique statues would (if I mistake not) seem to them something odd and insipid. The finest collection is not worth a groat where there is no one to admire and set a value on it, and our country seems to me the place in the world which is least furnished with virtuosi.

I have Sir, all the engagements in the world to think myself concerned in anything that in my apprehension may promote your interest, this it is that makes me pretend to advise you, how ill soever that office may become me. There is a person whose acquaintance and conversation I do earnestly recommend unto you as a thing of the greatest advantage: you will be surprised when I tell you it is yourself. Believe me, I am convinced there is nothing else wanting to complete your happiness, so much as a little more satisfaction in your own company, which might provoke you to spend regularly and constantly two or three hours of the morning in study and retirement. I do not take upon me to prescribe what you shall employ yourself about. I only propose the passing two or three hours of the twenty-four in private; and as for the subject of your reading or meditation I leave that to your own judgment. I have observed in you that you seem to prefer the improving ones self by conversation before private study. This proceeds either from an over modest opinion of your own parts (which fault I know is very incident to you) or else from a belief that the latter is not so profitable and pleasant as is pretended. For my part I am of a different opinion; and if you will show that regard for my judgment as to follow it in these two points, you will both do me a great honour and lay a new obligation on me, the most acceptable of all other.

I would not be thought to question your inclination for reading, who ever has the happiness of any degree of your acquaintance cannot but know you are conversant in books far above the ordinary rate of gentlemen of your rank, but this is what I am earnest with you for, viz. a fixed and settled method of study. And I press it the more earnestly at this time, because if you do not enter upon it before you marry it will be less practicable afterwards. Then to begin a habit of rising early and retirement may be ill interpreted by your lady, whereas if she knows you were used to it before, she can take no umbrage at it. Some there be who think the least reflection unbecoming men of business and action in the world. This notion may if I mistake not be easily impugned by a great number both of reasons and examples which I shall omit at this time. If you have any tincture of that notion, viz. the inconsistency of study with business, I shall take it as a favour if you will be pleased to communicate to me in a line or two your sentiments on that point, with your reasons for them. In the meanwhile I must desire you to pardon the long trouble I have given you in this letter, and am

    Sir,

    Your most humble & affectionate servant,

    Geo. Berkeley

5 PERCIVAL TO BERKELEY

EP, BL Add. MS 47025, fols. 135v–36.

London, 6 October 1709

Dear Sir,

I would have acknowledged your kind letter sooner, but for a cold and tooth ache, which keeps me still to my chamber. It was kind in several respects, but chiefly for reminding me how precious time is, and for furnishing me with an excuse for early rising against the time I marry: it is no improper caution to a young man bedded for a constancy to a pretty woman, as she shall be who I wed, or my eyes shall cheat me. Marriage is a voluntary confinement which I desire to make as agreeable as possible, the rather because it is a confinement for life. I therefore would have my roof well pitched and very clean, not one that had been lain in before, but fresh, new, and fashionable, otherwise the world would say I chose my lodging for cheapness or wanted judgment. So much for the walls. As for the furniture I cannot so well tell what I would have as what I would not, it being easier to say what displeases, than what one likes, besides we are more constant in our aversions than our pleasures. I would have no Latin sentences embroidered on my hanging like the narrow closets of great ladies who affect to be esteemed learned, neither should I like it to be of a changeable colour, for fear sometimes I should not know my room, nor should I desire it finely flowered, or wrought with smart repartees, but plain, even, and of one colour. I would have no pictures that should ruffle my mind with the ideas of storms and tempests, thunder or showers of rain, nor any representation of battles, civil wars, or domestic strifes, no Socrates and his wife, no Hooker[37] turning the spit while his wife corrects him with her ladle, nor anything suggesting resistance to the higher powers, but Portia swallowing live coals on Brutus's flight, Petus and Arie,[38] Sibylla wife of

[37] Most likely a reference to Richard Hooker (1554–1600), who was often parodied as being unusually meek.

[38] Rand corrects to "Cetus and Arie," but the context makes it clear that the reference is to Ceyx and Alcyone, a mythological story about a couple whose love was so strong that neither the gods nor death could keep them apart.

Robert Duke of Normandy, and such instances of conjugal affection. Nudities I banish for the story you told me of Lesley. In short, I must not have a thought a lewdness, foppery, affectation, or anything defective in my furniture, which so abounds in almost all the rooms I see. And so I leave this subject, only I must return to the walls and tell you they shall not be plastered and painted as is everywhere the fashion in France, and begins to be so in England, nor must (but here all allegory fails me) my wife be red haired. When I have found a room to my mind, you may expect to hear I keep much at home.

As to the employment of my time, I am resolved not to be altogether idle, but as well as I can inform myself of our Constitution, no study being so proper for a gentlemen to know as the measure of his obedience, and the length of their power who rule.

Which subject of government leads me to acquaint you, that very lately there is published a small octavo by one Higden,[39] a non-juror, but now convinced of his error. It has the reputation of being well put together, and to have wrought good effects on many of that party. The argument is, that oaths ought to be taken to kings *de facto* as readily as if they reigned *de jure*, which he proves not only from reason, but shows it to be the spirit of our Constitution from common and statute law, the rolls of parliament, and the opinions of many eminent judges. Lastly he proves this doctrine to be consistent with the opinion of our Church, with Scripture and the practice of the Jews, and ancient Christians. If this book has fallen in your way, you will oblige me with your sentiments of it. The title is 'A View of the English Constitution' etc. by W. Higdon.

I am

Your affect. & humble servt,

J. Percival

6 BERKELEY TO PERCIVAL

EP, BL Add. ms 47025, fols. 138–39.

Trinity College, Dublin, 21 October 1709

Dear Sir,

I return you my hearty thanks for the favour you did me in putting me on the perusal of a book, which is (I think) written with great solidity, and which I had

[39] William Higden (1662/63–1715). At the revolution of 1688 Higden became a nonjuror, but later took the oaths of allegiance to Queen Anne* at about 1708, publishing a defense of his actions in *A View of the English Constitution* (London, 1709).

not seen before. Mr. Higden[40] has in my mind clearly shown that the swearing allegiance to the king *de facto* (whether right or wrong) is comfortable as well to the laws of the land as to Scripture and reason, and the practice of nations. That it is agreeable to reason is so evident from the very nature and design of government, as one may justly wonder it was ever made a question, and particularly what Mr. Higden relates to have passed in Henry the Seventh's[41] reign, viz. the acknowledging the laws passed by Richard the Third,[42] the methods used in reversing his acts of attainder, and the statute made for the future security of all that should adhere to the king *de facto*, which he shows not to have been repealed since; all this I say demonstrates it to suit with our Constitution. Besides what he says of ancient custom, viz. that during the reigns of thirteen kings who came to the throne without hereditary titles, he does not know of any non-jurors, makes it seem surprising that those men should start up in our days. The reason I take to be that men having felt not long before the great mischief there was in forsaking the king, they now (as is usual to go from one extreme to another) thought they could not adhere too closely to his person, even when he was divested of all government, and utterly unable to protect them. For my part, when I consider what the difference is beween a king *de jure* and a king *de facto* I cannot easily find it. As for the right of inheritance, to me it seems a kingdom is not a property, but a charge; it is not therefore necessary that it go by the same rule as an estate or goods and chattels. But grant it be the property of a single person, and that the crown of right descend by inheritance, yet sure it is that no person who inherits can have by inheritance a better title to the thing inherited than he to whom he succeeds as heir. Now do but trace the present Royal line and you will end in William the Conquerour,[43] who by conquest had the same title to the crown that a highwayman has to your purse. So that after all, we are forced to place the right of kings in the consent and acquiescence of the people: whence it follows, that whoever has the crown in possession, and the people or their representatives, i.e. Lords and Commons concurring with him the same is rightful king. If therefore Cromwell[44] had taken the title of king, and got it confirmed to his posterity in a free Parliament, and they remained in

---

[40] William Higden (1662/63–1715). See Letter 5, note 3.
[41] Henry VII (1457–1509).
[42] Richard III (1452–85).
[43] William I, known as William the Conqueror, (1027/28–87).
[44] Oliver Cromwell (1599–1658).

possession of it, and the laws ran in their usual channel down to this time, it should seem to be wickedness in anyone to attempt to disturb the public peace, by introducing the family of the Stewarts. Because you desire my sentiments I speak freely what comes uppermost in my thoughts.

But to return to our author, two things there are that I scruple in his book: the first, is his retaining the distinction of kings *de jure* and kings *de facto* without giving any mark whereby we shall know the one from the other. I would ask him for example, how upon his principles it is possible to distinguish between the posterity of the usurper Cromwell (in case they had obtained and continued on the throne) and the posterity of the Conquerour, which is but a more specious name for an usurper. In the two first chapters he proves the legislative authority of the king for the time being and his two Houses of Parliament, to be acknowledged both by the common and statute law; and at the latter end of the sixth chapter he expressly says the right of the crown is under the direction of the legislative authority, i.e. of the king *de facto* and his Parliament. Whence it plainly follows that every king *de facto* is king *de jure*, and so the distinction becomes useless. The second thing I cannot approve of in Mr. Higden is, that he seems to be against all resistance whatsoever to the king *de facto* as is evident from chapter seven. Now by this it appears his principles do not favour the late Revolution, though indeed he is now for submission to the government established.

By this time I may reasonably suppose you are well nigh tired. I must nevertheless ask leave to add that nothing in my mind can be more becoming a gentleman and man of sense, than the resolution you are taking to know the measure of your obedience, and the bounds of their power who rule. As to the latter, I believe you may find some satisfaction in the last part of Mr. Locke's[45] *Treatise o[f] Government*, if you have not yet perused that piece. And with relation to the former, there is a dialogue of Plato's entitled *Crito*, wherein it is debated how far we are bound to the observance of the laws of our country, of which I would gladly know your opinion. It contains only about five or six leaves in 8° in the 2d vol. of Plato's works translated into English from the French of Mr. Dacier.[46] I believe Mr. Clerke[47] has the book. You are undoubtedly wise in resolving to have a beautiful lady: I wish she may be healthy too, that so you may be the father of a hardy race, for ever free from colds and toothaches.

---

[45] John Locke (1632–1704).

[46] André Dacier, *The Works of Plato, Abridged*, 2 vols. (London: A. Bell, 1701).

[47] An unknown acquaintance of Berkeley's. There were many Clerkes in Ireland at the time.

Dr. Lambert has lately published a defence of his letter:[48] it has the character of being smooth and trifling. The same person is said to have offended Mr. Tennison's[49] friends, because in his funeral sermon he charged him with ignorance in being against the money bill. I shall not add that the throwing away half an hour now and then on a correspondence with me is the greatest addition imaginable to the obligations you have already laid on.

Dear Sir,

Your most humble & affectionate servant,

Geo. Berkeley

7 BERKELEY TO MOLYNEUX

CCS D/M1/2. An incomplete photostat copy is available at TCD MS 4309.

Trinity College, Dublin, 26 November 1709

Dr. Molyneux,

I am lately entered into my citadel in a disconsolate mood, after having passd the better part of a sharp & bitter day in the damps & mustly [*sic*] solitudes of the library without either fire or any thing else to protect me from the injuries of the snow that was constantly driving at the windows & forcing its entrance into that wretched mansion, to the keeping of which I was this day sennight elected under an inauspiciary planet. What adds to my vexation is that the senior fellows have this evening nailed up my Lord Pembrook's[50] books in boxes; and so deprivd me of the only entertainment I could propose to my self in that place. But for my comfort preferment comes on a pace. Yesterday I was advancd a step higher by Dr. Edward's[51] being made senior fellow, upon a vacancy occasiond by Dr. Lloyd's[52] being made Dean of Connor. And I expect to be promoted two or three steps more

---

[48] Ralph Lambert* (1666–1732). The reference is to his *Partiality Detected: or, A Reply to a Late Pamphlet, Entituled, Some Proceedings in the Convocation, A.D. 1705. Faithfully Represented, etc.* (London: A. & J. Churchill, 1708).

[49] Henry Tennison (*c.* 1667–1709), son of the bishop of Clogher. His father Richard was later bishop of Meath. Henry was the Irish MP for Monaghan in 1695 and commissioner of the revenue 1703–04.

[50] Thomas Herbert* (1656/57–1733), eighth Earl of Pembroke and fifth Earl of Montgomery.

[51] Likely a copyist's mistake for "Elwood." John Elwood (?–1740), jurist. He was later vice-provost of Trinity College and served as its MP to the Irish Parliament.

[52] Owen Lloyd (?–1738), was professor of divinity at Trinity College, Dublin, and was appointed dean of Connor in 1709.

in a little time for the Bishop of Cork[53] died the other day of a purple fever in this town, the Dean of Cork also is dead, and as some say the Bishop of Kilmore.[54] It seems by the letter I had the honour to receive from you, that your expectations are not answered with relation to the magnificence of Kilkenny; believe me child that ancient & delightful city is not so remarkable for a splendid outside as for intrisic [*sic*] worth the rich marble that covers the houses and even the streets not being distinguishable by the eye from the vilest stone until by trial you have discovered its hardness and the polish & lustre it is capable of receiving. As for the piece of my drawing which you sought in the Duchess's closet, I am inclined to be of your mind, that it was translated with the rest of the most precious moveables to adorn the Duke's House in St. James's Square. The Cave of Dunmore if I was to see it now, I know not whether it would strike me with the like horrour & surprise, and fill my mind with the same images that it did when I saw it about ten years agone; I need not tell you a child is easier surprised and his little mind sooner filled with wonder & amazement than that of a man so well read in the history of nature and of such a daring spirit as you are. Ho[w]ever I should gladly be informed in your next how you were affected with the sight of that place, or what adventures you might have had in it. I am

> Dr. Molyneux
> your affectionate friend & servant,
> Geor: Berkeley

The other day I had a letter from Tom Prior[55] containing some objections or difficulties with respect to the *Theory of Vision*, wherein he gives his service to you.

8 PERCIVAL TO BERKELEY

EP, BL Add. MS 47025, fols. 142–43v.

London, 29 November 1709

Dear Sir,

I was extremely entertained with reading that excellent discourse of Socrates before his death, which you recommended to me, and I agree readily

---

[53] Dive Downes (1653–1709) was bishop of Cork from 1699 to 1709. He was succeeded by Peter Browne in 1710, at which time Benjamin Pratt (1669–1721) became provost of Trinity College, Dublin.

[54] Edward Wetenhall (1636–1713), bishop of Kilmore, survived several more years. He was succeeded in 1715 by Timothy Godwin (1670?–1729).

[55] Thomas Prior* (1681–1751).

with the Prefacer that in our days we should hardly find an instance of the like kind, and yet I remember to have read of some of the regicides that judged King Charles[56] to death though they well foresaw what was coming upon them, and had fair opportunity to escape, refused to stir, reputing it no less than a desertion of God and their country, to refuse laying down their lives in justification of the good old cause. But this was the force of enthusiasm which ever works strongest on the weakest minds, and when judgment is wanting hurries men often on to mistake vice for virtue and overact themselves. He is truly praiseworthy who can submit to evils after a wise and sober examination, when the passions are calm and undisturbed, as he is bravest that will resent an injury in cold blood. This Socrates did, and though it was common in those ages and in the beginning of Christianity for men to suffer for their opinions, yet there is something particular in his case which I think entitles him more to our admiration than any other. In most instances that history gives us of this sort of magnanimity, we may observe ambition, vanity, despair, or such like failings to have been a great incitement to if not the foundation of the action. Empedocles would be thought a god, and threw himself into Etna, and Cuxtius leaped into the chasm,[57] to have a year's enjoyment of the fairest women, which is no such strange thing for a heathen to do, when even Christians who are better convinced of a future state are seen to make themselves away often because disappointed of a single woman. Then if you come down to the first Christians who suffered in such numbers, we shall less wonder at their resolution when we consider how near they lived to the Apostles, whose example being fresh, must have had great influence, besides the assurance they had of immortality, and being for the very sake of suffering promised happiness hereafter, but above all when God was so favourable to many of them as (if we may believe the writers) to permit they should feel no pain when under the most violent execution. You will own it was no difficult matter then to be a martyr. Lastly many have suffered for religion who would have changed to save their lives. We know that Cranmer[58] recanted that he might not suffer, yet the law proceeded against him, so he was forced to death, when changing will do no good a

---

[56] Charles I (1600–49).

[57] This is most likely a reference to a (mythical) Roman story about a chasm that opened up in the Forum in Rome. A seer prophesied that the gap could only be closed by sacrificing the most precious thing Rome possessed. A famous Roman warrior named Marcus Curtius then mounted a horse and jumped into the crevice, whereupon the chasm promptly closed.

[58] Thomas Cranmer (1489–1556), archbishop of Canterbury.

man is a martyr in spite of his teeth, which surely is not very meritorious, though it is commendable to die in the faith we always professed.

But whoever considers the circumstances of Socrates as no doubt you have done, will find the greatest temptations before him to live that could be, and few inducements to the contrary. He will find that he consented to die merely for the good of others, even of those who wrongfully put him to death, so that he had a double aim in dying, the justifying truth, and preserving the laws of his country inviolable. A martyr dies for the good of his soul, Socrates of his soul and country too, and yet the greatest assurances his philosophy could give him of a future state were not comparable to the clear evidence revelation afterwards brought us, neither could Athens have been much hurt if so good a man had withdrawn himself from suffering under an unjust judgment; but Socrates adored truth and justice so much, that he would not give a pretence to any that were to come after for disobedience to the laws they once had owned, and in dying had no private aim, no vanity to satisfy, but showed that the best use we can make of life is to part with it in defence of truth.

If you remember when in Dublin I discoursed you about Mr. Whiston,[59] who writ an explication of several Scripture prophecies. He is now in great danger of losing a small living (which is all he has to subsist a large family with) for declaring publicly and in print that adoration or prayer is not due to God the Son, nor Holy Ghost. He owns that the Scriptures apply the divinity to them, but he says it is none of our business to draw consequences, and afterward make prayers, where not peremptorily enjoined, and example in Scripture is wanting. But really I think he is mistaken very much; for in my reading the New Testament, I thought nothing plainer than that our Saviour was prayed to, and he without whom nothing was made that was made, he that is in the father and the father in him, he that when you see him you see the father too, he that declared I and the father are one, he that could forgive sins, in short he that hath these powers and attributes given him in Scripture has a title to our prayers and adoration. Mr. Whiston therefore is absent always upon Litany days which he leaves to his curate, and some other passages he leaves out in our common prayer, for which he is threatened very hard; but he despises the worst they can do him, and says they cannot hurt him, though they may the body; thus he speaks like a philosopher, but like an enthusiast too. When they tell him his wife and children will starve he is not moved at all, but says God will help them. He is very positive and warm; I do not know whether he is within the act N & M that makes it punishable to deny the godhead of our Saviour, for as

[59] William Whiston* (1667–1752).

I told you before he owns whatever the text says of him, but either explains it differently or rejects the consequences we draw.

I have tired you and will therefore conclude, etc.,

Percival

9 BERKELEY TO MOLYNEUX

CCS D/M1/2. A photostat is available at TCD MS 4309.

Trinity College, Dublin, 8 December 1709

Dr. Molyneux,

You desire to know my thoughts, first, whether the ideas laid up in the imagination are all images of what they represent, and secondly whether we can reason without ideas, and if not how comes it that we can reason about a chiliag[o]n whereof we cannot frame an idea? This if I take you right is the substance of what you propose. To the first I answer, That the ideas laid up in the imagination need not be images, strictly speaking of what they represent, for example, in demonstrating the proposition which says, that the sum of the angles of any polygon is equal to twice as many right ones, as there be sides in the figure, bating four. You may make use of any one polygon, e.g. a pentagon to represent all the infinite variety of regular and irregular polygons that may possibly exist. Again when you recollect in your thoughts the idea of any house or city, for instance it is certain that idea does very rudely resemble the thing it represents, and not in each circumstance accurately correspond with it. And yet it may serve to most interests and purposes as well as if it did. To the second, I answer, that we may very well, and in my opinion often do, reason without ideas but only the words used, being used for the most parts as letters in algebra, which though they denote particular quantities, yet every step do not suggest them to our thoughts, and for all that we may reason or perform operations entirely about them. Numbers we can frame no notion of beyond a certain degree, and yet we can reason as well about a thousand as about five, the truth on it is numbers are nothing but names. Hence you may reason about a chiliagon with regard to the number of its sides and angles, though the idea you have of it be not different from that of a figure of 999 sides. I am of your opinion that Descartes[60] flounders often in his *Meditations* and is not always consistent with himself. In *Med.* 2. he says the notion of this particular

---

[60] René Descartes (1596–1650).

wax is less clear than that of wax in general, and in the same *Med.* a little before, he forbears to consider bodies in general because (says he) these general conceptions are usually confused. In *Med.* 3 and in the answer to the 3rd objection of Hobbes he plainly distinguisheth betwixt himself & cogitation, betwixt an extended substance & extension, and nevertheless throughout his principles he confounds those things as do likewise his followers. But it would take up too much time to observe to you all the like blunders that appeared to me when I formerly read that treatise. I know not whether I have hit your mind, if you explain me your thoughts more at large perhaps I may say something more pertinent. Last Saturday Caldwell[61] went along with J. Bligh[62] for London, where they intend to stay till a peace, and then proceed to make the tour of Europe. I am Dr. Molyneux,

    yours most affectionately,

    G: Berkeley

I have lately had much talk with Dr. Elwood[63] about my notion, I have communicated my design & papers to him & am glad I have done so, for I find he is a man of very good sense.

10 BERKELEY TO MOLYNEUX

CCS D/M1/2.

Trinity College, Dublin, 19 December 1709

Dr. Molyneux,

You desire to know what a geometer thinks of when he demonstrates properties of a curve formed by a ray of light as it passes through the air. His imagination or memory (say you) I can afford him no idea of it, and as for the rude idea of this or that curve which may be suggested to him by fancy that has no connexion with his theorems & reasonings. I answer first, that in my opinion he thinks of the various density of the atmosphere the obliquity of the incidence and the nature of refraction in air by which the ray is bent into a curve, it is on these he meditates and from these principles he proceeds to investigate the nature of the curve.

---

[61] Little mention is made of this Caldwell, who might be of the Caldwell family from Fermanagh (associated with Castle Caldwell). It is possible it is Henry Caldwell* (?–1726), second Baronet. See Letters 128, 133, 142, and 164.

[62] John Bligh* (1687–1728).

[63] John Elwood (?–1740), jurist. He was later vice-provost of Trinity College and served as its MP to the Irish Parliament.

Secondly, it appears to me that in geometrical reasonings we do not make any discovery by contemplating the ideas of the lines whose properties are investigated. For example, in order to discover the method of drawing tangents to a parabola, it is true a figure is drawn on paper & so suggested to your fancy, but no matter whether it be of a parabolic line or no, the demonstration proceeds as well though it be an hyperbole or the portion of an ellipsis, provided that I have regard to the equation expressing the nature of a parabola wherein the squares of the ordinates are every where equal to the rectangles under the abscissae & parameters, it being this equation or the nature of the curve thus expressed and not the idea of it that leads to the solution.

Again you tell me that if, as I think, words do not at every turn suggest the respective ideas they are supposed to stand for it is purely by chance our discourse hangs together, and is found after two or three hours jingling & permutation of sounds to agree with our thoughts. As for what I said of algebra, you are of opinion the illustration will not hold good because there are no set rules except those of the syllogisms whereby to range & permute o[u]r words like to the algebraic process. In answer to all which I observe first, that if we put our words together any how and at random then indeed there may be some grounds for what you say, but if people lay their words together with design and according to rule then there can be no pretence so far as I can see for your inference. Secondly, I cannot but dissent from what you say, of there being no set rules for the ranging and disposition of words but only the syllogistic, for to me it appears that all grammar & every part logic contain little else than rules for discourse & ratiocination by words. And those who do not expressly set themselves to study those arts do nevertheless learn them insensibly by custom. I am very sleepy & can say no more but that I am

yours etc.,

G. Berkeley

11 BERKELEY TO PERCIVAL

EP, BL Add. MS 47025, fols. 146–47v.

Trinity College, Dublin, 27 December 1709

I was glad to find the small piece I recommended to your perusal entertained you so well. I did indeed believe that anything of that excellent philosopher, whose divine sentiments are preserved to us by Plato and Xenophon, could not fail of being agreeable to a man of sense and virtue. Your reflections on

Socrates' behaviour gave me a great deal of pleasure, though not without some concern, in making me more sensible of the loss I sustain in being deprived of the conversation of one who has a taste of those things which (though formerly the chiefest heads of discourse among the politer heathen) are now almost grown out of fashion, and banished the conversation of well bred Christians. Socrates spent his time in reasoning on the most noble and important subjects, the nature of the gods, the dignity and duration of the soul, and the duties of a rational creature. He was always exposing the vanity of Sophists, painting vice and virtue in their proper colours, deliberating on the public good, enflaming the most noble and ungenerous tempers with the love of great actions. In short his whole employment was the turning men aside from vice, impertinence, and trifling speculations to the study of solid wisdom, temperance, justice, and piety, which is the true business of a philosopher. And this great man died as he lived; he went out of the world with the same indifference that a man rises from an ill play. He spent his last minutes in his usual exercise. In the morning of the last day of his life, you know he made that excellent discourse concerning the obligation that men have to obey the laws of their country, and Plato's dialogue entitled *Phaedon* contains an account of his discourse and behaviour during the rest of the day wherein he drank the poison prepared him by the executioner. It is now years since I read this dialogue, but I remember it entertained me very agreeably, as I believe it will you if you can find leisure to peruse it. It is in the same volume with *Crito*, and it would be a great favour to let me know your opinion of it. I must own it looks something impertinent to be still troubling you with one amusement or other; but when I call to mind how unmercifully you suffered me to devour your time when here, I flatter myself that I have a sort of right to the disposal of some few of your minutes even at this distance. But here is a particular reason why I could wish you would give yourself the trouble of looking over the *Phaedon*; for (besides that you will there find the thoughts of the wisest heathen on that subject which the most deserves our consideration, I mean the immortality of the soul) Socrates does therein explain his opinion of self-murder, which is a point I remember to have heard you discourse on more than once, and you appeared something fond of discussing it. But if you need any motive to peruse a discourse of Socrates, I know none more apposite than the authority of Squire Bickerstaff,[64] a man I think of excellent sense and whom you may have observed on all occasions to

---

[64] A pseudonym employed first by Jonathan Swift* (1667–1745), but adopted by Sir Richard Steele (1672–1729). The reference is most likely to Steele's *nom de plume*, which he used from 1709 to 1711 as editor of *The Tatler*.

express a very high esteem of that philosopher. For my own part, so far as I can judge by what notions of his I have seen, I cannot forbear thinking him the best and most admirable man that the heathen world produced.

It was with great concern I read that part of your letter which relates to Mr. Whiston.[65] He has been (as appears by his writings) a man of great industry and parts; but I must own myself very much surprised to find him espouse such an odd paradox, as adoration and prayer are not due to the Son and Holy Ghost, though he acknowledges their divinity. You tell me he says it is none of our business to draw consequences from Scripture, whereas in my opinion several parts of Scripture would be of little or no use, if we were not allowed to apply them and draw consequences from them. Whatever has an evident connexion with any part of revelation seems to me equally binding with it, otherwise all use of reason in points of the Christian religion must be quite laid aside. I agree with you entirely that we have express warrant in Scripture for praying to our Saviour; and if we had not, yet it is so clearly deducible from thence as sufficiently justifies the conduct of our Church in that point. This notion of Mr. Whiston's is, I believe, of a new sort, for the Socinians allow our Saviour may be prayed to, though according to them he is not God. But though I look on this thought of Mr. Whiston's as an error in point of judgment, yet I must confess the account you gave me of it, noways lessened but rather increased my opinion of the man; inasmuch as it is easier to find those who conform in the externals of worship and agree to the tenets of our Church, than to meet with one that has attained in so eminent a degree, that great perfection and badge of Christianity, the generous contempt of the things of this life, which as it is the most severe and least practised duty of our religion, so it is the surest mark of a true Christian, being the very root of all the heroical virtues recommended in the gospel. The large family of Mr. Whiston which you mention (for before I did not know he was married) are indeed to be pitied, but as for Mr. Whiston himself I do not think him any object of pity on account of the temporal misfortunes he is threatened with; there is a secret pleasure in suffering for conscience sake, which I doubt not is sufficient to overbalance whatever calamities may be inflicted on him on that score.

This obscure corner of the world furnishes no occurrences worth your notice. All things are in a dull state of mediocrity. Only the other day there came out a pamphlet in answer to Mr. Stoughton's[66] sermon. It was written by a young

---

[65] William Whiston* (1667–1752).

[66] William Stoughton (?–1718), prebendary of St. Patrick's (1681–1718). Stoughton's sermon was printed in Dublin and reprinted in London in 1709.

clergyman of my acquaintance that was formerly a member of our college. The thing seems to me to have some sense and pleasantry in it. You have here enclosed part of it and the remaining part I defer sending till next post.

Pray remember me to Mr. Clerke.[67]

I am, Dear Sir,

Your affectionate humble servant,

G. Berkeley

12 BERKELEY TO PERCIVAL

EP, BL Add. MS 47026, fols. 3v–5.

Trinity College, Dublin, 1 March 1709/10

Dear Sir,

I take this opportunity of Mr. Molyneux's[68] departure to give you the trouble of a letter, though I must own this corner furnishes scarce any that deserves to be communicated. We are a nation as it were in its nonage, put under the guardianship of a people who do everything for us, and leave us the liberty of transacting nothing material ourselves or having any part in the affairs of Europe, yet for all that we are not free from faction and discord any more than our neighbours. The feast at the Tholsel[69] on the Queen's birthday has occasioned much talk in this city and given offence to many on account of certain Whiggish healths which was there proposed, one whereof I am informed was the bringing in of Presbytery, and another that Dr. Sachervell[70] and his friends may meet with Greg's fate.[71] The said Dr. is entirely the subject of discourse, and everyone is engaged either for or against him. His sermon has been printed here, as well as some pamphlets of our own growth against it. I send you one which is thought to come from Mr. Daniel a famous Whig-clergyman and pretender to poetry in this town. I would not have you think by my sending it that I set any great value on it, for it seems to me writ with an affectation of more wit than in truth it has. The controversy occasioned by Mr. Boyle's sermon against

---

[67] An unknown acquaintance of Berkeley's. There were many Clerkes in Ireland at the time.

[68] Samuel Molyneux* (1689–1728).

[69] Dublin's city hall, a place for banquets and exchange.

[70] Henry Sacheverell* (1674–1724).

[71] William Greg (Gregg) (?–?), Lord Harley's secretary and intelligence agent. He was tried for treason and executed after offering military information to the French war minister. See *A Complete Collection of State Trials and Proceedings for High Treason and Other Crimes and Misdemeanours*, compiled by T. B. Howell, vol. XIV (London: Hansard, 1816), pp. 1372–96.

episcopacy is not yet ended. I hear he has a large volume of above three-score-sheets ready for the press. Archdeacon Percival's[72] answer to Dr. Lambert[73] is likewise suddenly expected. I know not whether my last came to your hands, it was directed under cover to Mr. Southwell[74] and enclosed a piece of controversy with Mr. Stoughton on the subject of his sermon. Sir Richard Bulkeley[75] and one Whitterow[76] an imposter whom he brought over along with him are lately gone from hence. They distributed a great deal of money and victuals to the poor while they were here, and set a stranger free who had been arrested for forty pounds which sum they paid. In short Sir Richard was resolved to sell his estate and give all to the poor. But I am told the Chancery opposed him as *non compos*.[77] Whitterow is said to have run away with a young woman. Some clergymen would fain have discoursed him on his mission but he carefully avoided it.

The bookseller who printed the *Essay on Vision*, imagining he had printed too few, retarded the publication of it on that side the water till he had finished this second edition whereof be pleased to accept one which I have sent you by Mr. Molyneux. I have made some alterations and additions in the body of the Treatise, and in an appendix have endeavoured to answer the objections of the Archbishop of Dublin.[78] There still remains one objection with regard to the uselessness of that book: but in a little time I hope to make what is there laid down appear subservient to the ends of morality and religion in a treatise I have now in the press,[79] the design of which is to demonstrate the existence and attributes of God, the immortality of the soul, the reconciliation of God's fore-knowledge with freedom of men, and by showing the emptiness and falseness of several parts of the speculative sciences, to reduce men to the study of religion and things useful. How far my endeavour will prove successful, and whether I have been all this time in a dream or no, time will manifest.

---

[72] William Percival* (?–?), cousin to Sir John Percival. William was a Tory and prolocutor of convocation. He received an honorary degree for defending the franchise of Trinity College (see the College Register, 8 February 1714). See Rand, p. 72n.

[73] Ralph Lambert* (1666–1732).

[74] Edward Southwell* (1671–1730).

[75] Sir Richard Bulkeley (1663–1710), great-grandson of Launcelot Bulkley, archbishop of Dublin. An avid experimentor and inventor, he was also a millenarian who supported the "French prophets," three men who came to England in 1706 claiming powers of prophecy. Bulkeley became involved with the group late in 1706, and in *An Answer to Several Treatises Lately Publish'd on the Subject of the Prophets* (1708) he defended the prophets' claims through Scriptural argument and based on his personal experiences.

[76] Abraham Whitrow (?–?) a follower of the "French prophets" and confederate of Sir Richard Bulkeley.

[77] Presumably Berkeley means *non compos mentis*: "not of sound mind."

[78] William King* (1650–1729).

[79] A reference to the *Principles of Human Knowledge*, published roughly eight weeks later.

Pray if Mr. Clarke[80] be alive give my humble service to him. I am in pain for him having not heard from him this long time. I met with some who supporting themselves on the authority of the Archbishop of Dublin's sermon concerning the prescience of God, denied there was any more wisdom, goodness, or understanding in God than there were feet or hands, but that all are to be taken in a figurative sense; whereupon I consulted the sermon and to my surprise found his Grace asserting that strange doctrine. It is true he holds there is something in the divine nature analogous or equivalent to those attributes. But upon such principles I must confess I do not see how it is possible to demonstrate the being of God: there being no argument that I know of for his existence, which does not prove him at the same time to be an understanding, wise, and benevolent Being, in the strict, literal, and proper meaning of those words. About the same time I wrote to Mr. Clarke and desired he would favour me with his thoughts on the subject of God's existence, and the proofs he thought most conclusive of it, which I imagined would prove a grateful entertainment while his sore eyes prevented his reading. But never since have I heard one word from him, either on that or any other subject. I am often inquired of about his character, and I would fain add the love of letters and study to the rest of his good qualities.

All friends here are well. The other night Archdeacon Percival, Dan. Dering[81] and myself were drinking your and Dr. Sachervell's healths at your brother's.

I am,

Your most obliged humble servant,

G. Berkeley

P.S.: This was to have gone by Mr. Molyneux[82] who, some time since, was in full haste setting about his journey to the Congress, but now finding he is not likely to continue his resolution I chose rather to resume the letter out of his hands and send it by post, then that you should escape the trouble of reading it, which trepass I depend upon your good nature to forgive. My Lady Roydon is just giving up the ghost, her goods are all seized and the bailiffs lodging in her house won't suffer her to die in peace.

---

[80] Luce speculates that this is a reference to Samuel Clarke* (1675–1729), but that is unlikely given that Percival reports that he is not acquainted with Clarke (see Letter 20) and neither is Berkeley. See *Works*, vol. IX, p. 8.

[81] Daniel Dering* (?–1730).

[82] Samuel Molyneux* (1689–1728).

13 BERKELEY TO KING[83]

TCD MS 2167, fol. 1.

Trinity College, Dublin, 18 April 1710

May it please your Grace,

It was with great concern and surprise that I understood my being fallen so far into the displeasure of your grace, as that you should order me to be prosecuted in your Grace's court, especially without any fault of mine that I knew of. For I do assure your Grace, that if the manner of my ordination was in me a fault, it was a fault of ignorance, as will appear from the following account which I humbly submit to your Grace's consideration. The time drawing nigh at which I was obliged by the Statutes of the College to take on priest's orders, I resolved to make use of the first opportunity that should offer, and being informed that a gentleman of my acquaintance had applied to the Bishop of Clogher[84] to be ordained by him, I thought it proper for me likewise to address his Lordship in my own behalf, and the rather for that his relation (as vice-chancellor) to our society entitled me in a particular manner to expect that favour from him. But, my Lord, as I was a stranger to the nature and extent[85] of your grace's jurisdiction, I did not apprehend it was my business to examine how far your Grace's licence may be necessary to his Lordship's holding an ordination. Whether the Bishop of Clogher would ordain me or no, or what licence he had to do it, I left entirely to his Lordship's [text damaged] to determine not thinking it became me to inter-meddle in [text damaged] of that nature, since I was [text damaged][86] and his Lordship might be presumed best to know on [what ?] grounds he proceeded. But least of all did it enter into my thoughts that in case there had been any irregular act of his, it would bring me under the resentment of your grace, or be interpreted in me an encroaching on your Grace's authority, which I never meant to lessen or dispute. This, my Lord, is the true state of the matter, which I presume to lay before your Grace, in hopes it may (if not justify me altogether) at least make my error appear the more pardonable. I have already engaged to the Dean of St. Patrick's[87] (who has been pleased to suspend the prosecution), as I do now to your Grace, that I shall not exercise any

---

[83] Addressed to Archbishop King near St. James's in London.
[84] St. George Ashe* (1658–1718), bishop of Clogher 1697–1717.
[85] Luce has "intent."
[86] Luce suggests "ignorant," but there are probably two missing words, and the last letters of the latter word are "-asine," which makes his speculation unlikely.
[87] John Stearne* (Sterne) (1660–1745).

ecclesiastical function in your diocese until I have first obtained licence from your grace. I am, my Lord,

>your Grace's
>most dutiful
>& most obedient
>servant,
>Geor: Berkeley

14 PERCIVAL TO BERKELEY

EP, BL Add. MS 47026, fols. 12–13v.

London, 20 April 1710

Dear Sir,

I act the most inconsistently in the world in not answering more punctually your letters, for nothing gives me a greater pleasure than to hear from you, and yet I risk that happiness by my silence. I could wish you would think I have had a great deal of business on my hands that prevented me, but I won't categorically affirm it, for fear you should think it no more than that tame and commonplace excuse. I find Dr. Sacheverell[88] has his partisans in Dublin as well as here, and see you are something altered from your former notion of the two parties, which indeed I did expect for I knew you such a lover of truth that you could not bear the wresting of men's words by innuendoes and forced constructions to different senses. We have people here that will not be convinced by any protestations the Dr. could make that he was not designedly guilty of the crimes laid to his charge, and for my own part his reflecting on the ministry I think was as plain as the sun, which he does not deny in his speech. This was no doubt a crime that ought to be followed by some punishment, but as for the others laid to his charge indeed I am not able to discern them in his sermons.

It must needs grieve to the heart all good men who love their country and have nothing to get by changes at court to see the divisions now amongst us. For my share I look upon the differences between Whig and Tory to proceed only from a desire of the one to keep in and the other to get into employment. This their ambition, avarice, and personal pique being but ill inducement for to obtain followers, one party pretends we are in danger of anarchy or presbytery, and the other of tyranny and popery, all which is only to beguile the

---

[88] Henry Sacheverell* (1674–1724).

multitude and support their interests. I cannot think that the Whigs (on one hand) who are most of them of the Church of England and have good fortunes and know the excellency of our constitution can have in view the destruction of it, though they enforce their party by the junction of dissenters and commonwealth men; nor can I on the other hand believe that the Torys are not entirely satisfied with a limited monarchy and the succession as established by law, for the bulk of them are true professors of the Church of England, and very distant from popery, though Papists and Jacobites [enroll?] under that name. The mighty feuds do therefore rise in my opinion from desire of places, which begets personal hatred, and that slander and defamation, after which follows jealousy, distaste and fears, which being for matters of importance, namely the conservation of liberty, constitution, and the established religion, no wonder if well meaning men rank themselves on each side according as the different parties can make impression on them and so become zealous tools to the aims of the cunning few. But though I cannot believe either party desires the destruction of the constitution, yet I do not pretend to say that an ill man will not in single instances, for the preservation of his place and bettering his fortune, sometimes venture to act too boldly and rashly, so as to give the opposite party (who will be sure to watch his behaviour) a pretence to cry out against him as if he intended certainly to overturn every thing, but this being the fault of a depraved mind, it may be common to both parties, in either of which it must be owned there are too many men of corrupt and wicked lives, and therefore we are not immediately to be in agonies for our constitution and think of shifting hands immediately, for worse men may come in their places. In this case therefore an honest man that has a share in the legislature ought to know the limits which belong to each part thereof, and never transgress them on any account. He ought to serve the king to his utmost as far as the interest of his country and the law of the land give leave, and act with either party as he finds them agree to his own opinion, for this reason he must be free from two passions, fear and avarice; from fear because he will be sure to be called a trimmer, and that by the art of party men is grown a scandalous name though naturally a commendable one; and from avarice because he must expect to get no thanks nor reward for preferring his duty and conscience to the service of those in power. It is no argument against this that so few men will be found thus staunch, that instead of doing service to his country such a man incapacitates himself from it by having no followers; for it is not natural that good should come of evil, and the tide of party carries men often into a whirlpool when once they lose their anchor, and then how miserable it is when good men who should at such times stand firm to rectify things are carried together with the rest into errors and evil actions.

> I am
>
> etc.,
>
> Percival

15 BERKELEY TO PERCIVAL

EP, BL Add. MS 47026, fols. 20v–21.

Trinity College, 29 June 1710

Dear Sir,

Suffer me to interrupt your joys by a short congratulation. I am heartily glad to find you are married to a lady who, by all the accounts I can hear, is just such a one as (had it been at my choice) I should have chosen to be your wife.[89] The first lines of your letter to your brother persuade me that I cannot make you a more agreeable wish than that you and my Lady Percival may spend together a long life in pleasure equal to that you have enjoyed this week past, that as the fury of love abates, the sweetness and tenderness of conjugal affection may increase, together with that unknown delight which springs up in the soul of a parent from the thought of a happy and well educated offspring.

> This Sir is the hearty prayer of
>
> Your most humble and obliged servant,
>
> Geo. Berkeley

P.S.: How unmannerly soever it may be to give you any trouble at this time, yet my affairs so fall out that I cannot possibly avoid it. I have some time since published a book which is dedicated to my Lord Pembroke.[90] It is necessary that one of them be forthwith presented to his Lordship, and I know not one that is capable of doing me that service but yourself. The book I have delivered to Mr. Conderon who has promised me that it shall be left at your lodging in London by a gentleman who is going thither. By the next opportunity I will send you one for yourself; though I cannot flatter myself you will find time to read it. If I ask an absurd or unreasonable thing, I beg you will excuse one who has good intentions but not the best judge of decorum.

---

[89] John Percival* (1683–1748) married Catherine Parker* (1687/88–1749), daughter of Sir Philip Parker (*c.* 1650–*c.* 1698), on 20 June 1710.

[90] Berkeley is referring to his *Principles of Human Knowledge* (1710). The dedication to Thomas Herbert* (1656–1733), eighth Earl of Pembroke, was omitted from the second edition.

16 BERKELEY TO PERCIVAL

EP, BL Add. MS *47026, fols. 21v–22.*

Trinity College, Dublin, 29 July 1710

Dear Sir,

The readiness you express to serve me in my affair with the Lord Pembroke[91] has drawn on you this second trouble, viz. that you will do me the favour to let me know if the book I sent to be presented to him, be not yet come to your hands. Mr. Conderon gave it one Mr. Hoar,[92] a parliament [sic] man of this kingdom, about a month since, he then went for England and promised to take care of it. I have likewise directed one to be left at your lodging in Pall Mall* for yourself. It goes with some more of the same sort, which my bookseller sends to London; from the conversation I have had with you on that subject, I flatter myself you will not be adverse to the notions contained in it, and if when you receive it you can procure me the opinion of some of your ingenious acquaintances who are thinking men and addicted to the study of rational philosophy and mathematics, I shall be extremely obliged to you.

You could not have conferred a more sensible obligation on me, than was the favour you did in imparting what gave me some idea of the reasonable and sweet rapture you taste in your new state. I have often heard that men are apt to set the best outside on their condition of life, particularly in what relates to matrimony; but there appears such an unaffected air of truth and passion in what you say, that it will not suffer me to entertain the least doubt of your being in earnest. You must give me leave to tell you, you are mistaken in that part of your letter, where you insinuate it to be your thought that I lie under a prejudice (as I am a bachelour) against marriage; for whatever reasons I may have to think that state not eligible to one in my own present circumstances, humour, and manner of life; yet I assure you I cannot easily imagine a more happy condition than that of man and wife, who abide in mutual love and harmony of temper. As for what commonly shocks young men, the being confined only to one and that for life, I am so far from thinking the worse of matrimony on this account that on any other conditions I am convinced it could never be happy. The impossibility which I have heard some men say there was in finding a woman accomplished in all those perfections that are necessary to the making a happy husband

[91] Thomas Herbert* (1656/57–1733), eighth Earl of Pembroke and fifth Earl of Montgomery.
[92] Most likely Edward Hoare (1678–1765), an Irish MP for Cork City from 1710 to 1713, and from 1715 to 1727. See C. M. Tenison, B.L., M.R.I.A, "Cork MP's [sic] 1559–1800," *Journal of the Cork Historical and Archaeological Society*, 1, 2nd series (1895): 425.

(and which you have so well enumerated in your letter) is what gave me greatest prejudice against matrimony. However I still thought there was such a one somewhere to be found, and I sincerely rejoice with you that you have lit on her. Pray give my service to Mr. Clerke.[93]

I am, Dear Sir,

Your most affectionate and most humble servant,

Geo. Berkeley

17 PERCIVAL TO BERKELEY

EP, BL Add. MS 47026, fol. 25–25v.

London, 26 August 1710

Dear Sir,

Four days ago Col. Percival[94] who came from Ireland brought me your book concerning the principles of human knowledge, which he saw by accident on a bookseller's stall in Dublin made up and directed for me, and so brought it a way, till when I had not seen it, for that you designed for my Lord Pembroke[95] never came to my hands, however it won't come too late for he is yet in the country.

It is incredible what prejudices can work on the best geniuses, nay and even on the lovers of novelty, for I did but name the subject matter of your book to some ingenious friends of mine and they immediately treated it with ridicule at the same time refusing to read it, which I have not yet got one to do, and indeed I have not yet been able to discourse myself on it because I had it so lately, neither when I set about it may I be able to understand it thoroughly for want of having studied philosophy more. A physician of my acquaintance undertook to describe your person, and argued you must needs be mad, and that you ought to take remedies. A Bishop pitied you that a desire and vanity of starting something new should put you on such an undertaking, and when I justified you in that part of your character, and added the other deserving qualities you have, he said he could not tell what to think of you. Another told me an ingenious man ought not to be discouraged from exercising his wit, and said Erasmus was not the worse thought of for writing in praise of folly, but that you are not gone so far as a gentleman in town who asserts not only that there is no such thing as matter

---

[93] An unknown acquaintance of Berkeley's. There were many Clerkes in Ireland at the time.

[94] Charles Percival (1674–1713), governor of Denia in Spain (south of Valencia), cousin of John Percival.* For his services he obtained a regiment. He was killed on 6 May 1713 in a duel in Lisbon.

[95] Thomas Herbert* (1656/57–1733), eighth Earl of Pembroke and fifth Earl of Montgomery.

but that we have no being at all. My wife,[96] who has all the good esteem and opinion of you that is possible from your just notions of marriage happiness, desires to know if there be nothing but spirit and ideas, what you make of that part of the six days' creation which preceded man.[97]

I have given you a plain account as I believe you would have me do what success the name of your book has had here, for I can hardly say they know any more of it, and shall endeavour to persuade people to read it, but by what they have already shown can scarce believe they will do it impartially.

I am, Sir,

Your affectionate friend & humble servant,

J. P.

18 BERKELEY TO PERCIVAL

EP, BL Add. MS 47026, fols. 27v–30.

Trinity College, Dublin, 6 September 1710

Dear Sir,

I am extremely obliged to you for the favourable representation you made of me and my opinions to your friends and the account you have given me of their judgments thereupon; and am not at all surprised to find that the name of my book should be entertained with ridicule and contempt by those who never examined what was in it, and want that common justice of trying before they condemn. But my comfort is that they who have entered deepest into the merits of the cause, and employed most time and exactness in reading what I have written, speak more advantageously of it. If the raillery and scorn of those that critique what they will not be at the pains to understand had been sufficient to deter men from making any attempts towards curing the ignorance and errors of mankind, we should have been troubled with very few improvements in knowledge. The common cries being against any opinion seems to me so far from proving it false that it may with as good reason pass for an agreement of its truth. However I imagine whatever doctrine contradicts vulgar and settled opinion had need been introduced with great caution into the world. For this reason it was I omitted all mention of the non-existence of matter in the titlepage, dedication, preface, and

---

[96] Catherine (*née* Parker) Percival* (1687/88–1749).

[97] This question that Percival advances on behalf of his wife concerning the Mosaic account of the Creation is addressed by Berkeley not only in his next letter to Percival, but also a few years later in *Three Dialogues Between Hylas and Philonous* (see *Works*, vol. II, pp. 255–58).

introduction, that so the notion might steal unawares on the reader, who possibly would never have meddled with a book that he had known contained such paradoxes. If, therefore, it shall at any time lie in your way to discourse your friends on the subject of my book, I entreat you not to take notice to them that I deny the being of matter in it, but only that it is a treatise of the principles of human knowledge designed to promote true knowledge and religion, particularly in opposition to those philosophers who vent dangerous notions with regard to the existence of God and the natural immortality of the soul, both which I have endeavoured to demonstrate in a way not hitherto made use of.

Two imputations there are which (how unjust soever) I apprehended would be charged on me by censorious men, and I find it has happened accordingly. The first, that I was not myself convinced of the truth of what I writ, but from a vain affectation of novelty designed imposing on the world:—whereas there is nothing I esteem more mean and miserable, I may add more wicked, than an intention to cheat men into a belief of lies and sophisms merely for the sake of a little reputation with fools. God is my witness that I was, and do still remain, entirely persuaded of the non-existence of matter, and the other tenets published along with it. How desirous soever I may be to be thought well of, yet I hardly think that anyone in his wits can be touched with a vanity to distinguish himself among wise men for a mad man. This methinks should satisfy others of my sincerity at least, and that nothing less than a full conviction not only of the truth of my notions but also of their usefulness in the most important points, could have engaged me to make them public. I may add that the opinion of matter I have entertained some years, if therefore a motive of vanity could have induced me to obtrude falsehoods on the world, I had long since done it when the conceit was warm in my imagination, and not have stayed to examine and revise it both with my own judgment and that of my ingenious friends. The second imputation, I was afraid of is, that men rash in their censures, and that never considered my book, would be apt to confound me with the sceptics, who doubt of the existence of sensible things and are not positive as to any one truth, no not so much as their own being (which I find by your letter is the case of some wild visionists no[w?] in London), but whoever reads my book with due attention will plainly see that there is a direct opposition betwixt the principles contained in it and those of the sceptics, and that I question not the existence of anything that we perceive by our senses.

As to your Lady's[98] objection, I am extremely honoured by it, and as I shall reckon it a great misfortune, in case any prejudice against my notions should lessen

---

[98] Catherine (*née* Parker) Percival* (1687/88–1749). For the objection, see Letter 17.

the good thoughts, you say, she is pleased to entertain of me, so I am not a little careful to satisfy her in point of the creation's consistency with the doctrine in my book. In order to which I must beg you will inform her Ladyship that I do not deny the existence of any of those sensible things which Moses says were created by God. They existed from all eternity in the Divine intellect, and then became perceptible (i.e. were created) in the same manner and order as is described in Genesis. For I take creation to belong to things only as they respect finite spirits, there being nothing new to God. Hence it follows that the act of creation consists in God's willing that those things should be perceptible to other spirits, which before were known only to Himself. Now both reason and Scripture assure us there are other spirits (as angels of different orders, etc.) besides men, who, it is possible, might have perceived this visible world according as it was successively exhibited to their view before man's creation. Besides, for to agree with the Mosaic account of the creation it is sufficient if we suppose that a man, in case he was then created and existing at the time of the chaos, might have perceived all things formed out of it in the very order set down in Scripture, which is no ways repugnant to our principles. I know not whether I express myself so clearly as to be understood by a lady that has not read my book. Much more I might say to her objection, if I had the opportunity of discoursing her, which I am sorry to hear we may not expect before next summer. I have a strong presumption that either I should make a proselyte of her Ladyship, or she convince me that I am in error. My reason is, because she is the only person of those you mentioned my book to, who opposed it with reason and argument.

As for the physician I assure him there are (besides several others) two ingenious men of his own profession in this town, who are not ashamed to own themselves every whit as mad as myself, if their subscribing to the notions contained in my book can make them so. I may add that the greatest Tory and greatest Whig of my acquaintance agree in an entire assent to them, though at this time our party men seem more enflamed and stand at a wider distance than ever.

This puts me in mind to tell you a pleasant accident that befell me about ten days since. I was just come into the coffeehouse when a drunken gentleman I had never seen before comes up to me and asks me whether I would pledge him in Dr. Sacheverell's[99] health; to be brief he obliged me whether I would or no to drink the Dr.'s health in a glass of brandy in the middle of the coffeehouse and when I had done he fell on his knees and swore and prayed for the Dr. and the Church. Then getting up he swore that all the coffeehouse round should drink the same health, and upon a gentleman's refusing it drew his sword, whereupon

[99] Henry Sacheverell* (1674–1724).

I made what haste I could out of the house. I understood afterwards that one or two more were obliged to drink it, the one of whom was a Parliament man. This occasioned Mr. Caulfield[100] to complain of it as a breach of privilege next day in Parliament; but all the effect his complaint had was that it set the whole house a laughing. I am told this involuntary act of mine is like to gain me the reputation of being a great admirer of Dr. Sacheverell's, which is a character I am not at all fond of. I like indeed very well the events which his preaching may have brought about; for (if I may judge of such things) it seems to me the Government had been much too long in the hands of a party. But for the sermons or conduct of the Dr., I confess I have a very moderate esteem of either.

The book for my Lord Pembroke[101] is delivered to Mr. Hoffman, Mr. Southwell's[102] gentleman, who will give it you as soon as he comes to London.

I am, Sir,

Your most humble and affectionate servant,

G. Berkeley

19 BERKELEY TO PERCIVAL

EP, BL Add. MS 47026, fols. 34–35.

Trinity College, Dublin, October 1710

Dear Sir,

I find by the last you favoured me with, that there is talk of my Lord Pembroke's[103] being employed in the new ministry. I know not whether upon the delivery of the book you will think it proper to intimate to his Lordship that it was printed off (as indeed it was) the beginning of May, but that I wanted opportunity to present it sooner, by this it will appear that I meant to address him in his retirement, and not upon any prospect of his returning into favour at Court which I could not foresee. You are, I know, too public spirited not to have your thoughts and conversations taken up with the occurrences of this busy time, which makes me that I can scarce tell how to desire you should lay out any part of them on the perusal of my book. Though I am sure there is no one whose free and deliberate opinion I should be more desirous of than yours.

---

[100] John Caufield (Caufeild) (?–?), son of William Caufeild (1625–71), Viscount of Charlemont. John was the Irish MP for Charlemont starting in 1703.

[101] Thomas Herbert* (1656/57–1733), eighth Earl of Pembroke and fifth Earl of Montgomery.

[102] Edward Southwell* (1671–1730).

[103] Thomas Herbert* (1656/57–1733), eighth Earl of Pembroke and fifth Earl of Montgomery.

It is the observation of a wise man (Sir Will Temple[104]) that solitude and leisure are the greatest advantages that riches can give those who possess them above other men; and yet these are what rich men least of all make use of. He that is equally fitted for thought and meditation in his closet, or for business and conversation in the world is certainly the best able to serve his country, and can pass with the greatest evenness through all scenes of life. It is thought which governs the world, and all the states in it, and produces whatever is great and glorious in them. Stirring and action is but the handmaid of thought, without which the former can do no good, but may a great deal of harm. Whatever therefore improves the thinking faculty surely ought to be practised. Now, thought is to the mind what motion is to the body; both are equally improved by exercise and impaired by disuse. In order therefore to obtain health and strength of mind it is useful that we employ our thoughts, though it should be even on useless subjects. How much rather ought we then to exercise them on the grounds and certainty of knowledge, the being and attributes of God, and the nature of our own soul. I mean not by this to persuade you that what I have written deserves much heed, but only to show you that the subjects I have chosen are worth thinking on.

I am, Sir,

Your most humble and affectionate servant,

Geo: Berkeley

20 PERCIVAL TO BERKELEY

EP, BL Add. MS 47026, fol. 36–36v.

London, 30 October 1710

Dear Sir,

There are here two clergymen who have perused your last book, Dr. Clarke,[105] and Mr. Whiston,[106] both deservedly esteemed men of excellent learning, though the last is a little different from the orthodox in some points, inclining as it is said to Arianism. Not having any acquaintance with these gentlemen I can only report to you by second hand that they think you a fair arguer, and a clear writer, but they say your first principles you lay down are

---

[104] William Temple (1628–99), English diplomat and author.

[105] Samuel Clarke* (1675–1729).

[106] William Whiston* (1667–1752). Whiston reports of Berkeley's attempts to draw Clarke into correspondence. See William Whiston, *Historical Memoirs of the Life of Dr. Clarke*, 2nd edn. (London, 1730), pp. 79 ff.

false. They look on you as an extraordinary genius, and profess a value for you, but say they wished you had employed your thoughts less on metaphysics, ranking you with Father Malebranche,[107] Norris[108] and another whose name I have forgot, all whom they think extraordinary men, but of a particular turn, and their labours of little use to mankind for their abstruseness.

This is what I believe you are armed against as foreseeing the objection which possibly may proceed merely from a largeness of disposition, not caring to think after a new manner which would oblige them to begin their studies anew, or else it may be the strength of prejudice. For my part I don't design their opinion shall prevent my reading this book which though small in bulk is great for the matter. I doubt indeed my want of philosophy and ignorance of that sort of learning will make me less capable of understanding it than another.

My Lord Pembroke[109] is not yet in town, and now there is no thought of employing him. I have your book by me to give him.

I am, etc.,

J. Percival

21 BERKELEY TO PERCIVAL

EP, BL Add. MS 47026, fols. 41–42.

Trinity College, Dublin, 27 November 1710

Dear Sir,

Your last (which came to hand after having been stopped for several posts by contrary winds) obliged me with the account that my *Treatise of the Principles* etc., had been perused by Dr. Clarke[110] and Mr. Whiston.[111] As truth is my aim, there is nothing I more desire than being helped forward in the search of it, by the concurring studies of thoughtful and impartial men: on both which accounts no less than for their uncommon learning and penetration those gentlemen are very deservedly much esteemed. This makes me very solicitious to know particularly what fault they find in the principles I proceed upon; which at this time cannot but be of great advantage to me in that it will either convince me of an error, and so prevent my wasting any more time and pains that way, or else it

---

[107] Nicolas Malebranche (1638–1715).
[108] John Norris (1657–1712).
[109] Thomas Herbert* (1656/57–1733), eighth Earl of Pembroke and fifth Earl of Montgomery.
[110] Samuel Clarke* (1675–1729).
[111] William Whiston* (1667–1752).

will prove no small confirmation of the truth of my opinions, in case nothing solid can be objected to them by those great men. This makes me trouble you with the two enclosed letters to be sealed and sent by you to those gentlemen respectively, if you shall think it convenient, or if not I must entreat you to get your friend to obtain from them the particulars which they object, and that you will transmit them to me; which will in truth be a deed of charity, much greater than that of guiding a mistaken traveller into the right way, and I think either good office may be with like reason claimed by one man from another.

As to what is said of ranking me with Father Malebranche[112] and Mr. Norris,[113] whose writings are thought too fine spun to be of any great use to mankind, I have this to answer: that I think the notions I embrace are not in the least coincident with, or agreeing with, theirs, but indeed plainly inconsistent with them in the main points, insomuch that I know few writers whom I take myself at bottom to differ more from than them. Fine spun metaphysics are what I on all occasions declare against, and if anyone shall show me anything of that sort in my *Treatise* I will willingly correct it.

I am sorry that I am not yet favoured with your own free thoughts on this subject. Would you but think away a few leisure hours in the morning on it, I dare say no one would understand it better. And, whether I am in a mistake or no, I doubt not but your own thoughts will sufficiently recompence your labour.

> I am, Dear Sir,
> Your most obliged humble servant,
> G. Berkeley

22 BERKELEY TO PERCIVAL

EP, BL Add. MS 47026, fols. 44–45v.

Rathmore, 20 December 1710

Dear Sir,

The last post brought me your letter of the fourth[114] instant which informs me what obligations I have to you on account of your care in providing that my book should be delivered to my Lord Pembroke,[115] for which I return you my hearty thanks, and I shall reckon myself farther obliged to you if you will please to let me

---

[112] Nicolas Malebranche (1638–1715).
[113] John Norris (1657–1712).
[114] There is no remaining record of this letter.
[115] Thomas Herbert* (1656/57–1733), eighth Earl of Pembroke and fifth Earl of Montgomery.

know whether my Lord has returned it (which you say is customary with him), or if by any other means his approbation or dislike of it shall come to your notice.

I am now at Mr. Blithe's[116] house in the County of Meath. It is a large and fair building and has very fine improvements about it. The young gentleman lives very well and since his father's death has behaved himself so in all respects as to have and gained the reputation of a very hopeful and prudent man. He is now building a poor house for the maintenance of the poor of his estate, and intends to assign for that purpose a hundred pounds per annum. I tell you this because I know such news can be to no one more agreeable than to yourself.

The day before I left Dublin (which was something more than a week agone) I chanced to meet at the Provost's house with one Mr. Langton a curate in the County of West-Meath, who had formerly been a Dominican friar. He came to complain of one of our College who together with several other of his Whig-parishioners had most grossly abused him during the time of Divine Service for preaching passive obedience. The sermon Mr. Langton saith was one of Dr. Scot's[117] which he had transcribed. The said Mr. Langton hath like-wise given in information upon oath to the government concerning an associ-ation or conspiracy on foot amongst the Whig-inhabitants of the County of West-Meath in order to oblige the Queen to restore the late ministry. The Council hath thought fit to take notice of it, and sent up for some persons whose testimony Mr. Langton made use of, but what has been since done in it I know not. I was acquainted with this Langton when I went to school in Kilkenny, and thought him to be somewhat silly. This mighty undertaking of the Whigs of West-Meath is certainly very ridiculous; but there are some who imagine the project extends farther than that county.

I purposed to have sent by Mr. Percival[118] half a dozen of my books to you, to be presented to such of your friends as are most conversant in those studies, but it happened that his things were then packed up and on shipboard. By that means I hoped the book would become public and known. I must therefore beg the favour of you that you will let any that are curious that way know that both my books are to be sold by Mr. Churchil[119] in Pater-Noster Row. I should not have given you this trouble but that Mr. Churchil (who is my bookseller's correspondent) has neglected to publish them in the usual forms. Mr. Pepyat[120] suspects the ground

---

[116] John Bligh* (Blithe) (1687–1728).

[117] Most likely a reference to Patrick Scot (?–?, but wrote most of his major works between 1618 and 1625), a Tory clergyman and defender of conformity in the Church of England.

[118] Most likely Philip Percival (?–1748).

[119] Awnsham Churchill (1658–1728), bookseller and politician.

[120] Jeremy Pepyat (?–after 1715), a Dublin bookseller.

of this backwardness in Mr. Churchil to be his apprehending that the encouragement of a printing trade in this kingdom would interfere with his interest; since there are yearly exported great sums of money to him and other booksellers in London for books, which if that trade were encouraged might be printed cheaper in Dublin because there is not here so great an impost on paper. Besides the trial of Dr. Sacheverell[121] and several other things that have been lately printed in Dublin there are now in the press twenty thousand prayer-books and an edition of Erasmus's *Colloquies*, which for print, paper, and correctness will I believe match any of the Dutch editions. This flourishing of the printing trade, more than ever was known in this kingdom, will I hope bring some benefit to poor Ireland, which consideration will I doubt not prove with you sufficient apology for my troubling you with this narrative of it.

It remains that I acknowledge the favour you do me in sending your thoughts of my Introduction. It would greatly rejoice me to find you thought the whole worth your careful perusal. As for anything requisite to the understanding of it, I am sure to the making it I found little else useful than the plain common sense God hath given me together with an application and eagerness to discover the truth. And if you will take my word for it, I assure you there are not those great flights and difficulties in it that you seem to imagine, nothing more being necessary to a thorough comprehending and judging of it than a little exercise of your native faculties, which I am persuaded the Author of Nature never intended should be wholly employed in the little bustling affairs of this spot of earth.

 I am,

Sir,

Your most humble & affectionate servant,

G. Berkeley

23 PERCIVAL TO BERKELEY

EP, BL Add. MS 47026, fol. 49–49v.

London, 28 December 1710

Sir,

 Yesterday my friend was with me who delivered your book to my Lord Pembroke[122] and said my Lord had been with him the day before to desire he

---

[121] Henry Sacheverell* (1674–1724).
[122] Thomas Herbert* (1656/57–1733), eighth Earl of Pembroke and fifth Earl of Montgomery.

would return you his thanks for it. He added you were an ingenious man and ought to be encouraged, but that he could not be convinced of the non-existence of matter, however your book was entertaining. Not being acquainted with the two gentlemen you addressed your letters to, I gave them to two friends of theirs, who I suppose delivered them; for Mr. Whiston[123] is lately come to town, and Dr. Clarke[124] told his friend that he did not care to write you his thoughts because he was afraid it might draw him into a dispute upon a matter which was already clear to him. I replied to the gentleman that if he did not care for exchanging many letters with you, I would engage for you that you would be content if he writ you once for all what were his objections. To which he answered that Dr. Clarke thought your principles you go on are false, and that Mr. Whiston had formerly told him the same, though both conceived a great opinion of you. Then he declined further speaking to Dr. Clarke, who he said was a modest man, and uninclined to shock any men whose opinion in things of this nature differed from his own.

I shall inquire Mr. Whiston's opinion more particularly of my other acquaintance and send it you.

I am,

etc.,

J. Percival

24 BERKELEY TO PERCIVAL

EP, BL Add. MS 47026, fol. 56–56v.

Trinity College, Dublin, 19 January 1710/11

Dear Sir,

Being just returned from the County of Meath I received not so soon as otherwise I should have done your last wherein I am informed of my Lord's favourable acceptance of my book. I am very sensible of the obligations I have to Mr. Southwell[125] for the trouble he has given himself in that affair, but since I have not the honour to be known by him, I doubt whether it be proper to return him thanks for the same. I leave it to you (who can best tell) whether it is or no, and if it be must beg the favour of you to do it for me. Dr. Clarke's[126]

---

[123] William Whiston* (1667–1752).
[124] Samuel Clarke* (1675–1729).
[125] Edward Southwell* (1671–1730).
[126] Samuel Clarke* (1675–1729).

conduct seems a little surprising. That an ingenious and candid person (as I take him to be) should declare I am in an error, and at the same time out of modesty refuse to show me where it lies, is something unaccountable. For my own part, as I shall not be backward to recede from the opinion I embrace when I see good reason against it, so on the other hand, I hope to be excused if I am confirmed in it, the more upon meeting with nothing but positive and general assertions to the contrary. I never expected that a gentleman otherwise so well employed should think it worth his while to enter into a dispute with me concerning any notions of mine. But being it was so clear to him that I went on false principles, I hoped he would vouchsafe in a line or two to point them out to me that so I may more closely review and examine them. If he but once did me this favour he need not apprehend I would give him any further trouble, or offer any the least occasion for drawing him into a dispute with me. If you should happen to meet with his friend by chance (for I have already given you too much trouble in this matter) I shall be obliged to you in case you will let him know this was all my ambition. I am very thankful to you for endeavouring to inform me more particular in Mr. Whiston's[127] opinion. For there is nothing I more desire than to know thoroughly all that can be said against what I take for truth.

> I am
> Dear Sir
> Your most obliged humble servant,
> G. Berkeley

25 BERKELEY TO PERCIVAL

EP, BL Add. MS 47026, fols. 57–58v.

Trinity College, Dublin, 13 February 1710/11

Dear Sir,

Having so often troubled you with my impertinencies I know not now what else to say, but that I leave it to your own good nature to apologise for my repeating the trespass in making this new request to you, viz. that you will take care the enclosed letter be delivered to my Lord Pembroke,[128] either by yourself or by the hands of some friend, or if you shall not think fitting to use one of these

---

[127] William Whiston* (1667–1752).
[128] Thomas Herbert* (1656/57–1733), eighth Earl of Pembroke and fifth Earl of Montgomery.

methods in the delivery of it, that you will send a servant who will be sure to leave it at my Lord's. I send it unsealed that if you or your friend please to deliver it you may see what it contains; but you will remember to seal it if upon reading it you think there is anything improper in it (which you are best judge of) as I would not have it delivered at all.

Of late we have been alarmed with several reports of the plagues being landed in this kingdom, but they have proved to have nothing in them. Dr. Synge[129] has put forth an answer to Archdeacon Percival's reply to Dr. Lambert's[130] vindication of the letter, I mean to such part of it as concerns himself. I hear too that the Bishop of Cork[131] is about an answer in his own behalf, so that the paper war is likely to prove violent and of long continuance. The new Lord Chancellor[132] is much liked and well spoken of by all parties without seeming to interest himself in any. Your friends here are well, but we all long to see you and my Lady Percival, together with your little son (for such I hope it will prove) arrived safe on this side the water.

> I am
> Dear Sir,
> Your most obliged humble servant,
> G. Berkeley

P.S.: The ends that I propose in writing to my Lord are first to thank him for his acceptance of my book and secondly to give him to understand by the most gentle and couched intimation possible that I should gladly know the particular grounds of his dissent from me in point of matter's existence, or the faults he finds in the arguments on that head. But I have conceived a great scruple and suspicion that it is not proper for me to address his Lordship in a letter. It would therefore be a great satisfaction to me if those ends could be obtained by word of mouth from some friend especially yourself (if you are yet introduced into the acquaintance of my Lord). But whether this can be done or not, I beg the favour of you to suppress the letter if you think there is anything in it in the least presumptuous, unmannerly, or apt to give offence, and to let me know your thoughts in a line or two.

---

[129] Edward Synge* (1659–1741).
[130] Ralph Lambert* (1666–1732).
[131] Peter Browne* (?–1735).
[132] Sir Constantine Phipps* (c. 1656–1723). He was lord chancellor of Ireland (December 1710–September 1714).

26 BERKELEY TO PERCIVAL

EP, BL Add. MS 47026, fol. 60v.

Trinity College, Dublin, 6 March 1710/11

Dear Sir,

This moment yours of the 27 of Feb. came to my hands. I heartily congratulate you upon your being blessed with a new sort of pleasure which bachelors cannot form a just notion of: something it is reported there is in the tender passion of a father to his child so different from all other enjoyments. And this I doubt not is considerably heightened by the circumstances that attend it, as first the safe condition of my Lady Percival (which though you mention not, yet you[r] letter assures me of it), and secondly the infant's proving of the nobler sex. It is true, your son and heir comes into the world at a factious and turbulent time, but I am not without hopes that he may spend the greater part of his life in the millennium, since from some modern interpretations we may expect it will be far gone before he comes to age. May he inherit your good qualities as well as your estate in order to which I entreat you will read Mr. Locke's book of Education[133] that abounds with excellent maxims. And, believe me, the foundations of a useful and healthy man cannot be laid too early.

> I am
> Sir,
> Your most humble and affectionate servant,
> G. Berkeley

27 BERKELEY TO LE CLERC[134]

University of Amsterdam Library, Le Clerc Papers J3a.

28 March 1711

Eruditissime & Clarissime Domine,

Tractatum de Principiis Cognitionis Humanae Anglice conscriptum, quem anno praeterito in lucem emisi, Bibliopolae ut ad te transmittendum curaret in mandatis dedi. Unaque literas ad te exarassem nisi veritus fuissem obscurus homuncio virum Celeberrimum rebusque literariis undequaque occupatissimum

---

[133] John Locke's (1632–1704) *On Education* appeared in 1693.

[134] Luce was only aware of the draft of this letter, which he published (*Works*, vol. VIII, p. 48). That draft and translation follows (Letter 28). See Peter Bellemare and David Raynor, "Berkeley's Letters to Le Clerc (1711)," *Hermathena* 146 (1989): 7–23.

ultro interpellare. Quod vero jam hoc facere sustineam, id tuae Humanitati ingenuoque veritatis Studio quod Scripta tua luculenter prae se ferunt acceptum referri debet. Te quippe, cum iis dotibus inclarescas etiam Philosophandi rationem multum excolueris, si opem tuam sive ad castigandas lucubrationes nostras sive ad illas uberiori luce donandas rogarem haud aegre laturum exist-imavi. Proinde abs te peto, Vir clarissime ut locum libro nostro praedicto (modo non indignus videatur) in Bibliotheca tua concedere, simulque sententiam tuam de Doctrina inibi tradita aperte declarare digneris. Vel si hoc minus placuerit Epistola saltem privatim ad me missa errores meos (si qui tibi deprehensi fuerint) patefacere ne detrectes.

Cur vero id impensius optem, in causa est quod tractatus iste (uti nec alter de Visione anno 1709 typis mandatus) vix cuiquam extra hanc Insulam quantum intelligo hactenus innotuit. Etsi plurima exemplaria ad Dominum Churchil Bibliopolam Londinensem transmissa fuerant. Unde fit ut Doctorum de Scriptas meis judicia (exceptis solummodo amicis quibusdam heic loci degenti-bus qui opiniones nostras amplectuntur) ad me non pervenerint. Id quod magno mihi Studiorum impedimento est, utpote qui primam tractatus nostri partem Eruditorum examinis seorsim subjectam voluerim eo fine ut vel ipsorum suf-fragiis confirmatus me alacrius ad consectaria inde deducenda partemque secundam pertexendam accingerem, vel siquid erratum esset tempestive corri-gerem, vel denique falsis Principiis Dogmata nostra inniti monitus ea prorsus [a]bnuerem meque istis adornandis haud ultra incassum fatigarem.

Quod reliquum est, rogo Vir Doctissime ut hanc epistolam, aequi & boni consulas, cre[dasque][135] me Studia tua haud fuisse interpellaturum, nisi nostra ista qualiacunque visa essent [amicis me]is alicuius momenti ad Veritatem dele-gendam componendos non modo Phi[losophic]os verum etiam Religiosos: adeo-que rei literariae nonnihil interesse si in [publicu]m prodirent, et habebis tui.

Observantissimum

G: Berkeley

E Museao nostro in Collegio Trinitatis juxta Dublinium

Martii die 28 Anno Dom. 1711

Trinity College, Dublin, 28 March 1711[136]

---

[135] The last paragraph is defective. In general I follow Bellemare and Raynor's transcription.

[136] This translation deviates from that provided by Raynor and Bellemare in minor respects. As a general rule, it is more literal and follows the Latin grammar more closely at the expense of elegance.

Most Learned and Distinguised Sir,

When I published my English *Treatise Concerning the Principles of Human Knowledge* last year, I asked my bookseller to see that a copy was sent to you. I would have written you a letter at that time were it not that I was afraid, little known and humble as I am, of bothering someone so famous and so busy with all kinds of literary projects. The fact that I take it upon myself to do so now must be credited to the kindness and the open-minded-zeal for truth that your writings so splendidly exhibit. Indeed, I thought that you, because you are famous for these qualities and have so cultivated the liberal style of philosophy, would not take it ill if I asked for your help, either to correct my efforts, or to give them more public exposure. Therefore I ask you, most distinguished Sir, to grant a place for my aforementioned book (provided that it does not appear unworthy of it) in your *Bibliothèque Choisie*,[137] and at the same time that you do me the favour of giving public expression to your opinion of the doctrine expounded therein. Or, if you should not deem that fitting, that you not refuse to communicate to me, at least by private letter, my errors (if you found any).

The reason why I wish this so earnestly is that this treatise to date, like the *Essay of Vision*, that I published in 1709, so far as I can judge, has hardly become known to anyone outside this island, although many copies were delivered to Master Churchil, a London bookseller. Consequently, the judgments of scholars about my writings have not reached me except for those of some friends living in this corner of the world who agree with my opinions. This is a great hindrance to my studies inasmuch as I should like to subject the first part of my treatise on its own to the examination of the learned, so that either, strengthened by their approval, I can equip myself to derive more quickly conclusions from it and to put together the second part, or else that I can correct whatever errors there are in a timely manner, or lastly, being warned that my ideas derive from false principles, so that I can withdraw from them straightaway, and not tire myself out anymore in vain by embellishing them.

As for the rest, I beg of you, most learned Sir, that you receive this letter favourably and with benevolence and that you [be assured] that I would not at all have interrupted your studies if it had not seemed [to my friends] that my own work (whatever its real value may be) was of some importance for the pursuit of truth [and] for composing both [philosophical] and religious [treatises]; and that,

---

[137] *Bibliothèque Choisie* (1703–13) was one of a number of series of periodicals, authored by Le Clerc, consisting of reviews and digests of recently published books.

if published, it would constitute a real contribution/it would be of no little importance to Letters.

And I will remain,

> Your most respectful (servant),
> G: Berkeley

The Library, Trinity College, near Dublin
March 28 1711 A.D.

28 BERKELEY TO LE CLERC (DRAFT)

BL MS 39304, fols. 76v–77v.

1711

Eruditissime Domine,

Tractatum de Principiis Cognitionis Humanae Anglico idiomate conscriptum quem anno proxime elapso in lucem emisi Bibliopolae ut ad te transmittendum curaret in mandatis dedi. Unaque litteras ad te exarassem, nisi veritus essem obscurus homuncio celeberrimum virum rebus literariis undequaque occupatissimum ultro interpellare. Quod vero jam hoc facere sustineam, id tuae humanitati ingenuoque veritatis studio quod scripta tua luculenter prae se ferunt acceptum referri debet.

Quippe te cum ejus modi [dotibus?] inclarescas liberamque praeterea philosophandi rationem multum excolueris, si opem tuam sive ad castigandas meditationes nostras sive ad eas uberiori luce donandas rogarem, haud aegre laturum existimavi.

Hoc igitur abs te peto vir clarissime, ut libro nostro praedicto locum (modo non indignus videatur) in bibliotheca tua selecta concedas, simulque sententiam tuam de doctrina inibi tradita aperte declarare ne detrectes.

Vel si hoc minus placuerit epistola privatim ad me missa errores meos (si qui ubi deprehensi fuerint) patefacere digneris. Cur vero id impensius optem in causa est quod tractatus iste (uti nec alter cui titulus An Essay etc. qui anno 1709 typis mandatus erat) vix cuiquam extra hanc insulam quantum intelligo hactenus innotuit, etsi plurima exemplaria ad dominum Churchil transmissa fuerant.

Unde fit ut doctorum de scriptis meis judicia [*sic* iudicata?] exceptis solummodo amicis quibusdam hoc loco degentibus (qui opiniones nostras amplectuntur) ad me hactenus non pervenerint, id quod magno mihi studiorum impedimento est quippe qui primam tractatus nostri partem eruditorum examini seorsim subjectam voluerim eo fine ut vel ipsorum suffragiis confirmatus me alacrius ad consentania[138] inde deducenda partem que secundam praetexendam accingerem, vel si quid erratum esset tempestive corrigerem, vel denique falsis principiis dogmata nostra inniti monitus ea prorsus relinquerem meque in istis adornandis haud ultra incassum fatigarem.

Most Learned Lord,

I have charged my Bookseller with sending to you my treatise in English, *Concerning the Principles of Human Knowledge*, which I published last year. I would have written you a letter at that time, if I, a little known and humble person, were not afraid, without being asked, of bothering someone so famous and so thoroughly busy with his literary projects. The fact that I take it upon myself to do so now must be credited to the kindness and the open-minded zeal for truth that your writings so splendidly exhibit.

Indeed, I thought that you, because you are famous for qualities of this kind and in addition you have so cultivated the liberal style of philosophy, would not take it ill if I asked for your help either to correct[139] my thoughts or to give them more public exposure. Therefore, most distinguished sir, I ask this of you: that you grant a place for my aforementioned book (provided that it does not appear unworthy of it) in your select library, and at the same time you not refuse to give public expression to your opinion of the doctrine expounded therein.

Or if this is not agreeable, that you [deign to] disclose in a letter sent to me privately, my errors (if any are found). The reason why I wish this so earnestly is that this treatise to date, like the one published in 1709, whose title was *An Essay...*, so far as I can judge, has hardly become known to anyone outside this island, although very many copies were sent to Master Churchil.[140]

Consequently, the judgments[141] of scholars about my writings to date have not reached me except for those of some friends who live in this corner of the world (here in this place) who agree with my opinions, which is a great hindrance to my studies, since I should like to subject the first part of my

---

[138] Berkeley has "consentania," not "consentanea," as Luce has it.
[139] The Latin word *castigandas* can also mean "proofreading" in the eighteenth century.
[140] Awnsham Churchill (1658–1728), bookseller and politician.
[141] Emending to "iudicata."

treatise on its own to the examination of the learned so that either, strengthened by their approval, I can equip myself to derive more quickly conclusions [literally "harmonizing things"] and to provide the second part, or else that I can correct whatever errors there are in a timely manner, or lastly, being warned that my ideas derive from false principles, that I can abandon them straightaway, and not tire myself out anymore in vain by embellishing them.

29 BERKELEY TO PERCIVAL

EP, BL Add. MS 47026, fol. 66–66v.

Trinity College, Dublin, 14 April 1711

Dear Sir,

   The very day I received the favour of your last, I returned you my thanks for the same in a letter of congratulation on that happy circumstance of your life, you were pleased to impart to me. Whether my letter came to your hands or no, I know not. I shall at present trouble you only with the perusal of the enclosed relation the facts it contains are attested in several letters from very good hands that were present at the Trial. Some of which I have seen. Particularly Dr. Coghil[142] Judge of the Perogative [*sic*] Court has received an account of the whole sent him by Dr. Tisdal[143] a very ingenious divine who was in Court while the evidence upon oath of several credible persons were given in. So that you may depend upon it this paper though but sorrily writ has nothing in it which was not sworn to and after the nicest examination thought true by the Court. The letters mention some other circumstances which still make the story more surprising, and are not to be accounted for without some preternatural power. This is certain that the eight women are condemned. The judges were Upton [and] Macartney, of whom the former is said to be greatly prejudiced against all belief of witches, and Dr. Tisdal (who had been a Fellow of our College) seems to me the most unlikely man in the world to be imposed on in an affair of that nature, into which he has strictly inquired. I know not what credit this is like[ly] to meet with in London. For my own part as I do not believe one in a thousand of these stories to be true, so neither on

[142] Marmaduk Coghill* (1673–1739).
[143] William Tisdall (1669–1735), Anglican clergyman and controversialist.

the other hand do I see sufficient grounds to conclude peremptorily against plain matter of fact well attested.

    I am

    etc.,

    G. Berkeley

30 BERKELEY TO PERCIVAL

EP, BL Add. MS 47026, fol. 69–69v.

Trinity College, Dublin, 3 June 1711

Dear Sir,

    I was given to expect that even this [*sic*?] I should have had an opportunity of returning you my thanks here by word of mouth, but missing of that I cannot forbear any longer troubling you with a letter to express my acknowledgments for the care you were pleased to take of that I sent to my Lord Pembroke.[144] I am very glad that your generous endeavours in behalf of our country have succeeded. Your friends here are well pleased upon their first finding by the printed notes that you stood up in opposition to the bill for a further impost on Irish yarn. I need not mention their sentiments on that occasion being persuaded that you think the inward satisfaction of having served your country a sufficient recompence for whatever trouble you were at on that account. This affair confirms me in a thought I formerly had, viz. that if some Irish gentlemen of good fortunes and generous inclinations would constantly reside in England, there to watch for the interest of their own country, they may at such conjunctures bring it far greater advantage than they could by spending their incomes at home.

    Dan. Dering[145] presents his humble service to you. He would be well in all respects if he had an employment suitable to his merit, since the late ministry did not. I hope the new will do something for him, they cannot place their favours on a more deserving young gentleman. I am

    Sir,

    Your most humble and affectionate servant,

    G: Berkeley

Pray give my service to your brother and to Mr. Clerke.[146]

---

[144] Thomas Herbert* (1656/57–1733), eighth Earl of Pembroke and fifth Earl of Montgomery.

[145] Daniel Dering* (?–1730).

[146] An unknown acquaintance of Berkeley's. There were many Clerkes in Ireland at the time.

31 BERKELEY TO PERCIVAL (DRAFT)[147]

BL Add. MS 39304, fol. 104v.

[Before 3 June 1711]

I [?] that to find this time I should have had an opportunity of returning you my thanks here by word of mouth, but failing of that I am obliged to trouble you with a line to express my acknowledgement for your care of my letter to the Lord Pembroke.[148] I am glad for you that your growing endeavors in behalf of our poor country have succeeded, your friends here were all very well pleased when first found by the printed notes that you stood up in opposition to the bill for a further impost on Irish yarn. I need not mention their sentiments on that occasion being sensible that you think the inward satisfaction of having served your country sufficient recompense for the trouble you were at on that account.

Since the Judges came up to town men have talked variously of the witches, it is said Judge Upton was for acquitting them and Judge Macartney and the jury for finding, which they accordingly did, guilty. I hear the afflicted woman is dead of her [disorders?] a sign she did not [feign?]. There was last [assizes?] at Cork a man convicted of murder by means of an apparition. And there are several other stories related with a wonderful confidence that I know not how to believe, I therefore shall not [trouble you with?] any account of them until I have the happiness of seeing you together with my Lady Percivale and your [young son] having here safely arrived in this kingdom. I wish you a refreshing voyage and am [. . .]

32 BERKELEY TO LE CLERC[149]

University of Amsterdam Library, Le Clerc Papers J3b.

14 July 1711

Celeberrimo Viro Johanni Clerico

[147] A draft of Letter 30, Percival to Berkeley, 3 June 1711. The letter is written in haste, with gaps and illegible words. I include it here because it contains content not present in the letter actually sent to Percival. Luce reprints the second half of the letter in a note (*Works*, vol. IX, pp. 15–16) with a few minor errors.

[148] Thomas Herbert* (1656/57–1733), eighth Earl of Pembroke and fifth Earl of Montgomery.

[149] Luce was only aware of the draft of this letter, which he published (*Works*, vol. VIII, pp. 49–50). That draft and translation follows (Letter 33). The front of the letter is addressed: "A Monsieur, Monsieur Jean Le Clerc Professeur en Theologie à Amsterdam." For additional details see Peter Bellemare and David Raynor, "Berkeley's Letters to Le Clerc (1711)," *Hermathena* 146 (1989): 7–23.

Georgius Berkeley SPD[150]

Nuper mihi in manus venit Bibliothecase tuae Selectae tomus vicesimus secundus cui insertam reperio Epitomen Tentaminis mei de Visione Anno 1709 editi. Porro te veritatis amantem ratus eumque adeo esse qui scripta tua quam emendatissiam velis prodire haud inique laturum spero si errores unum & alterum indicavero quas vel Typographo vel etiam tibi, Vir Doctissime, festinanti scilicet & multiplici literarum genere occupato excidisse non est quod quis admiretur.

p. 59 1.19 B.S.[151] pro plus convergens legere oportet moins divergens

p. 60 1.5 pro his verbis ce qui fait que nous appercevons la distance est premierement l'etressissement ou l'elargissement de la prunelle selon l'eloignement ou la proximite des objets, legendum ce qui fait que nous appercevons la distance est premierement la sensation qui accompagne l'etressissement ou l'elargissement de l'interval qui est entre les deux prunelles selon la proximite ou l'eloignement des objets.

p. 62 1.4 pro l'objet leg. le point visible.

p. 63 leguntur convergens & convergence pro divergens et divergence et vice versa usque ad 1.12.

Alios, siqui sunt, minoris notae lapsus facile praetermiserim; isti autem cum sensum a vero nimis quam dissentaneum lectori exhibeant, & proinde cogitata nostra apud eos qui Anglice non intelligunt erroris immerito possint arguere, necessum habui ut ad te scriberem, eo nempe fine ut Bibliothecae tuae parte illa quam typis proxime mandaturus es eorum emendatio inseratur, quod quin tu libenter feceris nullus dubito.

Animadversionibus utique tuis, quae extensionis & figurarum ideas abstractas spectant, quod sequitur duxi reponendum. Primum, ad id quod innuis p. 81, me viz. efformaturum ujusmodi ideas ope Intellectus puri si modo Facultatem istam caute distinxerim ab Imaginatione, respondeo me nullo modo posse effingere ideam abstractam Trianguli aut alius cujuscumque Figurae. Nec quidem capio qua ratione id exsequi quaeam distinguendo Intellectum purum (ut Metaphysici vulgo solent) ab Imaginatione, quod adhibita omnis mentis meae, qualiscunque tandem sit[152] illa aut quocunque nomine insignata, Vi ac. Facultate frustra saepe conatus fuerim. Secundo, etiamsi admittatur distinctio illa Intellectus tamen purus videtur versari solummodo circa res spirituales,

---

[150] i.e. Salutem Dicit Plurimum

[151] i.e. *Bibliothecase Selectae*, the *Bibliothèque Choisie* (Select Library) of Le Clerc.

[152] Raynor and Bellemare read "fit," which is understandable as Berkeley's "f's" and "s's" are often indistinguishable. The same letter formation for "s" occurs repeatedly in this piece, as with "solummodo" a few lines later. I thus correct to "sit," which I believe makes better sense of the text.

quae cognoscuntur per meditationem in mentem ipsam introversam, ideas vero ex Sensatione ortas, qualis est Extensio, nullatenus attingere. Id sane pro certissimo habeo, me non alias posse concipere rem ullam aut qualitatem sensibilem, adeoque nec Extensionem, quam sub imagine rei sensibilis: ut nec ulla mentis vi ideas earum rerum sensibilium disjungere distinctasque animo exhibere quae plane impossibile & repugnans sit ut distinctae ab invicem atque separatae sensum ingrediantur. Tertio illud praeterea animadvertendum est, quod aliud sit attendere ad unam tantum qualitatem, aliud, ejus ideam exclusa omni alia re aut qualitate in animo formare. Possum ego, exempli gratia, in Motus natura & legibus inquirendis, animum tantum ad ipsum motum praecipue advertere atque intendere, nequeo tamen illius ideam efformare quin simul mente comprehendatur etiam res mota. Porro haec uberius tractare supervacaneum faciunt quae disseruimus in Introductione, in Sect: 126 etc. libri de Principiis Cognitionis Humanae Anglice conscripti.

Quod reliquum est, ad ea quae habes p. 86 de objecto Geometriae Notandum, quod vox tangibilis duplicem admittat sensum, vel enim stricte sumitur pro eo duntaxat quod palpari manibusque attrectari possit: vel laxiori Significatu ita ut complectatur non modo res quae per Tactum utcumque percipi possint, ut Quies & Inane quae non sunt palpabiles, verum etiam ideas a mente ad similitudinem tactu perceptarum fictas. Cum igitur assero: Objectum Geometriae esse Extensionem Tangibilem, id posteriori sensu accipiendum est. Nimirum figura, angulus, linea, punctum, quae mente contemplatur Geometra, licet ipsa sub Sensum non cadant, tamen ad Tactum referuntur cui originem aliquo modo debent, quum per operationem mentis formentur ad speciem Idearum Tactui primitus impressarum. Vale, Vir Clarissime quodque te, intempestive forsan, Solicitare ausus sim aequi & boni consule.

Dabam in Academia juxta Dublinium sita, Julii die 14. 1711.

To the most distinguished Jean Le Clerc
George Berkeley sends his greetings[153]

The twenty-second volume of your *Bibliothèque Choisie*, containing an abstract of my *Essay on Vision* published in 1709, has recently come into my hands.

Knowing you as someone who loves truth so much that he wishes to publish his own writings in as faultless a state as possible, I hope that you will not take it amiss if I point out to you one or two errors which escaped the notice of your

---

[153] This translation deviates from that provided by Raynor and Bellemare in a few respects. As a general rule, this translation is more literal and follows the Latin grammar more closely at the expense of elegance.

typographer or (what would surprise nobody) of yourself, most learned Sir, who must evidently work quickly, engaged as you are in so many different directions in the literary field.

p. 59 1.19 of the *Bibliothèque Choisie. converging more* should read *diverging less.*

p. 60 1.5. Instead of the words *that make us perceive the distance, it is in the first place the contracting or the enlarging of the pupil according to the distance or proximity of the objects,* one should read *that make us perceive the distance, it is in the first place the sensation that accompanies the contracting or enlarging of the interval that is between the two pupils according to the proximity or the distance of the objects.*

p. 62 1.4. Instead of *the object* read: *a visible point.*

p. 63. *convergens & convergence* should be read instead of *divergens et divergence* and vice versa up to line 12.

If there are other faults of a minor kind, I shall easily let them pass. But I consider that these convey a sense which disagrees too much with the true one and that, as a result, readers who do not understand English might unjustly accuse my notions of error. I therefore thought it necessary to write to you so that these corrections could be inserted in the next issue of your *Bibliothèque* that you publish. I do not doubt but that you will agree to do so.

As for your remarks concerning the abstract ideas of extension and figure, I consider that I must answer the following.

First, to what you say on page 81, viz. that I could form that sort of idea by means of the pure intellect, if only I carefully distinguished this faculty from the imagination, I reply that I cannot in any way form an abstract idea of a triangle or of any other figure whatsoever. And I cannot understand in what manner I could achieve this by distinguishing (as metaphysicians commonly do) the intellect from the imagination, which is something that I have often attempted to achieve but to no avail, employing to that end the power and capacity of all my mind, whatever this may be or by whatever name one calls it.

Second, even if one admitted this distinction, it seems that the pure intellect has to do only with spiritual things, which are known through a meditation within the soul itself, and does not, by any means, pertain to ideas arising from sensation, for example extension. I regard it as most certain that I cannot conceive any thing or any sensible quality—and therefore extension—otherwise than as a representation of a sensible thing. Nor can I, by any power of the mind, separate the ideas from these sensible things and display them to the soul as things distinct from them. And it is plainly impossible and repugnant to reason that they enter the senses as distinct and separate from each other.

Third, it must also be remarked that it is one thing to think of one quality only, another to form its idea in the soul to the exclusion of any other thing or quality. I can, for example, while inquiring into the nature and the laws of motion, turn and direct the attention of my soul principally or exclusively towards motions itself, but I cannot form an idea of it without, at the same time, apprehending in my mind a thing which is moving.

Furthermore, my arguments set forth in the introduction, in section 126 etc. of my book *The Principles of Human Knowledge* make it superfluous to discuss this topic any further.

As for the rest, with respect to what you say on page 86 concerning the object of geometry, it must be noted that the word *tangible* admits of a double sense. In the strict sense, it designates only what can be stroked and touched by the hands. In a wider sense, it embraces not only things that can be perceived by touch in one way or another, but also ideas fashioned by the mind on the basis of things perceived by touch. So, when I assert that 'the object of geometry is tangible extension', this must be understood in the latter sense. Assuredly, figure, angle, line, point, (all objects) which geometers contemplate in their mind, although they themselves are not objects of sensory perception, are nevertheless referred to touch, to which, in some way, they owe their origin, when by an operation of the mind they are formed on the pattern of ideas that were originally imprinted by means of that sense.

Farewell, distinguished Sir, and I pray you to receive this perhaps importunate and unseasonable address with kindness.

Written in the Academy near Dublin, July 14, 1711

33 BERKELEY TO LE CLERC (DRAFT)

BL Add. MS 39304, fols. 102v, 103v, 105, 105r.

1711

Clarissime Vir,

Nuper ad hasce oras appulit Bibliothecae tuae Selectae Tomus vicesimus secundus, cui insertam reperio epitomen Tentaminis mei de Visione anno 1709 editi. Porro te veritatis amantem ratus adeo qui scripta tua quam emendatissima velis prodire, haud inique laturum spero, si errores unum alterumne indicavero, quos vel typographo vel etiam tibi, vir doctissime, festinanti scilicet et multiplici librorum [*sic*, laborum?] genere occupato, excidisse non est quod admirandum.

Alios si qui sint minoris notae lapsus facile praetermiserim, isti autem quos memoravi, cum sensum a vero nimis quam dissentaneum lectori exhibeant et proinde cogitata nostra apud eos qui anglice non intelligunt, erroris immerito possint arguere, necessarium habui ut ad te scriberem eo utique fine, ut Bibliothecae tuae parte illa, qua[m][154] proxime typis mandaturus es, corrigantur, quod quin tu libenter feceris, nullus [?] dubito.

P. 59, l. 19, B.S. (Bib. Sel.),[155] pro *plus convergens* legere oportet *minus divergens* v. S.6 Tentaminis de visione.

P. 60, l. 5, B.S. pro his verbis ce qui fait que nous appercevons la distance, est premierement l'etressissement ou l'elargissement de la prunelle selon l'eloignement ou la proximité des objets lege ce qui fait nous appercevons la distance, est premierement la sensation qui accompagne l'etressissement ou l'elargissemment de l'interval, qui est entre les deux prunelles selon la proximité ou l'eloignement des objects; v. S. [15?][156] Tentaminis.

P. [52?][157] l. 4 pro l'objet lege un point visible; v. S.34 Tentaminis.

P. 62[158] B.S. legitur convergens et convergence pro divergens et divergence et vice versa.

Animadversionibus utique tuis quae extensionis[159] et figurarum ideas [abstractas] spectant quod sequitur duxi reponendum.

Primum igitur ad id quod invenio p. 81 me utique efformaturum istius modi ideas ope intellectus puri, si modo eum caute disjunxerim ab imaginatione, respondeo me nullo modo posse effingere ideam abstractam trianguli aut aliuscujuscunque figurae. Nec quidem capio qua ratione id exsequi queam [*sic*, quaeam?] distinguendo intellectum purum (ut metaphysici vulgo solent) ab imaginatione, quod adhibita omni mentis meae, qualiscunque tandem sit aut quocunque nominee insigniatur, vi et facultate, frustra saepe conatus fuerim.

Secundo, etiamsi admittatur distinctio illa, tamen intellectus purus mihi videtur versari tantum circa res spirituales, quae cognoscuntur per reflexionem in ipsam animam, ideas vero ex sensatione ortas, qualis est extensio, nullatenus [?] attingere.

---

[154] Luce has "quam," the text has "qua" with a dash mark above the "a" and slightly to the right.

[155] i.e. *Bibliothecase Selectae*, the *Bibliothèque Choisie* (Select Library) of Le Clerc.

[156] Original text has "16," a mistake for "15."

[157] Original text has "62," a mistake for "52."

[158] Text immediately above (struck out) has "63."

[159] "abstractas" appears to be crossed out. The text above with "ideas abstractas" is corrupt and not to be trusted. The text cannot be clearly made out. Another word follows "ideas" but is not clear.

Tertio, illud praeterea animadvertendum est quod aliud sit attendere solummodo ad unam qualitatem, aliud ejus ideam exclusa omni alia re aut qualitate in animo formare; v.g. possum ego in motuum natura et legibus inquirendis animum tantum ad ipsum motum [praecipue?] advertere atque intendere, nequeo tamen illius ideam efformare, nisi simul mente comprehendatur etiam res mota. Id sane pro certissimo habeo me non alias [aliam?] posse concipere rem aut qualitatem sensibilem adeoque nec ipsam extensionem quam sub imagine rei sinsibilis, uti nec ulla mentis vi ideas earum rerum sensibilium disjungere distinctasque animo exhibere. Quae plane impossibile et repugnans sit ut sensum discretae ac invicem feriant atque ingrediantur.[160] Porro haec uberius tractare supervacaneum faciunt quae disseruimus in introductione, in sect 126 etc. libri de Principiis Cognitionis Humanae, qui haud ita pridem luce donatus est.

Quod reliquum est, ad ea quae, p. 76 habes de objecto geomentriae, notandum quod vox *tangibilis* duplicem admittat sensum vel enim sumitur stricte pro eo solummodo quod palpari aut manibus attrectari possit. Vel laxiori significatu ita ut complectatur non modo res quae per tactum actumque [utcumque?][161] percipi possint, ut quies et inane, quae nequeunt palpari, verum etiam ideas a mente ad similitudinem tactu perceptarum fictas. Cum igitur assero objectum geometriae esse extensionem tangibilem, id posteriori sensu accipiendum est. Nimirum figura, angulus, linea, punctum, quae mente contemplatur geometria, etsi ipsa sub sensum non cadant, tamen ad tactum referuntur, unde originem aliquot modo habent, quum per operationem mentis formentur ad speciem idearum tactui primitus impressarum.

Vale, Vir Clarissime, quodque te intempestive forsan solicitavimus, aequi et bone consule.

Most Illustrious Sir,

Recently there arrived on these shores the twenty-second volume of your Select Bibliography in which I find inserted the epitome of the 1709 edition of my *Essay on Vision*. Having earlier judged you to be so much a lover of truth that you would wish your writings to go forth as free from faults as possible, I hope that you will not at all bear it ill if I indicate one or another errors, which it is not

---

[160] Text has an "X" for an insertion starting "porro haec ..." *before* the paragraph starting "Quod reliquum." Luce places the insertion after the paragraph. The mistake is understandable as Berkeley adds with a quick division line the closing after this addition.

[161] In the letter actually sent to Le Clerc, Berkeley has "utcumque." I have left the translation of the draft with "actumque," but the change in meaning is significant.

surprising have slipped in, [attributable] to either typographical error or even to yourself, most learned man, making haste in the midst of so many labours.[162]

Even if I should have passed over other errors of minor note, those however that I have recounted, since they exhibit to the reader a sense so disagreeable to the truth and thus are able to make our thoughts clear with no fault of error to those who do not understand English, I have held it to be necessary to write to you by all means with this end, that in the part of your Library that you are about to send [for setting] in type, those things be corrected, a thing you would gladly do, I have no doubt.

P. 59, 1. 19, B.S. (Bib. Sel.), for *converging more* it is necessary to read *diverging less*. See S. 6 of Essay on Vision.

P. 60, 1. 5, B.S. For these words *that make us perceive the distance, it is in the first place the contracting or the enlarging of the pupil according to the distance or proximity of the objects* READ *that make us perceive the distance, it is in the first place the sensation that accompanies the contracting or enlarging of the interval that is between the two pupils according to the proximity or the distance of the objects*; see S. 15 of Essay.

P. 52, 1. 4. For the object READ a visible point; see S. 34 of Essay.

P. 62, B.S. *convergens* and *convergence* are read for *divergens* and *divergence*. I thought that what follows must by all means be replaced by your observations that look at both the abstract shape and abstract ideas of extension.[163]

First, therefore, to that which I find on page 81, [the idea] that I at any rate would shape ideas of that form with the support of the pure intellect, provided that I will have separated it cautiously away from the imagination, I respond that in no way am I able to fashion an abstract idea of a triangle or any other figure. Nor indeed do I take by any reasoning that thing I am able to follow by separating pure intellect (as the metaphysicians are usually accustomed [to do]) from imagination, on the grounds that with all of my mind having been applied, whatever kind [of thing] it [i.e. the abstract idea] be in the end or by whatever name it is distinguished, by power and mental capacity, in vain I have often tried.[164]

---

[162] Reading "laborum" for "librorum." The original might mean something like "making haste in working on so many books," but the Latin does not – aside from the word "librorum" – support this reading.

[163] Adding "et" between "figuram" and "ideas" to make sense of the text.

[164] The Latin is difficult and unclear. I have opted for a more literal – if ungainly – translation. One might object that "qualiscunque" is not neuter (and hence using "thing" is a mistranslation), but the word *ideas* is not neuter and the use of the English word *thing* is just for stylistic flow. The phrase *omni mentis meae* ("all of my mind") I treat, in the absence of a better translation, as a partitive genitive. Lucretius uses *omni* as a neuter noun to mean "the universe" or "everything" (here "all" as "the entirety") and I am following that construction. I can make no other good sense of the sentence.

Second, even if that distinction be admitted, a pure understanding seems to me to be turned so much around spiritual matters, which are known through reflection into the soul itself, that it [the pure intellect] does not at all reach the ideas that have arisen from sensation, just like extension.

Third, one must in addition pay attention to that thing which is something else, to attend to only one quality, another is to form in the mind an idea of it, every thing else or every quality excluded; for example, in inquiring about the laws and nature of things moving, I am able particularly to turn and direct my mind to attend to movement itself; I am nevertheless not able to form an idea of it unless at the same time the thing that has moved is comprehended by my mind. This of course I hold as most certain that I am not able to conceive another thing or a sensible quality and furthermore neither an extension itself as under the image of a sensible thing, so as to separate by any force of the mind the ideas of those sensible things and to exhibit them as distinct to the mind. Which ideas of sense it would be clearly impossible and repugnant, that they, separated and in turn, be at rest [idle] and in motion [commencing].[165] Hence they make it superfluous to treat these things more richly, the things we discussed in the introduction, in section 126, etc. of the book about the Principles of Human Knowledge, which not that long ago has been made public.

With respect to what is remaining, to those things that, on p. 76, you hold about the object of geometry, it must be noted that the term *tangibilis* admits of a double sense. For either it is taken strictly as that which alone can be stroked or touched [lit. "groped"] by hands, or [it is taken in] a wider meaning such that it embraces not only things that are able to be perceived through touch and through being moved,[166] but also [things] like quiet and emptiness, which are not able to be stroked, but even ideas invented by the mind to a likeness of things perceived by touch. When therefore I assert that an object of geometry is a tangible extension, this must be accepted in the latter sense. Truly a figure, an angle, a line, a point, which is contemplated geometrically by the mind, even if they themselves do fall under a sense, nevertheless they are referred to touch, whence they sometimes now have their origin, when they are formed through an operation of the mind to the appearance of ideas that are impressed on touch for the first time.

---

[165] Another difficult sentence. I treat the opening "quae" as a relative pronoun pushing forward to the *ut* clause (i.e. reading *quae* like *illa*). I have no clear sense of how to read "sensum" in the sentence without doing violence to the grammar. Fortunately we have the more polished final version (see Letter 32).

[166] See above note about the Latin. Berkeley corrects "actumque" to "utcumque" in the letter he actually sends to Le Clerc.

Farewell, most illustrious Sir, and what we have perhaps asked of you in an untimely way, consider evenly and kindly.

34 BERKELEY TO PERCIVAL

EP, BL Add. MS 47026, fols. 120–21v.

Trinity College, Dublin, 17 May 1712

Dear Sir,

Your friends here are beholding to Mrs. Parker[167] for letting us know by her letter to Mrs. Donnellan that you are all arrived safe at your journey's end. And I am very glad that the worst accident we have to condole with you upon, is your being obliged to make a meal at the barracks on cold meat. Burton[168] I find pleases beyond expectation; and I imagine it myself at this time one of the finest places in the world. And indeed the month of May with the much more enlivening circumstance of good company would make a more indifferent place delicious. Dunckarney, however, is not without its beauties; and as I believe no news can be more agreeable to you than that which brings some account of its lonely inhabitants, I shall give a narrative of a visit I made them this evening.

I took a solitary walk that way, and upon my coming was informed that the little Lady and Esquire were withdrawn to their apartment. Miss indeed was in her dishabille, but for all that I was admitted to visit her, and she entertained me with a familiarity and frankness greater than I had observed before. Both her complexion and carriage are altered for the better, the one being very fair, and the other free from those stately and affected airs which methought she had in Capell Street.[169] In a word she is grown a very charming and conversible Lady, and seemed not at all displeased at my visit. But good manners obliged me to shorten it, so after a little discourse about her absent friends I left her, and my entertainment fell to the young Esquire's share who acquitted himself very obligingly. We took a turn in the gallery and then walked in the gardens and avenue. You must not now imagine a child held by leading strings that has not a word to say, but a brisk young gentleman who walks alone and bears his part in conversation. I told what news I had heard of my Lady,[170] Mrs. Parker and

---

[167] Mary Parker* (1692–1731).
[168] John Percival's* house and estate in County Cork, Ireland.
[169] John Percival* (1683–1748) owned a house on Capell Street in Dublin.
[170] Catherine (*née* Parker) Percival* (1687/88–1749).

yourself, with which he was very much pleased. But I observed his discourse ran chiefly on my Lady, whom he often mentioned, and seemed to long for her company to that degree, that if you still think of making the same stay you intended, I don't know but that he may send you a letter to desire you to hasten your return. He shall not want an amanuensis to write what he dictates in case he cannot do it himself.

I must not forget to tell you the following instance of his sagacity. As we were walking in the avenue Mr. Percival being taken with the sight of a fine silver holly must needs touch it, but as soon as he felt the prickles drew back his hand. And upon my insulting him and asking whether he would venture to touch it again, he very orderly borrowed my handkerchief and putting it about his hand touched the holly two or three times, to let me see he had wit enough to find out a way of doing what I dared him to, without any inconvenience to his fingers.

He kisses still with open mouth, and has the same comical sneer with his nose. A child that shows such early and pregnant signs of good nature and good sense it is impossible I should not have a fondness for, even though he had not been your son. Yesterday I heard of a flaming beauty lately come from England who in Mrs. Parker's absence attracts the eyes of our gentleman, but I foresee her reign is not to last longer than four months at farthest, and it is in the power of some at Burton to make it as much shorter as they please. But I forget myself, you are a grave married man, and I a sort of monk or recluse in a college; it doth not therefore become me to talk to you of gallantry. So I conclude.

    Sir,

Your most affectionate and humble servant,

Geo: Berkeley

Pray give my humble service to my Lady, and Mrs. Parker. All friends are as well here as you can suppose them to be in the absence of so much good company.

35 BERKELEY TO PERCIVAL

EP, BL Add. MS 47026, fol. 126–26v.

Trinity College, Dublin, 5 June 1712

Dear Sir,

You are grown so distrustful that I doubt you won't believe me, if I should tell you that I no sooner informed your son of the caution you gave him against women, but he fell a laughing, said it was all banter, and swore he would never make his father a liar (alluding, you may suppose, to the predictions you used to make of him in Capel Street), and upon that fell to kissing his sister and nurses with all the eagerness imaginable. That he kissed them heartily is literally true. But what more pretty things he said and did, how he called himself brave boy, and played on the fiddle etc. you shall know nothing of from me, since you gave so little to the adventure of the handkerchief, which was really as I reported it. Miss has two teeth in sight, and is every day so much altered for the better, both in features and complexion, that I am sure she will appear a perfect little stranger to all of you when you see her next. Both she and her brother, being very pretty, hearty give their duty to you, their mother, and their aunt.

Dan. Dering[171] and I design to visit your paradise, and are sure of finding angels there, notwithstanding what you say of their rarity. In plain English we are agreed to go down to Burton together, and rejoice with the good company there. I give you this timely warning that you may hang up two hammocks in the barn against our coming. I never lie in a feather bed in the college, and before now have made a very comfortable shift with a hammock. I conclude in haste. Sir

> Your most humble and affecionate servant,
> Geo: Berkeley

Last nigh[t] a servant of one Mr. Alcock over the water hanged himself for the love of a coachman's daughter.

36 BERKELEY TO PERCIVAL

EP, BL Add. MS 47026, fols. 127–28.

Trinity College, Dublin, 18 August 1712

Dear Sir,

On Saturday night we came safe to town. I know not whether it is worth while to tell you, that the day I set out, being already half dead with the thoughts of leaving so much good company, it seemed as if the weather would have given the finishing stroke to my life; but the two following days were more favourable. Last night's pacquets have brought nothing remarkable that I can find, though

---

[171] Daniel Dering* (?–1730).

at my first coming I met with a hot rumour in everybody's mouth of an action between the Dutch and French, whereof the event was uncertain. It is believed by some of our college politicians that the Duke of Ormond[172] stays in Flanders with a design to compel the Dutch to a peace in case they obstinately stand out. His Duchess, I hear, has been complimented by the Queen and ministers upon his Grace's conduct in securing Ghent etc. There is some talk of a triple alliance between Britain, France and Sweden. I am informed by a gentlemen of my acquaintance just come from London that the account of my Lord Albemarle's[173] defeat was publicly cried about the streets by the title of good and joyful news. God grant that we have not a war with the Dutch.

I should have sent you the 4th part of *John Bull*[174] but that Dan. Dering[175] told me he sent it you by last Tuesday's post. My Lord Bolingbroke[176] is expected suddenly from France, whether [whither?] I suppose you know he lately went along with Mr. Prior.[177] The other day two malefactors were publicly pilloried and afterwards burnt alive in Felster's shop[178] for having offered some affront to the memory of King William,[179] which for ever ought to be held (at least by all Protestants of these nations) glorious and immortal as are his actions.

My best news I keep for the last. The two children are both very well. Master was ill indeed but is at present very easy, and his eye teeth are in sight which makes us think him past all danger. I gave your and my Lady's blessing to him; told him you were all well and designed to see him soon. He has made a new sort of a language for himself which I am not acquainted with, and as he is neither yet a perfect master of the English tongue, it is impossible for us exactly to understand one another. However, what with words and what with other signs and tokens he let me see his meaning. I am afraid to tell you the secret, but if I do, be sure do not let my Lady know it, least it might prevent her ever spending another summer at Burton. To be plain the child seems not to care a farthing for you both. Long absence seems to have produced in him a perfect indifference for his parents. And a little longer stay will probably make him forget you quite. In all other respects he is the same (with improvement) that he was before; the

---

[172] James Butler* (1665–1745), second Duke of Ormond.
[173] Arnold Joost van Keppel (1669/70–1718), first Earl of Albemarle. Keppel commanded the allied garrison at Denain which was stormed and overwhelmed by the French under Marshal Villars on 24 March 1712.
[174] *Law is a Bottomless Pit, or the History of John Bull*, a serial that appeared in four parts in 1712. The work is attributed to John Arbuthnot* (1667–1735).
[175] Daniel Dering* (?–1730).
[176] Saint-John Henry* (1678–1751), first Viscount Bolingbroke.
[177] Matthew Prior (1664–1721), poet and diplomat.
[178] A large building on Lower Abbey Street in Dublin.
[179] William III (1650–1702).

same pleasant, sensible, good natured boy. Miss Kitty at first sight methought was grown unwieldily fat, but upon examination I found it to be a plump and firm flesh, which in a very sufficient quantity covers her cheeks and arms, betokening much nourishment and good digestion. She is as brisk and lively as you could wish, and is without dispute the most agreeable young lady that I have seen on this side Burton. Nevertheless if I may be allowed to be a judge of beauty I should give it master for features and miss for complection.

Robin[180] stays impatiently for my letter which makes me conclude in haste with my most humble service to my Lady and Mrs. Parker.[181] Dear Sir,

Your most humble and most affectionate servant,

G: Berkeley

My humble service to Mr. Brereton.[182] I delivered his letter, his wife and family are all well. I have made his excuses for not coming up.

37 BERKELEY TO AN ENGLISHMAN

BL Add. MS 39306, fols. 16–17.

c. 1712

Some thoughts upon alliances in war in a letter to a friend.

Sir,

I do not at all wonder that you or any true Englishman should be no less jealous for the honour than the safety of his country, and offended at anything which hath the face of baseness or treachery however advantageous it may be thought to the public; nor, by consequence, that you should scrupulously inquire into the justice of a separate peace, as being apprehensive the necessity of our affairs, together with the backwardness of the allies, may possibly oblige our Ministry to enter upon some such measures. But I was surprised that you should write to me to know my thoughts concerning an affair of that nature since you cannot be ignorant how foreign it must needs be as well to my retired way of life, as that particular sort of employment I have always chosen. And as I am an utter stranger to the treatys and engagements between Her Majesty[183]

---

[180] Likely a reference to Berkeley's brother Robert (1698–1787).
[181] Mary Parker* (1692–1731).
[182] Brereton is one of the Breretons of Carrigslaney, an agent for Percival.
[183] Queen Anne* (1665–1714).

and the high allies and but little skilled in the interests of the several states of
Europe; so I am persuaded there is nothing more misbecoming and unworthy a
wise man than to pretend to give a judgment on things he is not acquainted
with. Nevertheless since I hold myself obliged to show a particular regard to
your commands, I shall give you[184] all the satisfaction I am able; by laying down
some general theoremes [sic] and reasonings upon the sacredness of treatys and
alliances between nations; and considering upon or on what accounts they may
be broken without guilt. The application of which to the present juncture of
affairs I leave to yourself who having an exact knowledge of the engagements
and interests of your country and want nothing requisite to the forming a fine
and impartial judgment on the point you are pleased to consult me upon, when
you have inquired into the moral part of the question and considered in[185] [. . .]
the obligations imposed by reason and religion on a [. . .] engaged in an alliance
for the prosecution of a war [. . .] Therefore with all the brevity and plainness I
can, I lay it [. . .] in the first place for a fundamental axiom, that no Law of [. . .]
ought to be violated either [. . . for] the obtaining any [advantage or escaping any]
inconvenience whatever [. . . of . . . to observe in . . . do . . . obtain . . . equal force
our . . . the public intercourse . . . between nation and nation.]

From these principles it clearly follows that Public Faith ought not to be
sacrificed to private regards, nor even to the most pressing [?][186] of a whole
People. The violation therefore of a compact with foreign states can never be
justified upon any pretext of that kind. Hence one nation having solemnly
entered into articles of alliance with another, in case they afterwards perceive
it highly for their advantage to break these articles; yet a breach upon that score
must certainly be looked upon as unjust and dishonourable. Nor doth it alter the
case that the alliance having been made under a former ministry is disliked and
condemned by the succeeding. For though the administration of affairs pass
through several hands, yet the Prince and nation continue still the same. Every
ministry therefore is in duty bound to preserve sacred and intire the faith and
honour of their Prince or country by standing firm to all alliances contracted
under former ministrys. But with this difference, that in case the evils attending
such an alliance shall appear to be fortuitous, or such as, at the making of it,
could not have been foreseen, then the conditions of that disadvantageous
alliance ought to be fulfilled at the public charge; whereas if the Treaty shall
appear originally and in itself prejudicial to the Public, then the fortunes of

---

[184] Luce has "them" in error for "you."
[185] The remainder of the paragraph is defective.
[186] Illegible, torn page.

those ministers who made it ought to go towards defraying the expenses which, through rashness or treachery, they had engaged their country in.

Hitherto I have proceeded upon supposition that the foundation of the alliance was just, or included nothing contrary to the laws of nature and religion. But in case several States enter into an agreement for commencing and carrying on the war upon unjust motives, [no sooner] shall any of those States be satisfied of the injustice of the cause on which the alliance is grounded, but they may with honour look upon themselves as disengaged from it. For example, suppose a parcel of Popish Potentates should, out of a pretence of doing right to the Pretender, engage in a war for placing him upon the throne of Great Britain, and some one of them was afterwards convinced [?][187]

It is also to be esteemed an unwarrantable procedure in case divers Potentates enter into a confederate war against an adjacent State for no other reason but because they apprehended it may otherwise become too powerful, and consequently too formidable a neighbour. For example, suppose the Dutch, jealous of that accession of strength to the British nation which will follow upon its union with Hannover, should engage themselves and friends in a war in order to force us to alter our succession; we would, I presume, think this unlawful, and that it was the duty of any one of the confederates, so soon as he became sensible of the injustice of his cause, to cease from all hostilities, and (in case his allies were for continuing them) to enter into a separate peace with us. The truth of these positions is plain from the two principles at first laid down.

Further, it cannot be denied that one party may, without consent of the rest, break off from an alliance in war originally founded upon just and honourable motives, upon conviction that the ends for which the war was begun and in consideration whereof it was esteemed just, are sufficiently answered; although his allies, whether blinded by passion or finding their advantage in carrying on the war, or by what principle soever actuated, should not concur with him in the same judgment. For it is no excuse for a man's acting against his conscience that he made a bargain to do so. But here you'll demand what must be thought in case it was a fundamental article of the alliance, that no one party should hearken to proposals of peace without consent of the rest. I answer that any such engagement is in itself absolutely void, forasmuch as it is sinful, and what no Prince or State can lawfully enter into, it being in effect no less than binding themselves to the commission of murder, rapine, sacrilege, and of violence, so long as it shall seem good to their [. . .] what else I beseech you is war abstracted from the

---

[187] Manuscript defective for eight lines.

[…] but a complication of all these [?][188] one the most hateful […] But as it is the […] I can do for you […] I hope you will […] it to be a […] of that respect with which I am […]

P.S.: Another obvious indisputable case there is which absolves a party from fulfilling the conditions of any contract, namely, when those with whom the contract was made fail to perform their part of it. Lastly, in case two or more States, for their mutual security, enter into a league to deprive a neighbouring Prince of some part of his possessions and add them unto those of another in order to constitute a ballance of Power. Allowing the grounds whereon the war is founded to be just, yet if, during the progress of it, the Prince whose territories were to be enlarged shall, by some unexpected turn, grow far more great and powerful than he was at the making of the treaty, it should seem the aforesaid [*sic*] States are disengaged from their contract to each other, which, having been originally by all parties introduced and understood only as a means to obtain a ballance of power, can never be of force to oblige them to act for a direct contrary purpose.

38 BERKELEY TO PERCIVAL

EP, BL Add. MS 47027, fols. 8v–11.

London, 26 January 1712/13

Dear Sir John,

In a fortnight after I left Dublin I arrived here having made easy journeys and stayed some time at Chester. The road from Coventry to London was very bad, the rest of the way tolerable enough. I was surprised to find the country in the depth of winter look incomparably pleasanter than most parts of Ireland in midsummer. But if the country outdid my expectation, the towns fell short of it; even London itself seems to exceed Dublin not so much in the stateliness or beauty of its buildings as in extent. I wrote from Hol[l]yhead to an acquaintance of mine to provide me a lodging, which he did in the same house with the Provost[189] and Mr. Molyneux.[190] We generally see one another in the morning,

---

[188] Manuscript defective for three or four lines.
[189] Benjamin Pratt (1669–1721) was Provost of Trinity College, Dublin, but spent much of his time in London, perhaps attempting to smooth relations between the college and the government.
[190] Samuel Molyneux* (1689–1728).

but for the rest of the day are dispersed about the town, and I loving early hours am gone to bed before either of them come home at night. Upon my first coming I was confined for some days, till my portmanteaux came by carriage from Chester. In the meantime Mr. Clerke[191] hearing I was in town came to see me, and next day engaged Charles Dering[192] and me to dine at his house with him, which is very neat and convenient. He is as I always found him very obliging and good natured, and seems in as good health as ever I knew him. He went with me to Mr. Southwell,[193] who received me very civilly, and with great willingness introduced me two days since to my Lord Pembroke,[194] who is a man perfectly good natured as well as very learned, and with whom I have the prospect of passing some part of my time as much to my satisfaction as anything can be in the absence of my friends in Ireland. As I troubled you to ask this favour of Mr. Southwell, so I must again trouble you to thank him for it the first time you write to him. There is lately published a very bold and pernicious book entitled a *Discourse on Free Thinking*.[195] I hear the printer of it is put into Newgate, as is likewise a woman for selling a ballad on the Duke D'Aumont[196] as being a wine merchant.

For want of other news you must give me leave to tell you a very remarkable story I heard the other morning from the Provost and Mr. Molyneux. Mr. Tickel,[197] fellow of Oxford, an ingenious, credible and sober person, author of the poem on the approaching peace, gave them the following account. That there is in a forest in Hampshire an oak which buds and shoots forth leaves every Christmas day. A year or two ago he went himself to make the experiment. He saw it in a light night about two hours before day, at which time it had not the least appearance of bud or leaf, but when day came was covered with both: several of the leaves about as large as sixpence he plucked and carried to Oxford, where above forty persons saw them. A gentleman, who was present when the Provost and Mr. Molyneux were telling this fact, added he had seen some of the leaves gathered by another.

The first news I heard upon coming to town was that Mr. Steele[198] did me the honour to desire to be acquainted with me: upon which I have been to see him. He is confined with the gout, and is, as I am informed, writing a play since he gave over

---

[191] An unknown acquaintance of Berkeley's. There were many Clerkes in Ireland at the time.
[192] Charles Dering* (?-?).
[193] Edward Southwell* (1671-1730).
[194] Thomas Herbert* (1656/57-1733), eighth Earl of Pembroke and fifth Earl of Montgomery.
[195] Authored by Anthony Collins (1676-1729), a deist and friend of John Locke.
[196] Luce reports this Duke as the French Ambassador in London. *Works*, vol. IX, p. 21.
[197] Thomas Tickell (1686-1740). He authored the poem "On the Prospect of Peace" in 1711.
[198] Richard Steele* (1672-1729).

the *Spectator[s]*.[199] This gentleman is extremely civil and obliging, and I propose no small satisfaction in the conversation of him and his ingenious friends, which as an encouragement he tells me are to be met with at his house. The Bishop of Dromore[200] is dead: yesterday in the afternoon the French Ambassador's house was burnt down to the ground by the carelessness of his servants. They say fine pictures and other moveables of the Duke of Powis's[201] are burnt in it, being locked up in the garrets to the value of forty thousand pounds. The other day dining at a tavern with two or three Irish clergymen, I found it a very difficult matter to persuade them you were no Whig: I venture however to send you the enclosed *Examiners*,[202] as well knowing you are no enemy to wit and humour, though in a Tory. Of late they are written by some new hand, and much better than formerly; I speak not with regard to the party debates, but the style and spirit, which is all we moderate sort of men mind in those sort of papers.

Your most affectionate & most obliged humble servant,

Geo. Berkeley

This day I dined again at Mr. Clerk's[203] where we drank your health. He talks of seeing you in Ireland this summer, and says Dublin is the finest city in the world.

My letters are directed to the Pall Mall Coffee-House in the Pall Mall.*

39 BERKELEY TO PERCIVAL[204]

EP, BL Add. Ms 47027, fols. 12–14.

London, 23 February 1712/13

Dear Sir John,

This night Mr. Bligh[205] is to have a ball at the late Duke Hamilton's[206] house in St. James's Square. The Marlborough family and one Mrs. Warburton

---

[199] One of the several newpapers founded and run by Steele. The *Spectator* ended in December 1712.

[200] Tobias Pullen (1648–1713), bishop of Dromore since 1695. He was succeeded by John Stearne* (1660–1745) on 13 May 1713.

[201] William Herbert (1657/61?–1745), second Marquess of Powis and Jacobite second Duke of Powis, Jacobite sympathizer. Herbert built Powis House in Great Ormond Street, London. Leased in 1712 to the French ambassador, the Duc d'Aumont, it mysteriously burned down on 26 January 1713.

[202] A Tory weekly. Jonathan Swift* (1667–1745) wrote a number of articles for it.

[203] An unknown acquaintance of Berkeley's. There were many Clerkes in Ireland at the time.

[204] In the margin a note says this letter was answered 14 March, but that letter is not present in the letterbook.

[205] John Bligh* (Blithe) (1687–1728).

[206] James Hamilton (1658–1712), fourth Duke of Hamilton and first Duke of Brandon. He died on 15 November 1712 after fatally wounding his adversary, Lord Mohun (1675–1712), in a duel.

and Mrs. Duncomb make part of his company. Sir Philip[207] is at length come to town. I find in him that frank good humour and other good qualities which might be expected in my Lady's and Mrs. Parker's brother:[208] he is very obliging.

Mr. Addison[209] and Mr. Steele[210] (and so far as I can find, the rest of that party) seem entirely persuaded there is a design for bringing over the Pretender; they think everything looks that way, and particularly three of the best Papist officers, Lieutenant General Mackoni, Major General Laules, and Brigadier Skelton, being now all in London. Laules, Mr. Addison assured me, was discovered by an officer at the Queen's birth night, the other two came over, one on pretence of sueing for his wife's or sister's fortune, the other of being in love with a lady here. All these are Irishmen, that have followed the fortunes of King James. I have heard another general officer of the same gang mentioned as being here, but forgot his name; and that the Duke of Berwick's[211] aunt was known to say, her nephew would soon be in London. Some Jacobite Tories too whom I have happened to converse with seem full of the same expectations. I must desire you will not quote me for this, not caring to be thought the spreader of such news. But I tell this to my Lady, Mrs. Parker, and yourself, that you may take proper measures against that time.

The value you always shewed for the *Spectator* makes me think it neither impertinent nor unwelcome news to tell you that by his mother-in-law's death he [i.e. Richard Steele] is come into an estate of five hundred pounds a year; the same day his wife was brought to bed of a son. Before she lay down the poor man told me he was in great pain and put to a thousand little shifts to conceal her mother's desperate illness from her. The tender concern he showed on that occasion, and what I have observed in another good friend of mine, makes me imagine the best men are always the best husbands. I told Mr. Steele if he neglects to resume his writings, the world will look on it as the effects of his growing rich. But he says this addition to his fortune will rather encourage him to exert himself more than ever; and I am the apter to believe him, because there appears in his natural temper something very generous and a great benevolence to mankind. One instance of it is his kind and friendly behaviour

---

[207] Philip Parker* (1682–1741).
[208] Mary Parker* (1692–1731).
[209] Joseph Addison* (1672–1719).
[210] Richard Steele* (1672–1729).
[211] James FitzJames (1670–1734), Duke of Berwick-upon-Tweed.

to me (even though he has heard I am a Tory). I have dined frequently at his house in Bloomsbury Square, which is handsome and neatly furnished. His table, servants, coach and everything is very gentile [genteel, *sic*], and in appearance above his fortune before this new acquisition. His conversation is very cheerful and abounds with wit and good sense. Somebody (I know not who) had given him my treatise of the *Principles of Human Knowledge* and that was the ground of his inclination to my acquaintance. For my part I should reckon it a sufficient recompence of my pains in writing it, that it gave me some share in the friendship of so worthy a man. But though the conversation of him and other new friends is very agreeable, yet I assure you it all falls short of Capel Street.[212]

I hear a sudden and general rumour that the peace has proposed[213] the seals and will be proclaimed next week. News from your fireside (would you but oblige me so far) would be infinitely more acceptable than from any court in Europe. My most humble service to my Lady and Mrs. Parker. I am

Sir

Your most affectionate and obliged humble servant,

G. B.

40 BERKELEY TO PERCIVAL

EP, BL Add. ms 47027, fols. 15–16v.

London, 7 March 1712/13

Dear Sir John,

I know not by what accident yours of the 11th February came not to my hands till the last post. Your presages of my good fortune I look on rather as kind wishes that deserve my thanks, than real prophecies that may raise my hopes. Happiness, whether in a high or low degree, is the same thing. And I desire no more; and this perhaps is more within anybody's reach than is vulgarly imagined.

In my last I gave you some intimation of Mr. Bligh's[214] ball. The Marlborough's family being there disgraced him with the Tories, his friends at

---

[212] Percival's house in Dublin was on Capel Street.
[213] Rand has "passed," but the text is clear, likely a copyist's error.
[214] John Bligh* (Blithe) (1687–1728).

the Cocoa-tree,[215] whither he constantly goes. And soon after it there was an advertisement published in one of the printed papers, giving an account that the Duchess of Marlborough[216] had left a hundred guineas to be laid out in a ball at Duke Hamilton's house, as a triumph over his Grace's memory.[217] This affront, which robbed him of the glory of his ball, could not but be uneasy to Mr. Bligh. Dr. Swift[218] (whom I met by chance at my Lord Pembroke's[219] two nights agone) told me Mr. Bligh had applied to the author of the *Post-boy*, to publish contradiction to his former advertisement; but that he refused to do it without the Duchess of Hamilton's consent. Mr. Bligh prevailed with Dr. Swift to introduce him to the Duchess in order to obtain it. But her Grace being a smart woman, and the Dr. (as he says himself) very ill naturedly taking part with her against Mr. Bligh, they proved to him the unreasonableness of his request, and sent him away in no small confusion.

It is expected we shall have the peace proclaimed this week. Both Whigs and Tories give out either that six new peers are to be created, or more than that number of young noblemen called up into the House of Lords.

You will soon hear of Mr. Steele[220] under the character of the *Guardian*; he designs his paper shall come out every day as the *Spectator*. He is likewise projecting a noble entertainment for persons of a refined taste. It is chiefly to consist of the finest pieces of eloquence translated from the Greek and Latin authors. They will be accompanied with the best music suited to raise those passions that are proper to the occasion. Pieces of poetry will be there recited. These informations I have from Mr. Steele himself. I have seen the place designed for these performances: it is in York buildings, and he has been at no small expence to embellish with all imaginable decorations. It is by much the finest chamber I have seen, and will contain seats for a select company of two [hundred][221] persons of the best quality and taste, who are to be subscribers. I had last night a very ingenious new poem upon Windsor Forest given me by the author, Mr. Pope.[222] This gentleman is a Papist, but a man of excellent wit and learning, and one of those Mr. Steele mentions in his last paper as having writ some of the *Spectators*.

---

[215] The Cocoa-tree Club was a chocolate house and social club frequented by Tories.

[216] Sarah (*née* Jenyns) Churchill, duchess of Marlborough (1660–1744).

[217] James Hamilton (1658–1712), fourth Duke of Hamilton and first Duke of Brandon. He died on 15 November 1712 after fatally wounding his adversary, Lord Mohun (1675–1712), in a duel.

[218] Jonathan Swift* (1667–1745).

[219] Thomas Herbert* (1656–1733), eighth Earl of Pembroke.

[220] Richard Steele* (1672–1729).

[221] Rand corrects from "two" to "two hundred" (and Luce follows Rand), a reasonable correction of a likely copyist error.

[222] Alexander Pope* (1688–1744).

I am extremely honoured by my Lady and Mrs. Parker[223] that they have not quite forgot me. Pray give my dearest[224] humble service to them, and let them know that notwithstanding the great distance between us they are every day present to my thoughts. Sir Philip[225] and Mr. Clerke[226] are very well. We were a day or two agone at Mr. Clerke's remembering our friends in Ireland. I am

> Dear Sir John
>
> Your most humble & affectionate servant,
>
> G. Berkeley

41 MISATHEUS (BERKELEY) TO THE GUARDIAN

Guardian, 9 (21 March 1713). Works, vol. VII, pp. 175–76.

16 March 1713

Sir,

By your paper of Saturday last you give the Town hopes that you will dedicate that day to religion. You could not begin it better than by warning your pupils of the poison vented under a pretence to *free-thinking*. If you can spare room in your next Saturday's paper for a few lines on the same subject, these are at your disposal.

I happened to be present at a publick conversation of some of the defenders of this *Discourse of Free-thinking*[227] and others that differed from them; where I had the diversion of hearing the same men in one breath persuade us to freedom of thought, and in the next offer to demonstrate that we had no freedom in anything. One would think men should blush to find themselves entangled in a greater contradiction than any the *Discourse* ridicules. This principle of *free fatality* or *necessary liberty* is a worthy fundamental of the new sect; and indeed this opinion is in evidence and clearness so nearly related to *transubstantiation* that the same genius seems requisite for either. It is fit the world should know how far reason abandons men that would employ it against religion; which intention, I hope, justifies this trouble from,

> Sir, your hearty well-wisher,
>
> Misatheus

---

[223] Mary Parker* (1692–1731).
[224] Rand has "best," but the first letter is clearly a *d*.
[225] Philip Parker* (1682–1741).
[226] An unknown acquaintance of Berkeley's.
[227] Authored by Anthony Collins (1676–1729).

42 BERKELEY TO PERCIVAL[228]

EP, BL Add. MS 47027, fols. 20–21v.

London, 27 March 1712/13

Dear Sir,

I received your letter about three days since. Your opinion of Mr. Steele[229] I take to be very just, and am persuaded a man of his discernment and insight into men will know how to value an acquaintance so much to be courted as that you design to honour him with. His wit, natural good sense, generous sentiments, and enterprising genius, with a peculiar delicacy and easiness of writing, seem those qualities which distinguish Mr. Steele. Mr. Addison[230] has the same talents in a high degree, and is likewise a great philosopher, having applied himself to speculative studies more than any of the wits that I know.

After what I have formerly told you of the apprehensions those gentlemen had, I think myself obliged to let you know that they are now all over. Mr. Steele having told me this week that he now imagines my Lord Treasurer[231] had no design of bringing in the Pretender,[232] and in case he had, that he is persuaded he could never perform it; and this morning I breakfasted with Mr. Addison at Dr. Swift's[233] lodging. His coming in whilst I was there, and the good temper he showed, was construed by me as a sign of an approaching coalition of parties, Mr. Addison being more earnest in the Whig cause than Mr. Steele (the former having quitted an employment, rather than hold it under the Tories, which by a little compliance he might have done), and there having passed a coldness, if not a direct breach, between those two gentlemen and Dr. Swift on the score of politics. Dr. Swift's wit[234] is admired by both of them, and indeed by his greatest enemies; and if I were not afraid of disobliging my Lady and Mrs. Parker[235] I should tell you that I think him one of the best natured and agreeable men in the world.

Mr. Steele's entertainment at York buildings only waits the finishing of two pictures, the one of truth, the other of eloquence, which are designed as part of the ornaments of the place where it is to be. He tells me he has had some discourse

---

[228] A note in Percival's letterbook says answered 21 April, but there is no record of that response.
[229] Richard Steele* (1672–1729).
[230] Joseph Addison* (1672–1719).
[231] Robert Harley* (1661–1724), first Earl of Oxford.
[232] James Francis Edward Stuart* (1688–1766).
[233] Jonathan Swift* (1667–1745).
[234] Rand mistakenly reads "will" for "wit."
[235] Mary Parker* (1692–1731).

with the Lord Treasurer relating to it, and talks as if he would engage my Lord Treasurer in his project, designing that it shall comprehend both Whigs and Tories. A play of Mr. Steele's, which was expected, he has now put off to next winter. But *Cato*, a most noble play of Mr. Addison's, and the only one he writ, is to be acted in Easter week. The town is full of expectation of it, the boxes being already bespoke, and he designing to give all the benefit away among the actors in proportion to their performing. I would send you the *Guardians* and two very fine poems, one of them being writ by an Irish Clergyman, Dr. Parnell,[236] if you would direct me how.

My humble service to my Lady and Mrs. Parker.

Your most humble servant,

G. Berkeley

43 BERKELEY TO PERCIVAL

EP, BL Add. MS 47027, fols. 25v–27v.

London, 16 April 1713

Dear Sir,

If I had sooner known of my Lady's being delivered of a daughter,[237] I should sooner have congratulated you upon that good fortune. I say this that you might not think me insensible of your happiness, though you were not pleased to impart it to me.

For public news I suppose the public papers sufficiently inform you as to that. However I shall tell you two or three particulars which I believe you have not heard. About three weeks ago my Lord Treasurer[238] was at a meeting of Whigs at my Lord Halifax's[239] house. The Duke of Argyle[240] and some other Tory Lords who were jealous of this taxed my Lord Treasurer with it in a private company, and were curious to know what was the business of that conference; to which he answered no more than this: What! am I not fit to be trusted? I would not be understood to apprehend a change by this, but only tell it as an instance of that man's secrecy, and to show that he is not on such violent terms with those of the other party as may be imagined. I was informed of this by a gentleman that was

---

[236] Thomas Parnell (1679–1718), poet.

[237] Catherine "Kitty" Percival (1712–48), born 11 January 1712 in Dublin.

[238] Robert Harley* (1661–1724), first Earl of Oxford.

[239] Charles Montagu (1661–1715), first Earl of Halifax, founder of the Bank of England.

[240] John Campbell* (1680–1743), second Duke of Argyll.

present at what passed between my Lord and the Duke of Argyle etc. The same person is very acquainted with all the ministers and with my Lady Masham[241] and declared to me that he never heard the least expression drop from any of them (and he makes one in almost all their partys of private meetings) that looked like an inclination to the Pretender.

On Tuesday last Mr. Addison's[242] play entitled *Cato* was acted the first time. I am informed the front boxes were all bespoke for nine days, a fortnight before the play was acted. I was present with Mr. Addison, and two or three more friends in a side box, where we had a table and two or three flasks of burgundy and champagne, with which the author (who is a very sober man) thought it necessary to support his spirits in the concern he was then under; and indeed it was a pleasant refreshment to us all between the acts. He has performed a very difficult task with great success, having introduced the noblest ideas of virtue and religion upon the stage with the greatest applause, and in the fullest audience that ever was known. The actors were at the expence of new habits, which were very magnificent, and Mr. Addison takes no part of the profit, which will be very great, to himself. Some parts of the prologue, which were written by Mr. Pope,[243] a Tory and even a Papist, were hissed, being thought to savour Whiggism, but the clap got much the hiss. My Lord Harley,[244] who sat in the next box to us, was observed to clap as loud as any in the house all the time of the play. Though some Tories imagine his play to have an ill design, yet I am persuaded you are not so violent as to be displeased at the good success of an author (whose aim is to reform the stage) because his hero was thought to be a Roman Whig.

This day I dined at Dr. Arbuthnot's[245] lodging in the Queen's palace. The Dr. read part of a letter from a friend in France, which gave an account that the French king is now forming a company of merchants to whom he will grant great privileges and encouragements to import into his kingdom sixty thousand head of black cattle alive. The gentleman who wrote the letter (whose name I am obliged not to mention) says that he was offered to be made director of this affair but that he refused it, being of the opinion it would prove very prejudicial to Her Majesty's dominions, and particularly to Ireland, whence they propose to import the greatest part of the cattle. This looks as if the stock of France was exhausted, and perhaps it may not be amiss if the Council of Ireland would enter on some measures to prevent the exhausting the stock of their own country by supplying France.

---

[241] Abigail Masham (?–1734), cousin of Sarah, the Duchess of Marlborough.
[242] Joseph Addison* (1672–1719).
[243] Alexander Pope* (1688–1744).
[244] Robert Harley* (1661–1724), first Earl of Oxford.
[245] John Arbuthnot* (1667–1735).

This Dr. Arbuthnot is the first proselyte I have made by the Treatise I came over to print, which will be soon published. His wit you have an instance of in his *Art of Political Lying*, and the tracts of *John Bull* of which he is the author. He is the Queen's domestic physician, and in great esteem with the whole Court. Nor is he less valuable for his learning, being a great philosopher, and reckoned among the first mathematicians of the age. Besides which he has likewise the character of very uncommon virtue and probity.

D. Dering[246] is so full of business that I can hardly ever see him. My humble service to my Lady and Mrs. Parker.[247] Pray inform me of the children in your next.

> Your most humble servant,
> G. Berkeley

44 ULYSSES COSMOPOLITA (BERKELEY) TO IRONSIDE[248]

Guardian, 35 (21 April 1713).

21 April 1713

To Nestor Ironside, Esq.

Sir,

I am a man who ha[s] spent great part of that time in rambling through foreign countries, which young gentlemen usually pass at the university; by which course of life, although I have acquired no small insight into the manners and conversation of men, yet I could not make proportionable advances in the way of science and speculation. In my return through France, as I was one day setting forth this my case to a certain gentleman of that nation with whom I had contracted a friendship, after some pause, he conducted me into his closet, and, opening a little amber cabinet, took from thence a small box of snuff, which he said was given him by an uncle of his, the author of *The Voyage to the World of Descartes*;[249] and, with many professions of gratitude and affection, made me a

---

[246] Daniel Dering* (?–1730).

[247] Mary Parker* (1692–1731).

[248] This letter and the next (Letter 45) may be treated as one extended letter in two parts.

[249] *Voyage du Monde de Descartes* (Paris, 1690) was a Jesuit parody of Cartesian philosophy by G. Daniel. It was translated into English and published as *Voyage to the World of Cartesius* in 1692.

present of it, telling me at the same time, that he knew no readier way to furnish and adorn a mind with knowledge in the arts and sciences than that same snuff rightly applied.

You must know, said he, that Descartes was the first who discovered a certain part of the brain, called by anatomists the *pineal gland*, to be the immediate receptacle of the soul, where she is affected with all sorts of perceptions, and exerts all her operations by the intercourse of the animal spirits which run through the nerves that are thence extended to all parts of the body. He added, that the same philosopher having considered the body as a machine or piece of clockwork, which performed all the vital operations without the concurrence of the will, began to think a way may be found out for separating the soul for some time from the body, without any injury to the latter; and that, after much meditation on that subject, the above-mentioned virtuoso composed the snuff he then gave me; which, if taken in a certain quantity, would not fail to disengage my soul from my body. Your soul (continued he) being at liberty to transport herself with a thought wherever she pleases, may enter into the *pineal gland* of the most learned philosopher, and, being so placed, become spectator of all the ideas in his mind, which would instruct her in a much less time than the usual methods. I returned him thanks, and accepted his present, and with it a paper of directions.

You may imagine it was no small improvement and diversion to pass my time in the *pineal glands* of philosophers, poets, beaux, mathematicians, ladies, and statesmen. One while to trace a theorem in mathematics through a long labyrinth of intricate turns and subtilties of thought; another, to be conscious of the sublime ideas and comprehensive views of a philosopher, without any fatigue or wasting of my own spirits. Sometimes, to wander through perfumed groves, or enamelled meadows, in the fancy of a poet: At others, to be present when a battle or a storm raged, or a glittering palace rose in his imagination; or to behold the pleasures of a country life, the passion of a generous love, or the warmth of devotion wrought up to rapture. Or (to use the words of a very ingenious author) to

Behold the raptures which a writer knows,
When in his breast a vein of fancy glows,
Behold his business while he works the mine,
Behold his temper when he sees it shine.[250]

---

[250] From Thomas Parnell's (1679–1718) *Essay on the Different Stiles of Poetry*, published anonymously in 1713.

These gave me inconceivable pleasure. Nor was it an unpleasant entertainment sometimes to descend from these sublime and magnificent ideas to the impertinences of a beau, the dry schemes of a coffee-house politician, or the tender images in the mind of a young lady. And as, in order to frame a right idea of human happiness, I thought it expedient to make a trial of the various manners wherein men of different pursuits were affected; I one day entered into the pineal gland of a certain person who seemed very fit to give me an insight into all that which constitutes the happiness of him who is called a *man of pleasure*. But I found myself not a little disappointed in my notion of the pleasures which attend a voluptuary, who has shaken off the restraints of reason.

His intellectuals, I observed, were grown unserviceable by too little use, and his senses were decayed and worn out by too much. That perfect inaction of the higher powers prevented appetite in prompting him to sensual gratifications; and the outrunning natural appetite produced a loathing instead of a pleasure. I there beheld the intemperate cravings of youth, without the enjoyments of it; and the weakness of old age, without its tranquility. When the passions were teased and roused by some powerful object, the effect was, not to delight or sooth the mind, but to torture it between the returning extremes of appetite and satiety. I saw a wretch racked, at the same time, with a painful remembrance of past miscarriages, a distaste of the present objects that solicit his senses, and a secret dread of futurity. And I could see no manner of relief or comfort in the soul of this miserable man, but what consisted in preventing his cure, by inflaming his passions and suppressing his reason. But though it must be owned he had almost quenched that light which his Creator had set up in his soul, yet in spite of all his efforts, I observed at certain seasons frequent flashes of remorse strike through the gloom, and interrupt that satisfaction he enjoyed in hiding his own deformities from himself.

I was also present at the original formation or production of a certain book in the mind of a Free-thinker, and, believing it may be not unacceptable to let you into the secret manner and internal principles by which that phaenomenon was formed, I shall in my next give you an account of it. I am, in the mean time,

your most obedient humble servant,
Ulysses Cosmopolita

N.B.: Mr. Ironside has lately received out of France ten pound averdupoise weight of this philosophical snuff, and gives notice that he will make use of it, in order to distinguish the real from the professed sentiments of all persons of eminence in court, city, town, and country.

45 ULYSSES COSMOPOLITA (BERKELEY) TO IRONSIDE[251]

Guardian, *39 (25 April 1713).*

25 April 1713

Mr. Ironside,

On the 11th day of October, in the year 1712, having left my body locked up safe in my study, I repaired to the Grecian coffee-house, where, ent[e]ring into the pineal gland of a certain eminent Free-thinker, I made directly to the highest part of it, which is the seat of the Understanding, expecting to find there a comprehensive knowledge of all things human and divine; but, to my no small astonishment, I found the place narrower than ordinary, insomuch that there was not any room for a miracle, prophesy, or *separate spirit*.

This obliged me to descend a story lower, into the imagination, which I found larger, indeed, but cold and comfortless. I discovered *Prejudice* in the figure of a woman standing in a corner, with her eyes close shut, and her fore-fingers stuck in her ears; many words in a confused order, but spoken with great emphasis, issued from her mouth. These being condensed by the cold-ness of the place, formed a sort of mist, through which methought I saw a great castle with a fortification cast round it, and a tower adjoining to it that through the windows appeared to be filled with racks and halters. Beneath the castle I could discern vast dungeons, and all about it lay scattered the bones of men. It seemed to be garrisoned by certain men in black, of gigantic size, and most terrific forms. But, as I drew near, the terror of the appearance vanished, and the castle I found to be only a church, whose steeple with its clock and bell-ropes was mistaken for a tower filled with racks and halters. The terrible giants in black shrunk into a few innocent clergymen. The dungeons were turned into vaults designed only for the habitation of the dead, and the fortification proved to be a churchyard, with some scattered bones in it, and a plain stone wall round it.

[251] This letter and the previous one (Letter 44) may be treated as one extended letter in two parts. Ironside writes as a preamble in the *Guardian*, "My correspondent, who has acquired the faculty of entring into other men's thoughts, having, in pursuance to a former letter, sent me an account of certain useful discoveries he has made by the help of that invention, I shall communicate the same to the public in this paper."

I had not been long here before my curiosity was raised by a loud noise that I heard in the inferior region. Descending thither I found a mob of the passions assembled in a riotous manner. Their tumultuary proceedings soon convinced me, that they affected a democracy. After much noise and wrangle, they at length all hearkened to *Vanity*, who proposed the raising a great army of notions, which she offered to lead against those dreadful phantoms in the imagination that had occasioned all this uproar.

Away posted *Vanity*, and I after her, to the store-house of ideas; where I beheld a great number of lifeless notions confusedly thrown together, but upon the approach of *Vanity* they began to crawl. Here were to be seen, among other odd things, sleeping deities, corporeal spirits, and worlds formed by chance; with an endless variety of heathen notions, the most irregular and grotesque imaginable. And with these were jumbled several of Christian extraction; but such was the dress and light they were put in, and their features were so distorted, that they looked little better than heathens. There was likewise assembled no small number of phantoms in strange habits, who proved to be idolatrous priests of different nations. *Vanity* gave the word, and straightway the *Talopoins*, *Faquirs*, *Bramines* and *Bonzes* drew up in a body. The right wing consisted of ancient heathen notions, and the left of Christians naturalized. All these together, for numbers, composed a very formidable army; but the precipitation of *Vanity* was so great, and such was their own inbred aversion to the tyranny of rules and discipline, that they seemed rather a confused rabble than a regular army. I could, nevertheless, observe, that they all agreed in a squinting look, or cast of their eyes towards a certain person in a masque, who was placed in the centre, and whom by sure signs and tokens I discovered to be *Atheism*.

Vanity had no sooner led her forces into the imagination, but she resolved upon storming the castle, and giving no quarter. They began the assault with a loud outcry and great confusion, I, for my part, made the best of my way and re-entered my own lodging. Some time after, inquiring at a bookseller's for *A Discourse on Free-thinking*, which had made some noise, I met the representatives of all those notions drawn up in the same confused order upon paper. Sage *Nestor*, I am

your most obedient humble servant,
Ulysses Cosmopolita

N.B.: I went round the table, but could not find a wit or mathematician among them.

46 BERKELEY TO PERCIVAL

EP, BL Add. MS 47027, fols. 31–32v.

London, 7 May 1713

Dear Sir,

I am very glad to hear that Miss has pleased the world so well upon her first appearance in it, and foresee there is not a pair in the Queen's dominions to whom the public will have greater obligations for propagating a healthy and beautiful race, than to my Lady[252] and yourself.

By the account I gave you in my last, I did not apprehend that the French would be able to rival us in our beef trade, but the danger that I and others apprehended from their project was, that the exporting so many head of black cattle out of Ireland might lessen the stock there, and by that means occasion an effect in its consequences much more prejudicial to the kingdom, than the present pistoles they would import might be of advantage to it.

Mr. Molyneux[253] has been this considerable time gone for Utrecht, whence he designs to continue his travels into Italy etc., and Mr. Bligh[254] is gone to France.

Mr. Addison's[255] play has taken wonderfully, they have acted it now almost a month, and would I believe act it a month longer were it not that Mrs. Oldfield[256] cannot hold out any longer, having had for several nights past, as I am informed, a midwife behind the scenes, which is surely very unbecoming the character of Cato's daughter. I hear likewise that the principal players are resolved for the future to reform the stage, and suffer nothing to be repeated there, which the most virtuous persons might not hear, being now convinced by experience that no play ever drew a greater concourse of people, than the most virtuous.

Pray let my Lady and Mrs. Parker[257] know that I converse much with Whigs. The very day on which the peace was proclaimed, instead of associating with Tories, I dined with several of the other party at Dr. Garth's,[258] where we drank the Duke of Marlborough's[259] health, though they had not the heart to speak one word against the peace, and indeed the spirit of the Whigs seems quite broken, and is not likely to recover.

[252] Catherine (*née* Parker) Percival* (1687/88–1749).
[253] Samuel Molyneux* (1689–1728).
[254] John Bligh* (Blithe) (1687–1728).
[255] Joseph Addison* (1672–1719).
[256] Ann Oldfield (1683–1730), actress.
[257] Mary Parker* (1692–1731).
[258] Dr. Samuel Garth (1661–1719), Whig physician and poet.
[259] John Churchill* (1650–1722), first Duke of Marlborough.

I believe, as you do, that I shall stay longer here than I at first designed, and am much obliged to you for your kind offer, but, I thank God, that way of life which best suits with my circumstances is not disagreeable to my inclinations. There is here a Lord of my name,[260] a man of letters and a very worthy man, from whom I have received great civilities; I dine two or three times a week at his table, and there are several other places where I am invited, which lightens my expence and makes it easier living here than I expected. I saw Sir Philip Parker[261] yesterday. He is resolved upon going to Ireland the latter end of this or the beginning of next month. My humble service to my Lady and Mrs. Parker.

I am, Dear Sir,

Your most obliged & most humble servant,

G. Berkeley

47 PERCIVAL TO BERKELEY

EP, BL Add. MS 47027, fols. 33v–34v.

Dublin, 14 May 1713

Dear Mr. Berk[e]ley,

I hear your new book is printed though not yet published, and that your opinion has gained ground among the learned, that Mr. Addison[262] is come over to you, and now what seemed shocking at first is become so familiar that others envy you the discovery and make it their own. This is a great progress for so short a time, and will I fear make you think England a more kindly soil for such productions than the country of your birth. However, we on this side will insist on it that the plant is our own, and owes her sprouting up so quick in England, not so much to the nature of that soil, as to the advantage of being transplanted into fresh ground. So if you come back to us altered in your taste and sense of things, we will still pride ourselves that you are of Irish growth, and any improvement you receive shall be owing only to the new ideas raised in you, which your own native genius has by reflection turned to good use, not in the excellency of things that offer themselves. So the rude ore has nothing in appearance delightful or useful till an artist by his skill extracts the silver.

---

[260] William Berkeley (?–1741), fourth Baron Berkeley of Stratton. Lord Berkeley was master of the rolls in Ireland between 1696 and 1731 and held political office as chancellor of the Duchy of Lancaster (1710–14) and as first lord of trade (1714–15). Berkeley dedicates the *Three Dialogues Between Hylas and Philonous* to Lord Berkeley.

[261] Philip Parker* (1682–1741).

[262] Joseph Addison* (1672–1719).

You have now an opportunity of gratifying one piece of curiosity which I have heard you very inquisitive about when on this side, I mean the surprise of a person born blind, when made to see. One Grant,[263] an oculist, has put out advertisement of his art this way, with whom I believe you would find satisfaction in discoursing.

I have desired Daniel Dering[264] when he comes to bring me a perspective glass five feet long, and beg you will assist him in the choice of a good one, to be bought of the best artist that way. I am

Sir etc.

To Mr. Berk[e]ley in London.

48 BERKELEY TO PERCIVAL

EP, BL Add. MS 47027, fols. 36v–38.

London, 2 June 1713

Dear Sir,

Your letter wherein you desire me to assist Mr. Daniel Dering[265] in the choice of a telescope for you came to my hands after his departure for Ireland. If in that or any other affair you will lay your commands upon me, I hope I need not tell you that I should be glad to serve you. As to what you mention of a dispute on foot here, concerning the invention of some notions that I have published, I do not know anything which might give ground for that report, unless it be that a clergyman of Wiltshire[266] has lately put forth a treatise, wherein he advances something which had been published three years before in my *Treatise concerning the Principles of Human Knowledge*. D. Dering brings you one of the books I printed the other day. I shall be very glad to hear your opinion of it, and that you thought it worth your perusal. I have discoursed with Mr. Addison,[267] Dr. Smalridge,[268] and several others since my coming hither, upon the points I have endeavoured to introduce into the world. I find them to be men of clear understandings and great candour.

---

[263] Roger Grant (?–1724). Grant, known as a Baptist preacher, proclaimed himself an "oculist" after having lost an eye himself while serving as a soldier. He published a broadsheet in 1712 claiming miracle cures to improve sight; Percival is presumably referring to this advertisement.

[264] Daniel Dering* (?–1730).

[265] Daniel Dering* (?–1730).

[266] A reference to Arthur Collier (1680–1732), philosopher and clergyman. Collier published *Clavis Universalis* in 1713, where he defends a version of immaterialism. He might well have read Berkeley, but a manuscript of the *Clavis* has been found dated January 1708 – before the appearance of Berkeley's own works. Collier studied both Malebranche and Norris, so it is not unreasonable to suppose that any similarities are attributable to a common indebtedness to Malebranche.

[267] Joseph Addison* (1672–1719).

[268] George Smalridge* (1662–1719).

Having mentioned Dr. Smalridge I cannot but take notice to you that I think myself very happy in the acquaintance I have made with him. He is a man no less amiable for his cheerfulness of temper and good nature, than he is to be respected for his piety and learning. He and Bishop Atterbury[269] are mentioned for the Bishopric of Rochester and Deanery of Westminster, which go together. If Atterbury is preferred before him, people will look on it as owing to a division between that Dean and the Canons of Christchurch, Oxon, which the government is willing to put an end to.

The Scotch are in a great ferment, occasioned by the malt tax, insomuch that they have proposed the breaking of the Union. And it is now in the mouth of everyone that the Duke of Argyle[270] and the rest of them are fallen off from the Court interest. It is reported that they had lately a meeting with the Whigs at the Duke of Devonshire's,[271] wherein they promised to vote with them for bringing over the heir of Hanover, and running down the Treaty of Commerce, in case the Whigs would join them in taking off the malt tax. This trafficking for votes looks very dishonourable. Love of their country is pretended to be the motive that stirs up the Scots, but others think it is love of places and pensions which they propose to get by bullying the Court.

My most humble service to my Lady and Mrs. Parker.[272]

I am, in haste,

Your most humble & affectionate servant,

George Berkeley

49 IRONSIDE TO A GENTLEMAN (BERKELEY)[273]

Guardian, 40 (24 June 1713).

23 June 1713

Sir,

I have received the favour of yours with the enclosed, which made up the papers of the two last days. I cannot but look upon myself with great contempt

---

[269] Francis Atterbury* (1663–1732).

[270] John Campbell* (1680–1743), second Duke of Argyll.

[271] William Cavendish (1670/71–1729), second Duke of Devonshire, politician and art collector.

[272] Mary Parker* (1692–1731).

[273] Ironside writes as a preamble: "I shall end this paper with a letter I have just now written to a gentleman, whose writings are often inserted in the *Guardian* without deviation of one tittle from what he sends me."

and mortification, when I reflect that I have thrown away more hours than you have lived, though you so much excel me in everything for which I would live. Till I knew you, I thought it the privilege of angels only to be very knowing and very innocent. In the warmth of youth to be capable of such abstracted and virtuous reflexions (with a suitable life) as those with which you entertain yourself, is the utmost of human perfection and felicity. The greatest honour I can conceive done to another, is when an elder does reverence to a younger, though that younger is not distinguished above him by fortune. Your contempt of pleasure, riches, and honour, will crown you with them all, and I wish you them, not for your own sake, but for the reason which only would make them eligible by yourself, the good of others.

I am, dearest youth,

your friend and admirer,

Nestor Ironside

50 PERCIVAL TO BERKELEY

EP, BL Add. MS 47027, fols. 39v–41.

Dublin, 18 July 1713

Dear Sir,

I have directed this to London, though I believe you are now at Oxford, but my letter might miss you there.

I hope you will be so kind as to give us some account of the Act,[274] and how that noble University has entertained you, where the aspect of the place and way of life is different from anything I believe you have seen before.

You will not want that I should inform you of what passed two days ago in your college in relation to the expulsion and degrading of Forbes.[275] Therefore I will say no more but give you some sense of the matter, that as far as the master's attempt

---

[274] A reference to the Ceremony of Inception, or Commencement, at which degrees are conferred.

[275] The reference is to Edward Forbes, who graduated BA from Trinity College, Dublin on 7 July 1705 and MA from Trinity on 10 July 1708. At the Proctor's Feast the day before the 1708 Commencements, the health of King William was proposed and Forbes not only refused to honor the toast, he insulted the sensibilities of those present by proposing a toast to a notorious robber executed in Dublin. That same month, on 21 July 1708, Forbes was publicly stripped of his degrees and expelled from the college. The event caused considerable debate as to the administration of the college and who had what powers. The senate of the college sought to reverse the sentence of degradation on multiple occasions over the succeeding years. There is no record of Berkeley commenting on the Forbes case.

could though in consequence reflect on the memory of King William and countenance a Jacobite principle, I rejoice that they miscarried, for I am still, as I hope ever to be, a grateful acknowledger of that man's services to our religion and liberties.

I heard the other day from a collegian that you have writ some friends word, you do not intend to come back, and he said if you did not come in four months, you of course would lose your fellowship, unless the Queen[276] gave you liberty in that point. Perhaps the late advancement of two junior fellows to be seniors will make you think it worth your while not to quit the college, you are so near a senior fellowship, but if you are otherwise determined, I shall not doubt but it is on a very good account, and I shall be very glad to hear of your advancement in England.

I can now tell you I have read your last book through and through,[277] and I think with as much application as I ever did any. The new method you took by way of dialogue, I am satisfied has made your meaning much easier understood, and was the properest course you could use in such an argument, where prejudice against the novelty of it was sure to raise numberless objections that could not anyway so easy as by dialogue be either made or answered. It is not common for men possessed of a new opinion to raise so many arguments against it as you have done, whether it be for want of ingenuity, and a partiality to themselves, that they won't set their notions in all lights to be viewed, or else because they are blinded, and really do not perceive the weight and number of reasons against them; but I speak with all sincerity, I am equally surprised at the number of objections you bring and the satisfactory answers you give afterwards, and I declare I am much more of your opinion than I was before. The least I can say is, that your notion is as probable as that you argue against, and when prejudice is wore off it must bear down the balance, towards which there is nothing contributes more than arguing the point, as I did lately on one occasion, where finding I was able to make my party good, though I had not then gone through your book, I began to think it unreasonable to favour an old opinion more than a new one, when there was as much to say for the one as the other, and at least equal difficulties against both.

I hear Dr. Swift[278] has said you have not made a convert of Dr. Arbuthnot.[279]

In short, prejudice to the understanding is like a mist to the sight, the fault is not in the object, neither is it in the eye, but a thick vapour arises from the irregularity of our wills which obscures for a while the things we would see, till the sunshine of reason disperses it.

---

[276] Queen Anne* (1665–1714).
[277] Berkeley published *Three Dialogues Between Hylas and Philonous* in 1713.
[278] Jonathan Swift* (1667–1745).
[279] John Arbuthnot* (1667–1735).

I have writ you a long letter, and it is time to conclude. I am
   etc.,
   J. Percival

My wife and sister desire their services, and because they know you wish us all well, bid me tell you the children are all well and thriving.

51 BERKELEY TO PERCIVAL

EP, BL Add. MS 47027, fols. 41v–42v.

Oxford, 19 July 1713

Dear Sir,

I have been now almost a month in this town and think it to be the most delightful place that I have ever seen, as well as for the pleasantness of its situation, as that great number of ancient and modern buildings which have a very agreeable effect on my eye, though I came from London and visited Hampton Court and Windsor by the way.

It may perhaps be some entertainment to give you an account of the solemnity with which the Act[280] has been celebrated in this place. For several days together we have had the best music of all kinds in the theatre performed by the most eminent persons of London, from the Opera, the Queen's Chapel etc., joined with some belonging to the choirs of Oxford; and with the music there were intermixed public exercises as disputations in the several faculties, speeches, declamations, and verses. These performances drew together a great concourse both from London and the country, amongst whom were several foreigners, particularly about thirty Frenchmen of the Ambassador's company, who (it is reported) were all robbed by one single highwayman as they were coming from London, who is since taken. The town was so crowded that lodgings at other times not worth half a crown were set for a guinea the week. It was computed that at once there were two thousand ladies in the theatre. During the time of the Act and since, there was nothing but feasting and music in the several colleges. Plays are acted every night, and the town is filled with puppet-shows and other the like diversions. But there is no part of the entertainment so agreeable to me as the conversation of Dr. Smalridge,[281] who is in all respects a

---

[280] A reference to the Ceremony of Inception, or Commencement, at which degrees are conferred. See Letter 50.
[281] George Smalridge* (1662–1719).

most excellent person. Two days since he was installed Dean of Christ Church. The same day a young gentleman of Christ Church College was found drowned in the public house of office. He fell in about four days before, through the holes which were too wide, and by some groans that were heard it is computed that he lived about five hours in that miserable condition.

The weather is extremely bad, I think no better than we had last summer at Burton. And indeed in this particular I have been very much disappointed ever since my coming into England.

My most humble respects to my Lady, Mrs. Parker,[282] your little son and daughters. I should be glad to hear how Mr. Johnny speaks, and what he says. If you favour me with a line, direct to Mr. Ives's over against All Souls College,

> I am
> Sir
> Your most humble & affectionate servant,
> G. Berkeley

52 BERKELEY TO PERCIVAL[283]

EP, BL Add. MS 47027, fols. 43–44.

Oxford, 7 August 1713

Dear Sir,

It makes me have a better opinion of my book that you have thought it worth your while to read it through, and not dislike the notions it contains the more for having attended to them. As it was my intention to conceal or smother nothing that made against me I endeavoured to place all objections in the fairest light, and if either you or any other ingenious friend will communicate any which are not answered, I shall not fail to consider them with all the impartiality I can.

As to what you write of Dr. Arbuthnot's[284] not being of my opinion, it is true there has been some difference between us concerning some notions relating to the necessity of the laws of nature, but this does not touch the main point of the non-existence of what philosophers call material substance, against which he has acknowledged he can object nothing.

---

[282] Mary Parker* (1692–1731).
[283] A note in Percival's letterbook indicates this letter was answered on 9 September 1713 (Letter 54).
[284] John Arbuthnot* (1667–1735).

I cannot imagine what should give occasion to the report of my not designing to go back for Ireland, since I have never written one word to that purpose to any friend there. I thank you for your kind concern for my advancement in the world, though I assure you it is not any prospect of that kind that detains me here. The steps I have taken since my coming hither, having been rather in order to make some acquaintance with men of merit, than to engage myself in the interests of those in power. Besides the greatest satisfaction which I proposed by living in England, I am utterly disappointed in, I mean fair weather, which we have had as little of here as ever I knew in the worst season in Ireland. And this circumstance makes me more in love with my own country than I was before. There is another motive which would give the preference in my thoughts to Ireland, viz. the conversation of yourself and the good company you have with you; but when I consider it is likely you will spend as much of your time here as there, I look on that point as making for neither side. The more I think on it, the more I am persuaded that my happiness will not consist in riches and advancement. If I could prosecute my studies in health and tranquility, that would make me as happy as I expect to be in this life, but in the College I enjoyed neither in that degree I do at present.

Pray give my most humble service to my Lady and Mrs. Parker,[285] and her nephew and nieces. I am, Dear Sir,

> Your most affectionate & most obliged humble servant,
> Geo. Berkeley

53 BERKELEY TO PERCIVAL

EP, BL Add. MS 47027, fols. 46–47.

London, 27 August 1713

Dear Sir,

Last night I came hither from Oxford. I could not without some regret leave a place which I had found so entertaining, on account of the pleasant situation, healthy air, magnificent buildings, and good company, all which I enjoyed the last fortnight of my being there with much better relish than I had done before, the weather having been during that time very fair, without which I find nothing can be agreeable to me. But the far greater affliction that I sustained about this time twelvemonth in leaving Burton[286] made this seem a small

---

[285] Mary Parker* (1692–1731).
[286] John Percival's* home and estate in County Cork.

misfortune. The first news I heard upon my coming to town was that two or three nights since Mr. Bligh[287] was married to the Lady Theodosia Hide,[288] daughter of the Earl of Clarendon.[289] I am told she is a great beauty, and has to her fortune about two thousand pound per annum: but I believe this is magnified. She is Baroness of Clifton, which title will descend to her son. I went to see him this morning when it was past ten o'clock, but he was not then stirring. Mr. Bligh has not been above ten days come from France, so that the match must have been very sudden. The Provost[290] who knows Lady Theodosia says she is of a very brisk and lively temper. I hardly find anyone that I used to converse with in town. But I was obliged to come here in order to solicit a licence for absence from the College,[291] at the Secretary's Office, the house thinking themselves obliged to put me to the expence and trouble of it. Mr. Clerke[292] I am informed went yesterday to the Bath. Pray give my humble respects to my Lady, Mrs Parker,[293] Sir Philip,[294] and the little pledges of your and my Lady's love. I am

Dear Sir,

Your most humble & most affectionate servant,

G. Berkeley

54 PERCIVAL TO BERKELEY

EP, BL Add. ms 47027, fols. 47v–49.

Dublin, 10 September 1713

Dear Mr. Berkeley,

I have two of yours lying by me to answer; in the first you desired I would let you know how my children come on in understanding; to which I answer that (in the first place) you could not enquire of one that minded children less than I. My wife[295] I believe may be able to say a thousand finer things of them than my poor observations can furnish you with; however to answer in some measure

---

[287] John Bligh* (Blithe) (1687–1728).

[288] Theodosia Hide (Hyde) (1695–1722). She married Bligh on 24 August 1713.

[289] Edward Hyde, third Earl of Clarendon (1661–1724).

[290] Benjamin Pratt (1669–1721). He was provost of Trinity College, Dublin from 1710 to 1717.

[291] Berkeley's leave of absence from the college and his duties there was set to expire. Berkeley sought (and obtained) royal permission to continue to hold his fellowship *in absentia*, renewed every two years. He renewed the permissions five times with royal letters dated 9 September 1713, 9 September 1715, 17 August 1717, 6 May 1719, and 6 May 1721.

[292] An unknown acquaintance of Berkeley.

[293] Mary Parker* (1692–1731).

[294] Philip Parker* (1682–1741).

[295] Catherine (*née* Parker) Percival* (1687/88–1749).

your desire, I will let you know that all three are generally taken to be handsome and lively children. We think they show good nature, because they're always kissing one another; we think Johnny will make a wise man, because he makes remarks & holds his tongue, that Kitty will prove a well bred, affable & sociable Lady, because she is always curtseying & dancing; & lastly that little Molly will be the occasion of forty duels.

And now to leave children, & talk of men & their wise actions, I must tell you that Mr. Blith[296] has occasioned as much discourse here as he could wish. We have cut out a Peerage for him, & the sale of his Irish Estate; he must now be taken notice of; let him look to his actions. I am very sorry that you are put to the trouble of suing for further leave to be absent;[297] I know it must be a charge, pray command me in it; you know I am ready & desirous to serve you.

The great thing that now employs heads & tongues is the treaty of commerce; I own I don't like it & believe I never shall. I have read a great deal concerning the trade with France, & think it pernicious, model it how you will, or rather how you can, for things are not now in your power. The Papists here are insolent, some have said, if the Whigs & we fall out, the Papists will be on our side; a great comfort that. The great cause of the city was heard last Friday before our board, & it went against the aldermen in favour of the Lord Mayor:[298] we sat from 10 in in [sic] the morning till 11 at night without rising.

My wife & sister are in good health, & much your humble servants, as is

> Dear Mr. Berk[e]ley
> Your affectionate friend,
> John Percival

55 BERKELEY TO PERCIVAL

EP, BL Add. MS 47027, fols. 50v–51v.

London, 2 October 1713

Dear Sir,

The description you favoured me with of your little offspring was very entertaining, and though slightly amiable has, I am persuaded, nothing of a father's fondness in it: what shall we think of your family which had before the

---

[296] John Bligh* (Blithe) (1687–1728).
[297] On Berkeley's petition to extend his absence from the college, see Letter 53.
[298] Sir Samuel Cooke (?–1758?), lord mayor of Dublin (1712–14 and 1740–41).

greatest charms of any that I ever knew, when it is enriched by the accession of these growing wits and beauties. As I cannot but think your condition to be envied for the present, since you have so much good company within your own walls, so I am troubled when I consider, that you must lose it in a little time; your son will distinguish himself in the University, and at Court, and your daughters will be forced from you by men of the greatest merit and fortune in England.

Lady Theodosia Bligh[299] is I think the most airy young creature that I ever saw: she detests the thought of going to Ireland, and Mr. Bligh[300] is about taking a house, and purchasing the furniture of it from my Dr. Stairs.

I am informed that the Queen and Council at Windsor have decided the affair in dispute between the Government and city of Dublin in favour of the latter,[301] to me it is surprising that you should begin a contest with the aldermen which you were not able to go through with.

I have good hopes that the public welfare will be better provided for by our treaty of peace and commerce than you seem to apprehend. My reason for this is, that on all hands it is agreed the Tories have incomparably the majority in the elections for parliament men, which could hardly be, in case they were thought to pursue methods destructive of the nation. Since I have been obliged to get a licence from the Queen for absence from the College, I shall probably stay longer than I intended, and do not now think of returning before Christmas.[302]

Mr. Steele[303] having laid down his employments, because (as he says) he would not be obliged to those to whom he could not be grateful, has of late turned his head towards politics and published a pamphlet in relation to Dunkirk, which you may perhaps have seen by this time.

My humble service to my Lady and Mrs. Parker.[304] I am

Dear Sir,

Your most humble & affectionate servant,

G. Berkeley

---

[299] Theodosia (*née* Hide [Hyde]) Bligh (1695–1722). She married Bligh on 24 August 1713.
[300] John Bligh* (Blithe) (1687–1728).
[301] The dispute concerned the election of the lord mayor of Dublin. The lord chancellor, Constantine Phipps* (*c.* 1656–1723), tried to insist that the election should be from a panel of names selected by him (including his own). Queen Anne* resolved the dispute in favor of the city.
[302] On Berkeley's petition, see the two preceeding letters, Letters 53 and 54.
[303] Richard Steele* (1672–1729).
[304] Mary Parker* (1692–1731).

56 BERKELEY TO PERCIVAL

EP, BL Add. MS 47027, fol. 52–52v.

London, 15 October 1713

Dear Sir,

I have just time to take my leave of you and let you know that I am now on the point of going to Sicily, where I propose seeing the new king's coronation. I go Chaplain to my Lord Peterborough,[305] who is the ambassador extraordinary sent thither on this occasion. We take France, etc. in our way. There is not any place that I have a greater curiosity to see than Sicily. I cannot now make a certain judgment of things, how they are likely to go with me, but when I am there in case I find myself pressed I shall have recourse to the kind offer you have often made me. This notion is very sudden. Pray give my respects to my Lady, Mrs. Parker,[306] etc. I am

> Dear Sir,
> Your most affectionate & obedient servant,
> George Berkeley

57 BERKELEY TO PERCIVAL[307]

EP, BL Add. MS 47027, fols. 53–55v.

Paris, 24 November 1713

Dear Sir,

On the 25 Oct. O.S.[308] I set out from London in company of a Frenchman, a Spaniard, and a Flandrian, with three English servants of my Lord's. I was glad of this opportunity of going before with Col. Du Hamel, my Lord's aide-de-camp, that I may have time to see Paris etc. before my Lord's arrival; besides I found a great benefit in travelling with foreigners, which obliged me to speak the French language. The 29th about four in the morning after a very narrow escape we landed at Calais. Here my Lord's chariot, which brought the Colonel and me from London to Dover, was to wait his coming; and it was left to my choice either to ride

---

[305] Charles Mordaunt* (1658?–1735), third Earl of Peterborough and first Earl of Monmouth.

[306] Mary Parker* (1692–1731).

[307] A note in Percival's letterbook indicates that this letter was answered on 17 December 1713, but there is no record of that letter.

[308] "Old Style." On the European continent many countries still used the Julian calendar as opposed to the newer Gregorian one. Berkeley explicitly adopts the reformed style. An act of Parliament in 1751 officially set the first of the new year as 1 January starting in 1752.

post with the Colonel (who was obliged to go before to provide lodgings etc. in Paris), or stay till the stage coach went. I chose the latter, and on the 12th November N.S. embarked in the stage-coach with a company who were all perfect strangers to me. There happened to be one English gentleman and two Scotch, among whom was Mr. Martin,[309] the author of *The Voyage to St. Kilda*. He also published an account of the other western islands of Scotland. We were very cheerful on the road, and the inhabitants of St. Kilda did not a little contribute to our diversion. For certain reasons I omit saying anything of the country, the towns, or the people that we saw in our seven days' journey from Calais to Paris, where we arrived on the 17th N.S. in the evening. The next day I dined with the Ambassador of Sicily, where there were several Sicilian and Piedmontese persons of quality. Since that I have visited Mr. Prior,[310] and am to dine with him today. He is a man of good sense and learning, and lives magnificently as becomes the Queen's Plenipotentiary. My time is thus divided between foreigners and statesmen, and the intervals of time are filled up with thinking on my absent friends, and viewing the noble buildings and pieces of painting and statuary, which are here very numerous, and so far as I can judge excellent.

I have here met with a pleasant and ingenious gentleman, Monsr l'Abbé d'Aubigne, Chevalier of the Order of St. Lazarus,[311] who has undertaken to show me everything that is curious. I have spent the two last days entirely with him; today he is to introduce me to Father Mallebranche [sic],[312] a famous philosopher in this city, and tomorrow we go together to Versailles. It were endless to recount particulars, all I shall say is, that the magnificence of their churches and convents surpasses my expectation. The day before yesterday I visited the place de Vendome, le place de Victoire, and le place Regale, and the Louvre, le convent des Capucins, le Feuillant, l'Eglise des Minims, l'Eglise des Celestins, where are the tombs of the ancient kings.[313] Yesterday we saw the monastery of St. Genevieve, with its library and cabinet of rarities; the English college where the body of King James and that of his daughter are still to be seen exposed in their coffins. The people who take the king for a saint have broke off several pieces of the coffin etc., for relics. We saw likewise the Irish college, and

---

[309] Martin Martin (?–1718), traveler and author. He penned *The Late Voyage to St. Kilda* in 1698, which was well received, and the more compendious *Description of the Western Islands of Scotland* in 1703.

[310] Matthew Prior (1664–1721), poet and diplomat.

[311] The Order of St. Lazarus is an ancient order founded in Jerusalem in the twelfth century to combat leprosy and defend the Christian faith. By the end of the Crusades it was almost exclusively a hospitaller order. Addressing the Abbé as "Chevalier" indicates that he held a rank of "Knight" or above in the order. Little is known about him.

[312] Nicolas Malebranche (1638–1715).

[313] In the original Berkeley does not include all of the French accents.

the Sorbonne, where we were present at their Divinity disputations. All is wonderfully fine and curious, but the finest of all is the Chapel in the Church of the Invalides, which the Abbé d'Aubigne assured me was not to be surpassed in Italy. We now expect my Lord every minute in Paris; so that I am in a great hurry, being willing to profit of the little time I stay here; however, I snatched the present moment to write you this scrawl, which I hope you will excuse, in

Dear Sir,

Your most humble & most affectionate servant,

G. Berkeley

My most humble service to my Lady and Mrs. Parker.[314]

58 BERKELEY TO PRIOR

LR, *pp. 74–77. Stock, pp. xxix–xxx.*

Paris, 25 November 1713

Dear Tom,

From London to Calais I came in the company of a Flamand, a Spaniard, a Frenchman, and three English servants of my Lord. The three gentlemen being of those different nations obliged me to speak the French language (which is now familiar), and gave me the opportunity of seeing much of the world in a little compass. After a very remarkable escape from rocks and banks of sand, and darkness and storm, and the hazards that attend rash and ignorant seamen, we arrived at Calais in a vessel which, returning the next day was cast away in the harbour in open daylight (as I think I already told you). From Calais, Colonel du Hamel left it to my choice either to go with him by post to Paris, or come after in the stage-coach. I chose the latter; and, on November 1, O.S., embarked in the stage-coach with a company that were all perfect strangers to me. There were two Scotch, and one English gentleman. One of the former happened to be the author of the *Voyage to St. Kilda* and the *Account of the Western Isles.*[315] We were good company on the road; and that day se'ennight came to Paris.

I have been since taken up in viewing churches, convents, palaces, colleges, etc., which are very numerous and magnificent in this town. The splendour and riches of these things surpasses belief; but it were endless to descend to particulars. I was present at a disputation in the Sorbonne, which indeed had much of

[314] Mary Parker* (1692–1731).
[315] Martin Martin (?–1718). See Letter 57.

the French fire in it. I saw the Irish and the English colleges. In the latter I saw, inclosed in a coffin, the body of the late king James. Bits of the coffin, and of the cloth that hangs the room, have been cut away for relics, he being esteemed a great saint by the people. The day after I came to town, I dined at the ambassador of Sicily's; and this day with Mr. Prior.[316] I snatched an opportunity to mention you to him, and do your character justice. Tomorrow I intend to visit Father Malebranche,[317] and discourse him on certain points. I have some reasons to decline speaking of the country or villages that I saw as I came along.

My Lord is just now arrived, and tells me he has an opportunity of sending my letters to my friends tomorrow morning, which occasions my writing this. My humble service to Sir John Rawdon,[318] Mrs. Rawdon, Mrs. Kempsy, and all other friends. My Lord thinks he shall stay a fortnight here. I am, dear Tom,

> your affectionate humble servant,

> G. Berkeley

I must give you the trouble of putting the inclosed in the penny-post.

59 BERKELEY TO PERCIVAL[319]

EP, BL Add. MS 47027, fols. 62–63v.

Lyons, 28 December 1713

Dear Sir,

Lyons has been all this day filled with rejoicings of all sorts, on account of the king's statue, which was placed this morning on its pedestal in the middle of the great place. Some part of the solemnity was pretty singular, the mayor, aldermen, and sheriffs were drawn out in their formalities, and bare-headed to salute the statue. The mayor made a speech to it, I am told it will be printed. The fireworks are now beginning to play, but I have more pleasure in snatching the present opportunity of writing to you than I should in seeing that spectacle. This is a very noble city, and more populous and rich in proportion than Paris. It has several fine buildings and antiquities, which made the week I have spent here pass very agreeably. The opera here is magnificent enough, but the music bad. I was introduced to the Assembly of Madame d'Intendante; when I was there I could not but observe, in my thoughts, how much her apartments and furniture as well

---

[316] Matthew Prior (1664–1721), poet and diplomat.
[317] Nicolas Malebranche (1638–1715).
[318] Sir John Rawdon* (1690–1723).
[319] A note in Percival's letterbook indicates the letter was received on 16 March 1714 and answered on 8 April 1714 (Letter 64).

as her person were inferiour to those of my Lady Percival. The month I spent at Paris was not so entertaining as I hoped on account of the extreme sharpness of the weather, which however did not prevent my visiting the king's palaces and country seats etc., though it must be owned it spoiled my relish and made them appear worse than they would have done in a better season.

I had forgot to tell (what seems odd to strangers) that the clergy game in these public assemblys. Play is the general humour of the French, and it runs high. Mr. Oglethorpe,[320] an ingenious English gentleman that goes with us to Sicily, lost fifty guineas last night at the Intendants. He and Col. du Hamel and I set forward tomorrow morning for Turin, and thence to Genoa, where we meet my Lord, who goes by sea from Toulon. For my own part I am glad of this opportunity of seeing Italy, though it be at the expence of passing the Alps in this rude season. I go armed with furred gloves, a furred bag to put my legs in, and the like necessaries to withstand the prodigious cold we must expect in this journey, which has already pretty well hardened my constitution.

I will not congratulate with you, but with your country, that has you for its representative in Parliament. I am sure it were to be wished there were many such representatives at this time when the parties there run so high, and are so much incensed against each other, though (God knows) at bottom for little reason, and to no other purpose than to hurt their country. I have only time to add my humble respects to my Lady and Mrs. Parker[321] (perhaps now Mrs. Domville, my Lady Poorscourt, or some other name) and remain,

>   Dear Sir,
>   Yr most humble & affectionate servant,
>   G. Berkeley

60 BERKELEY TO PRIOR

LR, pp. 77–79. Stock, pp. xxx–xxxi.

Turin, 6 January 1713/14

Dear Tom,

At Lyons, where I was about eight days, it was left to my choice whether I would go from thence to Toulon, and there embark for Genoa, or else pass

---

[320] Theophilus Oglethorpe (1684–c. 1737), son of Theophilus Oglethorpe (1650–1702), army general. The younger Theophilus succeeded his brother as MP for Haslemere (1708–13) and became aide-de-camp to the duke of Ormond (1712). He was in Peterborough's retinue on the embassy to Sicily. He would later retire to the Jacobite court at St. Germain-en-Laye.

[321] Mary Parker* (1692–1731).

through Savoy, cross the Alps, and so through Italy. I chose the latter route, though I was obliged to ride post, in company of Colonel du Hamel and Mr. Oglethorpe[322], Adjutant-General of the Queen's forces, who were sent with a letter from my Lord to the King's mother at Turin.

The first day we rode from Lyons to Chambery, the capital of Savoy, which is reckoned sixty miles. The Lionnois and Dauphiné were very well; but Savoy was a perpetual chain of rocks and mountains, almost impassible for ice and snow. And yet I rode post through it, and came off with only four falls; from which I received no other damage than the breaking my sword, my watch, and my snuff-box.

On New Year's Day we passed Mount Cenis, one of the most difficult and formidable parts of the Alps which is ever passed over by mortal men. We were carried in open chairs by men used to scale these rocks and precipices, which in this season are more slippery and dangerous than at other times, and at the best are high, craggy, and steep enough to cause the heart of the most valiant man to melt within him. My life often depended on a single step. No one will think that I exaggerate, who considers what it is to pass the Alps on New Year's Day. But I shall leave particulars to be described by the fireside.

We have been now five days here, and in two or three more design to set forward towards Genoa, where we are to join my Lord, who embarked at Toulon. I am now hardened against wind and weather, earth and sea, frost and snow; can gallop all day long, and sleep but three or four hours at night. The court here is polite and splendid, the city beautiful, the churches and colleges magnificent, but not much learning stirring among them. However, all orders of people, clergy and laity, are wonderfully civil, and everywhere a man finds his account in being an Englishman, that character alone being sufficient to gain respect. My service to all friends, particularly to Sir John and Mrs. Rawdon,[323] and Mrs. Kempsy. It is my advice that they do not pass the Alps in their way to Sicily. I am, dear Tom,

     yours, etc.,

     G. B.

---

[322] George Monck Berkeley (1763–1793) adds a footnote in the *Literary Relics*, "The celebrated General Oglethorpe," confusing the younger Theophilus Oglethorpe (1684–1737?), for his father, who held the rank of bridgadier-general in 1688 but died in 1702.

[323] John Rawdon* (1690–1723).

61 BERKELEY TO PERCIVAL

EP, BL Add. MS 47027, fols. 70v–71v.

Genoa, 4 February 1714

Dear Sir,

I stayed about a month at Paris, eight days at Lyons, and eleven at Turin, and I have been now almost three weeks at Genoa. I writ to you from each of the fore mentioned places, but know not whether my letters came to your hands, being in some doubt that the posts are not yet regulated, between France and England. This makes my letter shorter than otherwise it would be; for I have a thousand things to tell you of my travels by sea and land, by coach, horse, boat chaise, and in all kind of companies. I have not seen any town that pleased me more than this. The churches, palaces, and indeed the ordinary houses are very magnificent. It has nevertheless one fault, that the streets are generally very narrow, but I should not pretend to describe it to you, believing you have been here yourself.

I made it my business to visit the colleges, libraries, and booksellers' shops, both at Turin and here, but do not find that learning flourishes among them. Nothing curious in the sciences has of late been published in Italy. Their clergy for the most part are extremely ignorant; as an instance of it, they shewed me in a library of the Franciscans in this town a Hebrew book, taking it to be an English one.

My Lord Peterborough[324] joined us here, about a week since. He came by water from Toulon. He is a man of excellent parts, and frank cheerful conversation. We are to set out to-day in a felucca[325] for Leghorn, where we are to embark for Sicily in two Maltese vessels, the man-of-war and yacht with my Lord's equipage not being yet arrived.

I reckon it is now time that I congratulate you and my Lady on the birth of a new son,[326] and Mrs. Parker on her marriage.[327] I long to hear some news from your fireside and am with the truest respect to those that sit about it,

> Dear Sir,
> Your most obedient & affectionate servant,
> G. Berkeley

---

[324] Charles Mordaunt* (1658?–1735), third Earl of Peterborough and first Earl of Monmouth.
[325] A sailboat typically consisting of one or two lateen sails.
[326] Berkeley is anticipating the birth of Philip Clarke Percival, born 21 June 1714. He died an infant.
[327] Mary Parker* (1692–1731). Berkeley is misinformed; she did not marry until 1719, although apparently she had suitors.

62 BERKELEY TO PERCIVAL[328]

EP, BL Add. MS 47027, fols. 74v–77.

Leghorn, 19 February 1713/14

Dear Sir,

Ireland is certainly one of the finest countries and Dublin one of the finest cities in the world; the further I go, the more I am convinced of this truth. But if you have the advantage of these countries in point of plenty, government, and religion, it must be owned you fall infinitely short of them, in respect of concord, and unanimity. By nature and constitution you should be happy, but faction and jealousy make you miserable in spite of both. These reflections are occasioned by my seeing the newspapers filled with an account of the dissensions at present reigning between the citizens, lords, commons, and clergy of Ireland. I now fancy that your estate is converted into a ship filled with all necessaries for the voyage to Mascarenes,[329] and that you and our friends of that party are on the point of embarking. I beg you will turn aside to the left and take me up at Leghorn, though if I were not afraid of diverting you from such an agreeable project, I could assure you that the French nation is so impoverished and dispeopled by the war, that we need not entertain any apprehensions of having a Pretender[330] imposed upon us by their power. I speak this of my own knowledge having passed through the heart of France, and been an eyewitness of its misery.

I shall not pretend to give you any description of Italy, who know it so much better than myself. There is nothing in it that pleases me more than the clear sky and warm weather so universal with us in this season. This town is the neatest and most regular that I have seen in Italy. It is very populous and a place of great trade. There are several English families of merchants, who are very rich and live at a much greater rate than the Italian nobility.

My Lord Ambassador,[331] who is a man of excellent parts and good humour, not thinking fit to wait the arrival of his equipage, which is coming by sea from London, parted from hence about ten days since on board a Maltese

---

[328] A note in Percival's letterbook says this letter was answered 29 June 1714, but there is no record of the response.

[329] An old collective title for the islands of Mauritius, Réunion, and Rodriguez in the Indian Ocean.

[330] A reference to the Old Pretender, James Francis Edward Stuart* (1688–1766).

[331] Charles Mordaunt* (1658?–1735), third Earl of Peterborough and first Earl of Monmouth.

vessel bound to Palermo, where he designs to stay but a short time, and put off his public entry till his return. He has taken with him but two or three servants, and left orders for my diet and lodging here with his secretary, and some others of his retinue. The secretary is an Italian and a very good-natured gentleman, as well as a man of sense. There are already no less than nine different nations among my Lord's domestics. This gives me a good opportunity of improving myself in French and Italian. They are very civil to me, and in that respect make me as easy as I hope to be in any company besides those who used to rejoice my heart in Dublin.

A thought comes into my head that the restless state of affairs at home may put you (like Atticus)[332] upon seeking repose in Italy, till the storm is over-blown. This climate I am sure would contribute very much to your health as well as to that of my Lady and the children. Though in this suggestion I know I consult my own satisfaction more than the public interest. I shall probably stay a considerable time in this town or hereabouts, and should be overjoyed to hear you were on this side the Alps. I writ to you when I was at Paris, at Lyons, at Turin, and at Genoa, at each of which places I made a considerable stay. I long to see a line from you. When you do me that favour pray be particular, and rather with respect to domestic than public affairs. I can read in the *Gazette* that the Bishop of Raphoe[333] is made Primate, and the Lord Chancellor under the displeasure of the Commons;[334] but it says nothing of my Lady's health, your son's learning, your daughter's beauty, Mrs. Parker's being married,[335] Mrs. Dering's being recovered of the gout, or Mrs. Percival's breeding, or Mr. Dering's getting a good employment. If you send your letter to the Secretary's office in London to be enclosed in my Lord Peterborough's pacquet, or (in case there be a ship coming from Dublin to Leghorn) direct it for me, to be left at the English consul's here, it will come to my hands. I am, Sir,

　　　Your most humble & affectionate servant,
　　　G. Berkeley

---

[332] Atticus was a relative and correspondent of Cicero.

[333] Thomas Lindsay (1656–1724), a Tory clergyman. He was translated to Armagh in December 1713.

[334] The lord chancellor was Constantine Phipps* (c. 1656–1723), a Tory suspected at the time of Jacobite sympathies.

[335] Mary Parker* (1692–1731). Berkeley is misinformed; she did not marry until 1719.

63 BERKELEY TO PRIOR

LR, p. 80. Stock, pp. xxxii–xxxiii.

Leghorn, 26 February 1713/14

Dear Tom,

Mrs. Rawdon is too thin, and Sir John[336] too fat, to agree with the English climate. I advise them to make haste and transport themselves into this warm clear air. Your best way is to come through France; but make no long stay there; for the air is too cold, and there are instances enough of poverty and distress to spoil the mirth of any one who feels the sufferings of his fellow creatures. I would prescribe you two or three operas at Paris, and as many days amusement at Versailles. My next recipe shall be, to ride post from Paris to Toulon, and there to embark for Genoa; for I would by no means have you shaken to pieces, as I was, riding post over the rocks of Savoy, or put out of humour by the most horrible precipices of Mount Cenis, that part of the Alps which divides Piedmont from Savoy. I shall not anticipate your pleasure by any description of Italy or France; only with regard to the latter, I cannot help observing, that the Jacobites have little to hope, and others little to fear, from that reduced nation. The king indeed looks as he neither wanted meat nor drink, and his palaces are in good repair; but throughout the land there is a different face of things.

I stayed about a month at Paris, eight days at Lyons, eleven at Turin, three weeks at Genoa; and am now to be above a fortnight with my Lord's secretary (an Italian) and some others of his retinue, my Lord[337] having gone aboard a Maltese vessel from hence to Sicily, with a couple of servants. He designs to stay there incognito a few days, and then return hither, having put off his public entry till the yacht with his equipage arrives.

I have wrote to you several times before by post. In answer to all my letters, I desire you to send me one great one, close writ, and filled on all sides, containing a particular account of all transactions in London and Dublin. Enclose it in a cover to my Lord Ambassador, and that again in another cover to Mr. Hare at my Lord Bolingbroke's[338] office. If you have a mind to travel only in the map, here is a list of all the places where I lodged since my leaving England, in their natural order: Calais, Boulogne, Montreuil, Abbeville, Poix, Beauvais, Paris, Moret, Ville Neufe le Roi, Vermonton, Saulieu, Chany, Mâcon, Lyons, Chambery, St. Jean de Moridune,

---

[336] John Rawdon* (1690–1723).
[337] Charles Mordaunt* (1658?–1735), third Earl of Peterborough and first Earl of Monmouth.
[338] Saint-John Henry* (1678–1751), first Viscount Bolingbroke.

Lanebourg, Susa, Turin, Alexandria, Campo Maro, Genoa, Lestri di Levante, Lerici, Leghorne. My humble service to Sir John, Mrs. Rawdon, and Mrs. Kempsy, Mr. Digby,[339] Mr. French,[340] etc. I am, dear Tom,

>your affectionate humble servant,
>
>G. Berkeley

Leghorn, Feb. 26, N.S. 1713/14

64 PERCIVAL TO BERKELEY

EP, BL Add. MS 47027, fols. 86v–87v. Letter copied in Percival's diary:
EP, BL Add. MS 47087, fol. 64–64v.

London, 8 April 1714

Since I came hither I received both your letters from Lyons and Genoa, and am sincerely glad to hear that travelling agrees with your inclinations and health. The instances you give me of the effects of tyranny in France and popery in Italy are so very extraordinary that I cannot but cry out with Cato: O Liberty! O my country! and add, O happy Englishmen, who may own without offence to God or man, that princes and priests are like men with themselves. What is more deplorable than to see a prince reduce even the minds of his subjects to such a degree of slavery, that they shall affect by a sort of impious wit to pay devotion with their flattery, and raise their king to a god, by making processions before his statue. What more unhappy than that a people should leave that important affair, the salvation of their souls, to the guidance of a man, who to support his pretensions to infallibility, makes fools of mankind, and deprives them of the chiefest happiness a reasonable creature can aspire to, free exercise of the understanding. Their showing you at Genoa a Hebrew for an English book, is of a piece with another instance which I was witness of at Bologna, where in a gallery belonging to a convent (I think of Austin Friars) one of their Order showed me the head of Friar Bacon, who, said he, was one of the most eminent reformers under Henry VIII.

Now to write you of my family, in a word, they are all well as far as I know, for I left the two girls in Ireland. Of news, I have only this to say, there is an outcry

---

[339] Luce speculates that this is Robert Digby (?–?), a correspondent of Alexander Pope* (*Works*, vol. IX, p. 32).
[340] Luce speculates that this might be either Matthew French (?–1714), fellow of Trinity College, Dublin, or Matthew French, Jr. (?–?), who was one year senior to Berkeley at Trinity (mentioned in the *Notebooks* at entry 569).

upon the ministry that they design to bring the Pretender[341] in, and so great is the persuasion that due care has not been taken of the succession by law established, that peers and commons fall daily off. Lord Anglesea,[342] Abington,[343] Cartwright,[344] Archbishop[345] of York,[346] and others have followed my Lord Nottingham's[347] steps, and my Lord Treasurer[348] cannot hold long the staff. The other day the Lords voted an address that by proclamation a price might be put on the Pretender's head, in case he ever set foot on her Majesty's dominions.

I am, etc.

65 BERKELEY TO POPE

The Correspondence of Alexander Pope, *ed. George Sherburn (Oxford: Clarendon Press, 1956), addendum to vol. I, pp. 59–61. Stock, pp. xxxiii–xxxv.*

Leghorn, 1 May 1714

As I take ingratitude to be a greater crime than impertinence, I chose rather to run the risk of being thought guilty of the latter, than not to return you my thanks for the very agreeable entertainment you just now gave me. I have accidentally met with your *Rape of the Lock* here, having never seen it before.[349] Style, painting, judgment, spirit, I had already admired in your other writings; but in this I am charmed with the magic of your invention, with all those images, allusions, and inexplicable beauties which you raise so surprisingly, and at the same time so naturally out of a trifle. And yet I cannot say that I was more pleased with the reading of it, than I am with the pretext it gives me to renew in your thoughts the remembrance of one who values no happiness beyond the friendship of men of wit, learning, and good nature.

---

[341] James Francis Edward Stuart* (1688–1766).
[342] Arthur Annesley (*c.* 1678–1737), fifth Earl of Anglesey.
[343] Probably Willoughby Bertie (1692–1760), third Earl of Abingdon. He was elected MP for Westbury, but after a petition the election was overturned in June 1715 and Bertie lost his seat.
[344] Probably Thomas Cartwright (1671–1748), English MP for Northamptonshire (1695–98 and 1701–48).
[345] Rand has "a Bishop of" for "A'bishop," the latter of which was a common abbreviation for "Archbishop."
[346] William Dawes (1671–1724), third Baronet, was appointed archbishop of York by Queen Anne* on 20 February 1714 and consecrated on 9 March of the same year.
[347] Daniel Finch (1647–1730), second Earl of Nottingham and seventh Earl of Winchilsea.
[348] Robert Harley* (1661–1724) was lord treasurer under Queen Anne from 29 May 1711 until 27 July 1714.
[349] Pope's* *Rape of the Lock* first appeared in 1712. Another version "with additions" appeared in March 1714.

I remember to have heard you mention some half formed design of coming to Italy. What might we not expect from a muse that sings so well in the bleak climate of England, if she felt the same warm sun, and breathed the same air with Virgil and Horace?

There are here an incredible number of poets that have all the inclination, but want the genius, or perhaps the art of the ancients. Some among them who understand English, begin to relish our authors; and I am informed that at Florence they have translated Milton into Italian verse. If one who knows so well how to write like the old Latin poets came among them, it would probably be a means to retrieve them from their cold trivial conceits, to an imitation of their predecessors.

As merchants, antiquaries, men of pleasure, etc., have all different views in travelling, I know not whether it might not be worth a poet's while to travel, in order to store his mind with strong images of nature.

Green fields and groves, flowery meadows and purling streams, are nowhere in such perfection as in England; but if you would know lightsome days, warm suns, and blue skies, you must come to Italy; and to enable a man to describe rocks and precipices, it is absolutely necessary that he pass the Alps.

You will easily perceive that it is self interest makes me so fond of giving advice to one who has no need of it. If you came into these parts, I should fly to see you. I am here (by the favour of my good friend the Dean of St. Patrick's)[350] in quality of chaplain to the Earl of Peterborough,[351] who about three months since left the greatest part of his family in this town. God knows how long we shall stay here. I am

yours, etc.

66 BERKELEY TO PERCIVAL

EP, BL Add. MS 47027, fols. 103–04.

Leghorn, 1 May 1714

Dear Sir,

Since my last to you dated from this town, I have had an opportunity of seeing Pisa, Lucca, Pistoia, Florence etc. But I have not seen anything that should make me desirous to live out of England or Ireland. The descriptions that we find in the Latin

---

[350] Jonathan Swift* (1667–1745).
[351] Charles Mordaunt* (1658?–1735), third Earl of Peterborough and first Earl of Monmouth.

poets make me expect Elysian fields and the golden age in Italy. But in my opinion England is a more poetical country, the spring there is forwarder and lasts longer, purling streams are more numerous, and the fields and groves have a cheerfuller green, the only advantage here, is, in point of air, which as you know is warmer and dryer than with us, though I doubt whether it be generally more wholesome.

There is here together in a family about a dozen of my Lord's[352] domestics, among whom is the secretary (an Italian) and myself. Last week I received a letter from my Lord, dated at Palermo. He talks of coming soon to Leghorn. We have so long waited the vessel that brings the coaches and equipage, that (though it be now arrived here) yet I doubt whether we shall have a public entry in Sicily. As my Lord is Plenipotentiary to all the Courts in Italy, I know not whither we shall go next. I wish it may be homewards. I have already seen enough to be satisfied, that England has the most learning, the most riches, the best government, the best people, and the best religion in the world. Amongst two thousand clergymen that are reckoned in this town, I do not hear of any one man of letters worth making an acquaintance with. The people here are much dissatisfied with the hard government of the Grand Duke.[353] The family of the Medici is now on the point of being extinct, and they know not to whom they shall be next a prey. But in that matter they are easy, being sure they cannot fall into worse hands.

This letter I suppose will find you at London, where I hope to see you together with my Lady, and Mrs. Parker,[354] to whom pray give my humblest respects. I am,

Sir, your most humble

& most obedient servant,

G. Berkeley

67 BERKELEY TO PERCIVAL

EP, BL Add. MS 47027, fols. 141v–42v.

Paris, 13 July 1714

Dear Sir,

I am just come from Mr. Southwell,[355] who told me the joyful news of your being in London and my Lady being delivered of a son.[356] As I have a sensible

---

[352] Charles Mordaunt* (1658?–1735), third Earl of Peterborough and first Earl of Monmouth.

[353] Cosimo III (1642–1723).

[354] Mary Parker* (1692–1731).

[355] Edward Southwell* (1671–1730).

[356] Philip Clarke Percival, born 21 June 1714. He died an infant.

pleasure in all your good fortune I could not defer congratulating with you on that happy event till my seeing you, which I hope will be very soon. Nothing could have pleased me more than the hearing of your family's being in London, with a purpose of continuing there twelve months. I am sure it will be a strong motive for doing so too. I parted with my Lord Peterborough[357] at Genoa where I embarked with Mr. Molesworth[358] the late envoy at Florence, and the Colonel his brother, and have had a very pleasant journey in their company to Paris, where I came about three days agone. My Lord took post for Turin, and thence designed passing over the Alps, and so through Savoy and France in [sic] his way to England.

I have here met with an Irish gentleman of my acquaintance who designs returning to England through Flanders and Holland: being glad of an opportunity to see those countries, I have taken a place in the Brussels' coach with him. We are to set out next week.

I know not whether you received my letters from Paris, Lyons, Turin, Genoa, Leghorn, Florence. Last month I received one of yours dated in November last, being then in Italy, whence I answered it. I shall trouble you with no more at present, but with my humble respects to my Lady and Mrs. Parker,[359] I am

Dear Sir,

your most humble & affectionate servant,

G. Berkeley

68 BERKELEY TO PERCIVAL

EP, BL Add. MS 47028, fols. 32–33.

London, 6 July 1715

My Lord,

I am in hopes that this letter will find your Lordship[360] and my Lady safe arrived in Dublin. Things has [sic] been pretty much at a stand here since your departure. This by many is imputed to the difficulty which the Duke of Shrewsbury's[361] case gave the impeaching party. If this be all, the difficulty is now over, that peer being displaced from his office of Lord Chamberlain, which

---

[357] Charles Mordaunt* (1658?–1735), third Earl of Peterborough and first Earl of Monmouth.

[358] Most likely John Molesworth (1679–1726), second Viscount, diplomat and son of Robert Molesworth (1656–1725), first Viscount. John Molesworth was envoy to the Duke of Tuscany in 1710.

[359] Mary Parker* (1692–1731).

[360] John Percival* (1683–1748) was made Baron Percival of Burton, County Cork, on 21 April 1715.

[361] Charles Talbot* (1660–1718), Duke of Shrewsbury.

speaks him deserted by the Court. It had indeed been hard that a person who was so deep in the late measures, and concluded the peace with France, should be employed and favoured at Court, while others against whom nothing appears lie under a disgrace, e.g. Lord Peterborough.[362]

I promised your Lordship some Tory news, not doubting but that you are sufficiently furnished with Whig reports by other hands. But the truth is I hear little news at present to be depended on. People speak uncertainly, and seem to be in a suspense. As to my own opinion, men seem tired of baiting one another, the spirit of party begins to cool among us, and in a little time there is hopes we may be a quiet and united people. I am persuaded a little address[363] at this juncture might make the Tories all what they ought to be, true friends to the King, which would put an end to our fears, but this advice must come from cooler heads than those who advise infringing Charters of Universities for the extravagances and crimes of a few young lads.[364] I need not tell you what I hint at. You know what hath passed with regard to our university better than myself. All I can say is that the thing is represented here much to the disadvantage of the Court, and I am credibly informed that Oxford and Cambridge are both alarmed at it.

Of late I have had some symptoms of a return of my ague,[365] but am now upon the point of going to Gloucestershire, for about a fortnight or three weeks, which will I hope entirely cure me. Mrs. Parker[366] and Mr. Phill[367] are both, as I suppose you know, much better than when you left them. For the rest, all friends are as well as could be expected in your and my Lady's absence. For my own part I comfort myself with the thought that I shall see you soon there or here. In the meantime, I am

> My Lord,
> your Lordship's
> most obedient and most
> obliged servant,
> G. Berkeley

---

[362] Charles Mordaunt* (1658?–1735), third Earl of Peterborough and first Earl of Monmouth.

[363] Presumably a reference by Berkeley to his anonymously published *Advice to the Tories who have Taken the Oaths* (London, 1715).

[364] Between March and June 1715 several incidents occurred at Trinity College, Dublin, including the defacing of a statue of King William I. A number of students were reprimanded or expelled as a result. The lords justices in the king's name intervened to stop the election of fellows due to happen that June. The stop on college activities was not lifted until the following April. See *The Book of Trinity College Dublin* (Belfast: Marcus Ward & Co., 1892), pp. 66–67.

[365] A fever.

[366] Mary Parker* (1692–1731).

[367] Philip Parker* (1682–1741).

69 BERKELEY TO POPE

> The Correspondence of Alexander Pope, *ed. George Sherburn (Oxford: Clarendon Press, 1956), addendum to vol. I, pp. 101–02 (extract).*

7 July 1715

... Some days ago three or four gentlemen and myself, exerting that right which all the readers pretend to over authors, sat in judgment upon the two new translations of the first *Iliad*. Without partiality to my countrymen, I assure you they all gave the preference where it was due; being unanimously of opinion that yours was equally just to the sense with Mr.—'s,[368] and without comparison, more easy, more poetical, and more sublime. But I will say no more on such a threadbare subject as your late performance at this time ...

I am, etc.

70 BERKELEY TO PERCIVAL

> *EP, BL Add. MS 47028, fols. 43–44.*

Flaxley, 28 July 1715[369]

My Lord,

I have now spent about a fortnight in Gloucestershire in a very agreeable place, and with the most entertaining company that I know out of your family, and propose going to London next week. The news of that place I doubt not you are well informed of. But I may perhaps give you some account of riots in the neighbouring counties, Worcester, Stafford etc. the particulars whereof are not published in the papers. A servant of the Lady with whom I am, having gone to receive some money at Bromingham,[370] gives a dismal relation of tumults there. He says there have been twenty-eight of the rioters slain. He saw seven of their bodies lying unburied in the fields. There are likewise eight of the principal dissenters missed. He met in one squadron above five hundred rioters in a field. And says that being in the town of Bromingham he saw a man on horseback ride through the streets with a horn, which he publicly sounded to raise the mob, whereof four thousand immediately got together and joined him. They obliged

---

[368] Thomas Tickell (1685–1740), poet and government official. Tickell had contracted in May 1714 to translate the *Iliad* – nearly at the same time as Pope had agreed to do the same – but never finished the translation. Pope was aggrieved by the competition. He eventually reconciled with Tickell, but never forgave Addison,* who backed Tickell's project.

[369] Luce mistakenly lists the date as 23 July 1715 (*Works*, vol. VIII, p. 87).

[370] A variant for Birmingham.

the constable who at first came to seize the horseman to go with them and join in pulling down a meeting-house. Of a great number of meeting-houses there are now but three left standing in Worcestershire and Staffordshire. In a neighbouring town he says the dissenters, who guarded the meeting-house with firearms, got one of the Tory mob, and upon his refusing to curse Dr. Sacheverel[l][371] they slit his mouth from ear to ear, and gave him other wounds of which he died, and that this hath terribly incensed the riotry and increased their numbers. That an eminent Presbyterian's son is now in gaol at Bromingham for having proffered sixty pounds to some fellows to pull down the meeting-house, and that a dissenter assured him that he himself doubted these insurrections were at bottom set on foot and favoured by Whigs for a pretence to ruin the Tory party. Whether this be so or no, God knows. But I can tell you of my own knowledge that the mob of Gloucester would have pulled down the meeting-houses there, if they had not been dissuaded by the principal Tories of that town, who use all possible methods to keep them quiet, as knowing these riots can in no wise advantage their cause. It is said there are above twenty thousand men of Bromingham and the parts adjacent ready to take arms against the government if there was any one to head them. This falls out the more unluckily because of the vast number of firearms and all sorts of weapons which make the great trade of that town. It is the opinion of most people that the nation is ready to break out into a flame, and to do the Tories justice (with whom I principally converse here) they express an honest detestation of these proceedings, as I hope I need not tell you I do myself. This with my humble respects to my Lady is all I shall trouble you with at this time.

My Lord,

your Lordship's most obedient & most obliged servant,

Geo: Berkeley

71 PERCIVAL TO BERKELEY[372]

EP, BL Add. MS 47028, fols. 47v–49. Letter copied in Percival's diary: BL Add. MS 47087, fols. 105v–07.

Dublin, 2 August 1715

Sir,

I find by yours from Flaxley that you have not received a letter I writ you in answer to the first you was so kind to send me, but perhaps you may by this

---

[371] Henry Sacheverell* (1674–1724).

[372] Rand apparently missed this letter; it is not included in his *Berkeley and Percival*.

time being as I suppose returned to town. I directed it to the Pall Mall Coffee-House.

I am deeply afflicted at the news you send me in your last, and though I do you the justice to believe you heartily detest this rebellion, yet I cannot acquit the Torys in general of it. [I]t consists of Torys and has been fomented & is supported undoubtedly by them. For many of them, and I hope great numbers will now the fire is light help to extinguish it, yet it is to be expected likewise that number will appear in it, according as the success is like to prove; and this will be allow'd against them all that they concurred in a scheme of terrifying the King into a change of ministry, by fomenting the minds of the people. How detestable a thought this must be in a Church of England man's breast, and of how danger-ous consequence to the peace of the kingdom, how contrary to true allegiance and serviceable to the Pretender's[373] interest, I need not repeat, you know as well as I. But this I must declare which perhaps you are not so much concerned of as I am, that the behaviour of the inferior clergy during the last ministry, and even since the King came in, has much contributed to the present rebellion. Wise men feared only what since appears, and therefore thought it necessary to unite the minds of all, but the clergy never preached so much division as then, at present, when necessity is so apparent, we hear of a loyal sermon but very accidentally. Sanderson[374] in one of his sermons lays it down as a sin in a minister not to suit[e] his discourse to the necessity of the times. I can't find that among us now, the clergy think so.

As I can't acquit the clergy, so neither can I the laity, I mean the chief of them, which I presume are those that now sit in Parliament. How have they in the Commons house endeavoured to stifle the questioning those men who are now known to have betrayed their country, and how have the Torys in the house of Lords endeavoured to render our army useless. As to the middling sort of Torys, it will be consented by you that in general they have been more ready to invent and spread vile stories, pamphlets, and lampoons against the government than to discourage them, & have not failed of excusing at any rate the proceedings of their party, though at the expense of their honour reason & truth. Thus it shall be said the Duke[375] only went away for fear of his life, yet we find he declares for

---

[373] James Francis Edward Stuart* (1688–1766).

[374] A reference to Robert Sanderson (1587–1663), Bishop of Lincoln, whose sermons were influential into the eighteenth century. See *Sermons by the Right Reverend Robert Sanderson, Late Lord Bishop of Lincoln*, 2 vols. (London: Ball, Arnold & Co., 1841), vol. II, "Sermon I."

[375] James Butler* (1665–1745), second Duke of Ormond. Impeached for high treason and other misdemeanors in June 1715, he fled to France in July of that year.

the Pretender, and knew he might at any time make his peace with honour[376] with the King. Thus this infamous rebellion shall be charged upon Whigs as a design to ruin the Torys, when God knows the Pretender is the thoughts of the villains and his health drunk publicly every where by them. I would not have any body so weak as to give into this excuse, which you only have heard from a common servant, and was a discourse between him and another ordinary man in the heart of the rioters.

We have known an eminent Presbyterian parson, and a great Quaker Jacobites [*sic*], but did any body say the dissenters were so, much less shall it the Whigs would raise the rebellion, the Whigs are not dissenters, though the last side with them for their preservation against the rage of a persecuting high Church spirit, or if it must needs be that they are so, we must affirm it of the majority of Lords and Commons. But at this time of day when rebellion has set up her horn, and an invasion threatens us, when great men fly to the Pretender and own his pretended right, is it consistent with reason to believe that insurrections are occasioned by Whigs and not by Jacobites, or can a man be sincerely for the King and encourage the thought. I know you will not be deceived by such false appearances, and therefore I hope you will discourage so vile a belief in others, which can only tend to weaken our common defence by stifling that zeal, which is this day necessary for our preservation; and this I am assured that as no wise man will credit it, the believers and publishers will be suspected. I am now coming to the end of a long letter, but I must add this more that though I think neither the body of Torys in Parliament nor the body of the inferiour clergy have behaved themselves well, and that numbers of other Torys have been too apt to encourage our divisions and inculcate an indifference for the King's person and government, yet I am still so favourable in my opinion of them, as to hope and believe that now things have come to a crisis, and they have hurried us to the brink of a precipice, they will seriously reflect that they have families and fortunes and lives and religion to lose as well as others, and therefore will join heartily to prevent a common destruction. If not, much blood will be shed, for they must expect no quarter, as I am sure they will give none. I don't expect this behaviour from all, but I hope the generality will be so wise. I am just now informed the clergy begin to open their eyes, if they will open their mouths as Sanderson advises, I shall yet think well of as many as do so.

I am etc.,

Percival

---

[376] "[W]ith honour" in the diary only.

72 BERKELEY TO PERCIVAL

EP, BL Add. MS 47028, fols. 53v–55. Letter copied in Percival's diary: BL Add. MS 47087, fols. 112–13.

London, 9 August 1715

My Lord,

I am now to thank your Lordship for the favour of two letters which I received since my coming to town. I will endeavour to return it by sending you an account of such news as is current here. Mr. Kennedy, secretary to the Duke of Ormond,[377] and Col. Butler, uncle to the Lord Ikerin [Ickerin/Ikerrin],[378] were both seized at Dover as they were going to the Duke. They have been before the Council and are released from[379] custody.

The High-gate cobbler was whipped on Thursday last, and notwithstanding the act against riots,[380] there was a mob of several thousands got together on the occasion, who threatened to pull the executioner to pieces in case he did not perform his office gently.

I hear my Lord Peterborough[381] left the Kingdom on Friday last with the King's pass. I do not know the occasion, having had no discourse with his Lordship since my coming to town. On the same day articles of high treason and high crimes and high misdemeanours against the Duke of Ormond were exhibited and agreed to in the House of Commons. They are six in number, in substance as follows: Acting against orders. Corresponding with the enemy. Not concurring in the siege of Quesnoy. Informing M. Villars[382] what foreign troops withdrew with him. Advising the Queen to disappoint the Dutch in their design on Newport and Furnes. Imposing on her Majesty by a double letter to Lord Bolingbroke.[383]

I was in the house during part of the debate. General Lumley[384] made a long speech in defence of the Duke, shewed that what he did was pursuant to orders, and that had it been his own case, he would have followed the same measures. Mr. Spencer Cooper[385] in answer alleged that the orders were not valid, as not having been signed by the Queen, and added that if Lumley had done the same

---

[377] James Butler* (1665–1745), second Duke of Ormond.
[378] Thomas Butler (1683–1719), sixth Viscount Ikerrin.
[379] Diary has "out of."
[380] The Riot Act of 1715.
[381] Charles Mordaunt* (1658?–1735), third Earl of Peterborough and first Earl of Monmouth.
[382] Claude Louis Hector de Villars (1653–1734), Prince de Martigues, Marquis and then Duc de Villars, Vicomte de Melun, general in the French Army under Louis XIV.
[383] Saint-John Henry* (1678–1751), first Viscount Bolingbroke.
[384] Henry Lumley (c. 1658–1722), an army officer.
[385] The reference is clearly to Spencer Cowper (1669–1728), judge. Cowper was one of the managers of the Sacheverell* trial in 1710.

things he should have met with the same fate. Mr. Bromley[386] spoke much in honour of his Grace, and in the close of his speech said that the Duke's noble qualities had endeared him to all the nation, except those who envied him the having those qualities which they themselves wanted. He was answered with great warmth by Lord Coningsby.[387] Those who spoke against the Duke insisted on his flight into France, upon which the Speaker[388] interposed saying that was a point that did not appear to the House and which they were not to take notice of. Mr. Bromley added that flight was no certain argument of guilt, and instanced Lord Clarendon[389] and the Earl of Danby,[390] who formerly withdrew themselves (as he said), not out of guilt but from the violence of the times. Several others spoke, but some lord appearing in the gallery we were all ordered to withdraw. Upon the division on the first article, the Tories left the house.

The reason assigned for the Duke of Montrose's[391] laying down is that the Duke of Argyle[392] got himself made Lord Lieutenant of that shire where his interest and estate lay. It is said Lord Islay[393] will succeed him. Lord Oxford[394] continues very ill in the tower. I have it from a good hand that the Court have discovered an association amongst several great men here to bring over the Pretender.[395] It is talked too that the French king is to dismiss all the Scotch and Irish forces in his service, and to give them six months' pay as a reward for past service. And that one Fitzgerald an Irish merchant at St. Malo's will furnish four men of war at his own charges. A little time will show what there is in these reports.

What your Lordship observes that the clergy should open their mouths as well as eyes is certainly very just. For my part I think it my duty to disclaim perjury and rebellion on all occasions. Nothing surely can give a deeper wound to the [C]hurch than that her pretended sons should be guilty of[396] such foul practices. What advantage some great men here out of employ may purpose from the Pretender's

---

[386] William Bromley (1663–1732), MP for Oxford University, Speaker of the House of Commons (1710–13), and Secretary of State (1713–14).

[387] Thomas Coningsby (1656–1729), first Earl Coningsby, MP, and privy councillor to Queen Anne.*

[388] Spencer Compton* (c.1674–1743), Earl of Wilmington. Compton was voted Speaker of the House in March 1715.

[389] Henry Hyde (1638–1709), second Earl of Clarendon.

[390] Thomas Osborne (1632–1712), first Duke of Leeds, best known under his earlier title of Earl of Danby.

[391] James Graham (1682–1742), fourth Marquis and first Duke of Montrose, promoter of the Union and Secretary of State for Scotland (1714–15).

[392] John Campbell* (1680–1743), second Duke of Argyll and Duke of Greenwich.

[393] Archibald Campbell (1682–1761), Earl of Ilay (Islay), later third Duke of Argyll, younger brother of John Campbell.*

[394] Robert Harley* (1661–1724), first Earl of Oxford.

[395] James Francis Edward Stuart* (1688–1766).

[396] Diary says "should give occasion for" instead of "should be guilty of."

coming among us, they best know; but it is inconceivable what shadow of an advantage an Irish Protestant can fancy to himself from such a revolution.

I cannot well leave this country for Ireland before next month, when I hope to find you there. I cannot imagine why they should murmur at my absence in the College, considering all the persons absent. I am the only one who has the royal authority to be so, not to mention that I am no Senior Fellow, nor consequently concerned in the material part of governing the College.

The other day when I saw the children they were very well, except Philly who is much worn away. Mr. Bligh[397] lost his son last Saturday.

My humble respects to my Lady.

I am, My Lord,

> your Lordship's most obedient humble servant,
> G: Berkeley

73 BERKELEY TO PERCIVAL

EP, BL Add. MS 47028, fols. 60v–61. Letter copied in Percival's diary: BL Add. MS 47087, fol. 114v.

London, 18 August 1715

My Lord,

This is to inform you of two remarkable pieces of news that I heard this day. The French King is either[398] dead or at least past hopes of recovery, of which an express from Lord Stairs[399] has brought advice this morning, gangrene having begun in the leg and thigh of that prince. What I am further to tell you is that the rumour of the Pretender's[400] invasion is revived and credited more than ever. And indeed it does not seem improbable that the Anjou-faction in France should incline to give England a diversion at this juncture to prevent their assisting the Duke of Orleans[401] in his claim to the regency. My Lord Mar's,[402] Sir William Wyndham's,[403] Sir Thomas Hanmer's[404] and several others withdrawing into the country seems to strengthen the suspicion. At least I know it strengthens the hopes of the only Jacobite I am acquainted with here.

---

[397] John Bligh* (Blithe) (1687–1728). His son George died in infancy.
[398] The diary version has "actually" for "either."
[399] John Dalrymple (1673–1747), second Earl of Stair. He was aide-de-camp to Marlborough and serving as ambassador to Paris. In 1715 he managed to secure the expulsion of the Pretender* from Paris.
[400] James Francis Edward Stuart* (1688–1766).
[401] Charles Philippe (1674–1723). Philippe did serve as Regent of France from 1715 to 1723.
[402] John Erskine* (1675–1732), twenty-second or sixth Earl of Mar and Jacobite Duke of Mar.
[403] William Wyndham (c. 1688–1740), third Baronet.
[404] Thomas Hanmer* (1677–1746), fourth Baronet.

If this news prove true, and the Tories openly engage in the attempt, I shall think them guilty of as barefaced perjury and dishonesty as ever could be imputed to any set of men.

I am very sorry to hear of my Lady's illness. I hope it is only what owes it original to you. The most comfortable prospect I have in Ireland is that I shall find her Ladyship and you there. I am

> My Lord,
>
> your Lordship's most affectionate humble servant,
>
> G: Berkeley

74 BERKELEY TO PERCIVAL

EP, BL Add. MS 47028, fols. 69–70. Letter copied in Percival's diary: BL Add. MS 47088, fol. 2v.

London, 8 September 1715

My Lord,

I agree with your Lordship that there never was a more important juncture, or that justified a curiosity after news more than the present. It was my province to inform you what the Tories say. For Whig news, I doubt not you have enough from other hands. They say that Col. Paul,[405] who you must have heard is committed to Newgate, was always known to be a Whig, and consequently is innocent of what is laid to his charge. They add that the Sergeant, his accuser, is a noted villain, who suffered thirteen years' imprisonment in Dublin on account of former crimes, and so not to be depended on. But notwithstanding all this, the discovery of many others engaged in the same black design makes me think him guilty, which seems more probable because I am assured he is a silly man, and one likely to be prevailed on by the hopes of commanding the second battalion of guards, which is said was promised him by the Pretender.[406] There could not certainly have been a more subtle and mischievous project set on foot by the Jacobites, and I doubt it has spread further than is commonly imagined: I mean tampering with the soldiers and new levies. This occasions my calling to mind what I observed about a fortnight agone. As I walked through St. James's park, there was an odd looking fellow in close conference with one of the sentinels. I heard him mention the words, *hereditary right*; and think the entire sentence was: *But sure you are for hereditary right.* I observe likewise that the few I suspect for Jacobites are not so dispirited or desperate, as the late accidents

---

[405] An unknown reference, but not to be confused with William Paul (1679–1716), the Jacobite nonjuror.
[406] James Francis Edward Stuart* (1688–1766).

of the French King's death and the succession of the Duke of Orleans[407] in the regency would incline one to think they should be. Add to this the general ferment in men's minds, the artifice with which it is kept up by those that wish ill to the present establishment, and the indiscretion of some of its well wishers, which perhaps may no less contribute to the same effect, and our prospect must seem very dismal. I once little imagined that any considerable number of Church of England-men could be moved either by passion or interest to so wicked an undertaking as that must be which includes both rebellion and perjury. For my part I condemn both them and their practices.

The best on it is, that the vigilant measures taken at Court and the perfect seeming good disposition of France gives hopes that any impious design to embroil the nation may be soon defeated and turned on the heads of the contrivers. There is now a strict inquiry making into the characters of all persons in the army, private men as well as officers. And tomorrow the Duke of Argyle,[408] Duke of Roxburgh,[409] and Lord Sutherland[410] are to set out for Scotland. There must have been some pressing reason for this, it having been much against the inclination and endeavours of the Duke of Argyle. The Bishop of Bristol[411] assured me the other day that the Court expect the Duke of Orleans[412] would, in case of need, supply them with forces against the Pretender. And I myself have seen two letters, one from the Duke Regent, the other from the new King of France to the Prince of Wales, containing assurance of friendship and affection.

I reckon it is no news to tell you the two pretty children[413] are well and grow every day more like their mother and father; that is more pretty and wise. Mrs. Parker[414] is well. Mr. Dering[415] goes this day to meet his mother at Chester. I am

> My Lord,
>
> your Lordship's most
>
> humble and most
>
> affectionate servant,
>
> G. Berkeley

Argyle and Sutherland are set out today.

---

[407] Charles Philippe (1674–1723).

[408] John Campbell,* second Duke of Argyll (1680–1743).

[409] John Ker, fifth Earl and first Duke of Roxburghe (c. 1680–1741), Scottish politician, keeper of the Privy Seal (1714–16).

[410] John Gordon, sixteenth Earl of Sutherland (c. 1661–1733), army officer and politican.

[411] George Smalridge* (1662–1719).

[412] Charles Philippe (1674–1723).

[413] The diary version ends here abruptly, but includes the closing line below the signature.

[414] Mary Parker* (1692–1731).

[415] Either Daniel Dering* (?–1730) or, less likely, his brother Charles Dering* (?–?).

75 BERKELEY TO PERCIVAL

EP, BL Add. MS 47028, fols. 72v–74. Letter copied in Percival's diary:
BL Add. MS 47088, fol. 11–11v.

London, 22 September 1715

My Lord,

We are in a very ill condition, the rage and resentment of the Tories having at length broke out into an open flame. You are I doubt not already well informed of this. Be pleased however to take things as I hear them. The rebellion in Scotland is differently represented as to the force and number of the rebels. Some reckon twenty-eight thousand, others seventeen thousand, and others ten thousand. The last account came three days ago by an express from the Duke of Argyle,[416] who complains much of the disparity of numbers, having only fifteen hundred to oppose ten thousand that were then come within thirty miles of Edinburgh, and designed proclaiming the Pretender[417] at Dundee, yesterday was sennight. The Duke was then in suspense whether he should retire towards Berwick, or intrench near Stirling. The unhappy misunderstanding between our courtiers, particularly the Duke of Marlborough[418] and Argyle, prevents the Court from forming any resolute judgment on these informations, many being of an opinion that Argyle magnifies the force of the rebels with a design to oppose and distress the Duke of Marlborough, who is they say of a humour inclined to starve any service wherein he is not employed himself. On the other hand other well wishers of the King[419] are afraid the Duke of Marlborough's jealousy might make him propose such measures as may destroy the Duke of Argyle. Thus as in most other cases the public is neglected while ministers pursue and indulge their private piques and passions.

This account you may depend on for I had it from a very good hand who knows the Court, and whose interest and inclinations engage him to be heartily zealous for the King's safety. We are informed that the rebels increase daily, that they have seized and plundered the custom house of Leith, and that they have taken three companies of the King's forces, the major part whereof have listed under them. They have with them the Generals Dillon[420] and Hamilton,[421] and

---

[416] John Campbell* (1680–1743), second Duke of Argyll.

[417] James Francis Edward Stuart* (1688–1766).

[418] John Churchill* (1650–1722), first Duke of Marlborough.

[419] George I* (1660–1727).

[420] Arthur Dillon (1670–1733), Jacobite Earl Dillon.

[421] Richard Hamilton (?–1717), a Jacobite army officer and son of Sir George Hamilton, first Baronet (?–1679).

some say the Duke of Berwick.[422] Expresses come to Court thick one upon another, and their being kept secret makes one suspect they bring no good news. But the worst sign of all is the cheerful insolent behaviour of the Jacobites, and the downcast melancholy looks of the loyal party, which last was very observable yesterday in the House of Commons. It is not doubted that the rebels will march directly into England, and then it is very much feared that there will be a general insurrection in all parts of the land. It is this general bent of the people towards Jacobitism that occasions the raising of so few forces at home, which might prove to be raising the King's enemies. However, this is certain, that Brigadier Preston[423] is sent into Holland to demand the ten thousand soldiers which they were to furnish by the Barrier Treaty, and they talk here of listing several thousand French refugees under Lord Galloway.[424]

Yesterday the Lords Landsdowne[425] and Duplin[426] were seized here; Lord Jersey[427] was likewise sought for, but made his escape. There are warrants said to be issued for the seizing twenty lords more, and six commoners.

I wish your Lordship, my Lady and a dozen more friends safe at Mascarenes[428] out of this corrupt part of the world, where the resentment, the perjury, and breach of faith of one side, and the private piques and interested views of the other, are in a fair way of ruining our King and country, if providence does not interpose in a manner we nowise deserve. It is believed the Pretender is in England. I am

> My Lord,
>
> your Lordship's most obedient and affectionate humble servant,
>
> G: Berkeley

---

[422] James FitzJames (1670–1734), Duke of Berwick.

[423] Might be George Preston (1659?–1748), army officer. He was appointed governor of Edinburgh with the outbreak of the rebellion in 1715.

[424] James Stewart (?–1746), fifth Earl of Galloway.

[425] George Granville* (1666–1735), Baron Lansdowne and Jacobite Duke of Albemarle.

[426] George Hay (1689–1758), eighth Earl of Kinnoull. Made Viscount of Dupplin in 1709, he and Granville were two of the twelve peers created by Queen Anne.* Hay was made Baron Hay of Penwardine, Herefordshire, in the British peerage at the end of 1711 to defend the Tory stance on the Treaty of Utrecht. During the Jacobite rising of 1715, Dupplin, like his father, was detained in London on suspicion of support for the Stuart cause, being held until June 1717.

[427] Edward Villiers (1655?–1711), first Earl of Jersey.

[428] An old collective title for the islands of Mauritius, Réunion, and Rodriguez in the Indian Ocean.

76 BERKELEY TO PERCIVAL

EP, BL Add. MS 47028, fol. 78–78v. Letter copied in Percival's diary: BL Add. MS 47088, fol. 12v.

London, 26 September 1715

My Lord,

My last, according to the intelligence I then had, gave you a dismal prospect of our affairs. This is to make amends by assuring you there is ground to hope that all the bloodshed and desolation which then threatened us will be prevented by the discovery the Court has made of the persons and designs of the conspirators.

Mr. Harvey of Comb, a man of 7,000 pounds a year, has been taken up and examined before a Committee of Council. At first he spoke resolutely and denied all that he was charged with, but upon Lord Townshend's[429] producing his own handwriting he was struck dumb, and being sent away in custody of a messenger he soon after stabbed himself with a penknife in three places. I hear that Lord Nottingham,[430] his uncle, was with him today, and that he seemed desirous to live, but it is thought, if he be not dead already, that he will soon die of his wounds.

You have heard that Sir William Wyndham[431] made his escape out of the hands of a messenger; there is a report about town that he is again taken, but I do not find it gains credit. It was rumoured likewise yesterday that a warrant was issued out to apprehend the Bishop of Rochester,[432] but I hear nothing of it since. Lord Duplin[433] is in the hands of a messenger. Lord Landsdowne[434] is committed to the Tower. Our great security is that the Duke of Orleans[435] seems steady to the interest of the King, and that our last advices from Lord Stairs[436] bring assurances of the Pretender's[437] continuing still at Bar-le-duc.

---

[429] Charles Townshend* (1674–1738), second Viscount Townshend, politician, diplomatist, and agricultural innovator. He was briefly lord lieutenant of Ireland (1716–17).

[430] Daniel Finch (1647–1730), second Earl of Nottingham and seventh Earl of Winchilsea. In 1721 he published a lengthy vindication of orthodox trinitarianism in response to William Whiston.*

[431] William Wyndham (c.1688–1740), third Baronet. Wyndham, a close ally of Bolingbroke, was arrested for complicity in a Jacobite plot in 1715, but was never tried.

[432] Francis Atterbury* (1662–1732).

[433] George Hay (1689–1758), eighth Earl of Kinnoull, earlier Viscount Dupplin. See Letter 75.

[434] George Granville* (1666–1735), Baron Lansdowne and Jacobite Duke of Albemarle.

[435] Charles Philippe (1674–1723).

[436] John Dalrymple (1673–1747), second Earl of Stair. He was aide-de-camp to Marlborough and serving as ambassador to Paris. In 1715 he managed to secure the expulsion of the Pretender* from Paris.

[437] James Francis Edward Stuart* (1688–1766).

For my part I see no hopes for him or his pretensions.[438] His shyness in point of danger will sacrifice them, and their being sacrificed will discourage others from rising in his favour. What better could be hoped from so wicked management; but the most lamentable evil is the great dishonour they have done to the Church and religion by public perjury and rebellion.

This is so clear and plain a case now, that no honest man can pretend to justify them.

It is very late and I have only time to say, I am

My Lord,

your Lordship's most obedient and affectionate humble servant,

Geo: Berkeley

My humble respects to my Lady. I suppose I need [not] tell you Mrs. Dering is recovered, and that Mrs. Parker[439] and the children are well.

77 BERKELEY TO PERCIVAL

EP, BL Add. MS 47028, fols. 89–90. Letter copied in Percival's diary: BL Add.
MS 47088, fols. 21v–22.

London, 20 October 1715

My Lord,

I have but little inclination to write to your Lordship at present upon politics: the scene every day opening and discovering new cause to apprehend a popish power, and all the dismal consequences of it. You will therefore excuse me if I am backward to be the messenger of ill news. In a late letter to you I was of opinion we had no more to fear from the intended conspiracy. But things have since taken a different turn from what I then expected.

The rebellion in Northumberland is said to be two thousand men strong and daily increasing. It is not doubted that as many more have passed the Firth under General Hamilton.[440] The Court indeed gives them out to be a thousand only, but the other account is most credited. The Dutch forces, which I thought would set all things right, are not likely to be here until the game is over. It is at least certain that the Jacobites make a jest of them, saying, that if they do come, they will prejudice King George's affairs more than anything that has been done yet.

---

[438] The diary says "partisans" instead of "pretensions."
[439] Mary Parker* (1692–1731).
[440] Richard Hamilton (?–1717), a Jacobite army officer and son of Sir George Hamilton, first Baronet (?–1679).

Some say the Dutch have been threatened by the Duke of Ormond[441] and a certain foreign court[442] in case they furnish us with any forces. But whatever the cause is you may depend on it, they are not expected here by any body in a fortnight. I must own I cannot account for these dilatory proceedings. The seizing Lord Landsdowne[443] and Sir William Wyndham[444] has not given all the light I at first imagined. Sir William, when he was asked by the Council whether he knew anything of an association, answered that he knew of no association but that of the whole nation against the present ministry, upon which he was sent to the tower, and this, I know not why, is resented by the old Duke of Somerset,[445] his father-in-law. It is thought the Duke of Ormond is landed in Scotland. In a word the chief cause of my apprehensions is the pert confidence of the Jacobites, who are now more spirited than ever.

If my Lady and your Lordship continue thoughts of Mascarenes[446] I will gladly become one of your subjects, for I assure you I ever did and ever shall abhor a popish government.

I thought to have seen you before now, but have been prevailed with some friends to stay here a little upon a prospect of something in England, so that I believe I shall see you here again. I am

yours and my Lady's
most obedient and most humble servant,
Geo: Berkeley

78 BERKELEY TO PERCIVAL

EP, BL Add. MS 47028, fol. 99–99v. Letter copied in Percival's diary: BL Add. MS 47088, fols. 26v–27.

London, 3 November 1715

My Lord,

There is a high Tory (which is now reckoned the same thing with a Jacobite) of my acquaintance, who used to serve me instead of a political weather glass.

---

[441] James Butler* (1665–1745), second Duke of Ormond.

[442] Luce has a typo, reading "count" for "court," and the copy in the diary says "court" as well.

[443] George Granville* (1666–1735), Baron Lansdowne and Jacobite Duke of Albemarle.

[444] William Wyndham (c. 1688–1740), third Baronet.

[445] Charles Seymour (1662–1748), sixth Duke of Somerset, known as the "Proud Duke." He was appointed Master of the Horse by King George I,* but resigned in October 1715 when his offer to give surety for the release of his son-in-law William Wyndham was refused.

[446] An old collective title for the islands of Mauritius, Réunion, and Rodriguez in the Indian Ocean.

When his spirits were high I concluded our affairs went wrong, and the contrary when they were low. I never knew him so high in spirit as he was when I writ last to your Lordship; but since that time things are altered, and we have now reason to thank God that the enemies of our constitution hang down their heads. Whatever I might have apprehended of late, at present I think their game desperate.

Your Lordship will be of my mind when I tell you that the Duke of Ormond[447] is gone back to France, after having lain one night ashore at one Cary's in Devonshire. My Lord Stairs[448] has sent to Court a letter intercepted from him to the Pretender,[449] wherein the Duke tells his pretended Majesty that he would embark and make his signals on the coast of England, which if answered he did not doubt being at the head of a body of his subjects able to do him justice, otherwise he would be himself the messenger of the ill news to his Majesty. In the same letter he exhorts the Pretender to be in a readiness to embark in case occasion should serve.

For the future I shall never be scared at the vauntings of a few fellows who have all the villany, without the sense or courage necessary to carry on a conspiracy. The forces under Lord Mar[450] nobody doubts will languish and disperse in a little time. To do my Lord Peterborough[451] justice, this was the opinion he always declared himself to have of the rebels and their project.

Dr. Friend,[452] who got the £20,000 prize in the lottery,[453] is disposed to give up a living in the presentation of his Lordship. By what I hear he will resign it in a few months in which case it may be worth my acceptance. I wish your Lordship[454] a good voyage and hope to see you here in less than a month.

---

[447] James Butler* (1665–1745), second Duke of Ormond.

[448] John Dalrymple (1673–1747), second Earl of Stair.

[449] James Francis Edward Stuart* (1688–1766).

[450] John Erskine* (1675–1732), twenty-second or sixth Earl of Mar and Jacobite Duke of Mar.

[451] Charles Mordaunt* (1658?–1735), third Earl of Peterborough and first Earl of Monmouth.

[452] William Freind (1668/69–1745), Church of England clergyman. Berkeley and others frequently misspell the name.

[453] On 14 February 1715, it was reported in the newspapers that Freind had won the first prize of £20,000 in "The Adventure of £1,400,000" by statute 13 Anne c. 18. The "Adventure" was in fact a government loan disguised as a lottery with prizes: all subscribers won an annuity proportionate to their subscription, or, in the case of prize winners, the value of the prize. The lump sum of the prize was retained by the government for thirty-two years, during which time interest would be paid. Freind therefore had won an annuity of £800 per year until 1747, while both the annuity and the capital value of the prize provided security for borrowing. Berkeley apparently knew Freind and his two brothers John and Robert. Luce reports, "No doubt it was Robert that won the prize" (*Works*, vol. IX, p. 39), although the historical record indicates it was William.

[454] The diary version adds "and my Lady."

Two days ago I saw the children very well in the Pall Mall,* as are Mrs. Parker[455] and Mr. Dering.* I am

>My Lord,
>
>your Lordship's most obliged
>
>most humble and affectionate
>
>servant,
>
>G. Berkeley

79 BERKELEY TO PERCIVAL

EP, BL Add. MS 47028, fols. 104v–05. Letter copied in Percival's diary:
BL Add. MS 47088, fols. 29v–30.

London, 17 November 1715

My Lord,

I wish your Lordship and my Lady Percival joy of the victory which his Majesty's forces have gained over the rebels in Preston,[456] the particulars whereof the newspapers tell you. I hope this blow hath put an end to or prevented the calamities we had too much cause to apprehend from an obstinate and bloody civil war. The want of spirit and conduct in the rebels deserves our scorn, as much as the injustice of their cause and the mischiefs they were going to involve us in did our abhorrence.

They seem to have been intimidated and struck from heaven, which, it is to be hoped, will speedily open the eyes of their accomplices, and teach their own and the nation's true interest.

I reckon it none of the least misfortunes of these troublesome times that books and literature seem to be forgotten, conversation being entirely turned from them to more disagreeable and less innocent topics. Even the most retired men and who are at the bottom of fortune's wheel are too much interested in our public broils to be attentive to other things. This makes me doubt your application to the classics hath been intermitted since your going to Ireland. If it hath not and you are at leisure, I would much rather correspond with you on the beauties of the Latin authors, than on the subject of news of which the public papers tell you all that is certain, and for other surmises they

---

[455] Mary Parker* (1692–1731).

[456] A small skirmish between government and Jacobite forces occurred at Preston in Lancashire, 9–14 November 1715. It was heralded as a great victory for the Hanoverians.

are hardly worth troubling. But what do I talk, you have perhaps left Dublin already.

I wish you and my Lady a good voyage and long to see you safe in London.

My Lord,

your Lordship's most obedient and most obliged servant,

Geo: Berkeley

80 BERKELEY TO PERCIVAL

EP, BL Add. MS 47028, fol. 151–51v.

London, May 1716

My Lord,

I am sorry to hear you pass the time so pleasantly at Bath. I am afraid it may keep you too long from us. However, I hope to see you before I go Ireland, which is likely to be soon, the Prince[457] having recommended me to the Lords Justices to succeed Charles Carr[458] in the Living of St. Paul's, in Dublin. I suppose you have heard that Mr. Carr is named to the Bishopric of Killaloe, that the Bishop of Killaloe[459] is removed to Raphoe, and the Bishop of Raphoe[460] to the Archbishopric of Tuam. The letter from the Prince is enclosed and seconded by Mr. Secretary Stanhope,[461] so that I think it cannot fail of success. The living is reckoned to be worth about a hundred a year, but I put the greater value on it because it is consistent with my fellowship.

We had yesterday a very remarkable piece of news. An express arrived at Court from Constantinople with proposals to the King to mediate a peace between the Turk and the Venetians. This falls out very unexpectedly, and gives some credit to the opinions of the Bishop of Worchester,[462] and the rest

---

[457] George Augustus (1683–1760), Prince of Wales and later King George II.*
[458] Charles Carr (?–1739) was consecrated bishop of Killaloe in June 1716, vacating St. Paul's Church in Dublin. Berkeley apparently expected to receive the parish of St. Paul's, but did not.
[459] Nicholas Forster* (1672–1743) was translated to the bishopric of Raphoe.
[460] Edward Synge* (1659–1741) was made archbishop of Tuam in June 1716.
[461] James Stanhope (1673–1721), first Earl Stanhope. In 1716 Stanhope was secretary of state and largely guiding English foreign policy.
[462] William Lloyd (1627–1717). Lloyd was renowned for his long-standing study of biblical chronology and prophecy, relating the texts of Daniel and Revelation to current events. Berkeley's remark alludes to this work.

of our expositors who judged it inconsistent with their scheme that the Grand Seignoir should carry his arms any farther westward.

I hope the waters agree well with my Lady, Mrs. Parker,[463] and the children. Pray give my humble service to them all. I am

My Lord,

your Lordship's most obedient and most affectionate humble servant,

G: Berkeley

81 BERKELEY TO PERCIVAL

EP, BL Add. MS 47028, fol. 153–53v.

London, 26 May 1716

My Lord,

If it be what your Lordship can properly do I beg the favour of you to write a letter next post to the Duke of Grafton,[464] imparting your acquaintance with me, and your confidence of my being well affected to his Majesty's government. Were it necessary I might produce several instances of this, as well as from my endeavours to serve the present establishment by writing, which are more than I care to mention, as from the offer I refused in the times of the late ministry. I make you this request because I have some reason to think my competitors have wronged my character on the other side of the water.

The government of Ireland have yet made no answer to the recommendation of the Prince[465] and Secretary Stanhope,[466] which if they refuse to comply with I am assured it will be taken very ill, I am likewise told that their not complying may prove an advantage to me. But be that as it will, I cannot but be solicitous to have my character cleared to the Lords Justices and others there, who are probably misled by the calumny of interested persons who are strangers to me.

This is all that I desire of your Lordship. As for recommending me, or desiring any favour for me from his hands, I ask no such thing, because I do not think I want it, having been so well recommended already.

---

[463] Mary Parker* (1692–1731).
[464] Charles Fitzroy* (1683–1757), second Duke of Grafton.
[465] George Augustus (1683–1760), Prince of Wales and later King George II.*
[466] James Stanhope (1673–1721), first Earl Stanhope.

Please to give my humble service to Lady Percival and Mrs. Parker.[467] I am glad to hear from your Lordship that they and the children are well, and hope to see you all in town next week. I am

My Lord,

your Lord's most obedient

and most affectionate servant,

G. Berkeley

82 BERKELEY TO PERCIVAL[468]

EP, BL Add. MS 47028, fols. 169v–71.

Turin, 24 November 1716

My Lord,

I did not think it prudent to make reflections of the state of France while I was in the country, but now I am got out of it I may safely impart my mind to your Lordship and assure you that it is in a very bad condition: the [R]egent is generally misliked by the people, and his alliance with England has perhaps contributed to make him so as much as any other article of his conduct.

The French seemed to have recovered their tongues, and speak with a freedom unusual in the late king's reign. They scruple not to say the Duke[469] hath done more mischief in two, than his predecessor in seventy years. They exclaim against the demolition of Mardyke[470] as a thing dishonourable to their nation; and against his recoining their money as a project that has ruined them, and has cut off all correspondence with foreigners who are sure to lose four livres in the pound on the present foot of exchange. This project, however, hath filled the Regent's coffers by robbing the subjects of a fourth part of the money.

I was assured there appeared a disposition in several, as well clergy as laity, to embrace the [P]rotestant communion.

---

[467] Mary Parker* (1692–1731).

[468] A note in Percival's letterbook indicates this letter was answered on 11 December [1716] (Letter 83).

[469] The Duke of Orleans, Charles Philippe* (1674–1723), then regent of France.

[470] A fort in northern France by Dunkirk. Bought in 1662 from the English, the destruction of the fortifications was a provision of the Treaty of Utrecht.

We travel with all the ease and convenience possible. Mr. Ashe[471] is a modest, ingenious, well natured, young gentleman, whom the more I know the more I esteem, and we have unlimited letters of credit so that we want for nothing. I never thought I should pass Mount Cenis[472] a second time in winter. But we have now passed in a worse condition than it was when I saw it before. It blew and snowed bitterly all the time. The snow almost blinded us and reached above the waists of the men who carried us. They let me fall six or seven times, and thrice on the brinks of horrid precipices, the snow having covered the path so that it was impossible to avoid making false steps. The porters assured us they never in their lives had passed the mountain in such an ill road and weather. However, blessed be God, we arrived safe at Turin two nights ago, and design to set out from hence towards Milan tomorrow.

I forgot to tell you that we saw two avalanches of snow (as the men called them) on the mountain: I mean huge quantities of snow fallen from the side and tops of rocks, sufficient to have overwhelmed a regiment of men. They told us of fourteen, and about fifty mules that were some time since destroyed by an accident of that kind. I must not omit another adventure in Dauphine. A huge dark coloured alpine wolf ran across an open plain when our chaise was passing, when he came near as he turned about and made a stand with a very fierce and daring look, I instantly drew my sword and Mr. Ashe fired his pistol. I did the same too, upon which the beast very calmly retired looking back ever and anon. We were much mortified that he did not attack us and give us an opportunity of killing him.

The route we design to take is through Milan, Parma, Modena, Bologna, Florence, Siena, Rome etc., which will be a means of seeing the best part of the cities of Italy. We hear of banditti, rivers overflown, mountains covered with snow, and the like difficulties in this winter expedition, but our resolution is fixed.

Whatever becomes of me and wherever I am you may assure yourself I shall always be most sincerely,

My Lord,

your Lordship's most obliged and most affectionate humble servant,

G. Berkeley

My humble service to the ladies.

[471] St. George Ashe* (1698–1721).
[472] The copy in Percival's letterbook says "Senis."

83 PERCIVAL TO BERKELEY

EP, BL Add. MS 47028, fols. 173v–74v.

London, 11 December 1716

Dear Sir,

Your letter from Turin is very pleasing to me as it assures me of your having safely passed through many dangers and that you find yourself in heart and ability to encounter what yet remains before your arrival at the wished for resting place. There is something resembling between your unpleasant and painful journey and a deathbed sickness, which, though in itself uncomfortable and terrible, is yet cheerfully supported by men of your fortitude, for the prospect of that happy region to which it leads, and which restores men to their original innocence, as Naples will I hope Mr. Ashe[473] to his health.

The account you gave me of the misery and discontents in France is confirmed by many that come from thence. An instance of the ill state of their commerce is the high exchange from my part of Ireland to this place, which I have known at 1 and ½ at this time of year, and now is £10 per cent.

We have had a violent hard frost this week past, which prevents us from Holland mails, but I hope it will not continue so long as to hinder the King's[474] return by the sitting of Parliament, which is to be the 8th of next month.

It is so lately that you left us I have little to write you of public matters. I believe you will meet the public prints when this letter finds you, and they contain all that is material to know, besides you are now I guess in Naples, where the climate, prospects, villas, antiquities, and variety of liberal entertainments, will render you very little inquisitive after news, and ought to engross all your moments during absence which I hope will be but short. I believe therefore I shall please you much better if, setting public matters aside, I confine myself to let you know that all your friends here are well, and especially my small family who desire to be remembered to you, and that I am with all truth

your affectionate friend and humble servant,
Percival

My humble service to Mr. Ashe.

---

[473] St. George Ashe* (1698–1721). The young St. George was sickly.
[474] George I* (1660–1727).

84 BERKELEY TO PERCIVAL

EP, BL Add. MS 47028, fols. 182–83v. The penultimate paragraph (only) is copied in Percival's diary: BL Add. MS 47088, fol. 66.

Rome, 1 March 1716/17

My Lord,

It is with a great deal of pleasure that I hear my Lady hath been safely delivered of a daughter.[475] I wish you and her Ladyship joy of this happy event, and hope it may facilitate your projected journey into these parts this summer. I can give you no temptations to effect this design so long talked of, but what you know by your own experience better than I can possibly describe them to you. The climate, the music, the pictures, the palaces etc. are things so enchanting that I am afraid if my Lady sees them she will be more backward to return than ever she was to come abroad.

Though I would not pretend to inform you of anything to be seen in Italy, yet a picture in the gallery of the Duke of Parma, at Parma, may possibly have escaped your observation. I mean the original of your Danae, which is esteemed one of the finest pieces that ever Titian did. We have stayed at Rome much longer than we intended, being constrained partly by the extreme rigour of the season for about 3 weeks together, and since that by the illness of our valet de chambre. As soon as ever he can travel we design for Naples where I long to be. I have got eyes but no ears. I would say that I am a judge of painting though not of music. Cardinal Ottoboni[476] has let off his entertainments, and Prince Rospoli[477] is the man who now gives music every week to strangers, where I am sure to fall asleep as constantly as I go. Perhaps when I reach Naples I may be able to tell you of something you have not seen.

In the meantime give me leave to inform you of a piece of secret history that I learned the other night from one who I doubt not knew the truth, and I have reason to think told it me. In England there are now seven hundred clergymen in all of the Church of Rome, of which one hundred Jesuits, three hundred priests, and the rest friars of several orders. In Wales there are 50 clergy, in the west 10, in the north 200. In London and the environs 150, of which in London 20 Jesuits, 12 Benedictines, 5 Capuchins, 3 Carmelites.

---

[475] Mary, born 28 December 1716, died an infant.

[476] Pietro Ottoboni (1667–1740), Italian cardinal and grandnephew of Pope Alexander VIII. Ottoboni was a great patron of both music and art.

[477] Most likely Francesco Maria Marescotti Ruspoli (1672–1731), Prince di Cerveteri, first Marchese di Riano and sixth Conte di Vignanello.

The Jesuits have at least £8,000 a year terra firma in England (some say 30,000). The secular priests have £3,000 per annum. The number of Papists in England is 70,000.

Pray give my humble service to my Lady, Mrs. Parker,[478] Mrs. Dering (whose health I should gladly be informed of), Mrs. Minshull and Mr. Dering, with the rest of those friends who are so good as to remember me. I am

My Lord
your Lordship's most
obliged and most
humble servant,
G. Berkeley

85 BERKELEY TO PERCIVAL

EP, BL Add. MS 47028, fols. 186v–87v.

Naples, 6 April 1717

My Lord,

I know not whether I ought to reckon it to your good or ill fortune that when you were abroad you missed seeing the Kingdom of Naples. This in itself one of the worst accidents and disappointments of your life may become by prudent management a great piece of good fortune to you and your whole family. I mean, in case it should be the occasion of your wisely resolving to visit again the regions on this side of the Alps, and bring them with you. Your Lordship hath many motives of pleasure to invite you to home; but I have now solid reasons for bringing [you] further southward. The health of all that is most dear to you, my Lady and the pretty children, and yourself depend on it. The air of this happy part of the world is soft and delightful beyond conception, being perfumed with myrtle shrubs and orange groves; that are everywhere scattered throughout the country; the sky almost constantly serene and blue; the heat tempered to a just warmth by refreshing breezes from the sea. Nor will this serene and warmth of the climate have a better effect on the spirits, than the balsamine particles of sulphur which you breathe with the common air will have on your blood, correcting those sharp scorbutic humours that molest the inhabitants of these bleak islands. If enchanting prospects be a temptation, surely there are not more

---

[478] Mary Parker* (1692–1731).

and finer anywhere than here, rude mountains, fruitful hills, shady vales, and green plains, with all the variety of sea as well as land—prospects are the natural ornaments of this Kingdom. *Nullus in orbe locus Baiis praelucet amoenis*[479] was the opinion of one who had a very good taste. It would fill a volume to describe the wonders of nature and antiquity that adorn that whole coast. Every hill, rock, promontory, creek, and island, is sung by Homer and Virgil, and renowned as well for having been the scene of the travels of Ulysses and Aeneas as for having been the delicious retreat of all the great men among the Romans, whenever they withdrew from the fatigue of public affairs. The Campania felecie is a different scene; but surely nothing can be more beautiful than the wild Apennine on one hand and the boundless plain without enclosures on the other covered with a most delightful verdure and crowned with fruit trees scattered so thinly as not to hinder the prospect of the wide-extended green fields. Here grew the famous Falernian wine, and in the same plain stands the once famous city of Capua whose pleasures were destructive to Hannibal. To describe the antiquities and natural curiosities of these places would perhaps seem tedious to you, and I would not forestall the pleasure you will take in seeing them yourself.

It may be perhaps a more prevailing tune with my Lady, the informing you that there is here a very numerous nobility, who think of nothing but how to amuse themselves agreeably, and are very civil in admitting strangers to share with them in their entertainments of music and refreshments, though to say the truth they are not the politest people in the world. Today I had the honour to dine with three princes, besides half a dozen counts and dukes, the first nobility in the land, and I assure you it was not without some surprise that I found myself to be one of the politest persons at table. You will believe me disinterested and sincere in what I have said, when I tell you that I cannot propose to myself the happiness of seeing you here during my own stay in this country.

My humblest respects to my Lady, Mrs. Parker[480] and the rest of our friends.

My Lord,

your Lordship's

most obedient humble servant,

G: Berkeley

---

[479] The line is from Horace (*Epistles*, I.I.83), but Berkeley alters the line, perhaps for his own purposes. Horace originally had: "Nullus in orbe sinus Bais praeluct amoenis" ("No bay [curve, in context: a shoreline] on earth surpasses charming Baiae"). Berkeley's alteration translates as "No place on earth surpasses charming Baiae."

[480] Mary Parker* (1692–1731).

86 BERKELEY TO PERCIVAL

EP, BL Add. MS 47028, fol. 192–92v.

Naples, 18 June 1717

My Lord,

I am lately returned from a tour through the most remote and unknown parts of Italy.

The celebrated cities your Lordship is perfectly acquainted with. But perhaps it may be new to you to hear that the most beautiful city in Italy lies in a remote corner of the heel. Lecce (the ancient Aletium) is the most luxuriant in all ornaments of architecture of any town that I have seen. The meanest houses are built of hewn stone, have ornamented doors, rustics. Doric, Corinthian, are ornaments about the windows, and balustrades of stone. I have not in all Italy seen so fine convents. The general fault is they run into a superfluity of ornaments. The most predominant are the Corinthian, which order is much affected by the inhabitants, being used in the gates of their city, which are extremely beautiful.

The town being inland and consequently without trade hath not above 16,000 inhabitants. They are a civil polite people, and seem to have among them some remains of the delicacy of the Greeks who of old inhabited these parts of Italy.

You know that in most cities of Italy the palaces indeed are fine, but the ordinary houses of an indifferent gusto. It is so even in Rome, whereas in Lecce there is a general good gout, which descends down to the poorest houses. I saw many other remarkable towns, amongst the rest five fair cities in one day, the most part built of white marble, whereof the names are not known to Englishmen. The season of the year (which was much more moderate than I expected) together with the various beautiful [landscapes][481] throughout Apulia, Peucetia, and the old Calabria, made this journey very agreeable. Nor should I pass over the antiquities that we saw in Brundisium, Tarentum, Venusia (where Horace was born), Cannae famous for the great victory obtained by Hannibal, and many other places in all which we were stared at like men dropt from the sky, and sometimes followed by a numerous crowd of citizens, who out of curiosity attended us through the streets. The fear of bandits which hinders strangers from visiting these curiosities is a mere bugbear.

Upon my return to Naples I found Vesuvius in a terrible fit which is not yet over.

---

[481] The text has "landskips."

I beg your Lordship to let me know what way you, my Lady, and Mrs. Parker[482] design to take, that I may continue to meet you in our return. My humble service to them.

> I am,
>
> your Lordship's most obedient servant,
>
> G: Berkeley

87 PERCIVAL TO BERKELEY[483]

EP, BL Add. MS 47028, fols. 195v–96.

Kew, 25 July 1717

Dear Sir,

I am always extremely pleased to hear from you, and know by your own hand how you do, and where you are. This satisfaction I lately received from Naples dated 18 June whether you was [sic] lately returned from a tour through the most remote and unknown parts of Italy. The account you give me of that expedition is so delightful that I wonder our travellers into Italy have generally omitted to see those parts; and though I cannot accuse myself of wanting so much curiosity when I was at Rome, because I could not obtain leave even to see Naples which was then in French hands, yet I blame the tribe of governors who decline carrying young gentlemen into so fine a country as you have described.

Whatever design I might have formed of visiting you in Italy, I am now obliged by the expectation of another child to lay it aside, and I must rest satisfied for the present with the entertaining accounts you give me and I hope will continue to do of your own travels. But I often please myself with the resolution of going abroad again when it shall please God to give me a convenient opportunity.

We pass our time at Kew as we did the summer before, Miss Minshull and Daniel Dering,[484] is with us, but Charles Dering[485] left us some time ago and is

---

[482] Mary Parker* (1692–1731).

[483] The letter was apparently overlooked by Rand (and Luce does not publish the letters from Percival to Berkeley). It is not addressed to Berkeley and there is no marginalia indicating it is to Berkeley, but the content of the letter so closely follows that of Berkeley's previous one that the attribution is unmistakeable.

[484] Daniel Dering* (?–1730).

[485] Charles Dering* (?–?).

now returned to Ireland. I don't design to go there this summer, I hear from thence that all our friends are well, but Mr. Savage is dead which I write you that you may tell Mr. Ashe,[486] his brother-in-law Sir Ralph Gore[487] succeeds him in the Chancellorship of the Exechequer. Pray present my service to him and let him know I am very glad to find he is able to take tours of pleasure. I hope and don't doubt he will be perfectly established in his health when he returns.

My family are all well and much your humble servants, as is

> Dear Sir,
>
> etc.,
>
> Percival

I writ you a day or two before the Bishop of Derry[488] went to Ireland and sent it to his house to be conveyed to you.

88 BERKELEY TO PERCIVAL[489]

EP, BL Add. MS 47028, fols. 199–200.

Testaccio in the Island Inarime, 1 September 1717

My Lord,

Your Lordship's letter found me very ill in the Island Inarime,[490] a remote corner of the world where we have now spent three months. When we go to Naples or Rome I shall make it my business to provide the prints etc., there being nothing more agreeable to me than your Lordship's commands. My illness, a flux, after about six weeks continuance, hath now quite left me, and in a better state of health than it found me. I am thank God very well.

Though your Lordship is well acquainted with other parts of Italy perhaps you may be a stranger to the Island Inarime (now vulgarly called Ischia). It is situate about six leagues from the city of Naples to the southwest: about eighteen miles in circuit, containing sixteen thousand souls, the air temperate and wholesome, the

---

[486] St. George Ashe* (1698–1721).

[487] Sir Ralph Gore (*c.* 1675–1733), fourth Baronet. Gore was appointed in 1717 to the office of chancellor of the Irish exchequer. He would later be selected as Speaker of the Irish House of Commons in 1729.

[488] St. George Ashe* (1658–1718), the father of Berkeley's pupil.

[489] A note next to the text in the letterbook indicates the letter was received on the 28th, presumably of that same month, September 1717.

[490] The island of Ischia, known in the ancient world as Arime. Berkeley's use of the name "Inarime" follows Virgil, who perhaps takes poetic license by adding the preposition εἰν- to Homer, who refers to "the country of the Arimi" (*Iliad*, II.783).

soil extremely fertile. Apples, pears, plums, and cherries, are not worth the naming, besides apricots, peaches, almond[s], figs, pomegranates, and many other fruits that have no English names, together with vines, wheat, and Indian corn, cover almost every spot in the island. The fruit lying everywhere exposed without enclosures makes the country look like one great fruit garden, except some parks which are covered with chestnut groves and others that produce nothing but thickets of myrtle. Nothing can be conceived more romantic than the forces of nature, mountains, hills, vales, and little plains, being thrown together in a wild and beautiful variety. The hills are most of them covered to the top with vines, of which you will believe there is a prodigious abundance in the island, when I assure you there are no less than sixty thousand hogsheads of wine made every year in so small a spot. Here are also mountains very high, having towns and villages on their sides placed in steep situations one above another, and making a very odd prospect. And though the roads among the hills are often steep and unequal, yet the asses of the island (the only *voiture*[491] used here) carry us everywhere without danger. We have two considerable towns or cities, one of which contains six thousand souls: the rest are villages. The houses are real and lasting, being everywhere built of lime and stone, flat roofed.

As riches and honours have no footing here, the people are unacquainted with the vices that attend them, but in lieu thereof the[y] have got an ugly [habit] of murdering one another for trifles. The second night after our coming to the island a youth of 18 years was shot dead by our door; but we have had several instances of the like since that in several parts of the island. Last year thirty-six murders were compounded for by the governour; the life of man being rated at ten ducats.

In old times Inarime was inhabited by a Grecian colony from the Euboea. And Hiero, King of Syracuse, resided here some years, but the volcanoes and eruptions of fire in several parts of the island obliged the ancient inhabitants to quit it. We see the remains of these eruptions in many places, which gave occasion to the poets feigning that Typhoeus lay under it:

Inarime Jovis imperiis imposta Typhoeo. Virgil[492]

My humble service to my Lady, Mrs. Parker,[493] Miss Kitty,[494] Master Johnny,[495] the little stranger, Mrs. Dering, Miss Minshull, Daniel Dering,[496]

---

[491] A carriage.
[492] Virgil, *Aeneid*, IX.716. "Ischia, placed upon Typhoeus at the commands of Jupiter."
[493] Mary Parker* (1692–1731).
[494] Catherine Percival* (1712–48), Percival's eldest daughter.
[495] John Percival,* (1711–70), Percival's eldest child.
[496] Daniel Dering* (?–1730).

Charles Dering,[497] the two Mr. Shutes, Sir David, etc. I writ a long letter to Daniel Dering but never had an answer.

> My Lord,
>
> your Lordship's most obliged etc.,
>
> G: Berkeley

Mr. Ashe[498] gives his humble service to your Lordship.

89 BERKELEY TO ARBUTHNOT[499]

Philosophical Transactions 354 (Oct.–Dec. 1717): 708–13 (extract). Stock, pp. xxxvii–xlii.

October 1717

April 17, 1717. With much difficulty I reached the top of Mount Vesuvius, in which I saw a vast aperture full of smoke, which hindered the seeing its depth and figure. I heard within that horrid gulf certain odd sounds, which seemed to proceed from the belly of the mountain; a sort of murmuring, sighing, throbbing, churning, dashing (as it were) of waves, and between whiles a noise, like that of thunder or cannon, which was constantly attended with a clattering, like that of tiles falling from the tops of houses on the streets. Sometimes, as the wind changed, the smoke grew thinner, discovering a very ruddy flame, and the jaws of the pan or crater streaked with red and several shades of yellow. After an hour's stay, the smoke, being moved by the wind, gave us short and partial prospects of the great hollow, in the flat bottom of which I could discern two furnaces almost contiguous; that on the left, seeming about three yards in diameter, glowed with red flame, and threw up red-hot stones with a hideous noise, which, as they fell back, caused the fore-mentioned clattering.

May 8, in the morning, I ascended to the top of Vesuvius a second time, and found a different face of things. The smoke ascending upright gave a full prospect of the crater, which, as I could judge, is about a mile in circumference, and an hundred yards deep. A conical mount had been formed since my last visit, in the middle of the bottom. This mount, I could see, was made of the

---

[497] Charles Dering* (?–?).

[498] St. George Ashe* (1698–1721).

[499] The letter is reprinted, with minor changes, in *Gentleman's Magazine* 20 (April 1750): 161–62 and again in *Edinburgh Magazine* (July 1790): 57 ff. Immediately prior to the letter appears the following: "Extract of a letter of Mr. Edw. [sic] Berkeley from Naples, giving several curious observations and remarks on the eruptions of fire and smoke from Mount Vesuvio. Communicated by Dr. John Arbuthnot, M.D. and R.S.S."

stones thrown up and fallen back into the crater. In this new hill remained the two mouths or furnaces already mentioned; that on our left hand was in the vertex of the hill which it had formed round it, and raged more violently than before, throwing up, every three or four minutes, with a dreadful bellowing, a vast number of red-hot stones, sometimes in appearance above a thousand, and at least 300 foot[500] higher than my head as I stood upon the brink. But, there being little or no wind, they fell back perpendicularly into the crater, increasing the conical hill. The other mouth to the right was lower in the side of the same new-formed hill. I could discern it to be filled with red-hot liquid matter, like that in the furnace of a glasshouse, which raged and wrought as the waves of the sea, causing a short abrupt noise like what may be imagined to proceed from a sea of quicksilver dashing among uneven rocks. This stuff would sometimes spew over and run down the convex side of the conical hill, and appearing at first red-hot, it changed colour, and hardened as it cooled, showing the first rudiments of an eruption, or, if I may so say, an eruption in miniature. Had the wind driven in our faces, we had been in no small danger of stifling by the sulphurous smoke, or being knocked on the head by lumps of molten minerals, which we saw had sometimes fallen on the brink of the crater, upon those shots from the gulf at the bottom. But, as the wind was favourable, I had an opportunity to survey this odd scene for above an hour and a half together; during which it was very observable that all the volleys of smoke, flame, and burning stones, came only out of the hole to our left, while the liquid stuff in the other mouth wrought and overflowed, as hath been already described.

June 5th, after a horrid noise, the mountain was seen at Naples to spew a little out of the crater. The same continued the 6th.

The 7th, nothing was observed till within two hours of night, when it began a hideous bellowing, which continued all that night and the next day till noon, causing the windows, and as some affirm, the very houses in Naples to shake. From that time it spewed vast quantities of molten stuff to the south which streamed down the side of the mountain like a great pot boiling over. This evening I returned from a voyage through Apulia, and was surprised, passing by the north side of the mountain, to see a great quantity of ruddy smoke lie along a huge tract of sky over the river of molten stuff, which was itself out of sight.

The 9th, Vesuvius raged less violently: that night we saw from Naples a column of fire shoot between whiles out of its summit.

---

[500] Stock has "3000 feet" instead of "300 foot." The *Literary Relics* has "three thousand feet." I use 300, preserving the version in the *Philosophical Transactions*, which makes better sense of the text.

The 10th, when we thought all would have been over, the mountain grew very outrageous again, roaring and groaning most dreadfully. You cannot form a juster idea of this noise in the most violent fits of it, than by imagining a mixed sound made up of the raging of a tempest, the murmur of a troubled sea, and the roaring of thunder and artillery, confused all together. It was very terrible as we heard it in the further end of Naples, at the distance of above twelve miles. This moved my curiosity to approach the mountain. Three or four of us got into a boat, and were set ashore at *Torre del Greco*, a town situate[d] at the foot of Vesuvius to the south-west, whence we rode four or five miles before we came to the burning river, which was about midnight. The roaring of the volcano grew exceeding loud and horrible as we approached. I observed a mixture of colours in the cloud over the crater, green, yellow, red, and blue; there was likewise a ruddy dismal light in the air over that tract of land where the burning river flowed; ashes continually showered on us all the way from the sea-coast: all which circumstances, set off and augmented by the horror and silence of the night, made a scene the most uncommon and astonishing I ever saw; which grew still more extraordinary as we came nearer the stream. Imagine a vast torrent of liquid fire rolling from the top down the side of the mountain, and with irresistible fury bearing down and consuming vines, olives, fig-trees, houses; in a word, every thing that stood in its way. This mighty flood divided into different channels, according to the inequalities of the mountain. The largest stream seemed half a mile broad at least, and five miles long. The nature and consistence of these burning torrents hath been described with so much exactness and truth by Borellus in his Latin treatise of Mount Aetna[501], that I need say nothing of it. I walked so far before my companions, up the mountain along the side of the river of fire, that I was obliged to retire in great haste, the sulphureous stream having surprised me, and almost taken away my breath. During our return, which was about three-a-clock in the morning, we constantly heard the murmur and groaning of the mountain, which between whiles would burst out into louder peals, throwing up huge spouts of fire and burning stones, which falling down again, resembled the stars in our rockets. Sometimes I observed two, at others three, distinct columns of flames, and some-times one vast one that seemed to fill the whole crater. These burning columns and the fiery stones seemed to be shot 1,000 feet perpendicular above the summit of the volcano.

The 11th, at night, I observed it, from a terrass in Naples, to throw up incessantly a vast body of fire, and great stones to a surprising height.

[501] Giovanni Alfonso Borelli (1608–79), *Historia et Meteorologia Incendii Aetnaei Anni 1669* (Reggio di Calabria: Domenico Ferro, 1670).

The 12th, in the morning, it darkened the sun with ashes and smoke, causing a sort of eclipse. Horrid bellowings, this and the foregoing day, were heard at Naples, whither part of the ashes also reached. At night I observed it throw up flame, as on the 11th.

On the 13th, the wind changing, we saw a pillar of black smoke shot upright to a prodigious height. At night I observed the mount cast up fire as before, though not so distinctly, because of the smoke.

The 14th, a thick black cloud hid the mountain from Naples.

The 15th, in the morning, the court and walls of our house in Naples were covered with ashes. In the evening flame appeared on the mountain through the cloud.[502]

The 16th, the smoke was driven by a westerly wind from the town to the opposite side of the mountain.

The 17th, the smoke appeared much diminished, fat and greasy.

The 18th, the whole appearance ended, the mountain remaining perfectly quiet without any visible smoke or flame. A gentleman of my acquaintance, whose window looked towards Vesuvius, assured me that he observed this night several flashes, as it were of lightning, issue out of the mouth of the volcano. It is not worth while to trouble you with the conjectures I have formed concerning the cause of these phenomena, from what I observed in the *Lacus Amsancti*, the *Solfatara*,[503] etc., as well as in Mount Vesuvius. One thing I may venture to say, that I saw the fluid matter rise out of the centre of the bottom of the crater, out of the very middle of the mountain, contrary to what Borellus imagines,[504] whose method of explaining the eruption of a volcano by an inflexed syphon and the rules of hydrostaticks, is likewise inconsistent with the torrent's flowing down from the very vertex of the mountain. I have not seen the crater since the eruption, but design to visit it again before I leave Naples. I doubt there is nothing in this worth showing the Society: as to that you will use your discretion.

E.[505] Berkeley

---

[502] This sentence is not in the Stock original edition nor in *LR*, but *is* present in the published version that appeared in *Philosophical Transactions*.

[503] "the lake of Amsantus, the Solfatara." The former is a sulphorous lake, the latter is a dormant volcano, both near Naples.

[504] The eruption of Mt Etna in 1669 reported by Borelli was not actually witnessed by him. He took issue with the notion that there were vast caverns of lava beneath the earth's surface, for which volcanoes were a safety valve. Borelli thought instead that local combusion inside the mountain caused rocks and sand to melt, and this vitrified rock erupted as lava.

[505] A misprint for "G."

90 BERKELEY TO POPE

The Correspondence of Alexander Pope, *ed. George Sherburn (Oxford: Clarendon Press, 1956), addendum to vol. I, pp. 121–24. Stock, pp. xxxv–xxxvii.*

Naples, 22 October 1717

I have long had it in my thoughts to trouble you with a letter, but was discouraged for want of something that I could think worth sending fifteen hundred miles. Italy is such an exhausted subject that, I dare say, you'd easily forgive my saying nothing of it; and the imagination of a poet is a thing so nice and delicate that it is no easy matter to find out images capable of giving pleasure to one of the few, who (in any age) have come up to that character. I am nevertheless lately returned from an island where I passed three or four months; which, were it set out in its true colours, might, methinks, amuse you agreeably enough for a minute or two.

The island Inarime[506] is an epitome of the whole earth, containing within the compass of eighteen miles, a wonderful variety of hills, vales, ragged rocks, fruitful plains, and barren mountains, all thrown together in a most romantic confusion. The air is, in the hottest season, constantly refreshed by cool breezes from the sea. The vales produce excellent wheat and Indian corn, but are mostly covered with vineyards intermixed with fruit-trees. Besides the common kinds, as cherries, apricots, peaches, etc., they produce oranges, limes, almonds, pomegranates, figs, water-melons, and many other fruits unknown to our climates, which lie every where open to the passenger. The hills are the greater part covered to the top with vines, some with chesnut groves, and others with thickets of myrtle and lentiscus. The fields in the northern side are divided by hedgerows of myrtle. Several fountains and rivulets add to the beauty of this landscape, which is likewise set off by the variety of some barren spots and naked rocks. But that which crowns the scene, is a large mountain rising out of the middle of the island (once a terrible volcano, by the ancients called *Mons Epomeus*). Its lower parts are adorned with vines and other fruits; the middle affords pasture to flocks of goats and sheep; and the top is a sandy pointed rock, from which you have the finest prospect in the world, surveying at one view, besides several pleasant islands lying at your feet, a tract of Italy about three hundred miles in length, from the promontory of Antium to the Cape of Palinurus: the greater part of which hath been sung by

---

[506] The island of Ischia off the coast of Naples, Italy.

Homer and Virgil, as making a considerable part of the travels and adventures of their two heroes. The islands Caprea, Prochyta, and Parthenope, together with Cajeta, Cumae, Monte Miseno, the habitations of Circe, the Syrens, and the Laestrigones, the bay of Naples, the promontary of Minerva, and the whole Campagnia felice, make but a part of this noble landscape; which would demand an imagination as warm and numbers as flowing as your own, to describe it. The inhabitants of this delicious isle, as they are without riches and honours, so are they without the vices and follies that attend them; and were they but as much strangers to revenge as they are to avarice and ambition, they might in fact answer the poetical notions of the golden age. But they have got, as an alloy to their happiness, an ill habit of murdering one another on slight offences. We had an instance of this the second night after our arrival, a youth of eighteen being shot dead by our door: and yet by the sole secret of minding our own business, we found a means of living securely among those dangerous people.

Would you know how we pass the time at Naples? Our chief entertainment is the devotion of our neighbours. Besides the gaiety of their churches (where folks go to see what they call *una bella Devotione*, i.e. a sort of religious opera), they make fireworks almost every week out of devotion; the streets are often hung with arras out of devotion; and (what is still more strange) the ladies invite gentlemen to their houses, and treat them with music and sweetmeats, out of devotion: in a word, were it not for this devotion of its inhabitants, Naples would have little else to recommend it beside the air and situation.

Learning is in no very thriving state here, as indeed nowhere else in Italy; however, among many pretenders, some men of taste are to be met with. A friend of mine told me not long since that, being to visit Salvini[507] at Florence, he found him reading your Homer: he liked the notes extremely, and could find no other fault with the version, but that he thought it approached too near a paraphrase; which shows him not to be sufficiently acquainted with our language. I wish you health to go on with that noble work; and when you have that, I need not wish you success. You will do me the justice to believe, that whatever relates to your welfare is sincerely wished by

 your, etc.

---

[507] Antonio Maria Salvini (1633–1729), Italian philologist and professor of Greek. He was known for his translations and annotations of ancient texts.

91 BERKELEY TO CAMPAILLA

Preface to Thomas Campailla, L'Adamo, ovvero il Mondo Creato (1728).

Messanae, 25 Februarii 1718

Clarissime Vir,

Ex itinere per universam insulam instituto jam tandem, favente numine, reversus, animum jucundissima memoria Siculorum hospitum, atque amicorum, praesertim quos ingenio atque eruditione praestantes inviserim, subinde reficio. Porro inter illos quanti te faciam, vir doctissime, facilius mente concipi, quam verbis exprimi potest. Id unum me male habet, quod, exaudito tuo colloquia diutius frui per itineris festinationem non licuerit. Clarissimos ingenii tui fructus, quos mihi impartiri dignatus sis, quam primum Londinium pervenero, aequius illiusmodi Rerum Aestimatoribus distribuendos, curabo. Si quid interim aliud occurrat, quod ad Societatem Regiam Londiniensem transmitti cupias, id, modo mittatur ad D. D. Portem. Hoare & Allen Anglos, negotii causa Messanae commorantes, ad me, ubicunque tandem sim, perveniet; Porro Neutoni nostri Naturalis Philosophia Principia Mathematica, si quando in patriam sospes rediero ad te transmittenda dabo, vel si qua alia ratione commodis tuis inservire possim, reperies me, si minus potentem, promptum tamen, omnique ossequio.

Humillimum servum,

G. Berkeley

Most Illustrious Sir,

Having now at last returned, by God's favour, from a journey undertaken through the whole island, I am refreshing my mind from time to time with the most pleasant memory of my Sicilian hosts and friends, especially those, superior in genius and learning, whom I visited. Henceforth how highly I shall prize you among them, most learned sir, is able to be conceived more easily in my mind, than expressed by words. I felt badly about this one matter—that because of the speed of the journey it was not permitted to me to enjoy hearing your discourses for a longer time. As soon as I shall first arrive in London, I shall take care that the most illustrious fruits of your genius, which you have deemed worthy to share with me, will be more fairly distributed to those who esteem things of this sort. If something else should occur meanwhile, which you should like transmitted to the London Royal Society, this once sent to the Englishmen D.D. Portem Hoare and Allen (who are staying at Messina for the sake of business) will in the end reach me wherever I may be. Moreover, our

Newton's[508] *Mathematical Principles of Natural Philosophy*, if ever I shall return safe to the fatherland, I shall have sent to you, or if by some other means I am able to of service to your advantage, you will find me, if less able, nevertheless prompt and entirely in compliance.

Your most humble servant,

G. Berkeley.

92 PERCIVAL TO BERKELEY[509]

EP, BL Add. MS 47028, fols. 227v–28. Letter copied in Percival's diary:
BL Add. MS 47088, fols. 82v–83.

London, 13 March 1717/18

Dear Sir,

I would not be the first to send you the account of your good friend the Bishop of Derry's[510] death. I suppose this misfortune will if Mr. Ashe's[511] health permit, bring you sooner to England than you otherwise designed, where if you come this summer or winter you will see me deeply engaged in building the house you have often heard me talk of which I design to make very convenient for holding my family which is now increased by another daughter; so that now I have three daughters and one son. The two eldest of my children have very lately escaped the danger attending the small pox and I am in hopes they will not only remain without marks, but that their health, which is of far more importance, will be better established for the future. I have got them a French master, which language they take to, especially my boy, but Kitty excels him in dancing as it is fit she should.

My sister Percival and brother with their family are to be in England next month, and I hope will spend some time with us at Kew where we propose to go about midsummer.

You desired me when you went on your travels not to write you news, and now if I would I have nothing to send you of that sort.

There is lately erected a commission for receiving and disbursing charity to proselytes from Popery of which I am an unworthy member. The good we do and mischief we hinder is so great that I heartily wish our fund were greater.

---

[508] Sir Isaac Newton (1642–1727).
[509] The letter was first published by Luce, who noted that Rand missed the letter. See A. A. Luce, "More Unpublished Berkeley Letters and New Berkeleiana," *Hermathena* 23 (1933): 28–29.
[510] St. George Ashe* (1658–1718), bishop of Derry, died 27 February 1718.
[511] St. George Ashe* (1698–1721).

We have lately received a book from France which I believe was not published when you was [sic] there. *The Memoires of Cardinal de Retz,*[512] an eminent, intriguing man in the minority of Lewis the 14.[513] I could be angry with him for discovering so much of the corrupt nature of man, but that he pays you with good sense and useful instruction, and one thing appears through the whole work, that the greatest turns in state affairs are owing to minute and often accidental causes, and that men may talk what they please of the public, but their own private interest is the secret spring of their most gallant and popular actions.

My family are all well at present and give you their affectionate service; Daniel Dering[514] does the same, and I am ever

your affectionate friend and humble servant,

Percival

93 BERKELEY TO PERCIVAL

EP, BL Add. MS 47028, fols. 229v–30.

Rome, 26 April 1718

My Lord,

Upon my arrival here I had the good fortune to meet with Mr. Hamilton[515] who brought me a letter from your Lordship, which was very agreeable as everything is that assures me of the welfare of your family. Among the many obligations I have to your Lordship I must reckon your making me acquainted with a gentleman of Mr. Hamilton's merit. I gave him a recommendation to some friends of mine in Naples where he intends to make a short stay, and upon his return I hope to enjoy more of his company.

It would I believe be no news to your Lordship to give you an account of the functions of the Holy Week, which has drawn a great confluence of strangers from all parts of Europe, particularly several of the nobility and gentry of Great Britain, enough to fill two coffee-houses. The well affected part meet at that in Piazza d'Espagna; and the rebels have another part to themselves. Among the latter are the Lords Mar,[516] Southesk[517] etc. Methinks it is no ill sign to see them

---

[512] Jean François Paul de Gondi (1613–79), Cardinal de Retz. His *Memoires* first appeared in 1717.
[513] Louis XIV (1636–1715).
[514] Daniel Dering* (?–1730).
[515] Possibly John Hamilton (?–1729). He later would be dean of Dromore (1724–29). See Letter 184.
[516] John Erskine* (1675–1732), twenty-second or sixth Earl of Mar and Jacobite Duke of Mar.
[517] James Carnegie (1692–1730), fifth Earl of Southesk.

loiter about town as if they had nothing to do. Though it must be owned, men of good sense, understanding, and friends to King George, are in these parts alarmed with apprehensions more from divisions at home than from any power or foreign foes. Your Lordship hath seen too much of Italy not to know that every indifferent man who travels must be heartily concerned at any accident that should seem to make way for introducing among us, that sort of government and religion that hath made the inhabitants of these parts the greatest fools and slaves from the wisest and bravest men in the world. But I hope the breach is not so wide, nor the consequences likely to prove so fatal, as is commonly feared or imagined at this distance.

During the functions of the Holy Week and the Easter holidays it was impossible to look out for prints or books; but my next shall bring your Lordship an account of what I have procured for you, in which I hope my gusto will show itself somewhat improved since coming abroad.

I must beg your Lordship to give my humblest respects to my Lady, Mrs. Parker,[518] the children, and all friends who are so kind as to remember me, and to believe, that I am

> My Lord,
>
> your Lordship's most obedient and most humble servant,
>
> Geo: Berkeley

The general talk here is of a peace between the Emperor and King Philip.[519]

94 BERKELEY TO PERCIVAL

EP, BL Add. MS 47028, fols. 241v–43.

Rome, 28 July 1718

My Lord,

My last to your Lordship I have some suspicion might not have come to your hands, but having now got a correspondent at Leghorn to forward our letters I am in hopes this will. Upon the ill news of my Lord Bishop's death[520] we were

---

[518] Mary Parker* (1692–1731).

[519] Charles VI (1685–1740), Holy Roman Emperor of the Habsburg Empire (Austria), and King Philip V of Spain (1683–1746) were engaged in a complicated conflict involving territories in the Mediterranean and the succession of the French and Spanish thrones. The conflict led to the War of the Quadruple Alliance (1718–20).

[520] St. George Ashe* (1658–1718), bishop of Derry, died 27 Feburary 1718.

resolved to go directly homewards, but a few days after Mr. Ashe[521] received letters from his friends with directions to continue longer this side the Alps, which together with the extreme heats that render travelling insupportable hath determined us to stay some months longer at Rome, where we have at present about thirty English gentlemen and noblemen, most of them men of good sense and very sober, which makes the *séjour*[522] as agreeable as it is possible to be out of England, whither I long for liberty to return on many accounts, particularly that I may have a part in the contrivance of the house you design to build this winter, for you must know I pretend to an uncommon skill in architecture, as you will easily imagine when I assure your Lordship there is not any one modern building in Rome that pleases me, except the wings of the capitol built by Michael Angelo and the colonnade of Berninies [sic] before St. Peter's. The church itself I find a thousand faults with, as indeed with every other modern church here. I forget the little round one in the place where St. Peter was beheaded built by Bramante, which is very pretty and built like an ancient temple. This gusto of mine is formed on the remains of antiquity that I have met with in my travels, particularly in Sicily, which convince me that the old Romans were inferior to the Greeks, and that the moderns fall infinitely short of both in the grandeur and simplicity of taste.

I have bought for your Lordship prints of the churches, palaces, and statues of Rome, a great number. I had likewise bought those of the Colonne Trajana and Antonina, which in many large sheets display the Roman antiquity, but showing them to a judicious friend here who informed me that the plates are much worn out, and very coarsely retouched, which had spoiled the prints, I returned them. The rest are sent on board an English ship, safe packed up with some things of Mr. Ashe's, with directions to lie at the custom house in London till our return.

As for books there is no sort of learning flourishes here but civil and canon law. Not but there is enough too of divinity and poetry, but so very bad that I can meet with nothing in either kind worth buying. The truth is the Italians of the last and present age are not worth importing into England. Those of the golden age of Pope Leo the tenth[523] are scarce, and very hard to be met with. But those I presume you are already provided with. However, if there be any particular authors or editions that you want, please to let me know, and when I come to Padua or Venice, I shall make it my business to enquire for them.

---

[521] St. George Ashe* (1698–1721).

[522] French: "a visit or stay."

[523] Giovanni di Lorenzo de' Medici (1475–1521) was Pope Leo X from 1513 until his death. Famous for his response to Martin Luther's ninety-five theses and the use of indulgences to rebuild St. Peter's Cathedral, he was equally renowned for his patronage of the arts and classical literature.

I have had several letters from Lord Pembroke[524] with directions to enquire for about thirty books of which I have not in a years time with my utmost diligence been able to procure above three. If at Venice which is the great mart for books I meet with anything new worth buying, I intend to purchase it for your Lordship. As to old authors I would gladly know which you want, that I might not buy those you have already.

Your Lordship's letter under cover to George Ashe Esq., and directed to Messrs. Bates Campion and Mitchel at Leghorn, will at any time come safe to me, and can never bring any news more agreeable than that of the welfare of yourself and family.

My best respects to my Lady and Mrs. Parker[525] and the rest of those who remember me, particularly Mrs. Dering. I beg your Lordship to believe me, my Lord,

> your Lordship's most obedient and most obliged servant,
>
> G. Berkeley

95 BERKELEY TO PERCIVAL

EP, BL Add. MS 47028, fols. 254v–55.

Rome, 13 November 1718

My Lord,

I know not by what accident the letter your Lordship favoured me with from Paris came to my hands, being enclosed in a cover to Mr. St. George instead of Mr. Ashe.[526] My surprise to hear your Lordship and the ladies were at Paris was attended with no small mortification to think I should miss the happiness of seeing you there.

The Pretender[527] is hourly expected in this city where he designs to make his residence. The greatest part of his followers are already come and swarm in all public places, which must make Rome an uneasy place to men of different principles. So we are now in a hurry proposing to set out from hence in a day or two, which makes me fear I shall not have time to enquire about the medals and other things your Lordship mentioned in your last. But I design to leave directions with a friend here to inform himself as to the price of them and where they may be had. He is one who, having an excellent genius for painting, designs

---

[524] Thomas Herbert* (1656–1733), eighth Earl of Pembroke.
[525] Mary Parker* (1692–1731).
[526] St. George Ashe* (1698–1721).
[527] James Francis Edward Stuart* (1688–1766).

to continue a year longer at Rome, and will gladly serve me in anything that lies in his power.[528] So that by his means I hope to procure anything your Lordship shall have occasion for. I remember to have heard your Lordship speak of certain models in plaster of Paris cast from busts at Florence which miscarried in their way home, and having met with a man in the Villa Medici who has some moulds taken from celebrated antique busts, I have got him to form eight of them in terra cotta (as they call it), which is much more durable than plaster of Paris or giesso, being as hard as brick. Two painted after bronze antique are Julius Caesar and the Antinous in the Vatican, the other six busts have their names on billets affixed to them and are painted of a leaden colour, which seems to me more natural, though perhaps I had done better not to have had them painted at all. These I have seen carefully boxed up and sent to Leghorn, with directions from Mr. Ashe to his correspondents there to send them to London to Mr. Cairns (Sir Alexander's brother) with orders to deliver them to your Lordship, wishing they may in any measure repair the loss of those who had ordered yourself. You will have nothing to pay Mr. Cairns but the carriage from Leghorn to London.

I find the outside of your Lordship's house is finished and doubt not it will answer your fine taste. Within I hope to find a stone staircase, tiled floors, and vaulted roofs, with oval or square oblong pictures in the middle.

We are going to Venice in our way homewards and hope to kiss your Lordship's hands this spring in London. I am

My Lord,

your Lordship's most obedient humble servant,

Geo: Berkeley

My humble respects to the ladies.

96 BERKELEY TO PERCIVAL

EP, BL Add. MS 47029, fols. 37v–38v.

Florence, 9/20 July 1720

My Lord,

I have at length the pleasure to let you know of having procured for you what they called *serie mezana*[529] of brass medals from Julius Caesar down to Galienus, which they tell me is the period of the good work. They are fifty odd heads fair,

---

[528] Luce reasonably speculates that the reference of the person having "an excellent genuis for painting" is John Smibert* (1688–1751), who we know was in Italy at least by 1719.
[529] "middle series."

about a dozen copies. I have never studied medals so was obliged to follow the judgment of others. I hoped to have been able to have sent you this advice long since, having employed an English gentleman who passed this way to Rome (for my friend who I left there was returned to England). That gentleman after a long delay wrote me word he could get a series at a reasonable rate, but the heads would be very blind, and the sizes unequal. This put me upon trying what may be done here, and employing persons to pick up what originals may be had in Florence and making copies of the rest: but you know how tedious it is to deal with Italians. I never knew people so ready to promise and so slow to perform.

It is not Magnolfi but one Bianchi who hath care of the painters' heads. But upon enquiry I find it impracticable to have them copied, the great Duke being very jealous in that point lest they should be made public.

I have been with Soldani to know what the busts were which he did for you, but having at different times done things for English gentlemen, he remembers nothing in particular which he did for you.

Since the making those busts I sent you, I had got some others much finer being made of scaglione (a hard composition that looks and shines like marble). These packed up with the greatest care to prevent breaking I ordered to be sent to Mr. Cairns at London, but find they are gone without my knowledge to Lisbon with some things of Mr. Ashe's[530] in order to embark there for Ireland; but I have desired Mr. Ashe to write to his merchant in Dublin to send them back to London.

You wrote to me for a series of marbles. I have been told this was the proper place to get them in; accordingly I have made it my business to enquire for them, but could find only one set in the whole town. It contains about one hundred sorts, being small oval pieces. I shall either send them or bring it myself.

As to the figured stones which you wrote for, when I was here before, I bought several of them which I designed for you. They are now in London; but these as well as the prints are put up promiscuously with Mr. Ashe's things, so that I can give no directions for coming at them till we come to London, which I hope will be before the cold weather comes on. I have indeed been detained so long against my expectations and wishes on this side the Alps that I have lost all patience. Every month these six months we have designed to begin our journey and have been as often disappointed. We are now resolved to set out in two days, but shall travel slowly because of the heats which are intolerable except a few hours in the morning and evening.

---

[530] St. George Ashe* (1698–1721).

The advice you were so kind as to forward to me, and for which I return my hearty thanks, having by mistake lain many months at Brussels, came too late to be of any use. This and the like disappointments have had the good effect to harden me against any future mishaps. I hope to find that yourself and other friends there, particularly Mrs. Parker[531] and Mrs. D. Dering, have had better fortune in the general scramble for the wealth of the nation;[532] nothing else can reconcile the French projects now on foot in England to

>My Lord,
>
>Your Lordship's most obedient and most humble servant,
>
>George Berkeley

Mr. Ashe presents his humble service to your Lordship, and I must desire you to present mine to the Ladies and all friends. I was particularly obliged for the account you was pleased to give me of your hopeful offspring, which must be very entertaining to one who by inclination as well as gratitude thinks himself interested in all that concerns your family. Your Lordship cannot do a better service to the public than to get and breed up sons like your self and daughters like my Lady.

97 POPE TO BERKELEY

Printed in The Correspondence of John Hughes, Esq., *2 vols. (Dublin: Thomas Ewing, 1773), vol. I, pp. 53–54; and in LL, pp. 89–90.*

Sunday [1721?][533]

Dear Sir,

My Lord Bishop [Atterbury][534] was very much concerned at missing you yesterday; he desired me to engage you and myself to dine with him this day, but I was

---

[531] Mary Parker* (1692–1731).

[532] A reference to the South Sea* affair.

[533] The letter is undated. The editor of *The Correspondence* dates the letter between April and September 1713 by its placement between letters with those dates. The work also identifies the bishop as Atterbury in a footnote, but gives no evidence for the attribution. We do know that Berkeley and Atterbury were acquainted. There is no clear indication from the letter itself when it was authored, although it must have been before 1722, when Atterbury was arrested. Fraser idly speculates that the letter dates to 1721 (*LL*, p. 89), and Sherburn, following Warton, does the same, on the supposition that Berkeley was likely in London in the summer of 1721, returning from his Continental tour. Both dates, however, are possible. I correct some of Fraser's minor errors, taking the Hughes to be the more reliable. A previous set of correspondence, *Letters, by Several Eminent Persons Deceased, Including the Correspondence of John Hughes Esq.*, 3 vols. (London: J. Johnson, 1772), has the identical letter and notes (vol. II, p. 1). See Sherbum, ed., *Correspondence of Pope*, vol. II, p. 62.

[534] Francis Atterbury* (1663–1732).

unluckily pre-engaged. And (upon my telling him I should carry you out of town tomorrow, and hoped to keep you till the end of the week) he has desired that we will not fail to dine with him next Sunday, when he will have no other company.

I write you this, to intreat you will provide yourself of linen and other necessaries sufficient for the week; for, as I take you to be almost the only friend I have that is above the little vanities of the town, I expect you may be able to renounce it for one week, and to make trial how you like my Tusculum, because I assure you it is no less yours, and hope you will use it as your own country villa in the ensuing season.

I am, faithfully yours,

A. Pope

98 BERKELEY TO PERCIVAL

EP, BL Add. MS *47029, fols. 72–73.*

Trinity College, Dublin, 12 October 1721

My Lord,

I have been now a month in Ireland without writing to your Lordship, not that I am in the least insensible of many favours received from you and good Lady Percival, and the acknowledgments I ought to make for them. But the truth is I deferred it every post, in hopes I should have been able before the following to let you know, I was in possession of the preferment which of all those in the Lord Lieutenant's[535] gift would have been the most agreeable to me, which the goodness I have constantly experienced in your Lordship made me flatter myself would have proved welcome news; but his Grace still imagining himself obliged in point of policy to keep that affair in suspence, I can no longer delay what I should otherwise have done upon my first arrival.

I had no sooner set foot on shore, but I heard that the Deanery of Dromore was become vacant, which is worth about £500 a year and a sinecure: which circumstance recommends it to me beyond any preferment in the kingdom, though there are some Deaneries of twice that value. I instantly applied to his Grace, and put him in mind of his promises. He answered me very civilly, but in general terms, saying that he meant to do more than he cared to say, and more to the same purpose, from which I could gather that he designed to dispose of nothing during the session, in order to create a dependence, though at the same time he create much trouble to himself and others by encouraging more hopes

---

[535] Charles Fitzroy* (1683–1757), second Duke of Grafton.

and solicitations than he can satisfy. I have represented this matter in a letter to my Lord Burlington,[536] but can hardly hope his Lordship will write to the Duke, since he told me in England that he was willing to serve me in any other instance, but that he thought it below him to solicit his Grace any further.

The Duchess[537] is very civil, and, were this affair in her disposal, would I believe bestow it to my liking which I owe to my Lady Percival. Mr. Fairfax[538] also befriends me much. But notwithstanding all these things, and the Duke's repeated promises, it must be owned the importunities he exposeth himself to on all hands by this unnecessary delay make me uncertain of the event. One thing I believe is pretty sure, that it will not be determined before the recess, which can hardly be these three weeks yet, it being probable the debates about the bank will hardly be over before that time. I do not find that this new project meets with many partisans here besides those who are immediately interested in it, and I am inclined to think it may come to nothing.

I cannot conclude without recommending to you and your family a preservative against the plague, which I am told alarms you much at present, it is no more than the Jesuits bark taken as against the ague. This I had from Dr. Arbuthnot[539] just before I left London, who is resolved his whole family shall make use of it, and I cannot but think for the reasons he gave me, too long to be repeated, it would be of great benefit.

Mr. Dering,[540] who has gathered flesh and mended his complection very sensibly in the little time that I have been here, has given me the agreeable news of my Lady Percival's being well. God grant that she may continue so, and bring forth to your Lordship another fine boy, which I hope shortly to hear.

If there be any nonsense in this letter I beg your Lordship will have the goodness to excuse it: the truth is, I am more than half asleep as I write, having been up very early this morning. Pray present my humble service to my Lady, to her sister, and to Mrs. Dering, and believe me to be, my Lord,

> your Lordship's most obedient and most humble servant,
> G. Berkeley

If I get this Deanery I hope to see your Lordship soon.

---

[536] Richard Boyle* (1694–1753), third Earl of Burlington and fourth Earl of Cork.
[537] Henrietta (*née* Somerset) Fitzroy* (1690–1726), Duchess of Grafton.
[538] Probably Charles Brandon Fairfax (1684–1723). Fairfax was in the Duke of Grafton's retinue in Ireland and would be made dean of Down in 1722.
[539] John Arbuthnot* (1667–1735).
[540] Likely Daniel Dering* (?–1730).

99 PERCIVAL TO BERKELEY

EP, BL Add. MS 47029, fol. 73–73v.

Charlton, 21 October 1721

Dear Sir,

I was thinking to write to you, when last post your letter came to my hands, whereby I find you are in a fair prospect of what I heartily wish you may obtain, since it answers so well your desires, and would suffer you to visit England. I do not wonder you should be impatient till actually in possession of a preferment that differs in such circumstances from others, because accidents unforeseen may rise and disappoint you, but they must be very unforeseen indeed, considering how well you were recommended to his Grace,[541] how respectful he is to you, and let me add because it is truth, how well you deserve his favour. His Grace's policy, though perhaps ill judged and needless at this time, to defer the disposal of this preferment till the recess, ought so little to cause you apprehension, that I think it a sign that he intends it for you, because your interest lying on this side and little in Ireland, where that of the other candidates is all together, he apprehends disgusting for the present their friends there, whose service he is obliged to make use of, and therefore defers the disobliging them till their resentment will come too late to hurt him or the public affairs. We are all of this judgment, and the more so from a great opinion we have of his Grace's honour and discretion, believing that he will consider that the friends he obliges here are such as he passes most his time with, as his residence is in England. I am very glad you are so well with the Duchess,[542] and my wife hath writ to thank her Grace for her civilities to you. You will do well to cultivate your interest there.

I find the erecting of a Bank in Dublin is yet very uncertain. I am for my own part very indifferent, though it would certainly lower exchange, and consequently be advantageous to us who live here and have estates in Ireland, and I believe if wisely managed might be a benefit to that kingdom. If I thought there were any danger from it of our raising funds for a long term of years, and thereby bringing the nation into constant debt by anticipating any part of the additional supplies that are used to be raised within the year (which probably is apprehended by those who now oppose it), I should be as much against a bank as any man. In the meantime I am glad to find the government so indifferent about it,

[541] Charles Fitzroy* (1683–1757), second Duke of Grafton.
[542] Henrietta (*née* Somerset) Fitzroy* (1690–1726), Duchess of Grafton.

for it shows that if it pass, there is no private design from that quarter lurking underneath.

I thank you for your receipt against the plague: our apprehensions are not over, though less than a week ago, the story of the Dutch ship being groundless.

With services to you from my wife, and brother, and sister Dering,[543] I am

Dear Sir,

your most affectionate humble servant,

Percival

100 BERKELEY TO PERCIVAL

EP, BL Add. MS 47029, fol. 76.

Trinity College, Dublin, 23 October 1721

My Lord,

I remember to have read with a great deal of pleasure a very clear and instructive piece of your Lordship's concerning the bank, or rather concerning banks in general.[544] I must now make it my request to your Lordship to favour me with a copy of it. It may be sent conveniently in two covers. I cannot but think your discourse would be very serviceable to the public at this time, when men's thoughts and conversation are almost entirely turned towards a subject they are generally speaking very ignorant of. It would even have its use if it were shown only to two or three leading men in manuscript. I must therefore beg leave to press you on this head, the rather because the bank scheme is not quite laid aside, and may still one way or other be very important.

The love of your country will I doubt not be a sufficient motive to your Lordship to comply in this particular with, my Lord,

your Lordship's

most obedient and most humble servant,

G. Berkeley

I long to hear how my Lady does and the rest of your family, to all whom pray give my humble service. The affair which I mentioned last is not yet come to an issue.

---

[543] Mary (*née* Parker) Dering* (1692–1731).

[544] *Some Thoughts Touching an Irish Bank*, BL Add. MS 47029, fols. 80v–86.

101 PERCIVAL TO BERKELEY

EP, BL Add. MS 47029, fol. 80–80v.

Charlton, 9 November 1721

Dear Sir,

Your opinion that what I put together touching an Irish bank might furnish a reader with topics for reflection and discourse prevailed on me to comply with your desire of sending you those sheets, as I did a post ago under two covers directed for you at Trinity College, Dublin. The better part of them is taken from books of that sort that I had by me, wherein I found many things I did not well comprehend, and others I thought not rightly judged which I omitted, and substituted in their place what my own reflections suggested, applying the whole to the particular circumstances of Ireland. This is all the hand I properly had in that paper, nor should I have meddled at all in it, but that the gentlemen employed at that time to solicit a bank desired me to give them my thoughts thereof. I never showed it to any but them, yourself, and my brother Dering,[545] and am very desirous that you lend it only to such as will make no other use of it than you design yourself to do, for I am far from thinking so well of it as you seem to do, and know how weak a composure it must appear at this time when [the][546] subject of it is so canvassed and warmly contended for and against by the gentlemen in Parliament.

I am obliged to you for often acquainting me with what relates to your private concern. I am still of opinion the Deanery will be yours, and that not only from an aptness to credit my own wishes, but for the reasons I writ you in my last.

I am amusing myself with alterations in my garden, though another man's land, which by that time they come to perfection will be no longer mine; but if any man shall condemn my copying after the Duke of Buckingham,[547] who for his pleasure planted another man's fields, I will answer with him: blame me when I do ill, but suffer me in that which is good. When my trees are in my ground, I shall go for the winter to town, where all my family with pleasure expect your return about the time the government leaves Ireland.

---

[545] Daniel Dering* (?–1730).
[546] Following Rand, who reasonably replaces "so" from the letterbook with "the."
[547] John Sheffield (1647–1721), first Duke of Buckingham and Normandy.

Our family are much your humble servants. My wife is, as she always is at such times, very uneasy, but under no dangerous circumstances. I am

etc.,

I know not whether I mentioned one indispensable caution about the bank; it is, that they be obliged not to lend the government any money but by consent of Parliament. Without such restriction I should be absolutely against it, and will require an Act of Parliament for that purpose. Pray inculcate this to your friends. The Bank of England is so bound up.

[Addendum (not reproduced here): John Percival, *Some Thoughts Touching an Irish Bank*, BL Add. MS 47029, fols. 80v–86.]

102 BERKELEY TO PERCIVAL

EP, BL Add. MS 47029, fol. 91v.

Trinity College, Dublin, December 1721

My Lord,

I just now received the favour of your Lordship's letter, together with your dissertation on the bank,[548] for which I most heartily thank your Lordship. After a long dearth of news we have had ten packets this evening at once, which alone could occasion my being so late in my acknowledgment. I shall make the use you prescribe of what you have been pleased to send me, and must ask your pardon if I persist in thinking very differently of it from what you seem to do. And to say no more, this I will venture to affirm, that I never saw anything so proper as to give one[549] an easy insight into the several sorts of banks as your Lordship's papers. We have had two or three things printed here about the late project, particularly one by Mr. Maxwell,[550] and an answer to it by Mr. Rowley,[551] both Parliament men, the first for, the latter against the bank, which I would have sent to you, had I judged such large pamphlets worth the postage. But that affair

---

[548] *Some Thoughts Touching an Irish Bank*, BL Add. MS 47029, fols. 80v–86.

[549] Rand and Luce have "me." The words "one" and "me" are often hard to distinguish in script, but in this case it is clearly "one," which additionally makes better sense of the sentence.

[550] Henry Maxwell, MP, *Reasons Offer'd for Erecting a Bank in Ireland; In a Letter to Hercules Rowley, Esq.* (Dublin, 1721).

[551] Hercules Rowley, MP, *An Answer to a Book, Intitl'd, Reasons Offer'd for Erecting a Bank in Ireland. in a Letter to Henry Maxwell, Esq.* (Dublin, 1721).

is in such a declining way, that it is to be questioned whether it will be resumed this session, which commences next week.

The Deanery still continues in suspense, and is likely to remain so till the Parliament is up, which probably will not be before middle of January.

Your Lordship's amusement in planting trees for the use of a stranger is so far from culpable, that it shows a refined taste and a disinterested benevolence to mankind, a thing not the less excellent because it is rare and perhaps ridiculous in this corrupt age.

Three days hence we are to have the honour of entertaining the Duke of Grafton[552] at the College, and I am appointed to make the Latin speech to him, which employs my thoughts for the present, so I shall give you no further trouble, but concluding with my best good wishes for yourself, my good Lady Percival, and all the rest of your family. I remain,

> My Lord,
>
> your Lordship's most obedient & most humble servant,
>
> G. Berkeley

103 BERKELEY TO PERCIVAL

EP, BL Add. MS 47029, fol. 95v.

Trinity College Dublin, 9 January 1721/22

My Lord,

It is very obliging in your Lordship to think of me and my interests in the kind manner you do. This makes me think it will not be altogether impertinent to lay before you a short account of our Irish vacancies in the Church. There are vacant besides the Bishopric of Leighlin and Fernes, the Deaneries of Downe, Dromore, Limerick and Cork, and also some smaller benefices.[553] I applied at first for that of Dromore, and have not since altered my application, the Bishopric and rich Deanery of Downe being above my desires, and the others below them. The

---

[552] Charles Fitzroy* (1683–1757), second Duke of Grafton.

[553] All of the vacancies mentioned were filled by the end of 1722. Josiah Hort (c. 1674–1751) succeeded Bartholomew Vigors (1643–1721) as bishop of Leighlin and Ferns, Charles Fairfax (1684–1723) succeeded Benjamin Pratt (1669–1721) as dean of Down, Thomas Bindon (?–1740) succeeded G. W. Storey (1664?–1721) as dean of Limerick, and Robert Carleton (?–1735) succeeded Rowland Davies (1649–1731) as dean of Cork.

Deanery of Dromore exactly suits my wishes, and I have had encouragement to hope for it. At first I forced myself to be a pretty constant courtier, but of late have remitted somewhat of my diligence, being tired out with delays. I do nevertheless still see the Duke[554] and Duchess[555] once in ten days. The truth is, the assurances I have had from both ought in good manners to make me easy till the time comes when things can be declared, which cannot be far off if the Parliament rises in a fortnight.

For news I hear none, but that the Commons have been uneasy at their bills being altered in the Council here. This it was thought would have produced some resolutions, but their heat I am now told is now over. For some time past I have been afflicted for the death of poor Mr. Ashe[556] who died at Brussels.

I am glad to hear your family are all well, and am in hopes when you next favour me to have an account of my Lady's safe deliverance. So wishing you and all yours all happiness I remain

My Lord,

your Lordship's most obedient and most humble servant,

G. Berkeley

104 BERKELEY TO PERCIVAL

EP, BL Add. MS 47029, fol. 103.

Trinity College, 10 February 1721/22

My Lord,

Your Lordship hath been always so partial to my interests, that I persuade myself it will be welcome news to you that my patent is now passing the seals for the Deanery of Dromore. As upon all other accounts so especially on my Lady Duchess'[557] favour and friendly interposition on my behalf, I am very sensible of the obligations I have to my good Lady Percival. I shall be in pain till I hear she is well delivered of a child, that from my heart I wish may rival

---

[554] Charles Fitzroy* (1683–1757), second Duke of Grafton.
[555] Henrietta (*née* Somerset) Fitzroy* (1690–1726), Duchess of Grafton.
[556] St. George Ashe* (1698–1721).
[557] Henrietta (*née* Somerset) Fitzroy* (1690–1726), Duchess of Grafton.

Mr. Johnny[558] in learning, or Miss Helena[559] in beauty, and I can hardly wish more. I shall then request another favour from her Ladyship, and that is to acknowledge those I have received from my Lady Duchess. I believe I have formerly told your Lordship the Deanery of Dromore is worth £500 per annum. It is what were I in possession would please me beyond anything, but the worst on it is the Bishop, pretending a title, hath put in a presentee of his own, which unavoidably engages me in a lawsuit; but if I succeed, my pains will be abundantly recompensed.[560] I am my Lord,

> your Lordship's most obedient servant,
>
> G. Berkeley

105 BERKELEY TO PERCIVAL

EP, BL Add. MS 47029, fol. 105v.

Trinity College, 13 February 1721/22

My Lord,

As among all your friends there is nobody hath better reason to be pleased with any good fortune that befalls your Lordship or good Lady Percival than I have, so I beg leave to assure you there is no one employs more sincere and constant wishes for your prosperity. You will therefore do me the justice to believe it was most agreeable news to me which I heard this day of my Lady's being safely delivered of a fine boy.[561] I could not omit congratulating your Lordship on this happy event, and at the same time wishing you may live to procure many of the same kind to your own comfort, and the joy of all your friends, particularly of my Lord

> your Lordship's most obedient & most humble servant,
>
> G. Berkeley

---

[558] John Percival* (1711–70), Percival's eldest child.

[559] Helena Percival (1718–46).

[560] The Duke of Grafton had promised Berkeley a preferment. When the deanery of Dromore became vacant in 1721, Berkeley applied for it and received his patent on 16 February 1722. The bishop of Dromore, Ralph Lambert* (1666–1732), however, put in his own nominee, Henry Leslie (?–?), forcing Berkeley to take legal action to secure the position. Berkeley's case defending the prerogative of the Crown was never strong, never went to trial, and dragged on for several years.

[561] George Percival was born 28 January 1722. The Prince of Wales, later King George II,* was his godfather. George died a child in 1726.

106 PERCIVAL TO BERKELEY

EP, BL Add. MS *47029, fol. 108v.*

London, 3 March 1721/22

Dear Sir,

I yesterday waited on the Duke of Grafton[562] to thank him for his favours to you. He expressed very great respect for you and is only sorry you meet with such opposition from your Bishop.[563] He said that he is told the B—p's Patent is very strong in favour of his pretensions to name a dean, but that you had been allowed £50 out of the concordation to carry on the suit. I wondered how it should be made now a dispute, to which he replied that the last Dean had been long in the place, and that the matter had been compromised the time before. I heartily hope you will overcome this difficulty, which I fear is like to detain you from us this summer.

I find he is not well pleased at the resistance Bishop Hort[564] meets with from some of that bench. He was, he said, many years chaplain to the late Bishop of Ely,[565] and a sober gentlemanlike man. He expected however that last Sunday the bishops in commission would ordain him. My wife went out yesterday for the fifth time to see my sister Dering who has miscarried. I am ever

etc.,

Percival

107 BERKELEY TO PERCIVAL

EP, BL Add. MS *47029, fols. 109v-10.*

Dublin, 15 March 1721/22

My Lord,

It was very kind in your Lordship to wait on the Lord Lieutenant[566] and acknowledge the favour his Grace has been pleased to confer on me, which I

---

[562] Charles Fitzroy* (1683-1757), second Duke of Grafton.

[563] Dr. Ralph Lambert* (1666-1732), bishop of Dromore (1717). Lambert favored another candidate for the position of dean of Dromore. We do not know the reasons Lambert opposed Berkeley's candidacy.

[564] Josiah Hort (1674-1751), later archbishop of Tuam. Percival places the following note in the margin: "Mr. Hort, a Dean before, made Bishop of Leighlin and Ferns. He had been a Presbyterian teacher but came over to our Church, but was not ordained, as the Archbishop of Dublin, of Tuam, and Bishop of Clogher alleged. P."

[565] John Moore (1646-1714), the "late Bishop of Ely." The bishop of Ely at the time (1722) was William Fleetwood (1656-1723).

[566] Charles Fitzroy* (1683-1757), second Duke of Grafton.

am very sensible was in great goodness designed for my advantage, though in the event it may possibly prove otherwise. I had indeed £50 concordation money given towards carrying on the suit at the last council the Duke held. Twenty-five of that is gone already in seeing lawyers, and making searches and extracts in several offices, though the suit be not yet commenced; which upon enquiry I find will be more tedious, and the event much more doubtful, than I was at first aware of, but with a sure expense on my side, if I am informed right, of several hundred pounds besides what I am likely to get from the government, which will go but a little way to fee eight lawyers (for so many I have engaged), and defray all other expenses of a suit against a man who is worth £1,200 per annum beside the Deanery which he is in actual possession of, and who hath been practised in lawsuits five and twenty years together. This being the case, my friends think it would be no unreasonable request for me to desire the chantership of Christ Church now vacant by the death of the Dean of Armagh,[567] and said to be worth somewhat more than one hundred pounds per annum. This chantership is consistent with my fellowship, and might enable me to carry on the suit with ease, and perhaps recover the right of the Crown. And as it is in his Grace's gift, who hath on all occasions shown great humanity and goodness, I have hopes he may comply with my request, if it be speedily laid before him in a proper manner. As there is no one can do this better than your Lordship, so there is no one on whose friendship and protection I can better depend. I must likewise recommend myself to good Lady Percival whose speaking to the Duchess[568] will be of service, her Grace having been always favourable to me on her account. If your Lordship could speak yourself, or (if unacquainted with him) could get another to speak to Mr. Hopkins,[569] it would be very proper and useful on this occasion.

Your Lordship will do me the justice to believe, that as I have the sincerest gratitude for the favour his Grace hath already conferred upon me, so I should not presume to solicit for a new one, if I were in possession of that, and not under just apprehensions of a long, uncertain, and expensive suit, in no sort proportioned to my circumstances, which nevertheless I may be enabled to prosecute to the utmost by the addition of this small preferment.

---

[567] Peter (Pierre) Drelincourt, (1644–1722), Dean of Armagh. Again Berkeley did not receive the position, which was filled by Richard Daniel (*c.* 1681–1739).

[568] Henrietta (*née* Somerset) Fitzroy* (1690–1726), Duchess of Grafton.

[569] Edward Hopkins (?–1736), an English parliamentarian who came with the Duke of Grafton to Ireland as chief secretary. Appointed the Master of Revels in Ireland for life, he was ridiculed by Jonathan Swift in the poems *Epilogue to Mr. Hoppy's Benefit Night at Smock Alley* and *Billet to the Company of Players*. See *The Correspondence of Jonathan Swift*, ed. Harold Williams, 5 vols. (Oxford University Press, 1963), Swift to the Duke of Grafton, 24 January 1722/23, and *Works*, vol. IX, p. 48, n. 77.

I should be glad to hear your family are all well, and that Mrs. Dering[570] was out of danger.

You see, my Lord, the trouble your good natured inclination to serve your friends has drawn upon you. I have a particular reason why I would not trouble my Lord Burlington[571] in this affair, and I thought it would be more respectful to get a friend to state the case to the Duke than to write myself to him upon it. If in desiring this from your Lordship I ask anything improper, you are the best judge in what manner to act or whether to act at all; so begging ten thousand pardons, I conclude,

> your Lordship's most obedient and most obliged servant,
> Geo. Berkeley

108 PERCIVAL TO BERKELEY

EP, BL Add. MS 47029, fol. 111.

London, 27 March 1722

Dear Sir,

Though it is now some time since I received your last, I could not answer it before, for the Duke of Grafton[572] was out of town, and returned but a few days since. Thursday I communicated your desire to him in the properest manner I could, and added of my own that upon the termination of the suit you would surrender the chantership for his Grace to dispose of as he pleased. He replied that I knew very well the great value he had for you, and that you should still be supplied out of the concordation to carry on the suit as you wanted it, you making it appear how you disposed of the same, but that the chantership must go another way. I thanked his Grace, but said the Archbishop of Dublin[573] was not much your friend, to which he replied he believed it, for that he said he did not know you, but it signified nothing, the other two Justices would do as he directed.

My wife and Daniel[574] both think this is sufficient from his Grace, and truly I think so too, though I always shall wish your desires may be answered in your own way. We all wonder why you employ eight lawyers, both for the expense,

---

[570] Might be Mary (*née* Parker) Dering,* but the reference is not clear (1692–1731).
[571] Richard Boyle* (1694–1753), third Earl of Burlington and fourth Earl of Cork.
[572] Charles Fitzroy* (1683–1757), second Duke of Grafton.
[573] William King* (1650–1729).
[574] Daniel Dering* (?–1730).

and that we think you can hardly find so many good ones, supposing the other party to have engaged the best he could. I am ever

etc.,

Percival

109 BERKELEY TO PERCIVAL

EP, BL Add. MS 47029, fol. 115–15v.

Trinity College, 14 April 1722

My Lord,

I humbly thank your Lordship for the trouble you have taken on my account, not doubting but you have laid my affair before his Grace[575] in the properest and kindest manner that good nature and good sense could[576] suggest.

I make no question that the Duke will think it reasonable my cause should be supported out of the treasury during his Lieutenancy, but I much fear it will survive his government.

Your Lordship is surprised at the number of my lawyers, and truly so am I myself, having at first little thought that I should have occasion for so many. They are six counsellors, two attorneys, and a civilian. The former are Rogerson, Marlow, Malone, Nuttley, Stannard, and Howard. The attorneys are Mr. Smith of the King's Bench, and Mr. Stanton who is my solicitor. My civilian is Dr. Hawkshaw. The cause is a great cause, and I was told that fewer would not do. My adversary, if I am informed right, hath as many, and had the advantage to pre-engage the best, before I had got my patent.

Tuesday last I had a meeting of my lawyers, who direct that I should proceed by *quare impedit*,[577] and I am to serve my adversaries the Bishop[578] and Dr. Lesley[579] with a writ this week.

God preserve your Lordship from law and lawyers. Had the Deanery been disposed of when first vacant, I had been in possession and avoided all this trouble, but now the Bishop's clerk is in, I fear it will be a very difficult matter to

---

[575] Charles Fitzroy* (1683–1757), second Duke of Grafton.

[576] Rand and Luce mistakenly have "should" for "could."

[577] A legal term (literally: "why he hinders") from English ecclesiastical law. It is the name for a writ that empowers a monarch to present fit persons to positions in the Church when the defendants hinder the monarch.

[578] Dr. Ralph Lambert* (1666–1732).

[579] Henry Leslie (?–?), the Bishop of Dromore's candidate for (and *de facto* holder of) the deanery of Dromore.

dispossess him: so difficult and so doubtful that I heartily wish instead of my present patent I had a promise of the next Deanery that falls.

One of the most disagreeable effects of my lawsuit is that it detains me from England, and consequently from Charlton,* where I proposed being happy this summer, and where I hope your Lordship, my good Lady Percival and your delightful offspring now enjoy all those domestic pleasures which constitute the true and solid comforts of life. I am my Lord,

etc.,

G. Berkeley

110 BERKELEY TO PERCIVAL

EP, BL Add. MS 47029, fols. 126v–27.

Dublin, Trinity College, 29 July 1722

My Lord,

Not having had the honour of a line from your Lordship since my last, I am well pleased to find by Mr. Percival[580] that you and my Lady and the rest of the family are well.

Your Lordship knows this barren bleak island too well to expect any news from it worth your notice. The most remarkable thing now going on is a house of Mr. Conolly's[581] at Castletown. It is 142 feet in front, and above 60 deep in the clear, the height will be about 70. It is to be of fine wrought stone, harder and better coloured than the Portland, with outhouses joining to it by colonnades etc. The plan is chiefly of Mr. Conolly's invention, however, in some points they are pleased to consult me. I hope it will be an ornament to the country.

On Thursday next the King's equestrian statue is to be uncovered and exposed to view; the several companys will ride the fringes on that day, and our magistrates appear in their utmost magnificence. I hear six guineas are given for a floor to see the show. I was desired to make the Latin inscription for the statue, which I did, being willing to distinguish my zeal for his Majesty, and in consequence thereof had the honour to dine at my Lord Mayor's on last great day.

I heartily wish my lawsuit was at an end, that I may pay a visit to my friends in England, especially yourself and my good Lady, whom I long to see; but as it is, it

---

[580] There are several members of the Percival family to whom this might refer, including John the younger, now aged 11.
[581] William Conolly* (1662–1729), MP in Ireland and Speaker of the Irish House of Commons.

unluckily detains me here from seeing my friends, or prosecuting my interest in England. I do nevertheless conceive hopes it may be cut short by a project contained in the enclosed, which when you have read, I must entreat you to seal and deliver or send to Mr. Molyneux.[582] I take the liberty to give you this trouble, having cause to suspect that some former letters of mine to him might have miscarried, and as this is of importance, I would fain have it go sure and speedy. My Lord, I am out of countenance for the trouble I have given you, and remain with a hearty sense of all your favours,

> your Lordship's
> most obedient & most humble servant,
> Geo: Berkeley

111 PERCIVAL TO BERKELEY

EP, BL Add. MS 47029, fol. 129–29v.

Tunbridge, 5 August 1722

Dear Sir,

I received your letter with the other enclosed for Mr. Molyneux last Sunday, and sent it immediately under a cover to Kew.[583] I writ at the same time to him in hopes to have an answer, and thereby the satisfaction of knowing the letter came safe to his hands. I think the expedient you have proposed is extremely reasonable and proper, and the Duke[584] must be strangely overseen, or under very strong obligations of promise to some other person, if he do[es] not close with it and thereby preserve the right of the Crown, which by his negligence is so much in jeopardy.

I have been to blame that I did not answer your former letter till now, but to say the truth I had nothing to send you material, and I have not style to make something out of nothing, which is so easy to some.

I think it is now nine weeks in all since we came here, and my wife by reason of the bad weather and cholic has drunk the waters but twelve days only; but she is now very well and will pursue a regular course with them for three weeks, when we shall return to Charlton.* We have often wished you with us, and now more especially that we propose to pass the winter there.

---

[582] Samuel Molyneux* (1689–1728). At this time Molyneux was secretary to the Prince of Wales.
[583] Samuel Molyneux* (1689–1728) was an MP representing Kew.
[584] Charles Fitzroy* (1683–1757), second Duke of Grafton.

I am glad that for the honour of my country, that Mr. Conolly[585] has undertaken so magnificent a pile of building, and your advice has been taken upon it. I hope that the execution will answer the design, wherein one especial care must be to procure good masons. I shall be impatient until you send me a sketch of the whole plan and of your two fronts. You will do well to recommend to him the making use of all the marbles he can get of the production of Ireland for his chimneys, for since this house will be the finest Ireland ever saw, and by your description fit for a Prince, I would have it as it were the epitome of the kingdom, and all the natural rarities she afford should have a place there. I would examine the several woods there for inlaying my floors, and wainscot with our own oak and walnut: my stone stairs should be of black palmers stone, and my buffet adorned with the choicest shells our strand afford. I would even carry my zeal to things of art: my hangings, beds, cabinets and other furniture should be Irish, and the very silver that ornamented my locks and grates should be the produce of our own mines. But I forget that I write to a gentleman of the country who knows better what is proper and what the kingdom affords. I am

Dear Sir,

your affectionate friend & humble servant,

Percival

112 BERKELEY TO PERCIVAL

EP, BL Add. MS *47029, fol. 132v.*

Trinity College, Dublin, 7 September 1722

My Lord,

I am to return my thanks to your Lordship for your obliging letter, and your care in conveying mine to Mr. Molyneux,[586] though as it happens I might have spared my friends and myself that trouble. I flatter myself with hopes of seeing your Lordship in London this winter, if I can steal so much time from my lawsuit; which besides that it gives me but a very discouraging prospect (the only way of getting possession of the Deanery being I am fully persuaded to make Dean

---

[585] William Conolly* (1662–1729). He was building an impressive, large stone mansion. Berkeley's familiarity with architecture from his Continental trips was apparently widely enough known and respected such that Conolly consulted Berkeley on some of the design for his house. See Letter 110 and *Works*, vol. IX, pp. 49–50, 71.

[586] Samuel Molyneux* (1689–1728).

Lesley[587] bishop) hath this inconvenience, that it keeps me from my friends in England, though I have a letter of absence.

I shall then give you the best account I can of Mr. Conolly's[588] house; in the meantime you will be surprised to hear that the building is begun and the cellar floor arched before they have agreed on any plan for the elevation or facade. Several have been made by several hands, but as I do not approve of a work conceived by many heads so I have made no draught of mine own. All I do being to give my opinion on any point, when consulted.

We are much alarmed here by the seizing of the Bishop of Rochester,[589] which makes men think the plot more considerable than was at first imagined. Providence hath hitherto baffled all schemes for introducing popery and arbitrary power, and I trust in God will continue to do so. I am sorry and ashamed to see a Protestant bishop accused of so foul a conspiracy.

I remain with my humblest services to Lady Percival and best wishes to all your family. My Lord

your Lordship's most obedient and most obliged servant,

Geo. Berkeley

113 BERKELEY TO PERCIVAL

EP, BL Add. MS 47029, fol. 138v.

Trinity College, Dublin, October 1722

My Lord,

I have still hopes of seeing your Lordship this winter, when I flatter myself with the prospect of rejoicing by your fireside, where I have spent so many agreeable hours.

The information you were so good to send me about the Bishop of Rochester[590] was very acceptable: it is an affair that holds us all in suspense, everyone longing to see the event and know his accomplices.

As to my own affair,[591] I could wish it were one brought to any conclusion, being prepared for the issue, be it what it will, and I think as indifferent about it as one can well be supposed to be on a like occasion.

---

[587] Henry Leslie (?–?), then in possession of the deanery of Dromore, a position which Berkeley was suing to obtain, having a patent from the Duke of Grafton* for the same position.

[588] William Conolly* (1662–1729). See Letter 110 and *Works*, vol. IX, pp. 49–50, 71.

[589] Francis Atterbury* (1663–1732).

[590] Francis Atterbury* (1663–1732).

[591] The dispute over the deanery of Dromore.

My Lord Duke[592] hath taken one step of late that pleases every one, I mean the presenting Dr. Bolton[593] to the Bishopric of Clonfert. He could not possibly have pitched upon a person more universally esteemed and unenvied. There is another of that name Dean of Derry, who lieth dangerously ill of a palsy, and is indeed past hopes of recovery. My friends think that in case of a vacancy I may have some pretensions to my Lord Lieutenant's favour, especially if his Grace shall not think fit to recommend my adversary to a bishopric, without which I have little or no prospect of succeeding to the Deanery of Down [Dromore?].[594]

As to Mr. Payzant's copying pieces out of our Library, it is at present so old and ruinous, and the books so out of order, that there is little attendance given;[595] beside it is unusual for strangers to be admitted to copy in it. The only way is for me to borrow in my own name, and under caution any book that you would have copied, and so for Mr. Payzant to transcribe it at home, which I will gladly do. Let me therefore know what your Lordship would have, and I will enquire if it be in our MS. library, which to speak the truth is but indifferently furnished. This with my respects to my good Lady Percival, your Lordship and all your family, not forgetting Mr. Dering[596] and Mrs. Dering,[597] is what occurs from,

> your Lordship's, etc.,
> G. Berkeley

114 PERCIVAL TO BERKELEY

EP, BL Add. MS 47029, fol. 140–40v.

Charlton, 22 November 1722

Dear Sir,

You write with such indifference about your Deanery, that one would think the old times are returning, when the clergy fled into the wilderness to avoid a bishopric. I am sure there is much of that spirit appears in the resignation you show to the issue of Providence in this particular affair, a preferment which of

---

[592] Charles Fitzroy* (1683–1757), second Duke of Grafton and lord lieutenant of Ireland.

[593] Theophilus Bolton (1677/78–1744). Bolton became bishop of Clonfert in 1722. In April 1724 he was translated to Elphin and in January 1730 was appointed archbishop of Cashel.

[594] The letter says Down, but this is likely a transcription error in the letterbook, since Berkeley hopes in an earlier letter to have his rival Henry Lesley (Leslie), the *de facto* dean of Dromore, promoted to a bishopric to free the deanery for himself. See Letter 112.

[595] A new library at Trinity College was at that time under construction. Begun in 1712, it was completed in 1732. Mr. Payzant is referenced only one other time that I can find, in a 9 November 1723 letter from Philip Percival to John Percival (see Rand, pp. 213–14).

[596] Daniel Dering* (?–1730).

[597] Mary (*née* Parker) Dering* (1692–1731).

all others pleased you most[598] as most agreeable to your health, studies, and the enjoyment of your friends. What encouragement the lawyers have given you to proceed in your suit since your last to me I know not, but I suspect it not to be great, as well from your way of writing, as from what a gentleman told me some time ago, that he heard you begun to think you had not the right of your side.

Your hint of the Deanery of Derry is good, if my Lord Burlington,[599] Leinster,[600] or other of your friends here, who have the best interest with the Duke,[601] would propose it to his Grace; but surely it would be well worth your while to come over and animate their friendship in person. It would not retard your suit in Ireland, but would certainly promote any new project you entertain. Besides, by assuring yourself of the earliest intelligence from that side of any dignity worth your acceptance that shall fall in your absence, you will be upon the spot to make a sudden application yourself to the Duke, which is the likeliest means to get it, for the first applier generally succeeds, and it is much harder to resist a personal application when not unreasonable, than that made by another in behalf of his friend.

The interest I have with his Grace was, you know, not able to serve you in that small request you made him by me to give you a small living to help out the expenses of the suit;[602] and yet if it were greater, my brother Percival's affair, which I solicited long before your acquaintance with the Duke and lies yet unfinished, prevents me from urging the concerns of any other in that effectual manner which I could wish I had the liberty or credit with him to do; not to mention likewise another thing, which I beg you to keep secret because it was his Grace's commands to me that I should, my promotion to the rank of a Viscount, which without my asking, or in truth desiring, he told me he had asked of the King. This reason for secrecy was the application that others might make for a like mark of the King's favour, and therefore pray say nothing of it till you see it in the prints.[603] I take notice of it to you, to make you sensible that by this and my brother's affair I am not at so great liberty as others to ask favours, were my interest with him before as great as theirs, which I am far from pretending to. But pray consider what I now and in my former letters did propose, that you should come over and in person take care of your affairs.

---

[598] Rand has "your mood" instead of "you most." His transcription might be right from the original if he had access to it. Percival's letterbook (which is all that remains to us) reads "you most."

[599] Richard Boyle* (1695–1753), third Earl of Burlington and fourth Earl of Cork.

[600] Most likely a reference to Robert Fitzgerald, (1675–1744) nineteenth Earl of Kildare and Viscount of Leinster.

[601] Charles Fitzroy* (1683–1757), second Duke of Grafton.

[602] A reference to Berkeley's suit to obtain the deanery of Dromore.

[603] In December 1722 John Percival* (1683–1748) was made Viscount Percival of Kanturk, having been promoted to Baron of Burton in April 1715 by Queen Anne.*

I am now at Charlton,* where I thought to stay the winter, if my wife's cholic which is returned upon her with very great severity did permit, but it obliges us to go to the bath, as we shall do in about ten days or a fortnight. She has it every day and night, and I do not find that the physicians are of much use to her, other than now and then to give her a little ease, but they all advise her to these waters.

My children I thank God are all well and so are our other friends. I am pleased to hear that you enjoy your health and am ever,

> your affectionate friend & humble servant,
> Percival

115 BERKELEY TO PERCIVAL

EP, BL Add. MS 47029, fol. 142v.

London, 16 December 1722

My Lord,

After so dangerous a voyage, and so long a journey, it is a great mortification to find myself disappointed of the principal pleasure I proposed in London, by your Lordship's and my Lady's absence at Bath. But the occasion is still more mortifying. I hope my good Lady finds the benefit she expected from those waters. If the bath doth not perfect her cure, I know a place within a thousand leagues that I am persuaded will, if I can persuade her Ladyship to go thither.[604] But more of this when I have the happiness to see you.

For the present I have made an excursion into England, partly to see my friends, and partly to inform myself in some points of law which are not so well known in Ireland. I am heartily sorry that my suit is likely to call me back before your return to London, but if it should, I shall not be long without making another attempt to see you.

I know not whether you have heard of our abandoned condition at sea. For thirty-six hours together we expected every minute to be swallowed by a wave, or dashed in pieces against a rock. We sprung and split our mast, lost our anchor, and heaved our guns overboard. The storm and the sea were outrageous beyond description, but it pleased God to deliver us.

I have services to you and my Lady from Mr. Percival and Mrs. Percival, as also an Irish prayer-book which your brother sends as a specimen of our good printing.

The first house I went to was yours in Pall Mall,* where I found the children very well, and was particularly well pleased with my new acquaintance, your

---

[604] Luce speculates that the place "within a thousand leagues" is Bermuda. See *Works*, vol. IX, p. 51.

youngest son, who is as fine a boy as the sun shines on.[605] My humble service to my Lady and Mrs. Dering. I am,

> My Lord,
>
> your Lordship's most obedient & affectionate servant,
>
> G. Berkeley

116 PERCIVAL TO BERKELEY[606]

EP, BL Add. MS 47029, fol. 143v.

Bath, 21 December 1722

Dear Sir,

You may believe I was very uneasy to hear you was [sic] on board the yacht, when at the same time we had no account of her but believed her lost. I congratulate [you on] your escape most heartily, and share in the pleasure your safe arrival in London gives your friends. It is an addition to the trouble of a long winter's journey hither that I do not see you, and more so that, by what you write me, you propose to be gone again for Ireland before my return to London. I hope you have had frequent opportunities of seeing his Grace[607] and improving his good intentions towards you. There are very few things would give me equal pleasure to that of hearing you had overcome this vexatious business of the Deanery.[608] I was alarmed two posts ago with a report that the Duke was to quit his government, but to-day I had letters from those that ought to know that it is not true. I hope at least he will keep it until you either get your point, or have satisfaction made you some other way to your mind.

My wife finds herself better within these few days from a vomit she took, but her cholic is too obstinate to yield presently. Here are several Irish gentry, as Lord Barrimore,[609] Sir Pierce Butler[610] and his Lady, Mr. Mathew Ford[611] and his family, Mr. Butler, Lord Montgarret's son,[612] cousin Oliver and his Lady, Mr. Stafford, Mrs. Hambleton, etc.; and some Scots, as the Duke of Queensbury,[613]

---

[605] George Percival, born 28 January 1722.

[606] This letter is not in Rand.

[607] Charles Fitzroy* (1683–1757), second Duke of Grafton.

[608] A reference to Berkeley's suit to obtain the deanery of Dromore.

[609] James Barry (1667–1748), fourth Earl of Barrymore, politician and Jacobite conspirator.

[610] Pierce Butler (1652–1740), third Viscount Galmoye and Jacobite Earl of Newcastle.

[611] Mathew Ford (?–1729), MP of the Irish Parliament from 1703 to 1714.

[612] Edmund Butler (1663–1735), sixth Viscount Mountgarret. The son is likely Richard Butler (1685–1736), seventh Viscount Mountgarret.

[613] Charles Douglas (1698–1778), third Duke of Queensberry and second Duke of Dover.

Lord Dunbarton[614] and others: but I have no great acquaintance with any of them, and consequently am not here in full delight. I hope you received a letter I writ you to Dublin, wherein I enclosed one that came from beyond seas.

We have little news here. Lady Blantyre[615] died here two days ago, and Mr. Rolt, Parliament man from Chipenham, lies dangerously ill of the small-pox,[616] which is pretty rife among us. My wife and sister give you their affectionate service, and I am ever,

> Dear Sir,
>
> your humble & obedient servant,
>
> Percival

117 BERKELEY TO PERCIVAL

EP, BL Add. MS 47029, fols. 156v–58.

London, 4 March 1722/23

My Lord,

It is now about ten months since I have determined with myself to spend the residue of my days in the island of Bermuda, where I trust in Providence I may be the mean instrument of doing good to mankind.[617] Your Lordship is not to be told that the reformation of manners among the English in our western plantations, and the propagation of the Gospel among the American savages, are two points of high moment. The natural way of doing this is by founding a college or seminary in some convenient part of the West Indies, where the English youth of our plantations may be educated in such sort as to supply the churches with pastors of good morals and good learning, a thing (God knows!) much wanted. In the same seminary a number of young American savages may be also educated till they have taken their degree of Master of Arts. And being by that time well instructed in Christian religion, practical mathematics, and other liberal arts and sciences, and early endued with public spirited principles and inclinations, they may become the fittest missionaries for spreading religion, morality, and civil life, among their

---

[614] George Douglas (1687–1749), second Earl of Dumbarton.

[615] Anne Hamilton (1658–1722), second wife of Alexander Stewart, fifth Lord Blantyre, who died in 1704.

[616] Edward Rolt (1686–1722), MP from St. Mawes, Grantham, and finally Chippenham. A note from Percival in his letterbook reads: "deceased soon after."

[617] Berkeley proposed the founding of St. Paul's College in Bermuda. For an account of the project, see Luce, *Life of Berkeley*, chapters 7–9. See also Berkeley's *Proposal for the Better Supplying of Churches in our Foreign Plantations, and for Converting the Savage Americans to Christianity* (1724/25), in *Works*, vol. VII, pp. 335–61.

countrymen, who can entertain no suspicion or jealousy of men of their own blood and language, as they might do of English missionaries, who can never be so well qualified for that work. Some attempts have been made towards a college in the West, but to little purpose, chiefly I conceive for want of a proper situation wherein to place such college or seminary, as also for want of a sufficient number of able men well qualified with divine and human learning, as well as with zeal to prosecute such an undertaking. As to the first, I do think the small group of Bermuda islands the fittest spot for a college on the following accounts. 1. It is the most equidistant part of our plantations from all the rest, whether in the continent, or the isles.[618] 2. It is the only Plantation that holds a general commerce and correspondence with all the rest, there being sixty cedar ships belonging to the Bermudians, which they employ as carriers to all parts of the English West Indies, in like manner as the Dutch are carriers in Europe. 3. The climate is by far the healthiest and most serene, and consequently the most fit for study. 4. There is the greatest abundance of all the necessary provisions for life, which is much to be considered in a place of education. 5. It is the securest spot in the universe, being environed round with rocks all but one narrow entrance, guarded by seven forts, which render it inaccessible not only to pirates but to the united force of France and Spain. 6. The inhabitants have the greatest simplicity of manners, more innocence, honesty, and good nature, than any of our other planters, who are many of them descended from whores, vagabonds, and transported criminals, none of which ever settled in Bermudas. 7. The islands of Bermuda produce no one enriching commodity, neither sugar, tobacco, indigo, or the like, which may tempt men from their studies to turn traders, as the parsons do too often elsewhere.

It would take up too much of your Lordship's time minutely to describe the beauties of Bermuda, the summers refreshed with constant cool breezes, the winters as mild as our May, the sky as light and blue as a sapphire, the ever green pastures, the earth eternally crowned with fruits and flowers.[619] The woods of cedars, palmettos, myrtles, oranges etc., always fresh and blooming. The beautiful situations and prospects of hills, vales, promontories, rocks, lakes and sinuses of the sea. The great variety, plenty, and perfection of fish, fowl, vegetables of all kinds, and (which is in no other of our Western Islands) the most excellent butter, beef, veal, pork, and mutton. But above all, that uninterrupted health and alacrity of spirit, which is the result of the finest weather and gentlest

---

[618] The claim of equidistance is more or less true, but Bermuda lies approximately 600 miles from the nearest point on the North American mainland.

[619] It should be noted that Berkeley in fact never traveled to Bermuda. It is not clear to what sources Berkeley is appealing in his descriptions.

climate in the world, and which of all others is the most effectual cure for the cholic, as I am most certainly assured by the information of many very credible persons of all ranks who have been there.

In case I carry [the] Deanery (as I have good hopes I shall) I design to erect a charity school in Dromore, and to maintain ten savages and ten whites in the Bermudan University. But whatever happens, go I am resolved if I live. Half a dozen of the most agreeable and ingenious men of our college are with me in this project.[620] And since I came hither I have got together about a dozen English men of quality, and gentlemen, who intend to retire to these islands, to build villas and plant gardens, and to enjoy health of body and peace of mind, where they have a soft freestone like that at Bath, and a soil which produces everything that grows in America, Europe, or the East, and where a man may live with more pleasure and dignity for £500 p. annum than for £10,000 here: in short where men may find, in fact, whatsoever the most poetical imagination can figure to itself in the golden age, or the Elysian fields.

I have been proposing every day this month past to trouble you with this narrative, and have at last ventured to do it, though I run the risk of being thought mad and chimerical. But I beg your Lordship not to determine anything of me or my project till I have the honour of seeing you at Charlton, which I hope for this summer, and there to lay before you a thousand things relating to the scheme, the method of carrying it on, and answering objections against it. In the meantime I am going to Ireland, for three months, or four at most, by which time my lawsuit will probably be ended. If I can make a convert of your Lordship to Bermuda, I doubt not my Lady will be pleased to pass a few years there for the perfect recovery of her health, to which that climate will contribute beyond anything in the world. My heartiest good wishes and best respects to her Ladyship. I am, etc.,

G. Berkeley

118 BERKELEY TO PERCIVAL

EP, BL Add. MS 47030, fols. 5v–6v.

Trinity College, Dublin, 4 June 1723

My Lord,

The kind concern you have always shewn for my interests hath made it become my duty to inform you of any great advantage that should befall me.

---

[620] Robert Clayton* (1695–1758), a fellow of Trinity College, was second-in-command. William Thompson, Jonathan Rogers, and James King are named in the charter. See *Works*, vol. IX, p. 52.

Some thing of that sort is just now come to pass, that probably will surprise your Lordship as much as it doth me. Mrs. Hester van Omry,[621] a Lady to whom I was a perfect stranger, having never in the whole course of my life, to my knowledge, exchanged one single word with her, died on Sunday night. Yesterday her will was opened, by which it appears that I am constituted executor,[622] the advantage whereof is computed by those who understand her affairs to be worth three thousand pounds, and if a suit she had depending be carried,[623] it will be considerably more. But this is only a confused gross reckoning; in a little time I hope to see more distinctly into the state of her affairs. If this had not happened, I was determined to write to your Lordship by this post on my Lady's account. I am heartily sorry to hear she is not so well recovered of her cholic by the bath as I could wish, and do therefore repeat and insist on the advice I formerly gave her Ladyship to go and drink the waters of Geronster near Spa. If this does not perfect her cure, there is nothing left but your and her going to Bermuda, where to enjoy the company of you all in good health, would be as great a blessing as I can figure to myself upon earth.

I know not what your thoughts are on the long account I sent you from London to Bath of my Bermuda scheme (which is now stronger on my mind than ever, this providential event having made many things easy in my private affairs which were otherwise before). But I hear that Mr. Moore reports that you are terrified with the apprehension of earthquakes. Upon the word of a priest, I am thoroughly convinced that an earthquake was never known to have happened in Bermuda. The Summer Islands[624] are all to my certain knowledge freer from earthquakes than that on which you now live. There is not (I may say without vanity) a man in the world, who never was in the Summer Islands, that knows so much of them as I do; and this of the earthquakes is a most villa[i]nous calumny, set about by somebody who wants objections against the scheme, as I could easily prove by arguments and

---

[621] Typically spelled Hester (sometimes Esther) Van Homrigh (and pronounced "vanummery," according to Lord Orrey), the elder daughter of Bartholomew Van Homrigh (?–1703), once lord mayor of Dublin. She is the "Vanessa" of Jonathan Swift's *Cadenus and Vanessa*. The poem was written in 1713 and published in 1726, after her death in 1723. For an account of the relationship between Swift and Van Homrigh, see Luce, *Life of Berkeley*, pp. 87–93; and Margaret Anne Doody, "Swift and Women," in *The Cambridge Companion to Jonathan Swift*, ed. Christopher Fox (Cambridge University Press, 2003), pp. 87–111.

[622] Berkeley was named coexecutor of Vanessa's will along with Robert Marshall* (c. 1690–1772).

[623] Vanessa had a lawsuit pending against Peter Partinton* (?–?), the executor of her father and brother, which proved to be the major obstacle in resolving her will.

[624] A popular name at the time for the Bermuda Islands.

testimonies to your Lordship; but that I am in a prodigious hurry, the Lady being to be buried in a little more than an hour's time. Her funeral is under the direction of the king at arms, where I am to act I know not what part, which puts an end to this hasty scrawl.

I am, my Lord,

your Lordship's most obedient and most humble servant,

Geo. Berkeley

119 PERCIVAL TO BERKELEY

EP, BL Add. MS 47030, fol. 7–7v.

Spa, 30 June 1723

Dear Sir,

I arrived here two days ago, and yesterday had the pleasure of receiving your letter, dated 4th inst., which gives me an account of the convincing proof that a deceased lady has given of her value for you when living.[625] I congratulate you upon it from the bottom of my heart, and all the company with me received an inexpressible pleasure at the account. I hope it is only an earnest of the good things Providence has in store for a person so disinterested as you have ever been, and who will make so good use of the favours it shall bestow.

We all conclude that you will now persist in your thoughts of settling in Bermuda, and prosecute that noble scheme, which if favoured by our Court may in some time exalt your name beyond that of St. Xavier, or any the most famous missioners abroad; but without the protection and encouragement of the government you will meet with difficulties of sundry sorts from governors abroad, and from persons in office at home, as the Commissioners of the Plantation, the Society de propaganda Fide, and even the Bishop of London,[626] under whom the care of the Plantations in religious matters lies as you know.[627] Not that any of them can oppose the design you go upon, in general, but they may perplex you in the manner of carrying it on, unless you first settle every thing with them in part, and procure an assured protection from the supreme power. But both your own wisdom and the piety of the design will I am sure conduct it through, and

---

[625] A reference to Berkeley's being named coexecutor of the estate of Hester Van Homrigh* (1688–1723). See Letter 118.

[626] Edmund Gibson* (1669–1748).

[627] The bishop of London had responsibility for the Anglican churches in the American colonies.

then you will have the honour of wiping off the reproach, which Papists cast on us, of not having the care of infidels' souls at heart. But whether you go, or stay, in whatever station you are placed, and whatever scheme of life you resolve on, you have my best wishes to attend you.

My wife has to this hour the cholic, and but for laudanum, which more or less she takes every day, would be very miserable; even with it she can but barely support herself. It was the disappointment she met with in the several waters at home, and the number of medicines prescribed her (all without effect), that determined her to leave her children and take your advice of coming to Geronster.[628] We shall in a few days see what we are to expect from these waters, but at present the season is so wet we cannot begin them. I pray God they may prove successful, for after this, if she should not recover, I know not what she can do, but give herself up to laudanum for life. I am,

Dear Sir,

your affectionate & humble servant,

Percival

120 BERKELEY TO CAMPAILLA

Preface to Thomas Campailla, L'Adamo, ovvero il Mondo Creato (1728).

Londinii Kalendis Julii 1723

Clarissime Vir,

Post longam quinque ferme annorum peregrinationem, variosque casus, et discrimina, nunc demum in Angliam redux, nihil antiquius habeo, quam fidem meam tibi quondam obligatam. Deus bone! Ab illo tempore quot clades, quot rerum mutationes, tam apud vos, quam apud nos! Sed mittamus haec tristia. Libros tuos, prout in mandatis habui, viro erudito e Societate Regia tradidi, qui, cum solertiam, et ingenium tuum pro meritis extimet [*sic*], tum id plurimum miratur, tantum scientiae lumen in extremo Siciliae angulo tam diu delituisse. Telescopium quod attinet catoptricum, e metallo confectum, id quidem olim aggressus est Neutonus; verum res ex voto non successit; nam impossibile erat, nitidum chalybis splendorem usque eo conservare, ut stellarum imagines distincte exhiberet; proinde hujusmodi telescopia nec in usu sunt, nec unquam fuere; nec praeter unicum illud, quod Author experimenti causa fabricavit, ullum factum esse unquam, vel fando accepi. Hodie certe apud nostrates non

---

[628] Geronstere, a spa town near Spa in modern Belgium.

reperiuntur. Caeterum librum clarissimi istius philosophi juxta ac mathematici, quem spondebam missurum, ad te mitto, quem tanquam sincerae amicitiae pignus accipias, quaeso. Tu, interim, vir clarissime, promovere rem litterariam pergas; artesque bonas et scientias in ea insula serere et propagare, ubi felicissimae terrae indoles frugibus, et ingeniis apta ab omni aevo aeque fuit. Scito me tibi semper futurum

addictissimum et humillimum servum,

G. Berkeley

London Kalends of July [1 July] 1723

Most Illustrious Sir,

After a long journey of almost five years, and various accidents and risks, having returned at last to England, I consider nothing more important than my previously pledged loyalty to you. Good God, from that time, how many disasters, how many changes of affairs—as many for you as for us! But let us dismiss these sad things. Your books, to the extent that I hold them in my charge, I have handed over to a learned man from the Royal Society, who, when he will have esteemed your shrewdness and genius for their merits, will very much marvel at this: that so much light of knowledge has for so long lain hidden in a far corner of Sicily. The telescope which has a mirror, made from metal, is indeed the one Newton[629] once approached; but the thing did not succeed as promised; for it was impossible to preserve the shining splendour of steel to the point that it might distinctly show the images of stars; therefore telescopes of this kind are not in use nor were they ever; nor, except for this one, which the Authority made for the sake of an experiment, was any ever made, or so I have heard it said. Surely today among our people they are not found. Another book of that most illustrious philosopher and equally [illustrious] mathematician, which I was promising to send, I am sending to you, which I ask that you receive as a pledge of sincere friendship. You, meanwhile, most illustrious sir, continue to influence the literary world and to sow and propagate good arts and sciences on this island, where from every age there has been equally the inborn quality of a land most blessed in fruits and fitted with geniuses. Know that I shall always be your

Most humble obedient servant,

G. Berkeley

[629] Sir Isaac Newton (1642–1727).

121 BERKELEY TO PERCIVAL

EP, BL Add. MS 47030, fols. 16v–17.

Trinity College, Dublin, 19 September 1723

My Lord,

I heartily congratulate your and good Lady Percival's safe arrival at Charlton,* though I must own the pleasure this incident would otherwise have given me is not a little allayed by the account I hear of her Ladyship's not receiving all the benefit she expected from the Spa waters. I hope however that she is considerably eased, but for a perfect cure of so rooted a disorder, it must I believe under God be the effect of time and change of air. Besides my best wishes and prayers for her Ladyship's health, I will venture to contribute my mite of advice, how extravagant however it may seem, and that is to try the air of the Summer Islands which I am thoroughly satisfied is the best in the world, and particularly good for the cholic. And in good earnest what is a year's or two years' confinement there in competition with her health, which I am sure your Lordship can never be easy without.

In my last I gave an account of a legacy left me by a lady.[630] Since that, looking into her affairs we find her debts to have been considerably greater than we imagined. I am, nevertheless, still likely to make two thousand pound clear, not reckoning in the law suit depending between the executors and Mr. Partinton.[631]

As to the suit about the Deanery of Dromore, I despair of seeing it end to my advantage. The Deanery of Down is now vacant, but there is such a crowd of competitors for everything, that I cannot promise myself success without such assiduity and attendance as I hardly think it deserves.[632] The truth is, my first purpose of going to Bermuda sets me above soliciting anything with earnestness in this part of the world, which can now be of no use to me, but as it may enable me the better to prosecute that design: and it must be owned that the present possession of something in the Church would make my application for an establishment in these islands more considered. I mean a charter for a college there, which of all things I desire, as being what would reconcile duty and inclination, making my life at once more useful to the public and more agreeable to myself than I can possibly expect elsewhere. And as I am to run

---

[630] Hester Van Homrigh* (1688–1723).

[631] Peter Partinton* (?–?).

[632] Charles Fairfax (1684–1723), dean of Down, died 27 July 1723. He was succeeded by William Gore (?–1732).

into visions on this subject, I have sometimes thought it not quite impossible that you and my Lady may sometime or other take a fancy to retire to that part of the world. But I dare only think this possible, and if it be otherwise should be sorry to be undeceived. I am with all respect,

> My Lord,
>> your Lordship's most obedient most humble & affectionate servant,
>> Geor. Berkeley

122 PERCIVAL TO BERKELEY

EP, BL Add. MS 47030, fol. 19–19v.

London, 8 October 1723

Dear Sir,

It is always with great pleasure I hear from you, and especially when you inform me of anything falling out to your advantage or satisfaction. The legacy you write me of, you was so kind to let me know before, and I congratulated you upon it, as I do again, heartily wishing the lawsuit may end in your favour.[633] I know no body deserves it better, as on other accounts, so for the good use you will make of it. I could only wish this Providence had come a year later, that you might not be so negligent as you appear to be in your pursuits at court, where you know nothing is to be had without strong soliciting, especially when such a number of competitors show themselves, and in a time of Parliament. Surely the Deanery of Down is worth all lawful ways of obtaining, and he who is most deserving of it ought to make the strongest pushes, because he seems to have a moral right to it. I can say no more but that I earnestly wish it you.

I am extremely obliged to you for your concern for my wife, who is returned from the Geronster[634] without finding the good effects from those waters she expected; but that journey gave her the opportunity of consulting foreign physicians, particularly the famous Dr. Boerhaave of Leyden,[635] who upon a full knowledge of her case has ordered her some pills, a drink, and constant exercise on horseback. This will oblige her to stay the winter at Charlton,*

---

[633] The legacy refers to that of Hester Van Homrigh* (1688–1723), who named Berkeley coexecutor of her will. See Letter 118.

[634] Geronstere, a spa town in Belgium.

[635] Herman Boerhaave (1668–1738), Dutch physician, botanist, and chemist of international repute. He allegedly was famous enough to be known and sought out by nobility in China in his own day.

where she may go all day long in her riding habit, and not be prevented in her course by impertinent visits, or frightened by coaches and carts. I need not tell you how agreeably your company there would make us pass our time, but since we cannot hope for it speedily, pray make it up in part by letting us hear from you.

My wife gives you her affectionate service, and desires me to tell you that while she follows Boerhaave's prescription to ride, she cannot think of going to Bermuda, where she understands there are nothing but rocks and rugged paths. I am ever

Dear Sir,

your affectionate & humble servant,

Percival

123 BERKELEY TO PERCIVAL

EP, BL Add. MS 47030, fols. 64v–65.

Trinity College, Dublin, 5 May 1724

My Lord,

After a long silence which was purely occasioned by my not knowing what to say, and expecting every day to be able to say something with certainty of my affairs (which I flattered myself might not be disagreeable to one from whom I have received so many instances of favour and goodness), I can now tell your Lordship, that yesterday I received my patent for the best Deanery in this kingdom, that of Derry. The affair of Dromore[636] is still undecided, and likely to be so for some years, but it is now in other hands, God be praised.

I have had powerful competitors, who used many arts to undermine me: but two livings worth £700 per annum happening to fall in the gift of the College, which the House, to further my promotion, was so kind as to put into the disposal of my Lord Duke,[637] this gave a strong turn in my favour. I am very sensible how much the Duchess[638] hath been my friend, and as sensible how much I am indebted for that to good Lady Percival.

---

[636] In the margin Percival has a note: "the Crown had presented Dr. Berkeley to it, but the Bishop [of Dromore] contested it with him at law."

[637] Charles Fitzroy* (1683–1757), second Duke of Grafton.

[638] Henrietta (*née* Somerset) Fitzroy* (1690–1726), Duchess of Grafton.

This Deanery is said to be worth £1,500 per annum, but then there are four curates to be paid, and great charges upon entering, for a large house and offices, first fruits, patent, etc. which will consume the first year's profits, and part of the second. But as I do not consider it with an eye to enriching myself, so I shall be perfectly contented if it facilitates and recommends my scheme of Bermuda, which I am in hopes will meet with a better reception when it comes from one possessed of so great a deanery. I am the fonder of Bermuda because I take it to be the likeliest means under heaven to re-establish my Lady's health, which I know your just tenderness for her will put you on restoring by all possible methods. I intend tomorrow for the north in order to my instalment and taking possession. When that is over I may trouble your Lordship with another letter, till when, I conclude, my Lord,

> your most, etc.,
> George Berkeley

124 PERCIVAL TO BERKELEY

EP, BL Add. MS 47030, fol. 67–67v.

Charlton, 26 May 1724

Dear Sir,

I cannot easily express the satisfaction I received in the account you lately sent me of your promotion to the Deanery of Derry.[639] I was very uneasy to see your preferment held so long in suspense, and knowing your desert every way far exceeded that of the other pretenders (so that there ought to have been no deliberation whom to prefer) I grew fearful that some powerful interest had prevailed or rather necessitated the Duke[640] to give that most honourable and profitable vacancy to some other person, and the rather because he never actually promised it [to] you. But now he has shown the world he has a regard to merit, and also that those friends who applied to him in your favour have some interest with him; and it is a great pleasure to me to find I was not mistaken in his character, when I pronounced him a man of discernment and honour.

---

[639] Berkeley received his patent for the deanery of Derry on 4 May 1724.
[640] Charles Fitzroy* (1683–1757), second Duke of Grafton.

I waited on her Grace[641] to thank her for her sincerity to you. She spoke a great deal in your commendation and expressed her satisfaction in having as she believes been some way assisting to you in this affair; for she said you had some pretended friends who undertook to serve you with the Duke, and yet did all the hurt they could; but she discovered their false dealing to him, and set all matters right. She did not name them, but seemed full of indignation, and could not forbear mentioning the same again to my wife.

I see you persist in your Bermuda scheme, which if it go on must owe its success to the Christian and disinterested view of the projector. But unless the government encourage it, it will certainly be impossible for you to go through with it; for no private subject can support such a work when begun, unless the King commands the governours in those parts to favour and protect it. I suppose when your affairs are settled in Ireland, this business will bring you over, and then I shall hope for the pleasure of your company at Charlton, where you have I can assure you as many friends as there are persons under my roof.

My wife is much obliged to you for your constant concern for her health, but says she must consider the Bermuda scheme over and over before she can fix her resolution to go so far, even for the recovery of health, which indeed is far from well. The rest of my family is I thank God in a good state, and my children proceed well in their studies. All give their service to you, and I am ever

 etc.,

 Percival

125 BERKELEY TO PERCIVAL

EP, BL Add. MS 47030, fols. 68v–69.

Elphin,[642] 8 June 1724

My Lord,

I am now on my return from Derry, where I have taken possession of my Deanery, and farmed out my tithe lands, etc. for £1,250 a year. I am assured they are worth two hundred pounds per annum more, but thought it better to have men of substantial fortunes engaged for the punctual payment of the foregoing sum, than by keeping them in my own hands to subject myself to all that

---

[641] Henrietta (*née* Somerset) Fitzroy* (1690–1726), Duchess of Grafton.
[642] Elphin is a small cathedral town in County Roscommon.

trouble, and all those cheats which dissenters (whereof we have many about Derry) are inclined to practice towards the clergy of our Church.

The city of Londonderry is the most compact, regular, well built town, that I have seen in the King's dominions; the town house (no mean structure) stands in the midst of a square piazza from which there are four principal streets leading to as many gates. It is a walled town, and has walks all round on the walls planted with trees, as in Padua. The Cathedral is the prettiest in Ireland. My house is a fashionable thing, not five years old, and cost eleven hundred pounds. The corporation are all good churchmen, a civil people, and throughout English, being a colony from London. I have hardly seen a more agreeable situation, the town standing on a peninsula in the midst of a fine spreading lake, environed with green hills, and at a distance the noble ridge of Ennishawen[643] mountains and the mighty rocks of Maghilligan[644] form a most august scene. There is indeed much of the *gusto grande*[645] in the laying out of this whole country, which recalls to mind many prospects of Naples and Sicily.

After all I may chance not to be two pence the richer for this preferment, for by the time I have paid for the house and first fruits, I hope I shall have brought the Bermuda project to an issue, which, God willing, is to be my employment this winter in London, where I long for the pleasure of waiting on your Lordship and good Lady Percival, to whom with the rest of the family I beg you to give my most humble and affectionate respects. I remain,

 etc.,

 Geo. Berkeley

126 BERKELEY TO PERCIVAL

EP, BL Add. MS 47030, fol. 95–95v.

Trinity College, Dublin, 9 September 1724

My Lord,

I am now, bless God, quite at ease from a cruel periodical cholic which seized me after my return from Derry. For several days it was very violent, but the loss of thirty-six ounces of blood with about a dozen purgings and vomitings, reduced both it and me to a very weak state. I have now and then inclinations of a relapse

---

[643] Today known as Inishowen, a peninsula in northern Ireland.
[644] Magilligan is in northwest Ireland near the mouth of Lough Foyle.
[645] Italian: "great taste."

which hath made me entertain thoughts of going to Bath, Bristol, or Tunbridge. I am not yet determined which, but propose going the first opportunity for England, where I hope to find your Lordship, my Lady, and all your good family, if not so well as I could wish, at least in a way of being thoroughly recovered and established in good health by a year or twos' residence in Bermuda, which I earnestly recommend to you. This I must own looks like a selfish proposal. But though I cannot deny that it would delight me beyond measure, yet I doubt not when I see you to prove by good arguments that your own and my Lady's interest is as much consulted in this project as my satisfaction. I have so many things to say on this head that if I once begun I should soon exceed the bounds of a letter, and shall therefore only add (with my best respects to your Lordship, my Lady, and all your family), that in the hopes of seeing you soon, I remain with the greatest sincerity, My Lord,

    your Lordship's most obedient and most obliged humble servant,
    Geo: Berkeley

Yesterday Wood's effigy was carried in procession by the mob through most of the streets of this town in order to be hanged or burnt, but it is given out by them that the Lord Mayor hath reprieved him till Wednesday. It is hardly possible to express the indignation which all ranks of men show on this occasion.[646]

127 BERKELEY TO PRIOR

LR, pp. 98–99.

London, 8 December 1724

Dear Tom,

    You wrote to me something or other, which I received a fortnight ago, about temporal affairs, which I have no leisure to think of at present. The L[ord] Chancellor[647] is not a busier man than myself; and I thank God my pains are not without success, which hitherto hath answered beyond expectation. Doubtless the English are a nation *très éclairée*.[648] I have only time to tell you,

---

[646] In July 1722 William Wood (1671–1730) secured a patent to supply halfpences and farthings for use in Ireland and America. The introduction of English coinage into Ireland without consulting the Irish produced a storm of outrage at all levels. The Irish Parliament voiced objections in September 1723 and Jonathan Swift famously published a series of pamphlets attacking Wood, starting with his *Letter to the Shopkeepers Tradesmen Farmers and Common People of Ireland by M. B. Drapier* (1724).

[647] Alan Brodrick (1655/56–1728), first Viscount Midleton.

[648] French: "very enlightened."

that Robin[649] will call on you for thirteen pounds. Let me know whether you have wrote to Mr. Newman[650] whatever you judged might give him a good opinion of our project. Let me also know where Bermuda Jones lives, or where he is to be met with.

I am,

Your, etc.,

G. Berkeley

I lodge at Mr. Fox's, an apothecary in Albemarle Street, near St. James's.

Provided you bring my affair with Partinton[651] to a complete issue before Christmas day come twelvemonth, by reference or otherwise, that I may have my dividend, whatever it is, clear, I do hereby promise you to increase the premium I promised you before by its fifth part, whatever it amounts to.

128 BERKELEY TO PRIOR

LR, *pp. 99–100.*

20 April 1725

Dear Tom,

Nothing hath occurred since my last worth writing; only Clarke affirms the jewels were part of the father's goods, to be divided as the rest. He saith they were claimed as such from Partinton by the daughters, and that this may appear by the writings.[652] I long to hear that Mr. Marshal[653] and you have agreed on what is due, and taken methods to pay it, etc.

Pray give my service to Caldwell;[654] and let him know that in case he goes abroad with Mr. Stewart,[655] Jaques,[656] who lived with Mr. Ashe,[657] is desirous to attend upon him. I think him a very proper servant to travel with a gentleman; but believing him sufficiently known to Caldwell, I shall forbear recommending him in more words.

---

[649] Robert Berkeley* (c. 1699–1787), Berkeley's younger brother.

[650] Henry Newman* (1670–1743).

[651] Peter Partinton* (?–?).

[652] Peter Partinton* (?–?). This is a reference to Berkeley's attempts to settle Hester Van Homrigh's* (1688–1723) estate.

[653] Robert Marshall* (c. 1690–1772).

[654] See note to Letter 9.

[655] An unknown reference.

[656] Probably a valet, perhaps the one who fell ill in Italy (see Letter 84).

[657] St. George Ashe* (1698–1721).

I have obtained reports from the Bishop of London,[658] the Board of Trade and Plantations, and the Attorney and Solicitor General, in favour of the Bermuda scheme, and hope to have the warrant signed by his Majesty this week.[659]

Yours,

G. Berkeley

129 BERKELEY TO PRIOR

LR, *pp. 101–02.*

3 June 1725

Dear Tom,

I have been this morning with Mr. Wogan,[660] who hath undertaken to inform himself about the value of our South Sea* stock, and what must be done in order to impower him to receive it. I have nothing more to add to my last letter; only to desire you to transact with Marshal[661] and Partinton[662] so as may dispose them to terminate all matters by a speedy arbitration, I care not before whom, lawyer or not lawyer. I very much wish that we could get the reversionary lands off our hands. If Partinton's own inclination for them should be a stop to the sale, I wish he had them. But the conduct of all these matters I must leave to your own care and prudence: Only I long to see them finished for our common interest. I must desire you to give yourself the trouble of sending me by the very next post a bill of forty pounds, payable here at the shortest sight. Pray fail not in this; and you will oblige, dear Tom,

yours sincerely,

G. Berkeley

Yesterday the charter passed the Privy Seal. This day the new chancellor began his office by putting the *Recepi* to it.

London, June 3, 1725

---

[658] Edmund Gibson* (1669–1748). As the bishop of London had ecclesiastical authority over the American colonies, Berkeley needed his permission to proceed with the Bermuda scheme.

[659] A favorable report on Berkeley's project was issued from the attorney general and solicitor general on 15 March 1725. See *Works*, vol. IX, p. 56 and Luce, "More Unpublished Berkeley Letters and New Berkeleiana," 32–34.

[660] Wogan* (?–?).

[661] Robert Marshall* (*c.* 1690–1772).

[662] Peter Partinton* (?–?).

130 BERKELEY TO PRIOR

LR, *pp. 102–04.*

London, 12 June 1725

Dear Tom,

I wrote to you some time since for forty pounds to be transmitted hither. I must now beg you to send me another forty pounds. I have had no answer to my last; so if you have not yet negotiated that bill, make the whole together fourscore pounds; which sum I shall hope for by the first opportunity. Mr. Wogan[663] hath not yet found out the South Sea* stock, but hath employed one in that office to inquire about it. As soon as I am informed myself, I shall let you know. He is also to make inquiry at Doctors' Commons* to know what must be done in order to prove the present property in us, and to empower him to receive it. In order thereunto, I have given him a memorial of what I knew. I hope, as soon as he sends these directions, they will be complied with on that side the water. It was always my opinion we should have such an agent here. I am sure, had he been appointed a year agone, our affairs would have been the better for it.

The charter hath passed all the seals, and is now in my custody. It hath cost me 130 pounds dry fees, besides expedition-money to men in office.

Mr. Percival writes that he hath given you the bonds. I must intreat you, dear Tom, to get the residue of last year's rent, with an account stated from Alderman M'Manus.[664] I am,

> yours sincerely,
> G. Berkeley

131 BERKELEY TO PRIOR

LR, *pp. 104–08.*

London, 20 July 1725

Dear Tom,

I have been of late in much embarrass of business, which, with Mr. Wogan's[665] being often out of town, hath occasioned your not hearing

---

[663] Wogan* (?–?).
[664] McManus* (?–?). *LR* has "M'Maurs," which I correct to M'Manus as Luce does.
[665] Wogan* (?–?).

from me for some time. I must now tell you that our South Sea* stock, etc., is confirmed to be what I already informed you, viz. 880 pounds, somewhat more or less. You are forthwith to get probates of Alderman Pearson's[666] will, Partinton's[667] will, and Mrs. Esther Van Homrigh's[668] will, in which names the Exchequer annuities were subscribed, transmitted hither, together with two letters of attorney, one for receiving the stock, the other for the annuities. You will hear from Mr. Wogan by this post, who will send you more particular directions, together with a copy of such letters of attorney as will be necessary. In case Pearson refuses to sign the letter, let him send over a renunciation to any right therein, which will do as well. It may suffice, without going through all the steps, to tell you that I have clearly seen it made out how the Exchequer annuities, subscribed in the name of the three forementioned persons, came (through various mutations incident to stock) to be worth this money, and likewise to have begot other annuities; which annuities, stock and dividends unreceived make up the sum. But before you get Partinton and Marshal[669] to sign the letters of attorney, or make the probates, nay, before you tell them of the value of the subscribed annuities, you should by all means, in my opinion, insist, carry and secure, two points; *first*, that Partinton should consent to a partition of this stock, etc. (which I believe he cannot deny): *secondly*, that Marshal should engage not to touch one penny of it till all debts on this side the water are satisfied. I even desire you would take advice, and legally secure it in such sort that he may not touch it if he would till the said debts are paid. It would be the wrongest thing in the world, and give me the greatest pain possible, to think we did not administer in the justest sense. Whatever therefore appears to be due, let it be instantly paid; here is money sufficient to do it. And here I must tell that Mrs. Hill hath been with me, who says the debt was the mother's originally, but that Mrs. Esther made it her own, by giving a note for the same under her hand, which note is now in Dublin. Mr. Clarke hath likewise shewn me a letter of Mrs. Esther's (writ by him, but signed by her), acknowledging the debt for her mother's funeral. And indeed it seems she must have necessarily given order for that, and so contract the debt, since the party deceased could

---

[666] Probably Philip Pearson* (?–?), an alderman in Dublin. Luce mistakes this Pearson for John Pearson (?–1725), an alderman and brewer who died in 1725 (see *Works*, vol. IX, p. 57).
[667] Peter Partinton* (?–?).
[668] Hester Van Homrigh* (1688–1723).
[669] Robert Marshall* (c. 1690–1772).

not be supposed to have ordered her own burial. These things being so, I would see Marshal brought to consent to the payment of them, or good reason assigned why they should not be paid. Mrs. Philips *alias* Barret (a very poor woman) is in great want of her dues. She saith Clarke and Baron can attest them, besides that they appear in Mrs. Esther's accompt-book. I must therefore entreat you, once for all, to clear up and agree with Marshal what is due, and then make an end, by paying that which it is a shame was not paid sooner. Query, Why the annuities should not have been subscribed in Prat's[670] name, if B.[671] V. Homrigh had a share in them? For God's sake, adjust, finish, conclude any way with Partinton; for at the rate we have gone on these two years, we may go on twenty. In your next, let me know what you have proposed to him and Marshal,* and how they relish it. I hoped to have been in Dublin by this time; but business grows out of business. I have wrote lately to Alderman M'Manus[672] to clear accounts with you. I am, dear Tom,

    yours sincerely,

    G. Berkeley

Bermuda prospers.

132 BERKELEY TO WAKE

Christ Church Library, Oxford, Wake correspondence, vol. 24, item 86.

10 August 1725

May it please your Grace,

In obedience to your Grace's commands I take the liberty to inform you that Sir Robert Walpole[673] is of opinion the petition relating to the lands formerly belonging to popish clergy in Sa[i]nt Christopher's* should be presented to the Lord Justices at their next meeting. Those lands contain somewhat more than seven hundred acres whereof five hundred and twenty or thereabouts are fit for sugar canes, the remainder are coarse and of small value. Three

---

[670] Benjamin Pratt (*c.* 1669–1721), former provost of Trinity College, Dublin. Hester Van Homrigh's* brother Bartholomew bequeathed her estate in part to him (and Partinton*), which passed to Partinton's son upon Pratt's death.

[671] Bartholomew Van Homrigh (?–?), Hester's deceased brother.

[672] McManus* (?–?). *LR* has "M'Maury," but I correct to "M'Manus."

[673] Sir Robert Walpole* (1676–1745), later first Earl of Orford.

hundred pounds per annum is all that the Public can propose to make of the abovementioned lands but they would be a great matter in the endowment of our College.[674] Your Grace's known concern for every thing that may promote the interests of Religion and Learning leaves me no room to doubt of your favour herein. I shall therefore add only that I am—with most profound respect My Lord

> Your Grace's
> most dutiful
> & most obedient
> servant,
> Geor: Berkeley

August the 10th, 1725

133 BERKELEY TO PRIOR

LR, *pp. 108–11.*

London, 3 September 1725

Dear Tom,

I suppose you have long since received the draughts of the letters of attorney, etc., from Mr. Wogan,[675] with his letter and mine. I must now add to what I there said, that it will be necessary for me to administer here in order to obtain the money out of the South Sea*. This is what Mr. Wogan tells me, and this is a step that I cannot think of taking till such time as the debts on this side the water are agreed on by Mr. Marshal[676] and you; for, having once taken out an administration on this side the water, I may be liable to be put to trouble here by the creditors more than I am at present. To be short, I expect the business of the debts will be ascertained before I take any steps on my part about the stock or annuities. I must further tell you, that in case Mr. Marshal does not send orders to pay all the debts really due, with particular mention of the same, I must even put them all (pretenders as well as just creditors) upon attaching or securing the whole effects here, in South Sea, etc., to their own use, wherein I

---

[674] Berkeley's proposed St. Paul's College in Bermuda.
[675] Wogan* (?–?).
[676] Robert Marshall* (*c.* 1690–1772).

shall think myself obliged to be aiding to the best of my power. Clarke hath brought me from time to time the pretensions of diverse creditors, all which I directed him to send to you; and he saith he hath sent them to you. I think Mr. Wogan should be constituted attorney for paying the debts here, as well as for getting the stock. If my brother Robin[677] calls upon you for ten pounds, you will let him have it. I am, dear Tom,

yours,

G. Berkeley

I wrote long since to Caldwell[678] about his going to Bermudas, but had no answer, which makes me think my letter miscarried. I must now desire you to give my service to him, and know whether he still retains the thoughts he once seemed to have of entering into that design. I know he hath since got an employment, etc.; but I have good reason to think he would not suffer in his temporalities by taking one of our fellowships, although he resigned all that. In plain English, I have good assurance that our college will be endowed beyond any thing expected or desired hitherto. This makes me confident he would lose nothing by the change; and on this condition only I propose it to him. I wish he may judge right in this matter, as well for his own sake as for the sake of the college.

134 BERKELEY TO PRIOR

LR, *pp. 111–13.*

Flaxley, 15 October 1725

Dear Tom,

It is an age since I have heard from you. You have long since received instructions from Mr. Wogan[679] and from me what is to be done. If these are not already complied with, I beg you will lose no more time, but take proper methods, out of hand, for selling the South Sea* stock and annuities. I have very good reason to apprehend that they will sink in their value, and desire you to let Van Homrigh, Partinton,[680] and Mr. Marshal,[681] know as much. The

---

[677] Robert Berkeley* (c. 1699–1787), Berkeley's younger brother.
[678] See note to Letter 9.
[679] Wogan* (?–?).
[680] Peter Partinton* (?–?).
[681] Robert Marshall* (c. 1690–1772).

less there is to be expected from them, the more I must hope from you. I know not how to move them at this distance but by you; and if what I have already said will not do, I profess myself to be at a loss for words to move you. I shall therefore only mention three points (often mentioned heretofore) which I earnestly wish to see something done in. 1*st*, The debts on this side the water stated, if not with concurrence of Mr. Marshal, without him; for sure this may be done without him, by the papers you have already seen, where Clarke saith they all appear. 2*d*, A commission of attorney sent to Wogan (who I am assured is an honest and capable man) to transact all affairs here. 3*d*, Matters somehow or other concluded with Partinton. You have told me he was willing to refer them to an arbitration, but not of lawyers, and that Marshal would refer them only to lawyers. For my part, rather than fail, I am for referring them to any honest knowing person or persons, whether lawyer or not lawyer; and if Marshal will not come into this, I desire you will do all you can to oblige him, either by persuasion or otherwise: particularly represent to him my resolution of going (with God's blessing) in April next to Bermuda, which will probably make it his interest to compromise matters out of hand; but if he will not, agree if possible with Partinton to force him to compliance in putting an end to our disputes. Partinton Van Homrigh,[682] I remember, expressed a desire to purchase the reversionary lands. I beg he may be allowed to do it, or any other means be used to bring him to consent to the sale of them.

I have been these five weeks in a ramble through England. I came hither two or three days since, and propose leaving this place in a day or two, and being in London by the time answer may come from you; but not being sure where I shall lodge, must desire you to direct to be left with Mr. Bindon,[683] at the Golden-glove in Jermyn's Street, near Piccadilly.

And now I must desire you to pay to my brother Robin[684] seventeen pounds, for which his receipt will be sufficient. I am, dear Tom,

> yours sincerely,
> Geor. Berkeley

Flaxley, October 15, 1725

---

[682] Partinton's son, who under the terms of Bartholomew Van Homrigh's will was to take the surname Van Homrigh.

[683] An unknown Bindon. See Letter 152.

[684] Robert Berkeley* (*c.* 1699–1787).

135 BERKELEY TO PRIOR

LR, *pp. 114–16.*

2 December 1725

Dear Tom,

I am just returned from a long ramble through the country to London, where I am settled in my old lodging at Mr. Fox's, and where I have met with two letters from you, after a very long and profound silence, which made me apprehensive of your welfare.

I presume you have by this time a commission for the administration of Mr. Marshal,[685] which was to have gone last post to you from Messrs. Wogan and Aspinwall.[686] I do think it necessary that Mr. Marshal should act, both as he hath acted hitherto and hath right to act, and as my attention to other affairs makes it more inconvenient for me. You will therefore take care that Mr. Marshal perform his part without delay. There is another point to be managed, without which no step can be taken towards transferring the stock, and that is, a full renunciation (since he will not act) from Mr. Pearson,[687] provided he be sole heir to his father: if not, the other heirs must concur therein. Was there any authentic paper or declaration by which it legally appeared that old Mr. Pearson was only a trustee concerned in the stock? This alone would do; but I knew of none such. I beg you to dispatch this affair of the stock, and the other points relating thereto, which I formerly recommended to you, and which I hope you have not forgot. I long to hear what you and Mr. Marshal have resolved about the creditors: it is a shame something is not done. The woman of St. James's coffee-house claims a debt upon the family, for coffee, tea, etc. I promised to acquaint you with it: the particular sum I do not know, but suppose you are not unacquainted with any of the debts. If this be a debt that we ought to pay, I desire it be immediately taken care of. I must repeat to you, that I earnestly wish to see things brought to some conclusion with Partinton,[688] both with respect to the suit and the sale of the reversion. Dear Tom, it requires some address, diligence, and management, to bring business of this kind to an issue, which should not seem impossible, considering it can be none of our interests to spend our lives and substance in law. I am willing to refer things to an arbitration, even vote, of lawyers. Pray push this point, and let me hear from you upon it. I am,

your affectionate humble servant,

G. Berkeley

---

[685] Robert Marshall* (*c.* 1690–1772).
[686] Wogan* (?–?) and Aspinwall* (?–?).
[687] Philip Pearson* (?–?).
[688] Peter Partinton* (?–?).

136 BERKELEY TO PRIOR

LR, *pp. 116–17.*

London, 11 December 1725

Dear Tom,

I have not time to repeat what I have said in my former letters. I shall now only say one thing, which I beg you to see dispatched by all means, otherwise we may be great losers. There must have been heirs to Alderman Pearson[689] (whether his son alone, or his son with others); but there must of necessity be heirs; and those heirs must have administered, otherwise they could not be entitled to his effects. Now, what you are to do, is to get a full renunciation (or declaration that they and the Alderman had no concern otherwise than as trustees in the South Sea* stock and annuities) from the said heir or heirs, with a proper proof that they are such heir or heirs to Alderman Pearson. It is now near three months since I told you there were strong reasons for haste; and these reasons grow every moment stronger. I need say no more—I can say no more to you. I am, dear Tom,

    yours,

    G. B.

London, December 11, 1725

137 BERKELEY TO PERCIVAL

EP, BL Add. MS 47031, fols. 61v–62v.

London, 28 December 1725

My Lord,

Nothing could be more elegant or suitable to my fancy than the present I have the honour to receive from your Lordship. I cannot pretend to thank you with the same politeness and good taste with which you confer your favours, and shall only say as often as I cast my eye on the great men of antiquity, I shall have the pleasure to think of your Lordship who was one of the few (*antiquis moribus*)[690] that can appear without disadvantage in such company.

---

[689] Philip Pearson* (?–?).
[690] "[A man] of ancient character." The phrase is in the ablative of character.

I wish your Lordship, my Lady, and all your good family, a happy new year, and as nothing can contribute to make it so more than her Ladyship's health, I shall for a new year's gift send you a receipt for curing or giving sudden ease to a fit of the cholic, which I learned the other day from the Bishop of St. Asaph.[691] He assured me a clergyman in Wales had tried it on forty or fifty persons in very violent fits and never knew it once to fail. It is only drinking a pint of good fresh coffee. A lesser quantity may give ease, but this is said entirely to take away the pain and put an end to the fit. I knew that coffee is commonly thought to cause a trembling in the nerves, and yet I have known some very good drinkers of it, who never were affected with any such symptom. But allowing it to be prejudicial, it can only be so upon habitual drinking of it; and there is no medicine whatsover that would not be prejudicial, if one was constantly to breakfast on it. Whereas if coffee be only taken medicinally now and then in a painful fit of the cholic, I am persuaded such a use of it cannot induce an ill habit on the nerves, nor be a hundredth part so dangerous as laudanum. This medicine was recommended in such strong terms, from so good a hand, and such manifold experience, that from the first moment I heard of it, I was resolved to send you this account. I heartily wish it may be found useful to my Lady.

My long stay in town and great hurry of business had made fresh air and exercise necessary for my health. In this view I set out in September on a journey through eight or nine counties of England. I never travelled in worse roads or worse weather, so that all the advantage I got must be imputed to the motion. I doubt the same may be said of my Lady who at Paris is (as to the air) but one remove from the dirt and fog and smoke of London. Fine air and proper diversions together cannot be hoped for on this side Bermuda. Now I have mentioned Bermuda, I must acquaint your Lordship (who is so good a friend to it) that the subscriptions amount to £3,400, though the town hath been very thin ever since I obtained the charter. On the meeting of Parliament I have good hopes of seeing our affairs thrive. The desiring of that and His Majesty's absence have been such drawbacks, that I begin to fear it will not be possible for me to visit the island this spring. I conclude with my humblest services and best wishes to you all. My Lord,

your Lordship's most obedient and most obliged servant,
Geo. Berkeley

---

[691] John Wynne (1665/66–1743), bishop of St. Asaph (1715–27) and of Bath and Wells (1727–43).

138 PERCIVAL TO BERKELEY

EP, BL Add. MS 47031, fols. 62v–63v.

Paris, 29 December 1725

Dear Sir,

I lately sent you the impressions of some seals in the French King's collection, which being most of them good, though trifles, there is some curiosity in them, and may give you some pleasure. You having expressed a liking to such things when I saw you at Charlton,* I ventured to send them to you. They are left for you at my house in Pall Mall.*

I have heard with more joy than I can express the good progress you daily make in your Bermuda design, and particularly the favourable intentions Mr. Lesley[692] has to encourage it by giving the greatest part of his fortune to it. I should be glad to know from yourself that this is true, and with it what encouragement you have hitherto received from others. I have not been idle to recommend your scheme to the English gentry here, though without success, but perhaps when they return to England and see how well it is approved there they may incline to do their parts.

We have passed here some months and shall remain till the spring when we propose to leave the kingdom and travel eastward, but whither is not yet settled. My wife spends her time as agreeably here as can be, considering she is at a distance from her relations and friends. Her cholic has been well to a miracle for two months past or more, so that she has laid aside her laudanum. But two colds, which seized her one after the other, confine her to her chamber.

If you are curious in the controversy now on foot concerning the validity of our English ordination, the book wrote by Father Courayer [on] our side, and the answer made by Father le Quient [*sic*] (both which I understand are translated into English), will entertain you.[693] The former tells me he shall reply to the

---

[692] Hone and Rossi quote from a letter from Knightly Chetwood to John Ussher dated 20 August 1726 that mentions a "Robin Lesley" who resolves to go to Bermuda with Berkeley. In any event, this Lesley is not to be confused with the dean of Dromore, Henry Leslie (?–?), who was a reverend and doctor, and would have typically been addressed as "Dr. Lesley" by Berkeley. See Hone and Rossi, p. 139.

[693] Pierre-François le Courayer* (1681–1776) was a Roman Catholic priest who wrote a dissertation (*Dissertation sur la Validité des Ordinations des Anglais et sur la Succession des Évêques de l'Eglise Anglicane, avec les Preuves Justificatives des Faits Avancés* [Brussels, 1723]) attempting to establish that there was no break in the line of ordination from the apostles to the present Anglican Church, thus defending the validity of Anglican orders. An English translation was made in 1725. Courayer was excommunicated and retired to England, where he was well received. By his own account, he always considered himself a Roman Catholic, despite rejecting a number of points of Catholic dogma, including the doctrine of transubstantiation. See *Works*, vol. IX, p. 77. Michel le Quien (1661–1733) was a Dominican, a French historian and theologian. He published *La Nullité des Ordinations Anglicanes* (2 vols., Paris, 1725) and *La Nullité des Ordinationes Anglicanes Démontrée de Nouveau* (2 vols., Paris, 1730), against le Courayer's apology for the Anglican orders.

other about May, and that the Archbishop of Canterbury[694] has furnished him with very good materials, and he does not at all doubt setting the account in so clear a light as to satisfy all reasonable men that our ordinations are good. Indeed his first book has done it sufficiently, but his answerers having raised several critical objections against the authorities which he made use of to prove his point, as mistake of places, days, etc., and withal trumped up an old scandal that the basis of all our proof, the Lambeth Registry, is a piece forged in King James' time to invalidate the Nag's Head Narration,[695] which our adversaries in Queen Elizabeth's reign maintained to be all the ordination our first Bishops had, Father Courayer thinks himself obliged to show the weakness of these objections.

We have no other public news here than the breach between the two great ministers, Monseigneur le Duc and the Bishop of Frejus.[696] It is patched up for the present, but probably will not hold long.

You have the affectionate service of my wife and children. And I am ever Dear Sir,

> Yours etc.,
> Percival

139 BERKELEY TO PRIOR

LR, pp. 118–21.

London, 30 December 1725

Dear Tom,

I received your letters, and have desired Messrs Wogan and Aspinwall[697] (for they act in concert in all things) to look into the act of Parliament you mention,

---

[694] William Wake* (1657–1737).

[695] The reference here is to a conspiracy theory concerning the Anglican apostolic succession. In order to ordain new bishops, three ordained bishops must be present to transmit holy orders (the line of proper ordination extends all the way back to the Apostles). According to the theory, in 1559 Matthew Parker was to be ordained as the archbishop of Canterbury under Elizabeth I. Unfortunately, only two ordained bishops were available. As a result, they found a deposed bishop, a man by the name of Story, to lay hands on Parker. As Story was deposed, the ceremony could not take place in a church or cathedral without profanation, so they performed the ceremony in a tavern, which happened to be called the Nag's Head, hence the name. The tale by most accounts is apocryphal and without merit. See Cobham Brewer, *The Reader's Handbook of Allusions, References, Plots and Stories* (Philadelphia, PA: J. B. Lippincott, 1889), p. 675.

[696] Luce has "Trejus," but this is most likely an error, the reference being to the Bishop of Fréjus, André Hercule Cardinal de Fleury (1653–1743). The handwriting (not Percival's) is such that capital T and capital F are quite similar. The duke is the Duke of Bourbon, Louis Henri (1692–1740), then first minister under the French king Louis XV. Fleury would replace Bourbon as first minister in 1726. See note to Letter 148.

[697] Wogan* (?–?) and Aspinwall* (?–?).

though I doubt it cannot be to any great purpose; for though, by the act, it should appear that Pearson[698] was a trustee, yet as that was passed long before the South Sea* subscriptions, it will not, I fear, thereby appear that the said subscriptions were part of his trust. You have informed us there will be no difficulty in obtaining Mr. Pearson's renunciation. If the time be expired since the old gentleman's (his father's) death that by law is limited for taking out letters of administration, then I am told such single renunciation may be sufficient, without troubling the sisters. This you will inform yourself in there. Since Mr. Marshal[699] is averse to it, he need not act at all; only send back the will and probate hither for me to administer by. I know not what trouble this may expose me to, but I see it is a thing must be done in justice one time or other. One thing, nevertheless, I must repeat and insist on; that is, that you must order matters so with Mr. Partinton Van Homrigh[700] so that Mr. Marshal's share and mine of the South Sea,* etc., may be applied to the payment of English debts (as you formerly have assured me it should). If it were not in this view, I might incur great difficulties by administering here, and this money's lying by undivided, as the Duchess of Tyrconnel's[701] reversion would quite disappoint this view. I have not yet been able to find Mr. Levinge at his lodgings in the Temple. I must desire you to pay the sum of fifty pounds to my brother Robin,[702] who will call on you for it. I must also desire you to send me an account of what money is in Mr. Synge's[703] hands and yours belonging to me, as likewise of the draughts that I have made for money upon either of you. You'll be so good as to call on Mr. Stanton, and pay his bill when in Dublin. I called several times, but could not find him, to know what it came to. You will also inform yourself whether Coll. Maccasland[704] demands any thing for the running of my horse, and pay it; as likewise whatever is due for the other horse belonging to me; and I make you a present of them both.

I am exceedingly plagued by these creditors, and am quite tired and ashamed of repeating the same answer to them, that I expect every post to hear what Mr. Marshal and you think of their pretensions, and that then they shall be paid. It is now a full twelve-month that I have been expecting to hear from you on this

---

[698] Philip Pearson* (?–?).

[699] Robert Marshall* (*c.* 1690–1772).

[700] Partinton's son, who took the surname Van Homrigh as a condition of Bartholomew Van Homrigh's will.

[701] Frances (*née* Jenyns) Talbot (1648–1731), Duchess of Tyrconnell. She acquired the title upon marrying Richard Talbot (1630–91), who was created Earl of Tyrconnell in 1685 and raised to a duke in 1689.

[702] Robert Berkeley* (*c.* 1699–1787), Berkeley's younger brother.

[703] Edward Synge* (1691–1762).

[704] Colonel Robert McCausland* (*c.* 1685–1734?).

head, and expecting in vain. I shall therefore expect no longer, nor hope nor desire to know what Mr. Marshal thinks, but only what you think or what appears to you by Mrs. V. Homrigh's[705] papers and accounts, as stated by Clarke, and compared with the claims of creditors long since transmitted from hence. This is what solely depends on you, what I sued for several months ago, and what you promised to send me an account of long before this time. I have likewise sent you several hints and proposals, tending, as I thought, to shorten our affair with Partinton,* which, at the rate it hath hitherto gone on, is never likely to have an end; but to these points I have never received any answer at all from you. I hope you have not overlooked or forgot them. Had I more time I would repeat them to you; but I have only time to add at present that I am, dear Tom,

> your affectionate humble servant,
> Geor: Berkeley

London, December 30, 1725

140 BERKELEY TO PRIOR

LR, pp. 122–26.

London, 20 January 1725/26

Dear Tom,

I am wearied[706] to death by creditors: I see nothing done, neither towards clearing their accounts, nor settling the effects here, nor finishing affairs with Partinton.[707] I am at an end of my patience, and almost of my wits. My conclusion is, not to wait a moment longer for Marshal,[708] nor to have (if possible) any further regard to him, but to settle all things without him, and whether he will or no. How far this is practicable, you will know by consulting an able lawyer. I have some confused notion that one executor may act by himself; but how far, and in what case, you will thoroughly be informed. It is an infinite shame that the debts here are not cleared up and paid. I have borne the shock and importunity of creditors above a twelvemonth, and am never the nearer; have nothing now[709] to say to them: judge you what I feel. But I have already said all that can be said on this

---

[705] Hester Van Homrigh* (1688–1723).
[706] Stock corrects to "worried" here. *LR* has "wearied."
[707] Peter Partinton* (?–?).
[708] Robert Marshall* (c. 1690–1772).
[709] Stock has "new" for "now."

head. It is also no small disappointment to find, that we have been near three years doing nothing with respect to bringing things to a conclusion with Partinton. Is there no way of making a separate agreement with him? Is there no way of prevailing with him to consent to the sale of the reversion? Let me entreat you to proceed with a little management and dispatch in these matters; and inform yourself particularly, whether I may not come to a reference or arbitration with Partinton, even though Marshal should be against it?—Whether I may not take steps that may compel Marshal to an agreement?—What is the practised method when one of two executors is negligent or unreasonable? In a word, Whether an end may not be put to these matters one way or other? I do not doubt your skill; I only wish you were as active to serve an old friend as I should be in any affair of yours that lay in my power. All the papers relating to Mrs. V. Homrigh's[710] affairs were in the closet; and this I understand you have broke open, as likewise my bed-chamber (which last, having none of these papers in it, but only things of another nature, I had given no directions for breaking it open); but I do not find the effect I proposed from it, viz. a clear account of the debts transmitted hither, though, by what Clarke tells me, it would not take up an hour to do it. Mrs. Hill is very noisy: I mention her as the last that was with me. Pray let me know your thoughts of her, and all the rest of them together. Clarke demands to be considered for service done, and for postage of letters. You know wherein, and how much, you have employed him (for I have not employed him), and will concert with Marshal and Partinton what he should have. Qu. Had not Mrs. Hill commenced a suit, and how that matter stands? But again, I desire to hear from you a distinct answer to the claim of every creditor sent over by Clarke. As to the money in the South Sea,* I have already told you, that the thing to be done, is the obtaining the renunciation from Pearson,[711] which may do in case the old gentleman be dead a year and a day (which you may inform yourself, whether it be the time after which no other body can set up for heir). I hope to have this by the next post. I must also repeat to you, that I very much desire to have my last letter answered, particularly as to the money matters; which, depending only on Synge[712] and you, I flatter myself you will not defer. I am, dear Tom,

your affectionate humble servant,
Geor: Berkeley

---

[710] Hester Van Homrigh* (1688–1723).
[711] Philip Pearson* (?–?).
[712] Edward Synge* (1691–1762).

By the next post I shall hope for an account of my own money, though it should require a day or two more before you can write satisfactory on the other points. My last letters I directed to the Free Mason Coffee-house, and enclosed as you ordered; but not hearing, am in doubt whether you received them.

141 BERKELEY TO PRIOR

LR, pp. 126–29.

London, 27 January 1725/26

Dear Tom,

I received yours of the 13th, a little after I had wrote my last, directed to the Custom-house coffee-house. You say the letter of attorney for subscribing the annuities into the South Sea* stock, show these annuities to have been old Van Homrigh's.[713] This would make all easy. I beg therefore that you would transmit that letter hither, or let us know how we may come at it. As to my administering to Pearson,[714] I do not understand the consequences of it; therefore hope it will not be necessary. You say that if you cannot prevail on Marshal[715] to come in to an allowance of the just debts, you will send me your opinion of them, that I may govern myself accordingly. As to me, I know not how to act or govern myself: I depend upon your compelling Marshal by legal methods and that you will take advice thereupon, and act accordingly. That was the advantage that I proposed by your undertaking to act for me, and as my attorney in the management of those affairs, viz. that you would see that justice was done to the creditors and to me by Mr. Marshal, to whom I was as much a stranger as to the business. I have said this and many other things to you in my last, which I suppose you have received ere now; and as I am very earnest and instant, I doubt not you will soon let me see that you exert yourself, and answer all my desires specified in that and the foregoing letters. Dear Tom, I am at present exceedingly embarrassed with much business of a very different kind. I shall nevertheless administer as soon as I see that nothing else is wanting in order to sell the stock, and pay the debts herewith: for every other step I shall depend on you. I need not tell you what I formerly hinted to you. You see I was too true a prophet, and that we have already lost considerably by this delay.

[713] Hester Van Homrigh* (1688–1723).
[714] Philip Pearson* (?–?).
[715] Robert Marshall* (c. 1690–1772).

I must desire you to pay forty pounds to my brother, Cornet William Berkeley,[716] quartered in Sligo, or to his order in Dublin, for which you will take a receipt, and place it to my account. You will, I presume, soon hear from him.

In your next, pray let me know your opinion about the way of transmitting about five hundred pounds hither, whether by bill or by draught, from hence, or if there be any other way more advantageous. I must once more entreat you, for the sake of old friendship, to pluck up a vigorous active spirit, and disincumber me of the affairs relating to the inheritance, by putting, one way or other, a final issue to them.

I thank God I find, in matters of a more difficult nature, good effects of activity and resolution; I mean Bermuda, with which my hands are full, and which is in a fair way to thrive and flourish in spite of all opposition. I shall hope to hear from you speedily; and am,

    dear Tom, yours affectionately,

    Geor: Berkeley

London, Jan. 27, 1725/26

142 BERKELEY TO PRIOR

LR, pp. 129–33.

London, 6 February 1725/26

Dear Tom,

Messrs. Wogan and Aspinwall[717] have not yet been able to see the act of Parliament, which I am pretty sure could be of little or no use if they had seen it; for as it passed several years before the South Sea* business, it would never prove that Pearson[718] acted as trustee in the subscriptions. But if there be any paper (as you seem to intimate in your last), that sets forth his trust in that particular, you need only procure the sight thereof, and the business is done; otherwise, for ought I can see, it is necessary that Mr. Alderman Pearson's heir or heirs renounce, and that I admininister as to his effects in this province; otherwise nothing can be done, as I suppose you see by the paper of instructions sent you from Doctors' Commons.* Now that I may see my way in this

---

[716] William Berkeley* (?–?), Berkeley's younger brother.
[717] Wogan* (?–?) and Aspinwall* (?–?).
[718] Philip Pearson* (?–?).

matter, I must desire you to inform me particularly what the nature of administering is, what it obliges one to, and to what it may expose a man. I have not yet taken out letters of administration to Mrs. V. Homrigh[719] here, nor shall I, until I see that it can be of use; that is, until I see that every other step is accomplished towards the immediate selling the stock, and applying it as it should be applied. What I wrote in my former concerning the year and a day for administering, etc., has, I find, nothing in it, as I am now told by Mr. Aspinwall, from whom I had it, and who, it seems, was mistaken. I think I ought to tell you these things, that you may see where the stop is, and that you may act accordingly. The affair of the creditors I must recommend to you of course; though I have nothing new to say, but only that I earnestly refer you to what I have already written upon that and other matters; which, after all that hath been said, I need not repeat. I hope, dear Tom, that you will exert yourself once for all, and give a masterly finishing stroke to the whole business of the executorship. If it be not such a stroke as one could wish at law, yet a finishing one of any sort, by arbitration of lawyers, or not lawyers, before I leave this part of the world, would be very agreeable.

My brother hath informed me that Dr. Ward[720] tells him Colonel M'Casland[721] is not inclined to add to the trouble of his other business that of taking any further care of my tithes, etc. I must desire, if you can find out the truth of this, to let me know it; for it will be time for me to look out for other farmers. I had once thought of employing a brother of my own, but have now no thought of that kind. I must desire you to send me fifty pounds by the next post.

I am in a fair way of having a very noble endowment for the college of Bermuda, though the late meeting of Parliament, and the preparations of a fleet, etc.,[722] will delay the finishing things, which depend in some measure on the Parliament, and to which I have gained the consent of the government, and indeed of which I make no doubt; but only the delay, it is to be feared, will make it impossible for me to set out this spring. One good effect of this evil delay, I hope, may be, that you will have disembarrassed yourself of all sort of business that may detain you here, and so be ready to go with us. In which case, I may have somewhat to propose to you that I believe is of a kind agreeable to

---

[719] Hester Van Homrigh* (1688–1723).

[720] Peter Ward* (?–?).

[721] Colonel Robert McCausland* (c. 1685–1734?).

[722] The meeting of Parliament was delayed by the presence of King George I* in Hanover. The "preparations of a fleet" likely refers to the escalating tensions over the Treaty of Vienna (7 June 1725) where Spain and Austria allied, threatening English trade. In response England entered into the Treaty of Hanover (3 September 1725). Fleets were sent into the Baltic to posture against the Russians and to blockade Porto Bello, a major Spanish naval base in Panama.

your inclinations, and may be of considerable advantage to you. But you must say nothing of this to any one, nor of any one thing that I have now hinted concerning endowment, delay, going, etc. I have heard lately from Caldwell,[723] who wrote to me in an affair in which it will not be in my power to do him any service. I answered his letter, and mentioned somewhat about Bermuda, with an overture for his being fellow there. I desire you would discourse him as from yourself on that subject, and let me know what your thoughts are of his disposition towards engaging in that design. I am, dear Tom,

   your affectionate friend and humble servant,
   Geor: Berkeley

London, Feb. 6, 1725/26

143 BERKELEY TO PERCIVAL

EP, BL Add. ms 47031, fols. 104–05.

London, 10 February 1725/26

My Lord,

   I am now in a great hurry of business preparing an interest in the House of Commons against[724] the introducing my affair to St. Christopher's* among them. The spirits of the ministry have been hitherto and are still so entirely possessed with fleets, subsidies, etc., that it hath not yet been thought proper to insist on that point, which however I hope will be soon carried, there being very good interest made among malcontents, and the Court being quite for it.

   It is this hurry (which hardly allows me a moment to myself) that hath so long delayed my acknowledgment of your Lordship's letter, etc. In it you desire to be informed by me what there is in the report you have heard of Mr. Lesley's[725] going to Bermuda and bestowing a good part of his fortune on that design. All I can say is that this gentleman upon reading the proposal was struck with it and expressed himself in words to that effect. His affairs are I understand, at present in some disorder. As soon as those are settled I believe he may entertain thoughts of going to Bermuda and be a benefactor. In the interim nothing is done of what you heard was performed.

---

[723] See note to Letter 9.
[724] i.e. "before," not "contra."
[725] See note to Letter 138.

The subscriptions amount to about four thousand pounds. Lord Palmerston[726] is desirous that nine hundred and odd pounds in his hands should be disposed of to this our college for breeding up young negroes agreeable to Mr. Delon's will. The trustees for directing the disposal thereof are your Lordship, Dr. Bray,[727] Mr. Hales,[728] his brother,[729] and Mr. Beleitha.[730] The majority of these are of Lord Palmerston's mind, and your Lordship's concurrence hath been applied for.

You have annexed a poem wrote by a friend of mine with a view to the scheme.[731] Your Lordship is desired to show it to none but of your own family, and suffer no copy to be taken of it.

I am glad to hear your family, and particularly my Lady, are so well. I am,

My Lord,

your Lordship's most obedient and most humble servant,

G. Berkeley

AMERICA OR THE MUSE'S REFUGE[732]

A Prophecy

The muse, offended at this age, these climes
Where nought she found fit to rehearse,
Waits now in distant lands for better times,
Producing subjects worthy verse.

In happy climes where from the genial sun
And virgin earth fair scenes ensue,
Such scenes as shew that fancy is outdone,
And make poetic fiction true.

In happy climes, the seat of innocence,
Where nature guides and virtue rules,
Where men shall not impose for truth and sense
The pedantry of Courts and Schools.

---

[726] Henry Temple (1672/73–1757), first Viscount Palmerston. Temple assisted Berkeley in his attempt to fund St. Paul's College on Bermuda through the sale of the lands on St. Christopher.

[727] Thomas Bray (1658–1730), Church of England clergyman, founder of the Society for Promoting Christian Knowledge and the Society for the Propagation of the Gospel in Foreign Parts. He also founded Dr. Bray's Associates, a charity group designed to found libraries and support negro schools.

[728] Stephen Hales* (1677–1761).

[729] Robert Hales (?–?), brother to Stephen Hales and clerk of the Privy Council.

[730] William Belitha, Esq. (?–?), An associate of Dr. Thomas Bray (1658–1730), Belitha would later work with Percival* on founding the Georgia colony.

[731] In fact Berkeley is the author.

[732] This poem is directly appended to the end of the letter.

There shall be sung another golden age,
The rise of Empire and of arts,
The good and great inspiring epic rage
The wisest heads and noblest hearts.

Not such as Europe breeds in her decay,
Such as she bred when fresh and young,
When heavenly flame did animate her clay,
By future poets shall be sung.

Westward the course of Empire takes its way,
The four first acts already past,
A fifth shall close the drama with the day,
The world's great effort is the last.

144 BERKELEY TO PRIOR

LR, *pp. 134–37.*

London,15 March 1725/26

Dear Tom,

I have wrote to you on several points to which I have had no answer. The bill indeed of fifty pounds I have received; but the answer to other points you postponed for a few posts. It is not yet come to hand, and I long to see it. I shall nevertheless not repeat now[733] what I have so often insisted on, but refer you to my former letters, which I hope are not forgotten, and that I shall be convinced they are not in a post or two.

In your last you mention your design of coming to London this summer. I must entreat you to let me know by the first opportunity whether you persist in that design, and in what month you propose to execute it, and as nearly as possible the very time. Pray fail not in this; I have particular reasons for desiring it.

There is one point that will not admit of any delay; I mean the setting my deanery to farm. I told you that Dr. Ward[734] had informed my brother that Col. M'Casland[735] (who hath his hands full of other business) cared not to be any farther concerned in it. I must desire you, without loss of time, to inform yourself whether this be so, and to let me know what instrument I must send to you to empower you to set it. This by all means I would be informed of the next post, that

---

[733] The *LR* version has "nay" set off with commas, but I follow Luce and use "now."
[734] Peter Ward* (?–?).
[735] Colonel Robert McCausland* (*c.* 1685–1734?).

it may be set either to the same persons who held it last, or else to Mr. Bolton,[736] or some other person of sufficient credit and substance and good reputation. I do not doubt your setting it to the best advantage; only there is one thing which I desire you to insist on, viz. that instead of the first of April and the first of June, the days of payment for the current year, be the first of December and the first of February, that so I may have the money against my voyage to Bermuda, which possibly may not be till this time twelvemonth. Whatever trouble you are at in this affair, I shall acknowledge in the proper manner, and show myself thankful for it. I thought I should be able to have gone to Ireland, and transacted this affair myself. I had even once thought I should be able to have set out for Bermuda this season; but his Majesty's long stay abroad, the late meeting of Parliament, and the present posture of foreign affairs, taking up the thoughts both of ministers and [P]arliament, have postponed the settling of certain lands in St. Christopher's* on our college, so as to render the said thoughts abortive. I have now my hands full of that business, and hope to see it soon settled to my wish. In the mean time, my attendance on this business renders it impossible for me to mind my private affairs. Your assistance, therefore, in them, will not only be a kind service to me, but also to the public weal of our college; which would very much suffer if I were obliged to leave this kingdom before I saw an endowment settled on it. For this reason I must depend upon you. So hoping to hear from you upon this article by the first post, I conclude, dear Tom,

> yours affectionately,
> Geor: Berkeley

London, March 15, 1725/26

I need not tell you the time for setting my deanery to farm is now so nigh that it is necessary something be done out of hand.

145 BERKELEY TO PRIOR

LR, pp. 137–38.

19 April 1726

Dear Tom,

Last Saturday I sent you the instrument empowering you to set my deanery. It is at present my opinion that matter had better be deferred till the Charter of

---

[736] Perhaps one of the three sons of John Bolton (1691?–1723/24), the previous dean of Derry.

St. Paul's College hath got through the House of Commons, who are now considering it. In ten days at farthest I hope to let you know the event hereof; which, as it possibly may affect some circumstance in the farming my said deanery, is the occasion of giving you this trouble for the present, when I am in the greatest hurry of business I ever knew in my life; and have only time to add that I am,

    yours,

    G. B.

April 19, 1726

146 BERKELEY TO PRIOR

LR, pp. 138–40.

London, 12 May 1726

Dear Tom,

    After six weeks' struggle against an earnest opposition from different interests and motives, I have yesterday carried my point just as I desired in the House of Commons, by an extraordinary majority, none having the confidence to speak against it, and not above two giving their negative; which was done in so low a voice as if they themselves were ashamed of it. They were both considerable men in stocks, in trade, and in the city: and in truth I have had more opposition from that sort of men, and from the governors and traders to America, than from any others. But, God be praised, there is an end of all their narrow and mercantile views and endeavours, as well as of the jealousies and suspicions of others (some whereof were very great men), who apprehended this College may produce an independency in America, or at least lessen its dependency upon England.

    Now I must tell you, that you have nothing to do but go on with farming my deanery, etc., according to the tenor of my former letter, which I suspended by a subsequent one till I should see the event of yesterday. By this time you have received the letters of attorney for Partinton's[737] signing, in which I presume there will be no delay. Dear Tom,

    yours, etc.,

    G. Berkeley

---

[737] Peter Partinton* (?–?).

London, May 12, 1726

What more easy than to cast an eye on the draught of the two sisters' debts as stated by Clarke? What more unaccountable than that this is not yet done?

147 BERKELEY TO PERCIVAL[738]

EP, BL Add. MS 47031, fols. 172v–73.

London, 17 May 1726

My Lord,

Your Lordship hath every way been so good a friend to St. Paul's College in Bermuda, that I think it my duty to acquaint you with the success which hath of late attended it, the Commons of Great Britain having last Wednesday voted an address to His Majesty that he would be pleased to make such grant out of the lands of St. Christopher's* for the endowment thereof as to him shall seem proper. This point was carried in a full house with but two negatives, and those pronounced in so low a voice as showed that the persons who gave them were ashamed of what they were doing. I am heartily tired of soliciting for many weeks this point with all the diligence, patience, and skill, that I was master of; and am not less pleased to see it carried contrary to all men's expectation, who thought it a hopeless affair, first, because the like step had never been taken in any reign for any college before, and secondly, because great interest and opposition had been made against it from several quarters and upon different principles, motives, and surmises, some whereof had got into the heads of very considerable persons.

I am exceedingly pleased at the good effects which the change of air hath had upon my Lady, not only as it hath bettered her health, but likewise as it must have improved her disposition towards Bermuda, by giving her Ladyship to understand what may be expected from the best air in the world. Let what will happen I am resolved not to quit the pleasing hopes that I shall one day see you both in that happy island. In the meantime it would be a great credit and ornament to our college, as well as a particular pleasure to myself, if we had a

---

[738] A note at the top of the letter indicates it was answered 6 June 1726 from The Hague (Letter 148).

youth of such an excellent genius as your eldest son to begin with; but if this may not be hoped for, I put in an early claim to Master George and beg and insist upon it, that you will not refuse me the pleasure and the joy of assisting and forwarding the fine parts which already shine forth in him, and the rather because he seems to be of a constitution that should be likely to improve much in that climate.[739]

I am (with my best respects and service to you all)

My Lord,

your Lordship's most obedient and most obliged servant,

Geo: Berkeley

This is my third since I had the honour to receive a letter from your Lordship.

I had almost forgot to tell your Lordship that yesterday a report was made of his Majesty's answer to the Commons Address. It is very gracious.

148 PERCIVAL TO BERKELEY

EP, BL Add. MS 47031, fols. 184v–85v.

The Hague, 6 June 1726

Dear Sir,

If frequently informing myself of you and your affairs, if the having you always in my mind and being more than ordinarily solicitous for the success of your excellent design, afford any apology for my not writing so long, I know nobody has more candour than yourself to allow it. You who can distinguish better than any one the difference between a fixed and unalterable esteem and friendship, and the outward profession of it, which whether by mouth or letter is often false and generally dubious. But when I consider that I am not now on even terms with you, but indebted for three letters running, I fear you have condemned me for my silence so long, and that I must reason your own way to recover your good opinion: that is, I must think it essential to our intimacy to write more punctually, and give that outward mark of my inward esteem.

---

[739] The eldest son is John Percival* (1711–70), the youngest is George Percival (1722–26), who was shortly to die in June of that same year.

The anxiety your affair gave me while depending in Parliament[740] is well paid by the pleasure I receive in hearing it has succeeded at last so well, and not only so well, but so honourably; for surely to have an address from all the Commons of Great Britain *nem. cont.*[741] in its favour is the greatest honour a matter of this nature can receive, wherein party or the private interest of those who concurred in it could have no sort of share.

As to my son George's going with you, get my wife's consent and you have mine.[742] I am very certain he will be better educated under you than anywhere, and I know his morals would run less hazard of being spoiled; you will then ask why he is not to go, his mother must answer, and I am afraid she will be obstinate enough to delay it till she hears you are settled there to your content and have opened school.

Now as to ourselves, we arrived from Flanders two days ago, something fatigued with irregular hours of travelling and the great heats, but I thank God are tolerably well. To-day we all dined with Mr. Finch,[743] our Ambassador, who told me last night a piece of news which may have great consequences: that the Duke of Bourbon had received a message from the King of France, importing His Majesty had no farther occasion for his service, but that he should forthwith retire to Chantilly without taking leave of the Queen.[744]

I leave you to reason on this sudden fall of a Minister well disposed to our interest, and with affectionate services of my family, which they desire me to send you, remain

    Dear Sir, etc.,

    Percival

---

[740] Berkeley's scheme to use some of the proceeds from the sale of lands on St. Christopher Island* (St. Kitts) to fund St. Paul's College in Bermuda was approved by the House of Commons in May 1726.

[741] i.e. *nemine contradicente*: "without contradiction."

[742] Berkeley had hoped that the new viscount and Lady Percival would visit Bermuda and the new St. Paul's College, but he additionally was recruiting students for the new enterprise. He had initially hoped the Percivals would send their eldest son John, or, failing that, their second son George. See Rand, p. 35 and Letter 147.

[743] Most likely William Finch (1691-1766), envoy-extraordinary to the Netherlands (1724-28). He was the second son of Daniel Finch, (1647-1730), second Earl of Nottingham.

[744] The Duke of Bourbon, Louis Henri (1692-1740), was elevated to the role of first minister under Louis XV in December 1723. His tenure included securing the marriage of Louis to Marie Leczinska, the daughter of the deposed king of Poland, and witnessed the renewal of the persecution of Huguenots that the Regent Orleans had stopped prior to the ascension of Louis. The duke was dismissed in 1726, when he was extremely unpopular and preparing for war against Spain and the Holy Roman Empire. He was replaced as first minister by Cardinal Fleury (1653-1743).

149 BERKELEY TO PRIOR

LR, *pp. 140–44.*

London, 9 June 1726

Dear Tom,

I am surprised to find there are any debts left unpaid in Ireland, having thought that debt of Henry's which you mention long since discharged. I am sure I concluded that, with what money was left with you, and what I laid out here (in discharge of debts whereof I acquainted you), my share of the remaining Irish debts would have been reduced to nothing.[745] You formerly told me Marshal[746] did not keep pace with me. I hoped you would not think of paying anything more until he had brought himself up to equality with me. I am also very much surprised at your proposing to me to pay money for Marshal there, which you say I may reimburse myself here, when I already told you that I would never have been at the pains to administer here, if the effects on this side the water were not allotted to pay English debts (which you made me believe, in a former letter, should be done). And I have reason to think that, after the payment of such English debts, nothing will be left of these effects wherewith to reimburse myself any payment you shall make for Marshal out of my money there. To your question, therefore, whether you shall make such payment? I do answer in the negative. I am at a loss to explain what you mean by promising to try to state the English debts from the materials you have before you. I ask two distinct questions: 1st, Is there not among Mrs. V. Homrigh's[747] papers a catalogue of her debts clearly stated, as I am told by Mr. Clarke? 2ndly, Why have I not a copy of such catalogue transmitted to me? Had I foreseen the difficulties I am reduced to for want of it, I would have cast my eye on the papers myself, and have known what the debts were before I left Ireland; but I left that matter wholly to you. You still do not stick to tell me that Marshal will do nothing; nay (which is worse), that he will not allow any English debts at all, without telling me one of his reasons. You (for example) averred to me in Ireland, that Mrs. Perkins's appeared a just demand from Mrs. V. Homrigh's own papers; and I have seen here a note of Mrs. Esther V. Homrigh, the younger, to Mr. Tooke,[748] for fifty pounds, together with interest of five per cent. Now I would fain know why are not these debts to be paid and acknowledged as well as those in Ireland? Moreover, I would fain know why

---

[745] A reference to Berkeley's efforts as the coexecutor of Van Homrigh's* will to resolve her estate.
[746] Robert Marshall* (*c.* 1690–1772).
[747] Hester Van Homrigh* (1688–1723).
[748] Benjamin Tooke (?–1716). Swift directs Hester (Vanessa) to borrow from Tooke or John Barber (1675–1741) on his credit. See Williams, ed., *Correspondence of Swift*, Swift to Van Homrigh, 8 July 1714; and Letter 161.

book debts should not be paid here as well as in Ireland? In a word, why in any case a difference should be made between English and Irish debts? I grant we should distinguish between the mother's and the daughter's debts; and it was to make this distinction that I so often (to no purpose) dunn'd you for a catalogue of the daughter's debts, drawn up by her order, in Clarke's hand. But I find it is to no purpose to write; I long to talk to you by word of mouth, either there or here.

Pray let me know next post when you design coming for England, for I would go over to Derbyshire to meet you, in case you do not come to London. On the other hand, I am very loath to be dragged to Ireland before the grant to our College is settled and perfected. I write in great hurry; but before I conclude must tell you, that the Dean of Raphoe[749] hath informed me of his desire to live in Derry: now I had rather he should live in my house for nothing than a stranger for a paltry rent. It is therefore my desire, that a stop may be put to any disposition thereof till such time as the Dean can hear whether a house be (pursuant to his order) already taken for him in Derry.

Dear Tom, write me something satisfactory about the debts by next post, or send me a flat denial, that I may no longer expect it. Last autumn you promised me a full state of my whole accounts what hath been received and what disbursed: having not received it, I must now put you in mind again of it. In my last I desired that my money for the last year of the deanery be put in the hands of Swift & Company.* I am,

> yours,
>
> G. Berkeley

150 BERKELEY TO PRIOR

LR, *pp.* 145–48.

London, 14 June 1726

Dear Tom,

I received Messrs M'Manus's[750] account, in which there are certain articles that I cannot approve of. First, The ferry Mr. M'Manus himself told me I should not pay; that charge having been for the late Dean's household, and the

---

[749] William Cotterell (1697/98–1744). He was dean of Raphoe from 1725 to 1743 and bishop of Ferns and Leighlin from 1743 to 1744.

[750] McManus* (?–?).

curates' passage when they were to preach his turns. But as I have no household there, and as I have otherwise provided for having my turns preached, there is no colour or occasion for my paying it; and I am the more surprised at his charging it, because it was against his own positive opinion as well as my orders. Secondly, I do not see why the repairing of the church windows should be charged to me. Thirdly, I should have been acquainted with the paving of the street, or any such matters, before he had laid out money on them. Fourthly, I know not what those charges are which Mr. Maccasland[751] is said to be at for schoolmasters. I write not this as if I valued either repairing the church windows or allowing somewhat to schoolmasters, provided those things had been represented to me for my consent; but to be taxed without my knowledge is what I do not understand. It is my duty not to suffer the Dean to be taxed at will, nor to connive at the introducing new precedents to the wrong of my successors. To be plain, Mr. M'Manus being desired by me to make a list of such constant charges as the Dean should be at, I subscribed and warranted him to pay the same. Since that time, by letter to him, I made some addition to the charity children; but what is not warranted by that list, or by some subsequent order or warrant of mine, should not be allowed by me. However, for what is in the account you have sent me, I refer myself to you; only must beg you to signify to them that I shall never allow anything for the time to come but what I am apprised of, and consent to beforehand. So that no vouchers will do (without an order under my own hand) for expenses not included in the list made by Mr. McManus, and approved by me at Derry. This I believe you will think a reasonable precaution, in order to prevent myself or successors being imposed on.

I am of opinion that you should immediately write to Messrs. Wogan and Aspinwall,[752] directing and empowering them to sell whenever, from the circumstance of affairs, we shall think it proper so to do. Sudden occasions happen which will not allow waiting for orders from Ireland. We have already been great losers by that, which I very well foreknew here, though you knew nothing of it there; though by this time you are convinced the information I sent you last autumn was true. In short, intelligence may be had here, but it can never there, time enough to be of use.

yours affectionately,
G. B.

---

[751] Colonel Robert McCausland* (*c.* 1685–1734?).
[752] Wogan* (?–?) and Aspinwall* (?–?).

151 BERKELEY TO PERCIVAL

EP, BL Add. MS 47031, fols. 193v–94.

London, 24 June 1726

My Lord,

I was truly grieved on all accounts by the late sad but common accident in your family which by this time I hope your Lordship's Christian temper and good sense have got the better of.[753] I am nevertheless apprehensive that my Lady (considering her weak nerves) may be much affected by it, though I dare say you will omit no topic either from religion or reason to induce her to bear it with proper resignation.

I have lately had the honour of a letter from your Lordship overflowing with that goodness which is so natural to you I have experienced too long to doubt of. My observing that I had writ two or three times without receiving any answer was not meant to upbraid your Lordship in any sort, but only to signify that I had not been unmindful of my duty in case my letters were not come to hand, as it sometimes happens in foreign posts. Your patronage of and concern for the Bermuda affair justified my troubling you now and then with some short account of its progress, which is at present at a stand, and likely to continue so till Sir Robert Walpole[754] returns from Norfolk, soon after which I hope the grant addressed for by the Commons will be perfected.

Several years since your Lordship was so good as to supply me with sixty guineas, which I am sensible should have been restored before this time, but the truth is, the effects of Mrs. Van Homrigh[755] are not yet disposed of, nor all her debts paid, there being a suit depending with Mr. Partinton[756] which puts a stop to that affair which will fall much short of what was expected. Moreover, I was obliged to pay about eight hundred pounds for my Deanery house, together with first fruits and other expenses upon my coming into that preferment: all which as likewise my having been long engaged at law, and lying under a necessity of providing for some who are

---

[753] The death of George, Percival's youngest son (1722–26).

[754] Sir Robert Walpole* (1676–1745), later first Earl of Orford. Berkeley is waiting for Walpole to direct the Treasury to issue payment to him from the proceeds of the sale of lands on St. Christopher Island* (St. Kitts) for the founding of St. Paul's College.

[755] Hester Van Homrigh* (1688–1723).

[756] Peter Partinton* (?–?).

very near to me and depend upon me, hath sunk my affairs lower than people imagine.

Your Lordship will be so good as to accept this plea for my not returning your favour sooner. I am now I thank God in a capacity of doing it without any inconvenience; and therefore beg a line from you to direct me where to pay the abovementioned sum, which I am ready to return with all acknowledgment, and thanks, from, my Lord,

your Lordship's most obedient and most obliged humble servant,

G. Berkeley

I beg the favour of a line by next post being impatient to know how my Lady bears her misfortune. Pray present my humble service to her Ladyship and to all your good family.

152 BERKELEY TO PRIOR

LR, *pp. 148–54.*

London, 19 July 1726

Dear Tom,

Yours of the 2nd and the 9th of July are come to my hands. What you say in your last of the receipts in full, and the caution to be used thereupon, had occurred to my own thoughts, and I acted accordingly. With respect to Mrs. Philips and Mrs. Wilton, I found the former a palpable cheat; but the latter still stands out, that she never received, at any time, any of Mrs. Mary's[757] money. I must therefore desire you to look a second time on the receipt you mention from her to Mrs. Mary; for you might possibly have been mistaken. I thought, when in Ireland, that you owned Mrs. Parkins's to be a true debt. Pray give me your thoughts particularly upon it. The same I desire on the charges for the mother's funeral, which, if in right they are to be paid by us, I cannot understand what you mean by the creditor's abating one half of his demand. I am glad to find that you will take advice upon the dubious debts. Pray do it soon: and when that is done, I shall hope for one list from you, containing your own judgment upon the whole, of what debts are to be discharged by the money here. The exact sum of the annuities received by Messrs. Wogan and

---

[757] Mary Van Homrigh (?–?), sister of Hester Van Homrigh* (1688–1723). Hester was living with her sister outside Dublin when she passed away.

Aspinwall[758] I do not remember, but it is about £190. The next time I write you may know exactly.

I have considered about the house, and am come to this resolution: If Dr. Ward[759] be in Dublin, pray give my service to him, and tell him my house is at his service, upon condition only that he keep it in repair, and rid me of all charges about it, as hearth-money[760] or the like. I had some time since a letter from him, desiring the use of it on these terms; but the offer I had made the Dean of Raphoe[761] disabled me for that time from giving him the answer I now desire you to do, because I know not where to write to him myself, he having been about to leave Chester for Ireland when I received his letter. But at present I think myself at liberty, it being about six weeks since the Dean was with me, since which time I have not heard from him, though I then desired he would let me have his answer forthwith. As to setting it, I am less inclined that way, because Dr. Ward, being subdean, is at some trouble on my account, and I would willingly oblige him. You may therefore drop it to him, that I prefer his having it rent-free to a rent of twenty pounds, which you think I may get from another.

As to the account you have sent me of receipts and disbursements, I must observe to you, with respect to one particular, that when I made you a proposal of being concerned in the affairs accruing to me by the death of Mrs. V. Homrigh, the terms which I proposed, and you agreed to, were these, viz. that if you would undertake the trouble of settling that whole matter, when it was settled I should allow you twelve pence in the pound out of the profits arising therefrom. I never designed, therefore, nor promised to allow any thing, till the whole was settled; nor was it reasonable, or indeed possible that I should: Not reasonable, because the main reason for which I made such proposal of 1s. per pound, was the difficulty of disembrangling our affairs with Partinton;[762] which difficulty seems hardly to have been touched hitherto, at least I do not find that any thing to the purpose hath been done since I left Ireland:—Not possible, because, till the debts are paid, and affairs settled with Partinton, I cannot know what doth, or what doth not, come to my share. It was my desire to have things concluded as soon as possible; and in order to this, I expected more would be done by you than by another.

[758] Wogan* (?–?) and Aspinwall* (?–?).
[759] Peter Ward* (?–?).
[760] i.e. the hearth tax.
[761] William Cotterell (1697/98–1744). He was dean of Raphoe from 1725 to 1743 and bishop of Ferns and Leighlin from 1743 to 1744.
[762] Peter Partinton* (?–?).

I chose therefore putting my affairs into your hands rather than into Mr. Dexter's or Mr. Donne's; one of whom, if you had declined it, I was resolved on. I was also willing, for that end, to allow more than is commonly allowed to solicitors or agents.

For these reasons, and especially because I shall have, on many accounts, pressing occasion for what money I can raise against my departure[763] (which I propose to be next spring), I must desire you to desist for the present from paying yourself, and to pay the whole of my money into the hands of Swift & Company,* by them to be transmitted to me in England upon demand; and I shall leave a note behind me with you, which shall intitle you in the fullest and clearest manner to the said twelve pence in the pound. I must desire you to let me know whether you have obliged the farmers of my deanery to make all future payments to my order in Dublin, as I directed. I should be glad to see a copy of the articles you concluded with them, which you may send me per post. I am surprised at what you tell me of Mr. Synge's[764] paying 111 pounds to Mr. Bindon[765] on my account, which, on a second inquiry, you must find a mistake. I had received only one hundred English from Mr. Bindon, who (because he wanted it in Ireland) let me have it on the same terms that the banker was to supply him there, by which I saved about 30 shillings in the exchange; and so I drew on Mr. Synge for one hundred and ten pounds odd money, Irish. I shall hope to hear from you next post, after the receipt hereof, and that you will then tell me your resolution about coming to England. For myself, I can resolve nothing at present, when or whether I shall see Ireland at all, being employed on much business here. I am, dear Tom,

> your affectionate humble Servant,
> G. Berkeley

London, July 19, 1726

I have heard from Mr. M'Manus;[766] and by this post have wrote an answer, insisting that I will not allow any thing for the ferry, it being a gross imposition, and contrary both to his own advice and my express orders.

---

[763] Berkeley's planned departure for Rhode Island and (ultimately) Bermuda to set up St. Paul's College.

[764] Edward Synge* (1691–1762).

[765] Perhaps Thomas Bindon (?–1740), dean of Limerick since 1721, or the unknown Bindon to whom Berkeley refers earlier in Letter 134.

[766] McManus* (?–?).

153 BERKELEY TO PRIOR

LR, *pp. 154–57.*

London, 4 August 1726

Dear Tom,

The stocks being higher than they have been for this long time, and, as I am informed, not likely to rise higher, I have consented to their being sold, and have directed Messrs. Wogan and Aspinwall[767] to write you word thereof as soon as they are disposed of, with an account of their amounts. I hoped you would have sent me a copy of the articles for farming my deanery, that I may see whether they are according to my mind; particularly whether the money is made payable to my order in Dublin, as I directed, for special reasons. I likewise expected a copy of the last balance, the deductions being larger than I can account for. I have spoke with Mr. Binden,[768] who tells me he received within a trifle, under or over, one hundred and eleven pounds from Ned Synge.[769] I have wrote to Ned Synge to let him know his mistake. I have also wrote to him and Mr. Norman to pay the money in their hands to Swift & Company,* in order to have it transmitted hither.

I desire to know whether you come to England, at what time, and to what place, that I may contrive to see you, for I may chance not to be in London, designing to pass some time in the country; but I would steer my course so as to be in your way in case you came on this side the water.

Mrs. Wilton persists that she never gave a receipt to Mrs. Mary.[770] I must therefore desire you to send me her receipt enclosed in your next. As to Mr. Tooke's[771] bond or note, you desire to know whether it be sealed; which particular I do not remember: but I remember that it mentions interest; and I desire to know whether, in point of right, such interest should not be paid; and whether it would not seem odd to propose defalcating[772] any part of a man's right for want of form, when it plainly appeared to be intended? In short, I would know upon what principles you proceed, when you say he may be contented with no interest, or with half interest. By this post I suppose you will receive from Mr. Aspinwall an account of the sum-total of the transfer, etc. I am plagued with

---

[767] Wogan* (?–?) and Aspinwall* (?–?).

[768] Perhaps Thomas Bindon (?–1740), dean of Limerick since 1721, or the unknown Bindon to whom Berkeley refers earlier in Letter 134.

[769] Edward Synge* (1691–1762).

[770] Mary Van Homrigh (?–?), sister of Hester Van Homrigh* (1688–1723).

[771] Benjamin Tooke (?–1716). Swift directs Hester (Vanessa) to borrow from Tooke on his credit. See Williams, ed., *Correspondence of Swift*, Swift to Van Homrigh, 8 July 1714.

[772] To misuse funds; embezzle.

duns, and tired with put-offs, and therefore long to see it applied to pay them: but, in order to this, must desire you to send me two distinct lists, one of the undoubted legal demands, another of the equitable, that so I may have your opinion, in distinct terms, of what should be paid in law, and what in conscience. This was not answered by your last letter's observations, which nevertheless show you may easily do it; and it is no more than what you had promised to do before. I shall therefore expect such lists from you in a post or two. I am, dear Tom,

your affectionate humble Servant,

G. Berkeley

London, Aug. 4, 1726

You mentioned a friend of Synge's who was desirous to be one of our Fellows. Pray let me know who he is, and the particulars of his character. There are many competitors; more than vacancies; and the fellowships are likely to be very good ones: so I would willingly see them well bestowed.

154 BERKELEY TO PRIOR

LR, *pp. 158–60.*

London, 24 August 1726

Dear Tom,

It is a long time since I have heard from you, and am willing to suppose that some of your letters are miscarried. I have quitted my old lodging, and desire you to direct your letters to be left for me with Mr. Smibert,[773] painter, next door to the King's Arms tavern, in the little piazza, Covent Garden.

I desired a copy of the articles concluded on with the farmers of my deanery. I likewise desired the receipt of Mrs. Wilton, and the particular catalogues of the debts, in the manner you promised. I must now repeat the same desires. As for the articles and bonds, I have thought proper to lodge them with Mr. Synge,[774] who hath a fixed abode in town, and will take care to place them securely among his own papers. You will therefore deliver them to him. As I have occasion for my money to be gathered in and placed with Mr. Swift and Company,* in order to be transmitted hither, I have wrote to M'Manus[775] and Mr. Norman; to the

[773] John Smibert* (1688–1751).
[774] Edward Synge* (1691–1762).
[775] McManus* (?–?).

former, to send me the balance of accounts for last year; to the latter, to pay the money you told me lay in his hands to Swift & Company: but hitherto I do not find either done. Mr. Aspinwall[776] hath some time since informed you that the total of the effects transferred by him amounts to eight hundred and forty pounds odd money, out of which charges are to be deducted. He hath showed me the bill of these in Doctors' Commons,* which amount to about fourteen pounds. Some other money laid out by him, together with the fees for his own trouble, I have not yet seen the account of. I think you had better write to him by the next post to transmit the third part of the overplus sum to Swift & Company, for the use of Partinton Van Homrigh;[777] who, when he hath got his share remitted, can have nothing to complain of; and, as you have hitherto treated in his behalf with Messrs. Wogan and Aspinwall, your orders will be followed therein by them more properly than mine. I had almost forgot to repeat to you, that I want to know what reason there is for disputing any part of the interest on the note to Mr. Tooke,[778] whether it be sealed or no.

Let me know in your next what you resolve about coming to England, and when. I shall trouble you with no more at present, from, dear Tom,

yours affectionately,

G. Berkeley

London, August 24, 1726

155 BERKELEY TO PRIOR[779]

BL Add. MS 39311, fol. 7.

London, 3 September 1726

Dear Tom,

I received your letter in which you send me a copy of Mrs. Wilton's receipt. I should be glad of the receipt itself, she pretending it must[780] be a forgery. I long for the lists you promised of certain and legal debts in the first place, of

---

[776] Aspinwall* (?–?).

[777] Peter Partinton's* (?–?) son, who under the terms of Bartholomew Van Homrigh's will was to take the surname Van Homrigh.

[778] Benjamin Tooke (?–1716). Swift directs Hester (Vanessa) to borrow from Tooke on his credit. See Williams, ed., *Correspondence of Swift*, Swift to Van Homrigh, 8 July 1714.

[779] Fraser omits this letter entirely from his *Life and Letters*. It is printed in A. A. Luce, "Some Unpublished Berkeley Letters with some New Berkeleiana," *Proceedings of the Royal Irish Academy* 41 (1932): 144–45.

[780] Luce has "might," but the text clearly has "must."

equitable in the second, with your reasons for docking any part of them. I shall not repeat what I said in my last which I suppose you might have received since you writ to me. Ned Synge[781] I understand is in the country, I must therefore desire you to pay out of the money in your hands the charges you tell me Dr. Helsham[782] hath been at in my brother's trial. Give my service to him and tell him I am obliged to him as he intended a service to me in advancing that money, without my knowledge, but that if I had been aware of it I would not have disbursed half the sum to have saved that villain from the gallows.[783] I must at the same time desire you to pay the sum of nine pounds to my Brother Robin.[784]

Mr. MacManus[785] hath sent me the accounts as stated by him for the two last payments, in which I observe that you mistook the ballance [*sic*] of the first account making it only 227 odd money (which you informed me of in your last letter but one as paid into Swift etc.* though I could not draw for it having no note of theirs or acknowledgment for the same) whereas MacManus makes it to be 312 pounds 10ish i.e. the full of Maccasland's[786] moiety from which he tells me nothing was deducted he himself having made all the payments on my behalf. In his second account he subducts not only for past payments but for future (a new method of accounting) whereby he reduces the balance of his moiety to 87: 8: 9½ which he says Mr. Curtis was to pay to you, and that Maccasland's £312: 10s.: 00d. is to be paid entire to me, so that their whole ballance stands thus

$$312: 10: 00 =$$
$$312: 10: 00 = 712: 8: 9\frac{1}{2}$$
$$87: \ 8: 9\frac{1}{2}$$

which sum I must desire you to see paid to Swift & company for my use and direct them to send a note for the sum to their correspondent here, because I shall have occasion to transfer what money I can raise to England.

I must desire you to send me in a letter a full state of the particulars of our pretensions upon Partinton,[787] that I may have a view of the several emoluments expected from this suit and the grounds of each expectation (these

[781] Edward Synge* (1691–1762).

[782] Richard Helsham (1683–1738), physician and natural philosopher. In addition to being a professor of mathematics and natural philosophy at Trinity College, Dublin, he was Jonathan Swift's* personal physician.

[783] Thomas Berkeley (1704–26?), his brother, was condemned for bigamy in 1726. We do not actually know if the sentence was carried out. See Hone and Rossi, pp. 4, 9, and 139.

[784] Robert Berkeley* (*c*. 1699–1787).

[785] McManus* (?–?).

[786] Colonel Robert McCausland* (*c*. 1685–1734?).

[787] Peter Partinton* (?–?).

affairs being at present a little out of my thoughts) that so having considered the whole I may take advice here and write thereupon to Marshal in order to terminate that affair this winter (if possible). It is worth while to exert for once. If this be done the whole partition may be made and your share distinctly known and paid you between this and Christmas. But I know it cannot be done unless you exert. As for Marshal[788] I had from the beginning no opinion of him (no more than you have) otherwise I should not have troubled anybody else. I am, dear Tom,

yours affectionately,

G: Berkeley

156 BERKELEY TO PRIOR

LR, *pp. 160–64.*

London, 13 September 1726

Dear Tom,

I received yours; and accordingly went to Messrs. Wogan and Aspinwall,[789] who promised to transmit the money drawn for by Partinton,[790] which I suppose is due. I desired them to let me have their bill of charges; which they also promised against the next time I saw them.

As for the clamour of the people of Derry, I have not, nor ever shall have, the least regard for it, so long as I know it to be unjust and groundless: it being so false to suggest that I am for allowing less than my predecessors, that I am now actually at seventy-six pound *per annum* constant expence more than any of them ever were, having just now directed Dr. Ward[791] to provide a new curate for Col. Sampson's island,[792] and having formerly appointed another additional curate in Derry to preach my turns, as likewise having added to the number of charity children, which are annual expences, not to mention repairing the chancel, etc.; nothing of which kind I ever was against. I did not indeed like

---

788 Robert Marshall* (c. 1690–1772).

789 Wogan* (?–?) and Aspinwall* (?–?).

790 Peter Partinton* (?–?).

791 Peter Ward* (?–?).

792 A reference to Inch Island in County Donegal (not to be confused with Inch Island in Lough Gara in County Sligo). The particular Sampson is not clear as there were three colonels in the British Army (in each of three successive generations) from the Sampson family, descended from Richard Sampson (?–1652), in County Donegal, who owned land on the island. See Colonel Colby, *Ordnance Survey of the County of Londonderry* (Dublin: Hodges & Smith, 1837), vol. I, p. 97.

(nor would any man in his senses) that people should make articles of expence without acquainting me, or dispose of my money (though it were to good uses) without my consent previously obtained. But all this while I have gainsaid nothing but the ferry, and that for reasons I formerly gave you; not that I valued the expence, which was a trifle, but that I would not be imposed on myself, nor entail an imposition on my successor: for there is no man so unknowing or negligent in affairs as not to be sensible that little impositions lead to great ones. But as to that matter, M'Manus[793] having informed me that Dr. Ward had engaged I would pay the ferry-money, I have wrote to Dr. Ward to know the truth of that, and his judgment whether the same should be continued, being resolved to comply therewith. As to what you write about my making a difficulty of leaving 58 pounds in M'Manus's hands for the curates, it is a mistake. The sum charged in his account is about 140 pounds, not for charges paid, but to be paid; and not only to curates, but for several other purposes. I never meant but the curates should be punctually paid; nobody need be at any pain about that: but I thought, as they were paid the first year (when the farmers had no money of mine in their hands), so they might have been paid the subsequent years out of the running income. I thought likewise, and still think, that the rents of the glebe, and the dues formerly farmed to the clerk, are sufficient to make the November payment, without M'Manus's advancing one penny, and without his retaining my income of the preceding year, especially when the tithes of the current become payable a little after. As my money is not at interest, it is much the same whether these payments be stopt now or next January; but it was necessary to observe what I thought wrong, to prevent people's growing upon me. I still want the lists you promised me of the debts (legal and equitable), in order to make the payments, that the business on this side the water (which hath already cost me much trouble) may be at length dispatched. In your next, I desire to be informed what the mistake is which you observe in M'Manus's account, and likewise what you say to his telling me there were no deductions made from the 650 pounds of Col. Maccasland's[794] moiety, as I observed to you already in my last.

As to what you say of matrimony, I can only answer, that as I have been often married by others, so I assure you I have never married myself. I am, dear Tom,

your affectionate humble servant,

G. Berkeley

London, Sept. 13, 1726

---

[793] McManus* (?–?).
[794] Colonel Robert McCausland* (c. 1685–1734?).

Before you went to the country, you told me about eight hundred pounds of the last year's income would be paid to Swift & Co.* I desire to know whether it be so, or what it is. In my last I sent you what appeared in M'Manus's letter to me; but you are of opinion he mistook in my prejudice.

157 BERKELEY TO PRIOR[795]

BL Add. MS 39311, fol. 9.

London, 14 October 1726

Dear Tom,

It is now a long time since I have had a line from you. So long that I apprehend you have forgot the purport of my last letters. I shall therefore repeat part of them.[796] I desired you would send me one full letter containing an explicit particular account of what profits remain to be made in Ireland by the sales which Partinton[797] puts a stop to and by the demands we have upon him, also what state the lawsuit is in i.e. what has been done these three years passed and what remains to be done in it. I desired to know what money hath been paid in to Swift etc.* on my account, and what mistake you observed in MacManus:[798] I suppose it must be in his charging what Maccasland[799] had charged before, for by his account the latter should have charged nothing and consequently paid more to you than by yours it appears he has done. I desired therefore to have that matter cleared but your answer, if any, has miscarried. I do therefore repeat these requests to you. I likewise once more desire to know whether the yearly income of my Deanery be by the bonds stipulated to be paid to my order in Dublin. This I desired you to stipulate at the making the agreement for particular reasons but find nothing of it in the articles. I desire you to send me enclosed the original receipt of Mrs. Wilton in her own hand, for she denies she ever gave any. I likewise desire you to send me your particular thoughts of Mrs. Dupee the milliner's demands. In your observations on it you say that what she furnished Mrs. Mary[800] with was on the mother's credit who charged the

---

[795] This letter is printed in Luce, "Some Unpublished Berkeley Letters with some New Berkeleiana," 145–46.

[796] See Letter 156.

[797] Peter Partinton* (?–?).

[798] McManus* (?–?).

[799] Colonel Robert McCausland* (c. 1685–1734?).

[800] Mary Van Homrigh (?–?), Hester Van Homrigh's* (1688–1723) sister.

daughter with it. I ask does it appear that the daughter in any account was charged therewith by the mother and paid the mother? Your other observations are expressed in such ambiguous terms that in very few of them I can know what your judgment is or what mine should be. As to the ferry-money[801] I consulted Dr. Ward[802] who writes me word that I ought in his opinion to pay nothing but for the curate's passage on holidays, this he thinks the outside and is clear in it. He likewise affirms that he knew nothing of the matter nor ever gave any advice about it. Though McManus wrote to me that Dr. Ward had advised his paying that money [he] promised to make it good himself if I would not allow it. Dear Tom let me have a satisfactory letter on the above points by the first opportunity directed to Smibert's[803] as year last.

yours,

G. B.

158 BERKELEY TO PRIOR

LR, *pp. 165–69.*

London, 5 November 1726

Dear Tom,

I have received your letter, and write you this in haste. I am much importuned by the creditors, and at a loss how to deal with them. Why should not Comyng's debt for the funeral be wholly paid? I have seen a letter under Mrs. Esther's[804] hand promising to pay it: this was wrote to one Lancaster. What you say of paying half of this and other debts I cannot comprehend: Either they are due and should be all paid, or not due and none paid. I have seen a promissory note of Mrs. Esther's to Mrs. Hill, whereof I send you subjoined a copy. Let me know your opinion, and take advice of others on the nature of a note so worded; and whether it obligeth absolutely, or only as far as the mother's assets will go. What shall I do with Mr. Fisher, who claims twenty-three pounds odd money from Mrs. Mary, and about six pounds for Mrs. Esther, all for goods delivered since the mother's death. A day or two before I received your letter, I had paid three pound odd money to Mrs. Wilton, being no longer able to withstand her

---

[801] The ferry was to the Isle of Inch, in County Donegal, which was served from the deanery of Derry.

[802] Peter Ward* (?-?).

[803] John Smibert* (1688–1751).

[804] Hester Van Homrigh* (1688–1723).

importunity, and despairing of seeing her receipt. The truth is, she showed me a letter wrote several months after the date of that receipt from Mrs. Mary, acknowledging herself indebted, but mentioning no sum. I therefore paid that bill, which was dated after the day of clearing, and no more. What must be done with Farmer? and, above all, what must be done with the milliner Mrs. Du Puis or Du Pee? I before mentioned her to you: she gives me great trouble. It would be endless to go through all. I desire a word in particular to each of these. To put them off till your coming in the spring, is utterly impracticable; they having been amused with hopes of seeing you all last summer: and it being rumoured that I intend to leave Europe next spring, what would such a put-off look like? In the account of demands you formerly sent me, you, or rather in your notes upon the demands, you often mentioned Mr. Clarke's catalogue, without signifying what catalogue that is, whether one sent from hence, or one wrote there for the use of Mrs. Esther, or Mrs. Mary in her lifetime. If the latter, pray let me know it; such a catalogue would be of great use to prevent impositions. I should be glad of a copy of it. You observe it differs frequently from accounts sent from hence; for instance, it contains about half of Fisher's demand from Mrs. Mary, if I take you right. It should follow therefore, that Fisher should be paid, at least so much— should it not? Send a copy of that catalogue, with the time when it was drawn up. You often mention an act of Parliament to prevent frauds, which you say makes for us. Pray send me a distinct abstract of that act, or at least of the substance and purport of it. The note showed me by Mrs. Hill is in the following words:

> '*London, January* 28, 1713–14.—I Esther Van Homrigh, junior, do promise to pay to Katharine Hill the sum of thirty-three pounds eleven shillings and sixpence, on the 28th day of April next, for my mother Mrs. Esther Van Homrigh, being her sole executrix, as witness my hand,
> E. Van. Homrigh
> Witness present
> *Wm. Brunlty.*
> *Anne Kindon.*'

I desire you will give me your opinion clearly upon this note. I likewise desire you to satisfy me in these three points; 1*st*, Whether Mrs. Mary was minor during the whole time of her living with her mother? 2*dly*, Whether the mother died indebted to Mrs. Mary, or had spent part of her fortune? 3*dly*, Whether the things which Mrs. Mary had during her minority were charged by the mother, and the mother satisfied for the same?

I entreat you satisfy me instantly as to the points contained in this letter; after which, I shall speedily expect an answer to the matters in my former letters, which now I have not time to repeat, or say any more but that I am, dear Tom,

yours affectionately,

G. Berkeley

London, Nov. 5, 1726

159 BERKELEY TO PRIOR

LR, *pp. 169–73.*

London, 12 November 1726

Dear Tom,

I have wrote to you often for certain *eclaircissements* which are absolutely necessary to settle matters with the creditors, who importune me to death. You have no notion of the misery I have undergone, and do daily undergo, on that account. I do therefore earnestly entreat you to answer all that I have queried on that head without delay, and at the same time resolve me in what follows.

Have you any letter or entry that takes notice of Mr. Collins as a creditor to Mrs. Esther, junior?[805] He hath produced to me two notes of hers, one for ten, the other for four pound odd money. Mrs. Farmer demands, for hosiers goods, near six pound from Mrs. Mary,[806] and one pound nineteen from Mrs. Esther. I have seen her books, and by them it appears something is due; but in some places it looks as if they had transferred the mother's debts to the daughter. Pray tell me distinctly and intelligibly what appears to you from the papers of this. You have told me that this, with many other demands, are only the mother's debts. Pray tell me withal your reasons for this, that the creditors themselves may be satisfied hereof, for they will not take your word or mine for it. *First*, Let me know what appears to you to have been supplied by each creditor for Mrs. Mary's use. *2dly*, Let me know upon what grounds you conceive that and no more to have been so supplied. *3dly*, Be distinct in giving your opinion, whether a minor be not chargeable for eatables and wearables supplied on the credit of another, or on their own credit, during the minority?

---

[805] Hester Van Homrigh* (1688–1723).
[806] Mary Van Homrigh (?–?), Hester Van Homrigh's* sister.

Whether it appears that Mrs. Mary was ever charged by her mother for those things? *Lastly,* Let me know what you think was distinctly supplied for Mrs. Mary's use, used by her, and never paid for; it being my opinion such debts should be discharged *in foro conscientiae*,[807] though perhaps the law might not require it, on score of minority or length of time.

For God's sake disembrangle these matters, that I may once be at ease to mind my other affairs of the college, which are enough to employ ten persons. You promised a distinct tripartite list, which I never got. The observations you have sent are all of them either so ambiguous and indecisive as to puzzle only, or else precarious; that is, unsupported by reasons to convince me or others. Now, I suppose where you give a positive opinion you have reasons for it; and it would have been right to have sent these reasons distinctly and particularly. I will not repeat what I have said in my former letters, but hope for your answer to all the points contained in them, and immediately to what relates to dispatching the creditors. I propose to make a purchase of land (which is very dear) in Bermuda, upon my first going thither; for which, and for other occasions, I shall want all the money I can possibly raise against my voyage. For this purpose, it would be a mighty service to me if the affair with Partinton[808] were adjusted this winter, by reference or compromise. The state of all that business, which I desired you to send me, I do now again earnestly desire. What is doing or has been done in that matter? Can you contrive no way for bringing Partinton to an immediate sale of the remaining lands? What is your opinion and advice upon the whole? What prospect can I have if I leave things at sixes and sevens when I go to another world, seeing all my remonstrances even now that I am near at hand, are to no purpose? I know money is at present on a very high foot of exchange: I shall therefore wait a little, in hopes it may become lower; but it will at all events be necessary to draw over my money. I have spent here a matter of six hundred pounds more than you know of, for which I have not yet drawn over.

As to what you write of Robin,[809] I am glad to find that others think he behaves well: I am best judge of his behaviour to me. There is a way of resenting past favours, and there is a way of asking future ones; and in both cases a right

---

[807] A legal phrase ("in the tribunal of the conscience") referring to situations where there are obligations of conscience even though there might be no strict legal obligations.
[808] Peter Partinton* (?–?).
[809] Robert Berkeley* (c. 1699–1787).

and a wrong. I had some other points to speak to, but am cut short, and have only time to add, that I am

> yours affectionately,
> G. Berkeley

London, Nov. 12, 1726

160 BERKELEY TO PRIOR

LR, *pp. 174–81.*

1 December 1726

Dear Tom,

I have lately received several letters of yours, which have given me a good deal of light with respect to Mrs. V. Homrigh's[810] affairs; but I am so much employed on the business of Bermuda, that I have hardly time to mind any thing else. I shall nevertheless snatch the present moment to write you short answers to the questions you propose.

As to Bermuda, it is now on a better and surer foot than ever. After the address of the Commons, and his Majesty's most gracious answer, one would have thought all difficulties had been got over, but much opposition hath been since raised (and that by very great men) to the design. As for the obstacles thrown in my way by interested men, though there hath been much of that, I never regarded it, no more than the clamours and calumnies of ignorant mistaken people: but in good truth it was with much difficulty, and the peculiar blessing of God, that the point was carried maugre[811] the strong opposition in the cabinet council; wherein, nevertheless, it hath of late been determined to go on with the grant, pursuant to the address of the House of Commons, and to give it all possible dispatch. Accordingly his Majesty hath ordered the warrant for passing the said grant to be drawn. The persons appointed to contrive the draught of the warrant are the Solicitor-General,[812] Baron Scroop[813] of the Treasury, and (my very good friend) Mr. Hutchenson.[814] You must know that in July last the Lords of the Treasury had named commissioners for taking an

---

[810] Hester Van Homrigh* (1688–1723).

[811] Notwithstanding; in spite of.

[812] Sir Clement Wearg (1686?–1726). He was appointed solicitor general on 3 February 1724.

[813] John Scrope* (c. 1662–1752). Scrope (sometimes referred to as "Scroop," as Berkeley does here) was made secretary of the Treasury in early 1724, remaining in that post until his death.

[814] Archibald Hutchenson (c. 1659–1740), MP for Hastings (1713–27).

estimate of the value and quantity of the Crown lands in St. Christopher's,* and for receiving proposals either for selling or farming the same for the benefit of the public. Their report is not yet made; and the Treasury were of opinion they could not make a grant to us till such time as the whole were sold or farmed pursuant to such report. But the point I am now labouring is to have it done without delay; and how this may be done without embarrassing the Treasury in their after disposal of the whole lands was this day the subject of a conference between the Solicitor-General, Mr. Hutchenson, and myself. The method agreed on is by a rent-charge on the whole Crown lands, redeemable upon the Crown's paying twenty thousand pounds, for the use of the president and fellows of St. Paul's,[815] and their successors. Sir Robert Walpole[816] hath signified that he hath no objection to this method; and I doubt not Baron Scroop will agree to it; by which means the grant may be passed before the meeting of Parliament, after which we may prepare to set out on our voyage in April. I have unawares run into this long account because you desired to know how the affair of Bermuda stood at present.

You also desire I would speak to Ned. You must know Ned hath parted from me ever since the beginning of last July. I allowed him six shillings a week besides his annual wages; and beside an entire livery, I gave him old clothes, which he made a penny of; but the creature grew idle and worthless to a prodigious degree. He was almost constantly out of the way; and when I told him of it he used to give me warning. I bore with this behaviour about nine months, and let him know I did it in compassion to him, and in hopes he would mend; but finding no hopes of this, I was forced at last to discharge him, and take another, who is as diligent as he was negligent. When he parted from me, I paid him between six and seven pounds which was due to him, and likewise gave him money to bear his charges to Ireland, whither he said he was going. I met him the other day in the street; and asking why he was not gone to Ireland to his wife and child, he made answer that he had neither wife nor child. He got, it seems, into another service since he left me, but continued only a fortnight in it. The fellow is silly to an incredible degree, and spoiled by good usage.

I shall take care the pictures be sold in an auction. Mr. Smibert,[817] whom I know to be a very honest, skil[l]ful person in his profession, will see them put into an auction at the proper time, which he tells me is not till the town fills with company, about the meeting of Parliament.

---

[815] Berkeley's proposed college in Bermuda.
[816] Sir Robert Walpole* (1676–1745), later first Earl of Orford.
[817] John Smibert* (1688–1751).

As to Bacon, I know not what to do with him. I spoke often to Messrs. Wogan and Aspinwall[818] about him. Mr. Aspinwall also spoke to him, and threatened him with bringing the affair into court; and he still promised, and always broke his promise. I always, for my part, insisted they should prosecute him; and, since your mentioning him in your letter, have done it in stronger terms than ever, but to no purpose; for, upon the whole, I find they decline meddling with it. They say the fellow is a knave, and skillful in delays of law and attorneys' tricks, and that he may keep us employed for several years; that it is a matter out of their sphere; in short, they do not care to be employed in this affair. When I saw the man, I did not like his looks nor manner, and am now quite at a loss what to do with him. The whole expense they charge for management in South Sea House,[819] and at Doctors' Commons,* together with their own trouble, amounts to thirty-nine pounds ten shillings and sixpence. I have bills of the particulars. Some of the creditors I have paid; but there are many more unpaid, whose demands I could not yet adjust. The first leisure I have I shall try to do it, by the help of the lights I have now got. As to M' Manus,[820] I am content to favour him so far as to forbear his paying that part of my income on the first of January which was stipulated to be then paid; but then the whole must be paid punctually on the first of February. I say I shall have necessary occasion for the whole income of the present year to be paid, without fail, on the first of February next; and I wish he may have timely notice from you of this. I formerly gave him warning myself; but since he has wrote to you, it is fit he know this answer. My affairs absolutely require this; and I expect that he will not, upon any pretext, disappoint me. You tell me what is to be done with Mr. Tooke's[821] note, in case it be a bond in form, or a simple promissory note, or a promissory note with interest sealed; but still you omit what (to the best of my remembrance) is the true case, *to wit*, a promissory note unsealed, to pay the principal with interest. Before I closed this letter, the bond was brought me, sealed, witnessed, and bearing interest, making, with the principal, eighty pound, which I have paid this moment; so that I was mistaken in thinking it a note, being a bond in form. In your last but one, you sent two opposite opinions of

---

[818] Wogan* (?–?) and Aspinwall* (?–?).

[819] The business headquarters for the South Sea Company* on Threadneedle Street, London.

[820] McManus* (?–?).

[821] Benjamin Tooke (?–1716). Swift directed Hester (Vanessa) to borrow from Tooke on his credit. See Williams, ed., *Correspondence of Jonathan Swift*, Swift to Van Homrigh, 8 July 1714.

Howard and Marshal[822] concerning Mrs. Hill's note, but promised to give your own, and to be more clear in the point in your next, which it seems you forgot to do. I have in a former letter desired you to send me over an abstract of the state of our case in dispute with Partinton,[823] and a full account of our demands upon him. You have told me indeed where the point sticks at present; but you may see that this does not fully answer my desire. I want to know (as if I had never heard anything of the matter) a full account of that whole affair stated, what our demands amount to in each particular, and what expectations there are of succeeding, and grounds for prosecuting, the said demands respectively. I remember to have told you I could know more of matters here than perhaps people generally do. You thought we did wrong to sell; but the stocks are fallen, and depend upon it they will fall lower. In a former letter, I acquainted you that I desired the bonds may be lodged with Ned Synge,[824] who will call for them.

yours,

G. Berkeley

161 BERKELEY TO PRIOR

LR, *pp. 182–85.*

London, 27 February 1726/27

Dear Tom,

The packets you speak of you may direct, under cover, to the right honourable Thomas, Earl of Pomfret,[825] in Hanover Square; but then you must take care that no one packet be above a certain quantity or weight, and thereby exceed the limits of franking: in which case the frank I know will not be regarded, and the papers may miscarry. What the precise limits are I know not; any body there can inform you.

I send you herewith an account of our affairs transacted by Wogan and Aspinwall.[826] You may observe in the account of Mr. Gyles (employed by them) a half guinea blotted out, which I paid separately for an extract of a Will relating

---

[822] Robert Marshall* (*c.* 1690–1772).

[823] Peter Partinton* (?–?).

[824] Edward Synge* (1691–1762).

[825] Thomas Fermor (1698?–1753), second Baron Leominster. He was created Earl of Pomfret on 27 December 1721.

[826] Wogan* (?–?) and Aspinwall* (?–?).

to Bermuda,[827] and which by mistake was inserted in this account, to which it had no relation.

The pictures were all sold for forty-five pounds, at an auction which was held last week in Covent Garden, at the house of one Mr. Russel, a painter. They were sold publicly and fairly among several other pictures. The truth of it is, that of late years the taste lies so much towards Italian pictures, many of which are daily imported, that Dutch pictures go off but heavily. Mr. Smibert[828] did not think they would have brought so much.

I have taken the utmost care to keep myself within the limits of your directions in the payments I have hitherto made, and shall continue to act with the same caution. Mr. Marshal* cannot long more than I do to put an end to this matter of my administration, which I was willing to have declined, if he had thought good to accept it. But the constant hurry of business I have on my hands, together with my not being able to find out some of the creditors, hath hitherto unavoidably delayed it. However, I have paid between two and three hundred pounds, and shall finish all as soon as possible. Mr. Clarke I have not seen this long time. I suppose he is ashamed for my having found out that he was to receive a sum of money from Mrs. Philips, whose unjust debt he had undertaken to get paid. This, and his not giving me the notice Alderman Barber[829] said he desired him to give before the sale of the jewels, makes me think very indifferently of him. Besides, there is no sort of consistency between the accounts of creditors, as given in by him, and their own demands, which still strengthens my suspicion of him. As to the sum to be paid into Swift & Company,* and the deductions to be made for curates, etc., I only desire that all may be done on the foot you told me you had agreed with Mr. M' Manus,[830] and whereof you stated the account in a letter I have by me, and which I need not transcribe, because I suppose you remember it. As to the sale of the reversionary lands, I desire it may be done as soon as possible; and not to stand out, but to take the best terms you can. As to the rest, I long to see it all finished by arbitration.

---

[827] The Report of the Law Offices mentions the will of Sir Nathanel Riche, who left land in the Bermudas for the establishment of a school. See *Works*, vol. IX, p. 69; and Luce, "More Unpublished Berkeley Letters and New Berkeleiana," 32–34.

[828] John Smibert* (1688–1751).

[829] John Barber (1675–1741), printer and local politician. The printer of the *Examiner*, he befriended Jonathan Swift* and apparently handled some loans to Hester Van Homrigh,* this one on the security of some of her jewels. See, Williams, ed., *Correspondence of Swift*, Swift to Van Homrigh, 4 August and 15 October 1720. For evidence that Barber had been used earlier for loans, see Swift to Van Homrigh, 8 July 1714.

[830] McManus* (?–?).

My going to Bermuda I cannot positively say when it will be. I have to do with very busy people at a very busy time. I hope nevertheless to have all that business completely finished in a few weeks. I am, dear Tom,

yours,

G. B.

162 BERKELEY TO PRIOR

LR, pp. 185–88.

London, 11 April 1727

Dear Tom,

In my last I made no mention of any sums of my money applied to the payment of debts, or other purposes common to Mr. Marshal[831] and me, because I suppose you have taken care that he keep equal pace with me: if he be deficient, this is the only time to right myself. As to those you call dubious debts, and those which, being contracted in the mother's lifetime, are payable by Partinton,[832] I should be glad to hear your opinion in a line or two, since I am not allowed to act otherwise than by strict legal justice. Thus much I think Mr. Marshal and myself are obliged to, viz. to pay those debts if nothing be stopped for them by Partinton; and if there be, to advertise the creditors thereof. Since my last, I paid what you allowed to be due to Mrs. Farmer (now Mrs. Reed). For this and all other payments I have receipts or notes which I propose bringing with me to Ireland.

And now I mention my coming to Ireland, I must earnestly desire you, by all means, to keep this a secret from every individual creature.[833] I cannot justly say what time (probably some time next month) I shall be there, or how long; but find it necessary to be there to transact matters with one or two of my associates (who yet I would not have know of my coming till I am on the spot), and, for several reasons, am determined to keep myself as secret and concealed as

---

[831] Robert Marshall* (*c.* 1690–1772).

[832] Peter Partinton* (?–?).

[833] Berkeley later explains his perceived need for secrecy in his travels leading up to his departure for Rhode Island. Had he stayed in England to secure the monies from the sale of the land on St. Christopher Island,* the delay would threaten the security of his private investors. If he left England, he would have been censured for leaving without the monies in hand to start the college. See Letter 187.

possible all the time I am in Ireland. In order to this, I make it my request that you will hire for me an entire house, as neat and convenient as you can get, somewhere within a mile of Dublin, for half a year. But what I principally desire is, that it be in no town or village, but in some quiet private place, out of the way of roads, or street, or observation. I would have it hired with necessary furniture for kitchen, a couple of chambers, and a parlour. As the same time, I must desire you to hire an honest maid servant, who can keep it clean, and dress a plain bit of meat: a man servant I shall bring with me. You may do all this either in your own name, or as for a friend of yours, one Mr. Brown (for that is the name I shall assume), and let me know it as soon as possible. There are several little scattered houses with gardens about Clantarfe, Rathfarnum, etc. I remember particularly the old castle of Ramines, and a little white house upon the hills by itself, beyond the Old Men's Hospital,[834] likewise in the outgoings or fields about St. Kevin's, etc. In short, in any snug private place within half a mile or a mile of town. I would have a bit of a garden to it, no matter what sort. Mind this, and you will oblige

    your affectionate humble Servant,

    G. Berkeley

163 BERKELEY TO PRIOR

LR, *pp. 188–89.*

London, 20 May 1727

Dear Tom,

    Things being as you say, I think you were in the right to pay only 100 pounds to Mr. Marshal[835] at present. I have drawn on you for 12 pounds, which my B[rother] Robin[836] will call for.

    I would by all means have a place secured for me by the end of June: it may be taken only for three months. I hope you will not have left Ireland before my arrival.

    I take it for granted you have paid what I directed for Mr. Partinton Van Homrigh's[837] share of the pictures. I sent the answer to his bill engrossed by

---

[834] The Royal Hospital, Kilmainham.

[835] Robert Marshall* (c. 1690–1772).

[836] Robert Berkeley* (c. 1699–1787).

[837] Partinton's* son, who under the terms of Bartholomew Van Homrigh's will was to take the surname Van Homrigh.

post, and shall be glad to hear you have got it. I long to hear the sale of lands (reversionary) perfected to Mr. Conolly.[838]

I am (God be praised) very near concluding the crown grant to our college, having got over all difficulties and obstructions, which were not a few.

I conclude, in great haste, dear Tom,

> yours,
>
> G. Berkeley

London, May 20, 1727

164 BERKELEY TO PRIOR

LR, *pp. 189–91.*

London, 13 June 1727

Dear Tom,

Poor Caldwell's[839] death I had heard of two or three posts before I received your letter. Had he lived, his life would not have been agreeable. He was formed for retreat and study, but of late was grown fond of the world and getting into business.

A house between Dublin and Drumcondra I can by no means approve of: the situation is too public; and what I chiefly regard is privacy. I like the situation of Lord's house much better, and have only one objection to it, which is your saying he intends to use some part of it himself; for this would be inconsistent with my view of being quite concealed; and the more so because Lord knows me, which of all things is what I would avoid. His house and price would suit me. If you can get such another, quite to myself, snug, private, and clean, with a stable, I shall not matter whether it be painted or no, or how it is furnished, provided it be clean and warm. I aim at nothing magnificent or grand (as you term it), which might probably defeat my purpose of continuing concealed.

You have more than once talked of coming to England without coming: perhaps you may alter your mind now as well as heretofore, but you are best

---

[838] William Conolly* (1662–1729), MP in Ireland and Speaker of the Irish House of Commons.

[839] Possibly Henry Caldwell* (?–1726), second Baronet. Given that he died in early November 1726, the date fits. See note to Letter 9.

judge of that. I desire to know when your business requires your being in England?—whether you come to London?—and how long you propose staying on this side of the water? I am sure it will be at least a full month before I can reach Dublin. If you come over immediately, and make but a very short stay, possibly I might defer my going, to attend you in your return. At all events, I should be sorry we missed of each other by setting out at the same time, which may occasion my seeing you neither there nor here.

 The bell-man calls for my letter, so I shall add no more but that I am
  your affectionate humble servant,
  G. Berkeley

London, June 13, 1727

Pray let me hear from you next post.

165 BERKELEY TO PRIOR

LR, p. 192.

London, 15 June 1727

Dear Tom,

 Yesterday we had an account of King George's death.[840] This day King George II was proclaimed.[841] All the world here are in a hurry, and I as much as any body; our grant being defeated by the King's dying before the broad seal was annexed to it, in order to which it was passing through the offices. I have *la mer à boire*[842] again. You shall hear from me when I know more. At present I am at a loss what course to take. Pray answer my last speedily.

  yours,
  G. B.

London, June '15, 1727

---

[840] King George I* (1660–1727) died on 12 June 1727.
[841] George Augustus (1683–1760), then Prince of Wales, was proclaimed King George II* on 15 June 1727. The coronation occurred on 11 October 1727.
[842] A French idiom. When used in the negative form (*ce n'est pas la mer à boire*) it means roughly "not a big deal," but here Berkeley clearly does not intend that sense. "I have again an ocean to cross" is a reasonable, if somewhat free, translation.

166 BERKELEY TO PRIOR

LR, *pp. 193–94.*

London, 27 June 1727

Dear Tom,

Yesterday I received your letter, containing an account of your design about coming to England. In a former letter, I gave you to know that my affairs were ravelled by the death of his Majesty.[843] I am now beginning on a new foot, and with good hopes of success. The warrant for our grant had been signed by the King, countersigned by the Lords of the Treasury, and passed the Attorney General. Here it stood when the express came of the King's death.[844] A new warrant is now preparing, which must be signed by his present Majesty, in order to a patent passing the broad seal.

As soon as this affair is finished, I propose going to Ireland. I cannot certainly say when that will be; but sure I am it will not be time enough to find you there, if you continue your scheme of coming over the next month. It is unlucky that we should both think of crossing the sea at the same time. But as you seem to talk doubtfully of your design, I hope it may suit with your conveniency to alter it; in which case we may probably come together to England.

The changes of ministry you talk of are at present but guessed at; a little time will show.

yours, etc.,

G. Berkeley

167 BERKELEY TO PRIOR

LR, *pp. 194–96.*

London, 6 July 1727

Dear Tom,

This is to inform you, that I have obtained a new warrant for a grant, signed by his present Majesty,[845] contrary to the expectations of my friends, who

---

[843] King George I* (1660–1727) died on 12 June 1727.
[844] See Letter 160 for an account of who signed the first warrant.
[845] King George II* (1683–1760).

thought nothing could be expected of that kind in this great hurry of business. As soon as this grant (which is of the same import with that begun by his late Majesty) hath passed the offices and seals, I purpose to execute my design of going to Ireland. In case, therefore, you continue your purpose of coming to England this summer, I must desire you to leave all papers relating to my affairs with Mr. Synge,[846] sealed up in a bag as things belonging to me, put into his hands for fear of accidents; but to say nothing to him of my going to Dublin, which I would have by all means kept secret from every one; my design being, in case I find you are absent, to make my arrival, after I am come, known to Synge; to look into the papers myself, and try if I can state matters so as to bring them to a conclusion with Partinton.[847] It would assist me much in this affair if you would do what I have long and often desired, viz. draw up a paper containing an account of my demands on Partinton or others in virtue of my executorship, with the several reasons supporting the said demands, and an account of the proceedings thereupon at law; what hath been done, and what remains to be done. I hoped to have heard of the sale of the reversion by this time. Let me hear by next post. I am

yours,

G. Berkeley

London, July 6, 1727

168 BERKELEY TO PRIOR

LR, pp. 196–99.

21 July 1727

Dear Tom,

In answer to your last letter, this is to let you know, that my grant is now got farther than where it was at the time of the King's death.[848] I am in hopes the broad seal will soon be affixed to it, what remains to be done in

---

[846] Edward Synge* (1691–1762).
[847] Peter Partinton* (?–?).
[848] King George I* (1660–1727) died on 12 June 1727.

order thereto being only matter of form; so that I propose setting out from hence in a fortnight's time. When I set out, I shall write at the same time to tell you of it.

I know not whether I shall stay longer than a month on that side of the water. I am sure I shall not want the country lodging (I desired you to procure) for a longer time. Do not therefore take it for more than a month, if that can be done. I remember certain remote suburbs called Pimlico and Dolphin's Barn, but know not whereabout they lie. If either of them be situate in a private pleasant place, and airy, near the fields, I should therein like a first floor in a clean house (I desire no more); and it would be better if there was a bit of a garden where I had the liberty to walk. This I mention in case my former desire cannot be conveniently answered for so short a time as a month; and, if I may judge at this distance, these places seem as private as a house in the country: for you must know, what I chiefly aim at is secrecy. This makes me uneasy to find that there hath been a report spread among some of my friends in Dublin of my designing to go over. I cannot account for this, believing, after the precautions I had given you, that you would not mention it directly or indirectly to any mortal. For the present, I have no more to add, but only to repeat my request that you will leave all papers relating to my executorship with Mr. Synge[849] sealed up in a bag, with directions to deliver them to my order. This I desired you to perform in my last, in case you leave Ireland before I arrive there. If with them you likewise leave what I formerly desired, it will save me some trouble. I am, dear Tom,

> your affectionate humble Servant,
> G. Berkeley

I observe you take no notice of what I said about selling the reversionary lands, though you formerly encouraged me to think I should have heard of their being sold before this time.

In case you do not make use of the power I gave you by letter of attorney to make sale of the reversionary lands before you come for England, I desire you would leave that said letter of attorney among the papers with Mr. Synge.

---

[849] Edward Synge* (1691–1762).

169 BERKELEY TO PRIOR

LR, *pp. 199–201.*

London, 20 February 1727/28

Dear Tom,

I agree that M'Manus[850] should retain for payment of the curates to the first of May. After so many delays from Partinton,[851] I was fully convinced the only way to sell the reversionary lands must be by compelling him to join in the sale by law, or by making a separate sale. This I proposed to you by word of mouth, and by letter, as much as I could; and I now most earnestly repeat it, entreating you to do the one or the other out of hand if it be not done already, as I have hopes it is by what you say in your last. Dear Tom, fail me not in this particular; but by all means order matters so that the purchase-money may be paid in to Swift & Co.* on the first of April, or at farthest ten days after; which ten days I am willing to allow to M'Manus as desired. I need not repeat to you what I told you here of the necessity there is for my raising all the money possible against my voyage, which, God willing, I shall begin in May, whatever you may hear suggested to the contrary; though you need not mention this.

I propose to set out for Dublin about a month hence; but of this you must not give the least intimation to any body. I beg the favour of you to look out at leisure a convenient lodging for me in or about Church-street, or such other place as you shall think the most retired. Mr. Petit Rose[852] writes me from Portarlington about renewing his lease, which he desires I would empower you to do. He mentions a promise I made on the last renewal, that I would another time allow him one year gratis. For my part, I absolutely deny that I know any thing of any such promise. If you remember any thing of it, pray let me know; for if there was such a thing, it must have been made by you, to whom I referred the management of that affair. As I do not design to be known when I am in Ireland, I shall comply with his desire in sending you a letter of attorney to perfect the renewal, agreeable to such draught as you transmit hither; provided still, that his proposal (which I have by this post directed him to send to you) be approved by you; to

---

[850] McManus* (?–?).
[851] Peter Partinton* (?–?).
[852] An unknown tenant of Berkeley's. See Letter 220.

whom I leave it, to do what to you shall seem fair and reasonable in that matter. I am,

> your affectionate humble Servant,
> Geor: Berkeley

London, Feb. 20, 1727/28

170 BERKELEY TO PRIOR[853]

BL Add. MS 39311, fol. 11.

London, 6 April 1728

Dear Tom,

I send you herewith the letter of attorney and that to Dr. Ward.[854] Four Irish pacquets are now due, one of which I expect brings an account of your having finished the sale of those lands which I have been pressing for these four years.

I have been detained from my journey partly in expectation of Dr. Clayton's[855] coming (who was doing business in Lancashire) and partly in respect to the excessive rains. The Doctor hath been several days in town, and we have had so much rain that probably it will be soon over. I am therefore daily expecting to set out, all things being provided.

Now it is of all things my earnest desire (and for very good reasons) not to have it known that I am in Dublin. Speak not, therefore, one syllable of it to any mortal whatsover. When I formerly desired you to take a place for me near the town, you gave out that you were looking for a retired lodging for a friend of yours; upon which everybody surmised me to be the person. I must beg you not to act in the like manner now, but to take for me an entire house in your own name, and as for yourself: for, all things considered, I am determined upon a whole house, with no mortal in it but a maid of your own putting, who is to look on herself as your servant. Let there be two bedchambers, one for you, another for me and, as you like, you may ever and anon lie there. I would have the

---

[853] Fraser omits the first paragraph (*LL*, pp. 148–50), which is printed (without the rest of the letter) in Luce, "Some Unpublished Berkeley Letters with some New Berkeleiana," 146.

[854] Peter Ward* (?–?).

[855] Robert Clayton* (1695–1758).

house, with necessary furniture, taken by the month (or otherwise, as you can), for I purpose staying not beyond that time: and yet perhaps I may. Take it as soon as possible, and never think of saving a week's hire by leaving it to do when I am there. Dr. Clayton thinks (and I am of the same opinion) that a convenient place may be found in the further end of Great Britain Street, or Ballibough-bridge[856]—by all means beyond Thomson's the Fellow's. Let me entreat you to say nothing of this to anybody, but to do the thing directly. In this affair I consider convenience more than expense, and would of all things (cost what it will) have a proper place in a retired situation, where I may have access to fields and sweet air, provided against the moment I arrive. I am inclined to think, one may be better concealed in the outermost skirt of the suburbs than in the country, or within the town. Wherefore, if you cannot be accommodated where I mention, inquire in some other skirt or remote suburb. A house quite detached in the country I should have no objection to provided you judge that I shall not be liable to discovery in it. The place called Bermuda[857] I am utterly against. Dear Tom, do this matter cleanly and cleverly, without waiting for further advice. You see I am willing to run the risk of the expence. To the person from whom you hire it (whom alone I would have you speak of it to) it will not seem strange you should at this time of the year be desirous, for your own convenience or health, to have a place in a free and open air. If you cannot get a house without taking it for a longer time than a month, take it at such the shortest time it can be let for, with agreement for further continuing in case there be occasion. I am, dear Tom

your affectionate humble Servant,

G: Berkeley

London, April 6, 1728

Mr. Madden,[858] who witnesses the letter of attorney, is now going to Ireland. He is a clergyman, and man of estate in the north of Ireland. Divide this letter from that of attorney.

---

[856] The word "bridge" is now obscured by a defect in the paper, but I follow Luce here.

[857] A reference to a house or estate near Dublin. Luce notes that such an estate can be found in Pembroke township. See *Works*, vol. IX, p. 73.

[858] Samuel Madden (1686–1765), writer, clergyman, and benefactor. He authored *Themistocles, the Lover of his Country: A Tragedy in Five Acts and in Verse* in 1729, which was performed at the Theatre Royal in Lincoln's Inn Fields. In 1731 Madden proposed instituting a system of prizes for students in the quarterly examinations at Trinity College, Dublin. The Madden prizes commenced in 1798 following a bequest from Madden's son Samuel.

171 BERKELEY TO FAIRFAX[859]

HSP, Ferdinand Dreer Collection, English Clergy, vol. I, p. 15. Photostat at TCD, MS 4309, fol. 3.

Dublin, 7 June 1728

Sir,

When I waited on you I took the liberty to inform you that my library was to be sent from Dublin to London in order to lie there till it might be conveniently shipped off again and I now give you this trouble to let you know that it is actually put on board the ship called William & James and consigned to the bearer hereof. The whole parcel amounts to fifty-eight boxes, whereof fifty-five contain only books; the other three beside books contain papers and mathematical instruments, all old except a water level which I take to be the only instrument made in this kingdom. The books printed here are very inconsiderable though I cannot punctually tell the number. I do verily think they are not worth ten pounds. The others which were either printed in England or came from thence (as all our books constantly used to do) may be presumed liable to no duty upon their return into England. But this is submitted to the Honourable board of Commissioners to whom I beg the favour of you to set forth this case, and that you will be pleased to give orders accordingly which will much oblige.

Sir,

your most obedient humble servant,

Geor: Berkeley

Dublin, June 7, 1728

172 BERKELEY TO PERCIVAL

EP, BL Add. MS 47032, fols. 81v–82.

Greenwich, 3 September 1728

My Lord,

I think myself obliged before I set sail from Europe to take leave of your Lordship and express my sincere gratitude for all your favours, my being

---

[859] The letter is addressed to Bryan Fairfax, Esq.* (1676–1749). This letter was published in A. A. Luce, "Berkeley's Bermuda Project and his Benefactions to American Universities, with Unpublished Letters and Extracts from the Egmont Papers," *Proceedings of the Royal Irish Academy* 42 (1933): 99.

withheld from doing this in person is no small mortification to me though perhaps it would have been greater to have done it, taking leave being in my opinion the most disagreeable instance of good manners that custom obliges us to. Tomorrow we sail down the river. Mr. James[860] and Mr. Dalton[861] go with me. So doth my wife,[862] a daughter of the late Chief Justice Forster,[863] whom I married since I saw your Lordship. I chose her for the qualities of her mind and her unaffected inclination to books. She goes with great cheerfulness to live a plain farmer's life, and wear stuff of her own spinning. I have presented her with a spinning wheel, and for her encouragement have assured her that from henceforward there shall never be one yard of silk bought for the use of myself, herself, or any of our family. Her fortune was two thousand pounds originally, but travelling and exchange have reduced it to less than fifteen hundred English money. I have placed that, and about six hundred pounds of my own, in the South Sea Annuities,* as your Lordship will perceive by the enclosed letter of attorney which I take the liberty to send you. I design to give your Lordship no farther trouble by it than one journey in a year into the city; and that only to such time as I can find means of laying it out to advantage where I am going. Your Lordship's goodness and readiness to serve your friends which I have so frequently experienced have drawn this trouble upon you and prevent any further apology.

My most humble respects and best wishes attend my Lady, your whole family, and the good company at your house. That God may preserve your Lordship in health and happiness is the sincere hearty prayer of

your Lordship's
most obedient humble servant,
G. Berkeley

If your Lordship should at any time favour me with a line please direct to Dean Berkeley at Rhode Island, near Boston, and enclose the letter in a cover to Thomas Corbett, Esq.[864] at the Admiralty Office in London, who will further it by the first opportunity.

---

[860] John James* (?–1741).

[861] Richard Dalton* (c. 1695–1769).

[862] The first mention in Berkeley's correspondence of Anne (*née* Forster) Berkeley* (?–1786), Berkeley's wife.

[863] John Forster (1668–1720), politician. John Forster was speaker of the Irish House of Commons from 1707 to 1709 and chief justice of the Irish Common Pleas from 1714 until his death.

[864] Thomas Corbett* (?–1751).

173 BERKELEY TO [GIBSON?][865]

MS unknown. Berkeley Studies (Berkeley Newsletter) 4 (December 1980): 14.

Gravesend, 5 September 1728

My Lord,

The small time I have been in London since my return from Ireland was spent in such hurry of business, that I could wait on none of my patrons or friends, which must be my apology for taking this method of paying my duty to your Lordship whom I beg leave to inform that to-morrow with the blessing of God I shall set sail to Rhode Island near new England. It is a place abounding in provisions where I design to purchase a piece of land with my own money in order to supply our college[866] with such necessaries as are not the product of Bermuda, which will in good measure remove one principal objection to the success of our design. The money contributed by Subscribers is left in Mr. Hoare[867] the Banker's hands and made payable to Dr. Clayton[868] with whom I have also left the patent for receiving the £20,000 from St. Christopher's.* I propose to continue at Rhode Island till such time as Dr. Clayton hath received that money and is come to Bermuda with the rest of my associates where I intend to join them. Going to Bermuda without either money or associates I could not think of. I should have made a bad figure and done no good. Staying here would have been no less disagreeable and to as little purpose, since all I could do here was finished except receiving the money which may be done by others. It should seem therefore that the intermediate time may be passed with more advantage in America where I can see things with my own eyes and prepare matters for the rendering our college more useful. I humbly recommend the undertaking & my self to your Lordship's protection & prayers and remain with all duty and respect,

> My Lord
> your Lordship's most
> obedient & most
> devoted humble
> servant,
> G. Berkeley

---

[865] David Berman published this letter in "Berkeley's Departure for America: A New Letter," *Berkeley Studies (Berkeley Newsletter)* 4 (December 1980): 14 and reported that it was auctioned on 10 May 1979 by Swann Galleries of New York. The letter was transcribed by him before its sale. It was sold to a private buyer and its location is unknown.

[866] The proposed St. Paul's College.

[867] Either Henry Hoare* (1705–85) or his uncle Benjamin Hoare* (1693–1749/50).

[868] Robert Clayton* (1695–1758).

174 BERKELEY TO PRIOR

LR, *pp. 202–04.*

Gravesend, 5 September 1728

Dear Tom,

To-morrow, with God's blessing, I set sail for Rhode Island, with my wife and a friend of hers, my Lady Hancock's daughter,[869] who bears us company. I am married since I saw you to Miss Forster,[870] daughter of the late Chief Justice,[871] whose humour and turn of mind pleases me beyond any thing that I know in her whole sex. Mr. James,[872] Mr. Dalton,[873] and Mr. Smibert,[874] go with us on this voyage. We are now all together at Gravesend, and are engaged in one view.

When my next rents are paid, I must desire you to inquire for my cousin Richard Berkeley,[875] who was bred a public notary (I suppose he may by that time be out of his apprenticeship), and give him twenty moidores[876] as a present from me, towards helping him on his beginning the world.

I believe I shall have occasion to draw for six hundred pounds English before this year's income is paid by the farmers of my deanery. I must therefore desire you to speak to Messrs. Swift, etc.,* to give me credit for said sum in London about three months hence, in case I have occasion to draw for it; and I shall willingly pay their customary interest for the same till the farmers pay it to them, which I hope you will order punctually to be done by the first of June. Give me advice of your success in this affair, viz. whether they will answer such draught of mine in London, on what interest, and on whom, and how I am to draw?

---

[869] Miss Hancock (?–?), the daughter of Sir William Hancock (1655–1701), recorder of Dublin, and Elizabeth Coddington (?–?). Of Hancock's three daughters, only the youngest, Jane, was unmarried at the time, making it likely the reference is to her.

[870] Anne (*née* Forster) Berkeley* (?–1786).

[871] John Forster (1668–1720), politician. Forster was Speaker of the Irish House of Commons (1707–9) and chief justice of the Irish Common Pleas from 1714 until his death.

[872] John James* (?–1741).

[873] Richard Dalton* (*c.* 1695–1769).

[874] John Smibert* (1688–1751).

[875] Nothing is known of this relation.

[876] A Portuguese gold coin minted from roughly 1640 to 1732. In the second edition of The *Querist*, the editor makes note of the flood of Portuguese coinage. See *Works*, vol. VI, p. 145n.

Direct for me in Rhode Island, and enclose your letter in a cover to Thomas Corbet, Esq.,[877] at the Admiralty office in London, who will always forward my letters by the first opportunity. Adieu. I write in great haste,

yours,

G. B.

I wrote by this post to M'Manus[878] to comply with all the points proposed in Dr. Ward's[879] memorial. A copy of my charter was sent to Dr. Ward by Dr. Clayton.[880] If it be not arrived when you go to London, write out of the charter the clause relating to my absence. Adieu once more.

175 NEWMAN TO BERKELEY[881]

SPCK MS D4/41, fols. 15–16.

Bartlett's Buildings, 25 October 1728

Revd Sir,

I hope this will find you & Messrs. James[882] and Dalton[883] safely arrived in New England and that you all find such a reception there as you deserve, and if it be true as the *Daily Journal* of the 12th current has told the town I hope that the ladies you carried with you are also happily arrived. I wonder you have been so long spared by our news writers this being the first account they have given of you since you went, and some things being awkward represented I suspend my belief of them till I hear from you.

The books you desired me to procure to be sent over with you, came according to the enclosed account to 22: 13: 7, of which I have received £20 from Messrs

---

[877] Thomas Corbett* (?–1751).

[878] McManus* (?–?).

[879] Peter Ward* (?–?).

[880] Robert Clayton* (1695–1758).

[881] Henry Newman* (1670–1743). The letter is addressed "To the Revd Mr. Dean Berkeley, at Newport, Rhode Island. By the Rebecca and Mary, Captn John Suckling." This letter was published in Luce, "Berkeley's Bermuda Project and his Benefactions to American Universities, with Unpublished Letters and Extracts from the Egmont Papers," 103.

[882] John James* (?–1741).

[883] Richard Dalton* (c. 1695–1769).

Hoare[884] and Company, and the remainder I am to receive when Lady Betty Hastings[885] has signified her allowance for last year.

I shall be glad to receive your commands how the remainder of your bill of £40 shall be applied when I do receive it.

I beg leave to refer you for news to the papers herewith sent. My humble service to Mr. James and Mr. Dalton to whom I beg this may be communicated & accepted as if I had wrote. Wishing you and them with the ladies all manner of prosperity at the same time I assure you of my being Revd Sir,

> your most obedient humble servant,
> H. N.

N.B.: sent 6 of the daily papers of yesterday and this day, with the *Craftsman* of the 26th Oct. 1728.[886]

176 BERKELEY TO PERCIVAL[887]

EP, BL Add. MS 47032, fols. 102–03.

Newport, in Rhode Island, 7 February 1728/29

My Lord,

Though I am at present in no small hurry and have been so ever since my landing with visits and business of several kinds, yet I would not omit the first opportunity of paying my duty to your Lordship, and acquainting you with our safe arrival in this island.[888] We came last from Virginia, where I received many unexpected as well as undeserved honours from the Governour and principal inhabitants.[889] The same civil kind treatment attends us here. We were a long time blundering about the ocean before we reached Virginia, but

---

[884] Henry Hoare* (1705–85) and his uncle Benjamin Hoare* (1693–1749/50).

[885] Lady Elizabeth Hastings (1682–1739), benefactor. "Lady Betty" became notable for her intelligence, her pious character, and her support of charitable causes. She provided financial support for the Society for Promoting Christian Knowledge.

[886] An additional appended note reads: "N.B.: sent 6 of the daily papers of yesterday and this day, with the Craftsman of the 28 October 1728."

[887] In the margin of Percival's letterbook: "Dean Berkeley received in April, answered 25 April" [Letter 181].

[888] Berkeley resided in Newport on Rhode Island in Narrangansett Bay. The isle is often referred to as Aquidneck Island to distinguish it from the colony of Rhode Island.

[889] Berkeley first landed at or near Williamsburg, Virginia.

our voyage from thence hither was as speedy and prosperous as could be wished. Mr. James[890] who proposeth to continue in Virginia till spring, and Mr. Dalton[891] who pursued his journey to this place by land, will both repent of their choice, when they find us arrived so long before them. I shall soon (I hope) be able to give your Lordship a more particular account of things. For the present I shall only say that this island wants only your Lordship's family and a few more of my friends to make it the most agreeable place I ever saw. And (that which pleases me beyond all things) there is a more probable prospect of doing good here than in any other part of the world. I am so fully convinced of this, that (were it in my power) I should not demur one moment about situating our College here. But no step can be taken herein without consent of the Crown, and I shall not apply for that till his Majesty's bounty from St. Christopher's* is paid to Dr. Clayton,[892] till which time this design should be kept private.

I took the liberty to trouble your Lordship with a letter of attorney which Dr. Clayton was to put into your hands relating to my stock in the South Sea Annuities.* It occurs to me that it is possible you may once more travel abroad into France or Italy, in which case I beg the favour of you to sell my said annuities and receive the dividend due thereupon at that time, and place the whole in some known banker's hands making it payable to my order. Mr. Hoare,[893] of all others, I should choose; but as the contributors' money belonging to our College of Bermuda is in his hands, and as I would have my private stock entered into the banker's books under a distinct article as my own money, in order to prevent any confusion, I must request your Lordship to be particular with him on that head, if the money be put into his hands. And you will be pleased to let me know his partner's names that I may draw in form, for I intend to purchase land in this country. Your Lordship's usual goodness will pardon this trouble.

The post is just going out so I conclude with my best wishes and respects to my Lady Percival and your whole family in which I include Mr. Dering.[894] My Lord,

      your most obedient and obliged humble servant,

      G. Berkeley

I shall hope for a line from your Lordship.

---

[890] John James* (?–1741).
[891] Richard Dalton* (*c.* 1695–1769).
[892] Robert Clayton* (1695–1758).
[893] Either Henry Hoare* (1705–85) or his uncle Benjamin Hoare* (1693–1749/50), bankers.
[894] Daniel Dering* (?–1730).

Since I wrote and sealed the enclosed I have heard something which makes it highly expedient for me to draw for the money which I left in the South Sea Annuities,* and must therefore request the favour of your Lordship to sell the same out of hand and place it together with dividend due thereupon in a sure banker's hand, and to send me as soon as possible directions how to draw for it. I shall ever acknowledge this with the many other obligations I owe your Lordship. If your Lordship will be so good as to send a duplicate of the said directions, one by the Admiralty and the other by Mr. Newman's[895] conveyance (to whom my humble service), it will be the likelier to come to my hands.

177 BERKELEY TO PERCIVAL[896]

EP, BL Add. MS 47032, fols. 106v–07.

Newport, 28 March 1729

My Lord,

Sometime I wrote to your Lordship requesting the favour of you to sell my South Sea Annuities* and place the money in a banker's hand making it payable to my order, and if in Mr. Hoare's[897] to see it put into a distinct article from the Bermuda accounts, to prevent confounding my private money with that of the College.[898] I know not whether my letter arrived, and therefore repeat the same request by the opportunity of a gentleman, who I am just told is going from Boston to be ordained in England.[899] As he intends to return I shall hope for a line from your Lordship by him with directions how to draw for my money. You see my Lordship the genuine effects of your great goodness is trouble to yourself and benefit to your friends; though if I had known what I now do, I should have avoided trespassing on your Lordship's good nature and brought my money in specie with me, which would have been more to my advantage.

I have now some experience of this place, and can tell your Lordship the climate is like that of Italy north of Rome, and in my opinion not quite so cold, though this season has been reckoned colder than ordinary. The land is

---

[895] Henry Newman* (1670–1743).

[896] In the margin of Percival's letterbook: "Dean Berkeley received 16 May, answered 14 June" [Letter 185].

[897] Either Henry Hoare* (1705–85) or his uncle Benjamin Hoare* (1693–1749/50).

[898] The money set aside for the founding of St. Paul's College, Bermuda.

[899] Anglican ministers in America were forced to travel to England for their ordination. Queen Anne* (1665–1714) attempted to create four new bishoprics in the Americas, but her efforts were blocked by forces keen on keeping the colonies dependent on England.

pleasantly diversified with hills, vales, and rising grounds. Here are also some amusing rocky scenes. There are not wanting several fine rivulets and groves. The sea, too, mixed with capes and adjacent islands, makes very delightful prospects. But I forget myself and am running the risk of being thought romantic, though I assure you I write much below the truth. The town is prettily built, contains about five thousand souls, and hath a very fine harbour. The people industrious, and though less orthodox, I cannot say they have less virtue (I am sure they have more regularity) than those I left in Europe. They are indeed a strange medley of different persuasions, which nevertheless do all agree in one point, viz. that the Church of England is the second best. Mr. Honyman,[900] the only Episcopal clergyman in this island, in whose house I now am, is a person of very good sense and merit on all accounts, much more than I expected to have found in this place.

I must send my letter by this morning's post to Boston, so have time to say no more but that I am and ever shall be, My Lord

your Lordship's most obliged and most obedient humble servant,

Geo: Berkeley

My best respects to my Lady and all your family. I long to know how you all do, Mr. Dering,[901] etc. and what is become of Père Courayer,[902] to whom pray my humble service.

178 BERKELEY TO BERNON[903]

LRIHS, Bernon Papers MS 294, pp. 86–87. Photostat at TCD, MS 4309.

Newport, 9 Avril 1729

Monsieur,

J'aurois repondu plutôt [plus tôt] a la lettre dont vous m'avez honoré si je n'etois empeché tantôt par des affaires tantôt par un indisposition laquelle me travailloit de tems en tems, mais ni l'un ni l'autre m'auroit [ne m'auroit] detourné d'avoir rendue cette [ce] service a l'eglise de Dieu que vous attendez de moy si j'avois quelque pouvoir de juger ou de decider sur cet affaire

---

[900] James Honeyman* (c. 1675–1750).
[901] Daniel Dering* (?–1730).
[902] Pierre-François le Courayer* (1681–1776).
[903] Gabriel Bernon* (1644–1736). Corrections to Berkeley's French to improve readability are made in square brackets. Luce published this letter without translation in "More Unpublished Berkeley Letters and New Berkeleiana," 37–38.

malheureuse dont vous m'avoit [m'avez] fait un recit si touchant & si pleine [plein] de zele pour la gloire de Dieu.

Il faut avouer, Monsieur, que je ne suis qu'un simple passager dans ce pais sans etre revetûe [reveftûe] d'aucune autorité ni jurisdiction sur les Eglises de cette colonie & que toute ma petite jurisdiction (telle [quelle?] qu'elle soit) est bornée par la [le] diocese de London-derry en Irlande. Vous voyez donc qu'il e[s]t impossible que j'apportasse aucune [aucun] remede a votres [vos] inconveniens les quelles [quels] neanmoins me touchant [touchent] au fond du coeur. Je puis cependant vous assurer que je ne doute gueres que Monseigneur l'Evêque de Londres & l'honorable Societé prendront des mesures tres justes & tres sages pour y remedier. C'est donc de leur conduite qu'il faut attendre la [le] remede que vous souhatez [souhaitez]. Je ne laisseroy pas pourtant de supplier le Bon Dieu de secourir & de protéger votre Eglise de Providence la quelle est si rudement secouée par cet [ce] triste evenement dont vous m'avez fait part & de vous consoler dans votre venerable viellesse par la decouverte de cette verité pour la quelle vous faites des voeus si ardens. Vous aurois [aurez] la bonte Monsieur de me pardonner ce [de ce] que j'ecris dans une langue que je n'ay pratiqué que tres rarement & de croire que je suis avec beaucoup de respect, Monsieur

votre tres humble & tres obeissant serviteur,

Geor: Berkeley

Sir,

I would have responded to your letter earlier with which you honoured me if I were not precluded sometimes by my affairs and sometimes by an indisposition that has bothered me from time to time, but neither one nor the other would have prevented me from having given service to the Church of God that you were expecting from me, if I had some power to judge or decide this unfortunate case, of which you related to me such a touching tale so full of zeal for the glory of God.[904]

To speak frankly, sir, I am nothing but a simple passenger in this country without any authority or jurisdiction concerning the Churches of this colony, and all of my small jurisdiction (as little as it is) is limited by the diocese of Londonderry in Ireland. You see, therefore, that it is impossible for me to bring any solution to your inconveniences that nevertheless touch the bottom of my

---

[904] For some suggestive details about the issue Bernon might have brought to Berkeley for his help, see Wilkins Updike, *A History of the Episcopal Church in Narrangansett Rhode Island*, 2nd edn., revised and enlarged by Daniel Goodwin (Boston, MA: Merymount Press, 1907), esp. pp. 41–60.

heart. I can, however, assure you that I have no doubt that the Bishop of London[905] and the honourable society will take very wise and just measures to solve the problem. It is thus on their acting that you must wait for the solution you desire. However, I would not restrain myself from supplicating the Good God to rescue and protect your church of Providence, which is so roughly shaken by this sad event of which you have informed me, and to counsel you in your venerable old age by the discovery of this truth for which you so ardently wish. You will kindly forgive me, sir, for what I am writing in a language I have practised only rarely and believe that I am, with much respect, sir,

> your very humble & respectful servant,
> Geor: Berkeley

179 BERKELEY TO BENSON[906]

Yale, MS Vault File Berkeley.

Newport, in Rhode Island, 11 April 1729

Dear Sir,

In compliance with your own desire I delayed writing till such time as I could say something from my own experience of this place and people. The inhabitants are a mixed kind containing many sects and subdivisions of sects. Here are four sorts of Anabaptists besides Independents, Quakers and many of no profession at all. These several sects do all agree in one point viz.: that each thinks our church the second best.

The climate is like that of Italy, though not quite so cold in the winter as I have known it in many places north of Rome. But the spring is later. The fields are now green and the trees budded but the leaves are not yet shot forth. To make amends I am told on all hands that they have the pleasantest summer and the longest and most delicious autumn in the world. The great plenty of melons, standard peaches, and wild vines etc. are a proof of this. The face of the country is pleasantly laid out in hills vales woods and rising grounds, watered with

---

[905] Edmund Gibson* (1669–1748). The bishop of London was responsible for all ecclesiastical affairs in the American colonies.

[906] The letter is addressed to "The Reverend Dr. Benson Prebendary of Durham to be left at the Bishop of Durham's house in Hannover Square, London." This letter was first published in A. A. Luce, "A New Berkeley Letter and the Endorsement," *Proceedings of the Royal Irish Academy* 51, sec. C (1945–46): 86.

several rivulets. Here are also in some parts very amazing rocky scenes, and fine landscapes [*sic*] of the sea intermixed with capes and islands. But I forbear for fear of being thought Romantic. Give me leave only to add that the town of Newport is exceeding pretty and hath the advantage of a very fine situation both for prospect and access, the harbour being very commodious. The people are industrious and not given to quarrel about Religious matters. Mr. Honeyman[907] the only Episcopal clergyman of this island is a scholar and every way a man of considerable merit. James[908] is not yet arrived from Virginia. Dalton[909] hath been here some time, he and Smibert[910] are now at Boston where they propose passing a few days. Your little friend hath been much embarrassed in dealing with a Quaker of this island for the hire of his farm. This affair is one of the greatest eclat and importance that for many years hath been transacted in this Rhodian Government the principal persons of the State having all interposed therein. I have purchased a pleasant farm of about one hundred acres with two fine groves and winding rivulet upon it.[911] Till such time as I hear of my associates being arrived with his Majesty's bounty money at Bermuda I do not think I could be so useful in any part of the world as in this place. The subject of our last conversation I am now convinced of more than ever. God keep it warm in your heart. I intended to have wrote by this same opportunity to Dr. Rundle,[912] but think it will do better to wait for another, not to overcharge you with two letters at once. I doubt not you have made the proper apologies to my friends which I desired. You will be so good as to make my humble service and best respects accepted of all our common friends: To mention particulars would be endless. Those in Hannover Square & Dover Street are always especially to be understood. Sir Philip York[913] & Mr. Talbot[914] who had been so useful in furthering our college patents and so very obliging to me might well have expected I should not have left the Kingdom without waiting on them. But you knew the reason. I have all the gratitude imaginable towards these gentlemen and a most particular respect for my Lady York[915] whom I look upon to be one of the most reasonable and valuable women in Europe. God protect and preserve

---

[907] James Honeyman* (*c.* 1675–1750).

[908] John James* (?–1741).

[909] Richard Dalton* (*c.* 1695–1769).

[910] John Smibert* (1688–1751).

[911] Whitehall, near present-day Newport, Rhode Island.

[912] Thomas Rundle* (1687/88–1743).

[913] Philip York* (or Yorke) (1690–1764), first Earl of Hardwicke. He was attorney general at this time (since 1724) and would be made lord chancellor in 1737.

[914] Charles Talbot* (1685–1737), first Baron Talbot of Hensol.

[915] Margaret (*née* Lygon) York (Yorke) (*c.* 1695–1761).

you Dear Archdeacon to the joy of all your friends among whom I am sure you will never forget those in this new world, who are most sincerely yours, but no body is or can be more than

Dear Sir,

your most affectionate humble servant,

Geor: Berkeley

I have not had a line from Europe (but one from Mr. Newman)[916] since my arrival. Nothing can be more welcome than a letter from you. Enclose in a cover to Thomas Corbet[917] Esqe at the Admiralty office.

His majesty's instructions meet with great opposition in the neighbouring government of New England. The Church of England men as many as are in the assembly or the council are all unanimous for complying in the most respectful manner with the Governor. Every impartial statesman who knows how things are carried in these parts must conclude it would be the most effectual, the cheapest, & on all accounts the most desirable way to promote and secure his Majesty's interests in these parts by planting an Episcopal Seminary in Rhode Island which I doubt not would greatly lessen that party which at present gives uneasiness in New England. You will know the proper use to be made of this hint, or whether any use should be made of it, before the St. Christopher's* money be paid or the mind of the court be declared further on that matter. I long to hear[918] what people say or mean to do.

180 BERKELEY TO PRIOR

LR, *pp. 209–12.*

Newport, in Rhode Island, 24 April 1729

Dear Tom,

I can by this time say something to you, from my own experience, of this place and people. The inhabitants are of a mixed kind, consisting of many sects and subdivisions of sects. Here are four sorts of Anabaptists, besides Presbyterians, Quakers, Independents, and many of no profession at all. Notwithstanding so many differences, here are fewer quarrels about religion than elsewhere, the people living peaceably with their neighbours, of whatever profession. They all

---

[916] Henry Newman* (1670–1743).
[917] Thomas Corbett* (?–1751).
[918] Inserted but stricken after "hear" is "something."

agree in one point, that the Church of England is the second best. The climate is like that of Italy, and not at all colder in the winter than I have known it every where north of Rome. The spring is late; but, to make amends, they assure me the autumns are the finest and longest in the world, and the summers are much pleasanter than those of Italy by all accounts, forasmuch as the grass continues green, which it doth not there. This island is pleasantly laid out in hills and vales and rising grounds; hath plenty of excellent springs and fine rivulets, and many delightful landscapes of rocks and promontories and adjacent islands. The provisions are very good; so are the fruits, which are quite neglected, though vines sprout up of themselves to an extraordinary size, and seem as natural to this soil as to any I ever saw. The town of Newport contains about six thousand souls, and is the most thriving flourishing place in all America for its bigness. It is very pretty and pleasantly situated. I was never more agreeably surprised than at the first sight of the town and its harbour. I could give you some hints that may be of use to you if you were disposed to take advice; but of all men in the world, I never found encouragement to give you any.

By this opportunity I have drawn on Messrs. Wogan and Aspinwall[919] for ninety-seven pounds, and shall soon draw for about five hundred pounds more. I depend on your taking care that my bills be duly paid. I hope you have well concerted that matter with Swift & Company,* as I desired you. My draughts shall always be within my income; and if at any time they should be made before payment thereof into their hands, I will pay interest. I doubt not you keep my farmers punctual.

I have heard nothing from you or any of my friends in England or Ireland, which makes me suspect my letters were in one of the vessels that wrecked. I write in great haste, and have no time to say a word to my brother Robin.[920] Let him know we are in good health. Once more take care that my draughts are duly honoured (which is of the greatest importance to my credit here); and if I can serve you in these parts, you may command

your affectionate humble servant,

Geor. Berkeley

Send the state of my accounts and affairs, directed and enclosed to Thomas Corbet,[921] Esq., at the Admiralty Office in London. Direct all your letters the same way. I long to hear from you.

---

[919] Wogan* (?–?) and Aspinwall* (?–?).

[920] Robert Berkeley* (*c.* 1699–1787).

[921] Thomas Corbett* (?–1751).

181 PERCIVAL TO BERKELEY

EP, BL Add. MS 47032, fols. 110v–11.

London, 25 April 1729

Dear Sir,

The news of your safe arrival at Rhode Island gives all your friends here unspeakable pleasure, and the more so that a current report had obtained that you were lost in your passage. I hope as Providence has preserved you so far you will live to perfect the great work you are upon, and with long health enjoy the satisfaction that will arise from it.

I suppose by your design of buying lands where you are that you are determined to fix the college in Rhode Island, which, by what I have heard of the dismal effects of a tempest some months ago on Bermudas, may be the most eligible place of the two, and I should hope the government will not scruple the change of the place, when you shall represent your reasons in the strong light you are so capable of doing.

I obeyed your commands as soon as I was able, and have sold your £2,000 South Sea Annuities* for £2,047. 10s. 0d. The charge of the brokerage came to £2. 10. 0, so I have placed the remaining £2,045. 0.0 with Mr. Benjamin Hoare[922] and Company, who told me he would make a separate article for you under the head of Dr. George Berkeley's private account of money, to distinguish it from the other articles entitled 'Subscription money to Bermudas'. There was no difficulty or objection I could see in it, or made by him, and he will pay this money to your order, drawing on Benjamin Hoare and Company and mentioning it to be the money on your private account. His partners are Henry Hoare[923] and Christopher Arnold.[924]

I believe you are very little solicitous how affairs go in Europe, other than what regards your college, and indeed I have little to send you. What I know is, that the Parliament have called for an account of the lands of St. Christopher* sold. So on another occasion you will be informed what progress has been made therein, and how near you approach to receiving your £20,000.

As to public affairs, there came an account this week that the King of Spain[925] is willing to come into our terms, provided the Allies of Hanover

---

[922] Benjamin Hoare* (1693–1749/50).
[923] Henry Hoare* (1705–85).
[924] Christopher Arnold (?–?), a goldsmith, made partner in the Hoare Bank in 1725.
[925] Philip V (1683–1746).

will prevail on the Emperor to consent that Don Carlos[926] be immediately agreed for successor to the State of Florence, supposing the present Duke should die issueless.

You have most affectionate services from all my family, who with me desire their humble service to Mrs. Berkeley,[927] and the rest of your fellow voyagers. If you have any further commands I desire you will not spare me, for on all occasions I shall be ready to the utmost to show myself what I ever was from the time of our first acquaintance to the end of my life.

> Dear Sir,
>
> Your, etc.,
>
> Percival

I must tell you that I cannot receive your dividend on the £2,000 bill until after the 23rd of May. When that is paid I will do by it as by the annuity I have sold.

I send you a duplicate of this letter by Mr. Newman's[928] packet.

182 NEWMAN TO BERKELEY[929]

SPCK MS D4/41, fols. 20–21.

Bartlett's Buildings, 29 April 1729

Revd Sir,

The news from Boston of your safe arrival after a perilous passage has happily delivered your friends here from the pain they were in upon the apprehension of your being lost. I shall be glad to hear that things answer your expectation, and that your main design may at length be accomplished if not in the manner you first proposed, yet in such a one as may be effectual. I believe you are now satisfied that if you had made a short voyage to America before you had published your *Proposal*[930] you would have very much altered your scheme, but I hope you will have it in your power to rectify your first project in whatever it was amiss, and

---

[926] Don Carlos (1716–88) was the son of Philip V of Spain and Isabella of Parma. He ruled as duke of Parma, by right of his mother (1732–34), was King of Naples (1734-59) and ascended to the throne of Spain as Charles III in 1759.

[927] Anne (*née* Forster) Berkeley* (?–1786).

[928] Henry Newman* (1670–1743).

[929] Addressed "To the Revd Dr. Geo. Berkeley, Dean of Derry in Rhode Island, By the Benjamin & William Brigantine, Captain Bennet Master to Rhode Island." A copy is published in W. O. B. Allen and Edmund McClure, *History of the Society for Promoting Christian Knowledge: 1698–1898* (New York: Burt Franklin, 1898 [reprinted 1970]), p. 244.

[930] Berkeley's *Proposal for the Better Supplying of Churches in our Foreign Plantations, and for Converting the Savage Americans to Christianity* (1724/25). For the text, see *Works*, vol. VII, pp. 335–61.

that your friends here may easily obtain a royal licence for such alterations as may be recommended by you.

My Lord Percival[931] does me the honour to call on me just now with the enclosed, which I embrace the first opportunity of forwarding. I shall be glad to hear that the climate agrees with you and your Lady[932] & that Mr. James[933] & Mr. Dalton[934] have their health and meet with their wishes after sharing so many perils with you. Pray give my humble service to them. I have received £20 of the £40 bill you gave me on Mr. Hoare[935] towards paying for the parcel of books you had from Mr. Downing, but wait your order for laying out the remainder before I receive it. The books you had came to 22:13:7 according to the account enclosed. I wish you all manner of prosperity and am,

    Revd Sir, your most humble servant,

    H. N.

If you should be induced to pitch your stakes in N. York government there is an Island called Fisher's Island of which Mr. Winthrop is proprietor,[936] who I believe would give you a good tract of land towards encouraging your settlement there. Mr. A. D. Benson[937] is well & sends his humble service to you.

183 BERKELEY TO BERNON[938]

LRIHS, Bernon Papers MS 294, pp. 88–89. Photostat at TCD, MS 4309.

30 Mai 1729

Monsieur,

    Le promt [prompt] retour du messager qui m'apportât la lettre dont vous m'aves honoré ne me permet pas de vous ecrire une response digne de votre belle prose & belle poesie: je vous remercie pour l'une & l'autre.

[931] John Percival* (1683–1748).

[932] Anne (née Forster) Berkeley* (?–1786).

[933] John James* (?–1741).

[934] Richard Dalton* (c. 1695–1769).

[935] Benjamin Hoare* (1693–1749/50).

[936] Fisher's Island lies at the eastern end of Long Island Sound near the Connecticut–Rhode Island border, not that far from Newport. In 1640 the General Court of the Massachusetts Bay Colony granted the island to John Winthrop the Younger (1606–76), later governor of Connecticut. It is unclear exactly which Winthrop Newman is referring to (perhaps John Winthrop [1681–1776], son of Wait-Stil Winthrop [1642–1717] and grandson of John Winthrop the Younger), but the island stayed in the Winthrop family into the nineteenth century.

[937] Presumably archdeacon Martin Benson* (1689–1752).

[938] Corrections to the French to improve readability are made in square brackets. Luce published this letter without translation in "More Unpublished Berkeley Letters and New Berkeleiana," 38.

Vos reflexions sur les evenemens de ce monde montrent une [un] zele tres louable pour la religion & pour la gloire de Dieu, qui dans le tems [temps] que bon semblera a sa sagesse infinie mettera fin aux schismes aux heresies a la tyrannie du Pape & aux scandales de tous [toutes] façons. Pour ce qui regarde le Monsieur qui se trouve chez vous permettez moy de vous dire que comme je n'ay aucun droit de decider sur son affaire je ne trouve pas a propos de m'y meler du tout. Je prie le bon Dieu de vous conduire & tous autres la dessus en sorte que tout scandale se puisse passer. On croit qu'il feroit bien de ne pas venir a Newport pour rencontrer le clergé jusque a ce qu'une response vien [vienne] de la part de Monseigneur l'Eveque de Londres sur son sujet.

Je vous prie de me croire avec beaucoup de respect, Monsieur,

votre tres humble & tres obeissant serviteur,

Geor: Berkeley

May 30 eme 1729

Sir,

The prompt return of the messenger who brought me the letter with which you honor me does not allow me to write to you an answer worthy of your beautiful prose and poetry: I thank you for both of them.[939]

Your reflections on the events of this world show a very laudable zeal for religion and the glory of God, who, when convenient[940] to his infinite wisdom, will put an end to schisms, to heresies, popish tyranny and to scandals of all kinds. As to what concerns the gentleman in your home, allow me to tell you that since I do not have any right to decide about his case I do not find it appropriate to interfere at all. I pray good God to guide you and all the others above in such a way that all this scandal may pass away. It is believed that he would do well not to come to Newport to meet the clergy until a response comes from monseigner the Bishop of London[941] about him.

I beg you to believe that I am with much respect, Sir

your very humble and very obedient servant,

Geor: Berkeley

---

[939] Literally "I thank you for the one and the other."
[940] Literally "In the time it will appear good ..."
[941] Edmund Gibson* (1669–1748).

184 BERKELEY TO PRIOR

LR, pp. 212-14.

Newport, in Rhode Island, 12 June 1729

Dear Tom,

Being informed that an inhabitant of this country is on the point of going for Ireland, I would not omit writing to you, and acquainting you that I received two of yours, dated September 23 and December 21, wherein you repeat what you formerly told me about Finney's legacy.[942] The case of Marshall's[943] death I had not before considered. I leave it to you to act in this matter for me as you would for yourself if it was your own case. I depend on your diligence about finishing what remains to be done, and your punctuality in seeing my money duly paid in to Swift & Company,* and sending me accounts thereof.

If you have any service to be done in these parts, or if you would know any particulars, you need only send me your questions, and direct me how I may be serviceable to you. The winter, it must be allowed, was much sharper than the usual winters in Ireland, but not at all sharper than I have known them in Italy. To make amends, the summer is exceedingly delightful; and if the spring begins late, the autumn ends proportionably later than with you, and is said to be the finest in the world.

I snatch this moment to write; and have time only to add, that I have got a son, who, I thank God, is likely to live. My wife joins with me in her service to you. I am, dear Tom,

> your affectionate humble Servant,
> G. Berkeley

I find it hath been reported in Ireland that we propose settling here. I must desire you to discountenance any such report. The truth is, if the King's bounty were paid in, and the charter could be removed hither, I should like it better than Bermuda: but if this were mentioned before the payment of said money, it may perhaps hinder it, and defeat all our designs.

As to what you say of Hamilton's[944] proposal, I can only answer at present by a question, viz. Whether it be possible for me, in my absence, to be put in possession of the Deanery of Dromore? Desire him to make that point clear, and you shall hear farther from me.

[942] Luce speculates that "Finney" is a relation of Jonathan Swift's.* See *Works*, vol. IX, p. 80.

[943] Presumably this is a speculation about what would happen were Robert Marshall* (c. 1690–1772), Berkeley's coexecutor of Hester Van Homrigh's* will, to die.

[944] John Hamilton (?–1729) was dean of Dromore (1724–29). Luce speculates that he proposed to Berkeley that they switch deaneries (Dromore for Derry). See *Works*, vol. IX, p. 80.

185 PERCIVAL TO BERKELEY

EP, BL Add. MS 47032, fols. 118v–19v.

London, 12 June 1729

Dear Sir,

The 25th of April last I writ you an account that your £2,000 South Sea Annuities* were sold and put into Mr. Hoare's[945] hands. I made a duplicate and sent one as you desired by Mr. Newman's[946] conveyance, and the other I gave to Mr. Corbett.[947] I cannot doubt their coming to you safe. I had for your annuities £2,045 exclusive of the charge of brokerage. I have since received the interest due on them, amounting to £80, which I likewise paid to Mr. Hoare, and is with the rest put into a separate article under the head of your private account to distinguish it from the subscription money. You are to draw on Benjamin Hoare and Company, and so mention it when you draw as money on your private account. His partners are Henry Hoare and Christopher Arnold.

Your second letter dated 23 March was delivered [to] me by the gentleman who came to take orders. You desired me to write by him when he returned, but there was too great uncertainty of our seeing one another, and therefore I told him I would not trouble him to call, but would write by Mr. Corbett or Newman's packet.

Your purchasing in Rhode Island is no secret, but I was the last to own it. A friend of yours mentioned it at Court to some company of which I was one, and was more particular in the acres bought and money laid out and profitableness of your bargain than I knew before.

The few I have conversed with on the subject of your voyage think Rhode Island a better place than Bermuda to fix your college in, but what prospect there is of getting the £20,000, your friends employed therein know best. A good deal of the St. Christopher* money is come in.

You write so agreeably of the face of the country and climate, and the manners of the people, that almost you persuade me to be a Rhodian. I hear you have already preached to the Quakers and that they come to our Church to hear you, acknowledging you to be an inspired man of God, who preach by the Spirit and are come so far without interest to pour out the word.[948] Should you

---

[945] Benjamin Hoare* (1693–1749/50).
[946] Henry Newman* (1670–1743).
[947] Thomas Corbett* (?–1751).
[948] Berkeley preached at Trinity Church in Newport on a number of occasions, starting shortly after his arrival in Newport on 26 January 1729. See Letter 189.

be able to do no more than bring them over, it were a service to religion worth your voyage, and what will be a consolation to you if your primary view should miscarry, but God forbid it should, and I cannot believe so great, and pious, disinterested undertaking will want the assistance of God or man.

Our Parliament have been up some time and passed a great many good laws: two for the relief of prisoners for debt who now come out to the number of £30,000 as the lowest reckoners put it, nor can new debtors be confined hereafter without a weekly allowance made them by their creditors. By another law we have regulated the number of attorneys and cut off the practice of those who are not regularly educated. We have passed also a law for better paving the streets, and lighting them, another good one against perjury and one to prevent bribery in elections which cuts it up by the roots. This last was hard fought and we carried it by two votes. Our committee for visiting the gaols[949] has got great honour, and we have detected[950] most crying abuses in the Fleet and Marshalsea prisons. Next year the committee will be revived and we shall go on with the others. Huggins[951] who was the warden of the Fleet has been tried for murder committed on a debtor there and a special verdict found against him. Bambridge[952] his successor was also tried for the murder of another debtor but acquitted. However he still lies in Newgate to be tried for robbery.

As to peace we are still under great uncertainty, but a large fleet under Sir Charles Wager[953] is speedily to sail and as we conceive to the Mediterranean, the Spaniards having got together a good number of ships for some design of importance. Nevertheless, it is believed that we shall have a peace before winter.

---

[949] John Percival* (1683–1748) was a member of the Committee of the House of Commons appointed to inquire into the State of Gaols. The committee was led by James Edward Oglethorpe* (1696–1785).

[950] Rand and Luce have "delicted" for "detected."

[951] John Huggins, Esq. (?–?) was a warden of Fleet prison. He was tried and convicted in 1729 of various crimes, including dereliction of his duties, cruelty, extortion, illegally selling his office to another, and the murder of a debtor in his charge. See *A Complete Collection of State Trials and Proceedings for High Treason and Other Crimes and Misdemeanors from the Earliest Period to the Year 1783*, compiled by T. B. Howell (London: Hansard, 1816), vol. XVII, pp. 297 ff.

[952] Thomas Bambridge (?–?) was Huggins's replacement as warden of Fleet prison and formerly its deputy-warden. Like Huggins, Bambridge was accused of various crimes (including extortion and murder), but he was acquitted on the charge of murder.

[953] Charles Wager (1666–1743), naval officer and politician. In May 1729 Wager was ordered to take command of thirty-three ships to be supplemented with some Dutch vessels. The squadron, however, never actually left port and was popularly ridiculed as the "stay-at-home fleet." The fleet remained in readiness until it was learned that Spain would sign a firm treaty. Wager then served as commander of the fleet that oversaw the implementation of the treaty provisions in Italy through 1731. He would be selected as the first lord of the Admiralty in 1733 and was elected MP for Westminster in 1734.

All my family desire their humble service to you and your Lady and the gentlemen with you; and I hope I may now wish you joy of Mrs. Berkeley's being safely delivered.[954] My sister Dering[955] has been long out of order and I know not what to think of it. Her case puzzles the doctors. Daniel is in the old way, making bloody water, and pursuing his interest at Court where yet he has got nothing; but he is in high grace with the Prince from which something must come.[956] My wife still complains of the cholic and uses her laudanum. We go this summer to the Scarborow [sic] waters in Yorkshire from which journey I hope she will find benefit.

Young Mr. Southwell is to be married to a daughter of my Lady Sands with [£]10000 portion down, and £1500 a year settled on him immediately beside her fortune.[957] I am

yours etc.,
Percival

186 BENSON TO BERKELEY

BL Add. MS 39311, fol. 12.

London, 23 June 1729

Dear Mr. Dean,

It was great joy to me to hear from your own hand, what I had before heard from others, that you were safely arrived in Rhode Island, and that Rhode Island is so agreeable to you; and I am the more pleased it is, as I find so little likelihood of the £20,000 being paid in order to remove you thence to Bermuda. I know how much it is your desire and design to be doing a great deal of good wherever you are, and I hope it may [be in] your power to do it in some other place if they will not permit you to do it where you at first proposed. [I said] to Ld. Pembroke[958] as a thought of my own whe[ther] they would give some part of the money if they [could not be] persuaded to pay in the whole. This he said it [would be dan]gerous to propose, because the offering to accept [a part] might be interpreted by them the giving up a right [to the whole], and that such an offer

---

954 Henry Berkeley* (1729–after 1756) was born around 12 June 1729 and baptised in Trinity Church in Newport on 1 September of the same year.

955 Mary (*née* Parker) Dering* (1692–1731).

956 The reference is to Daniel Dering* (?–1730). There is some evidence Dering had kidney stones. See Letter 206.

957 Edward Southwell (1705–55), son of Edward Southwell* (1671–1730), married Catherine Watson (?–1765), daughter of Lady Catherine Sondes, wife of Lewis Watson, (1655–1724), first Earl of Rockingham.

958 Thomas Herbert* (1656/57–1733), eighth Earl of Pembroke.

should come from them and not from [your] agents. The old Earl [Pembroke?] has been enquiring and rum [inating?] much about these affairs, but with what intention, [or with?] any or not I do not know. This I know, that if you do not take care to return an answer to the query I sent you enclosed in my former letter to you (which I hope came safe to your hands), you will be as much out of the good graces of the Earl as you are in them now. I have not been wanting to say everything which I thought might be proper in order to promote, and to be silent about everything which I feared might prejudice your good designs. As the Master of the Rolls[959] seems very well affected towards them, I have [talked?] a good deal with him, but as he told me the affair of [Rhode Is]land would be brought before the Parliament, I have [been very] cautious since in dropping anything of any [. . . ?] settling within the Government. So great is the [prejudice of?] some men, that a certain wise gentleman told [me he was] persuaded that you acted in concert with the [men of?] New England, and was fomenting the opposition [there] to settling a salary on the Governour. And so [. . .?] interested-ness of others, that the good example they hear your Lady is setting of beginning a manufacture which herself will wear, they look upon as a dangerous prece-dent, and what may prove in time prejudicial to the manufactures of England.[960] Thus you see your company and your designs are not inconsiderable in the eyes of the world. I acquainted you in my other letter that there is a likelihood of Dr. Clayton's being made a bishop in Ireland,[961] and by this means of that being really compassed by his mea[ns] which you projected in relation to another person. The [Clerk?] of the Council, to show you that the highest honours cannot secure men from sickness and human infirmities, [is so] mortified by a very severe fit of Rheumatism, and he is so much humbled that he has this day ac[tually] sworn in my Official of the Archdeaconry of Be[?]. [I have no] private news to write you, and I wish I could send [any] publick that is good, but those wise heads which [might be our de]fence against evils which might arise [?] from your going to Bermuda have not been [aware of those?] which were before their eyes, and which we are now so [much in dan]ger of feeling that war is ready everywhere.

I am going to Durham in a few days, and propose to [stay there] some months. My Brother Secker,[962] Dr. Rundle,[963] etc. are there. [I am] much delighted to hear

---

959 Sir Joseph Jekyll* (1662–1738).
960 Anne (*née* Forster) Berkeley* (?–1786), Berkeley's wife, advocated spinning as a cottage industry and promised to wear (some) clothes of her own making. See Letter 172.
961 Robert Clayton* (1695–1758). Clayton was appointed bishop of Killala and Achonry in 1729.
962 Thomas Secker* (1693–1768). Secker married Catherine Benson in October 1725, hence "brother Secker."
963 Thomas Rundle* (1687/88–1743).

of your health. I am desired from Ld. Pomfret,[964] the Bishop of Durham,[965] and many other places and persons, to make their compliments to you, and I desire you to make mine to James,[966] Dicky,[967] and Smibert,[968] and to the ladies too, for I look [on them as] my acquaintance though I had never the honour to see them. As Dicky is my vassal, my r[egal privileges?] will extend to all his possessions however far he flies from me, and therefore [I consider myself] a party concerned in the title he is making out to his new purchase.

Dear Mr. Dean, I have nothing more to add at present, than wishing health to yourselves and prosperity to all your designs. You need, you can say nothing more to recommend Rhode Island and make me wish myself there, than that you are there and the good company with you.

> I am, dear Mr. Dean,
> with the greatest esteem and truest affection,
> your most sincere and faithful friend and servant,
> M. B.

Sir John[969] has a project for propagating the race of blacks in Europe, which I suppose he has communicated to you.

187 BERKELEY TO PERCIVAL

EP, BL Add. MS 47032, fol. 122–22v.

Newport, in Rhode Island, 27 June 1729

My Lord,

As I had reason to believe that before this time the St. Christopher's* money would have been returned into the exchequer, and as we were alarmed in these parts with speedy expectation of a war, I intended to have drawn my money out of the South Sea Annuities* into this part of the world, which in that case would have been more convenient for my affairs. But the rumour of a war daily decreasing and no account being come that the St. Christopher* money is yet

---

[964] Thomas Fermor, second Baron Leominster (1698?–1753). He was created Earl of Pomfret on 27 December 1721.
[965] William Talbot* (1658–1730).
[966] John James* (?–1741).
[967] Richard Dalton* (c. 1695–1769).
[968] John Smibert* (1688–1751).
[969] The referent is unclear.

paid into the treasury, I think it more advisable to let my money remain where it was. In case therefore it is not already taken out, I desire it may remain in the South Sea Annuities.* The trouble I give your Lordship on this subject is I am confident more uneasy to myself than it is to you whose ready and obliging goodness I have so often experienced.

I am here in no small anxiety waiting the event of things. I understand that in Ireland they have been told it is my resolution to settle here at all events. This report I am concerned at and would have it by all means discouraged, for it may give a handle to the Treasury for withholding the £20,000, and at the same time disgust my associates. The truth is, I am not in my own power, not being at liberty to act without the concurrence as well of the Ministry as of my associates. I cannot therefore place the college where I please; and though on some accounts I did and do still think it would more probably be attended with success if placed here than in Bermuda, yet if the government and the gentlemen engaged with me should persist in the old scheme, I am ready to go thither, and with God's blessing actually shall do so as soon as I hear the money is received and my associates are arrived. This is the truth and I beg the favour of your Lordship to mention it as often as occasion offers. Before I left England I was reduced to a difficult situation. Had I continued there, the report would have obtained (which I found beginning to spread) that I had dropped the design after it had cost me and my friends so much trouble and expense. On the other hand, if I had taken leave of my friends, even those who assisted and approved my undertaking would have condemned my coming abroad before the King's bounty was received. This obliged me to come away in the private manner that I did, and to run the risk of a tedious winter voyage. Nothing less would have convinced the world that I was in earnest, after the report I knew was growing to the contrary.

For my amusement in this new world I have got a little son whom my wife nurses.[970]

I shall trouble your Lordship no farther than with my best wishes for yourself and family to whom I am,

> a most devoted and most humble servant,
> Geo: Berkeley

Under cover to your Lordship's most humble servant,
Henry Newman[971]

---

[970] Henry Berkeley* (1729–after 1756) was born around 12 June 1729 and baptised in Trinity Church in Newport on 1 September of the same year.
[971] Henry Newman* (1670–1743).

188 BERKELEY TO NEWMAN[972]

EP, BL Add. MS 47032, fol. 140–40v.

Rhode Island, Newport, 27 June 1729

Sir,

Since my arrival in this island I received the favour of a packet from you, which I long since acknowledged in a letter consigned to Mr. Marshall,[973] who I doubt not hath forwarded the same to you. It is needless to send you any account of this place or climate, which you are so well acquainted with.[974] I shall only observe that upon the whole it seems to me a proper situation for a college, though it must be owned that provisions are neither so plenty nor so cheap as I apprehended. And as to the inhabitants, I find them divided in their opinions, those in the country, or (as they are termed here) the men in the woods, being grossly ignorant and uneducated, are not a little alarmed at the coming of strangers, and form many fears and ridiculous conclusions thereupon. The inhabitants of the town of Newport, particularly the churchmen, are much better disposed towards us.

I have wrote to some friends in England to take the proper steps for procuring a translation of the college from Bermuda to Rhode Island as soon as the £20,000 arising by sale of lands in St. Christopher's* is paid to our order, and I have furnished them with the weightiest reasons that occured for so doing, but I don't think it advisable to make this proposition, or say anything about it before the money is received. In the meantime I am understood to remain here till I hear of the said payment, and the arrival of my associates in Bermuda where I am to join them, which indeed is the truth of the case, supposing I should not be able to bring about the translation before-mentioned.

Believing your packets are taken particular care of, I have enclosed some letters under your cover, which I beg the favour of you to forward as directed, which will be an obligation upon,

    Sir,

    your most obedient humble servant,

    Geo: Berkeley

---

[972] This is a transcription of a copy of the letter from John Percival's* letterbooks.

[973] This Marshall is an unknown person. It is unlikely to be Robert Marshall* (1690–1772), Berkeley's coexecutor, since that would have entailed him placing an enclosure for London in a letter to Ireland.

[974] Henry Newman* (1670–1743) was born in Massachusetts.

189 BERKELEY TO PERCIVAL

EP, BL Add. MS 47032, fols. 132–33v.

Rhode Island, 30 August 1729

My Lord,

I congratulate your Lordship in the share you had in redressing the villanies in the Fleet Prison,[975] and was much pleased to find you recorded in the monthly Register (which with us supplies the place of all other newspapers), as a principal agent in that most laudable piece of justice and charity. At the same time I return my humble thanks to your Lordship for the favour of your letter and your goodness in taking my money out of the fund and placing it in Mr. Hoare's[976] hands: mine which I wrote to prevent your Lordship's giving yourself that trouble having it seems been sent too late. I am ashamed to desire your Lordship to put it again into the Annuities, but if this were done I should think it a great favour and be very cautious how I gave you any further trouble.

The truth is we were alarmed here by accounts of a war with Spain and that the stocks would fall, which alarm being since abated I have altered my design, so that I am now desirous to have interest for my money, and the rather because I have been at great expense since I saw you. And I know no other way of laying out my money but in the public funds, which I am told will be as secure at least as any private bankers. Rather than to break the sum of £2,000 (which I would have secured for my family) I have got credit for 600 pounds at the legal interest, which Mr. Prior[977] is to pay out of my Deanery. This enables me to perfect the purchase of my land and house in this island, which purchase in case the college should not go on will be much to my loss. For lands within this island being very well cleared and near an excellent harbour are very dear, at an average about ten pounds sterling an acre, and it was expedient I should buy lands fit to produce provisions, and near a good seaport where they may be easily exported [to] Bermuda for the supply of our college. True it is that on the continent within this government uncleared lands may be bought very cheap, even for a twentieth part of the above-mentioned price; but the clearing of them would be very expensive, and require much time, and in the interim they produce nothing. Though if they were left to lie till the colony fills, without any pains or any expense bestowed upon them, they would in time grow very

---

[975] See Letter 185.
[976] Benjamin Hoare* (1693–1749/50).
[977] Thomas Prior* (1681–1751).

valuable, and I should think this the best way of laying out my money in case the college were settled in these parts. But where it will be settled, or when is a point still in the dark, nor by what I can find likely to be cleared during the present uncertainty of public affairs. I doubt not the Treasury is backward in all payments; but I cannot, I will not, understand that they can form any resolve to withhold a grant conveyed in such legal and authentic manner by His Majesty's patent under the broad seal, though it may possibly [be] postponed for some time.[978] In the interim I must patiently wait the event and endeavour to be of some use where I am.

For the first three months I resided at Newport and preached regularly every Sunday, and many Quakers and other sectaries heard my sermons in which I treated only those general points agreed by all Christians. But on Whit-Sunday (the occasion being so proper) I could not omit speaking against that spirit of delusion and enthusiasm which misleads those people: and though I did it in the softest manner and with the greatest caution, yet I found it gave some offence, so bigoted are they to their prejudices. Till then they almost took me for one of their own, to which my everyday dress, being only a strait-bodied black-coat without plaits on the sides, or superfluous buttons, did not a little contribute.

I live now in the country and preach occasionally sometimes at Newport, sometimes in the adjacent parts of the continent. Mr. James[979] and Mr. Dalton[980] have taken a house at Boston; in which town I have not yet been, though I have had several invitations and been visited in this island by many of the principal inhabitants thereof. My family I bless God are well. My little son thrives,[981] and we are already flattered by the neighbours upon his parts and person.

I heartily wish to your Lordship, and all that belong to you, increase of health and joy. My wife, who has a very sincere respect for your Lordship and my good Lady joins with me in these wishes, and her humble service with mine to both of you. I am with the greatest truth,

---

[978] Berkeley's frustration with the refusal of the Treasury to pay out the funds as directed by both the king and the House of Commons is understandable. The Treasury only required (1) the funds and (2) the permission of the prime minister (Robert Walpole*). Berkeley reasonably expected the latter since Walpole had actually pledged £200 to the Bermuda project. Eventually it had the former, but Walpole's cabinet included individuals who opposed any measure that might reduce the dependency of the colonies on England. Eventually they persuaded the prime minister that the scheme was not workable. See Luce, *Life of Berkeley*, p. 137.

[979] John James* (?–1741).

[980] Richard Dalton* (c. 1695–1769).

[981] Henry Berkeley* (1729–after 1756).

My Lord,

your Lordship's most obliged and most obedient servant,

G: Berkeley

What might have been formerly an inconvenience is now none at all. I must therefore desire your Lordship, before my money is replaced in the funds, to take sixty guineas out of it, which money I had long since from your Lordship, and for which with many other favours I shall always hold myself obliged to you.

190 JOHNSON TO BERKELEY[982]

CU, Spec. MS Coll. Samuel Johnson, Box 1.

Stratford, 10 September 1729

Rev'd Sir,

The kind invitation you gave me to lay before you any difficulties that should occur to me in reading those excellent books which you was pleased to order into my hands, is all the apology I shall offer for the trouble I now presume to give you. But nothing could encourage me to expose to your view my low and mean way of thinking and writing, but my hopes of an interest in that candor [*sic*] and tenderness which are so conspicuous both in your writings and conversation.

These books (for which I stand humbly obliged to you) contain speculations the most surprisingly ingenious I have ever met with; and I must confess that the reading of them has almost convinced me that matter as it has been commonly defined for an unknown Quiddity is but a mere non-entity. That it is a strong presumption against the existence of it, that there never could be conceived any manner of connection between it and our ideas. That the *esse* of things is only their *percipi*; and that the rescuing us from the absurdities of abstract ideas and the gross notion of matter that have so much obtained, deserves well of the learned world, in that it clears away very many difficulties and perplexities in the sciences.

---

[982] In Johnson's letterbook the following is added before the letter: "A Letter to the Revd. Dr. Berkeley Dean of London Derry, upon reading His Books – of *The Principles of Human Knowledge & Dialogues*." This letter is printed in Herbert and Carol Schneider, eds., *Samuel Johnson, President of King's College: His Career and Writings*, 4 vols. (New York: Columbia University Press, 1929), vol. II, pp. 263–70.

And I am of opinion that this way of thinking can't fail of prevailing in the world, be sure it is likely to prevail very much among us in these parts, several ingenious men having entirely come in to it. But there are many others on the other hand that cannot be reconciled to it; though of these there are some who have a very good opinion of it and plainly see many happy consequences attending it, on account of which they are well inclined to embrace it, but think they find some difficulties in their way which they can't get over, and some objections not sufficiently answered to their satisfaction. And since you have condescended to give me leave to do so, I will make bold to lay before you sundry things, which yet remain in the dark either to myself or to others, and which I can't account for either to my own, or at least to their satisfaction.

1. The great prejudice that lies against it with some is its repugnancy to and subversion of Sir I. Newton's[983] philosophy in sundry points; to which they have been so much attached that they can't suffer themselves in the least to call it in question in any instance. But indeed it does not appear to me so inconsistent therewith as at first blush it did, for the Laws of Nature which he so happily explains are the same whether matter be supposed or not. However, let Sir Isaac Newton, or any other man, be heard only so far as his opinion is supported by reason:—but after all I confess I have so great a regard for the philosophy of that great man, that I would gladly see as much of it as may be, to obtain in this ideal scheme.

2. The objection, that it takes away all subordinate natural causes, and accounts for all appearances merely by the immediate will of the supreme spirit, does not seem to many to be answered to their satisfaction. It is readily granted that our ideas are inert, and can't cause one another, and are truly only signs one of another. For instance my idea of fire is not the cause of my idea of burning and of ashes. But inasmuch as these ideas are so connected as that they seem necessarily to point out to us the relations of cause and effect, we can't help thinking that our ideas are pictures of things without our minds at least, though not without the Great Mind, and which are their archetypes, between which these relations do obtain. I kindle a fire and leave it, no created mind beholds it; I return again and find a great alteration in the fuel; has there not in my absence been all the while that gradual alteration making in the archetype of my idea of wood which I should have had the idea of if I had been present? And is there not some archetype of my idea of the fire, which under the agency of the Divine Will has gradually caused this alteration? And so in all other instances, our ideas are

---

[983] Isaac Newton (1642–1727).

so connected, that they seem necessarily to refer our minds to some originals which are properly (though subordinate) causes and effects one of another; insomuch that unless they be so, we can't help thinking ourselves under a perpetual delusion.

3. That all the phenomena of nature, must ultimately be referred to the will of the Infinite Spirit, is what must be allowed; but to suppose his immediate energy in the production of every effect, does not seem to impress so lively and great a sense of his power and wisdom upon our minds, as to suppose a subordination of causes and effects among the archetypes of our ideas, as he that should make a watch or clock of ever so beautiful an appearance and that should measure the time ever so exactly yet if he should be obliged to stand by it and influence and direct all its motions, he would seem but very deficient in both his ability and skill in comparison with him who should be able to make one that would regularly keep on its motion and measure the time for a considerable while without the intervention of any immediate force of its author or any one else impressed upon it.

4. And as this tenet seems thus to abate our sense of the wisdom and power of God, so there are some that cannot be persuaded that it is sufficiently cleared from bearing hard on his holiness; those who suppose that the corrupt affections of our souls and evil practices consequent to them, are occasioned by certain irregular mechanical motions of our bodies, and that these motions come to have an habitual irregular bias and tendency by means of our own voluntary indulgence to them, which we might have governed to better purpose, do in this way of thinking, sufficiently bring the guilt of those ill habits and actions upon ourselves; but if in an habitual sinner, every object and motion be but an idea, and every wicked appetite the effect of such a set of ideas, and these ideas, the immediate effect of the Almighty upon his mind; it seems to follow, that the immediate cause of such ideas must be the cause of those immoral appetites and actions; because he is born down before them seemingly, even in spite of himself. At first indeed they were only occasions, which might be withstood, and so, proper means of trial, but now they become causes of his immoralities. When therefore a person is under the power of a vicious habit, and it can't but be foreseen that the suggestion of such and such ideas will unavoidably produce those immoralities, how can it consist with the holiness of God to suggest them?

5. It is, after all that has been said on that head, still something shocking to many to think that there should be nothing but a mere show in all the art and contrivance appearing in the structure (for instance) of a human body,

particularly of the organs of sense. The curious structure of the eye, what can it be more than merely a fine show, if there be no connection more than you admit of, between that and vision? It seems by the make of it to be designed for an instrument or means of conveying the images of external things to the perceptive faculty within; and if it be not so, if it be really of no use in conveying visible objects to our minds, and if our visible ideas are immediately created in them by the will of the Almighty, why should it be made to seem to be an instrument or medium as much as if indeed it really were so? It is evident, from the conveying of images into a dark room through a lens, that the eye is a lens, and that the images of things are painted on the bottom of it. But to what purpose is all this, if there be no connection between this fine apparatus and the act of vision; can it be thought a sufficient argument that there is no connection between them because we can't discover it, or conceive how it should be?

6. There are some who say, that if our sensations don't depend on any bodily organs—they don't see how death can be supposed to make any alteration in the manner of our perception, or indeed how there should be (properly speaking) any separate state of the soul at all. For if our bodies are nothing but ideas, and if our having ideas in this present state does not depend upon what are thought to be the organs of sense, and lastly, if we are supposed (as doubtless we must) to have ideas in that state; it should seem that immediately upon our remove from our present situation, we should still be attended with the same ideas of bodies as we have now, and consequently with the same bodies or at least with bodies however different, and if so, what room is there left for any resurrection, properly so-called? So that while this tenet delivers us from the embarrassments that attend the doctrine of a material resurrection, it seems to leave no place for any resurrection at all, at least in the sense that word seems to bear in St. John 5: 28, 29.

7. Some of us are at a loss to understand your meaning when you speak of archetypes. You say the being of things consists in their being perceived. And that things are nothing but ideas, that our ideas have no unperceived archetypes, but yet you allow archetypes to our ideas when things are not perceived by our minds they exist in, i.e., are perceived by some other mind. Now I understand you, that there is a two-fold existence of things or ideas, one in the Divine Mind, and the other in created minds; the one archetypal, and the other ectypal; that, therefore, the real original and permanent existence of things is archetypal, being ideas in *mente Divina*,[984] and that our ideas are copies of them,

---

[984] "the divine mind."

and so far forth real things as they are correspondent to their archetypes and exhibited to us, or begotten in us by the will of the Almighty, in such measures and degrees and by such stated laws and rules as he is pleased to observe; that, therefore, there is no unperceived substance intervening between the divine ideas and ours as a medium, occasion or instrument by which He begets[985] our ideas in us, but that which was thought to be the material existence of things is in truth only ideal in the Divine Mind. Do I understand you right? Is it not therefore your meaning, that though the existence of our ideas (i.e., the ectypal things) depends upon our perceiving them, yet there are external to any created mind, in the all-comprehending Spirit, real and permanent archetypes (as stable and permanent as ever matter was thought to be), to which these ideas of ours are correspondent, and so that (though our visible and tangible ideas are *toto coelo*[986] different and distinct things, yet) these may be said to be external to my mind, in the divine mind, an archetype (for instance of the candle that is before me) in which the originals of both my visible and tangible ideas, light, heat, whiteness, softness, etc., under such a particular cylindrical figure, are united, so that it may be properly said to be the same thing that I both see and feel?

8. If this, or something like it might be understood to be your meaning, it would seem less shocking to say that we don't see and feel the same thing, because we can't dispossess our minds of the notion of an external world, and would be allowed to conceive that, though there were no intelligent creature before Adam to be a spectator of it, yet the world was really six days *in archetypo*, gradually proceeding from an informal chaotic state into that beautiful show wherein it first appeared to his mind, and that the comet that appeared in 1680 (for instance) has now, though no created mind beholds it, a real existence in the all-comprehending spirit, and is making its prodigious tour through the vast fields of aether, and lastly that the whole vast congeries of heaven and earth, the mighty systems of worlds with all their furniture, have a real being in the eternal mind antecedent to and independent on the perception of any created spirit, and that when we see and feel, etc., that that almighty mind, by his immediate fiat, begets in our minds (*pro nostro modulo*)[987] ideas correspondent to them, and which may be imagined in some degree resemblances of them.

9. But if there be archetypes to our ideas, will it not follow that there is external space, extention, figure and motion, as being archetypes of our ideas, to which we

---

[985] Manuscript is damaged here, but "begets" is most likely.

[986] "by the entire extent of the heavens."

[987] Literally "for our [small] measure." In context and more freely it means something like "in our own way, small as it might be."

give these names. And indeed for my part I cannot disengage my mind from the persuasion that there is external space; when I have been trying ever so much to conceive of space as being nothing but an idea in my mind, it will return upon me even in spite of my utmost efforts, certainly there must be, there can't but be, external space. The length, breadth, and thickness of any idea, it's true, are but ideas; the distance between two trees in my mind is but an idea, but if there are archetypes to the ideas of the trees, there must be an archetype to the idea of the distance between them. Nor can I see how it follows that there is no external absolute height, bigness, or distance of things, because they appear greater or less to us according as we are nearer or remote from them, or see them with our naked eyes, or with glasses; any more than it follows that a man, for instance, is not really absolutely six foot high measured by a two foot rule applied to his body, because divers pictures of him may be drawn some six, some four, some two foot long according to the same measure. Nobody ever imagined that the idea of distance is without the mind, but does it therefore follow that there is no external distance to which the idea is correspondent, for instance, between Rhode Island and Stratford? Truly I wish it were not so great, that I might be so happy as to have a more easy access to you, and more nearly enjoy the advantages of your instructions.

10. You allow spirits to have a real existence external to one another. Methinks, if so, there must be distance between them, and space wherein they exist, or else they must all exist in one individual spot or point, and as it were coincide one with another. I can't see how external space and duration are any more abstract ideas than spirits. As we have (properly speaking) no ideas of spirits, so indeed, neither have we of external space and duration. But it seems to me that the existence of these must unavoidably follow from the existence of those, insomuch that I can no more conceive of their not being, than I can conceive of the non-existence of the infinite and eternal mind. They seem as necessarily existent independent of any created mind as the Deity Himself. Or must we say there is nothing in Dr. Clarke's argument a priori, in his *Demonstration of the Being and Attributes of God*,[988] or in what Sir Isaac Newton says about the infinity and eternity of God in his *Scholium Generale* to his *Principia*? I should be glad to know your sense of what those two authors say upon this subject.

---

[988] Samuel Clarke* (1675–1729). *A Demonstration of the Being and Attributes of God: More Particularly in Answer to Mr. Hobbes, Spinoza and their Followers, Wherein the Notion of Liberty is Stated, and the Possibility and Certainty of it Proved, in Opposition to Necessity and Fate* was the first of his Boyle lectures delivered in 1704.

11. You will forgive the confusedness of my thoughts and not wonder at my writing like a man something bewildered, since I am, as it were, got into a new world amazed at everything about me. These ideas of ours, what are they? Is the substance of the mind the substratum to its ideas? Is it proper to call them modifications of our minds? Or impressions upon them? Or what? Truly I can't tell what to make of them, any more than of matter itself. What is the *esse* of spirits?—you seem to think it impossible to abstract their existence from their thinking. Princ. p. 143. sec. 98. Is then the *esse* of minds nothing else but *percipere*, as the *esse* of ideas is *percipi*? Certainly, methinks, there must be an unknown somewhat that thinks and acts, as difficult to be conceived of as matter, and the creation of which, as much beyond us as the creation of matter. Can actions be the *esse* of any thing? Can they exist or be exerted without some being who is the agent? And may not that being be easily imagined to exist without acting, e.g., without thinking? And consequently (for you are there speaking of duration) may he not be said *durare, etsi non cogitet,*[989] to persist in being, though thinking were intermitted for a while? And is not this sometimes fact? The duration of the eternal mind, must certainly imply some thing besides an eternal succession of ideas. May I not then conceive that, though I get my idea of duration by observing the succession of ideas in my mind, yet there is a *perseverare in existendo,*[990] a duration of my being, and of the being of other spirits distinct from, and independent of, this succession of ideas?

But, Sir, I doubt I have more than tired your patience with so many (and I fear you will think them impertinent) questions; for though they are difficulties with me, or at least with some in my neighbourhood, for whose sake, in part, I write, yet I don't imagine they can appear such to you, who have so perfectly digested your thoughts upon this subject. And perhaps they may vanish before me upon a more mature consideration of it. However, I should be very thankful for your assistance, if it were not a pity you should waste your time (which would be employed to much better purposes) in writing to a person so obscure and so unworthy of such a favor as I am. But I shall live with some impatience till I see the second part of your design accomplished, wherein I hope to see these (if they can be thought such) or any other objections, that may have occurred to you since your writing the first part, obviated; and the usefulness of this doctrine more particularly displayed in the further application of it to the arts and sciences. May we not hope to see logic,

---

[989] "to endure, even without thinking."
[990] "to persevere in existing."

mathematics, and natural philosophy, pneumatology, theology and morality, all in their order, appearing with a new lustre under the advantage they may receive from it? You have at least given us to hope for a geometry cleared of many perplexities that render that sort of study troublesome, which I shall be very glad of, who have found that science more irksome to me than any other, though, indeed, I am but very little versed in any of them. But I will not trespass any further upon your patience. My very humble service to Mr. James[991] and Mr. Dalton,[992] and I am with the greatest veneration,

> Rev'd Sir,
>
> your most obliged and most obedient humble servant,
>
> Samuel Johnson

191 NEWMAN TO BERKELEY[993]

SPCK MS D4/41, fols. 35–36.

Bartlett's Buildings 17 September 1729

Revd Sir,

My last to you was of the 29th of April, enclosing one from my Lord Percival,[994] by the Benjamen & William Brigantine Captain Bennet Master for Rhode Island, since which I have the honour of your letters of the 28th February & 27th of June last, by which I am glad to find the country & climate of N. England agree so well with you as they do. I had six letters & packets with your last which were all immediately forwarded as directed. My Lord Percival is at Charlton* & Archdeacon Benson[995] at Durham.

I have prepared a box of Hookers[996] and Chillingworths[997] works etc. as you ordered which shall be sent by the 1st Rhode Island vessel but if none such go

---

[991] John James* (?–1741).

[992] Richard Dalton* (c. 1695–1769).

[993] Addressed "To the Revd Dr. Berkeley at Rhode Island N.E. By the Dolphin Captain Alden." A copy is published in Allen and McClure, *History of the Society for Promoting Christian Knowledge: 1698–1898*, pp. 244–45. Luce republished the letter in "Berkeley's Bermuda Project and His Benefactions to American Universities, with Unpublished Letters and Extracts from the Egmont Papers," 103–04.

[994] John Percival* (1683–1748).

[995] Martin Benson* (1689–1752).

[996] Presumably Richard Hooker (1554?–1600), theologian, author of *Of the Laws of Ecclesiastical Politie* (1593).

[997] William Chillingworth (1602–44), theologian, most famous for *The Religion of Protestants* (1638).

this autumn they shall be sent to Boston, presuming you have the convenience of land carriage thence at a reasonable price. The letters herewith
sent are I suppose in answer to those I received. I can't yet learn that the
20 thousand pound is paid, though I have called on Dr. Clayton,[998] and sent
him word of this opportunity of writing but he was not at home either time. If
the government are in earnest to erect the college where it may be most
effectual to answer the purposes of it, I hope they will not refuse the leave
you desire of a translation, especially when they see such good reasons for it as
I doubt not but you have offered; but you know what it is to solicit at our
Court, and though a thing may not be refused yet by the delays given without a
vigorous solicitation a man's life wastes and all projects built upon dilatory
grants must suffer extremely in the execution though never so well designed.
If you could come over youself for 2 or 3 months next spring you would have a
better chance to succeed upon your own solicitations than I doubt can be
expected from your friends here though they wish heartily well to the Design,
but there is a great difference beween being a well-wisher and being the soul
of an under-taking.

I mentioned Mr. Winthrop[999] to you in my last, he is a vast landed man in
the province of Massachusets, Connecticut, & New York governments and if
he has any estate property situated for your purpose I believe he would let
you have what you want on as easy terms as you can desire. He is now here to
prosecute some complaints against Connecticut, where he has been treated
very scurvily considering him the grandson of the father of all the colonies in
N.E. but particularly of Connecticut. A usage but too common with us in that
part of America where the servants of the 1st planters are now become the
masters of their posterity and treat them with envy and scorn to avoid as they
think contempt, & the remembrance of their origin, whereas in truth they
confess the poverty of their descent, by their ingratitude to the memory of
their patrons & public benefactors: and if those public spirited men who first
planted the country had not acted on nobler principles, they that now boast
of having raised fortunes in a wild wilderness might at this time have commanded no better a din[n]er in one or other of the 3 Kingdoms than a half-
penny role, but such is the way of the world, and you must not be surprised if
you or your successor meet with the same treatment.

---

[998] Robert Clayton* (1695–1758).
[999] It is unclear exactly to which Winthrop Newman is referring. It might be John Winthrop
(1681–1776), son of Wait-Stil Winthrop (1642–1717) and grandson of John Winthrop the
Younger (1606–76).

But while I mention the brutality of some Americans I can't but with concern reflect upon our degeneracy at home, you would be surprised to see what progress infidelity has made here in a short time, notwithstanding the learned labours of some of our prelates & others to oppose it. So that some good men are apprehensive that the time is coming when the Gospel that has left the Eastern parts of the world to reside in the Western parts of it for some centuries past is now, by the just judgment of God, taking leave of us, to be received in America, but I tell such if it may be any consolation to them we are as wicked in America as they can be here.

It is true there are in America no masquerades, nor robbing on the highway etc. of wicked inventions here, but they are more addicted to pride, envy, uncharitableness, detraction, lying, cheating, hypocrisy & other vices that may be acted secretly then perhaps any people in Europe, & even their innocent huskings[1000] are not without some views that wont bear daylight, appointed to be in the dead of the night. So that all things considered I can't be so partial to my countrymen not to acquit them of being upon a balance in point of wickedness with their brethern in Europe. I rather think we are hastening to that period which our Saviour has predicted, when the Son of man comes shall he find faith upon earth.

May God direct us amidst the nonsense of a deceitful world to secure our own true interests by advancing his glory in our several stations in spite of all discouragements, till it shall please him to remove us to a better world. I am, Revd Sir,

> your most
> H. N.

My humble service to your Lady and to Messrs. James[1001] and Dalton[1002] to whom I have wrote a short letter, by this ship.

[Postscript added:]
23rd Sept. 1729

Rev. Sir,

I just now received the envelope from Lord Percival & must let you know what the New England men here say of you, that you are so complaisant

---

[1000] A footnote is added here in the letter printed in Allen and McClure's *History*: "Social meetings originally for husking corn, but degenerating afterwards into assemblies meriting Mr. Newman's strictures." See p. 245.

[1001] John James* (?–1741).

[1002] Richard Dalton* (c. 1695–1769).

to the Quakers that you even go to their meetings & preach among them and they in their turn go to Church, where you dispense with the use of the surplice and some other observances here particularly the 30th of January etc as would disgust weak people. I tell them I believe St. Paul would have done the same if he had been in your place. My humble service to Mr. Honeyman[1003] & please let him know I lately received his letter of 14th of April and am endeavouring to procure some books for him as he desires which I hope to send with yours.

192 PERCIVAL TO BERKELEY

EP, BL Add. MS 47032, fols. 138–39.

Charlton, 20 September 1729

Dear Sir,

I have just received yours of the 27 June. Your last was of the 28 March, which I answered the 14th following, before which I also writ you on the 23 April that I had sold your annuities as you directed me, and placed the money in Mr. Hoare's[1004] hands. You have doubtless by this time received my letters, of which I sent duplicates by Mr. Corbett's[1005] and Mr. Newman's[1006] packets. I find you had not sold them, and I wish so too, for the certainty of peace has made the stocks in general rise, but I had your peremptory orders for what I did, and to sell them even with speed. It is pity the money should lie dead in a banker's hands. I thought you had drawn for it long ago to pay the purchase of the land you had agreed for in Rhode Island. I am ready with much pleasure to obey your directions about it when you think fit to dispose of it any particular way whether in annuities or otherwise, and shall wait your orders and powers.

I am very glad you have instructed me with authority to declare your resolution of going to Bermuda when the £20,000[1007] shall be paid in, in case the government and your associates should persist in the choice of

---

1003 James Honeyman* (c. 1675–1750).
1004 Benjamin Hoare* (1693–1749/50).
1005 Thomas Corbett* (?–1751).
1006 Henry Newman* (1670–1743).
1007 A reference to Berkeley's scheme to use some of the proceeds from the sale of lands on St. Christopher Island (St. Kitts)* to fund St. Paul's College in Bermuda. The plan received royal support and was approved by the House of Commons in May 1726. Berkeley is still waiting for the Treasury to release the funds for his use.

that place preferable to any other and particularly the island where you are. It is certain the report of your settling on Rhode Island and preferring that place has universally obtained belief, both from your own accounts of it, and your purchasing lands there, which is known to everybody, to which I may add the general persuasion that Bermuda would not fit your purpose. But I have constantly said (and so I believe have your other friends) that you went to Rhode Island to show you were in earnest about your scheme, and to inform yourself of all the particulars necessary for carrying it on, to settle and prepare matters for beginning your work, and to be near at hand to pass to Bermuda when the government money should be paid in. But that you avoided going directly to that island, because by your patent, you was [sic] to vacate your Deanery a year after you had been there, and it would be a great imprudence to hazard that while you were uncertain of the moneys coming. As to this last particular, your friends employed to get it & without doubt inform you from time to time of their motions, but last week I was at Court, and Mr. Eccleshal[1008] the Queen's Secretary told me that none of the St. Christopher's money was yet paid into the treasury, though I think I heard Mr. Scroop[1009] tell the House of Commons last winter that there were lands already sold for £60,000.

I heartily congratulate you on the birth of your son,[1010] and I hope your Lady is well after it, and that the change of climate has agreed with all the company with you.

There is a report that Mr. Smibert[1011] is married to the Lady who accompanied Mrs. Berkeley,[1012] but if so I suppose you would have said something of it.

As to ourselves, my wife labours at times under very great cholic pains, and is forced to increase her dose of laudanum. Mrs. Dering[1013] is now at Bath where an exceeding bad state of health from a complication of distempers carried her some months ago. My brother writes me that the waters did her head and stomach good, but have thrown the humours down into her legs insomuch they more than fear she has the dropsy to which her physicians are free to own she has a tendency, and therefore my last letters from thence talk

---

[1008] John Eckersall (?-?) was secretary to Queen Caroline (1727-37).

[1009] John Scrope* (c. 1662-1752).

[1010] Henry Berkeley* (1729-after 1756) was born around 12 June 1729 and baptised in Trinity Church in Newport on 1 September of the same year.

[1011] John Smibert* (1688-1751).

[1012] The report was false. Smibert married Mary Williams (c. 1707/8-after 1760), the daughter of a Boston schoolmaster, on 30 July 1730.

[1013] Mary (née Parker) Dering* (1692-1731).

of her return to London, which is but melancholly news. I thank God my children are all well, and prove to my satisfaction.

I mentioned that there was very great likelihood of peace. Every post gives us more reason to expect it. Mr. Stanhope[1014] is set out Ambassador to Spain, and it will be about seven weeks before we can have any thorough confirmation. In the meantime great civilities pass, and the effects of the galeons are delivered out. This will put a final end to the Ostend Company,[1015] and England will be no more concerned in the jars of Europe; but whether the Emperor will be satisfied to let Don Carlos[1016] live peaceably in Italy is a question. They say he is marching troops thither.

Dr. Courayer[1017] is now with me and presents his service to you. He has been lately in Holland to see his last book printed, wherein he gives a narrative of the proceedings in France against him, and justifies his behaviour, adding with all the proofs. Since his return the Queen presented him with another £100, with intimation that she will continue this favour.

The Archbishop of Dublin is not yet appointed.[1018] It lies between the Bishop of St. David's and the Bishop of Salisbury's brother.[1019] London,[1020] Canterbury,[1021] and the Lord Lieutenant[1022] are for the former, but whether the Ministry are is the question. My Lord Lieutenant says it will disoblige all the Bishops there to have the Junior of their Bench put over their heads, but Salisbury insists that London promised it, which London denies. It is objected to St. David's that he is a man of too warm a temper, and not conversant enough in worldly matters to be Archbishop of Dublin. Whether the other is more so, or whether it is necessary that bishops should be men of this world, is a question, but I must wish for my old tutor, who is a virtuous, religious, and

---

[1014] William Stanhope* (1683?-1756), later first Earl of Harrington. Rand (p. 258n) claims the reference is to Philip Dormer Stanhope* (1694-1793), but Philip was serving in a diplomatic capacity in the Netherlands at the time.

[1015] In 1722/23 the Emperor of Austria formed the Ostend Company to try and gain a share of the lucrative East India trade.

[1016] Don Carlos (1716-88) was the son of Philip V of Spain and Isabella of Parma. He ruled as duke of Parma, by right of his mother (1732-34), was king of Naples (1734-59), and ascended to the throne of Spain as Charles III in 1759.

[1017] Pierre-François le Courayer* (1681-1776).

[1018] Archbishop of Dublin William King* (1650-1729) died on 8 May 1729. He was replaced by John Hoadly* (1678-1746), who would later become primate of Ireland in 1742.

[1019] The bishop of St. David's since 1723 was Richard Smalbroke (1672-1749). The bishop of Salisbury was Benjamin Hoadly (1676-1761), whose brother John Hoadly* (1678-1746) did in fact succeed William King* as archbishop of Dublin.

[1020] Edmund Gibson* (1669-1748).

[1021] William Wake* (1657-1737).

[1022] John Carteret* (1690-1763), second Earl Granville.

learned man. He has just finished his first volume in defence of our Saviour's miracles against Woolaston's tracts, who would turn them all into allegories.[1023] Some tell me it is heavy writ, but learned.

Dr. Clayton is by means of Mrs. Clayton in great favour at Court.[1024] My Lord Lieutenant spake to the Queen without his knowledge to grant him the Deanery of Dromore, but the Queen replied she designed better things for him. Probably if the Bishop of Salisbury's brother be made Archbishop of Dublin, he will succeed him.

> You have all services from hence, I am ever
> Dear Sir, etc.,
> Percival

193 NEWMAN TO BERKELEY[1025]

SPCK MS D4/20, fol. 60.

Bartlett's Buildings, 30 September 1729

Revd Sir,

According to your desire 28th February last I have shipped the books within mentioned on the Wm. & Sarach Captain Steel for Boston, and not knowing who is your correspondent there, they are consigned to Jonathan Belcher Esq. & Company by leave of Mr. Belcher[1026] himself who is here, but his partner Mr. Foy will follow any direction you please to give him for conveying them to you.

Please to give me humble service to Mr. Honyman[1027] & let him know that I have communicated his letter to the Society for Propagating the Gospel by Dr. Humphreys,[1028] but have not yet received their answer. In the meantime I have put up in your box a small parcel of little books such as I thought might be of use in your parts, and if you or he want more of the like please to signify

---

[1023] Richard Smalbroke (1672–1749) was a tutor to John Percival* at Magdalen College, Oxford. He authored *A Vindication of the Miracles of our Blessed Saviour* (2 vols., 1729 and 1731), a systematic refutation of the arguments of Thomas Woolston (1668–1733), a free-thinking controversialist.

[1024] Robert Clayton* (1695–1758). He was in such good favor that he would be announced as bishop of Killala and Achonry by the year's end.

[1025] Addressed to "Rev. Dr. Berkeley, Dean of Derry at Rhode Island."

[1026] Jonathan Belcher* (1682–1757).

[1027] James Honeyman* (c. 1675–1750).

[1028] David Humphreys* (1690–1740), secretary for the Society for the Propagation of the Gospel from 1716 until his death.

it. I have herewith sent 2 little tracts which I wish I had added some of to that parcel if think them proper for your parts pray signify your pleasure to Revd Sir

P.S.: You will excuse my making use of my clerk's hand, being straitened for time that I could not transcribe from my letterbook what is above; and for the same reason have not wrote to Mr. Honyman.

I congratulate you on your being blessed with a son,[1029] which my Lord Percival[1030] was so good as to inform me of. He is my countryman, and therefore pray make my humble service acceptable to him and his mamma who is so good as to nurse him.[1031] My humble service to Messieurs James[1032] and Dalton,[1033] and to Governor Jenks.[1034]

194 BERKELEY TO JOHNSON[1035]

MS *unknown. Printed in Schneider, vol. II, pp. 270–74.*

25 November 1729

Reverend Sir,

The ingenious letter you favoured me with found me very much indisposed with a gathering or imposthumation in my head, which confined me several weeks, and is now, I thank God, relieved. The objections of a candid thinking man to what I have written will always be welcome, and I shall not fail to give all the satisfaction I am able, not without hopes of convincing or being convinced. It is a common fault for men to hate opposition, and be too much wedded to their own opinions. I am so sensible of this in others that I could not pardon it to myself, if I considered mine any further than they seem to me to be true, which I shall the

---

[1029] Henry Berkeley* (1729–after 1756).

[1030] John Percival* (1683–1748).

[1031] Henry Newman* (1670–1743) was an American by birth, hence Berkeley's child is his "countryman."

[1032] John James* (?–1741).

[1033] Richard Dalton* (c. 1695–1769).

[1034] Joseph Jenckes (1656–1740). He was governor of the Rhode Island colony (1727–32).

[1035] The letter is also printed in *Works,* vol. II, pp. 279–83 and excerpted in Beardsley, pp. 71–72. Fraser also prints an excerpt of the letter (*LL*, pp. 179–81) and mistakenly dates it around 25 June, which probably is what tempted Beardsley into misleadingly saying the personal correspondence between Berkeley and Johnson begins "as early as June 25, 1729." Beardsley reproduces the letter in part, not otherwise dating it. As Schneider rightly notes (pp. 270–71n), there is no reason to believe a June letter exists. In Letter 197 Johnson refers explicitly to the letter of 25 November 1729 (Letter 194).

better be able to judge of when they have passed the scrutiny of persons so well qualified to examine them as you and your friends appear to be, to whom my illness must be an apology for not sending this answer sooner.

1. The true use and end of natural philosophy is to explain the phenomena of nature, which is done by discovering the laws of nature, and reducing particular appearances to them. This is Sir Isaac Newton's[1036] method; and such method or design is not in the least inconsistent with the principles I lay down. This mechanical philosophy doth not assign or suppose any one natural efficient cause in the strict and proper sense; nor is it, as to its use, concerned about matter; nor is matter connected therewith; nor doth it infer the being of matter. It must be owned, indeed, that the mechanical philosophers do suppose (though unnecessarily) the being of matter. They do even pretend to demonstrate that matter is proportional to gravity, which, if they could, this indeed would furnish an unanswerable objection. But let us examine their demonstration—it is laid down in the first place, that the momentum of any body is the product of its quantity by its velocity, *moles in celeritatem ducta*.[1037] If, therefore, the velocity is given, the momentum will be as its quantity. But it is observed that bodies of all kinds descend *in vacuo*[1038] with the same velocity; therefore, the momentum of descending bodies is as the quantity of moles, i.e., gravity is as matter. But this argument concludes nothing, and is a mere circle. For, I ask, when it is premised that the momentum is equal to the *moles in celeritatem ducta*, how the moles or quantity of matter is estimated. If you say, by extent, the proposition is not true; if by weight, then you suppose that the quantity of matter is proportional to matter: i.e., the conclusion is taken for granted in one of the premises. As for absolute space and motion, which are also supposed without any necessity or use, I refer you to what I have already published; particularly in a Latin treatise, *De Motu*,[1039] which I shall take care to send to you.

2. Cause is taken in different senses. A proper active efficient cause I can conceive none but spirit; nor any action, strictly speaking, but where there is will. But this doth not hinder the allowing occasional causes (which are in truth but signs), and more is not requisite in the best physics, i.e., the mechanical philosophy. Neither doth it hinder the admitting other causes besides God; such as spirits of different orders, which may be termed active causes, as acting

---

[1036] Isaac Newton (1642–1727).
[1037] Somewhat freely, "a mass having been made to move quickly."
[1038] "in a vacuum."
[1039] For the text of *De Motu* see *Works*, vol. IV, pp. 1–52.

indeed, though by limited and derivative powers. But as for an unthinking agent, no point of physics is explained by it, nor is it conceivable.

3. Those who have all along contended for a material world, have yet acknowledged that *natura naturans*[1040] (to use the language of the Schoolmen) is God; and that the divine conservation of things is equipollent to, and in fact the same thing with a continued repeated creation: in a word, that conservation and creation differ only in the *terminus a quo*.[1041] These are the common opinions of the Schoolmen; and Durandus,[1042] who held the world to be a machine like a clock, made and put in motion by God, but afterwards continuing to go of itself, was therein particular and had few followers. The very poets teach a doctrine not unlike the schools, *Mens agitat molem* (Virg. Aeneid VI).[1043] The Stoics and Platonists are everywhere full of the same notion. I am not therefore singular in this point itself, so much as in my way of proving it. Further, it seems to me that the power and wisdom of God are as worthily set forth by supposing Him to act immediately as an omnipresent, infinitely active spirit, as by supposing Him to act by the mediation of subordinate causes, in preserving and governing the natural world. A clock may indeed go independent of its maker or artificer, inasmuch as the gravitation of its pendulum proceeds from another cause, and that the artificer is not the adequate cause of the clock; so that the analogy would not be just to suppose a clock is in respect of its artist what the world is in respect of its creator. For aught I can see, it is no disparagement to the perfection of God to say that all things necessarily depend on Him as their conservator as well as creator, and that all nature would shrink to nothing, if not upheld and preserved in being by the same force that first created it. This, I am sure, is agreeable to Holy Scripture, as well as to the writings of the most esteemed philosophers; and if it is to be considered that men make use of tools and machines to supply defect of power in themselves, we shall think it no honor to the divinity to attribute such things to him.

4. As to guilt, it is the same thing whether I kill a man with my hands or an instrument; whether I do it myself or make use of a ruffian.[1044] The imputation therefore upon the sanctity of God is equal, whether we suppose our sensations to be produced immediately by God, or by the mediation of instruments and

---

[1040] "nature being nature" (i.e. nature behaving as it does).

[1041] "the point from which" (i.e. the starting point).

[1042] Durandus of Saint-Pourçain (*c.* 1275–1334?). See *In Petri Lombardi Sententias Theologicas Commentarium* (Venice, 1571), lib. II, dist. I, qu. v: "All that is necessary is that He [God] should act mediately by conserving the nature and power of the secondary cause."

[1043] From Virgil, *Aeneid*, VI, 727. In the context of Virgil's poem, *molem* refers back to the earth and universe, making a reasonable translation: "The mind rouses the mighty mass [body]."

[1044] See *Works*, vol. II, p. 236 (*Three Dialogues*).

subordinate causes, all which are his creatures, and moved by his laws. This theological consideration, therefore, may be waived, as leading besides the question; for such I hold are points to be which bear equally hard on both sides of it. Difficulties about the principle of moral actions will cease, if we consider that all guilt is in the will, and that our ideas, from whatever cause they are produced, are alike inert.

5. As to the art and contrivance in the parts of animals, etc., I have considered that matter in the *Principles of Human Knowledge*,[1045] and, if I mistake not, sufficiently shown the wisdom and use thereof, considered as signs and means of information. I do not indeed wonder that on first reading what I have written, men are not thoroughly convinced. On the contrary, I should very much wonder if prejudices, which have been many years taking root, should be extirpated in a few hours' reading. I had no inclination to trouble the world with large volumes. What I have done was rather with a view of giving hints to thinking men, who have leisure and curiosity to go to the bottom of things, and pursue them in their own minds. Two or three times reading these small tracts, and making what is read the occasion of thinking, would, I believe, render the whole familiar and easy to the mind, and take off that shocking appearance which hath often been observed to attend speculative truths.

6. I see no difficulty in conceiving a change of state, such as is vulgarly called death, as well without as with material substance. It is sufficient for that purpose that we allow sensible bodies, i.e., such as are immediately perceived by sight and touch; the existence of which I am so far from questioning (as philosophers are used to do) that I establish it, I think, upon evident principles. Now, it seems very easy to conceive the soul to exist in a separate state (i.e. divested from those limits and laws of motion and perception with which she is embarrassed here), and to exercise herself on new ideas, without the intervention of these tangible things we call bodies. It is even very possible to apprehend how the soul may have ideas of color without an eye, or of sounds without an ear.[1046]

And now, Sir, I submit these hints (which I have hastily thrown together as soon as my illness gave me leave) to your own maturer thoughts, which after all you will find the best instructors. What you have seen of mine was published when I was very young, and without doubt hath many defects. For though the notions should be true (as I verily think they are), yet it is difficult to

---

[1045] See *Works*, vol. II, pp. 1–113, especially sections 60–66 (pp. 66–70).
[1046] The Schneider text ends the paragraph with an ellipsis, but it is not clear why.

express them clearly and consistently, language being framed to common use and received prejudices. I do not therefore pretend that my books can teach truth. All I hope for is that they may be an occasion to inquisitive men of discovering truth by consulting their own minds and looking into their own thoughts. As to the second part of my treatise concerning the principles of human knowledge, the fact is that I had made a considerable progress in it, but the manuscript was lost about fourteen years ago during my travels in Italy; and I never had leisure since to do so disagreeable a thing as writing twice on the same subject.

Objections passing through your hands have their full force and clearness. I like them the better. This intercourse with a man of parts and a philosophic genius is very agreeable. I sincerely wish we were nearer neighbours. In the meantime whenever either you or your friends favor me with their thoughts, you may be sure of a punctual correspondence on my part. Before I have done I will venture to recommend three points: (1) To consider well the answers I have already given in my books to several objections. (2) To consider whether any new objection that shall occur doth not suppose the doctrine of abstract general ideas. (3) Whether the difficulties proposed in objection to my scheme can be solved by the contrary, for if they cannot, it is plain they can be no objection to mine.

I know not whether you have got my treatise concerning the principles of human knowledge. I intend to send it with my tract *De Motu*. If you know of a safe hand favour me with a line, and I will make use of that opportunity to send them. My humble service to your friends, to whom I understand I am indebted for some part of your letter.

    I am, your very faithful, humble servant,

    Geor. Berkeley

195 PERCIVAL TO BERKELEY

EP, BL Add. MS 47000, fols. 51–52.

London, 17 January 1729/30

Dear Sir,

Your letter of the 30 August came to my hands the 23 of last month, by which I find your family is well and your child in person and parts most promising, upon which I heartily congratulate you being (as I hope you are persuaded) much concerned in every thing that contributes to your happiness and satisfaction: you make apologies for giving me opportunities of serving you which I take unkindly.

I am sorry you sold your annuities[1047] because of the interest money you have lost and the advanced price they since are at. I was under a difficulty how to obey your last command of buying them over again, for want of a proper authority: for it seems, the first letter of attorney by which I sold them is no legal order to Wm. Hoar[1048] to pay me back the money which by your direction I lodged in his hands and which stands entered in his books to your account, neither could he do it on the authority of your private letter to me, but you must send me a fresh letter of attorney directing me to demand it of him and to dispose of it according to your pleasure: which I desire you will send me as soon as you can: in the mean time Mr. Hoar has been so kind as to buy the 2,000 S. Sea Annuities in his own name, and promises to let it rest so till your order shall arrive for transferring it to me for your use. It cost at 105 5/8 & 1/8 brokage two thousand one hundred and fifteen pound.

As to your payment from the Treasury I am wholly in the dark when it will come, but I fear your friends employed in it must have the greatest zeal and assiduity, and more interest at Court to obtain it than you imagine. Your account of the Quakers farsaking your sermons is what I did not at first expect: I thought they were really coming over, and that they could not be so stupid as to believe your preaching on topics common to all professors of Christ was any argument that you must be one of themselves, but reflecting afterwards that they don't know well what they are themselves, I don't wonder they should mistake you.

The peace with Spain being signed,[1049] the King laid it before the Parliament which met the 13 [instant?] and after a long debate, our House voted an address of thanks to his majesty for his great care in obtaining a just honourable and advantageous peace. The ante-ministerrians would not acknowledge it to be so, but we carried it 262 against 129.

The Bishop of Killalla Dr. Clayton[1050] kist hands the end of December last, and I believe the consideration of preferring him was one great reason for preferring

---

[1047] Berkeley owned South Sea annuities.*

[1048] An error, perhaps by the copyist, for Benjamin Hoare* (1693–1749/50). There were no William Hoares in the banking family until much later in the eighteenth century. The error is all the more clear because we have the letters exchanged between Percival and Benjamin Hoare about this issue. See Rand, pp. 260–61, Benj. Hoare to Percival, 31 December 1729, and Percival to Benj. Hoare, 2 January 1729/30.

[1049] A peace treaty with Spain was signed on 9 November 1729 in Seville, Spain.

[1050] Robert Clayton* (1695–1758).

Bishop Hoadly[1051] to the Archbishop of Dublin. I think you will not expect him after this in Bermuda, though he wishes as well to the design as any man who does not go. There is a vacant bishoprick for which Syng[1052] sollicits.

The lords of Ireland have displayed themselves very lately in a weekly paper called the Tribune: I am sorry to see it reprinted here, because of the jest they make of your notion of matter and of your Bermuda scheme.[1053] The author must needs have a worse design than to divert his fancy because he times his ridicule so unluckily. I would not acquaint you with this but that I know you are above being affected with other men's malice, and have long prepared yourself against the several sorts of opposition you expected for some time past to meet with in your great attempt. You are the subject of a whole paper, but I will only send you the last paragraph by which you may judge of the meaness of the rest.

> As our dreams give us incredible facility of transporting ourselves from place to place, so now me thought I was conveyed away over a vast track of ocean, and placed on an island at a great distance, on the shores of which I saw a great doctor handing a lady. The island was walled about with rocks and planted with huge lemons, but my glass quickly made this appear as great an enchantment as all the rest. The lady in a moment dwindled away into an agreeable spectre: the solid rock shrunk away into fugitive heaps of primary and secondary qualities, and the lemons became clusters of yellow imaginations. My heart was touched with compassion for the poor lady, but I very soon had my revenge, by seeing the doctor himself metamorphosed into a phantom resembling a clergyman, and kicking about the trammels of a much thiner gown than ever was worn by any of the Order.

In the close of your letter, you give me a title to sixty guineas.[1054] I have no sort of claim to them, but if you think so, I insist on it that you suffer me to present them to you again. My family join with me in most humble services to you and Mrs. Berkeley, and I am ever

> your most affectionate friend and obedient servant,
> Percival

[1051] John Hoadly* (1678–1746), made archbishop of Dublin in 1729 following the death of William King* (1650–1729).

[1052] Edward Synge* (1691–1762). Synge was appointed bishop of Clonfert in 1730.

[1053] The lampoon of Berkeley's immaterialist philosophy appeared in the *Tribune* 21 (1729) and was also published in a collection of the issues of the magazine (London: T. Warner, 1729), pp. 149–55.

[1054] See Letter 189.

196 NEWMAN TO BERKELEY[1055]

SPCK MS D4/41, fol. 46.

Bartlett's Buildings, 27 January 1729/30

Revd Sir,

Two or three days since I received the enclosed from my Lord Percival[1056] which I wish may carry to you some good news of the situation of your affairs here. The Bishop of London[1057] and other persons of note here seem to think it impracticable to prevail with the government to consent to a transfer of the settlement designed at Bermudas to Rhode Island. The objection made to Bermudas are with them so many good reasons for withdrawing the grant promised to the design in case it had gone on as first projected. Upon which considerations I believe you will think of returning to secure your deanery before it can be liable to forfeiture.

Dr. Clayton[1058] is nominated for Bishop of Killala, and when you return you will have a fair chance to be appointed to the first vacancy of that kind that you may be inclined to accept.

Mr. Winthrop,[1059] mentioned in my former letter, desires me to offer you the refusal of 2 or 3 islands belonging to him called Elizabeth Islands, which are between Rhode Island and Martha's Vineyard, if you should be inclined to make any more purchases in N. England, or if not perhaps Messrs James[1060] & Dalton[1061] may be disposed to purchase an estate so valuable as those islands are capable of being made, and though Mr. Winthrop did not set any price, he assured me if you was inclined to buy them, you should have them a penny-worth provided you signified your inclination before he treated with another person. My humble Service to your Lady[1062] & Messrs James & Dalton, who I hope do not repent their voyage though they underwent greater difficulties than most people do to visit America. May God Almighty direct you for the best in what remains to be done to accomplish your design is the wish of,

Revd Sir, your most obedient humble servant,

H. N.

[1055] Addressed "To the Revd Mr. Dean Berkeley at Rhode Island, by the Sarah Captain Erwin."
[1056] John Percival* (1683–1748).
[1057] Edmund Gibson* (1669–1748).
[1058] Robert Clayton* (1695–1758). He was named bishop of Killala in December 1729.
[1059] It is unclear to exactly which Winthrop Newman is referring. It might be John Winthrop (1681–1776), son of Wait-Stil Winthrop (1642–1717) and grandson of John Winthrop the Younger. See Letters 182 and 193.
[1060] John James* (?–1741).
[1061] Richard Dalton* (c. 1695–1769).
[1062] Anne (*née* Forster) Berkeley* (?–1786).

197 JOHNSON TO BERKELEY[1063]

BL Add. MS 39311, fols. 17–20. CU, Spec. MS Coll. Samuel Johnson, Box 1.

Stratford, 5 February 1729/30

Rev'd Sir,

Yours of November 25th, I received not till January 17th, and this being the first convenient opportunity I now return you my humblest thanks for it.

I am very sorry to understand that you have laboured under the illness you mention, but am exceeding glad and thankful for your recovery; I pray God preserve your life and health, that you may have opportunity to perfect these great and good designs for the advancement of learning and religion wherewith your mind labours.

I am very much obliged to you for the favorable opinion you are pleased to express at what I made bold to write to you and that you have so kindly vouchsafed so large and particular an answer to it. But you have done me too great an honor in putting any value on my judgment; for it is impossible my thoughts on this subject should be of any consequence, who have been bred up under the greatest disadvantages, and have had so little ability and opportunity to be instructed in things of this nature. And therefore I should be very vain to pretend any thing else but to be a learner; it is merely with this view that I give you this trouble.

I am sensible that the greatest part of what I wrote was owing to not sufficiently attending to those three important considerations you suggest at the end of your letter. And I hope a little more time and a more careful attention to and application of them, will clear up what difficulties yet lie in the way of our entirely coming into your sentiments. Indeed I had not had opportunity sufficiently to digest your books; for no sooner had I just read them over, but they were greedily demanded by my friends, who live much scattered up and down, and who expected I would bring them home with me, because I had told them before that if the books were to be had in Boston, I intended to purchase a set of them; and indeed they have not yet quite finished their tour. The *Theory of Vision* is still at New York and the *Dialogues* just gone to Long Island. But I am the better content to want them because I know they are doing good.

For my part I am content to give up the cause of matter, glad to get rid of the absurdities thereon depending if it be defensible, I am sure, at least, it is not in my power to defend it. And being spoiled of that sandy foundation, I only want now to

---

[1063] The original at the British Library is both damaged and incomplete, lacking the last two pages. The draft copy at CU seems complete and closely matches what we have of the letter in the BL. The entire draft is printed in Schneider, vol. II, pp. 274–82.

be more thoroughly taught how and where to set down my foot again and make out a clear and consistent scheme without it. And of all the particulars I troubled you with before, there remain only these that I have any difficulty about, viz., archetypes, space and duration, and the *esse* of spirits. And indeed these were the chief of my difficulties before. Most of the rest were such objections as I found by conversation among my acquaintance, did not appear to them sufficiently answered. But I believe upon a more mature consideration of the matter, and especially of this kind reply, they will see reason to be better satisfied. They that have seen it (especially my friend Mr. Wetmore)[1064] join with me in thankfully acknowledging your kindness, and return their very humble service to you.

1. As to those difficulties that yet remain with me, I believe all my hesitation about the first of them (and very likely the rest) is owing to my dullness and want of attention so as not rightly to apprehend your meaning. I believe I expressed myself uncouthly about archetypes in my 7th and 8th articles, but upon looking back upon your *Dialogues*, and comparing again three or four passages, I can't think I meant any thing different from what you intend.

You allow, *Dial.* p. 74, 'That things have an existence distinct from being perceived by us' (i.e., any created spirits), 'and that they exist in, i.e., are perceived by, the infinite and omnipresent mind who contains and supports this sensible world as being perceived by Him'. And p. 109, 'That things have an existence exterior to our minds, and that during the intervals of their being perceived by us, they exist in another (i.e., the infinite) mind'; from whence you justly and excellently infer the certainty of His existence, 'who knows and comprehends all things and exhibits them to our view in such manner and according to such rules as he himself has ordained'. And p. 113, 'That, e.g., a tree, when we don't perceive it, exists without our minds in the infinite mind of God'. And this exterior existence of things (if I understand you right) is what you call the archetypal state of things, p. 150.

From these and the like expressions, I gathered what I said about the archetypes of our ideas, and thence inferred that there is exterior to us, in the divine mind, a system of universal nature, whereof the ideas we have are in such a degree resemblances as the Almighty is pleased to communicate to us. And I cannot yet see but my inference was just; because according to you, the idea we see is not in the divine mind, but in our own. When, therefore, you say sensible things exist in, as being perceived by, the infinite mind I humbly conceive you must be understood that the originals or archetypes of our sensible things or ideas exist independent of us in the infinite mind, or that sensible things exist *in*

[1064] James Wetmore (1695–1760). Ordained in England in 1724, Wetmore served at Trinity Church in New York City briefly before moving to the parish of Rye in 1726.

archetypo in the divine mind. The divine idea, therefore, of a tree I suppose (or a tree in the divine mind), must be the original or archetype of ours, and ours a copy or image of His (our ideas images of His, in the same sense as our souls are images of Him) of which there may be several, in several created minds, like so many several pictures of the same original to which they are all to be referred.

When therefore, several people are said to see the same tree or star, etc., whether at the same or at so many several distances from it, it is (if I understand you) *unum et idem in Archetypo*, though *multiplex et diversum in Ectypo*,[1065] for it is as evident that your idea is not mine nor mine yours when we say we both look on the same tree, as that you are not I nor I you. But in having each our idea being dependent upon and impressed upon by the same almighty mind, wherein you say this tree exists, while we shut our eyes (and doubtless you mean the same also, while they are open), our several trees must, I think be so many pictures (if I may so call them) of the one original, the tree in the infinite mind, and so of all other things. Thus I understand you not indeed that our ideas are in any measure adequate resemblances of the system in the divine mind, but however that they are just and true resemblances or copies of it, so far as he is pleased to communicate his mind to us.

2. As to space and duration, I do not pretend to have any other notion of their exterior existence than what is necessarily implied in the notion we have of God; I do not suppose they are any thing distinct from, or exterior to, the infinite and eternal mind; for I conclude with you that there is nothing exterior to my mind but God and other spirits with the attributes or properties belonging to them and ideas contained in them.

External space and duration therefore I take to be those properties or attributes in God, to which our ideas, which we signify by those names, are correspondent, and of which they are the faint shadows. This I take to be Sir Isaac Newton's[1066] meaning when he says, *Schol. General. Deus—durat semper et adest ubique et existendo semper et ubique, durationem et spacium, eternitatem et infinitatem constituit.*[1067] And in his *Optics* calls space as it were God's boundless sensorium, nor can I think you have a different notion of these attributes from that great philosopher, though you may differ in your ways of expressing or explaining yourselves. However it be, when you call the deity infinite and eternal, and in that most beautiful and charming description, *Dial.* p. 71, etc., when you speak of the abyss of space and boundless extent beyond thought and imagination,

---

[1065] "One and the same in archetype," though "multiple and distinct in ectype."
[1066] Sir Isaac Newton (1642–1727).
[1067] "General Scholium. God – always remains and is present everywhere, and by existing always and everywhere, he constitutes eternal duration and infinite space." The quote comes from the general scholium to Book III of Newton's *Principia*.

I don't know how to understand you any otherwise than I understood Sir Isaac, when he uses the like expressions. The truth is we have no proper ideas of God or His attributes, and conceive of them only by analogy from what we find in ourselves; and so, I think we conceive His immensity and eternity to be what in Him are correspondent to our space and duration.

As for the *punctum stans*[1068] of the Schools, and the τὸ νῦν[1069] of the Platonists, they are notions too fine for my gross thoughts; I can't tell what to make of those words, they don't seem to convey any ideas or notions to my mind, and whatever the matter is, the longer I think of them, the more they disappear, and seem to dwindle away into nothing. Indeed they seem to me very much like abstract ideas, but I doubt the reason is because I never rightly understood them. I don't see why the term *punctum stans* may not as well, at least, be applied to the immensity[1070] as the eternity of God; for the word *punctum* is more commonly used in relation to extension or space than duration; and to say that a being is immense, and yet that it is but a point, and that its duration is perpetual without beginning or end, and yet that it is but a τὸ νῦν, looks to me like a contradiction.

I can't therefore understand the term τὸ νῦν unless it be designed to adumbrate the divine omnisciency or the perfection of the divine knowledge, by the more perfect notion we have of things present than of things past; and in this sense it would imply that all things past, present and to come are always at every point of duration equally perfectly known or present to God's mind (though in a manner infinitely more perfect), as the things that are known to us are present to our minds at any point of our duration which we call *now*. So that with respect to His equally perfect knowledge of things past, present or to come, it is in effect always now with Him. To this purpose it seems well applied and intelligible enough, but His duration I take to be a different thing from this, as that point of our duration which we call *now*, is a different thing from our actual knowledge of things, as distinguished from our remembrance. And it may as well be said that God's immensity consists in His knowing at once what is, and is transacted in all places (e.g., China, Jupiter, Saturn, all the systems of fixed stars, etc.) everywhere, however so remote from us (though in a manner infinitely more perfect), as we know what is, and is transacted in us and about us just at hand; as

---

[1068] Scholastic phrase meant to capture the "eternal now" or the eternality of God. Literally "standing point." From its particular point (of view, a standing point), God "sees" everything in human temporality all "at once." The same concept was often also captured by the phrase *nunc semper stans* ("now always standing").

[1069] Literally "the now" or "the present." When τό is affixed to a noun, it typically functions to make the modified word abstract. Thus the translation "the abstract now," as an eternal, timeless present.

[1070] Schneider has "immortality" for "immensity" (vol. II, p. 278).

that His eternity consists in this τὸ νῦν as above explained, i.e., in His knowing things present, past and to come, however so remote, all at once or equally perfectly as we know the things that are present to us now.

In short our ideas expressed by the terms immensity and eternity are only space and duration considered as boundless or with the negation of any limits, and I can't help thinking there is something analogous to them without us, being in and belonging to, or attributes of, that glorious mind, whom for that reason we call immense and eternal, in whom we and all other spirits, *live, move and have their being,*[1071] not all in a point, but in so many different points places or *alicubis,*[1072] and variously situated with respect one to another, or else as I said before, it seems as if we should all coincide one with another.

I conclude, if I am wrong in my notion of external space, and duration, it is owing to the rivetted prejudices of abstract ideas; but really when I have thought it over and over again in my feeble way of thinking, I can't see any connection between them (as I understand them) and that doctrine. They don't seem to be any more abstract ideas than spirits, for, as I said, I take them to be attributes of the necessarily existing spirit; and consequently the same reasons that convince me of his existence, bring with them the existence of these attributes. So that of the ways of coming to the knowledge of things that you mention, it is that of inference or deduction by which I seem to know that there is external infinite space and duration because there is without me a mind infinite and eternal.

3. As to the *esse* of spirits, I know Descartes held the soul always thinks, but I thought Mr. Locke had sufficiently confuted this notion, which he seems to have entertained only to serve an hypothesis. The Schoolmen, it is true, call the soul *Actus* and God *Actus purus;*[1073] but I confess I never could well understand their meaning perhaps because I never had opportunity to be much versed in their writings. I should have thought the Schoolmen to be of all sorts of writers the most unlikely to have had recourse to for the understanding of your sentiments, because they of all others, deal the most in abstract ideas; though to place the very being of spirits in the mere act of thinking, seems to me very much like making abstract ideas of them.

There is certainly something passive in our souls, we are purely passive in the reception of our ideas; and reasoning and willing are actions of something that reasons and wills, and therefore must be only modalities of that something. Nor

---

[1071] Acts 17:28. See also Nicolas Malebranche, *The Search After Truth*, ed. Thomas Lennon and Paul Olscamp (Cambridge University Press, 1997), III.II.6, p. 235.

[1072] "Somewhere."

[1073] "Pure act."

does it seem to me that when I say [something] I mean an abstract idea. It is true I have no idea of it, but I feel it; I feel that it is, because I feel or am conscious of the exertions of it; but the exertions of it are not the thing but the modalities of it distinguished from it as actions from an agent, which seem to me distinguishable without having recourse to abstract ideas.

And, therefore, when I suppose the existence of a spirit while it does not actually think, it does not appear to me that I do it by supposing an abstract idea of existence, and another of absolute time. The existence of John asleep by me, without so much as a dream is not an abstract idea. Nor is the time passing the while an abstract idea [*sic*], they are only partial considerations of him. *Perseverare in existendo*[1074] in general, without reflecting on any particular thing existing, I take to be what is called an abstract idea of time or duration; but the *perseverare in existendo* of John is, if I mistake not, a partial consideration of him. And I think it is as easy to conceive of him as continuing to exist without thinking as without seeing.

Has a child no soul till it actually perceives? And is there not such a thing as sleeping without dreaming, or being in a *deliquium*[1075] without a thought? If there be, and yet at the same time the *esse* of a spirit be nothing else but its actual thinking, the soul must be dead during those intervals; and if ceasing or intermitting to think be the ceasing to be, or death of the soul, it is many times and easily put to death. According to this tenet, it seems to me the soul may sleep on to the resurrection, or rather may wake up in the resurrection state, the next moment after death. Nay I don't see upon what we can build any natural argument for the soul's immortality. I think I once heard you allow a principle of perception and spontaneous motion in beasts. Now if their *esse* as well as ours consists in perceiving, upon what is the natural immortality of our souls founded that will not equally conclude in favour of them? I mention this last consideration because I am at a loss to understand how you state the argument for the soul's natural immortality; for the argument from thinking to immaterial and from thence to indiscerpible,[1076] and from thence to immortal don't seem to obtain in your way of thinking.

If *esse* be only *percipere*, upon what is our consciousness founded? I perceived yesterday, and I perceive now, but last night between my yesterday's and today's perception there has been an intermission when I perceived nothing. It seems to me there must be some principle common to these perceptions, whose *esse* don't

---

[1074] "To persist in existing."

[1075] Literally "a state of melting." A better translation here would be "a state of mental dissolution," i.e. a state where the mind is not properly functioning (and hence lacks thought).

[1076] Schneider has "indivisible" for "indiscerpible."

depend upon them, but in which they are, as it were, connected, and on which they depend, whereby I am and continue conscious of them.

Lastly, Mr. Locke's argument (B. 2. Ch. 19. Sec. 4.) from the intention and remission of thought, appears to me very considerable; according to which, upon this supposition the soul must exist more or have a greater degree of being at one time than at another, according as it thinks more intensely or more remissly.

I own I said very wrong when I said I did not know what to make of ideas more than of matter. My meaning was, in effect, the same as I expressed afterwards about the substance of the soul's being a somewhat as unknown as matter. And what I intended by those questions was whether our ideas are not the substance of the soul itself, under so many various modifications, according to that saying (if I understand it right) *Intellectus intelligendo fit omnia?*[1077] It is true, those expressions (modifications, impressions, etc.) are metaphorical, and it seems to me to be no less so, to say that ideas exist in the mind, and I am under some doubt whether this last way of speaking don't carry us further from the thing, than to say ideas are the mind variously modified; but as you observe, it is scarce possible to speak of the mind without a metaphor.

Thus Sir, your goodness has tempted me to presume again to trouble you once more; and I submit the whole to your correction; but I can't conclude without saying that I am so much persuaded that your books teach truth, indeed the most excellent truths, and that in the most excellent manner,[1078] that I can't but express myself again very solicitously desirous that the noble design you have begun may be yet further pursued in the second part. And everybody that has seen the first is earnestly with me in this request. In hopes of which I will not desire you to waste your time in writing to me (though otherwise I should esteem it the greatest favor), at least till I have endeavored further to gain satisfaction by another perusal of the books I have, with the other pieces you are so kind as to offer, which I will thankfully accept, for I had not *The Principles* of my own, it was a borrowed one I used.

The bearer hereof, Capt. Gorham, is a coaster bound now to Boston, which trade he constantly uses (except that it has been now long interrupted by the winter). But he always touches at Newport, and will wait on the Rev'd Mr. Honyman[1079] both going and returning, by whom you will have opportunity to send those books.

[1077] "Does the intellect [reason], through its own activity [reasoning], become everything?"

[1078] At this point in the original letter the words "Mr. Norris" oddly appear across the top of the page, crossed out. There is no apparent relation to the text of the letter nor any special reason to think it a reference to John Norris (1657–1712), the Malebranchian philosopher.

[1079] James Honeyman* (c. 1675–1750).

I am, Rev'd Sir, with the greatest gratitude, your most devoted humble servant,
S. Johnson

Stratford, Feb. 5, 1729/30

198 BERKELEY TO PRIOR

LR, pp. 204–08.

Rhode Island, 9 March 1729/30

Dear Tom,

My situation hath been so uncertain, and is like to continue so till I am clear about the receipt of his Majesty's bounty, and, in consequence thereof, of the determination of my associates, that you are not to wonder at my having given no categorical answer to the proposal you made in relation to Hamilton's[1080] deanery, which his death hath put an end to. If I had returned, I should perhaps have been under some temptation to have changed; but as my design still continues to wait the event and go to Bermuda as soon as I can get associates and money (which my friends are now soliciting in London), I shall in such case persist in my first resolution of not holding any deanery beyond the limited time.

I long to hear what success you have had in the law suit. Your account of the income of the deanery last paid in is come to my hands. I remember that one of Mrs. Van Homrigh's[1081] creditors (I think a stay-maker) was in France, and so missed of payment. I should be glad you could find some way of paying him, and any others if you find anything still due, even during the minorities of the young ladies, if in books of account charged to their credit. I suppose Mr. Marshall[1082] will agree to this; but whether he doth or no, I think it should be done. I do therefore leave that matter to be fully accomplished by you as you can find opportunity, as perhaps some affair might call you to London, or you may have some friend there. For, in the hurry of things, I should be sorry to have overlooked any, or that any should suffer who should make out their pretensions since. I now call to mind that for this reason I withheld that forty pounds which was paid Mr. Marshall when I was in Dublin; but this was then out of my thoughts, or

[1080] John Hamilton (?–1729), was dean of Dromore from 1724 until 1729. Luce speculates that he proposed to Berkeley that they switch deaneries (Dromore for Derry). See *Works*, vol. IX, p. 80 and Letter 184.

[1081] Hester Van Homrigh* (1688–1723) or her mother. Berkeley was coexecutor of Esther Van Homrigh's estate, which included debts incurred by her mother.

[1082] Robert Marshall* (c. 1690–1772).

I should not have ordered the payment thereof. I agree to what you propose about paying Finny's son, since it is agreeable to Mr. Marshall.

I live here upon land that I have purchased, and in a farmhouse that I have built in this island. It is fit for cows and sheep, and may be of good use for supplying our college at Bermuda.

Among my delays and disappointments, I thank God I have two domestic comforts that are very agreeable, my wife and my little son;[1083] both which exceed my expectations, and fully answer all my wishes. My wife gives her service to you; and, at her request, I must desire you to pay, on my account, two guineas yearly to her brother's wife, towards the support of a young girl, child of my wife's nurse. The girl's name is Betty Smith. Mrs. Forster lives in Henry-street. As this is a piece of charity, I am sure you will not neglect it.

I must also desire that out of the next payment made by M'Manus,[1084] you give one hundred pounds to brother Robin,[1085] to be disposed of by him as I have directed, in pursuance of a letter I had from him, and that the rest be paid into Swift & Company.

Messrs. James,[1086] Dalton,[1087] and Smibert,[1088] etc., are at Boston, and have been there for several months.[1089] My wife and I abide by Rhode Island, preferring quiet and solitude to the noise of a great town, notwithstanding all the solicitations that have been used to draw us thither. No more at present but that I am, dear Tom,

> your affectionate humble servant,
> Geor: Berkeley

As to what you ask about my companions, they are all at Boston, and have been there these four months, preferring that noisy town to this peaceful retreat which my wife and I enjoy in Rhode Island. Being in a hurry, I have writ the same thing twice.

I have desired M'Manus, in a letter to Dr. Ward,[1090] to allow twenty pounds *per annum* for me, towards the poor-house now on foot for clergymen's widows, in the diocese of Derry.

[1083] Henry Berkeley* (1729–after 1756).
[1084] McManus* (?–?).
[1085] Robert Berkeley* (c. 1699–1787).
[1086] John James* (?–1741).
[1087] Richard Dalton* (c. 1695–1769).
[1088] John Smibert* (1688–1751).
[1089] Luce has "these four months" for "several months," presumably because of the postscript.
[1090] Peter Ward* (?–?).

199 BERKELEY TO JOHNSON[1091]

MS unknown. Printed in Schneider, vol. II, pp. 282–84.

Rhode Island, 24 March 1730

Reverend Sir,

Yours of Feb. 5th came not to my hands before yesterday; and this afternoon being informed that a sloop is ready to sail towards your town, I would not let slip the opportunity of returning you an answer, though wrote in a hurry. I have no objection against calling the ideas in the mind of God archetypes of ours. But I object against those archetypes by philosophers supposed to be real things, and to have an absolute rational existence distinct from their being perceived by any mind whatsoever, it being the opinion of all materialists that an ideal existence in the divine mind is one thing, and the real existence of material things another.

1. As to space, I have no notion of any but that which is relative. I know some late philosophers have attributed extension to God, particularly mathematicians; one of whom, in a treatise, *De Spacio [sic Spatio] Reali*, pretends to find out fifteen of the incommunicable attributes of God in Space.[1092] But it seems to me, that they being all negative, he might as well have found them in nothing; and that it would have been as justly inferred from space being impassive, uncreated, indivisible, etc., that it was nothing, as that it was God.

Sir Isaac Newton[1093] supposeth an absolute space different from relative, and consequent thereto, absolute motion different from relative motion; and with all other mathematicians, he supposeth the infinite divisibility of the finite parts of this absolute space; he also supposeth material bodies to drift therein. Now, though I do acknowledge Sir Isaac to have been an extraordinary man and most profound mathematician, yet I cannot agree with him in these particulars. I make no scruple to use the word space, as well as other words in common use, but I do not mean thereby a distinct absolute being. For my meaning I refer you to what I have published.

By the τὸ νῦν[1094] I suppose to be implied that all things past and to come are actually present to the mind of God, and that there is in Him no change, variation,

---

[1091] The original is lost. The letter is also printed in *LL*, p. 176; *Works*, vol. II, pp. 292–94; and Beardsley, pp. 73–75.

[1092] Joseph Raphson (1648?–1715). His *De Spatio Reali*, published in 1697 as an annex to the second edition of the *Analysis Aequationum Universalis*, treats "real" space as mind-independent. Berkeley refers to Raphson elsewhere as well. See Berkeley's *Of Infinites* in *Works*, vol. IV, pp. 237–38 and the *Notebooks* entries 298 and 827.

[1093] Sir Isaac Newton (1642–1727).

[1094] Literally "the now" or "the present." When τό is affixed to a noun, it typically functions to make the modified word abstract. Thus the translation "the abstract now," as an eternal, timeless present.

or succession—a succession of ideas I take to constitute time and not to be only the sensible measure thereof, as Mr. Locke[1095] and others think. But in these matters every man is to think for himself, and speak as he finds. One of my earliest inquiries was about time, which led me into several paradoxes that I did not think fit or necessary to publish, particularly into the notion that the resurrection follows the next moment to death. We are confounded and perplexed about time. (1) Supposing a succession in God. (2) Conceiving that we have an abstract idea of time. (3) Supposing that the time in one mind is to be measured by the succession of ideas in another. (4) Not considering the true use and end of words, which as often terminate in the will as in the understanding, being employed rather to excite influence, and direct action than to produce clear and distinct ideas.

3. That the soul of man is passive as well as active I make no doubt. Abstract general ideas was a notion that Mr. Locke held in common with the Schoolmen, and I think all other philosophers; it runs through his whole book *Of Human Understanding*. He holds an abstract idea of existence exclusive of perceiving and being perceived. I cannot find I have any such idea, and this is my reason against it. Descartes proceeds upon other principles. One square foot of snow is as white as a thousand yards; one single perception is as truly a perception as one hundred. Now any degree of perception being sufficient to existence, it will not follow that we should say one existed more at one time than another, any more than we should say one thousand yards of snow are whiter than one yard. But after all, this comes to a verbal dispute. I think it might prevent a good deal of obscurity and dispute to examine well what I have said about abstraction, and about the true sense and significancy of words, in several parts of these things that I have published, though much remains to be said on that subject.

You say you agree with me that there is nothing within [*sic* without?] your mind but God and other spirits, with the attributes or properties belonging to them, and the ideas contained in them. This is a principle or main point from which, and from what I had laid down about abstract ideas, much may be deduced. But if in every inference we should not agree, so long as the main points are settled and well understood, I should be less solicitous about particular conjectures. I could wish that all the things I have published on these philosophical subjects were read in the order wherein I published them, once to take in the design and connection of them, and a second time with a critical eye, adding your own thought and observation upon every part as you went along.

[1095] John Locke (1632–1704).

I send you herewith ten bound books and one unbound. You will take yourself what you have not already. You will give *The Principles*, *The Theory*, and *The Dialogues*, one of each, with my service to the gentleman who is Fellow of New Haven College,[1096] whose compliments you brought me. What remains you will give as you please.

If at any time your affairs should draw you into these parts, you shall be very welcome to pass as many days as you can spend at my house. Four or five days' conversation would set several things in a fuller and clearer light than writing could do in as many months. In the meantime I shall be glad to hear from you or your friends when ever you please to favour,

> Rev. Sir,
>
> your very humble servant,
>
> Geor. Berkeley

Pray let me know whether they would admit the writings of Hooker[1097] and Chillingworth[1098] into the library of the College in New Haven.

Rhode Island, March 24, 1729–30

200 BERKELEY TO PERCIVAL

EP, BL Add. MS 47032, fol. 167–67v.

Rhode Island, 29 March 1730

My Lord,

About three weeks ago I had the honour of receiving one of your Lordship's of an old date. I am glad the public affairs go on so well, but sorry that the private account of your family is not equally agreeable. I long to hear that my good Lady Percival and Mrs. Dering[1099] get rid of their ailments, which I doubt will never be done but by change of air and exercise. If I should pretend to advise them to a long voyage my advice may be suspected, I can nevertheless affirm sincerely that I believe it would be the best remedy for them in the world. My wife, whose constitution had been much hurt and weakened by a long ague, found wonderful relief from sea sickness and even from the hardships and distresses of the voyage, and is now in health better than she had been for several years before.

[1096] New Haven College later became Yale University.

[1097] Richard Hooker (1554?–1600), theologian, author of *Of the Laws of Ecclesiastical Politie* (1593).

[1098] William Chillingworth (1602–44), theologian, most famous for *The Religion of Protestants* (1638).

[1099] Mary (*née* Parker) Dering* (1692–1731).

We have passed the winter in a profound solitude on my farm in this island, all my companions having been allured five or six months ago to Boston, the great place of pleasure and resort in these parts, where they still continue. After my long fatigue of business this retirement is very agreeable to me; and my wife loves a country life and books so well as to pass her time contentedly and cheerfully without any other conversation than her husband and the dead.

There is no truth in what your Lordship heard of Mrs. Handcock's being married, or about to marry.[1100]

I wait here with all the anxiety that attends suspense till I know what I can depend upon or what course I am to take. On the one hand I have no notion that the Court would put what men call a bite[1101] upon poor clergymen, who depended upon charters, grants, votes, and the like encouragements. On the other hand, I see nothing done towards payment of the money. All I can do is to continue to recommend it to those who are most likely and able to push this matter, and I could do no more if I were on the spot, which makes me not follow the advice of some who have lately wrote to me to return home and solicit myself. When the charter and grant were verified in legal form I thought all solicitation was at an end. One thing I am sure of, that if the Treasury will not issue the money in regard to his Majesty's command, subscribed by his own hand and sealed with the broad seal (which is in Dr. Clayton's[1102] custody), they will not be likely to pay it in regard to anything I can say or do. I have therefore hinted (in a letter I send by this same opportunity) to Dr. Clayton that it would be right to go in form with his Majesty's letter patent in his hands to the Treasury and there make his demand that we may obtain at least a public and direct answer from the proper persons. My views are still the same with regard to Bermuda, whither I am ready to set sail as soon as the money is paid.

I have many thanks to return your Lordship for your kind and friendly care in the concerns I presume to trouble you with, and hope the letter which I wrote several months ago containing my request that your Lordship will be pleased to replace my money in the South Sea* is arrived safe to your hands. Wherever I am I find my self always increasing my debt of obligations to your Lordship, a grateful sense of which I shall ever preserve, and on all occasions be glad to show how truly and faithfully, I am, My Lord,

> your Lordship's most obedient and most humble servant,
> Geo: Berkeley

[1100] See Letter 192.
[1101] i.e. a trick or hoax.
[1102] Robert Clayton* (1695–1758).

My wife joins in our best respects and humble service to your Lordship and good Lady Percival. I am glad to hear that P. Courayer[1103] is taken care of. Pray my humble service to him and Mr. Dering,[1104] etc.

201 BERKELEY TO NEWMAN[1105]

Yale MS Vault Berkeley, Box 1.

Rhode Island, 29 March 1730

Sir,

I thank you for the favour of yours with the box of books which arrived some time ago. I gave what was directed to Mr. Honeyman[1106] and may venture to assure you that whatever you send of that kind to him will be committed to the hands of a man of sense & merit who will not fail to make the best use thereof & distribute them where they may be of most service. If there remains any thing of the money you get from Mr. Hoare[1107] please to remit it in those two small pamphlets you sent for a specimen, the one an abstract of the bible, the other a small catechetical piece.

The delay that our affair depending in the treasury hath met with is no small discouragement & I very much apprehend it may cause an alteration in the minds of my associates. I have not failed to set this matter in its proper light & recommend it in the most earnest manner to such friends in England as I judged most able and willing to solicit at Court. But the same reasons which determined me to come away without taking leave of my friends or waiting on men in power are still as prevalent to hinder me from soliciting in person which should be my last shift and forelorn hope, being at present altogether of opinion that it may be solicited to better purpose by others than by myself.

What you observe of the growth of atheism and irreligion hath a fatal aspect upon England but it is no more than hath been carrying on for many years past by a set of men who under the notion of liberty are for introducing licence and a general contempt of all laws divine or humane. Political societies have their

---

[1103] Pierre-François le Courayer* (1681–1776).

[1104] Daniel Dering* (?–1730).

[1105] On the front in another hand is written: "Read 4 June 1730, ordered the books delivered on the terms of the Society. Answered 5 February 1733/34 vid. N.E.L.B." First published in *Yale University Library Gazette* 8.1 (July 1933): 26–27.

[1106] James Honeyman* (c. 1675–1750).

[1107] Benjamin Hoare* (1693–1749/50).

diseases as well as natural bodies and this seems that which will be the death of Great Britain. God governs the world and knows his own times and seasons: it is our duty to endeavour, not be unserviceable in this our day, and patiently leave the event to Providence. My wife is obliged to you for your kind compliment and joins with me in her respects to you. I am Sir,

your most obedient servant,

Geor: Berkeley

202 BERKELEY TO PRIOR

LR, *pp. 215–21.*

Newport, Rhode Island, 7 May 1730

Dear Tom,

Last week I received a packet from you by the way of Philadelphia, the postage whereof amounted to above four pounds of this country money. I thank you for the enclosed pamphlet,[1108] which in the main I think very seasonable and useful. It seems to me, that in computing the sum-total of the loss by absentees, you have extended some articles beyond the due proportion; e.g. when you charge the whole income of occasional absentees in the third class: and that you have charged some articles twice; e.g. when you make distinct articles for law suits £9,000 and for attendance for employments £8,000, both which seem already charged in the third class. The tax you propose seems very reasonable, and I wish it may take effect, for the good of the kingdom, which will be obliged to you whenever it is brought about. That it would be the interest of England to allow a free trade to Ireland, I have been thoroughly convinced ever since my being in Italy, and have upon all occasions endeavoured to convince English gentlemen thereof, and have convinced some, both in and out of Parliament; and I remember to have discoursed with you at large upon this subject when I was last in Ireland. Your hints for setting up new manufactures seem reasonable; but the spirit of projecting is low in Ireland.

Now, as to my own affair, I must tell you that I have no intention of continuing in these parts but in order to settle the college his Majesty hath

---

[1108] Thomas Prior,* *List of the Absentees of Ireland* (1729). Berkeley is listed in the second edition as an absentee dean. The pamphlet caused some consternation, especially amongst Prior's own class, since it advocated a 20 percent tax on any monies taken out of the country.

been pleased to found at Bermuda; and I wait only the payment of the King's grant to transport myself and family thither. I am now employing the interest of my friends in England for that purpose; and have wrote in the most pressing manner either to get the money paid, or at least to get a positive answer that may direct me what course I am to take. Doctor Clayton[1109] indeed hath wrote me word, that he hath been informed by a good friend of mine (who had it from a very great man), that the money will not be paid.[1110] But I cannot look upon a hearsay, at second or third hand, to be a proper answer for me to act upon. I have therefore suggested to the Doctor, that he ought to go himself with the letters-patent containing the grant in his hands, to the Treasury, and there make his demand in form. I have also wrote to others to use their interest at Court; though indeed one would have thought all solicitation at an end when once I had obtained a grant under his Majesty's hand and the broad seal of England. As to going to London and soliciting in person, I think it reasonable first to see what my friends can do; and the rather because I cannot suppose my own solicitations will be more regarded than theirs. Be assured I long to know the upshot of this matter; and that, upon an explicit refusal, I am determined to return home; and that it is not the least in my thoughts to continue abroad and hold my deanery. It is well known to many considerable persons in England, that I might have had a dispensation for holding it for life; and that I was much pressed to it, but I resolutely declined it: and if our design of a college had taken place as soon as I once hoped it would, I should have resigned before this time. A little after my first coming to this island, I entertained some thoughts of applying to his Majesty (when Dr. Clayton had received the 20,000 pounds, the patent for which I left with him), to translate our college hither; but have since seen cause to lay aside all thoughts of that matter. I do assure you, *bona fide*, that I have not the least intention to stay here longer than I can get a clear answer from the Government; for, upon all private accounts, I should like Derry better than New England. As to the reason of my coming to this island, I think I have

---

[1109] Robert Clayton* (1695–1758).

[1110] Stock reports the following reply from Robert Walpole* (1676–1745) when Edmund Gibson* (1669–1748), then bishop of London, asked him directly about the payment of the funds for the Bermuda scheme: "If you put this question to me as a minister, I must and can assure you, that the money shall most undoubtedly be paid, as soon as suits with public convenience: but if you ask me, as a friend, whether Dean Berkeley should continue in America, expecting the payment of £20,000, I advise him, by all means, to return home to Europe, and to give up his present expectations." Joseph Stock, *Memoirs of George Berkeley: Late Bishop of Cloyne in Ireland*, 2nd edn. (London: J. Murray, 1784), pp. 25–26. See also Letter 206, where Percival* relates a similar story about Walpole's intentions.

already informed you that I have been at great expence in purchasing land and stock here, which might supply the defects of Bermuda, and so obviate a principal objection that was made to placing a college there. To conclude, as I am here in order to execute a design addressed for by Parliament, and set on foot by his Majesty's royal charter, I think myself obliged to wait the event, whatever course is taken in Ireland about my deanery. I had wrote to both the bishops of Raphoe[1111] and Derry;[1112] but letters are of uncertain passage. Yours was half a year in coming; and I have had some a year after their date, though often in two months, and sometimes less. I must desire you to present my duty to both their Lordships, and acquaint them with what I have now wrote to you in answer to the kind message from my Lord of Derry, conveyed by your hands; for which I return my humble thanks to his Lordship.

I long to hear the success of our law suit with Partinton.[1113] What I hear from England about our college-grant you shall know.

My wife gives her service to you. She hath been lately ill of a miscarriage; but is now, I thank God, recovered. Our little son is great joy to us.[1114] We are such fools as to think him the most perfect thing we ever saw in its kind. I wish you all happiness; and remain, dear Tom,

yours affectionately,

G. Berkeley

Newport in Rhode Island, May 7, 1730

P.S. [Sent with the duplicate letter only]

This is a duplicate of a letter I sent you several months ago. I have not since had one line from the persons I had wrote to, to make the last instances for the 20,000 pounds. This I impute to an accident that we hear happened to a man of war, as it was coming down the river, bound for Boston, where it was expected some months ago, and is now daily looked for, with the new governor.

The newspapers of last February mentioned Dr. Clayton's[1115] being made bishop. I wish him joy of his preferment, since I doubt we are not likely to see him in this part of the world.

I know not how to account for my not hearing that the dispute with Partinton is finished one way or other before this time.

Newport in Rhode Island, July 20, 1730

[1111] Nicholas Forster* (1672–1743).
[1112] Henry Downes (?–1735). Downes translated from Meath in 1727.
[1113] Peter Partinton* (?–?).
[1114] Henry Berkeley* (1729–after 1756).
[1115] Robert Clayton* (1695–1758) was made bishop of Killala and Achonry in 1729/30.

203 PERCIVAL TO BERKELEY

EP, BL Add. MS 47032, fols. 203v–04.

Charlton, 9 July 1730

Dear Sir,

By yours of the 29 March last I perceive you had not received my letter dated 17 January, wherein I acquainted you that your £2,000 South Sea Annuities* were bought in again by Mr. Hoare[1116] in his own name; for want of a power in me to demand back the money arising from the sale of them, which by your direction I lodged in his hands. This money was entered in his books to your account, and he would not allow that your bare directions in a letter gave me sufficient authority to demand it from him again, because it did not empower me to give him a legal discharge. But to comply as far as he might with your directions he bought the Annuities again, as I have said for your use, but in his own name, and will deliver them up, when you send me a letter of attorney to demand them of him. They cost 105⅝ and ⅛ brokerage; in all £2,115.

It is great pleasure to hear you and your family keep your health, and that you can find agreeableness in so much solitude. However, you still show that you prefer to it a public and useful life, and that all the discouragement you have met with has not in the least abated your zeal for erecting your intended college. I wish to God I were able to acquaint you with anything satisfactory on that head, but I am still in the dark and in great despondency about the money.

Bishop Clayton[1117] went a considerable time since to Ireland, and who will advise or undertake to go to the treasury with your letters patent and make the demand in the manner you mention, I know not, nor can I see any good effect that would come from such a procedure, the delay not arising I believe from thence. If ordered they must pay it, and if not they will give that for a reason, and all you could get if you pursued that step would be a lawsuit with the Crown, which though successful would not advance your scheme, because without the civil protection and encouragement your college would fall to the ground. It is possible that in time it may be thought fit to pay it, but I think it must be by some miraculous influence from above, and your friends here despair of it, though my Lord

---

[1116] Benjamin Hoare* (1693–1749/50).
[1117] Robert Clayton* (1695–1758).

Townshend,[1118] who had some politic reasons against advancing learning in America (as I have heard), is retired from business.

Father Courayer[1119] is now with Mr. Duncomb[1120] in Wiltshire, but returns to me in the autumn. The Queen has paid him constantly a hundred pounds a year, only some months are now lapsed by accidents that happened, but not from any weariness to support him, for her Majesty has a very good and kind opinion of him. Father le Quien[1121] has lately published two other volumes against him, but they contain nothing new.

We now seem to be in earnest to fix Don Carlos[1122] in Italy; and troops are actually marching to Portsmouth to embark for that service. But the Emperor[1123] is determined to oppose it, and where the contest will end I believe the wisest cannot foresee. It is thought we shall attack Sicily out of hand which is ready to change masters.

My sister Dering[1124] has been greatly mended in her health by two journeys to Bath, but Daniel[1125] I think is in a bad state. It is now several months that he has not been a day right well, and lately he voided a stone as big as an olive stone. My wife ventured once more to Bath, and found so good success from those waters that we propose to return thither in September again. It is the opinion of Dr. Stenard that the Bath waters will do service in one time of life when it will not in another, and I hope my wife may find his observation true.

You have her humble service to you and your Lady, to whom pray present mine and believe me ever,

>Dear Sir,
>
>your, etc.,
>
>Percival

[1118] Charles Townshend* (1674–1738), second Viscount Townshend. Townshend promoted policies designed to keep the colonies dependent on England.

[1119] Pierre-François le Courayer* (1681–1776).

[1120] Perhaps William Duncombe (1690–1769), writer.

[1121] Michel le Quien (1661–1733) was a Dominican, a French historian, and a theologian. He published *La Nullité des Ordinations Anglicanes* (2 vols; Paris, 1725), and *La Nullité des Ordinationes Anglicanes Démontrée de Nouveau* (2 vols; Paris, 1730), against Le Courayer's apology for the Anglican orders.

[1122] Don Carlos (1716–88) was the son of Philip V of Spain and Isabella of Parma. He ruled as duke of Parma, by right of his mother (1732–34), was king of Naples (1734–59), and ascended to the throne of Spain as Charles III in 1759.

[1123] Charles VI (1685–1740), Holy Roman Emperor of the Habsburg Empire (Austria).

[1124] Mary (*née* Parker) Dering* (1692–1731).

[1125] Daniel Dering* (?–1730).

204 BERKELEY TO PERCIVAL[1126]

EP, BL Add. MS 47032, fols. 204–05.

Rhode Island, 20 July 1730

My Lord,

Your Lordship is entitled to more thanks than I know how to express for your kind care about my money. I waited this opportunity of a vessel going from hence, whereby I send the enclosed authorities drawn in the most authentic manner, and which I suppose will enable your Lordship to do what you are so good to take upon you.

I must beg leave to repeat and insist upon your Lordship's paying yourself out of the first money that shall become due on my South Sea Annuities,* and am concerned this was not done sooner. Be pleased therefore my good Lord to put your humble servant (who hath a thousand other favours to acknowledge) to no further confusion on this head.

I have not heard from Dr. Clayton since he was made Bishop.[1127] I take him to be a man of worthy views and heartily wish success to his endeavours of being useful in that station since we are not likely to see him in this part of the world.

The enclosed letter to Mr. Archdeacon Benson[1128] I entreat your Lordship to send by a careful hand as directed. I appoint him to take the care of our college affairs upon instead of the Bishop of Killala, and to take into his custody the patents and the college sea, and papers that were left with his Lordship. He is a true friend to me and the undertaking, and nobody hath better inclinations or more opportunity to do it service. I long to know the issue of his endeavour, and what course I am to take, or what to expect.

I already informed your Lordship that I hold myself in readiness to go to Bermuda, and I beg that you will take occasion to do me justice in that particular, because I understand the contrary hath been given out, though without any truth or foundation, since I have for this year past taken all possible pains to undeceive the people and contradict that report. Bermuda after all is the proper place, for, besides that the £20,000 were addressed for by Parliament and granted by the Crown for that individual spot, there are other reasons which lie against placing the college here, particularly the extreme dearness of labour and the difficulty of getting Indians, the number whereof is very inconsiderable in this part of America,

---

[1126] In the margin is a note: "Dean Berkeley received at Bath 12 December, answered 23rd."
[1127] Robert Clayton* (1695–1758).
[1128] Martin Benson* (1689–1752).

having been consumed by wars and strong liquors, not to mention some other particulars wherein I take Bermuda to have the advantage.

As for the raillery of European wits, I should not mind it if I saw my college go on and prosper; but I must own the disappointments I have met with in this particular have nearly touched me, not without affecting my health and spirits. If the founding of a college for the spreading of religion and learning in America had been a foolish project, it cannot be supposed the Court, the Ministers, and the Parliament, would have given such public encouragement to it; and if, after all that encouragement, they who engaged to endow and protect it, let it drop, the disappointment indeed may be to me, but the censure, I think, will light elsewhere.

My best wishes wait on your Lordship, my good Lady Percival, and all your family. I wrote to Mr. Dering[1129] but have not heard from him. I shall ever be glad to hear that good health and prosperity attend you all.

I am sorry that I live in a country that resembles England so much in its produce of every kind, that here is not any one curiosity worth sending; otherwise I should not have been unmindful of my duty to my Lady. Be pleased to accept of mine and of my wife's respects and believe that I am with the greatest truth and gratitude,

> your Lordship's most obedient and most humble servant,
> G. Berkeley

205 JOHNSON TO BERKELEY[1130]

> *Johnson Family Papers (MS 305). Manuscripts and Archives, Yale University, folder 175.*

24 July 1730

Revd Sir,

I take this opportunity again to thank you for the great kindness and [cond...?] you favoured me with when I had the honour to be at your house and the vast pleasure and advantage I enjoyed in your most engaging conversation. I think myself very unhappy that I am so remote from it: I design, however, if I can to pay me respects to you again before winter.

I have disposed of the books you was pleased to send by me into these parts according to your order and I am desired by the several gentlemen who have received your benefaction to return you their humblest thanks. Mr. Williams[1131]

[1129] Daniel Dering* (?–1730).

[1130] Appended to the letter is a tract, "A General View of Philosophy, or A Prolegomenon to the Arts & Sciences." Above the tract is written "A copy of what I sent to the Dean Berkeley."

[1131] Elisha Williams* (1694–1755). Berkeley made the sizable and valuable gift of eight cases of books.

designs to give you the thanks of the college for the share they have had of your goodness and will if possible give you a visit.

Hooker[1132] I have given to Mr. Caner[1133] and Chillingworth[1134] with one of your dialogues to Mr. Wilmore,[1135] whose letter of thanks to you is here enclosed. These two neighbours of mine are very worthy honest men, and I know of nobody that would make a better use of them. The other dialogue I gave to a very promising young man of the college that I have the care of. All in these parts who have any taste for learning and good sense are mightily enamoured with your philosophy. Twenty at least I know of who entirely fall in with it and many have got the booksellers of Boston to send for several sets of your books.

As for my self who have had so much the greatest share in your benefactions, I am not a master of words sufficient to tell you how much I esteem my self obliged to you and your Lady for the books you have enriched me with; and therefore I will not attempt it. I will only assure you that it shall be my utmost endeavor to answer your good ends in bestowing them by doing all the good I can with them, in promoting good sense knowledge and virtue as far as I am able both in my self and others.

206 PERCIVAL TO BERKELEY

EP, BL Add. MS 47032, fols. 256v–58.

Bath, 23 December 1730

Dear Sir,

Yours of the 20 July came last week and with a power enclosed to receive your annuities such as I suppose will content Mr. Hoare.[1136] I shall when I return to London take care of it, and that won't be long first for the Parliament meets the 21 of next month.

Your friend Mr. Stanhope[1137] is lately dead and Archdeacon Benson[1138] is at Durham. My brother Percival,[1139] to whom I enclosed the letters you sent me for

---

[1132] Richard Hooker (1554?-1600), theologian and author of *Of the Laws of Ecclesiastical Politie* (1593).
[1133] Most likely Henry Caner (1699?-1792), Johnson's pupil and missionary to Fairfield. See James Henry Stark, *The Loyalists of Massachusetts and the Other Side of the American Revolution* (Salem Press, 1910), pp. 346-49.
[1134] William Chillingworth (1602-44), theologian most famous for *The Religion of Protestants* (1638).
[1135] An unknown neighbor of Johnson's.
[1136] Benjamin Hoare* (1693-1749/50).
[1137] An unknown Stanhope. George Stanhope (1660-1728), dean of Canterbury, died in 1728, but there is no record of an acquaintance.
[1138] Martin Benson* (1689-1752).
[1139] Philip Percival (?-1748).

those two gentlemen, has forwarded the Archdeacon's to him, and keeps that for Stanhope for further order.

I don't wonder the disappointment you so long have met with in the settlement of your college, after the progress you had made, and the charge, labour, and hazard you have gone through to perfect it, should sensibly affect you; but the design seems too great and good to be accomplished in an age where men love darkness better than the light, and nothing is considered but with a political view. A very good Lord asked me whether I thought the Indians would not be saved as well as we? and if I considered that learning tended to make the plantations independent of their Mother Country?, adding that the ignorance of the Indians and the variety of sects in our plantations was England's security. He was even sorry that we had an university in Dublin. And yet the Lord is the ornament of the nobility for learning and sobriety, but he reduced all to policy.[1140] I am very sorry you should let this disappointment affect you so nearly; you know we can but propose, the disposal and event is in God's hands, who will when he thinks fit effectually bring about what tends to his own glory, I own I do not see at present great reason to hope success, but who knows what sparks of fire may yet remain among the ashes.

I discoursed it with the Speaker, who though he approves it not for the same reason the Lord above mentioned gave me, yet thinks the honour of Parliament engaged, and told me he on that account had spoken to Sir Joseph Jekyl[1141] not to let it drop. But on the other hand Sir Robert Walpole[1142] told Mr. Hutchinson[1143] in confidence, as he undoubtedly has writ you word, that the money would never be paid; so I confess I have very little hopes.

I have not spared to declare on every occasion, that your intention is, and has always been, to settle in Bermuda, and that you only went to Rhode Island to settle methods for furnishing your college with provisions.

There is a project on foot for settling a colony of a hundred English families on the river Savannah that bounds the north side of Carolina, by which it is proposed that a vast tract of good land uncultivated by reason of the incursion of the Indians will be protected and of course improved to the enriching that province, and to the great advantage of England.[1144] The King is to give the land, and the charges furnished by subscriptions, and 5 or £6,000 is all we think

---

[1140] This "very good Lord" is likely Charles Townshend* (1674–1738), second Viscount Townshend.
[1141] Sir Joseph Jekyll* (1662–1738).
[1142] Sir Robert Walpole* (1676–1745).
[1143] An unknown Hutchinson. Philip Percival writes from London of the Mr. Hutchinson who received a letter from Berkeley. See Rand, pp. 263–64, Philip Percival to John Percival, 4 July 1730.
[1144] A reference to the Georgia colony.

necessary for beginning it. This being entirely calculated for a secular interest meets with approbation, and the Board of Trade have agreed with the undertakers upon a favourable report to be made of it to His Majesty, who, with the Ministry, and the merchants of the city, commend the design.

Mr. Oglethorpe,[1145] a young gentleman of very public spirit and chairman of the late committee of gaols, gave the first hint of this project last year, and has very diligently pursued it. Several Parliament men, clergy, etc. are commissioners for executing it, myself among others. It is proposed the families there settled shall plant hemp and flax to be sent unmanufactured to England, whereby in time much ready money will be saved in this Kingdom, which now goes out to other countries for the purchase of these goods, and they will also be able to supply us with a great deal of good timber. It is possible too they may raise white mulberry trees and send us good raw silk. But at the worst they will be able to live there, and defend that country from the insults of their neighbours, and London will be eased of maintaining a number of families which being let out of gaol have at present no visible way to subsist.

I now come to a very melancholy part of my letter, to acquaint you with the loss of two of my nearest and dearest relations. My brother Dering[1146] after a year's struggle with the stone and a shattered constitution died at Leiden the 13 September last. He went thither to consult Dr. Boerhaave,[1147] but he was too far gone when he came, and only languished on for a few weeks. He had lately obtained the place of Auditor for the Duchy of Cornwall, but lived not to enjoy a penny of the profits for it was in great confusion, and I believe his solicitude to reduce it into order contributed to his end. If I were writing to another I should fill this sheet with his virtues, but to you who knew him I will say no more, than that to a religious and sober life he joined a Christian death, after acquitting himself of the duties of a good subject, husband, father, and friend. You may judge the affliction it is to us all, and particularly how near it has gone to my sister's heart who loses with him an income of £1,000 a year, and who I think is in a very ill way of health. The other relation we have lost is cousin Southwell,[1148] who died the 4th of this month, after having suffered greatly by an overturn in his coach, which occasioned much painful surgeon's work about his leg, which weakened him past recovery. He had a

---

[1145] James Edward Oglethorpe* (1696–1785).

[1146] Daniel Dering* (?–1730).

[1147] Herman Boerhaave (1668–1738), Dutch physician, botanist, and chemist of international repute. He allegedly was famous enough to be known and sought out by nobility in China in his own day.

[1148] Edward Southwell* (1671–1730).

year ago some slight hurt of the palsy, and after that a fit of the apoplexy, in one of which he died without a groan or convulsion like a child fallen to sleep.

Since you so peremptorily [insist] on my receiving out of your annuities the money you mention, rather than disoblige you by further refusal, as I find it would, I will comply with you; but I declare it shall go to some charitable use, or the furtherance of some good design, the merit of which will be in great part your own.

If my wife could recover of her cholic we should all be well, but I think it rather grows upon her, for nothing but greater quantities of laudanum relieves her, though we try everything, and have been here since August for the use of these waters. She joins with the rest in affectionate service to you. I beg my humble service to your Lady and hope she with your child are in perfect health. I am ever

> Sir,
>
> your, etc.,
>
> Percival

207 PERCIVAL TO BERKELEY

EP, BL Add. MS *47033, fol. 11–11v.*

London, 4 February 1730/31

Dear Sir,

Having an opportunity of writing to you given me by Mr. Newman[1149] I cannot lose it, though I am in prodigious hurry, just come to town, and perplexed with variety of business after six months absence from home, at Bath. I shall as soon as possible invest myself with your money in the funds as you desired, and be always ready to execute any other orders of yours.

We are in great affliction for the death of my sister Dering[1150] the 24 of last month at Bath, which has thrown my wife into her bad state of health from which we have so long laboured to set her free.

I hope you, and your Lady, and child are in perfect health, to whom my humble service, and am ever, etc.,

> Percival

[1149] Henry Newman* (1670–1743).
[1150] Mary (*née* Parker) Dering* (1692–1731). Her husband, Daniel Dering* (?–1730), had also just recently died (4 December 1730).

208 NEWMAN TO BERKELEY[1151]

SPCK MS D4/41, fols. 61–63.

Bartlett's Buildings, 5 February 1730/31

Revd Sir,

About 5 weeks ago I received two letters from the Bishop of London[1152] to be forwarded to you by different Ships, the first that should sail for N. England, and accordingly I have herewith sent one of them, and the other by another ship going home at the same time. I hope they contain advices of importance to direct your future resolutions which I pray God may be prosperous. I have this day received a letter from my Lord Percival[1153] which is herewith sent. His Lordship is just now returned with his Lady from Bath, where they have buried Mrs. Dering after a lingering illness said to be occasioned by grief for the death of Mr. Dering last summer in Holland in his way to the German Spa.[1154] Good Mr. Southwell,[1155] Clerk of the Council, is also lately dead, in whom His Lordship & you have lost a particular friend.

I received your letter of the 29th March last & bespoke the books you therein desired, but the bookseller not expecting the ships would depart so early has not yet sent them in.

My humble service to your Lady and to Messrs. James[1156] and Dalton[1157] and to Mr. Honeyman,[1158] and please to be assured that I am

> Revd Sir
>
> your most obedient humble servant,
>
> H. N.

P.S.: In December last I received your letter of the 18 of August[1159] & immediately forwarded your letter to the Bishop of London as I hope his Lordship acknowledges. I have acquainted several of your friends in our Society with your resolution to go to Bermuda as soon as the government are determined to comply with their grant under the great seal, but they seem to think the government will be

---

[1151] Addressed "To the Revd Mr. Dean Berkeley at Rhode Island." The letter is printed in Allen and McClure, *History of the Society for Promoting Christian Knowledge: 1698-1898*, pp. 246–47.
[1152] Edmund Gibson* (1669–1748).
[1153] John Percival* (1683–1748).
[1154] Mary (*née* Parker) Dering* (1692–1731).
[1155] Edward Southwell* (1671–1730).
[1156] John James* (?–1741).
[1157] Richard Dalton* (c. 1695–1769).
[1158] James Honeyman* (c. 1675–1750).
[1159] There is no record of this letter.

less inclined to such a determination upon the advices of the mutinous disposition of the inhabitants since the withdrawing of the independent companys from thence to the Bahama Islands. And that thereupon many of the inhabitants at Bermuda are gone & going to the Bahama Islands & South Carolina.

As to public affairs the newspapers with you I doubt not inform you of everything worth your notice. My Lord Wilmington[1160] is lately made President of the Privy Council, & the Duke of Dorset[1161] continues appointed Lord Lieutenant of Ireland, whither his Grace it is said will be going as soon as the Parliament is up. You will hear of a project vigorously espoused by Mr. Oglethorpe[1162] & several other active Members of Parliament, among which my Lord Percival is one, for sending a colony of our poor helpless people from hence furnished with all necessarys for a year's support under the direction of Captain Coram, a gentleman well known in your parts, to the southern parts of South Carolina, where his Majesty has some unappropriated lands to give them, a grant of which is now preparing.[1163] And a considerable Number of Swiss and Palatines are designed to follow them, to instruct them in the improvements of producing wine and raw silk, which the Climate they say is capable of equal if not beyond any part of Europe.

The great number and amicable dispositions of the Indians in those Parts, confirmed very lately by a solemn treaty here, is another inducem[en]t that has turned their thoughts on this project, in hopes it may succeed to the relief of many thousand of his Majesty's subjects that are now perishing in the streets of this city & its suburbs, or in the gaols of this Kingdom, leading a useless life.

209 BERKELEY TO PERCIVAL[1164]

EP, BL Add. MS 47033, fol. 32–32v.

Rhode Island, 2 March 1730/31

My Lord,

I was very much concerned at an account I met with not long since in the public papers of Daniel Dering's[1165] death and the disposal of his employments.

[1160] Spencer Compton* (c.1674–1743), Earl of Wilmington. Towards the end of December 1730 he was appointed lord president of the Privy Council.

[1161] Lionel Cranfield Sackville* (1688–1765), first Duke of Dorset. He was appointed lord lieutenant of Ireland 23 June 1730. He would serve in that role until 1737.

[1162] James Edward Oglethorpe* (1696–1785).

[1163] A reference to the founding of the Georgia colony.

[1164] In the margin: "Dean Berkeley intends to return received at Charlton 5 July 1731."

[1165] Daniel Dering (?–1730) had recently died (4 December 1730).

His good qualities and long intimate acquaintance (things that I myself shared in and was long a witness of) I doubt not endeared him to your Lordship as much as the nearness of relation. I am sincerely touched with everything that affects your Lordship and your family, but on this occasion I was sensibly affected on my own account.

I have received such accounts on all hands both from England and Ireland that I now give up all hopes of executing the design which brought me into these parts. I am fairly given to understand that the money will never be paid. And this long continued delay and discountenance hath (as I am informed by several letters) made those persons who engaged with me entirely give up all thoughts of the college and turn themselves to other views. So that I am absolutely abandoned by every one of them. This disappointment which long lay heavy upon my spirits I endeavour to make myself easy under[1166] by considering that we cannot know the times and the seasons of Providence, that we even know not what would be eventually good or bad, and that no events are in our power. Upon the whole my thoughts are now set towards Europe, where I shall endeavour to be useful some other way.

What they foolishly call free thinking seems to me the principal root or source not only of opposition to our College but of most other evils in this age, and as long as that frenzy subsists and spreads, it is in vain to hope for any good either to the mother country or colonies, which always follow the fashions of Old England. I am credibly informed that great numbers of all sorts of blasphemous books published in London are sent to Philadelphia, New York, and other places, where they produce a plentiful crop of atheists and infidels. I am apt to think more from an affectation of imitating English customs (which is very prevalent in America) than from any other motive.

My wife and child[1167] are both I thank God very well, and very much together with myself, humble servants to your Lordship and my good Lady. My wife is big with child and so far gone that we cannot safely put to sea least she should be brought to bed on shipboard. As soon as this event is over and that she and her infant can put to sea, I propose with God's blessing to return. I pray God preserve your Lordship and good family and remain with sincere affection and respect,

> My Lord
> your Lordship's most obedient
> and most obliged humble
> servant,
> Geo. Berkeley

[1166] From here until the comma omitted by Luce and Rand, but is present in the letterbook version.
[1167] Henry Berkeley* (1729–after 1756).

210 BERKELEY TO GIBSON[1168]

Lambeth, FP XVII, pp. 19–20.

Rhode Island, 15 March 1730/31

My Lord,

I beg leave to return my humble thanks to your Lordship for the favour of a letter just come to my hands wherein you have been pleased to send me Sir Robert Walpole's[1169] answer which leaves me no room to deliberate what I have to do. I shall therefore prepare to get back as soon as possible. I was prepared for this event by advices from other hands particularly some from Ireland which informed me that all my associates to a man had absolutely abandoned the design upon which I came and betaken themselves to other views having been tired out with discouragement and delay which hath proved as fatal to our college as an absolute refusal.

I have waited these two months in expectation that some vessel from Bermuda might possibly have touched at this island which would have better enabled me to send your Lordship an account of the present state of the Church and clergy there. But none having come I can only say what I formerly had upon the information of some credible persons, viz. that there are eight churches in those islands that are alternately served by three clergymen who have each of them a small glebe and two [of them] forty pounds *per annum*; the third, who is minister in the town of St. George, having fifty pounds *per annum* in that country many which I think is thirty per cent worse than English. I had heard that one of those three clergymen had left Bermuda for a living in the continent but if I mistake not by his place hath been since supplied by another provided by the present governor. Some year ago there was a [conventicle?] set up there by a very troublesome man, one Smith, who brought a dissenting teacher from Carolina, but it seems upon the rumour of our college they both thought fit to leave those islands. So that I believe the people there are now generally well affected to the Church.

Your Lordship will please to accept of this which is the best account can be given by

> My Lord
> your Lordship's most dutiful and most obedient servant,
> Geor: Berkeley

Rhode Island, March 15, 1730–1

[1168] Edmund Gibson* (1669–1748).
[1169] Sir Robert Walpole* (1676–1745). See note to Letter 202.

211 OGLETHORPE TO BERKELEY[1170]

EP, BL Add. MS 47033, fols. 94v–96v.

May 1731

Revd Sir,

Mr. Archdeacon Benson[1171] did me the honour of calling here, and acquainted me in a more particular manner with your most excellent design. I had heard in general of it before, and admired that extensive charity which had overcome the natural love men bear to their native country, and to those places and things which renew the pleasing ideas of youth. That Christian charity which had for the sake of the ignorant, barbarous Indians preferred labour and danger to ease and plenty, and chose study and abstinences in a wilderness, rather than the enjoyment of a plentiful fortune and large preferments in one of the most agreeable countries in Europe.

Mr. Archdeacon informed me of the many difficulties and obstacles you had met in that glorious design of establishing an university, where the students were by daily exercise to be instructed in Christianity, temperance, patience, fortitude, and other laborious virtues, as well as in arts and sciences.

When he told me there was no probability of your receiving the money voted by Parliament, I was not at all surprised, considering that in the paying to you the money no private views was [sic] to be gratified, no relation served, nor pander preferred, nor no depraved opposition indulged. Mankind it is true was to be benefitted, and learning and revealed religion extended, but these were not ministerial points, and consequently might be opposed without danger of losing other pensions or employments.

The reason Mr. Archdeacon spoke to me more particularly upon your affairs, was that there are several members of Parliament, and others (of whom I have the honour to be one), associated together for the carrying on some good designs. Mr. Archdeacon thought that we might be of some service towards effecting your truly Christian undertaking. He therefore desired that I would communicate to you an account of this new society.[1172]

[1170] James Oglethorpe* (1696–1785). Percival's* note in the margin: "Mr. Oglethorpe's letter to Dean Berkeley in Rhode Island, America, touching the Carolina Colony."

[1171] Martin Benson,* (1689–1752). In his journal Percival* notes on 10 March 1731 that archdeacon Benson* had heard from Berkeley a month prior about Berkeley's intended return to Europe. Percival also remarks on an "impertinent letter" written by the bishop of Down, Francis Hutchinson, (1660–1739), requiring Berkeley to return home and "calling his scheme idle and simple" (EP, BL Add. MS 47060, fol. 85).

[1172] The society planned to establish a colony in Georgia, drawing on prisoners (primarily debtors) from English gaols.

Charity and humanity is the motive that hath united them, and their end is the relieving the wants of their fellow creatures both in mind and body, therefore from their very destitution they are obliged to be assistant to your design, since your motives and ends are the same. Many of these gentlemen by visiting the gaols became acquainted with the miseries of the distressed. Compassion for those wretched objects worked so strongly upon them, that they could not be easy till they had given them liberty, and near 6,000 insolvents, who must otherwise have perished in prison, were restored to mankind. The merely releasing them they thought an imperfect charity, since those only who had friends to put them in a way of subsistence could reap a real benefit from it, since others whose credit, health, and perhaps morals, were impaired by a prison could have no advantage from the act, but the privilege of starving at large. They therefore thought of putting them in a Christian, moral, and industrious way of life, and instructing them how by labour to gain a comfortable subsistence for themselves and families. They resolved alone not to confine this charity to prisoners, but to extend it as far as their funds would allow to all poor families as would be desirous of it. And in case it would not extend to all to choose out from among the prisoners and others, such as were most distressed, virtuous, and industrious. By this means they hope to take so many wretches from the utmost misery and settle them in a comfortable way of living, and of providing well for their children, who otherwise must perish through want. At the same time that this rescues them from want it would preserve them from such strong temptations to vice as I fear they are scarce able to resist.

The Society have obtained the King's order for a grant of all the lands in South Carolina lying between the rivers Savannah and Alatamaha, and licence for collecting all charities, and receiving all the legacies and donations, as shall be given to them. They intend to lay out the money they shall receive in sending out colonies of poor families after the Roman method, and to provide them passage, clothes, arms, working tools, etc., and provisions for one year, during which time they shall be under such regulations as shall oblige them to fortify, build houses, clear lands, and raise provisions for themselves.

In the situation of the intended town, health, safety, fertility of soil, and commodiousness of access, will be considered. The Society will use their utmost endeavours to prevent luxury and oppression in the officers, and idleness and vice in the people. They intend to send no governour to prevent the pride that name might instil. The power of government they intend to invest in an overseer and council of honest and discreet men. The division of the people is to be into hundreds and tithings under constables and tithing men, the men to be regularly armed and exercised, yet the lands where they establish to be purchased from the Indians and all measures used to keep peace and friendship with them, for which purpose none of the English will be permitted to go up into the country, unless it be such as are sent on embassies to the Indians. No rum nor intoxicating liquors will be allowed to be sold to the Indians, but public fairs are to be appointed at stated times, to which the Indian nations shall be invited, where judges shall be nominated to keep order and settle the prices of goods. The Indians shall upon all occasions be treated with the strictest justice and utmost humanity.

Each poor family are to have as large farms allotted to them and their heirs for ever as will consist with contiguity, and the safety of the whole. All men from the very beginning are to be established as freemen and not as servants.

In return of the money laid out upon them, of their being rescued from poverty, and instead of rent for their lands each man is to give one day's labour in six, which day's labour is to be employed on lands to be reserved for the use of the charity. Out of the produce of those public lands the aged and sick are to be subsisted, and the people to be supported in case of the casualities of famine, pestilence, or war; and if there shall be any remainder it is to be applied by the Society to the sending over more poor families.

There are many other regulations designed by the associates, which are too long now to give you a detail of, which they have formed with a view to health, safety, society, assistance, easy commerce, instruction of youth, government of the people's manners, conveniency of religious assembling, and encouragement of mechanics.

The undertaking hath met with great encouragement, as well from the public as from private persons; the former being sensible that to this they will owe the preserving of their people, the increasing the consumption of their manufactures, and the strengthening their American dominions. Mankind will be obliged to it, for the enlarging civility, cultivating wild countries, and founding of colonies, the posterity of whom may in all probability be powerful and learned nations. And lastly Christianity may be benefitted by this species of charity, since the discipline established by a society of virtuous men will certainly reform the manners of those miserable objects who shall be by them subsisted; and the sending of proper men with such a colony will contribute greatly towards the conversion and preaching the Gospel to numberless nations who never yet heard the glad tidings of revealed religion.

212 WILLIAMS TO BERKELEY

HSP, Ferdinand Dreer Collection, American Clergy, vol. VII, p. 73.

New Haven, 6 August 1731

Reverend Sir,

I am obliged to ask your pardon that I haven't acknowledged the favour of yours long since received. Your pointing of me therein to the entertainment and satisfaction a visit I knew would afford me, occasioned me to defer the same till I should have the opportunity of waiting upon you at Newport, which I was fully resolved upon whenever Providence should give leave. Hitherto I have been inevitably disappointed of my purpose, yet ever flattering myself I should have that pleasure till Mr. Johnson[1173] brought me the undesirable[1174] tidings of your design to embark for London sometime this month. I can't but regret my disappointment you are in and reflect with sorrow upon the frustration of your good design of promoting learning and religion in America, which I suppose may be concluded from your return.

The wisdom of Providence we cannot fathom; but if (as I hope)[1175] your retirement from public business while you have been in New England has given you leisure to employ your pen in [efforts?] that most effectually [curtail?] the growing infidelity which is the scandal of the present age.[1176] And your return home may so provide the occasion of your being fixed in the most advantageous station for the cooking of it out and reviving religion in a sinful nation; though for the present your return be grevious, yet it may prove joyous in the end. This I earnestly pray God may be the case and that when you have lived long the promoter and ornament of the Christian religion and the honour of the nation you may eternally reap the happy fruits of a life spent for God.

And Sir, since it is your business and pleasure to promote the interests of learning and religion of which you have already given us such evidence as will never be forgotten by us. Suffer me to presume so far on your goodness as to pray we may have your smiles still on the college in someway or other if Providence may allow of it being persuaded it will give you pleasure to see the interest of learning promoted here and to be yourself the means thereof, where you will

---

[1173] Samuel Johnson* (1696–1772).

[1174] Above is written "disagreeable," perhaps marked to be inserted or to replace the word "undesirable."

[1175] Struck from inside the parenthetical remark: "as I may reasonably conclude from Mr. Johnson's recount."

[1176] This text replaced the following, which was struck: "has ... afforded a happy opportunity for your giving that ..." and "age ... the most fatal blow it has ever yet received."

have a lasting memorial, we having already the honour of being called after your name at least let me hope for your pardon of my freedom therein.[1177]

I conclude, Sir, with the tender of my best regard to your self and Madam your Lady and sincere prayers you may find the smiles of heaven upon you and yours in your return home and all many of happiness even after, and that my prayers above may not be in vain – who am

Revd Sir
your most obliged humble servant,
Elisha Williams

New Haven, Aug. 6, 1731

213 BERKELEY TO JOHNSON[1178]

MS unknown. Printed in Schneider, vol. I, p. 81.

Rhode Island, 7 September 1731

Rev. Sir,

I am now upon the point of setting out for Boston in order to embark for England. But the hurry I am in could not excuse my neglecting to acknowledge the favour of your letter. In answer to the obliging things in it, I can only say I wish I might deserve them.

My endeavours shall not be wanting, some way or other, to be useful; and I should be very glad to be so in particular to the college at Newhaven,[1179] and the more as you were once a member of it, and have still an influence there. Pray return my service to those gentlemen who sent their complements by you.

I have left a box of books with Mr. Kay,[1180] to be given away by you—the small English books where they may be most serviceable among the people, the others as we agreed together. The Greek and Latin books I would have given to such

---

[1177] This paragraph is partially overwritten in between the lines, with differing but similar language as already in the main paragraph.

[1178] Also printed in *LL*, p. 188 and in Beardsley, p. 78. Schneider has no record of the original manuscript.

[1179] The college adopted the name Yale in 1718.

[1180] Nathaniel Kay (?–1741?), collector of the king's customs in Newport and later founder of a parochial school in Newport.

lads as you think will make the best use of them in the college, or to the school at New Haven.

I pray God to bless you, and your endeavours to promote religion and learning in this uncultivated part of the world, and desire you to accept mine and my wife's best wishes and services, being very truly, Rev. Sir,

> your most humble servant,
> George Berkeley

Rhode Island, Sep. 7, 1731

214 NEWMAN TO BERKELEY[1181]

SPCK ms D4/23, fol. 59.

20 January 1731/32

Revd Sir,

I just now received a small ponderous packet from Boston by Captain Shepardson directed to your self to be left with Mr. Dalton[1182] or me. It seems to be too valuable to be trusted by the penny post but any person calling for it with a note from you. Though I had rather have the honour of seeing you, and so would our Society who meet here every Tuesday forenoon by 11 or 12 o'clock that they may have an opportunity of congratulating your safe return to Great Britain. Mr. Hoare[1183] telling me that you had come to a resolution to return the contributions he had received towards the design at Bermuda as perhaps you might be inclined to permit me to intercede with such as may happen to be known to me or any of my friends for applying what they had devoted to a charitable use towards assisting some one or more of the religious branches of the designs of our Society particularly the Protestant mission to East India which only wants money to be prosperous under the blessing God Almighty has already vouchsafed to the beginnings made by the Society. I am

> Revd Sir
> your most humble servant,
> Henry N.

[1181] Addressed "To the Revd Dean Barkley at May's Hill at Greenwich."
[1182] Richard Dalton* (c. 1695–1769).
[1183] Benjamin Hoare* (1693–1749/50).

215 NEWMAN TO BERKELEY[1184]

SPCK MS D4/24, fol. 40.

Bartlett's Buildings, 5 July 1732

Revd Sir,

I am sorry I was not at home last week when you did me the honour to call upon me; I have called several times at your lodgings near St. James's Market but have not been so happy as to call when you was in town to show you the enclosed letter from Mr. Cary[1185] of Bristol in answer to one I wrote to him some time since at your desire.

There were some other benefactions which came through my hands from Bristol which I paid to your self or Dr. Mayo[1186] deceased concerning which I have waited for the happiness of a conference with you rather than to give you the trouble of a long letter about them. If I could know beforehand when you would be in town or that I might be sure of finding you at home at Greenwich, I would do myself the honour of waiting on you as I you shall appoint, Reverend Sir

your most humble and obedient servant,

H—N—

I thank you for your edifying sermon at Bow[1187] last February which I hope will do great service to the Society for the Propagation of the Gospel.

Be pleased to accept the account herewith sent as a present from the Society for Promoting Christian Knowledge.[1188]

[1184] Addressed: "Dean Berkeley at May Hill Greenwich."

[1185] The exact reference is uncertain, but the extended Cary family of Bristol was landed and had connections with the colonies, especially in Rhode Island. See Seth Cooley Cary, *John Cary, the Plymouth Pilgrim* (Boston, 1911).

[1186] An unknown person.

[1187] Berkeley preached a sermon at Bow Church (St. Mary-le-Bow) on 18 February 1732 at the anniversary meeting of the Society for the Propagation of the Gospel in Foreign Parts. It was subsequently published and reprinted in the *Miscellany* in 1752. See *Works* VII, pp. 114–28.

[1188] The following appears in the letterbook added as a note by H. N. at the bottom of the page. "N.B. The enclosed letter abovementioned was the copy of a letter from Mr. Cary at Bristol dated 5 February 1731/32 to H. N. and the account mentioned in the P.S. was a Saltzburg account."

216 BERKELEY TO JOHNSON[1189]

MS *unknown. Printed in Schneider, vol. I, pp. 82–83.*

London, 25 July 1732

Rev. Sir,

Some part of the benefactions to the College of Bermuda, which I could not return, the benefactors being deceased, joined with the assistance of some living friends, has enabled me without any great loss to myself, to dispose of my farm in Rhode Island in favour of the college in Connecticut.[1190] It is my opinion that as human learning and the improvements of reason are of no small use in religion, so it would very much forward those ends, if some of your students were enabled to subsist longer at their studies, and if by a public trial and premium an emulation were inspired into all. This method of encourage-ment hath been found useful in other learned societies, and I think it cannot fail of being so in one where a person so well qualified as yourself has such influence, and will bear a share in the elections. I have been a long time indisposed with a great disorder in my head; this makes any application hurtful to me, which must excuse my not writing a longer letter on this occasion.

The letter you sent by Mr. Beach[1191] I received, and did him all the service I could with the Bishop of London[1192] and the Society. He promised to call on me before his return, but have not heard of him, so am obliged to recommend this pacquet to Mr. Newman's[1193] care. It contains the instrument of convey-ance in form of law, together with a letter for Mr. President Williams,[1194] which you will deliver to him. I shall make it my endeavour to procure a benefaction of books for the college library, and am not without hopes of success. There hath of late been published here a treatise against those who are called Free-thinkers, which I intended to have sent to you and some other friends in those parts, but on second thoughts suspect it might do mischief to have it known in that part of the world what pernicious opinions are boldly espoused here at home. My little family, I thank God, are well. My best wishes

---

[1189] Also printed in Beardsley, pp. 79–81. Schneider has no record of the original manuscript.

[1190] Yale.

[1191] The Revd. John Beach (?–1782) of Newton. He likely crossed the Atlantic to receive ordination in London, as so many colonial clergymen were compelled to do. He formally organized Christ Church in Roxbury, Connecticut, in 1740 and was active in the administration of the Anglican Church in the colonies.

[1192] Edmund Gibson* (1669–1748).

[1193] Henry Newman* (1670–1743).

[1194] Elisha Williams* (1694–1755).

attend you and yours. My wife joins her services with mine. I shall be glad to hear from you by the first opportunity after this hath come to your hands. Direct your letter to Lord Percival[1195] at his house in Pall Mall,* London, and it will be sure to find me wherever I am. On all occasions I shall be glad to show that I am very truly, Rev. Sir,

> your faithful humble servant,

> Geor. Berkeley

217 BERKELEY TO HUMPHREYS[1196]

> *SPG C/AM9, fol. 32. Imperfect copy at SPG A24 "Letters Received," p. 92.*

10 February 1732/33

Reverd Sir,

In answer to the favour of your letter, wherein you tell me the Society are pleased to refer themselves to me, for an account of Mr. Scot[1197] recommended by Mr. Honeyman,[1198] I must needs say that I know Mr. Scot, and am satisfied of his merits, both as a scholar, a man of good morals, and a diligent schoolmaster, and do sincerely think whatever encouragement, the Society shall think fit to give him, will be very usefully employed, there being great need of a schoolmaster[1199] so qualified in Rhode Island.

I lately received a letter from Mr. Honeyman himself relating to an additional salary of twenty pounds per annum for which he had applied to the Society. Whether his request be granted or no he is yet uncertain. I beg leave to say that as he is the oldest missionary in America, as he hath done long and excellent service in that station, and is a person of very good qualifications for life and learning, it would seem that both for his own and others' encouragment he may well be distinguished, but how far and in what manner the Society are proper judges. I take this opportunity to

---

[1195] John Percival* (1683–1748).

[1196] David Humphreys* (1690–1740), secretary for the Society for the Propagation of the Gospel from 1716 until his death.

[1197] David Scott (?–?), schoolmaster in Newport, Rhode Island. See Edwin Gaustad, *George Berkeley in America* (New Haven, CT: Yale University Press, 1979), p. 126.

[1198] James Honeyman* (c. 1675–1750).

[1199] The copy in SPG A24 omits "master," leaving it as "school."

declare my respect and zeal for the service of that venerable body and to subscribe myself.

Revd Sir

your obedient humble servant,

Geor: Berkeley

Feb: 10th 1732–3

218 BERKELEY TO PRIOR

LR, pp. 234–35.

Green-street, 13 March 1732/33

Dear Tom,

I thank you for the good account you sent me of the house, etc., in Arbor Hill. I approve of that and the terms; so you will fix the agreement for this year to come (according to the tenor of your letter) with Mr. Lesly, to whom my humble service. I remember one of that name, a good sort of man, a class or two below me in the college.[1200] I am willing to pay for the whole year commencing from the 25th instant; but cannot take the furniture, etc., into my charge till I go over, which I truly propose to do as soon as my wife is able to travel. But, as I told you in my last, my wife expects to be brought to bed in two months; and having had two miscarriages, one of which she was extremely ill of in Rhode Island, she cannot venture to stir before she is delivered. This circumstance not foreseen, occasions an unexpected delay, putting off to summer the journey I proposed to take in spring. Mr. Lesly, therefore, or whoever is at present in it, may continue there gratis for about three months to come.

I hope our affair with Partinton[1201] will be finished this term. We are here on the eve of great events, to-morrow being the day appointed for a pitched battle in the House of Commons.[1202] I hope to hear from you speedily, particularly on the subject of my two last letters. I have no objection to you setting the deanery to Messrs. Skipton and Crookshanks[1203] for two years, as you propose, provided

---

[1200] According to College records, Edmund Leslie was graduated from Trinity College, Dublin in 1709 and Peter Leslie in 1707.

[1201] Peter Partinton* (?–?).

[1202] The "pitched battle" is likely a reference to Robert Walpole's* attempt to pass the Tobacco Excise Bill.

[1203] Persons unknown, apparently successors to McManus* in farming the Derry benefice. There were many Skiptons and Crookshanks in Ireland at the time.

the security be good. My wife gives her service to you; and my son, who (I thank God) is very well, desires me to send his love and service to Mr. Puddleya. I am,

> your affectionate humble servant,
> G. Berkeley

Green-street, March 13, 1732/33

219 BERKELEY TO PRIOR

LR, pp. 240–42.

London, 27 March 1733

Dear Tom,

This comes to desire you'll exert yourself on a public account, which you know is acting in your proper sphere. It has been represented here, that in certain parts of the kingdom of Ireland, justice is much obstructed for the want of justices of the peace, which is only to be remedied by taking in dissenters. A great man hath spoke to me on this point. I told him the view of this was plain; and that, in order to facilitate this view, I suspected the account was invented, for that I did not think it true. Depend upon it, better service cannot be done at present than by putting this matter as soon as possible in a fair light, and that supported by such proofs as may be convincing here. I therefore recommend it to you to make the speediest and exactest inquiry that you can into the truth of this fact; the result whereof send to me. Send me also the best estimate you can get of the number of papists, dissenters, and churchmen, throughout the kingdom; an estimate also of dissenters considerable for rank, figure, and estate; an estimate also of the papists in Ulster. Be as clear in these points as you can. When the above-mentioned point was put to me, I said that in my apprehension there was no such lack of justices or magistrates except in Kerry and Connaught, where the dissenters were not considerable enough to be of any use in redressing the evil. Let me know particularly whether there be any such want of justices of the peace in the county of Londonderry; or whether men are aggrieved there by being obliged to repair to them at too great distances. The prime serjeant, Singleton,[1204] may probably be a means of assisting you to get light in these particulars. The dispatch you give this affair will be doing the best service to your country. Enable me to clear up the truth, and to support it,

---

[1204] Henry Singleton (1682–1759). He became prime serjeant, the chief law officer in Ireland, in 1726, and acted continuously as a justice of assize. He was appointed chief justice of the Irish Court of Common Pleas in 1740.

by such reasons and testimonies as may be felt or credited here. Facts I am myself too much a stranger to, though I promise to make the best use I can of those you furnish me with, towards taking off an impression which I fear is already deep. If I succeed, I shall congratulate my being here at this juncture.

yours,

G. Berkeley

220 BERKELEY TO PRIOR

LR, *pp.* 242–44.

Green-street, 14 April 1733

Dear Tom,

I thank you for your last, particularly for that part of it wherein you promise the numbers of the justices of the peace, of the Papists also, and of the Protestants, throughout the kingdom, taken out of proper offices. I did not know such inventories had been taken by public authority, and am glad to find it so. Your argument for proving Papists but three to one, I had before made use of; but some of the premises are not clear to Englishmen. Nothing can do so well as the estimate you speak of, to be taken from a public office; which therefore I impatiently expect.

As to the design I hinted, whether it is to be set on foot there or here I cannot say. I hope it will take effect nowhere. It is yet a secret. I may nevertheless discover something of it in a little time; and you may then hear more.

The political state of things on this side the water I need say nothing of. The public papers probably say too much; though it cannot be denied much may be said.

I would have Petit Rose's[1205] fine, and the deficiencies of the last payments of the deanery farms, paid into Swift & Company* to answer my demand. As soon as this is done, pray let me know, that I may draw accordingly.

I must desire you, in your next, to let me know what premium there is for getting into the public fund, which allows five *per cent* in Ireland; and whether a considerable sum might easily be purchased therein? Also, what is the present legal interest in Ireland? and whether it be easy to lay out money on a secure mortgage where the interest should be punctually paid?

[1205] An unknown tenant of Berkeley's. See Letter 169.

I shall be also glad to hear a word about the law suit.[1206] I am, dear Tom,
your affectionate humble Servant,

G. Berkeley

My wife and child's service to you.

221 BERKELEY TO PRIOR

LR, *pp. 245–46.*

19 April 1733

Dear Tom,

Not finding Mr. Percival[1207] at home, I got his valet-de-chambre and another Irish servant to witness to the letter of attorney; which herewith I send you back. You may farm the deanery to the persons mentioned, since you find their security to be good, for two years. I thank you for your last advices, and the catalogue of justices particularly; of all which the proper use shall be made. The number of Protestants and Papists throughout the kingdom, which in your last but one you said had been lately and accurately taken by the collectors of hearth-money,[1208] you promised, but have omitted to send. I shall hope for it in your next. The enclosed subpoena (as I take it to be) was left two days ago at my lodging by an unknown person. As I am a stranger to what hath been done or is doing in the suit with Partinton,[1209] I thought proper to transmit it unto you; who, upon perusal thereof, will know or take advice what is to be done, without delay, to avoid further expence or trouble, which may be incurred by neglect of this *billet doux*.[1210] In your next let me know your thoughts on this and the whole affair. My wife and child give their service. We are all glad to hear of your welfare. I am, dear Tom,

yours sincerely,

Geor: Berkeley

[1206] Most likely a reference to the Hester Van Homrigh* estate and the lawsuit involving Partinton.*

[1207] Perhaps John Percival* (Perceval) (1711–70), eldest son to John Percival* (1683–1748).

[1208] A tax on hearths was instituted on 19 May 1662. Householders were required to pay a charge of two shillings per annum for each hearth, with various exceptions for the poor and other special cases. The tax was predictably unpopular and was repealed by William III in 1689. It has ever since been used to estimate population.

[1209] Peter Partinton* (?–?).

[1210] Literally "sweet bill" and also a French idiom for a love letter.

222 BERKELEY TO PRIOR

LR, pp. 230–32.

London, 1 May 1733

Dear Tom,

I long for the numeration of Protestant and Popish families, which you tell me has been taken by the collectors.[1211] A certain person now here hath represented the Papists as seven to one; which, I have ventured to affirm, is wide of the truth.[1212] What lights you gave me I have imparted to those who will make the proper use of them. I do not find that any thing was intended to be done by act of Parliament here. As to that, your information seems right. I hope they will be able to do nothing anywhere.

I give my consent to your setting the deanery for three years, and for postponing the later payment to the first of July in consideration that it will, as you say, produce punctual payment. As to a gardener, I do not design to hire one into my service, but only employ him by the job. Your letter of attorney I sent back to you, signed and witnessed, the following post after I had received it.

The approaching act at Oxford is much spoken of.[1213] The entertainments of music, etc., in the theatre, will be the finest that ever were known. For other public news, I reckon you know as much as

> your affectionate humble servant,
> Geor. Berkeley

My wife sends her service. She is well for one in her circumstances; so is my little boy.[1214] Your letter came not to my hands before yesterday. Let me hear if you know any fair man, of a clear estate, that wants two or three thousand pounds at 5½ *per cent* on mortgage.

London, May 1, 1733

[1211] The collectors of the hearth tax. See Letter 221.

[1212] No reliable data exists on the proportion of Protestants to Catholics in Ireland at the time. The (in)famous Elphin census of 1749 (undertaken by Edward Synge* [1691–1762], bishop of Elphin) estimated that for the diocese of Elphin the ratio was 1:13 (the report indicates three Protestants per thirty-nine "Papists"), but there is nothing to indicate how the data was collected. The collectors of the hearth tax produced a census in 1740 and the only other official religious census for Ireland in the eighteenth century was taken in 1766, but most of the records for both censuses were destroyed in a fire at the Public Records Office in 1922.

[1213] The Ceremony of Inception, a medieval name for commencement activities where degrees are conferred.

[1214] Henry Berkeley* (1729–after 1756).

223 BERKELEY TO WILLIAMS[1215]

SPCK MS D4/42, fol. 32.

London, 31 May 1733

Revd Sir,

I thought I could not better apply the benefactions of certain persons who left them to my disposal than in purchasing a collection of useful books for the public library of your college, which books are contained in eight cases & accompany this letter. I earnestly hope that the pious intentions of the benefactors may be answered in the use of this gift for the increase of religion and learning. These cases of books are consigned by Mr. Henry Newman[1216] to Mr. Belcher[1217] (son of the Governor) merchant at Boston who will deliver them to your order; the freight to Boston hath been paid here. I wrote to you last summer by the same vessel which brought a deed for conveying the farm I formerly possessed in Rhode Island to the use of your college; but have not since heard from you. I remain with sincere wishes that true learning and piety may ever grow and flourish among you, Sir,

> your obedient humble servant,
> George Berkeley

224 BERKELEY TO JOHNSON[1218]

SPCK MS D4/42, fols. 32–34.

London, 31 May 1733

Revd Sir,

[B]eing desirous so far as in me lies to promote sound learning and true religion in your part of the world I judged that the purchasing a good

---

[1215] This letter is addressed "To the Revd Mr. Williams, Rector of Yale College at New Haven in Connecticut N.E." It was published in Luce, "Berkeley's Bermuda Project and his Benefactions to American Universities, with Unpublished Letters and Extracts from the Egmont Papers," 108–09.

[1216] Henry Newman* (1670–1743).

[1217] Andrew Belcher (1706–71), son of Jonathan Belcher* (1682–1757).

[1218] Addressed "To the Revd Mr. Samuel Johnson at Stratford in Connecticut New England." This letter was published in Luce, "Berkeley's Bermuda Project and his Benefactions to American Universities, with Unpublished Letters and Extracts from the Egmont Papers," 109-10.

collection of books for the library of Yale College might be a proper application of the liberality of certain public spirited persons who left it to my disposal accordingly I have sent herewith 8 cases of books, I think well chosen, which I heartily wish may shed a copious light in that remote wilderness, and answer the worthy intentions of the benefactors. The aforementioned cases of books are consigned by Mr. Hen Newman[1219] to Mr. Belcher,[1220] son of the Governor, at Boston. I had a letter from you dated in last December wherein you intimate some defect in the expression of the instrument conveying the farm in Rhode Island to the use of Yale College in which benefaction, as I told you before I had but a small share.[1221] I know not particularly wherein that defect consists; and as I have heard nothing from the President[1222] or college, I must desire you to place this matter in a clear light and show how it may be rectified. If you think a letter of attorney empowering certain persons there to make a conveyance in such terms as shall best answer the design would be the proper means, let me know; and name the persons you would have joined with yourself (for there should be 2 or 3 to provide in case of mortality or accidents) and I will send you such letter of attorney. In order to which it might be proper to send me a pattern thereof conformable to the advice of your own lawyers. Though I should be gone to Ireland, Mr. Henry Newman will forward any letters to me. This gentleman is I doubt not by reputation, if not by person, known to you and to all New England for the service of which as he is very zealous; so letters directed to him will be very safe. In order to preserve the books I doubt not the college [doubt not – *sic*] will think fit to make proper statutes and regulations; particularly in lending them out, it would seem convenient that the full price (if not the double) of the book lent should be lodged in the hands of the President by way of caution or security. I hope this will find you and your family well. My wife and I join our services to you. I thank God my health seems on the mending hand. I write by this same opportunity to Mr. Williams Rector of the College. Pray give my service to any friends in your

---

[1219] Henry Newman* (1670–1743).

[1220] Andrew Belcher (1706–71), son of Jonathan Belcher* (1682–1757).

[1221] Berkeley donated Whitehall and his land in Rhode Island to Yale College. There are two conveyances, one dated 26 July 1732 and a second dated 17 August 1733. The second presumably cleared up the "defect in the expression of the instrument."

[1222] Elisha Williams* (1694–1755). He was rector of Yale from 1726 to 1739. Yale did not formally employ the title of president until 1745, when Rector Thomas Clap* (1703–67) became president of the college.

colony not forgetting Mr. Elliot[1223] in particular. I am, Revd Sir, with great truth,

> your most faithful humble servant,
> George Berkeley

225 BERKELEY TO WADSWORTH[1224]

SPCK ms D4/42, fol. 34.

London, 31 May 1733

Revd Sir,

With this letter I take the liberty to introduce a box of books containing all the Latin classic authors in quarto being of the fairest editions and the best comments for the use of your society. This is owing to certain well disposed [*sic*] who having made me the steward of their liberality I thought it might in part answer their views for the encouragement of useful learning if I shou[l]d send to your college at new Cambridge the fore-mentioned books which as they seemed to me wanting in your public library so I am persuaded there are not wanting those in your society who will make the proper use of them.[1225] I remain with sincere wishes that piety and learning may flourish among you, Sir,

> your obedient humble servant,
> George Berkeley

The box is marked CC and consigned by Mr. Henry Newman[1226] to Mr. Belcher[1227] the Governor's son at Boston.

[1223] Mr. Elliot (?–?) was apparently a young divinity student who would later travel to England to receive ordination. For another mention of him see Letter 246.

[1224] Addressed "To the Revd Mr. Wadsworth, President of the College at Cambridge near Boston in New England." Benjamin Wadsworth* (1670–1737). This letter was published in Luce, "Berkeley's Bermuda Project and his Benefactions to American Universities, with Unpublished Letters and Extracts from the Egmont Papers," 110.

[1225] Berkeley would make a second book donation through the Society for the Propagation of the Gospel in 1747, sent in 1748, and acknowledged in 1749.

[1226] Henry Newman* (1670–1743).

[1227] Andrew Belcher (1706–71), son of Jonathan Belcher* (1682–1757).

226 BERKELEY TO WILLIAMS[1228]

HSP, Simon Gratz Collection, British Authors, Case 10, Box 26.

London, 27 August 1733

Revd Sir,

I am to thank you for the favour of your letter with the copy of a printed poem wherein the ingenious author has made me undue compliments. I am in good hopes that the donation to Yale College, in procuring whereof I was instrumental, will under the management of a person of your prudence and abilities be found to answer its end, to wit the encouragement of useful learning. In the former deed transmitted to you, containing that donation, I understand that there was some mistake in the titles or naming of the grantees: which mistake I have endeavoured to correct, and also made some small additions in another deed, that will be conveyed to you with this letter. It will be in your option which deed to abide by, and to cancel the other. I have sent herewith all the titles and papers relating to the estate which I had upon my purchase thereof. The library of books for your college is, I hope, safely arrived: the catalogue of them is sent by this conveyance.[1229] The disorder in my head and the short warning on which I write will permit me only to add my best respects to your self and the rest of your learned Society, and to assure you that

I remain,

your faithful humble servant,

G: Berkeley

[1228] Elisha Williams* (1694–1755). The original letter is addressed: "to the Revd. Mr. Williams, Rector of Yale College in New Haven, Connecticut New England" and marked as answered 19 December 1735. A copy of a letter from Newman to Williams dated August 1733 (SPCK MS D4/42, fol. 50) mentions the catalogue of books sent by Berkeley. Luce published the letter in "Berkeley's Bermuda Project and his Benefactions to American Universities, with Unpublished Letters and Extracts from the Egmont Papers," 110.

[1229] The catalogue did arrive and can be found in the archives at Yale University, MS Vault Section 17, "Early Yale Documents," Box 3, item 104. The catalogue is signed by Henry Newman* and listed as shipped on 30 May 1733 "by order of the Reverend Mr. Dean Berkeley." The catalogue contains nearly five hundred works and (with some duplicate copies) almost one thousand total books – a veritable fortune for the young institution.

227 NEWMAN TO BERKELEY[1230]

SPCK MS D4/42, fols. 48–49.

Bartlett's Buildings, 28 August 1733

Reverend Sir,

I wrote to Mr. Sandford according to your order and have received the enclosed answer by which he has paid the £22 on account of Mr. Kay[1231] to Mr. Hoare.[1232]

I hope to send the organ by Captain Cary but have not been able to see him yet to treat with him about it.[1233]

We have witnessed the deed herewith sent which should have been accompanied with the catalogue but I have not yet had time to examine them. If the gentlemen bearers go so suddenly as they talk of I doubt I must desire leave to forward the catalogues in your name. You will see by the enclosed poem printed 6 months ago how impossible it is to keep your name out of print which I hope you will excuse when it is done out of a sense of gratitude which they can not suppress, especially when they hope your generous example being known may animate others to follow it.

I am, Revd Sir

your most humble servant,

Henry Newman

P.S.: Mr. Bridge[1234] was with me today and I have ordered him to have the organ packed up in readiness for embarkation.

228 BERKELEY TO PERCIVAL

EP, BL Add. MS 47000, fol. 76.

London, Thursday noon [*c.* September 1733][1235]

My Lord,

This morning I endeavoured to have waited on your Lordship at your house in Pall Mall,* but was told there that you intend going tomorrow from Charlton* to

---

[1230] Addressed "To the Revd Mr. Dean Berkeley in Green Street near Grosvenor Square."

[1231] Nathaniel Kay (?–1741?), collector of the king's customs in Newport and later founder of a parochial school in Newport.

[1232] Benjamin Hoare* (1693–1749/50).

[1233] In the spring of 1733 Berkeley made arrangements to have a pipe organ made for Trinity Church in Newport. He is here making arrangements to have it shipped from Europe to the colony. Captain Cary would prove unwilling or unable to carry the burden, so Newman made alternate arrangements. The organ did arrive safely the following year. See Letter 229 and Gaustad, *Berkeley in America*, pp. 126–29.

[1234] Richard Bridge (Bridges) (?–1758), organ builder. He built the organ Berkeley commissioned for Trinity Church.

[1235] Luce dates the letter around 6 November 1733, but September is more accurate since Berkeley makes reference to his wife being about to give birth, which we know to be his second son, George* (1733–95), born 28 September 1733.

Bath, I therefore take this opportunity of congratulating your Lordship on your new honour, which I most heartily wish yourself and your posterity may long enjoy with the greatest prosperity.[1236] How just a title you have to it, I endeavoured to say in the preamble, a rough draught whereof I had some time since put into my young Lord Percival's[1237] hands to be perused by you, intending nevertheless when I had your Lordship's thoughts thereupon to have reviewed and corrected it. The theme was ample, but I was straightened by your Lordship's commands which I shall always think it my duty to obey. Whatever defects you observe in it I beg you to impute not to want of care or zeal, but to the disorder in my head which is very great and renders me more unfit for things of that kind than I have formerly been. I thank your Lordship for the American pacquet you were pleased to forward. My wife is still hourly expecting. I conclude with both our humble services and best wishes of health and happiness to yourself, and the good countess of Egmont.

My Lord, your Lordship's most obedient and most humble servant,
G: Berkeley

229 NEWMAN TO BERKELEY[1238]

SPCK MS D4/28, fol. 9.

Bartlett's Buildings, 6 October 1733

Revd Sir,

I have sent Captain Draper to know when I may ship the organ but have not yet received his answer though I daily expect it.[1239]

Mr. Jonathan Belcher[1240] the Governour's son is now residing at Trinity College in Cambridge where they have admitted him master of arts and a vacancy of a fellowship in Trinity Hall happening he is advised by his friends as he is qualified for it by the rules of the foundation to offer himself a candidate for the present or succeeding vacancy of which there is a prospect in a few months. The Duke of

---

[1236] On 6 November 1733 John Percival* (1683–1748) was formally made Earl of Egmont, but the announcement would have been public sooner.

[1237] John Percival* (Perceval) (1711–70).

[1238] Addressed to "the Revd Mr. Dean Berkeley at London."

[1239] When Captain Cary was unwilling or unable to carry the organ from Europe to Rhode Island, Newman found another captain and vessel to take the cargo.

[1240] Jonathan Belcher (1710–76) the son of Jonathan Belcher* (1682–1757), colonial governor of Masschusetts and New Hampshire. Jonathan Belcher the younger was graduated from Harvard and took an MA in mathematics from Cambridge in 1733.

Chandois[1241] and the bishops of London[1242] and Lincoln[1243] have given him assurance of their interest but in these cases the more friends can be made the better for securing a majority and therefore he has desired me to request your favour in his behalf with Dr. James or any other of the fellow electors with whom you may be acquainted and in granting which you will oblige the Governour of New England as well as Mr. Belcher[1244] and Revd Sir

> your most humble servant,
> Henry Newman

230 NEWMAN TO BERKELEY[1245]

SPCK ms D4/42, fol. 61. Incomplete copy at SPCK ms D4/28, fol. 18.

Bartlett's Buildings, 7 November 1733

Revd Sir,

I am sorry I was not at home the other day when you did me the honour of calling on me. I have herewith sent your contract with Mr. Bridge[1246] to be cancelled with your own hand, and also the account of the charges of insurance and freight paid for the organ with Captain Draper's bill of lading which you will please to preserve for fear of any misfortune to the organ as a voucher to satisfy the insurers;[1247] though I have also another bill which I keep with the policy because it is made in my name, but is transferrable to you whenever you please. I am

> Sir
> your most humble servant,
> Henry Newman

My most humble service to your Lady and my countrymen. I sent your letter to Mr. Honyman[1248] by Captain Draper.

[1241] James Brydges (1674–1744), first Duke of Chandos.
[1242] Edmund Gibson* (1669–1748).
[1243] Richard Reynolds (1674–1744), bishop of Lincoln (1723–43).
[1244] Jonathan Belcher* (1682–1757).
[1245] Addressed to "the Revd Dr. Berkeley, Dean of Derry in Green Street near Grosvenor Square."
[1246] Richard Bridge (Bridges) (?–1758), organ builder. He built the organ Berkeley commissioned for Trinity Church.
[1247] Henry Newman* (1670–1743) persuaded Berkeley to take the sensible precaution of insuring the organ he was shipping to Rhode Island (for £150). Captain Draper transported the organ safely on his ship *Godfrey*.
[1248] James Honeyman* (Honyman) (c. 1675–1750).

231 BERKELEY TO PRIOR

LR, *pp. 246–49.*

Green-street, London, 7 January 1733/34

Dear Tom,

I did not intend you should have made the proposal to the B. of D.;[1249] but since you did, am well enough pleased with his answer. Only I would have the matter understood as proposed and transacted by yourself, without my privity, as indeed it was. I had myself thought of a preferment, a sinecure in the north, formerly possessed by old Charles Lesly.[1250] I took it to be the chancellorship of Connor, and imagined it might have been in the gift of the Crown; but do now believe it to be that you mention, possessed by Dr. Wetherby, and in the Bishop's disposal. I must desire that your next step may be to inform yourself precisely what the deanery and that chancellorship are each at this present time actually set for; and not to say a word of the notion I have conceived (which is indeed an hypothetical one) to any mortal: but only, as soon as you have informed yourself, to send me an account of the foresaid values.

My family are, I thank God, all well at present; but it will be impossible for us to travel before the spring. As to myself, by regular living, and rising very early (which I find the best thing in the world), I am very much mended; insomuch, that though I cannot read, yet my thoughts seem as distinct as ever. I do therefore, for amusement, pass my early hours in thinking of certain mathematical matters, which may possibly produce something.[1251]

I doubt not you have done as I advised in settling accounts with M'Manus;[1252] at least that you have his bonds till he pay what is due. You say nothing of the law suit; I hope it is to surprise me in your next with an account of its being finished.

[1249] Either the bishop of Derry, Down or Dromore.

[1250] The reference is unclear. A number of Leslies held high ecclesiastical posts in Ireland and it is unlikely that Berkeley would be referring to Charles Leslie (1650–1722), the nonjuror, who held no post in the Church of Ireland, although Charles's father, John Leslie (1571–1671), was successively bishop of the Isles (1628–33), Raphoe (1633–61), and Clogher (1661–71).

[1251] Berkeley published *The Analyst* in 1734, a critical discussion of the underpinnings of Newton's calculus. See *Works*, vol. IV, pp. 55–102.

[1252] McManus* (?–?).

Perhaps the house and garden on Montpelier-hill may be got a good penny-worth; in which case, I should not be averse to buying it, as also the furniture of the bed-chambers and kitchen, if they may be had cheap. It is probable a tenement in so remote a part may be purchased at an easy rate. I must, therefore, entreat you not to omit inquiring in the properest manner about it, and sending me the result of your inquiry. You'll be so good as to take care of the inclosed letter. My wife's and son's services wait on you. I am, dear Tom,

> your affectionate humble servant,
>
> G. Berkeley

232 BERKELEY TO PRIOR

LR, *pp. 249–51.*

London, 15 January 1733/34

Dear Tom,

I received last post your three letters together; for which advices I give you thanks. I had at the same time two from Baron Wainwright[1253] on the same account.

That, without my intermeddling, I may have the offer of somewhat, I am apt to think, which may make me easy in point of situation and income, though I question whether the dignity will much contribute to make me so. Those who imagine (as you write) that I may pick and choose, to be sure think that I have been making my court here all this time, and would never believe (what is most true), that I have not been at the Court or at the minister's but once these seven years. The care of my health, and the love of retirement, have prevailed over whatsoever ambition might have come to my share.

I approve of the proposal you make from Mr. Nichols for my continuing the tenement upon Arbor Hill, at the same rent, till I go over and can make a judgment thereupon. As soon as any thing is done here, you shall be sure to hear from me; and if any thing occurs there (or even if there doth not), I should be glad to hear from you. We are all well at your service. I am, dear Tom,

> your affectionate humble servant,
>
> G. Berkeley

[1253] John Wainwright* (?–1741).

It was something odd that yours of January 1st should not come to my hands till the 13th at night.

Pray send me as particular an account as you can get of the country, the situation, the house, the circumstances of the bishopric of Cloyne; and let me know the charges of coming into a bishopric i.e. the amount of the fees and first-fruits. I remain,

yours, etc.

233 BERKELEY TO PRIOR

LR, *pp. 222–23.*

London, 19 January 1733/34

Dear Tom,

Since my last I have kissed their Majestys' hands for the Bishopric of Cloyne,[1254] having first received an account from the Duke of Newcastle's[1255] office, setting forth that his Grace had laid before the King[1256] the Duke of Dorset's[1257] recommendation, which was readily complied with by his Majesty. The condition of my own health, and that of my family, will not suffer me to travel in this season of the year. I must therefore entreat you to take care of the fees and patent, which Mr. Delafoy tells me will be perfected there in consequence of the King's warrant sent to Mr. Cary.[1258] Let me know what the fees amount to. There is some proper person who does business of that kind to whom you need only pay the fees; which I will draw for as soon as you let me know the sum. I shall be glad to hear from you what particulars you can learn about this Bishopric of Cloyne. I am obliged to conclude in haste, dear Tom,

your affectionate humble servant,

G. Berkeley

London Jan. 19, 1733/34

[1254] The kissing of hands for a bishopric was a mark of allegiance and considered the decisive act when receiving an appointment.

[1255] Thomas Pelham-Holles* (1693–1768), Duke of Newcastle upon Tyne and first Duke of Newcastle under Lyme.

[1256] King George II* (1683–1760).

[1257] Lionel Cranfield Sackville* (1688–1765), first Duke of Dorset.

[1258] Most likely Walter Cary (?–?), the new lord lieutenant's (i.e. Sackville's*) chief secretary.

234 BERKELEY TO PRIOR

LR, *pp. 223–36.*

London, 22 January 1733/34

Dear Tom,

On the sixth instant the Duke[1259] sent over his plan, wherein I was recommended to the Bishopric of Cloyne. On the fourteenth I received a letter from the secretary's office, signifying his Majesty's having immediately complied therewith, and containing the Duke of Newcastle's[1260] very obliging compliments thereupon. In all this I was nothing surprised; his Grace the Lord Lieutenant having declared, on this side the water, that he intended to serve me the first opportunity, though at the same time he desired me to say nothing of it. As to the A. B. D.[1261] I readily believe he gave no opposition. He knew it would be to no purpose; and the Queen[1262] herself had expressly enjoined him not to oppose me. This I certainly knew when the A. B. was here, though I never saw him. Notwithstanding all which I had a strong penchant to be Dean of Dromore, and not to take the charge of a bishopric upon me. Those who formerly opposed my being Dean of Downe, have thereby made me a bishop; which rank, how desirable soever it may seem, I had before absolutely determined to keep out of.

The situation of my own and my family's health will not suffer me to think of travelling before April. However, as on that side it may be thought proper that I should vacate the deanery of Derry, I am ready, as soon as I hear the bishopric of Cloyne is void, by Dr. Synge's[1263] being legally possessed of the see of Ferns, to send over a resignation of my deanery; and I authorize you to signify as much where you think proper. I should be glad you sent me a rude plan of the house from Bishop Synge's description, that I may forecast the furniture. The great man whom you mention as my opponent concerted his measures but ill; for it appears by your letter, that at the very time when my brother informed the speaker of his soliciting against me there, the Duke's plan had already taken place here, and the resolution was passed in my favour at St. James's. I am nevertheless pleased, as it gave me

---

[1259] Lionel Cranfield Sackville* (1688–1765), first Duke of Dorset.

[1260] Thomas Pelham-Holles* (1693–1768), Duke of Newcastle upon Tyne and first Duke of Newcastle under Lyme.

[1261] Archbishop of Dublin. At the time it was John Hoadly* (1678–1746).

[1262] Queen Caroline (Princess Caroline of Brandenburg-Ansbach) (1683–1737).

[1263] Edward Synge* (1691–1762). At the time of this letter he was bishop of Cloyne (since 1731) and was being translated to the bishopric of Ferns (1733).

an opportunity of being obliged to the speaker,[1264] which I shall not fail to acknowledge when I see him, which will probably be very soon, for he is expected here as soon as the session is up. My family are well, though I myself have gotten a cold this sharp foggy weather, having been obliged, contrary to my wonted custom, to be much abroad paying compliments and returning visits. We are all at your service; and I remain, dear Tom,

yours affectionately,

Geor: Berkeley

London, Jan. 22, 1733/34

235 BERKELEY TO PRIOR

LR, *pp. 226–28.*

London, 28 January 1733/34

Dear Tom,

In a late letter you told me the bishopric of Cloyne is let for 1,200 pounds *per annum*, out of which there is a small rent-charge of interest to be paid. I am informed by a letter of yours which I received this day, that there is also a domain of 800 acres adjoining to the episcopal house. I desire to be informed by your next whether these 800 acres are understood to be over and above the 1,200 pounds *per annum*, and whether they were kept by former bishops in their own hands?

In my last, I mentioned to you the impossibility of my going to Ireland before spring, and that I would send a resignation of my deanery, if need was, immediately upon the vacancy of the see of Cloyne. I have been since told that this would be a step of some hazard, viz. in case of the King's death, which I hope is far off. However, one would not care to do a thing which may seem incautious and imprudent in the eye of the world; not but that I would rather do it than be obliged to go over at this season. But, as the bulk of the deanery is in tithes, and a very inconsiderable part in land, the damage to my successor would be but a trifle upon my keeping it to the end of March. I would know what you advise on this matter.

[1264] Presumably the speaker of the Irish House of Commons, Henry Boyle (1682–1764). He was only recently elected speaker in October of 1733. He would be made the first Earl of Shannon in April 1756.

My wife and children are, I thank God, all well at present, and join in service to you. I am, dear Tom,

your affectionate humble servant,

G. Berkeley

Not long since I sent you inclosed a letter for my brother Robin,[1265] which I desired you to deliver to him. It contained a bill of forty pounds upon Swift & Company,* to be received and disposed of by him. But as you make no mention of this letter, and I have had no account of its coming to hand, I begin to apprehend it might have miscarried; in which case I desire you to inquire at Swift's, etc., to give warning. Pray let me hear next post.

236 NEWMAN TO BERKELEY[1266]

SPCK ms D4/29, fol. 14.

Bartlett's Buildings, 28 January 1733/34

Revd Sir,

I just received the enclosed letters and papers from Mr. President Williams[1267] and Mr. Johnson[1268] of Yale College, which I take the first opportunity of forwarding to your hands, leaving the rest to be signified when I have the honour of seeing you. In the meantime I take leave to congratulate you on your nomination to the bishopric of Cloyne as the papers have informed the town being [damaged text] [. . .] present [blotted text] [?] of your great service to religion and learning. I remain

Revd Sir

your most obedient humble servant,

H. N.

P.S.: I am glad to add that your organ is safe arrived in Portugal, and like to proceed directly thence to Rhode Island.[1269] [Damaged text] be able [damaged text]

[1265] Robert Berkeley* (c. 1699–1787).

[1266] Addressed to "the Revd Dr. Berkeley in Green Street near Grosvenor Square."

[1267] Elisha Williams* (1694–1755).

[1268] Samuel Johnson* (1696–1772). Johnson was technically no longer strictly affiliated with Yale, having converted to the Anglican Church and lost his position at the college. He did, however, continue to work with the institution and aid its endeavours. For instance, he helped secure Berkeley's donations.

[1269] See Letter 227.

237 BERKELEY TO PRIOR[1270]

BL Add. MS 39311, fol. 25.

London, 1 February 1733/34

Dear Tom,

The post is just going out, so I have time only to tell you that I have altered my mind about the house on Monpelier hill. To have two houses to furnish at once would be an indiscreet expence. If therefore you have not yet given my last answer to the landlord, I would have you say that I have no further thoughts of it. But if you have already told him that I will continue till I see it, I must abide by what I authorised you to say. However I hope and wish it may not be too late.

I am, dear Tom,

yours affectionately,

G: Berkeley

London, Feb. 1. 1733/34

238 BERKELEY TO PRIOR

LR, *pp. 229-30.*

London, 7 February 1733/34

Dear Tom,

This comes to tell you that I have been for several days laid up with the gout. When I last wrote to you I was confined; but at first knew not whether it might not be a sprain or hurt from the shoe: but it soon showed itself a genuine fit of the gout in both my feet, by the pain, inflammation, swelling, etc., attended with a fever and restless nights. With my feet lap'd up in flannels, and raised on a cushion, I receive the visits of my friends, who congratulate me on this occasion as much as on my preferment.

As to Bishop Synge's[1271] furniture, we shall be able to judge upon seeing it, which will be as soon as possible. His stock and his overseer will, I think, suit my purpose, especially if I keep the lands in my own hands; concerning which I would know your opinion; as also, whether that domain be reckoned in the

---

[1270] See Luce, "Some Unpublished Berkeley Letters with some New Berkeleiana," 147.
[1271] Edward Synge* (1691–1762). Synge is vacating Cloyne (held since 1731) and translating to Ferns (1733).

income of 1,200 pounds *per annum*. I conclude with my wife and son's compliments to you. Dear Tom,

> your affectionate humble servant,
>
> G. Berkeley

London, Feb. 7, 1733/34

239 BERKELEY TO PRIOR

LR, *pp. 251–52.*

London, 19 February 1733/34

Dear Tom,

Now I have been confined three weeks by the gout, an unusual length for the first fit; but my friends and physician think it will be of so much the more service to me in carrying off the dregs of my long indisposition, and clearing my head. I have had it successively in my feet, head, stomach, and one knee. It is now got into my feet again, but is comparatively very gentle. I hope to get soon abroad: but I shall have some business to do beside the taking leave of my friends, and preparing things for my departure for Ireland; where, I am sure, I long to be more than any one there can long to see me. I must, however, neither hurt my health, after the tenderness of a long confinement, nor neglect things absolutely necessary. And to make people concerned as easy as I am able, I by this post send inclosed to Baron Wainwright[1272] a formal resignation of my deanery.

> yours,
>
> Geor: Berkeley

240 BERKELEY TO PRIOR

LR, *pp. 252–54.*

London, 23 February 1733/34

Dear Tom,

In a late letter, you told me that the wardenship of Tuam, to which I had no title, was inserted in my patent. But some time since I received a letter from one Mr. Rugge, a class-fellow of mine in the college, dated from Youghall, of which

---

[1272] John Wainwright* (?–1741).

town he tells me I am warden. Now, it comes into my head that there may be a mistake in the patent of Tuam for Youghall, which mistake may deprive me of a considerable part of the bishop's income. I must therefore desire you to look into the patent in order to clear up this point, and let me know how to rectify it.[1273] Bishop Synge[1274] (from whom I have not yet heard) and Mr. Lingen[1275] can tell how this matter stands, and what is to be done. Pray send me the favour of a line by next post on this head.

I have not yet received M'Manus's[1276] account for the last year of his farming; so I cannot justly say, but I expected a much greater balance in his hands than 50 pounds. You perceive, by the 20 pounds overcharged for the widows, how requisite it is that his accounts be sharply looked after, especially in the great article of paying the curates, concerning which I already wrote you my thoughts. As I confide that affair to your care, I trust you will look sharp, and not suffer me to be imposed on. I need not mention that no deductions are to be made by Mr. Skipton[1277] for cures, since, in pursuance to your letter, I agreed they should be paid out of the profits of the foregoing year. Pray, in your next, let me know when I may expect Mr. Skipton's payments, that I may order my affairs accordingly; and whether my brother be gone to Cloyne. I have sent a resignation of the deanery to Baron Wainwright,[1278] witnessed by Dr. King,[1279] and in full form. I hope to get abroad in two days, and to be able to put on my gouty shoes. My family is well, and give their service.

    yours,

    G. Berkeley

[1273] When Charles Crow (?-1726) was made bishop of Cloyne in 1702, he was provost of Tuam. Crow retained his provostship when elevated to bishop and his successor to the bishopric, Henry Maule (1676-1758), mistakenly had the provostship included in his patent for Cloyne. The wardenship was hence later removed from the patent for the bishopric.

[1274] Edward Synge* (1691-1762).

[1275] William Lingen (?-?), secretary to the lord justices of Ireland. He was active in the 1740s and a painting of him resides in the National Portrait Gallery in London (NPG D37347; William Lingen).

[1276] McManus* (?-?).

[1277] Skipton and Crookshank, persons unknown, apparently succeeded McManus* in farming the Derry benefice. There were many Skiptons and Crookshanks in Ireland.

[1278] John Wainwright* (?-1741).

[1279] Luce speculates that this might be James King (?-1745). A 1720 fellow of Trinity College, Dublin (and co-opted senior fellow in 1728), King was named one of the first three fellows in the charter of Berkeley's planned St. Paul's College in Bermuda. Luce suspects this King on the grounds that he might have traveled to London to represent the college in the affair of the shooting of junior fellow Edward Ford. The shooting, however, occurred on 8 March 1734, a few weeks *after* the date of this letter, which makes Luce's explanation for the presence of King in London unlikely. King might have been in London on other business, of course, but the identification should be taken cautiously. See *Works*, vol. IX, p. 93. For an account of the Ford shooting, see *The Book of Trinity College, Dublin* (Belfast: Marcus Ward & Co., 1892), pp. 69-70 and W. Macneile Dixon, *Trinity College, Dublin* (London: Robinson & Co., 1902), p. 102.

241 BERKELEY TO PRIOR

MS *unknown. Stock, pp. lxx–lxxii (extract).*

London, 2 March 1734

Dear Tom,

As to what you write of the prospect of new vacancies, and your advising that I should apply for a better bishopric, I thank you for your advice. But, if it pleased God the Bishop of Derry[1280] were actually dead, and there were ever so many promotions thereupon, I would not apply, or so much as open my mouth to any one friend to make an interest for getting any of them. To be so very hasty for a removal, even before I had seen Cloyne, would argue a greater greediness for lucre than I hope I shall ever have. Not but that, all things considered, I have a fair demand upon the government for expence of time and pains and money, on the faith of public charters: as likewise because I find the income of Cloyne considerably less than was at first represented. I had no notion that I should, over and above the charge of patents and first fruits, be obliged to pay between £400 and £500, for which I shall never see a farthing in return; besides interest I am to pay for upwards of £300, which principal devolves upon my successor. No more was I apprized of three curates, viz. two at Youghal and one at Aghada, to be paid by me. And, after all, the certain value of the income I have not yet learned. My predecessor[1281] writes that he doth not know the true value himself, but believes it may be about £1,200 per annum, including the fines, and striking them at a medium for seven years. The uncertainty, I believe, must proceed from the fines; but it may be supposed that he knows exactly what the rents are, and what the tithes, and what the payments to the curates; of which particulars you may probably get an account from him. Sure I am, that if I had gone to Derry, and taken my affairs into my own hands, I might have made considerably above £1,000 a year, after paying the curates' salaries. And as for charities, such as school-boys,- widows, etc. those ought not to be reckoned, because all sorts of charities, as well as contingent expences, must be much higher on a bishop than a dean. But in all appearance, subducting the money that I must advance, and all expence of the curates in Youghal and Aghada, I shall not have

---

[1280] Henry Downes (?–1735). Downes died 14 January 1735 and was succeeded by Thomas Rundle* (1687/88–1743).

[1281] Edward Synge* (1691–1762).

remaining £1,000 *per annum*; not even though the whole income was worth £1,200, of which I doubt, by Bishop Synge's uncertainty, that it will be found to fall short. I thank you for the information you gave me of a house to be hired in Stephen's Green. I should like the Green very well for situation: but I have no thoughts of taking a house in town suddenly; nor would it be convenient for my affairs so to do considering the great expence I must be at on coming into a small bishopric. My gout has left me. I have nevertheless a weakness remaining in my feet, and, what is worse, an extreme tenderness, the effect of my long confinement. I was abroad the beginning of this week to take a little air in the park, which gave me a cold, and obliged me to physic and two or three days' confinement. I have several things to prepare in order to my journey, and shall make all the dispatch I can. But why I should endanger my health by too much hurry, or why I should precipitate myself, in this convalescent state, into doubtful weather and cold lodgings on the road, I do not see. There is but one reason that I can comprehend why the great men there should be so urgent; viz. for fear that I should make an interest here in case of vacancies; which I have already assured you I do not intend to do; so they may be perfectly easy on that score.

242 BERKELEY TO PRIOR

LR, *pp. 232–33.*

London, 9 March 1733/34

Dear Tom,

I think what my brother and you write about the impropriety and uselessness of his going now to Cloyne very reasonable, and must entreat you to give him the enclosed letter with your own hands. I have not yet seen Mr. Roberts,[1282] but am willing to do all the service I can in relation to the affair you mention;[1283] though I apprehend I am not likely to do much, for two

---

[1282] Robert Roberts* (?–?).

[1283] Benjamin Burton (?–1728) and Francis Harrison (?–1725) established a bank – popularly known as Burton's bank – in Dublin in 1700. The bank failed, and closed its doors on 25 June 1733. Following the collapse its creditors (including such notables as the archbishops of Armagh and Dublin) petitioned the House of Commons for relief (additional bills were advanced in 1735 and 1751). Presumably Prior was a creditor as well. See F. G. Hall, *History of the Bank of Ireland*

reasons: first, because I can hardly stir abroad without catching cold, such is my tenderness after so long confinement; secondly, because I apprehend there will be council heard, which makes it a judicial case, in which there is no room for favour. I shall, however, endeavour to speak for it in the best manner I can to the Lord Chancellor,[1284] Lord President,[1285] Lord Chief Justice,[1286] and to the Master of the Rolls;[1287] which four I take to be persons of the most weight, at least that I know, in the Privy Council. I shall attempt to find them at home; though in this busy time it is very difficult to come at them there: and as for going to the Parliament House in my present condition, I should run too great a risk to think of it. On Monday I shall have a useful servant, whom I shall employ in hastening things for my departure as soon as possible; for I sincerely long to be with you. My wife's service and mine. I am, dear Tom,

> your affectionate humble servant,
> G. Berkeley

243 BERKELEY TO PRIOR

LR, *pp.* 255–58.

London, 17 March 1733/34

Dear Tom,

I received your letter, containing M'Manus's[1288] account for the last year. I have not leisure to examine it at present; but, at first sight, it strikes me that he charges 20 pounds where he should have charged but ten, i.e. to the clergymen's widows. You'll inquire how this comes to pass.

I am *bona fide* making all the haste I can. My library is to be embarked on board the first ship bound to Cork, of which I am in daily expectation. I suppose it will be no difficult matter to obtain an order from the commissioners to the custom-

---

(Dublin: Hodges, Figgis & Co., 1949), pp. 6–8; and Robert Roberts, *A State of the Case of the Creditors of Burton's Bank* (Dublin, 1751).

[1284] Charles Talbot* (1685–1737), first Baron Talbot of Hensol.

[1285] Spencer Compton* (c.1674–1743), Earl of Wilmington.

[1286] Philip York* (or Yorke) (1690–1764), first Earl of Hardwicke.

[1287] Sir Joseph Jekyll* (1662–1738).

[1288] McManus* (?–?).

house officers there to let it pass duty-free, which, at first word, was granted here on my coming from America. I wish you would mention this, with my respects, to Dr. Coghill.[1289] After my journey, I trust that I shall find my health much better, though at present I am obliged to guard against the east wind, with which we have been annoyed of late, and which never fails to disorder my head. I am in hopes, however, by what I hear, that I shall be able to reach Dublin before my Lord Lieutenant leaves it. I shall reckon it my misfortune if I do not. I am sure it shall not be for want of doing all that lies in my power. I am in a hurry. I am obliged to manage my health, and I have many things to do.

I must desire you, at your leisure, to look out a lodging for us, to be taken only by the week; for I shall stay no longer in Dublin than needs must. I shall want three beds for men-servants, one bed for maid-servants,- two convenient bed-chambers, a dining room and parlour, utensils for the kitchen and table; for though I believe my wife and I shall dine seldom at home, yet my family must. I imagine the house in St. Mary's parish, where I first lodged in my solitude, when I was last in Dublin, might do, if it might be had. There was only a woman and a maid in it; and I should be glad to have as few of the people in the house as may be. Baron Wainwright[1290] I should like to be near; but in Stephen's Green[1291] I should not like to be. But, if the aforesaid conveniences are not easily to be had in William-street, you may probably find them on the other side the water without difficulty; and a coach soon carries me wherever I have a mind to visit. I would have the lodging taken for the 10th of April. But say nothing of this providing a lodging, nor of the time, except to my brother, who perhaps may be helpful in looking out for it.

You may remember that, upon my being made Dean of Derry, I paid the curates for the current year. The reason assigned why I should do this, will hold good for my successor, viz. because I was to have the whole tithes of the year. Pray be mindful of this. I am, dear Tom,

>your affectionate humble servant,

>G. Berkeley

London, March 17, 1733/34

You will also remember to take bonds for the money, to be reimbursed for the deanery-house.

[1289] Marmaduke Coghill* (1673–1739).
[1290] John Wainwright* (?–1741).
[1291] An area in Dublin not far from Trinity College.

244 BERKELEY TO PRIOR

LR, *pp. 236–39.*

20 March 1733/34

Dear Tom,

Last post I received one from you, wherein you mention orders sent to clear the curates till the 5th instant. I hope you will recollect, and see that I am done by as I myself did by my predecessor on first coming into the deanery. The same reason that was then assigned for my paying the curates for the year, though I came in so late as May, will surely hold for my successor's doing the same thing.

Your account of my income I should be glad to find true. It widely differs from what Bishop Synge writes;[1292] and both of your accounts differ from my brother's.[1293] I would fain know what I might depend on. There may be some uncertainty in the fines or tythes; but the rents regularly and annually paid must surely be known to the bishop. By this post I inform Bishop Synge of my design to employ the person recommended by him. As for the distance, I shall know by experience how far that is inconvenient. I wish you could get money from Skipton[1294] to make up what was wanting in your hands towards paying for the patents; for I have largely drawn of late, and shall draw again before I set out, on Swift & Company;* so that there will be little left in their hands. I shall have time to receive another letter from you before I leave this.

The agent you mentioned for the bill against the heirs of Burton and Harrison never came to me to state the case; so I have little to say: and by what I find, it is to no purpose, for the bill is not likely to pass. I reasoned as well as I could on the little and wrong lights which I had with my Lord President;[1295] but I found by him, that the Committee of Council have weighty reasons against passing it. I spoke also to another privy counsellor, but I doubt to no effect. There will be pleadings probably, as well as petitions, on both sides, which must determine, and in the mean time procrastinate, the fate of this bill.[1296]

[1292] Edward Synge* (1691–1762).

[1293] Most likely his brother "Robin," Robert Berkeley* (c. 1699–1787).

[1294] Skipton, about whom little is known, apparently succeeded McManus* in farming the Derry benefice.

[1295] Spencer Compton* (c.1674–1743), Earl of Wilmington.

[1296] In fact the bill did eventually pass (with alterations), being agreed to by the House of Lords on 29 April 1734. Two subsequent bills were also passed in 1735 and 1751. See Berkeley to Prior, 9 March 1733/34. For details of the bank failure, see Hall, *History of the Bank of Ireland* pp. 6–8 and Roberts, *A State of the Case of the Creditors of Burton's Bank.*

There is one Mr. Cox,[1297] a clergyman, son to the late Dr. Cox near Drogheda,[1298] who I understand is under the patronage of Dr. Coghill.[1299] Pray inform yourself of his character, whether he be a good man, one of parts and learning, and how he is provided for. This you may possibly do without my being named. Perhaps my brother may know something of him. I would be glad to be apprised of his character on my coming to Dublin. No one has recommended him to me; but his father was an ingenious man, and I saw two sensible women, his sisters, at Rhode Island, which inclines me to think him a man of merit, and such only I would prefer. I have had certain persons recommended to me; but I shall consider their merits preferably to all recommendation. If you can answer for the ingenuity, learning, and good qualities of the person you mentioned, preferably to that of others in competition, I should be very glad to serve him.

I must put you in mind of what I mentioned long since, viz. getting Dr. Helsham's[1300] note for 200 pounds under my hand, which I allowed to you, and you had allowed to Bishop Synge,[1301] who paid that sum out of my money long ago. You promised when you were here to see it cancelled, but I suppose you might have forgot it. I think the more of it at present, because I have, for want of exactness, paid the sum of sixteen pounds twice over; and a burnt child, you know, dreads the fire. My wife makes you her compliments. I am, dear Tom,

> yours affectionately,
> G. Berkeley

March 20, 1733/34

245 BERKELEY TO PRIOR

LR, pp. 258-61.

London, 2 April 1734

Dear Tom,

The other day Mr. Roberts[1302] called at my lodging; where, not meeting with myself, he left your letter, a full month after its date. I wish I had seen

---

[1297] Marmaduke Cox (1707?-62). In September 1736 he was licensed to the curacy of Inniscarra.
[1298] Thomas Cox (?-1719?). He was vicar of Carlingford and St. Peter's, Drogheda, and later dean of Ferns.
[1299] Marmaduke Coghill* (1673-1739).
[1300] Richard Helsham (1683-1738), physician and natural philosopher. In addition to being a professor of mathematics and natural philosophy at Trinity College, Dublin, he was Jonathan Swift's personal physician. The money relates to expenses concerning the trial of Berkeley's brother Thomas* (1704-26?), condemned for bigamy. See Letter 155.
[1301] Edward Synge* (1691-1762).
[1302] Robert Roberts* (?-?).

him, to have known more particulars of the case; though, on second thoughts, I imagine it was not needful, for all these points will be opened by lawyers before the Attorney-General[1303] and before the Committee of Council. I have, in compliance with your desire, talked of this affair with the Lord President,[1304] Lord Chancellor,[1305] and Master of the Rolls;[1306] to all whom I recommended it, as far as was decent to recommend a judicial affair wherein private property is concerned. I spoke also to one or two more of the Privy Council; all the members whereof I thought equally judges of the bill. But I find that the committee for Irish bills consists only of the Lords of the Cabinet and the Law Lords of the Council. I tried to find my Lord Hardwicke,[1307] the Chief Justice of the King's Bench, and shall try again. Tomorrow I propose to speak on the same subject to the Duke of Newcastle.[1308] I am in no small hurry, have many things to do, and many things to think of; but would not neglect or omit to throw in my mite towards forwarding an affair which you represent to be of national concern.

I hear of a ship going to Cork, on board of which I design to have my things embarked next week. But it will be impossible for me to go till after Easter; and if it was possible, would not be decent. I propose, therefore, without fail, to set out from hence either on the Tuesday or at farthest on the Wednesday after Easter-day; and if the lodging in Dublin be secured against that day se'ennight it will be time enough. We would either have a furnished house to ourselves by the week, or else a house with as few inhabitants as may be. I wrote to my brother Robin[1309] last week; which letter I directed to the College. Let him know this when you see him. I thank you for thinking of my library's passing easily through the custom-house. It is to be sent to Messrs. Harper and Morris, as Bishop Synge[1310] directed; who, I hope, hath apprised them of it, and recommended it to their care. I shall have occasion to draw for about a hundred pounds. I hope you'll urge Mr. Skipton[1311] to

---

[1303] Sir John Willes (1685–1761). He succeeded Philip York* (or Yorke) (1690–1764), first Earl of Hardwicke, as attorney general on 30 November 1733.

[1304] Spencer Compton* (c.1674–1743), Earl of Wilmington.

[1305] Charles Talbot* (1685–1737), first Baron Talbot of Hensol.

[1306] Sir Joseph Jekyll* (1662–1738).

[1307] Philip York* (or Yorke) (1690–1764), first Earl of Hardwicke.

[1308] Thomas Pelham-Holles* (1693–1768), Duke of Newcastle upon Tyne and first Duke of Newcastle under Lyme.

[1309] Robert Berkeley* (c. 1699–1787).

[1310] Edward Synge* (1691–1762).

[1311] Skipton, about whom little is known, apparently succeeded McManus* in farming the Derry benefice.

be early in his payment. My wife and son give their service to you. I am, dear Tom,

> your affectionate humble servant,
> G. Berkeley

246 BERKELEY TO JOHNSON[1312]

MS *unknown.* LL, *p. 221.*

London, 4 April 1734

Reverend Sir,

Your ordering matters so that every year one Scholar of the House be chosen, is quite agreeable to my intentions.. As to lending out the books of your library, I think there should be made some public statute by the proper authority, which same authority may alter it, if it prove upon trial to be so inconvenient. But this rests on the trustees or governors of the College. My private opinion is, that you may, for the present, lend out books to any persons residing in the Colony, who have studied either in that or any other College, but always under the caution mentioned in my former letter—upon forfeiture whereof the book is to be returned within a limited time.

As to the Bishop of Cork's book,[1313] and the other book you allude to, the author whereof is one Baxter,[1314] they are both very little read or considered here; for which reason I have taken no public notice of them. To answer objections already answered, and repeat the same things, is a needless as well as disagreeable task. Nor should I have taken notice of that Letter about

---

[1312] Only Fraser prints this letter (and Luce following him: *Works*, vol. VIII, pp. 236–37). The letter appears in neither the Beardsley nor the Schneider. There is no record of the original.

[1313] Peter Browne* (?–1735), bishop of Cork and Ross from 1710 until his death. He published *The Procedure, Extent and Limits of the Human Understanding* in 1728. Berkeley criticizes the work in his *Alciphron* (see *Works*, vol. III, pp. 163 ff.), which prompted Browne to add nearly two hundred pages of rebuttal to the final chapter of his 1733 work *Things Divine and Supernatural Conceived by Analogy*. Johnson is likely referring to the latter work, to which Berkeley never responded.

[1314] Andrew Baxter (1686/87–1750). He published the first edition of *An Enquiry into the Nature of the Human Soul* in October 1733. The book contains a strawman attack on Berkeley's metaphysical system.

Vision,[1315] had it not been printed in a newspaper which gave it course, and spread it through the kingdom. Beside, the *Theory of Vision* I found was somewhat obscure to most people; for which reason I was not displeased at an opportunity to explain it.

Of late I have been laid up with the gout, which hath hindered me hitherto from going to Ireland to be consecrated Bishop of Cloyne, to which his Majesty nominated me near three months ago.

The hurry I am now in, providing for my journey to Ireland, doth not allow me time to add any more than my service and best wishes to yourself, Mr. Williams,[1316] Mr. Elliot,[1317] etc.

> I am, Rev. Sir,
> Your faithful humble Servant,
> G. Berkeley

When you write next, direct for me at Cloyne in Ireland.

247 BERKELEY TO PRIOR

LR, *pp. 261–62.*

London, 16 April 1734

Dear Tom,

Last Friday evening I saw Mr. Roberts[1318] for the first time. He told me he apprehended opposition from Lord Hardwicke.[1319] Next day I attempted to find my Lord, but could not. This day I saw his Lordship, but to no purpose; for he told me the affair of the Banker's bill was finished last night. I then said nothing, but only asked him how it had gone. He told me they had made Harrison's[1320] estate liable to one moiety of the demands on the bank, and

---

[1315] Berkeley's *Theory of Vision ... Vindicated and Explained* was published in London in 1733 in response to an anonymous letter that appeared in the *Daily Post-boy* of 9 September 1732. See *Works*, vol. I, pp. 243–79.

[1316] Elisha Williams* (1694–1755).

[1317] Mr. Elliot (?–?) was apparently a young divinity student who would later travel to England to receive ordination. For another mention, see Letter 224.

[1318] Robert Roberts* (?–?).

[1319] Philip York* (or Yorke) (1690–1764), first Earl of Hardwicke.

[1320] Francis Harrison (?–1725), one of the founders of Burton's bank. See Letter 242.

that this was just: so the bill is passed, but with alteration; yet such as it is hoped will not defeat the intention of it. It is very late; and I have time only to add, that I am,

> your affectionate humble servant,
> G. Berkeley

I thought I should have set out tomorrow; but it is impossible before Monday. You shall soon hear again from me. My wife and son make their compliments.

248 BERKELEY TO PRIOR

LR, *pp. 262–65.*

St. Alban's, 30 April 1734

Dear Tom,

I was deceived by the assurance given me of two ships going for Cork. In the event, one could not take in my goods, and the other took freight for another port. So that, after all their delays and prevarications, I have been obliged to ship off my things for Dublin on board of Captain Leach. From this involuntary cause, I have been detained here so long beyond my intentions, which really were to have got to Dublin before the Parliament, which now I much question whether I shall be able to do; considering that, as I have two young children with me, I cannot make such dispatch on the road as otherwise I might.

I hope Skipton's[1321] first payment hath been made; so that you have got the money you returned, and that the rest is lodged with Swift & Company* to answer my draughts; otherwise I have overdrawn.

The lodging in Gervais-street, which you formerly procured for me, will, I think, do very well. I shall want, beside the conveniences I before mentioned, a private stable for six coach-horses; for so many I bring with me. I shall hope for a letter from you at the post-office in Chester, giving an account of the lodging, where and what it is, etc. My wife thinks that on breaking up of the Duke's[1322] kitchen, one of his under-cooks may be got; and that a man-cook would be a great convenience to us. If you can procure a sober young man, who is a good cook, and understands pickling and preserving, at a reasonable price, we shall be much obliged. The

---

[1321] Skipton, about whom little is known, apparently succeeded McManus* in farming the Derry benefice.

[1322] Most likely Lionel Cranfield Sackville* (1688–1765), first Duke of Dorset. He would remain lord lieutenant of Ireland until 1737, so the reason for the "break-up" of his kitchen is unclear.

landlady of the lodging must, in your agreement, be obliged to furnish linen and necessaries for the table, as also to dress our meat. This is to be included in the price that we pay by the week for the lodgings. In your last, you mentioned black cattle and sheep of Bishop Synge's,[1323] which I am resolved to purchase, and had long ago signified the same to my brother, if I remember rightly. If I meet with a good ship at Chester, I propose going from thence. As for sending a ship, I doubt this will not come time enough; and write sooner I could not, because of my uncertain situation. However, you can tell what passageships are on this side the water, and what is proper to be done. If a ship be sent, you will take care it is the best can be got. I have a coach and six to embark. We propose being at Chester on Saturday evening. I write this on Tuesday morning from St. Alban's. We are on the point of taking coach. So with my little family's compliments and my own, I remain

> your affectionate humble servant,
> George Berkeley

I hope to find a letter at the post-office in Chester, informing where the lodging is taken.

249 SECKER TO BERKELEY[1324]

BL Add. MS 39311, fols. 27–28.

1 February 1734/35

My dear Lord,

I return you my heartiest thanks for your very friendly congratulations:[1325] and we are all very happy that you consider us in the view of neighbours. For that relation gives us an undoubted right to a visit from you immediately upon our arrival at Bristol. And I take it Master Harry's[1326] obligations in point of gallantry to make Miss Talbot[1327] that compliment are quite indispensable. Then from Bristol we will beg leave to wait upon you to the palace of my good

---

[1323] Edward Synge* (1691–1762). Synge was Berkeley's predecessor as bishop of Cloyne, having been translated to Ferns (1733).

[1324] Thomas Secker* (1693–1768).

[1325] Secker* had just been consecrated bishop of Bristol a few weeks earlier, on 19 January 1735.

[1326] A reference to Berkeley's eldest child, Henry* (1729–after 1756).

[1327] After marrying Catherine Benson, Thomas Secker* and his wife lived with bishop of Durham William Talbot's* (1659–1730) widowed daughter-in-law and her daughter, the latter of whom is likely to be the "Miss Talbot" mentioned here.

Lord of Gloucester,[1328] who indeed, to do him justice, bears with tolerable composure his being restrained from the pleasures of street walking; but all his honours avail him not, so long as Dicky Dalton[1329] continues to beat him at chess. But perhaps, my Lord, before the time comes of receiving a visit from you, we may send an old acquaintance to pay you one. For I take it for granted Dr. Rundle[1330] will now be made an Irish bishop, and probably of Derry unless it can be filled up in such a manner as to vacate some good deanery for him here, which I believe he would rather choose. His health is much better than it was, and this new prospect seems to have done him great service. The pamphlet war about him is not quite extinguished, but the attention of the world is almost entirely turned from it to other matters. The parliament hath done nothing yet besides giving each side an opportunity of showing their numbers, which are sufficiently in favour of the court. The Queen[1331] is perfectly well again, and Sir R. Walpole's[1332] unseasonable gout is going off. It continues doubtful whether any petition will be brought in against the Scotch peers. And it does not appear that we shall have any Church work this session. Dr. Waterland[1333] was chosen prolocutor last week, but declines it, upon which Dr. Lisle,[1334] archdeacon of Canterbury, was chosen yesterday. There hath lately been a proposal made by the Bishop of London[1335] for reprinting by subscription the most considerable tracts against popery that were written in and about King James the Second's time, I think in two folios. Whether such a work would meet with any number of subscribers in Ireland I know not. Your friend Mr. Pope[1336] is publishing small poems every now and then, full of much wit and not a little keenness. Our common friend, Dr. Butler hath almost completed a set of speculations upon the credibility of religion from its analogy to the constitution and course of nature, which I believe in due time you will read with pleasure.[1337] And now, my good Lord, give me leave to ask what are you doing. As you seem to write with cheerfulness, and make no complaints

---

[1328] Augustus Berkeley (1715/16–55), fourth Earl of Berkeley. He was lord lieutenant of Gloucester (1737–55).
[1329] Richard Dalton* (c. 1695–1769).
[1330] Thomas Rundle* (1687/88–1743). He was indeed made bishop of Derry in 1735.
[1331] Queen Caroline (Princess Caroline of Brandenburg-Ansbach) (1683–1737).
[1332] Sir Robert Walpole* (1676–1745), later first Earl of Orford.
[1333] Daniel Waterland (1683–1740), theologian.
[1334] Samuel Lisle (1683–1749), prolocutor of the Lower House of Convocation in 1734, later bishop of St. Asaph (1744) and Norwich (1748).
[1335] Edmund Gibson* (1669–1748).
[1336] Alexander Pope* (1688–1744).
[1337] Joseph Butler (1692–1752). *The Analogy of Religion* would be published in May 1736. Thomas Secker* helped prepare the text.

of your health, we are willing to believe the best of it. And your diocese we hope cannot but leave you some intervals of leisure which you must allow the friends of religion and virtue to promise themselves publick advantages from.

My whole family desire to join their sincere assurances of the greatest respect and friendship to you and good Mrs. Berkeley, and their compliments to the young gentlemen, with those of,

> My Lord,
> your Lordship's most affectionate brother
> and most obedient servant,
> Tho. Bristol.

Feb 1. 1734/35

250 BERKELEY TO HOADLY[1338]

RCB Library D6/150/6.

Cloyne, 17 March 1734/35

My Lord,

Though upon receipt of your Grace's[1339] letter, I had ordered the proper inquiries to be made, yet I was not enabled before yesterday to return a satisfactory answer to it.[1340] But I believe the following account may be depended on. As for Ballihay, there is a Prebend so called in my Diocese, but no part thereof is impropriated: So here is a mistake in the gentlemen of the Choir. There is a like mistake, as I am informed, with regard to the parish of Temple-Robin, no part of which belongs to them. But the tithes of Temple-Bodane (which is not mentioned in your Grace's letter) are half in the vicar and half in the impropriator holding under the choir of St. Patrick's. The former share amounts from 25 to 30 pounds pannum, and the impropriated share is set at 23 pounds pannum. The tithes of Killalay are equally divided between the vicar and the impropriator. The former

---

[1338] The reverse reads "Temple Godare, County Corke," but the addressee is otherwise not named. Since the letter is directed to Berkeley's superior concerning the diocese, it is likely Archbishop Hoadly.*

[1339] John Hoadly* (1678–1746), then archbishop of Dublin. He became primate of Ireland (archbishop of Armagh) in 1742.

[1340] Archbishop Hoadly* was inquiring about the revenues of the vicars-choral of St. Patrick's, a corporate body which was an impropriator. "Impropriation" is a technical term for the holding by a layman (or corporate body) of an ecclesiastical tithe. The layman would then provide a vicar to perform the ecclesiastical duties.

share communibus annis is set for 20 pounds: the impropriator sets his for 16 pds pannum. The impropriated tithes of Carigleamleary were set to Mr. Causabon for sixteen pounds pannum. The vicar's moiety never exceeded twenty pounds pannum. This is the best information that could be procured by,

> My Lord, your Grace's
> most obedient humble servant,
> Geor: Cloyne

Cloyne March 17, 1734/35

251 BENSON TO BERKELEY

BL Add. MS 39311, fols. 29–30.

St. James' Street, 13 May 1735

My dear Lord,

I write to you immediately upon the receipt of yours, as I can give you the answer you wish to the chief part of your letter, that the person you mention is not to come over with the Bishop of Derry,[1341] and he is determined to bring no chaplain over with him. There is a cousin-german of his, who has a small living here, whom he thinks himself obliged to provide for, but he does not carry him over with him. If A. Bishop Goodwin's[1342] son shall take orders, he will, I believe, think himself obliged to take him for his chaplain preferably to any other in Ireland, but he tells me he goes over determined to prefer those educated in the country, with regard only to their merit and learning.

I heartily wish you joy of the birth of your son;[1343] this is one of the greatest blessings providence can send you, and you are so wise and happy as to understand the value of it. I hope I may by this time give you and Mrs. Berkeley joy on her entire recovery, and may God grant you both life and health to give your boys what is better than all the wealth which you or all the world can give them, a religious and good education.

I beg you to write a line to the Baron,[1344] and acquaint him with what I acquainted you at the beginning of my letter. I wish we had the Baron in our own Court of Exchequer, more for the clergy's than for his own sake. The

---

[1341] Thomas Rundle* (1687/88–1743).
[1342] Timothy Godwin (1670?–1729), archbishop of Cashel (1727–29).
[1343] John Berkeley was born on 11 April 1735 but died an infant on 16 October 1735.
[1344] John Wainwright* (?–1741).

clergy have been used extremely ill in that Court, and their only hope was in an appeal to the House of Lords. But the House on Monday was sennight passed such a decree upon an appeal in relation to Modus's,[1345] that all their hopes are gone there, and they have great reason to fear that the consequences of this decree will be very fatal. The clergyman who brought the appeal was a distinguished Tory, and he thought, I believe, he should find favour, and all thought at least he would have common justice from that quarter. But several lords of that party appeared in a cause in which I am not sure if any one even of the Scotch lords would appear. The case was exceedingly clear. But it was given out that the consequences of this case would affect every man that had an estate, and that it was time to put a stop to the growing wealth of the clergy. My Lord Chancellor[1346] and the Bishops of London[1347] and Salisbury[1348] spoke on one side, and Lord Bathurst[1349] and Lord Onslow[1350] on the other. Lord Hardwicke,[1351] unfortunately for the clergy,[1352] was obliged to attend a cause at Guildhall that day. When the House came to divide, about 15 of the lords present had the modesty to retire to the throne, and not vote at all, but enough stayed to make a majority, and the bishops had only the Chancellor and the Duke of Bedford[1353] with them. This affair makes a great deal of noise, as it affects the rights of all the parochial clergy, and as the injustice of the case is very notorious, the most notorious, perhaps, of any that has been decided for a hundred years past in the House of Lords. But Lord Bathurst did not seem to think that enough, but talked a great deal, though quite foreign to the purpose, about the clergy having raised their fines. I am sorry I have not a more agreeable subject to write to you upon, but, as it is at present the chief subject of

---

[1345] The reference is likely to a case, *Giffard* v. *Webb*, which started in the Court of the Exchequer and was appealed to the House of Lords. The rector of Stoke (John Giffard) complained that a modus of three shillings per lamb was not an appropriate tithe, it not representing the full value of the property. A *modus* is a monetary substitute for a traditional tithe. Instead of tithing a lamb, for instance, farmers would tithe a set amount instead per new lamb born. The House of Lords confirmed the modus, which was a blow to rights of the clergy to regulate their income. See F. K. Eagle and E. Younge, *A Collection of the Reports of Cases, the Statues, and Ecclesiastical Laws, Relating to Tithes* (London, 1826), esp. vol. II, pp. 615–16, and *The English Reports, House of Lords*, vol. III, ed. A. Wood Benton (London: Stevens & Sons, 1901), pp. 11–12.

[1346] Charles Talbot* (1685–1737), first Baron Talbot of Hensol.

[1347] Edmund Gibson* (1669–1748).

[1348] Thomas Sherlock (1677–1761). He was made bishop of Bangor in 1728, but promoted to Salisbury in 1734. He would translate to the bishopric of London in 1748 after the death of Edmund Gibson.*

[1349] Allen Bathurst (1684–1775), first Earl Bathurst.

[1350] Perhaps Denzil Onslow (?–1765?).

[1351] Philip York* (or Yorke) (1690–1764), first Earl of Hardwicke.

[1352] "for the clergy" omitted by Fraser.

[1353] John Russell (1710–71), fourth Duke of Bedford.

discourse, at least among the clergy here, I have made it the greatest part of my letter. I have only room to add many services from the Bishop of Bristol[1354] and his family to you and yours. My sister has been very ill, but is now better— I am, my dear Lord, your most affectionate faithful servant and brother, M. Glocester.

252 BERKELEY TO SMIBERT[1355]

MS *unknown.* Gentleman's Magazine *101 (February 1831): 100.*

Cloyne, 31 May 1735

Dear Mr. Smibert,

A great variety and hurry of affairs, joined with ill state of health, hath deprived me of the pleasure of corresponding with you for this good while past, and indeed I am very sensible that the task of answering a letter is so disagreeable to you, that you can well dispense with receiving one of mere compliment, or which doth not bring something pertinent and useful. You are the proper judge whether the following suggestions may be so or no. I do not pretend to give advice; I only offer a few hints for your own reflection.

What if there be in my neighbourhood a great trading city? What if this city be four times as populous as Boston, and a hundred times as rich? What if there be more faces to paint, and better pay for painting, and yet nobody to paint them? Whether it would be disagreeable to you to receive gold instead of paper? Whether it might be worth your while to embark with your busts, your prints, your drawings, and once more cross the Atlantic? Whether you might not find full business in Cork, and live there much cheaper than in London? Whether all these things put together might not be worth a serious thought? I have one more question to ask, and that is, whether myrtles grow in or near Boston, without pots, stoves,[1356] or greenhouses, in the open air? I assure you they do in my garden. So much for the climate. Think of what hath been said, and God direct you for the best.

I am, good Mr. Smibert,

Your affectionate humble servant,

Geor: Cloyne

[1354] Thomas Secker* (1693–1768).

[1355] Printed in *Gentleman's Magazine* in the "Original Communications" section.

[1356] Luce mistakenly corrects to "stones." A "stove" is a hothouse, often used for the cultivation of plants.

P.S: My wife is exceedingly your humble servant and joins in compliments both to you and yours. We should be glad to hear the state of your health and family. We have now three boys,[1357] doubtful which is the prettiest. My two eldest past well through the small-pox last winter. I have my own health better in Cloyne than I have either in Old England or New.

253 BERKELEY TO JOHNSON[1358]

MS *unknown.* LL, *p. 241.*

Cloyne, 11 June 1735

Reverend Sir,

It is very agreeable to find that the public examinations appointed in your College[1359] have not failed of their design in encouraging the studies of the youth educated therein. And I am particularly pleased that they have given to some of your own family an opportunity of distinguishing themselves. One principal end proposed by me was to promote a better understanding with the Dissenters, and so by degrees to lessen their dislike to our communion; to which methought the improving their minds with liberal studies might greatly conduce, as I am very sensible that your own discreet behaviour and manner of living towards them hath very much forwarded the same effect. The employing young men, though not in orders, to read a sermon, and some part of the Liturgy, in those places where they are unprovided with churches and ministers, I always thought a reasonable and useful institution; and though some among you were prejudiced against it, yet I doubt not their prejudices will wear off when they see the good effects of it. I should imagine it might be some encouragement to well disposed students to reflect that by employing themselves in that manner they not only do useful service to the Church, but also thereby recommend themselves in the properest manner to Holy Orders, and consequently to missions, whenever vacancies shall make way for them, or when the Society shall be enabled to found new ones.

[1357] Berkeley's three children at this time were Henry (1729–after 1756), George (1733–95), and the recently born John (1735–35), who would die on 16 October that same year. A fourth child, Lucia, died in infancy in Rhode Island in 1731.

[1358] Fraser and Luce print this letter (*Works*, vol. VIII, pp. 241–42), but neither Beardsley nor Schneider make mention of it.

[1359] Yale.

My wife is obliged to you for your kind remembrance, and sends her compliments to you. Our little family is increased to three boys, whereof the two eldest past the small pox last winter.

I wish you and yours all happiness, and pray God to forward your good endeavours for the advancement of true religion and learning, being very truly,

Reverend Sir,

Your faithful Brother and humble Servant,

George Cloyne.

When any from your College have encouragement to pass over to England in expectation of Holy Orders and a mission, I would have them, now I am absent myself, to apply to Dr. Benson,[1360] the bishop of Gloucester, as they were used to do to me.

He is a most worthy prelate, and attends the meetings of the Society; and in my present situation I cannot do better service than by recommending your candidates to his protection.

254 GIBSON TO BERKELEY

BL Add. MS 39311, fol. 31.

Fulham, 9 July 1735

My Lord,

I have now before me a letter from your Lordship of so old a date that I know not how to excuse the lateness of this answer, unless you will make allowance for the hurry of our winter campaign, and my removing hither, and my holding a Visitation in part of the months of May and June.

What your Lordship observes is very true, and appears to be so in experience here, that the men of science (a conceited generation) are the greatest sticklers against revealed religion, and have been very open in their attacks upon it. And we are much obliged to your Lordship for retorting their arguments upon them, and finding them work in their own quarters, and must depend upon you to go on to humble them, if they do not yet find themselves sufficiently humbled.

If there be a prospect of bringing the Irish to come to our churches, in case the Liturgy were read to them in their own language, the rest of your scheme will

---

[1360] Martin Benson* (1689–1752). He was made bishop of Gloucester in 1735.

bear no deliberation; nor are the abilities of the persons ordained deacons for that purpose to be regarded, so long as they are sober and virtuous. My great doubt is, whether the priests, by terror and persuasion, have not such influence upon the lower people, for whose sake chiefly it is intended, as to hinder them from joining in a Protestant service. And though it might prove so at last, I can see no inconvenience in making the experiment. But your Lordship and the Bench of Bishops there must be far better judges of what is prudent and practicable than we can be.

It is taken for granted here, that our Dissenters will bring their Bill for repealing the Test Act[1361] next winter, and that whether the Court encourage them or not. It is probable that they rely upon promises which have been made by candidates in the late elections, to secure the dissenting interest in cities and boroughs; but I cannot think that all these promises will be remembered if the Court should oppose it, nor that the Court will wantonly divest itself at once of the whole Church interest.

I find that a new Lord-Lieutenant[1362] has been talked of on that side the water, but on this side we hear nothing of it. And I have reason to believe, from a circumstance that happened to come lately to my knowledge, that my Lord-Lieutenant himself does not think of it at present.

I am, my Lord, Your Lordship's very faithful servant and brother,

Edm. London.

255 TAYLOR TO BERKELEY

EP, BL Add. MS 46986, fol. 88–88v.

Egmont, 8 October 1735

My Lord,

The enclosed letter came to me from the Principle Inhabitant of Canturk a very considerable man in character and circumstance whose word may be

---

[1361] The Test Acts were a series of laws (initially passed in 1673) that excluded from public office anyone who refused to take the oaths of allegiance and supremacy, who refused to receive Communion according to the rites of the Church of England, or who refused to renounce belief in the doctrine of transubstantiation. The acts were aimed primarily at Catholics, but also excluded many Protestants who did not conform to the beliefs of the Church of England. In 1678 the acts were extended to members of Parliament. The law was not fully repealed until 1828.

[1362] Lionel Cranfield Sackville* (1688–1765), first Duke of Dorset. He would remain lord lieutenant until 1737.

depended upon in any case he will give it. The speaks so fully its own purpose that I have little more to say but to vouch my entire belief of it and to acquaint your Lordship with the steps formerly taken.

In the Bishop of Dromore's time the inhabitants desired a chapel of ease which the Bishop encouraged them in and some way ordered it so that for about half a year they had service every fortnight in the markethouse. Upon this subscriptions were carried on and money enough subscribed to build a chapel of ease but for want of a settled provision for a parson to give divine services in it once a fortnight. The scheme was at a stand and when the present Bishop of Dromore[1363] succeeded it was laid aside.

That bishop when I spoke to him about it told me that he would encourage such a good work with all his heart but that he was at a loss how to provide for it. I hope your Lordship will pardon me if I repeat my answer to him which was that I knew of but two: one was the convent of the incumbent who must pay somebody for giving them service once a fortnight and the other was setting out some small sinecure such as Kilbrun for the service of that chapel. Neither of the methods were in his power nor do I know if he would have pursued either in case they were.

In case any thing can be done in it I am sure my Lord Egmont[1364] will do at least as much as he offered before which was ten pounds and the ground, and in case of building a house for the clergyman which the Bishop of Dromore was fond of my Lord offered four acres of ground. I dare say that when my Lord Egmont knows your sentiments he will co-operate very zealously in so good work.

The subject must plead my excuse for this trouble given your Lordship. This messenger will I hope bring me an account of an alteration in your health for the better which will give me great pleasure as I am with great respect

> My Lord
> your Lordship's most obedient and
> most humble servant,
> William Taylor

To the Rt Revd, the Bishop of Cloyne

[1363] The bishop of Dromore in 1735 was Henry Maule (1676–1758). "In the Bishop of Dromore's time" refers to Maule's tenure as bishop of Cloyne (1726–32).
[1364] John Percival* (1683–1748).

256 BERKELEY TO TAYLOR[1365]

EP, BL Add. MS 46986, fol. 89.

Cloyne, 9 October 1735

Sir,

I should be very glad there was a chapple of ease established at the place you mention in your letter, but how to endow it I am at a loss. The thing I shall readily agree to but the means I doubt are not in my power—at present I am confined by my disorder but in the spring purpose to visit those parts when I may have an opportunity of talking with you at large on this subject. In the meantime I question whether my authority extends so far as to set out a sinecure[1366] for the service of such chapel. I am

> Sir
>
> your most faithful humble servant,
>
> Ge: Cloyne

To William Taylor Esq.

257 TAYLOR TO BERKELEY[1367]

EP, BL Add. MS 46986, fol. 99–99v.

Dublin, 8 November 1735

My Lord,

I send your Lordship Swift's & Co* receipt for one hundred and fifty pounds. Your Lordship will please to send me your receipt in return to it in full to the time it discharges the interest due from Lord Egmont[1368] and please to include the seventy-five pounds paid formerly because I have no receipt for it and your Lordship's receipt must be my voucher.

I had a letter lately from my Lord Egmont in answer to one I wrote him about the chapel of ease at Canturk wherein he tells me that in case any

---

[1365] Luce first published the letter in "Some Unpublished Berkeley Letters with Some New Berkleiana," *Proceedings of the Royal Irish Academy*, 147. He did not publish Taylor's initial letter (Letter 255), nor his reply to Berkeley (Letter 257).

[1366] A sinecure (from the Latin "without care") is either a benefice without active responsibilities or an income derived from such a benefice.

[1367] On the back along the edge is written "8 Nov. 1735 copy of Mr. Taylor's letter to the B. of Cloyne."

[1368] John Percival* (1683–1748).

provision can be made for it he will give ground and fifty pounds, which is so handsome a subscription that I would engage to make up the rest to build a neat chapel; he was so kind also that if Mr. Brereton[1369] did not accept of the living of churchtown, to offer, to present my brother lately put into orders to it, in case your Lordship would approve him, and in case Mr. Brereton accepts it, has given me encouragement to mention my brother to your Lordship for Newmarket (if you had not fixed a person for it) as one that would serve both Newmarket Church and the chapel at Canturk. But my brother having the misfortune to be a stranger to your Lordship and for fear of being thought too presuming, I would not venture to mention him when I had the honour of visiting your Lordship at Cloyne, nor did I care to ask a letter from Lord Egmont, knowing how kind your Lordship had lately been to Mr. Cannon upon his recommendation. I should not have taken the liberty of doing it now, if he had not been so good to give me such an opportunity that I should be wanting to the affection my brother has a right to expect from me if I did not embrace it.

As far as I may have a right to speak of my brother I will beg leave to give him a character that he is a sober well principled young man and I hope will go through the business of his profession without being a disgrace to it. This I venture to speak with the more assurance as it is Lord Orrery's[1370] opinion of him to whom he has the honour to be chaplain.

Your Lordship will I hope forgive this liberty, it is what I must own I have no right to take and is what in my own case I could not bring my self to do.

I shall hope for an account of your Lordship's better health than when I had the honour to see you last and am

My Lord
your Lordship's most obedient faithful servant

[1369] Most likely Robert Brereton (1705–64), one of the Breretons of Carrigslaney. He graduated from Trinity College, Dublin, in 1727 and was rector of Burton and Brahenny from 1735 to 1764.
[1370] John Boyle* (1707–62), fifth Earl of Cork and fifth Earl of Orrery.

258 GIBSON TO BERKELEY

BL Add. MS 39311, fol. 32.

Whitehall, 7 February 1735/36

My Lord,

I hope this will find your Lordship perfectly at ease, and at liberty to attend your mathematical infidels;[1371] for, though I am not a competent judge of the subject, I am sure, from your espousing it with so much zeal, and against such adversaries, that, in pursuing the point, you are doing good service to religion. Here we have now little trouble from professed infidels, but a great deal from semi-infidels, who, under the title of Christians, are destroying the whole work of our Redemption by Christ, and making Christianity little more than a system of morality. But their design is so barefaced and shocking that they make little progress among serious people.

It has been a doubt for some time, whether the Dissenters would trouble this Session with their Bill for repealing the Corporation and Test Acts.[1372] But now it is said with some assurance that we are to expect it, though without any probability of success. The Court are [sic] openly and avowedly against them, and so are the Tories; and from what quarter their support is to come, we do not yet see or conceive. It is given out that they do it, to know their friends from their foes, and I believe they reckon that the beginning it now, though without success, will make the way for better quarter in some future Session. On the contrary, their bringing in the Bill is so much against the declared judgment of many members who otherwise wish them well, that we think they will provoke their friends, and lose much ground by the attempt. Whether they or we judge right, time must show.

I shall be glad to see the proportion between Protestants and Papists fairly stated; not only because the accounts have hitherto been represented very differently, but also because it is a point upon which great stress is laid, upon some occasions, both with them and us.[1373]

[1371] A reference to Berkeley's *The Analyst or a Discourse Addressed to an Infidel Mathematician* first published in 1734.

[1372] The Test Acts were a series of laws (initially passed in 1673) that excluded from public office anyone who refused to take the oaths of allegiance and supremacy, who refused to receive Communion according to the rites of the Church of England, or who refused to renounce belief in the doctrine of transubstantiation. The acts were aimed primarily at Catholics, but also excluded many Protestants who did not conform to the beliefs of the Church of England. In 1678 the acts were extended to members of Parliament. The law was not fully repealed until 1828. See Letter 254.

[1373] Berkeley had inquired earlier of Thomas Prior* (1681–1751) about the proportion of Protestants to Catholics in Ireland. See Letter 222.

I am, my Lord,
your Lordship's very faithful servant
and brother,
Edm. London

259 BERKELEY TO JOHNSON[1374]

MS *unknown.* LL, *pp. 245–46.*

Cloyne, 12 March 1735/36

Reverend Sir,

My remote distance from London deprives me of those opportunities which I might otherwise have of being serviceable to your missionaries, though my inclinations are still the same. I am very glad to find persons of Mr. Arnold's[1375] character disposed to come over to our Church, which, it is to be hoped, will sooner or later prevail over all their prejudices. It were indeed to be wished that the Society was able to establish new missionaries as often as candidates offer themselves; but I persuade myself that what their funds will allow them to do will not be wanting in favour of your natives. I have wrote to my friend the Bishop of Gloucester,[1376] desiring an allowance from the Society may be obtained for Mr. Arnold towards defraying the expenses of his voyage. But for a salary he must wait till provision can be made, or till a vacancy occurs.

It is no small satisfaction to me to hear that a spirit of emulation is raised in our scholars at Newhaven, and that learning and good sense are gaining ground among them. I do not wonder that these things should create some jealousy in such as are bigotted to a narrow way of thinking, and that this should produce uneasiness to you and other well-wishers of our Church. But I trust in God that the prudence and temper of yourself and your associates will, with God's

---

[1374] This letter is printed by Fraser and Luce, but neither Schneider nor Beardsley make mention of it. I cannot find any trace of the original, but the letter otherwise appears genuine.

[1375] Jonathan Arnold (?–1739) joined the Church of England in 1734 and was ordained in England in 1736. He perished on a second voyage to England in 1739. See Updike, *History of the Episcopal Church in Narrangansett Rhode Island*, pp. 182–83 and E. Edwards Beardsley, *The History of the Episcopal Church in Connecticut* (Boston: Houghton, Mifflin & Co. 1883), pp. 111–12.

[1376] Martin Benson* (1689–1752).

blessing, get the better of misguided and unruly zeal, which will never be a match for the wisdom from above.

I have passed this winter at Cloyne, having been detained from Parliament by my ill-health, which is now pretty well re-established. My family are all well, and concur with me in best wishes to you and yours.

I am, Reverend Sir,

your most faithful, humble servant and brother,

George Cloyne

As to your postscript, I can only say that Ireland contains ten times more objects of charity, whether we consider the souls or bodies of men, than are to be met with in New England. And indeed there is so much to be done (and so few that care to do it) here at home, that there can be no expectations from hence.

260 BENSON TO BERKELEY

Yale, Osborn Files "B" folder 1118.

St. James's Street, 20 May 1736

My dear Lord,

It is a great pleasure to me as all your friends here to hear that your health is better, for which we have been long in great pain. It will be for your good, as well as the good of your diocese, that you should move about it. Your having been so long confined by one illness is enough to create several others. Wherever you are, I know you are always contriving to do all the good you can. And what you tell me you are doing at Cloyne is a very wise and useful charity.[1377] Instead of promoting, people have been contriving here to put a stop to charity, as the Master of the Rolls,[1378] though a good man, is doing I think an unchristian thing.

A clause was added to this bill in the House of Lords for preventing the mischief it was feared it might do to Anne's country to the poor clergy.[1379] Lord Carteret[1380] offered a clause for repealing the statutes in the universities, whereby the fellows are obliged to go into orders. He, the Duke of Argyle,[1381]

[1377] For some details about Berkeley's charity projects, see Letter 263.

[1378] Sir Joseph Jekyll* (1662–1738).

[1379] On 5 April 1736 Jekyll* sponsored a "Bill to restrain the Disposition of Lands" that would make void all grants intended for charity unless executed by a will entered into a year before the death of the grantor. Petitions were then brought to the House of Commons by universities and other charitable organizations seeking exemption from the measure.

[1380] John Carteret* (1690–1763), second Earl Granville.

[1381] Archibald Campbell (1682–1761), third Duke of Argyll.

Lord Bathurst,[1382] Lord Chesterfield,[1383] and Lord Hervey,[1384] have been the warmest and bitterest in all these bills. Sir R. Walpole[1385] so strenuously opposed the bill for the repeal of the Test,[1386] that he was for a few days the greatest favourite of the bishops and clergy. But this was soon interrupted by the coming in of the Quakers bid.[1387] The bishops without consulting or acquainting the ministry wrote into their dioceses and got petitions presented from every county. This the ministry highly resented from all, and so particularly from the Bishop of London,[1388] that the friendship which has to[o?] many years subsisted is entirely broken between him and Sir R. Walpole. Sir Robert was silent upon that occasion in the House of Commons and the bid went through that house. But when it came up in the House of Lords, it was very strongly opposed by my Lord Chancellor[1389] and Lord Hardwick,[1390] and upon the second reading, after two days consideration and debate, near ten o'clock at night, it was carried against committing and for rejecting the bill by a majority of 54 against 35. Lord Bathurst was so far transported with passion upon this account, that he moved the orders might be given for preparing a bill against the next session for abrogating of the spiritual courts. And Bishop of Salisbury[1391] hath by his writing and speaking upon this occasion has [*sic*] done the greatest service.

My Lord Lempster[1392] is perfectly recovered and Lord Pomfret is much your humble servant. Sir John James[1393] I hear is certainly upon the ocean in his return home, he will hear of his father's death when he lands and the seamen will be informed of the dignity of the person they have brought over. I saw old Archibald in fine waistcoat, though perhaps not a new one, at Court on the day

---

[1382] Allen Bathurst (1684–1775), first Earl Bathurst.

[1383] Philip Dormer Stanhope* (1694–1773), fourth Earl of Chesterfield.

[1384] John Hervey (1696–1743), second Baron Hervey of Ickworth.

[1385] Sir Robert Walpole* (1676–1745), later first Earl of Orford.

[1386] For more about the Test Act, see Letters 254 and 258.

[1387] In the same session, on 30 April, a bill was advanced to force suits against Quakers for the nonpayment of tithes to be heard only by justices of the peace (removing said cases from the Spiritual Court). Quakers refused to pay tithes on the grounds of religious conscience. At the introduction of the bill, a number of Anglican bishops submitted petitions from their dioceses opposing it, thinking that the measure might undermine the income of the Church. The bill was defeated in the House of Lords. See *Papers Relating to the Quakers Tythe Bill* (3rd edn., 1736), pp. 31–32.

[1388] Edmund Gibson* (1669–1748).

[1389] Charles Talbot* (1685–1737), first Baron Talbot of Hensol.

[1390] Philip York* (or Yorke) (1690–1764), first Earl of Hardwicke.

[1391] Thomas Sherlock (1677–1761). He was bishop of Salisbury (1734–48) and then translated to London.

[1392] Thomas Fermor (1698?–1753), second Baron Leominster and first Earl Pomfret.

[1393] John James* (?–1741).

we were to compliment the Princess of Wales. I enquired after his health and we both talked of you. Though he was not so fine as many others, yet I esteem him more than most, I might say all, I saw there. I hope notwithstanding what the ministry say, the step taken by the bishops here is not to be thought an indiscrete one. But the step taken by one of your bishops and some of the clergy in Ireland is by all here thought to be a very imprudent one, and I fear it may be a means of doing the clergy of both kingdoms a good deal of harm. Dr. Maddox[1394] is at last made Bishop of St. Asaph. The Bishop of Landaff[1395] has his Deanery of Wells, and Dean [Cressat?] of your kingdom who has an estate in the diocese of Hereford of 2,000 a year, as it is said, is to be Dean of Hereford. The Parliament rose this day and I am very glad it is up. Out of seven divisions this session, five of them I have been against the Court, and there would have been one more, had not my attendance [to?] the address of the University of Oxford hindered my attendance yesterday in the House of Lords.

I must employ the room that is left in making my compliments to your good Lady. I am going as soon as ever I can to Glocester and I am in all places my dear Lord's

> most affectionately yours,
> M. Glocester

261 BERKELEY TO JAMES[1396]

MS *unknown.* Gentleman's Magazine *101 (February 1831): 99–100.*

Cloyne, 30 June 1736

Dear Sir,

In this remote corner of Imokilly, where I hear only the rumours and echoes of things, I know not whether you are still sailing on the ocean, or already arrived to take possession of your new dignity and estate.[1397] In the former case I wish you a good voyage; in the latter I welcome you, and wish you joy. I have a letter written and lying by me these three years, which I knew not whither or how to send you. But now you are returned to our hemisphere, I

[1394] Isaac Maddox (1697–1759). He would be consecrated bishop of St. Asaph in July 1736 and translate to Worcester in 1743.

[1395] John Harris (1680–1738), bishop of Llandaff (1729–38).

[1396] Published in *Gentleman's Magazine* under the heading "Original Communications."

[1397] John James* (?–1741) was made Sir John James of Bury St. Edmunds in 1736.

promise myself the pleasure of being able to correspond with you. You who live to be a spectator of odd scenes are come into a world much madder and odder than that you left. We also in this island are growing an odd and mad people. We were odd before, but I was not sure of our having the genius necessary to become mad. But some late steps of a public nature give sufficient proof thereof.

Who knows but when you have settled your affairs, and looked about and laughed enough in England, you may have leisure and curiosity enough to visit this side of the water? You may land within two miles of my house, and find that from Bristol to Cloyne is a shorter and much easier journey than from London to Bristol. I would go about with you, and show you some scenes perhaps as beautiful as you have seen in all your travels. My own garden is not without its curiosity, having a number of myrtles, several of which are seven or eight feet high. They grow naturally, with no more trouble or art than gooseberry bushes. This is literally true. Of this part of the world it may truly be said that it is –

Ver ubi longum, tepidasque praebet
Jupiter brumas.[1398]

My wife most sincerely salutes you. We should without compliment be over-joyed to see you. I am in hopes soon to hear of your welfare, and remain, dear Sir,
> your most obedient and affectionate servant,
> G. Cloyne

262 BENSON TO BERKELEY

BL Add. MS 39311, fols. 35–36.

St. James Street, 1 March 1736/37

My dear Lord,

I must first mention what is first in the thoughts and mouths of every one—the death of my Lord Chancellor.[1399] It is lamented so much as a public loss that it seems too selfish to bewail it as a private one. Never loss was so publickly and universally lamented. All degrees and orders and parties of men, however opposite in other respects, all unite in their sorrow upon this account, and none express a greater than the friends of the Established

---

[1398] From Horace, *Carmina*, II, 6. "Where Jupiter grants long springs and mild winters ..."
[1399] Charles Talbot* (1685–1737), first Baron Talbot of Hensol. He died on 14 February 1737.

Church. He had given so strong and late an instance of his affection to it, by getting the Bounty of the late Queen,[1400] which had been so violently attacked the end of the last session, so well settled by an Order of Council, and he was ready on all occasions so powerfully to have espoused the interests of the Church, and so able to have defended them, that none more than the clergy express their sorrow on this occasion, and among the clergy none more than the Bishop of London.[1401] The Bishop of Oxford[1402] will, I doubt not, make a very good Archbishop. Upon his promotion it was proposed to me to remove to Oxford, and that, besides the Commendam I already have, I should have a Canonry of Christ Church, which is vacant, added to it. I am, I thank God, so much contented where I am that I have no desire to move to Oxford, or any other place. My Brother Secker[1403] has since had an offer of the Bishoprick of Oxford, but he also has declined accepting it, and it is not as yet disposed of.

My Lord Bathurst,[1404] whom you mention, has lately said a great deal to me, to assure me of his good intention towards the Church and Universities, to both of which he has of late been looked on to be so great an enemy. [I] will hope his professions are real, though other persons are not inclined to think them so. My Lord Bolingbroke[1405] set himself up for an old Whig, a great patron of republican principles, and a great admirer of such religious ones as Thomas Chubb[1406] and some others have been advancing. His Lordship has endeavoured to proselyte as many of the Tories as he could, but he has made few disciples among them, and most of them, to their honour be it spoken, have declared their detestation of his new scheme, and have acted like honest and consistent men.

I am rejoiced to hear of the increase of your health and of your family. My best wishes attend them. [My] humble services wait upon Mrs. Berkeley. My sister is still at Bath, and there is little likelihood of her being able to come to London this Spring.

[1400] As Queen Caroline, queen to George II* (1683–1760), would not die until 20 November 1737, the reference must be to Sophia Dorothea, queen to George I* (1666–1726).

[1401] Edmund Gibson* (1669–1748).

[1402] John Potter, (1673/74–1747). He was bishop of Oxford (1715–37) and archbishop of Canterbury (1737–47) following William Wake* (1657–1737).

[1403] Thomas Secker* (1693–1768), bishop of Bristol. Although he declined the offer of translation to Oxford at first, he ultimately accepted the offer and translated later in 1737.

[1404] Allen Bathurst (1684–1775), first Earl Bathurst.

[1405] Saint-John Henry* (1678–1751), first Viscount Bolingbroke.

[1406] Thomas Chubb (1679–1747). Chubb was a controversial religious writer, tending towards a form of deism. He authored over fifty tracts, including *The Supremacy of the Father Asserted . . . Eight Arguments from Scripture* (1715) and *The Previous Question with Regard to Religion* (1725).

Mr. Walpole, the second son of Sir Robert, is appointed secretary to the Duke of Devonshire.[1407]

My Lord Hardwick[1408] has succeeded my Lord Talbot,[1409] as he was the only person in the kingdom capable of filling that post.

We have had an unhappy contest between the K[ing] and Prince, about settling an allowance for the latter.[1410] It has been moved in both Houses to address his Majesty to settle £100,000 per annum on his son, which was rejected by a majority of [. . .] [damaged text] against 204 in the House of Commons, and of 10 [. . .] [damaged text] in the House of Lords.

I have enclosed with this Mr. Tryon's[1411] account of his having received the money. He and his son are joint Treasurers of the Society.

I am, my dear Lord,

Most affectionately and faithfully yours,

M. Glocester

263 BERKELEY TO PRIOR

LR, *pp. 265–67. Stock, p. lxxiii (extract).*

Cloyne, 5 March 1736/37

Dear Tom,

I here send you what you desire. If you approve of it, publish it in one or more of our newspapers;[1412] if you have any objection, let me know it by the next post. I mean, as you see, a brief abstract; which I could wish were spread through the nation, that men may think on the subject against next session.

But I would not have this letter made public sooner than a week after the publication of the third part of my *Querist*, which I have ordered to be sent to you.

[1407] Edward Walpole (1706–84), son of prime minister Sir Robert Walpole* (1676–1745), was appointed the chief secretary of William Cavendish (1698–1755), third Duke of Devonshire, in September 1737. Cavendish was appointed lord lieutenant of Ireland in April of 1737 and would serve in that post until 1744.

[1408] Philip York* (or Yorke) (1690–1764), first Earl of Hardwicke.

[1409] Charles Talbot* (1685–1737), first Baron Talbot of Hensol.

[1410] King George II* (1683–1760) quarreled with his son, Frederick Lewis* (1707–51), Prince of Wales, over his allowance. A measure in the House of Commons to set the allowance at £100,000 was defeated, but Walpole* persuaded George II to give £50,000 to the Prince and an equal amount for use by his new wife, Princess Augusta of Saxe-Gotha (1719–72).

[1411] William Tryon (?–1742), treasurer to the Society for the Propagation of the Gospel in Foreign Parts (not to be confused with William Tryon [1729–88], colonial governor of North Carolina).

[1412] Prior did so, in *Pue's Occurrences* and the *Dublin Newsletter* of 2/5 April 1737. See Letter 264 below.

I believe you may receive it about the time that this comes to your hands; for, as I told you in a late letter, I have hastened it as much as possible. I have used the same editor (Dr. Madden)[1413] for this as for the foregoing two parts.

I must desire you to purchase for me six copies of the third part of the *Querist*, which I would have stitched in six pamphlets; so that each pamphlet shall contain the first, second, and third Parts of the *Querist*. I would have these pamphlets covered with marbled paper pasted on white paper, and the leaves cut and gilt on the edges; and you will let me know when they are done—the sooner the better.

Our spinning-school is in a thriving way. The children begin to find a pleasure in being paid in hard money; which I understand they will not give to their parents, but keep to buy clothes for themselves. Indeed I found it difficult and tedious to bring them to this; but I believe it will now do. I am building a workhouse for sturdy vagrants, and design to raise about two acres of hemp for employing them. Can you put me in a way of getting hemp-seed; or does your society distribute any? It is hoped your flax-seed will come in time.

Last post a letter from an English bishop[1414] tells me, a difference between the King and Prince is got into Parliament, and that it seems to be big with mischief, if a speedy expedient be not found to heal the breach. It relates to the provision for his Royal Highness's family.

My three children have been ill.[1415] The eldest and youngest are recovered; but George is still unwell. We are all yours truly.

> your affectionate humble servant,
>
> Geor: Cloyne

[Appended to this letter is a draft of Berkeley's *Letter on the Project of a National Bank*, in *Literary Relics* pages 268–71. For the printed letter, see Letter 264 below.]

To A. B. Esq.

Sir,

You tell me gentlemen would not be averse from a national bank, provided they saw a sketch or plan of such bank laid down and proposed in a distinct manner. For my own part, I intended only to put queries, and offer hints, not presuming to direct the wisdom of the public. Besides, it seemed no hard matter, if any one should think fit, to convert queries into propositions. However, since

---

[1413] Samuel Madden (1686–1765).

[1414] Martin Benson* (1689–1752). See Letter 262.

[1415] In addition to Henry* (1729–after 1756) and George* (1733–95), Berkeley now has a third son, William* (1736–51), born 10 December 1736.

you desire a brief and distinct abstract of my thoughts on this subject, be pleased to take it as follows.

I conceive that, in order to erect a national bank, and place it on a right foot, it may be expedient to enact

1. That an additional tax of ten shillings the hoghead be laid on wine, which may amount to about ten thousand pounds a year; or to raise a like sum on foreign silks, linens, and laces.
2. That the fund arising from such tax be the stock for a national bank; the deficiencies whereof to be made good by Parliament.
3. That bank-notes be minted to the value of one hundred thousand pounds in round numbers, from one pound to a hundred.
4. That these notes be issued either to particular persons on ready money or on mortgage, or to the uses of the public on its own credit.
5. That a house and cashiers etc. be appointed in Dublin for uttering and answering these bills, and for managing this bank as other banks are managed.
6. That there be twenty-one inspectors, one third whereof to be persons in great office under the Crown, the rest members of both houses, ten whereof to go out by lot, and as many more to come in once in two years.
7. That such inspectors shall, in a body, visit the bank twice every year, and any three of them as often as they please.
8. That no bills or notes be minted but by order of Parliament.
9. That it be felony to counterfeit the notes of this bank.
10. That the public be alone banker, or sole proprietor of this bank.

The reasons for a national bank, and the answers to objections, are contained in the *Querist*; wherein there are also several other points relating to a bank of this nature, which in time may come to be considered. But at present, thus much may suffice for a general plan to try the experiment and begin with: which plan, after a year or two of trial, may be further improved, altered, or enlarged, as the circumstances of the public shall require.

Every one sees the scheme of a bank admits of many variations in minute particulars; several of which are hinted in the *Querist*, and several more may easily be suggested by any one who shall think on that subject. But it should seem the difficulty doth not consist so much in contriving or executing a national bank, as in bringing men to a right sense of the public weal, and of the tendency of such bank to promote the same.

I have treated these points, and endeavoured to urge them home, both from reason and example, particularly in the third part of the *Querist* lately published; which, with the two former, contain many hints, designed to put men upon thinking what is to be done in this critical juncture of our affairs; which I believe may be easily retrieved and put on a better foot than ever, if those among us who are most concerned be not wanting to themselves. I am, Sir,

  your humble servant,

  the QUERIST

264 BERKELEY TO A. B.

  Dublin Newsletter, *2–5 April 1737*. Pue's Occurrences, *2–5 April 1737. BL 8227.a.12.*

26 March 1737[1416]

Sir,

  You tell me gentlemen would not be averse from the National Bank proposed in the *Querist*, provided they could see a distinct sketch or plan of such bank drawn up in one view. The *Querist* indeed only puts questions and offers hints, not presuming to direct the wisdom of the legislature.

  But it should seem no difficult matter to convert queries into propositions. However, since you desire a short abstract of my thoughts in this subject, take them as follows.

  I conceive that in order to erect a national bank it may be expedient to enact:

  I. That an additional tax be raised[1417] of ten shillings the hogshead on wine, or that such other tax be raised as shall seem good to the Legislature.

  II. That the fund arising from such tax be stock for a national bank, the deficiencies whereof to be made good by Parliament.

[1416] This letter appeared in a number of places, often with minor variances. Here I use the original publication and supplement it with notes from the version appended to the 1737 Dublin edition of *Queries relating to a National Bank, extracted from the Querist* (published by George Faulkner). The latter contains notes added later that were not present in the original publication in the *Dublin Newsletter* and *Pue's Occurrences*. See NLI microfilm 3141, p. 2761, and an original pamphlet with the letter and added notes (BL 8227. a.12).

[1417] *Dublin Newsletter* inserts here: ", for instance,"

III. That bank notes be minted (a)[1418] to the value of one hundred thousand pounds in round numbers from one pound to twenty.[1419] (b)[1420]

IV. That such notes be issued either to particular persons on cash, or security, or else to the uses of the public on its own securities.

V. That a house, treasurer,[1421] cashiers, and other officers, (c)[1422] be appointed in *Dublin* for the uttering and answering of bills, for the judging of securities, for the receiving and keeping of cash, and for the managing of this Bank as other banks are managed.

VI. That there be twenty-one visitors,[1423] one-third of these, persons in great office (d)[1424] for the time being; the rest, members of either house of Parliament, some whereof to go out by lot and as many to come in by ballot once in two years.

VII. That such visitors visit the bank in a body four times every year; (e)[1425] and any three of them as often as they please.

VIII. That no bills or notes be minted but by order of Parliament. (f)[1426]

[1418] Berkeley's note (a): No country has more natural advantages. Our wants therefore are mostly to be resolved into the want of skill and industry in our peoples; the proper encouragement whereof consist in ready payments. These payments must be made with money, and money is of two sorts, specie or paper. Of the former, we neither have a sufficient quantity, nor yet means of acquiring it. Of the latter sort, we may have what we want, as good and current as any gold for domestic uses. Why should we not therefore reach forth our hand, and take of that sort of money which is in our power; and which makes far the greater part of the wealth of the most flourishing states in Europe? This, by promoting industry at home, may advance our credit abroad; and in the event, multiply our gold and silver.

[1419] The *Dublin Newsletter* has "from one pound to an hundred."

[1420] Berkeley's note (b): It seems very evident that, be the fund what it will, or in case there was no fund at all; yet those notes would circulate with full credit, if they were sure to pass in al payments of the revenue. That is to say, the government itself could give more credit to that paper, than any other security now current among us.

[1421] "Treasurer" added; not in the *Dublin Newsletter* version.

[1422] Berkeley's note (c): Among these it is proposed, that there be two managers with salaries: one of whom always to attend; and that such officers be at first named in the act, and afterward replaced by the visitors.

[1423] "inspectors" in other editions, including the *Dublin Newsletter*.

[1424] Berkeley's note (d): No just jealousy can be conceived of the power of such visitors, inasmuch as they are to give no new directions, but only see that the directions of the legislature be observed.

[1425] Berkeley's note (e): It is objected, that this were too much trouble to be expected from visitors who have no salaries. But if four times be thought too often, twice may do. It is hardly to be supposed that gentlemen would begrudge the attendance of two days in the year gratis, for the service of their country; or if there be such gentlemen, it cannot be supposed that they would be chosen by ballot. But this may be provided against, by allowing persons, who cannot attend, leave to decline the office, and electing others in their stead.

[1426] Berkeley's note (f): Under the direction of the Parliament, the public weal will prescribe a limit to the bank notes, which will always preserve their use and value, provided they are multiplied only in proportion to industry, and to answer to the demands of

IX. That it be [a] felony to counterfeit the notes of this bank.

X. That as the public is at all the charge and makes good the credit of this bank, so the public be alone banker or sole proprietor of this bank;[1427] the profits whereof shall be accounted for in Parliament and applied under the direction of the legislature, to the promoting of public works and manufactures. (g)[1428]

For the better administering of this national bank to the content of all persons it will be thought expedient to add diverse regulations about the number and choice of visitors and other officers concerned in so great a trust, into some share whereof it may not perhaps altogether seem improper to admit the deputies of great corporations. For the same end, those several precautions by signatures, cyphers, strong boxes under diverse keys, and such like checks, which are used in other banks, would not be omitted in this.

A bank wherein there are no sharers would be free from all the evils of stockjobbing. A bank whereof the public makes all the profit, and therefore makes good all deficiencies, must be most secure. Such a bank prudently managed would be a mine of gold in the hands of the public. The bills therein minted would be equivalent to so much money imported into the kingdom. The advantages of such a bank in restoring credit, promoting industry, answering the wants, as well of the public as of private persons, putting spirit into our people and enlivening our commerce, will, I suppose, be evident to whoever shall consider the queries of late proposed to the public.

Reasons for a national bank and answers to objections are particularly insisted on in the *Querist*, wherein are contained also several other matters relating to such [a] bank; which in time may be further improved, altered and enlarged, as the circumstances of the public shall require.

---

industry. Paper credit can never be so secure of doing good to a state, as by making the demands of industry its measure and the increase of industry its end. The same holds also with regard to gold and silver. The not considering this seems to have been the great oversight.

[1427] The rest of this paragraph was added; it is not in the *Dublin Newsletter*.

[1428] Berkeley's note (g): Men disposed to object, will confound the most different things. We have had, indeed, schemes of private association formerly proposed, which some may mistake for national banks. But it doth not appear, that any scheme of this nature was ever proposed in these kingdoms. And among the foreign banks perhaps there will not be found one established on so clear a foot of credit, contrived for such a general and easy circulation; and so well secured from frauds and accidents as that which it is now hoped may, by the wisdom of our legislature, be modelled and erected in Ireland.

Everyone sees that the scheme of a national bank admits of many variations and minute particulars, diverse of which are hinted by the *Querist*, but the public will choose* what shall be judged most convenient.

It should seem the difficulty doth not consist so much in the contriving or executing of a national bank as in bringing men to a right sense of the public weal, and of the tendency of such [a] bank to promote the same.

To explain these points, and to urge them home, both from reason and example, hath been the aim of the *Querist*, particularly of the third part, just now published, which, with the two foregoing, contains many hints designed to put men upon thinking what is to be done in this critical state of our affairs, which perhaps, may be easily retrieved and placed on a better foot than ever if those among us who are most concerned be not wanting to themselves.

I am your humble servant,

The Querist.

265 SECKER TO BERKELEY

BL Add. MS 39311, fols. 37–38.

Gloucester, 29 June 1737

My very good Lord,

I return you my hearty thanks for your friendly letter of congratulation.[1429] I have made an exchange, to accommodate other persons, which I never thought an advantageous one to my self in point of interest and begin to fear too late it will prove the contrary. But I have some advantage in situation by removing from your neighbour-city of Bristol: and a good situation I think is well worth purchasing. But then one should stay in it and I assure you my Lord I have no views of removing. To tread in the steps of my predecessor[1430] is to be Bishop of Oxford two and twenty years. What fancies one may come to have by the end of that time I cannot foretell but when the Bishop of Glocester[1431] and I were at the late Archbishop's[1432] funeral we were clearly of opinion that breathing the air of Lambeth and

---

[1429] Thomas Secker* (1693–1768) had just been translated from Bristol to be bishop of Oxford.

[1430] Secker's* predecessor as the bishop of Oxford was John Potter (1673/74–1747). Potter was bishop of Oxford (1715-37) and made archbishop of Canterbury in February 1737 after the death of William Wake.*

[1431] Martin Benson* (1689–1752).

[1432] William Wake* (1657–1737).

being buried in the Church of Croyden are neither of them felicities that one would much disquiet ones self to attain. And now I have mentioned my Lord of Glocester I should tell you in the next place that I and my family are at present his guests. My poor wife was most deplorably ill all the last year at Bath and had too frequent occasion to practise your Lordships rule of early rising, the disorder of her spirits not permitting her either to sleep or lie in bed awake. She is now recovered enough to take small journeys and I have brought her from Bath hither in hopes she may receive great benefit from the neighbourhood of her native air and the chearful hospitality of our good brother. We have been here as yet somewhat less than a week but so far the experiment succeeds very well: and we enjoy bright days and cool evenings in a very entertaining tranquillity, quite unconcerned about what may befall either Church or State the next Session. The ministry I believe mean us of the clergy neither any harm nor much good. Many of those who would be thought their best friends indeed are vehement against us and so are many also of their most determined enemies. It doth not seem therefore that our strength lies in adhering to either party; as indeed I think it never can: but in the honest policy of acting uprightly between both and joining with neither to do wrong. They who act thus will either stand or fall with honour. I see very little prospect that any thing in the Established Church will be altered for the better: for ministers are against all changes and they who complain would be very sorry to see the things which they complain of, mended. Nor doth there appear any immediate danger of alterations for the worse. And yet considering the increasing disregard to Religion and every thing that deserves the name of principle, together with the strange growth of that wild spirit which calls it self zeal for liberty there would be no reason to wonder at any shock how great or sudden soever which might happen either to the ecclesiastical or the civil part of our Constitution. But sufficient for the day is the evil thereof. May the calm which you seem to have at present in Ireland continue and may we none of us ever needlessly bring storms upon our selves. The Clergy might do much towards laying those which are raised already if we had not our share of faults as well as our adversaries. But enough of these matters. Miss Talbot[1433] whom you are so good to mention particularly is grown a very fine girl and continues a very good one. Her Mama and she, the prelate and his sister desire you and Mrs. Berkeley to accept their

[1433] After marrying Catherine Benson, Thomas Secker* and his wife lived with bishop of Durham William Talbot's* (1659–1730) widowed daughter-in-law and her daughter, the latter of whom is the "Miss Talbot" mentioned here.

compliments and best wishes to you both and your whole family: With which I beg leave to joyn those of

My Lord

Your sincerely affectionate brother

And faithfull servt,

Tho. Oxford

Glocester, June 29. 1737

266 BERKELEY TO ECLES[1434]

TCD MS 2167, fol. 2.

Cloyne, 1 September 1737

Sir,

As I hold my visitation next week I shall have occasion for a buck out of my Lord Burlington's[1435] park: I must therefore use the privilege his Lordship has given me, and desire you will please to order it to be sent on Monday next, which will oblige,

Sir,

your very humble servant,

Geor: Cloyne

267 BERKELEY TO AN OFFICIAL OF TRINITY COLLEGE, DUBLIN[1436]

TCD MS 2167, fol. 3.

Cloyne, 14 September 1737

Revd. Sir,

Your letter found me confined to my bed by the cholic. A few days after I ordered the surveyor who is usually employed in these parts to be sent for.

[1434] Addressed "To Henry Ecles, Esq. at Lismore, or in his absence to the park-keeper." See Luce, "Some Unpublished Berkeley Letters with some New Berkeleiana," 148.

[1435] Richard Boyle* (1694–1753), third Earl of Burlington and fourth Earl of Cork.

[1436] The front of the letter indicates it is from the bishop of Cloyne, "about the survey of Rathcoursey in the County of Cork." Luce lists this as a letter to some official in Trinity College, Dublin. The grounds for the attribution, however, are not clear. I follow his lead simply out of lack of an alternative. See Luce, "More Unpublished Berkeley Letters and New Berkeleiana," 42–43.

He happened to be absent from the country. Soon after I procured another from the county of Lymeric, who set about the work; but was interrupted and hinderd by Mr. Smyth, from making an inward survey in small divisions, with the quality and value of each parcel distinctly noted, as I had ordered him to do in compliance with the desire of your board. Beside my illness I had several lets and delays thrown in my way, perhaps by some who are under Mr. Smyth's influence. Even my own agent is, I find, his tenant for two farms. The business I perceive is somewhat odious. However you have here enclosed what I could get done. If it be not as compleat as I could wish, I assure you it is not for want of zeal for the interest of your Society, which I shall always be ready to serve to the utmost of my power, being very truly their and your,

> Revd. Sir,
> most faithful humble servant,
> Geor: Cloyne

I have given Mr. Kelly twenty-five shillings. He hath measured the entire contents and the outline anew, and pretends his survey to be more accurate than the former. As I desire to live well with my neighbours, the less I am mentioned in this affair, the better.

268 BENSON TO BERKELEY

BL Add. MS 39311, fols. 39–40.

Berry Street, Westminster, 7 February 1737/38

My dear Lord,

I was much pleased to hear that you were come to Dublin and attended the session of Parliament there. For though I love to be in my Diocese as much as I can, and wish that some of my brethren loved it more, yet it is so necessary for supporting the interest of the Church that the Bishops should be present in Parliament, that it is our duty I think to appear there, and if we take care to show that it is not our private interest which brings us thither and rules us there, we may be able to do some good or at least to hinder a good deal of mischief. A great deal is designed against us, and every opportunity is watched and waited for to put it in execution. The Queen's death[1437] is a severe blow, and those who would not be persuaded while she lived how zealous a friend she was to our Church and Constitution, have, since her death, been fully convinced of it. Both the King[1438] and the Minister[1439] seem firmly resolved to suffer no innovation, and to keep things as they are both here and in Ireland. And the great man you mention is, I believe, in the same way of thinking; but there are so few others in it, that, notwithstanding this support we stand I fear upon very dangerous ground. Not that I think the danger so near as you apprehend. There are some few wise men who would be for saving the Church upon political considerations, and some few good men who would be for preserving it upon religious ones, and those who are for destroying it, though many, yet are so divided, that though they agree to pull down, yet they differ so much about what they would have erected in the place, that this may be a means of keeping the old building up. Though the memory of Cromwell[1440] is not publicly drank to on this as it is on your side the water, yet we have those who are silly enough to think that he was a Republican, and venerate him upon that account.

I made your compliments to my Lord Chancellor,[1441] who desired his in return to you, and spoke with great esteem and regard of you.

I have sent your letter to Mr. Wolfe's lodgings. He is not in town, but they promised it should be sent safely to him.

We are likely to do little in Parliament, and you will think I believe the less the better. The less harm it certainly is so, but when so many good things are so much wanted to be done, it is very shameful to see us sit so idle. It looks as if a power of doing harm only and none of doing good was lodged with us.

The King is still very disconsolate; he sees no company, nor is entertained with any diversions. He is very thoughtful and serious, and if serious people were about him, a great deal of good both to himself and the nation might come from the situation and turn of mind he is at present in. There has been talk of a reconciliation between the Prince[1442] and him, but I could never find there was any sufficient ground for it.

[1437] Queen Caroline died on 20 November 1737.
[1438] George II* (1683–1760).
[1439] Prime Minister Sir Robert Walpole* (1676–1745), later first Earl of Orford.
[1440] Oliver Cromwell (1599–1658).
[1441] Philip York* (or Yorke) (1690–1764), first Earl of Hardwicke.
[1442] Frederick Lewis* (1707–51), Prince of Wales.

Severe colds have been general here as well as in Ireland. I have escaped pretty well, but I am sorry to hear you and your family have had so large a share of this epidemical evil. My humble service and best wishes of health wait upon Mrs. Berkeley and always attend all your family. I am very exact in my diet and regular in my hours, and both agree very well with me. I am better, I thank God, both in my health and spirits now than I have been for many years. The Bishop of Derry's[1443] recovery is very surprising. But I wish that what some reckon the cure does not prove the ruin of his health, and that is, his return to flesh and wine. While the Queen lived I had fair hopes of seeing the Baron here. The prospect is since much clouded, but it perhaps may brighten up again. It would be great joy to myself and to the Bishop of Oxford's[1444] family to hear that you and yours design to visit England. James[1445] had deserted it before I got to London, and he does not talk of returning before I shall have left it again.

Our Lords have made a less important order in their House than that you mention to be made in yours, and that is, that I should print a sermon preached before them January 30th.[1446] The Bishop of Carlisle[1447] not coming up, it came to my turn sooner than it should. This order, however, ought to have weight enough to excuse me to my friends for troubling them with one of the sermons, above all, as the order does not extend so far as to oblige them to read it.

I am, my dear Lord, Ever most affectionately and faithfully yours,
M. Glocester

269 FORSTER TO BERKELEY[1448]

BL Add. MS 39311, fols. 41–42.

20 February 1737/38[1449]

My Lord,

I have the favour of your letter that came by last post, and hope your family, which, you say, have been twice laid down with colds, is up again,

---

[1443] Thomas Rundle* (1687/88–1743).

[1444] Thomas Secker* (1693–1768), recently translated from Bristol to Oxford in 1737.

[1445] Perhaps Sir John James* (?–1741).

[1446] Benson* preached a sermon before the House of Lords, published in 1738.

[1447] Sir George Fleming (1667–1747), second Baronet, bishop of Carlisle (1734–47).

[1448] Nicholas Forster* (1672–1743).

[1449] Luce has a typographical error for the date, listing "1731-8" instead of "1737/38."

and that the season of the year that is coming in, will bring you relief from your colic.

I am persuaded you have made a true representation of the present state of the Church, and, God knows, it is a melancholy one. When the laity form themselves into a party in opposition to the clergy, how can we expect any good success from our labours among them? Men will never receive instruction from those to whom they bear ill will, and their contempt of our labours will, I fear, bring an increase of vice and infidelity among us. However, it is our duty to be circumspect and give no offence; to be diligent in the discharge of our office, and moderate in the demands of our temporalties; that the laity may see that the cause of religion more at heart than any worldly gain. These are the likeliest means, with God's blessing, to allay those heats that are raised against us, but, if violent measures be taken on both sides, what hope can we have of a reconciliation. The clergy in this part of the country have had their share in the common calamity, but I find that angry spirit that has been artfully[1450] stirred up in the minds of the people against them begins to abate, and they receive their dues with less opposition than they did some time ago, and I have good hopes that time and patience on our side will bring the people to reason.

Your account of the new society of Blasters in Dublin, is shocking.[1451] The zeal of all good men for the cause of God should rise in proportion to the impiety of these horrid blasphemers.

I am glad to hear both the King[1452] and his ministry are determined to give no countenance to innovators in Church affairs; there is reason to believe they have ill designs against the State as well as the Church. I pray God give peace in our time on earth and bring us safe to heaven, where there is no contention. We are happily freed from those two pernicious bills you mention, and may be content now with a blank session.

[1450] Fraser has "awfully," but the text clearly has "artfully."

[1451] The Blasters was a society formed in Dublin that allegedly professed devil-worship and other impieties offensive to the establishment of the day. Berkeley penned *A Discourse Addressed to Magistrates and Men in Authority* (see *Works*, vol. VI, pp. 193–222), which is subtitled *Occasioned by the Enormous Licence and Irreligion of the Times*, in part as a response to the society. Little is known about the organization and some have speculated that the Blasters is in fact another name for the Hell-fire Club that met near Dublin. See William E. H. Lecky, *History of Ireland in the Eighteenth Century* (London: Longmans & Co., 1913), vol. I, p. 323. Stock reports that Berkeley's only known address to the Irish House of Lords occurred in connection with his denouncing this society. See Joseph Stock, *Memoirs of George Berkeley: Late Bishop of Cloyne in Ireland* (London: J. Murray, 1784), 2nd edn. p. 31n.

[1452] George II* (1683–1760).

I am, my Lord,
    your Lordship's
    most faithful brother and
    humble servant,
    N. Rapho

Rapho, Feb. 20 1737–38

If your lordship's health and leisure will allow, I should desire you would, on the return of the bills, favour me with an account of such of them as relate to the Church.

270 BENSON TO BERKELEY

BL Add. MS 46688, fols. 6–7v.

Berry Street, 28 April 1738

My Dear Lord,

Before I received the favour of yours with the corrected copy, an impression was printed off by Roberts,[1453] which I was very sorry for, and the more because the objections which I sent you word I heard might be made, I heard soon after actually made by the Master of the Rolls[1454] whom I saw at my Lord Chancellor's[1455] and by others. They acknowledge that there are several very good things in the tract,[1456] but they are so angry that the liberty of the press or of private judgment should be invaded that they are upon the whole more inclined to condemn than commend it, as the Reformation and Protestant religion they say are only to be defended upon the principles which are by you exploded. I need not say to you how much farther they stretch your words than your meaning. But whatever is said by a clergyman is immediately suspected, and a wrong interpretation will be very likely to be put upon it. Our friends among the laity are jealous of us, and the malice of our enemies is beyond all bounds. This should make us guard ourselves as

---

[1453] J. Roberts (?–?), a Dublin publisher.
[1454] Joseph Jekyll* (1662–1738).
[1455] Philip York* (or Yorke) (1690–1764), first Earl of Hardwicke.
[1456] A reference to Berkeley's *A Discourse Addressed to Magistrates and Men in Authority*, published in Dublin and then London in 1738. See *Works*, vol. VI, pp. 193–222.

cautiously as we can, though perhaps the utmost caution may not be sufficient to secure us. I and others of your friends here think it to be an excellent good pamphlet and that it might be a useful one too; they were desirous to have that occasion cut off, which would they knew be diligently searched for, of finding fault with some part of it. But notwithstanding this, it may I hope still do a great deal of good.

I was this morning with Lord Egmont,[1457] who has designed to give it to one Richardson, but before he could do it, Roberts he found had printed it off. I went to Roberts's yesterday but did not find him at home. He came to me this morning; when I asked him whether he would print a second edition, to which he answered that he had printed so many of the first that he thought there would be no occasion. If there were, he would acquaint me with it.

I have inquired about the book you mention. I have not found any one who has read it, but the miracles it mentions are ridiculous forgeries of the anti-constitutioners by which they attempt to confound their adversaries.

If the Primacy of Ireland[1458] were to be vacant, there could not be a fitter person to fill than one who is known to others much better than he is to himself. The best thing I can say of myself is that I know myself so well, that if others would give me a post which I thought to be very unequal to, I would not accept it. And I have still a greater satisfaction that I would not exchange the bishopric I have for any other in this kingdom.

My humble services and respects wait upon your good Lady, and I am my dear Lord

      most faithfully and affectionately yours,

      M. Glocester

The Jansenists are said to have entirely ruined their interest in France by this method they took to support it.

Mr. Bury has been with me and I promised to repeat my recommendation to Mr. Winnington.[1459] But I did not then reflect that Mr. Winnington has now nothing to do in the Admiralty, being advanced from that board to be a commission in the Treasury.

[1457] John Percival* (1683–1748).

[1458] The primacy of Ireland ("Primate of All Ireland") is held by the archbishop of Armagh.
The primate at this time was Hugh Boulter (1672–1742), archbishop of Armagh from 1724 to 1742.

[1459] Thomas Winnington (1696–1746). He was promoted to the Treasury in May 1736.

271 BERKELEY TO JOHNSON[1460]

MS unknown. LL, p. 258.

Dublin, 11 May 1738

Reverend Sir,

I should not have been thus long in arrear[s] in regard to my correspondence with you, had I not been prevented by ill health, multiplicity of business, and want of opportunities. When I last heard from you I was at Cloyne, and am returning thither now with my family, who, I bless God, are all well except myself, who for a long time past have been troubled with an habitual colic, nor am I yet freed from it. My wife sends you her compliments, and we both join in good wishes to you and your family. The accounts you sent me from the College at Newhaven[1461] were very agreeable, and I shall always be glad to hear from you on that or any other subject. I am sensible you have to do with people of no very easy or tractable spirit. But your own prudence will direct you when and how far to yield, and what is the proper way to manage with them. I pray God preserve you and prosper your endeavours. And I am,

> Reverend Sir,
> Your very faithful Servant and Brother,
> G. Cloyne

272 BERKELEY TO EVANS[1462]

MS unknown. LL, p. 259.

Cloyne, 7 September 1738

Sir,

Two nights ago I received the favour of your letter, but deferred answering it till I should have seen Dean Bruce[1463] at my visitation; from which the Dean

---

[1460] Luce (*Works* VIII, pp. 246–47) and Fraser both print this letter, but neither Schneider nor Beardsley make mention of it.

[1461] Yale.

[1462] Luce claims he was given the letter by the then archdeacon of Cloyne, but there is no trace of the letter at present. According to Luce, the recipient is Colonel Thomas Evans (?–?) of Milltowne, whose daughter was married to dean Bruce's son. See *Works*, vol. IX, p. 103.

[1463] Jonathan Bruce (1681–1758). A graduate of Trinity College, Dublin (1703), he held several cures and ended his life as dean of Kilfenora (1724–58). See W. M. Brady *Clerical and Parochial Records of Cork, Cloyne, and Ross* (London: Longman et al., 1864), vol. II, pp. 38–39.

happened to be detained by the illness of his son. I am very sorry there hath arisen any difference between you; but, as you have been silent as to particulars, and as the Dean hath mentioned nothing of it to me, either by word of mouth, letter, or message, I can do no more than in general terms recommend peace and good neighbourhood, for the providing of which my best endeavours should not be wanting.[1464] In the meantime give me leave to assure you that I have not the least reason to entertain ill thoughts of your conduct; and that where no blame is imputed all apology is useless. Upon the whole, since the Dean hath not stirred in this matter, I hope it may die and be forgotten. My wife presents her compliments, and

> I remain, Sir,
> Yr very obedient humble Servt,
> G. Cloyne

273 BERKELEY TO GERVAIS[1465]

CU, Spec. MS Coll. Edwin R.A. Seligman, Box Bas-Bon.

Cloyne, 25 November 1738

Reverend Sir,

My wife sends her compliments to Mrs. Gervais and yourself for the receipt etc. And we both concur in thanks for your venison. The rain hath so defaced your letter that I cannot read some parts of it. But I can make a shift to see there is a compliment of so high a strain, that if I knew how to read it I am sure I should not know how to answer it. If there was anything agreeable in your entertainment at my house, it was chiefly owing to yourself, and so requires my acknowledgment, which you have very sincere. You give so much pleasure to others, and are so easily pleased yourself, that I shall live in hopes of your making my house your inne whenever you visit these parts, which will be very agreeable to, etc.

> your faithful
> humble servant
> & brother,
> G. Cloyne

[1464] The nature of the dispute is unknown. Colonel Thomas Evans's daughter was married to dean Bruce's son. See *Works*, vol. IX, p. 103.

[1465] Isaac Gervais* (1680–1756). Stock only prints an extract of this letter (p. lxxxix), which was used by Luce.

274 JOHNSON TO BERKELEY[1466]

CU, Spec. MS Collection Samuel Johnson, vol. I, p. 69, fol. 4.

14 May 1739

May it please your Lordship:—

I humbly thank your Lordship for your obliging letter of May 11, 1738, which came not to my hands till precisely that day twelve months after it was written, and in the very interim when (having lately attended on the examination of the scholars at Yale College for your Lordship's premium) I was meditating to write to your Lordship and give you some account of the condition of things among us; which is as follows:

We had a good struggle this year for the scholarship, and it is very agreeable to see to what perfection classical learning is advanced in comparison with what it was before your Lordship's donation to this College, though I cannot say it has much increased for these two years past, and I doubt it is got to something of a stand. Another son of Mr. Williams[1467] has got it this year, who had manifestly the advantage of the rest; but I think none have ever performed to so great perfection as one Whittelsey[1468] last year, who is son of a neighbouring minister, whose performance was very extraordinary, not only for scholarship, but also for books purchased with some money that had been forfeited by the resignation of Leonard.[1469]

I am very sorry to tell your Lordship how ungrateful New Haven people have been to the Church after so many benefactions their college hath received from that quarter, in raising a mob and keeping Mr. Arnold[1470] *vis et armis*[1471] from taking possession of the land, which (as I told your Lordship in my last) one Mr. Gregson of London had given him to build a church on near the college.

Another instance of injurious treatment the Church has lately met with from this ungrateful country has been in the General Assembly denying a most reasonable petition we laid before them last year. The case was this: all the lands within

---

[1466] This letter is also printed in Schneider, vol. I, pp. 98–99. The volume is catalogued at CU, in its rare manuscript collection, as BK 811 J63 06.

[1467] Elisha Williams (1717/18–84) and Samuel Williams (1720–40) both received part of Berkeley's scholarship at Yale College in different years. The reference here is to the younger brother Samuel. See Franklin B. Dexter, *Biographical Sketches of the Graduates of Yale College* (New York: Holt & Co., 1885), pp. 547–48.

[1468] Chauncey Whittelsey (?–after 1778), who graduated from Yale College in 1738 and is remembered for his facility with ancient languages. See *Memorial of the Whittelsey Family in the United States* (Case, Tiffany & Co., 1855), p. 83.

[1469] Silas Leonard (?–1764). See Dexter, *Biographical Sketches of the Graduates of Yale College*, p. 565.

[1470] Most likely Jonathan Arnold (?–1739), who joined the Church of England in 1734 and was ordained in England in 1736. He perished on a second voyage to England in 1739. See Updike, *History of the Episcopal Church in Narragansett Rhode Island*, pp. 182–83 and Beardsley, *History of the Episcopal Church in Connecticut*, pp. 111–12.

[1471] "by force and arms."

the bounds of this government are by charter alike granted to all the inhabitants, without limitation to those of any particular denomination in matters of religion. Now of these lands there remained a sufficient quantity for seven new townships, which were lately laid out and ordered to be sold, and the money (amounting to above 70,000 pounds) to be considered as the common right of the whole community. When it was considered how to dispose of it, it was at length concluded that it should be divided proportionally to each town, according to their estates, for the support of dissenting teachers; whereby the church people, who had manifestly a right to their proportion of it, were excluded. Whereupon we presented an humble address to the Assembly, signed by every male of the Church in the government above sixteen years old, to the number of about 700, praying we might have our proportion in these public moneys. But they were pleased to pass a negative upon it; and I should be very thankful for your Lordship's advice whether it would be worth our while to apply to the King and Council on this affair.

I heartily rejoice with your Lordship in the health and prosperity of your Lady and family, and am no less grieved for the illness you labour under, in your own person. I earnestly[1472] pray, God remove it, and give you health.

Good Dr. Cutler[1473] is in great grief, having lately lost a very hopeful son, nigh of age for Orders. Mr. Honyman[1474] has been till lately very much indisposed with grief for the loss of his spouse, but is within these few months recovered and married again to one Mrs. Brown, an elderly gentlewoman, mother to Capt. Brown of Newport. With our humble duty to your lady, I remain

> May it please your Lordship, etc.,
>
> S. J.

275 JOHNSON TO BERKELEY[1475]

CU, Spec. MS Coll. Samuel Johnson, vol. I, p. 69, fols. 7v–8.

20 June 1740

My Lord:

I did myself the honour to write to you about a year ago, and most thankfully acknowledged yours of May 11, [17]38, and gave you some account of the

---

[1472] Fraser has "earnestly"; Schneider has "sincerely."

[1473] Timothy Cutler (1684–1765). Like Samuel Johnson,* he converted to the Church of England, leaving his position as rector of Yale College in 1722.

[1474] James Honeyman* (c. 1675–1750).

[1475] Also printed in Schneider, vol. I, pp. 101–02. The volume is catalogued at CU as BK 811 J63 06.

condition of things among us in this colony, and especially the College,[1476] which is so much indebted to your Lordship, that I think it is but fit that your Lordship should, at least once a year, have some account of the success of your generous donation to it; and this I hope will apologize for my troubling your Lordship once in a while with some account of our affairs which otherwise would not deserve your notice.

Our College has been in a very unsettled posture this last year, which perhaps may be the reason that there has not this May appeared quite so good a proficiency in classical learning as heretofore (though yet very considerable compared with what used to be), there having been an interregnum of seven or eight months wherein it has had no rector. Mr. Williams[1477] had been much out of health for some months, and last fall was persuaded it was owing to his sedantry life and the seaside air, and accordingly took up a resolution, from which he would not be dissuaded, to retire up into the country, where he has lived ever since, and where indeed he seems to have enjoyed his health better; though some people are so censorious as to judge that, considering the age and declining state of our Governor, his chief aim was to put himself in the way of being chosen for that post. But if this was his view, it is not unlikely that he may be disappointed, for upon a considerable struggle last election for a new governor he had but few votes, and Mr. E[l]liot had a vast many more than all other competitors put together, and will doubtless succeed whenever there is a new choice. However, Mr. Williams was a Representative and Speaker in their Assembly and was made one of the Judges of the Superior Court, and may possibly get to be one of the Council or Assistants, which is, I believe, the utmost he will attain to.

Upon his leaving the College, the trustees have appointed one Mr. Clap,[1478] late minister of Windham, to succeed, who seems to be a well tempered gentleman and of good sense and much of a mathematician, and though he is not so well acquainted with the classics as might be wished, I hope he will improve much in that and all other points of learning, and prove a good governor to the College.

We have again applied to the Assembly about the seven new townships, that I mentioned to your Lordship in my last, and nothing has been yet done. Next October will be the last time of asking, but I do not expect they

---

[1476] Yale College.
[1477] Elisha Williams* (1694–1755). He was rector of Yale, retiring from that post 31 October 1739.
[1478] Thomas Clap* (1703–67).

will finally grant our petition. However, the Church greatly increases, especially in the town. But I grow tedious, and will not add any further save my
earnest prayers for your Lordship's health and happiness and that of your
lady and family, to whom my very humble duty. I beg your prayers, and
remain, my Lord

    your Lordship's etc.,

    S. J.

276 BERKELEY TO PRIOR

LR, *pp. 272–74.*

Cloyne, 8 February 1740/41

Dear Tom,

    I should have complied with your desire sooner, but I was not so well able to
say what method I thought best to take in this epidemical bloody flux,[1479] that
distemper not having been rife in this town till very lately, though it had made
a great progress in other parts of this county. But this week I have cured several
by the following course; than which nothing is easier or cheaper. I give to
grown people a heaped spoonful of rosin powdered fine, in a little broth; and
this is repeated at the distance of six or eight hours till the blood is staunched.
To children I give a bare spoonful not heaped. A farthing's worth of rosin (if I
may judge by my own short experience) will never fail to stop the flux of blood,
with a regular diet. Broth seems to me the most proper diet; and that simple, of
mutton or fowl, without salt, spice, or onions. I doubt not clysters[1480] of the
same broth and rosin would likewise have a good effect; but this I have not yet
tried. In the first place, make some private experiments of this as you have
opportunity. If, after the bloody flux is over, a looseness remain, chalk in
boiled milk and water may remove it. I have also known tow,[1481] dipped in
brandy and thrust into the fundament, to be effectual in strengthening that
sphincter. What you call a felon is called in the books a phlegmon,[1482] and

---

[1479] A common name in the period for dysentery and related illnesses, where blood is found in the
stool.

[1480] An enema, often administered with a "clyster syringe."

[1481] An untwisted bundle of fibers.

[1482] In the period the word *felon* was primarily used to mean an inflammation or infection in the tip
of a finger. Phlegmon is a more general term for inflammation in connective tissue.

often is the crisis following a fever or other distemper. I believe tar water might be useful to prevent (or to perfect the cure of) such an evil; there being, so far as I can judge, no more powerful corrector of putrid humours. But I am making a farther enquiry, and more experiments, concerning the virtues of that medicine, which I may impart to you before it be long.

I find what you say of the two plain looms to be true, you having allowed me for them. I desire you not to forget the wheels; and to procure what seed you can, if not what I wrote for. My wife and all here join in wishing you all happiness, and hoping to see you here in May. Adieu, dear Tom,

>   your most faithful humble servant,

>   G. Cloyne

I thank you for thinking of the French book. Let me hear your success in using the rosin.

277 BERKELEY TO PRIOR

LR, pp. 274–75.

Cloyne, 15 February 1740/41

Dear Tom,

I must desire you to take up what money I have in Henry's[1483] and Alderman Dawson's[1484] hands, and lodge it in the bank of Swift & Company.*[1485] You have their notes, so I need not draw. Upon paying this money into Swift, you will send me his account balanced.

Our weather is grown fine and warm; but the bloody flux[1486] has increased in this neighbourhood, and raged most violently in other parts of this and the adjacent counties. By new trials, I am confirmed in the use of the rosin, and do therefore send you the following advertisement, which you will communicate to the printer. We are all yours, particularly

>   your affectionate

>   G. Cloyne

[1483] Hugh Henry & Co., a Dublin bank. The bank dissolved in September 1737, but the liquidation took several years to complete. See *Journal of the Cork Historical and Archeological Society* 3 (1894): 194.

[1484] Richard Dawson (?–1766). Dawson was a wealthy merchant and banker, establishing his bank in 1740. He was an alderman for Dublin and MP for Kilkenny (1727–60).

[1485] Berkeley is concerned about the continuing instability of the Irish banks. A number of Dublin banks failed, including most famously Burton's bank. See Letter 242 and Hall, *History of the Bank of Ireland*.

[1486] Dysentery or a similar illness where blood is found in the stool.

278 BERKELEY TO FAULKNER[1487]

Dublin Journal 1533 (17-21 February 1741). LR, pp. 275-76.

17 February 1741

Mr. Faulkner,

The following being a very safe and successful cure of the bloody flux,[1488] which at this time is become so general, you will do well to make it publick. Take a heaped spoonful of common rosin, powdered, in a little fresh broath, every five or six hours, till the bloody flux is stopt; which I always found to have happened before a farthing's worth of rosin was spent. If, after the blood is staunched, there remain a little looseness, this is soon carried off by milk and water boiled with a little chalk in it. This cheap and easy method I have tried of late, and never knew it fail. I am your humble servant,

A. B.

279 BERKELEY TO PRIOR

LR, pp. 276-77.

Cloyne, 24 February 1740/41

Dear Tom,

I find you have published my remedy in the newspaper of this day. I now tell you that the patients must be careful of their diet, and especially beware of taking cold. The best diet I find to be plain broth of mutton or fowl, without seasoning of any kind. Their drink should be, till they are freed both from dysentery and diarrhoea, milk and water, or plain water boiled with chalk, drunk warm, e.g. about a large heaped spoonful to a quart. Sometimes I find it necessary to give it every four hours, and to continue it for a dose or two after the blood hath been stopped, to prevent relapses, which ill management has now and then occasioned. Given in due time (the sooner the better), and with proper care, I take it to be as sure a cure for a dysentery as the bark[1489] for an ague. It has certainly, by the blessing of God,

---

[1487] George Faulkner* (1703?-75).
[1488] Dysentery or a similar illness where blood is found in the stool.
[1489] i.e. quinine, popularly known at the time as "Jesuit's bark."

saved many lives, and continues to save many lives in my neighbourhood. I shall be glad to know its success in any instances you may have tried it in. We are all yours. Adieu,

G. Cloyne

280 BERKELEY TO CLARKE[1490]

TCD MS 1186, fol. 2.

Cloyne, 16 April 1741

Revd Sir,

I have been this week very unwell with my habitual cholic, otherwise I should have sent the enclosed letters sooner. My own acquaintance in the universities is very little. At Cambridge I have never passed above two days. I passed as many months at Oxford, but so long ago as Queen Anne's reign.[1491] And all I then knew are since dead or gone.

If your curiosity shall lead you to Lambeth, you will go on one of the Archbishop's[1492] public days, be present at chapel, after that deliver your letter, and stay to dine with his grace.

I am sensible how far I am obliged and honoured by you and the rest of those gentlemen who think of me for vice-chancellor. But as my ill health and distance from the university would not permit me to serve it as I could wish, so to aim at the honour without discharging the duty is what I cannot think of.

I wish you good health and all the satisfaction you propose in your voyage, and am,

Revd. Sir,

your obedient humble servant,

Geor: Cloyne

[1490] The letter, a copy, is attached to a letter from Dean Jonathan Swift* to Clarke. The letter is not addressed, but the attribution to Berkeley as the author is reasonable on the strength of the fact that the letter has a note in Dr. Clarke's hand: "Letter from the Bp of Cloyne Dr. Berkeley 1741." Henry Clarke (?–1764) would later be vice-provost of Trinity College (1744–47). Clarke received a leave of absence for five months (dated 18 April 1741) and apparently wrote to Berkeley for introductions at Lambeth and the universities at Oxford and Cambridge. See Luce, "More Unpublished Berkeley Letters and New Berkeleiana," 43–44. See also Williams, ed., *Correspondence of Swift*, Swift to Clarke, 12 December 1734.

[1491] Queen Anne* reigned from 1702 until 1714.

[1492] John Potter, (1673/74–1747). He was bishop of Oxford (1715–37) and made archbishop of Canterbury in February 1737 after the death of William Wake.*

281 BERKELEY TO PRIOR

LR, *pp. 278–80.*

Cloyne, 19 May 1741

Dear Tom,

The physico-theology you mention of Dr. Morgan[1493] is not the book I want; but I should nevertheless be glad to have it, and therefore desire you to get it, with the French book of Mr. Bouillé.[1494]

Though the flax-seed came in such quantity and so late, yet we have above one half ourselves in ground; the rest, together with our own seed, has been given to our poor neighbours, and will, I doubt not, answer, the weather being very favourable.

The distresses of the sick and poor are endless.[1495] The havoc of mankind in the counties of Cork, Limerick, and some adjacent places, hath been incredible. The nation probably will not recover this loss in a century. The other day I heard one from the county of Limerick say that whole villages were entirely dis-peopled. About two months since I heard Sir Richard Cox[1496] say that five hundred were dead in the parish where he lives, though in a country I believe not very populous.

It were to be wished people of condition were at their seats in the country during these calamitous times, which might provide relief and employment for the poor. Certainly if these perish, the rich must be sufferers in the end.

Sir John Rawdon,[1497] you say, is canvassing for an English election. If he doth not lose it, I doubt his country will lose him.

Your journey hither is, it seems, put off for some time. I wish you would hasten: the sooner the better, both for your own health and the pleasure of your friends in this family, where we all expect you, and think we have an annual right in you.

[1493] Dr. Thomas Morgan (?–1743). A religious writer and controversialist, he authored *Physico-Theology* (1741).

[1494] Jean Bouillet (1690–1777), French physician. He published *Sur la Manière de Traiter la Petite Vérole* (*On the Method of Treating Small Pox*) in 1733.

[1495] Ireland was suffering from a famine in 1740/41.

[1496] Richard Cox (1702–66), grandson of Richard Cox (1650–1733), justice of the common pleas and lord chancellor of Ireland.

[1497] Most likely John Rawdon* (c. 1719–93).

You have not said a word this age about our suit with Partinton.[1498] Pray how stands that matter?

Adieu, dear Tom. I am

your affectionate humble Servant,

G. Cloyne

All here salute you.

We have tried in this neighbourhood the receipt of a decoction of briar-roots for the bloody flux[1499] which you sent me, and in some cases found it useful. But that which we find the most speedy, sure, and effectual cure, above all others, is a heaped spoonful of rosin dissolved and mixed over a fire with two or three spoonfuls of oil, and added to a pint of broth for a clyster;[1500] which, upon once taking, hath never been known to fail stopping the bloody flux. At first I mixed the rosin in the broth, but that was difficult, and not so speedy a cure.

282 BERKELEY TO JAMES[1501]

BL Add. MS 39306, fols. 19–23.

Cloyne, 7 June 1741

Dear Sir,

I would not defer writing though I write in no small confusion and distress, my family having many ill of an epidemical fever that rages in these parts, and I being the only physician to them & my poor neighbours. You have my sincere thanks for the freedom and friendship with which you are so good to communicate your thoughts. Your making the *unum necessarium*[1502] your chief business sets you above the world. I heartily beg of God that he would give me grace to do the same, a heart constantly to pursue the truth and abide in it wherever it is found.

No Divine could say, in my opinion, more for the Church of Rome than you have done.—

[1498] Peter Partinton* (?–?).

[1499] Dysentery or a similar illness where there is blood in the stool.

[1500] An enema, often administered with a "clyster syringe."

[1501] Luce entitles the letter "On the Roman Controversy to Sir John James, Bart." See *Works*, vol. VII, p. 143. The text is defective and incomplete.

[1502] "the one thing necessary."

Si Pergama dextra
Defendi possent, etiam hâc defensa fuissent.[1503]

The Scriptures and Fathers, I grant, are a much better help to know Christ and his Religion than the cold and dry writings of our modern Divines.[1504] Many who are conversant in such books I doubt have no more relish for the things of the Gospel, than those who spend their time in reading the immense and innumerable tomes of Scholastic Divinity with which the Church of Rome abounds. The dry polemical theology was the growth of Rome, begun from Peter Lombard the Master of the Sentences[1505] and grew and spread among the monks and friars under the Pope's eye. The Church of England is not without spiritual writers of her own—Taylor,[1506] Ken,[1507] Beveridge,[1508] Scot,[1509] Lucas,[1510] Stanhope,[1511] Nelson,[1512] the author of the words falsely ascribed to the writer of the *Whole Duty of Man*, and many more, whom I believe you will find not inferior to those of the Church of Rome. But I freely own to you that most modern writings smell of the age, and that there are no books so fit to make a soul advance in spiritual perfection, as the Scriptures and ancient fathers.

I think you will find no Popery in St. Augustine[1513] or St. Basil[1514] or any writers of that antiquity. You may see, indeed, here and there in the fathers a notion borrowed from Philosophy (as they were originally philosophers) for instance, something like a Platonic or Pythagorean Purgatory: But you will see nothing like indulgences or a bank of merits, or a Romish Purgatory

---

[1503] Virgil, *Aeneid*, II, 291. These are the words of Hector to Aeneas at the fall of Troy: "If Troy could have been saved by human hand, it would have been saved by mine." More literally "If Troy could have been defended by a right [hand], it would have been saved by this [hand]."

[1504] Added by Berkeley at the bottom of that page: "*l*. 16: Divines—*prima manu*, Whigs."

[1505] Peter Lombard (*c*. 1100–*c*. 1160), bishop of Paris, author of *Sententiarum Libri Quattor*, a collection of the opinions of the Church Fathers, which crystallized sacramental doctrine.

[1506] Jeremy Taylor (1613–67), bishop of Down and Connor, author of *The Rule and Exercise of Holy Living* (1650) and *Holy Dying* (1651).

[1507] Thomas Ken (1637–1711), bishop of Bath and Wells, author of hymns and devotional works.

[1508] William Beveridge (1637–1708), bishop of St. Asaph's, author of *Exposition of the XXXIX Articles* (1710).

[1509] Daniel Scot (1694–1759), theological writer.

[1510] Richard Lucas (1648–1715), prebendary of Westminster, author of *Enquiry after Happiness* (1685).

[1511] George Stanhope (1660–1728), dean of Canterbury, author of *Paraphrase and Comment upon the Epistles and Gospels* (vols. I and II, 1705; vol. III, 1706; vol. IV, 1708).

[1512] Robert Nelson (1656–1715), wrote *Companion for the Festivals and the Fasts of the Church of England* (1704).

[1513] Aurelius Augustine (354–430), bishop of Hippo, author of *De Civitate Dei* and many other works.

[1514] Basil (330–79), bishop of Caesarea founder of monastic institutions.

whereof the Pope has the Key. It is not simply believing even a Popish tenet or tenets that makes a Papist but believing on the Pope's authority. There is in the fathers a divine strain of piety and much of the spiritual life. This we acknowledge all should aspire after, and I make no doubt is attainable and actually attained in the communion of our Church at least as well as in any other.

You observe very justly that Christ's religion is spiritual, and the Christian life supernatural; and that there is no judge of spiritual things but the spirit of God. We have need, therefore, of aid and light from above. Accordingly we have the Spirit of God to guide us into all truth. If we are sanctified and enlightened by the Holy Ghost & by Christ, this will make up for our defects without the Pope's assistance. And why our Church and her pious members may not hope for this help as well as others I see no reason. The Author of our faith tells us, He that will do the will of God, shall know of the doctrine, whether it be of God.[1515] I believe this extends to all Saving Truths.

There is an indwelling of Christ and the Holy Spirit, there is an inward light. If there be an *ignis fatuus*[1516] that misleads wild and conceited men, no man can thence infer there is no light of the sun. There must be a proper disposition of the organ, as well as a degree of daylight to make us see. Where these concur no body doubts of what he sees. And a Christian soul wherein there is faith, humility, and obedience, will not fail to see the right way to salvation by that light which lightens the Gentiles and is a glory to Israel.

There is an invisible Church whereof Christ is the head, the members of which are linked together by faith, hope, & charity. By faith in Christ, not in the Pope. Popes are no unerring rule, for Popes have erred: witness the condemnation and suppression of Sixtus Quintus's bible by his successor.[1517] Witness the successions of Anti-popes for a long tract of time.[1518]

There is a secret unction an inward light and joy that attends the sincere fervent love of God and his truth, which ennables men to go on with all

---

[1515] John 7:17.

[1516] A "foolish fire" or "foolish passion."

[1517] Pope Sixtus V (1521–90), began in 1589 a revision of the Vulgate that was completed under his successor, Clement VIII (1535–1605). Clement suppressed the Sixtine edition.

[1518] In 1378 Urban VI was elected Pope; but the cardinals had doubts as to the validity of his election. Eventually they decided that he was an intruder, and proceeded to elect Clement VII. The schism, known as the Great Schism, lasted from 1378 to 1417 and came to an end with Martin V, who reigned as Pope from 1417 to 1431.

cheerfulness and hope in the Christian warfare. You ask how I shall discern or know this? I answer much more easily than I can that this particular man or this particular society of men is an unerring rule. Of the former I have an inward feeling jointly with the interior as well as exterior λόγος[1519] to inform me. But for the later I have only the Pope's word and that of his followers.

It is dangerous arguing from our notion of the expediency of a thing, to the reality of the thing it self. But I can fairly argue from facts against the being of such an expedient. In the first centurys of the church when heresies abounded, the expedient of a Pope or Roman oracle was unknown, unthought of. There was then a Bishop of Rome, but that was no hindrance or remedy of Divisions. Disputes in the Catholic church were not ended by his Authority. No recourse was had to his infallibility: an evident proof they acknowledged no such thing! The date of his usurpations and how they grew with his secular power, you may plainly see in Giannoni's history of Naples:[1520] I do not refer you to a Protestant writer.

Men travelling in day-light see by one common light, though each with his own eyes. If one man should say to the rest, "Shut your eyes and follow me who see better than you all." This would not be well taken. The sincere Christians of our communion are governed or led by the inward light of God's grace, by the outward light of his written word, by the ancient and Catholic traditions of Christ's church, by the ordinances of our National Church which we take to consist all and hang together. But then we see, as all must do, with our own eyes, by a common light but each with his own private eyes. And so must you too or you will not see at all. And not seeing at all how can you choose a Church? Why prefer that of Rome to that of England? Thus far, and in this sense every man's judgment is private as well as ours. Some indeed go farther and without regard to the holy Spirit or the word of God, or the writings of the primitive fathers, or the universal uninterrupted traditions of the Church, will pretend to canvass every mystery, every step of Providence, and reduce it to the private standard of their own fancy, for reason reaches not those things. Such as these I give up and disown as well as you do.

I grant it is meet the Law of Christ should like other laws have magistrates to explain and apply it. But then as in the civil State a private man may know the law enough to avoid transgressing it, and also to see whether the magistrates deviate from it into tyranny: Even so, in the other case a private Christian may know and ought to know the written law of God and not give himself up blindly

---

[1519] *Logos*: reason, rational principle, or word. It is typically associated in Christian contexts with the Word of God.
[1520] Pietro Giannone (1676–1748), Italian historian, author of *Storia Civile del Regno di Napoli* (1723), which was placed on the Index.

to the dictates of the Pope and his assessors. This in effect wou'd be destroying the law and erecting a despotic government instead thereof. It wou'd be deserting Christ and taking the Pope for his master.

I think it my duty to become a little child to Christ and his Apostles, but not to the Pope and his courtiers. That many honest well-meaning men live under such thraldom, I freely admit and am sorry for it. I trust that God will have compassion on them, as knowing how they were educated, and the force of first impressions. But one who never had their education cannot plead their prejudices.

Light and heat are both found in a religious mind duly disposed. Light in due order goes first. It is dangerous to begin with heat, that is with the affections. To balance earthly affections by spiritual affections is right. But our affections should grow from inquiry and deliberation else there is danger of our being superstitious or Enthusiasts. An affection conceived towards a particular Church, upon reading some spiritual authors of that communion which might have left a bias in the mind is I apprehend to be suspected. Most men act with a bias. God knows how far my education may have biased me against the Church of Rome, or how far a love of retreat and a fine climate may bias me towards it. It is our duty to strive to divest our selves of all bias whatsoever.

Whatever unguarded expressions may be found in this or that Protestant Divine, it is certainly the Doctrine of our Church that no particular church or congregation of Believers is infallible. We hold all mankind to be peccable and errable, even the Pope himself with all that belong to him. We are like men in a cave in this present life seeing by a dim light through such chinks as the divine goodness hath open'd to us. We dare not talk in the high unerring positive style of the Romanists. We confess that we see through a glass darkly:[1521] and rejoice that we see enough to determine our practice and excite our hopes.

An humble devout penitent Believer, not biased by any terrene affections but sincerely aiming and endeavouring by all the means God hath given him to come at truth, need not fear being admitted into the Kingdom of God without the Pope's passport. There is indeed an invisible Church, whereof Christ is head, linked together by charity, animated with the same hope, sanctified by the same Spirit, heirs of the same promise. This is the universal church militant and triumphant: the militant dispersed in all parts of Christendom partaking of the same word and sacraments. There are also visible, political or national churches: none of which is universal. It would be a blunder to say particular universal. And yet I know not how, the style of Roman Catholic hath prevailed. The members of

[1521] I Corinthians 13:12.

this universal church are not visible by outward marks, but certainly known only to God whose Spirit will sanctify and maintain it to the end of time.

The church is a calling ἐκκλησία.[1522] Many are called but few are chosen.[1523] Therefore there is no reckoning the elect by the number of visible members. There must be the invisible grace, as well as the outward sign; the spiritual life and holy unction to make a real member of Christ's invisible church. The particular churches of Jerusalem Antioch Alexandria Rome etc. have all fallen into error.[1524] And yet in their most corrupt and erroneous state I believe they have included some true members of that body whereof Christ is head, of that building whereof He is the corner stone.[1525] Other foundation shall no man lay, but on this foundation there may be superstructures of hay stubble[1526] and much combustible trash without absolutely annihilating the Church. This I take to have been evidently the case. Christ's religion is spiritual and super-natural, and there is an unseen cement of the faithful, who draw grace from the same source, are enlightened by the same father of lights[1527] and sanctified by the same Spirit. And this, although they may be members of different political or visible congregations, may be estranged or suspected or even excommunicate to each other. They may be loyal to Christ however divided among themselves. This is the charitable belief of the true sons of our Church howsoever contrary to the damning temper of Rome and the sour severity of Dissenters.

To explain this by a familiar instance. When King Charles the Second[1528] was at Brussels he had friends in England of different factions, and suspected or even hated each by other who yet alike wished the King well, and corresponded with him though not with one another. The King knew his loyal subjects though they were not known owned or trusted mutually. They all promoted his return though by different schemes; and when he came to his kingdom, they all rejoiced with him.

But perhaps you will say there is need of an infallible visible guide for the soul's quiet. But, of what use is an infallible guide without an infallible sign to know him by?[1529] We have often seen Pope against Pope and Council against Council. What or whom shall we follow in these contests but the written word of God, the Apostolical traditions, and the internal light of the

---

[1522] *Ekklesia*: an assembly, used to describe the Church.
[1523] Matthew 22:14.
[1524] *Articles of Religion*, No. XIX.
[1525] Ephesians 2:20.
[1526] I Corinthians 3:11, 12.
[1527] James 1:17.
[1528] King Charles II (1630–85).
[1529] See Edmund Gibson,* *A Preservative Against Popery*, 3 vols. (1738), vol. I, Tit. IV, Cap. 3, and G. Salmon, *The Infallibility of the Church* (1888).

λόγος that irradiates every mind but is not equally observed by all? If you say notwithstanding these helps and lights that we are still weak, and have weak eyes; in a word that we may err. I say So may you. Man is fallible, and God knows it, and God is just. I am more easy on these principles, and this way of thinking than if I tamely and slothfully gave myself up to be ridden & hoodwinked by the Pope or by any other visible Judge upon earth.

The security and repose of souls is pretended or promised to be had in the Bosom of the Roman Church: But I think least of all to be hoped for in a Church which, by her doctrine of the priest's intention being necessary to the efficacy of Sacraments must raise in every thinking member infinite and indissoluble scruples. Since it is acknowledged that many Infidels and Jews and Mahometans have been ordained and possessed all degrees of dignity and administred all Sacraments, in the Church of Rome. Therefore all Sacraments derived either mediately or immediately from such were ineffectual. Therefore no particular member can know upon the principles of the Church of Rome whether he is a Christian or no. Therefore that very church which sets up above all others for making men easy and secure within her communion, is, indeed, more than any other calculated for producing doubts and scruples; such as I do not see possible how they shou'd be solved or quieted upon her principles.

You seem to think the numerousness of her sons one argument of her truth. But it is admitted the Mahometans are more numerous than the Christians; and that the Arians once upon a time were more numerous than the Orthodox. Therefore the argument concludes nothing.

As for her miracles which you think so well attested that thinking Protestants dare not deny them. I declare honestly that the best attested of Her miracles that I have met with, and the only that seemed to have any verisimilitude were those said to be performed at the tomb of Abbé Paris[1530] and those are not admitted by the Church of Rome her self. I have read, inquired, and observed myself, when abroad, concerning their exorcism and miracles, and must needs say they all appeared so many gross impositions. As for the miracles said to be performed in foreign missions I can give no credit to them (I judge by what accounts I have seen) and if you will be at the trouble of perusing the *Lettres édifiantes et curieuses écrites des missions étrangères*[1531] printed at Paris, perhaps you may think of them as I do.

[1530] François de Pâris (1690–1727), French Jansenist theologian at whose grave in the cemetery of St. Medard miracles were said to have occurred.

[1531] *Edifying Letters and Curious Writings of Foreign Missions*. The letters appeared between 1717 and 1776.

As for Romish saints and martyrs, please to read their legends or even read the canonizations of the last century, since Rome hath been enlightened and something reformed by our reformation, for those of St. Pietro d' Alcantara and St. Magdalena de Pazzi. I believe you never read of any thing like them and their marvellous wonders which nevertheless were admitted for authentic by Pope & cardinals. I my self saw and conversed with a woman at Genoa, a reputed Saint, whose head I met three years after encircled with rays to be sold among other pictures in the great square of Leghorne. This same Saint appeared to me very manifestly a vile lying hypocrite though much extolled and admired.

I never saw any character of a Popish Martyr that came up to that of Jerome of Prague[1532] one of the first Reformers for which I refer you to Poggius & Aeneas Sylvius,[1533] who was eye-witness to his behaviour and afterwards became Pope. Cranmer,[1534] Ridley[1535] and Latimer[1536] were, I think, good men and acted on good motives. So was Jewell[1537] a very good man. I wish you'd read his little Latin book in defence of the Reformation. I have not seen it these thirty years but remember I liked it well. Hooker,[1538] Usher,[1539] Dodwell,[1540] Fell,[1541] Hammond,[1542] and many more Protestants of our Church had piety equal to their learning. Basil Kennet,[1543] chaplain to the factory at Leghorne in Queen Anne's reign was esteemed and called a Saint by the papists themselves as the English merchants there assured me. On the other hand in so many convents and such a numerous clergy that there may be found sundry good and learned men I make no doubt whose learning and piety are skillfully made use of and applied by the Court of Rome to extend her influence and credit.

[1532] Jerome of Prague (?–1416), Bohemian reformer and friend of Hus, condemned and burnt at the stake by the Council of Constance.

[1533] Aeneas Sylvius (1405–64), poet, novelist, historian, and Pope Pius II (1458–64).

[1534] Thomas Cranmer (1489–1556), archbishop of Canterbury, burnt at the stake on 21 March 1556.

[1535] Nicholas Ridley (1500?–55), bishop of London, burnt at the stake with Latimer at Oxford on 15 October 1555.

[1536] Hugh Latimer (1485?–1555), bishop of Worcester, burnt at the stake with Ridley at Oxford on 15 October 1555.

[1537] John Jewel (1522–71), reformer and bishop of Salisbury; wrote *Apologia pro Ecclesia Anglicana* (1562).

[1538] Richard Hooker (1554?–1600), theologian; author of *Of the Laws of Ecclesiastical Politie* (1593).

[1539] James Ussher (Usher) (1581–1656), theologian and chronologist, archbishop of Armagh, and vice-chancellor of Trinity College, Dublin.

[1540] Henry Dodwell (1641–1711), scholar, theologian, and writer on religious issues.

[1541] John Fell (1625–86), dean of Christ Church, bishop of Oxford, and editor of classical texts and religious books.

[1542] Henry Hammond (1605–60), Anglican divine and chaplain to Charles I; author of *Practical Catechism* (1644) and many other works.

[1543] Basil Kennett (1674–1715), chaplain to the British Factory at Leghorn, where Berkeley preached for him in 1714; author of miscellaneous works, amongst them *The Antiquities of Rome* (1696).

You mention monasteries to have been antiently regarded as schools of Divine Philosophy. But there is by what I can find no similitude between ancient and modern monks. Compare what St. Bernard[1544] in his treatise *de vita solitaria* saith of the monks of Thebais with what you'll see in the monasterys of Flanders. I fear there is no corruption or perversion worse than that of a monastic life.

It seems very expedient that the world should have among the many formed for action some also formed for contemplation, the influence whereof might be general & extend to others. But to get men & women to a contemplative life who are neither fitted nor addicted to contemplation is a monstrous abuse. To assist the λύσις & φυγή[1545] of the soul by meditation was a noble purpose even in the eyes of pagan philosophers, how much more so in the eyes of Christians, whose philosophy is of all others the most sublime and the most calculated to wean our thoughts from things carnal, and raise them above things terrestrial.

That the contemplative and ascetic life may be greatly promoted by living in communities and by rules I freely admit. The Institution of the Essenes among the Jews, or the republic of philosophers that was to have been settled in a city to have been built by the direction of Plotinus[1546] in the territory of Capua if the Emperor Gallienus had not changed his mind; such institutions as these give delightful images but very different from any thing that I could ever see in a popish convent, and I have seen and known many of them.

I should like a convent without a vow or perpetual obligation. Doubtless a College or monastery (not a resource for younger brothers, not a nursery for ignorance laziness & superstition) receiving only grown persons of approved piety, learning, and a contemplative turn would be a great means of improving the divine philosophy, and brightening up the face of religion in our church. But I should still expect more success from a number of Gentlemen living independently at Oxford who made divine things their study, and proposed to wean themselves from what is called the world.

You remark on the badness of men and views that seem to have concurred in the reformation. That there may be some truth in this charge, I will not deny. But I deny that this can be an argument against the reformation, since you seem to grant your self that the Church of Rome hath been reformed on occasion of our reformation

---

[1544] St. Bernard (1090–1153), abbot of Clairvaux and founder of the Cistercian Order; he wrote on dogma, asceticism, monasticism, and ecclesiastical government.

[1545] *Lusis*: setting free. *Phuge*: flight or exile. Thus Berkeley intends the setting free and flight of the soul from the body.

[1546] Plotinus (204–70), founder of a school of philosophy at Rome, the culmination of Neoplatonism, and a bridge from pagan to Christian thought. His lectures were edited by Porphyry in the *Enneads*.

which yet you condemn. Evil men and councils may sometimes be the occasion of good. And it is on all hands admitted that God knows how to extract good from evil.

The charge of Idolatry on the Church of Rome (which you make so light of) is, I fear, not without foundation. For although the learned may and do distinguish between a relative respect for images and an absolute worship of them, yet it cannot be doubted that the use made of them becomes a great snare to the multitude. I my self by talking to some common people in Italy found they worshiped images with an adoration as formal and stupid as any heathen idolater. And both I and every other traveller must see (and the best men among themselves are scandalized to see it) that the B. Virgin is oftener prayed to and more worship'd than God himself.

You speak of the unity and peace of the Church of Rome as an effect of the Spirit of God presiding in it and of the doctrine of an infallible head. But the fact is denied. Successions of Anti-popes with horrible dissensions violent measures & convulsions ensuing thereupon sufficiently shew the contrary. The court of Rome it must be owned hath learned the Venetian policy of silencing her sons and keeping them quiet through fear. But where there breathes a little spirit of learning and freedom as in France, or where distance lessened respect as in China there have often appeared and ever and anon continue to appear great struggles parties and divisions both in matters of faith and discipline. And where they are quiet their union seems, so far as I can judge, a political union founded in secular power and arts, rather than an effect of any divine doctrine or spirit.

Those who are conversant in history plainly see by what secular arts and stages the Papal power was acquired. To history therefore I refer you. In the mean time I cannot forbear making one remark which I know not whether it hath been made by others. Rome seems to me to have cut her own throat by the forgery of Constantine's Donation[1547] in which there is this remarkable clause—*Decernentes sancimus, ut [Romana Ecclesia] principatum teneat tam super quatuor sedes Alexandrinam Antiochenam Hierosolymitanam ac Constantinopolitanam quam etiam super omnes in universo orbe terrarum Dei Ecclesias.*[1548] Doth not this look like an acknowledgment that the see of Rome oweth her preheminence to the appointment of Constantine the great, and not to any divine right?

[perhaps several missing pages, text continues . . .]

[1547] "The Donation of Constantine," a ninth-century forgery, attributed to Isidore.
[1548] "Pronouncing, we decree that just as the Roman Assembly [Church] has dominion over the four seats Alexandria, Antioch, Jerusalem, and Constantinople, so too [it has dominion] over all the Assemblies [churches] of God in all the world."

many innovations are in theirs which we account repugnant to the word of God, and the primitive traditions. Therefore a Papist of any tolerable reason, though bred up in the Roman Church, may nevertheless with a good conscience occasionally join in our worship; and I have known this done. May I not therefore hope that you will continue to do it, and not in perfect complaisance to the Pope renounce and damn us all. In the mean time you may deliberate, continue your impartial inquiry, and well weigh your steps before you range under the Pope and receive his mark.

I had forgot to say a word of Confession which you mention as an advantage in the Church of Rome which is not to be had in ours. But it may be had in our communion by any who please to have it; and I admit it may be very usefully practised. But as it is managed in the Church of Rome, I apprehend it doth infinitely more mischief than good. Their casuistry seemeth a disgrace not only to Christianity, but even to the light of nature.

As Plato thanked the gods that he was born an Athenian, so I think it a peculiar blessing to have been educated in the Church of England. My prayer nevertheless and trust in God is, not that I shall live and die in this church, but in the true church. For, after all, in respect of religion our attachment should be only to the truth. I might therefore, own my self a little surprised upon observing that you concluded your letter with declaring—You trust by God's grace to live and die in the church of Rome.—I can easily suppose that expression was a slip; but I can never suppose that all [the] skill and arts of Rome can destroy your Candor.

You will pardon the freedom of an old friend who speaks [his] thoughts bluntly, just as they come, to one who used to be [a man] of frankness without forms. If I have exceeded in this kind, impute it to haste, as well as my repetitions, inaccuracies, and want of order. You set me a time and I have obeyed as I could, hoping that your own thought will give give [sic] clearness and method to my broken and indigested hints.

To your own thoughts I appeal trusting that God will give you grace to think for your self, and to exert that sharpness of judgment which He has given you, with double diligence in this most weighty affair. There are some writings of my Lord Falkland's[1549] concerning the Infallibility of the Roman Church bound up in the second volume of Doctor Hammond's works together with some learned arguments in behalf of the Church of Rome. I have not read those writings but on the reputation of Lord Falkland venture to recommend to your perusal.

[1549] Lucius Cary (1610?–43), second Viscount Falkland. Educated at Trinity College, Dublin, and killed at the battle of Newbury, he wrote *Of the Infallibilities of the Church of Rome* (1645).

The importance of the subject, together with my esteem and affection for you have run me into a greater length than I intended: which if you are so good to pardon this once, I promise to be more succinct and methodical another time, if you think fit to favour me with an answer. In which case I would intreat you to number your paragraphs with figures prefixed, which will govern and shorten my answer.

The years I have lived, the pains I have taken, and the distempers I labour under make me suspect I have not long to live. And certainly my remnant of life, be it what it will, could be spun out delightfully in the sun and the fresco, among the [fountains?][1550] & grottos, the music, the antiquities, the fine arts and buildings of Rome, if I could but once reconcile myself to her religion. But I trust in God, those [. . .] [text damaged] things shall never bribe my Judgment. Dress therefore your batteries against my reason attack me by the dry light and assign me some good reason why I should not use my reason, but submit at once to his holiness's will and pleasure. Though you are conqueror, I shall be a gainer. In the [pursuit?] of truth I am ready to hear and canvass with the best of my skill whatever you shall be so good to offer.

To your kind inquiry about my health I can say that, though I am not well, yet I am less bad than I was a year ago and that [. . .] disorders seem to quit me though with a leisurely pace. [My fa]mily is a great comfort to me. My wife, who is just recovered from an illness, always remembers you with the highest esteem & interests her self in your welfare. She sends her compliments but knows nothing of the subject of our correspondence. If she did, I doubt it would make her think better of the Church of Rome in which she liked some things when she was in France. She is become a great farmer of late. In these hard times we employ above a hundred men every day in agriculture of one kind or other all which my wife directs. This is a charity which pays it self. At least the Domaine of this See will gain by it. Oh! that you had a farm of a hundred acres near Oxford, what a pleasure it would be to improve and embellish the face of nature, to lead the life of a patriarch rather than a friar, a modern cloistered friar! My wife finds in it a fund of health & spirits, beyond all the fashionable amusements in the world. Dear Sir you have the best wishes and most hearty prayers of

    your most obedient & affectionate servant,

    G: Cloyne

[1550] I cannot make out the word, but am reasonably certain it is not "fountains," as Luce has it. As I cannot supply a better replacement, I follow Luce's transcription but with this caveat.

283 JOHNSON TO BERKELEY[1551]

CU. Spec. MS Coll. Samuel Johnson, vol. I, p. 69, fols. 10v–11.

3 October 1741

My Lord:

This comes to your Lordship upon occasion of our recommending to the Society, Mr. Richard Caner[1552] (brother to my good neighbour Mr. H. Caner,[1553] missionary to Fairfield, of whom you may possibly retain some remembrance), who well deserves the Society's notice. On this occasion I have the pleasure to inform your Lordship that upon the occasion of our new rector, Mr. Clap,[1554] and his application to the business of the college, we have the satisfaction to see classical as well as mathematical learning improve among us; there having been a better appearance the last May than what I gave your Lordship an account of before; for this gentleman proves a solid, rational, good man, and much freer from bigotry than his predecessor.

But this new enthusiasm, in consequence of Whitefield's[1555] preaching through the country and his disciples', has got great footing in the College, as well as throughout the country. Many of the scholars have been possessed of it, and two of this year's candidates were denied their degrees for their disorderly and restless endeavours to propagate it. Indeed Whitefield's disciples have in this country much improved upon the foundations which he laid; so that we have now prevailing among us the most odd and unaccountable enthusiasm that perhaps ever obtained in any age or nation. For not only the minds of many people are at once struck with prodigious distresses upon their hearing the hideous outcries of our itinerant preachers, but even their bodies are frequently in a moment affected with the strangest convulsions and involuntary agitations and cramps, which also have sometimes happened to those who came as mere spectators, and are no friends to their new methods, and even without their minds being at all affected. The Church, indeed, has not, as yet, much suffered,

---

[1551] Also printed in Schneider, vol. I, pp. 102–03. The volume is catalogued at CU as BK 811 J63 06.

[1552] Richard Caner (?–1745). Caner was accepted into the Society and appointed missionary to Norwalk, Connecticut.

[1553] Henry Caner (1699?–1792). He was Johnson's pupil and missionary to Fairfield. See James Henry Stark, *The Loyalists of Massachusetts and the Other Side of the American Revolution* (Salem Press, 1910), pp. 346–49.

[1554] Thomas Clap* (1703–67).

[1555] George Whitefield (1714–70). Whitefield was a Church of England minister (ordained by Martin Benson* [1689–1752], bishop of Gloucester) who became itinerant and started preaching dissenting views. His religious enthusiasm is associated with the "Great Awakening" in America. He preached all over the colonies, arriving in New England for the first time in the fall of 1740.

but rather gained by these commotions, which no men of sense of either denomination have at all given in to, but it has required great care and pains in our clergy to prevent the mischief. How far God may permit this madness of the people to proceed, He only knows. But I hope that neither religion nor learning will in the whole event of things much suffer by it.

I humbly beg an interest in your Lordship's prayers and blessing, and remain,

Etc.,

S. J.

284 BERKELEY TO [WOLFE?][1556]

BL Add. MS 39306, fol. 24.

[1741]

Dear Sir,

I have lived[1557] long in this Irish nook, by ill health as well as situation cut off from the ways of men and sequestered from the rest of the world,[1558] which nevertheless hath not effaced the memory of my friends, and good wishes for them.

You will therefore pardon me if, having no news to send, I send you instead thereof a letter of advice. Our friend Mr. Dalton[1559] is, I hear, married the third time, which shews him to be a prudent man as well as a laudable patriot. Such an example is indeed a public benefit, when the nation is drained by war and hard times, and when our gentlemen conspire to put marriage out of countenance. It is to be wished you may profit by this example, not only for the public good but for your own. Though you are far from being an old man, I will take the freedom to say you are bordering on what we call an old bachelor, a character not the most useful to the public, nor the most agreeable to him that wears it. The former point needs no common place to clear it. For the other, give me leave to

---

[1556] The addressee is uncertain. On the strength of a reference in Letter 288, Luce speculates that it might be James Wolfe (1727–59), later the "hero of Quebec" (see *Works*, vol. IX, pp. 107–08). It is unlikely to be James, however, as Berkeley refers to him in this letter as "an old bachelor" and as a godparent. James would have been 14 years of age in 1741. The addressee is thus likely another member of the Wolfe family.

[1557] Luce inserts "so" before long, but it is not in the text.

[1558] Following "world" and placed in brackets is "[of business and intelligence (which makes me an . . .) all which I . . .]." The bracketed text was probably intended to be omitted and is undecipherable; the letter is a draft.

[1559] Richard Dalton* (*c.* 1695–1769).

say, Mr. Dalton and I are better judges than you. Health and affluence may bear you up for some years, but when age and infirmities come on (your life will not be tolerable without a family),[1560] you will feel and bewail the want of a family of your own, and the comforts of domestic life. A wife and children are blessings invaluable, which as a man cannot purchase for money, so he would sell them for no price. The privation of these that *orbitas* the disgrace as well as disaster both to Jews and Pagans it is miraculous that it should be fashionable or affected in a Christian country. Fear is unmanly, I will not therefore suppose you are afraid of a woman of your own choosing. But how shall you choose? Choose her by reputation. The quicksightedness and malice of the world will not keep the faults of a woman concealed from those eyes that are not already blinded by love. Therefore choose first and love after. But I fear you are already tired of this impertinent letter, which yet (odious as advice is) defends a good construction as it springs from a good will and is agreeable to the sincere opinion of etc.

Before I have done give me leave to add one hint, viz., that Plato (who you know was a wise man for a Gentile) sacrificed to nature as an atonement for his not having children. Your godson exceeds my hopes. I wish I had twenty [like] George.[1561] I assure you I would rather have them than twenty thousand pounds a year.

285 BERKELEY TO JAMES[1562]

BL Add. MS 39306, fol. 24.

[1741]

Your letter refreshed me like a shower after a drought. I thought you had been in foreign lands, but am glad to find you have been so long in England, and your health not the worse for it. Give me leave to reckon it at least among the possibilities, that you may sometime or other come to Bath, and from thence take it in your head to make a short trajet[1563] to our coast, where you

---

[1560] Luce leaves out the parenthetical phrase; it might have been omitted from the transmitted letter.

[1561] Berkeley's second son, George* (1733–95).

[1562] Addressee is likely James in part because of the claim that Mr. Dalton* is likely abroad with him. James and Dalton were frequent travel companions. The letter is unsigned and undated.

[1563] A crossing.

will find me with a wife, three sons, and daughter (of starlike beauty) rejoicing liberally under our fig trees.

Your patriots surely are the most profound or the most stupid of politicians. Why they should freely and with open eyes make such a step seems a most inexplicable riddle. I have long wished well to the public, but my wishes have been so often disappointed, that public affairs are grown more my amusement than concern. But news will always be entertaining.

Stultorum regum et populorum continet aestus.[1564]

I thank you for what you told me. What you sent was very agreeable, as, indeed, a line from you always will be. Here we have no news; but this, in all this province of Munster great devastations are made by bloody fluxes, fevers, and want, which carry off more than a civil war.

Our well-bred friend whom you call the Abbé acts a becoming part; I wish we had many more such Abbés among his brethren.[1565] Mr. Dalton,[1566] who I expected was abroad with you, is, it seems, made happy the third time (*O terque quaterque beatus*);[1567] I wish you would once [marry to have that natural comfort of children] dare to do what he does so often. Without that expedient you will lose the comforts of domestic life, that natural refuge from solitude and years which is to be found in wife and children. Mine are to me a great joy [the chief of the good things of this world], and alone capable of making a life tolerable so much embittered by sickness as mine has been for several years. I had many symptoms of the stone, and for a long time suspected my cholic to be an effect thereof. But of late I am satisfied that it is a scerbutic cholic, and that my original disease is the scurvy.[1568] At the same time I have hit on what I take to be the best cure for the scurvy and begin to be sensibly better for it. I am heartily glad that your temperate regular life has been rewarded with good health and good spirits which that [*sic*] you may long enjoy is the sincere wish of Geor[1569]

[1564] From Horace's *Letters*, I.2. "[The story] contains the passions of foolish kings and people."

[1565] The reference is unknown. It has been suggested to me that the Abbé is Msgr. l'abbé d'Aubigne, Chevalier of the order of St. Lazarus, mentioned by Berkeley in Letter 57 in 1713, but the temporal distance is great and there is no additional evidence to suggest a connection.

[1566] Richard Dalton* (*c.* 1695–1769).

[1567] "O three and four times blessed [one]." *Beatus* should be in the vocative case *beate*.

[1568] What follows was omitted in the Luce lying on the facing page and clearly belongs with this letter.

[1569] The closing word is unclear and overwritten, as if written in haste.

286 BERKELEY TO DALTON[1570]

BL Add. MS 39306, fol. 25.

[1741]

When I expected to have heard you were an exile at Rome or Paris I am agreeably surprised to hear you are the happiest man in London, married to a young and beautiful nymph. *O terque quaterque beate*,[1571] in this degenerate age; when so many are afraid to marry once, you dare to do it a third time. May all happiness and success attend your courage. Were I a dictator there should be a *jus trium uxorum*[1572] allowed for those who so magnanimously endeavour to repair the late breaches made upon the public by famine, sickness, and wars.

Without compliment, my wife and I do sincerely congratulate your nuptials, and wish your example may prevail with those worthy bachelors Sir John[1573] and Mr. Wolfe,[1574] who have not much time to lose. A long continuance of ill health has weaned me from the world, and makes[1575] me look with indifference on the most dazzling things in it. But, so long as I live, I shall retain good wishes for my friends, and a sense of their happiness.

I look upon you now as a man who may one day be my neighbour, and take it for granted that your roving spirit is fixed in your native land, which I was heartily sorry to think had been forsaken by you and Sir John James, and am as much pleased to think myself mistaken. Sir John tells me his health can stand the climate, and for everything else I imagine he will give the preference to his country which, with all its faults about it, I take to be the goodliest spot of Europe.

I hope all your family are well and thriving. My little ones are so, amidst a raging epidemical fever and bloody flux[1576]—three sons and a daughter. But such a daughter! so bright a little gem! that to prevent her doing mischief among the illiterate squires, I am resolved to treat her like a boy and make her study eight hours a day.

[1570] Although not explicitly addressed, from the preceding two letters it is clear that this letter is to Dalton.* This and Letters 284 and 285 are copied together in a letterbook in order. Only the date is uncertain.

[1571] "O three and four times blessed [one]."

[1572] "right of [having] three wives."

[1573] John James* (?–1741).

[1574] An unknown member of the Wolfe family. See note to Letter 284.

[1575] Correction from Luce, who has "made."

[1576] Dysentery or a similar illness where there is blood in the stool.

287 BERKELEY TO [UNKNOWN] [1577]

BL Add. MS 39306, fol. 25v.

[1741]

My Register[1578] who puts this letter into your hands will make my compliments also to your colleague, with my request that you would both honour me with lodging at my house which will hardly be out of your way. I am at present confined by a gentle fit of the gout which is some relief to my cholic and your visit will put me in high spirits. I have many things to say to you *tête à tête*. And shall no further intrude on your busy hours at present than to add that I shall reckon the greatest favour if you give me what moments you possibly can at Cloyne which will always be thankfully acknowledged by etc.

Let me know when you come and I will do myself the honour to go as far as I am able or can venture to meet you.

288 BERKELEY TO [BENSON?] [1579]

BL Add. MS 39306, fol. 25v.

[1741]

I had in my late desired your Lordship to let me know what was become of James[1580] & Dalton.[1581] I received a letter from Sir John James by which I found they are both in England that Mr. Dalton is married a third time to a young and beautiful damsel. I cannot wish better to all my good unmarried friends than that they should follow his example who is a delicate connoisseur as to the ease and comforts of life. I will not throw away my artillery on your Lordship who have the Church and the State to take care of, [and beside

---

[1577] For more about this letter see Luce, "More Unpublished Berkeley Letters and New Berkeleiana," 44–45.

[1578] The register of the diocese in 1752 was James Hanning (?–?), who witnessed Berkeley's will. He arrived in Cloyne in 1709 and allegedly lived to be 105 years of age.

[1579] A draft of a letter without an addressee, but the content makes it plausible to suppose that it is to Martin Benson* (1689–1752). Luce first published this letter in "More Unpublished Berkeley Letters and New Berkeleiana," 45, and did not make a claim about its addressee. When he included the letter in his edition of the *Works* (vol. VIII, p. 256), he speculated that the recipient was Benson. As I do not have a better alternative and the mention of parliamentary actions at the end is suggestive of Benson, I cautiously follow Luce's attribution here.

[1580] Sir John James* (?–1741).

[1581] Richard Dalton* (c. 1695–1769).

your own way of thinking. I would not give one of my sons][1582] though in my humble opinion the care of a family would interfere with neither. Besides Mr. Dalton who is a better judge than your Lordship of that matter can tell you marriage lessens and divides care. I will only say to you that my greatest want is children. I have but three boys and a daughter. And even this little daughter I would not give for the Duke of Bedford's[1583] estate. Wolfe[1584] is a grave regular man, I endeavour to make him a proselyte to marriage. I think he would educate his children well.

My friend Sir John applauds your and the Bishop of Oxford's[1585] conduct in Parliament. I congratulate you both upon it. You could not have the applause of a more sincere and incorrupt heart. At the same [*sic*] it was no surprise to me who knew you that you behaved well. I should be surprised if it were otherwise. The malcontents were I think beside them selves in this last step. I beg the favour of your Lordship to send the enclosed letters not knowing where to direct them.

289 BERKELEY TO GERVAIS[1586]

MS unknown. Stock, pp. lxxxix–xc.

Cloyne, 12 January 1741/42

Revd Sir,

You forgot to mention your address, else I should have sooner acknowledged the favour of your letter, for which I am much obliged, though the news it contained had nothing good but the manner of telling it.

I had much rather write you a letter of congratulation than of comfort; and yet I must needs tell you for your comfort, that I apprehend you miscarry by having too many friends. We often see a man with one only at his back pushed on and making his way, while another is embarrassed in a croud of well-wishers.

The best of it is, your merits will not be measured by your success. It is an old remark that the race is not alwaies to the swift. But at present who wins it,

---

[1582] The bracketed text is marked off to be removed.
[1583] John Russell (1710–71), fourth Duke of Bedford.
[1584] An unknown member of the Wolfe family. See note to Letter 284.
[1585] Thomas Secker* (1693–1768).
[1586] Luce indicates (*Works*, vol. IX, p. 109) that the letter is held privately and that he viewed it in 1955. The current location of the letter is unknown.

matters little. For all Protestant clergymen are like soon to be at par; if that old priest[1587] your countryman continues to carry on his schemes with the same policy and success he has hitherto done.

The accounts you send agree with what I hear from other parts. They are all alike dismal. Reserve your self however for future times, and mind the main chance. I would say, shun late hours, drink tar water, and bring back (I wish a good deanry at least) a good stock of health and spirits to grace our little parties in Imokilly, where we hope, 'ere it be long to see you and the sun returned together.

My wife, who values her self on being in the number of your friends, is extremely obliged for the Italian psalms you have procured, and desires me to tell you, that the more you can procure, the more she shall be obliged. We join in wishing you many happy new years, health, and success,

    I am, Revd Sir,

    your most faithful & obedient servant,

    Geor: Cloyne

290 BERKELEY TO GERVAIS[1588]

TCD MS 2167, fol. 4.

Cloyne, 19 January 1741/42

Revd. Sir,

The pleasure you take in serving your friends is apt to encourage their importunity. We address our selves to you as a virtuoso, a lover of music, and one who converses with musical men, in hopes it may fall in your way to hear of a great four-string bass violin with a fine sounding base, approved by a good master. Such a one if you meet with, be so good as to agree for at any price you shall think reasonable, and I have wrote to Mr. Prior[1589] in Bolton Street to pay for it and to send it hither. We are contriving a concert for your entertainment the next time you favour us at

---

[1587] Most likely this is a reference to Cardinal André Hercule de Fleury (1653–1743), then 87 years of age. Dean Gervais* (1680–1756) was a native of Montpellier and carried out of France as an infant on the revocation of the Edict of Nantes in 1680. See Stock, note to p. lxxxix.

[1588] The letter is printed in Luce, "Some Unpublished Berkeley Letters with Some New Berkeleiana," 148.

[1589] Thomas Prior* (1681–1751).

Cloyne, and in the mean time intreat you accept our compliments and excuse this trouble from,

> Revd Sir,
> your most faithful humble servant,
> G: Cloyne

Not knowing your address I enclosed my last as I do this to Mr. Prior.

291 BERKELEY TO PERCIVAL (SON)[1590]

EP, BL Add. MS 47012B, fols. 110–11.

Cloyne, 24 January 1741/42

My Lord,

Though by the want of five pacquets I have not yet seen it certified from England, I venture on the credit of a general report to congratulate your Lordship on your late success.[1591]

I do not congratulate you merely from the long and intimate attachment I have to you and your family which claims and will always be entitled to my best wishes, because I do not look on a place in Parliament as a private perquisite to a family.

Nor yet do I congratulate your Lordship on the prospect of an approaching change of hands, which God knows whether it will be for better or worse; though worse I think our affairs can hardly be.

But what I congratulate you upon is the being nearer to execute your excellent scheme of an agrarian law, for want of which we are undone by luxury and avarice.

If you suffer not your vertue to cool with years, but persist and succeed in that scheme which you imparted to me at Cloyne, you will do a thing at once most beneficial to the public and most glorious to your self, by cutting out the core of our evil, the very root of all corruption, which I fear will otherwise only change hands, but never be remedied.

That God would preserve you and yours and keep this generous spark alive in your breast, and conduct and prosper all your endeavours for the public good is the sincere wish and hearty prayer of my good Lord

---

[1590] See Luce, "Some Unpublished Berkeley Letters with some New Berkeleiana," 148–49.

[1591] John Percival* (Perceval) (1711–70), son of John Percival* (1683–1748), the Earl of Egmont, was elected to Parliament from Westminster in 1741.

your Lordship's most obedient faithful servant,

Geo: Cloyne

292 BERKELEY TO GERVAIS

Stock, pp. xc–xci (extract).

Cloyne, 2 February 1742

I condole with you on your cold, a circumstance that a man of fashion who keeps late hours can hardly escape. We find here that a spoonful, half tar and half honey, taken morning, noon, and night, proves a most effectual remedy in that case. My wife, who values herself on being in your good graces, expresses great gratitude for your care in procuring the psalms, and is doubly pleased with the prospect of your being yourself the bearer. The instrument she desired to be provided was a large four-stringed bass violin: but, besides this, we shall also be extremely glad to get that excellent bass viol which came from France, be the number of strings what it will. I wrote indeed (not to overload you) to Dean Browne[1592] to look out for a six-stringed bass viol of an old make and mellow tone. But the more we have of good instruments, the better; for I have got an excellent master, whom I have taken into my family, and all my children, not excepting my little daughter, learn to play, and are preparing to fill my house with harmony against all events: that if we have worse times, we may have better spirits. Our French woman is grown more attentive to her business, and so much altered for the better, that my wife is not now inclined to part with her, but is nevertheless very sensibly obliged by your kind offer to look out for another. What you say of a certain pamphlet is enigmatical; I shall hope to have it explained *viva voce*.[1593]

As this comer furnishes nothing worth sending, you will pardon me if, instead of other news, I transcribe a paragraph of a letter I lately received from an English bishop. 'We are now shortly to meet again in Parliament, and by the proceedings upon the state of the nation Sir Robert's[1594] fate will be determined. He is doing all he can to recover a majority in the House of Commons, and is said to have succeeded as to some particulars. But in his

---

[1592] Jemmett Browne* (1703–82), then dean of Ross.

[1593] Literally "with living voice." Here he means something like "by word of mouth," i.e. in person.

[1594] Sir Robert Walpole* (1676–1745), later first Earl of Orford. Walpole had a slim majority in the House of Commons after the election in December 1741. He would be defeated on a minor matter a few weeks later and resign.

main attempt, which was that of uniting the Prince[1595] and his court to the King's,[1596] he has been foiled. The Bishop of Oxford[1597] was employed to carry the proposal to the Prince, which was, that he should have the £100,000 a year he had demanded, and his debts paid. But the Prince, at the same time that he expressed the utmost respect and duty to his Majesty, declared so much dislike to his minister, that without his removal he will hearken to no terms.'

I have also had another piece in the following words, which is very agreeable. 'Lady Dorothy,[1598] whose good temper seems as great as her beauty, and who has gained on every one by her behaviour in these most unhappy circumstances, is said at last to have gained over Lord Euston, and to have entirely won his affection.'

I find by your letter, the reigning distemper at the Irish Court is disappointment. A man of less spirits and alacrity would be apt to cry out, *spes et fortuna valete*,[1599] etc., but my advice is, never to quit your hopes. Hope is often better than enjoyment. Hope is often the cause as well as the effect of youth. It is certainly a very pleasant and healthy passion. A hopeless person is deserted by himself; and he who forsakes himself is soon forsaken by friends and fortune: both which are sincerely wished you by, etc.

293 BERKELEY TO GERVAIS[1600]

CU, Spec. MS Coll. David Eugene Smith Historical, Box Ba-Bin.

19 February 1741/42

Revd Sir:

We are glad to find the spring is likely to bring you to us with other good things. My wife with her thanks and service desires me to send you word that she is resolved not to suffer that choice instrument (which you will tell is the history of all Cloyne) to escape her hands leaving you to make as good a purchase as you can, be it ten pounds, or rather than [fail] ten guinea. She is likewise much obliged for the four-stringed bass violin, of which you say you have three or four

---

[1595] Frederick Lewis* (1707–51), Prince of Wales.

[1596] George II* (1683–1760).

[1597] Thomas Secker* (1693–1768).

[1598] Dorothy Boyle* (1724?–41) was the daughter of Richard Boyle* (1694–1753), third Earl of Burlington and fourth Earl of Cork. She married George Fitzroy, Earl of Euston (1715–47), son of Charles Fitzroy* (1683–1757), the Duke of Grafton, on 10 October 1741. She died of smallpox shortly thereafter, in May 1742.

[1599] "farewell hope and fortune!"

[1600] The letter is addressed "To the Reverend Mr. Gervais at Mrs. Greenway's in the lower Castle yard, Dublin."

in view, and depends on your choosing that which has the best tone. I told you before that Mr. Prior[1601] in Bolton Street will pay for both instruments and take care to convey them to Corke. For want of other news I send you a scrap of a private letter I received this day from a man of quality in London.

There will be many [removes?], but what and to give place to whom, we shall not know nor have the opposition agreed it, for you may be assured there are many expectants. When that is done the prince will come to court and not till then. The country party have plainly got a majority which will daily increase, and the Lords are falling off.

So far the words of my letter I leave you to make your own reflexions on this changeable scene of things, and at the same time assure that I am with unalterable regard

> Revd sir
> your most
> faithful humble servant,
> G. Cloyne

294 BERKELEY TO PRIOR

LR, pp. 281–83. Stock, pp. lxxv–lxxvi.

Cloyne, 26 February 1741/42[1602]

Dear Tom,

I believe there is no relation that Mr. Sandys[1603] and Sir John Rushout[1604] have to Lord Wilmington[1605] other than what I myself made by marrying Sir John Rushout's sister to the late Earl of Northampton,[1606] who was brother to Lord Wilmington. Sandys is nephew to Sir John. As to kindred or affinity, I take it to have very little share in this matter; nor do I think it possible to foretell whether the ministry will be Whig or Tory. The people are so generally and so much incensed, that (if I am rightly informed) both men and measures must be changed before we

---

[1601] Thomas Prior* (1681–1751).

[1602] Stock dates the letter 1741, likely an error with the old style date system given that the LR agrees with 1742.

[1603] Samuel Sandys (1695–1770), MP for Worcester. Made first Baron Sandys of Ombersley in 1743, Sandys was a vigorous opponent of Walpole* (1676–1745). After Walpole's fall he became chancellor of the exchequer.

[1604] Sir John Rushout (1685–1775), fourth Baronet, MP for Evesham (1722–68). LR has "Rushent" for "Rushout."

[1605] Spencer Compton* (c.1674–1743), Earl of Wilmington.

[1606] George Compton (1664–1727), fourth Earl of Northampton, married Elizabeth Rushout on 3 July 1726. George was the elder brother of Spencer Compton* (c.1674–1743), Earl of Wilmington.

see things composed. Besides, in this disjointed state of things, the Prince's[1607] party will be more considered than ever. It is my opinion there will be no first minister in haste; and it will be new to act without one.[1608] When I had wrote thus far, I received a letter from a considerable hand on the other side the water, wherein are the following words: 'Though the Whigs and Tories had gone hand in hand in their endeavours to demolish the late minstry, yet some true Whigs, to show themselves such, were for excluding all Tories from the new ministry. Lord Wilmington and Duke of Dorset[1609] declared they would quit if they proceeded on so narrow a bottom; and the Prince, Duke of Argyle,[1610] Duke of Bedford,[1611] and many others, refused to come in, except there was to be a coalition of parties. After many fruitless attempts to effect this, it was at last achieved between eleven and twelve on Tuesday night; and the Prince went next morning to St. James's. It had been that very evening quite despaired of; and the meeting of the Parliament came on so fast, that there was a prospect of nothing but great confusion.' There is, I hope, a prospect now of much better things. I much wanted to see this scheme prevail, which it has now done; and will, I trust, be followed by many happy consequences. We are all yours. Adieu.

>your affectionate humble servant,
>G. Cloyne

You say that Swift & Co.* acquainted me by letter of their receipt of Purcel's bill;[1612] but I have got no such letter.

295 BERKELEY TO GERVAIS

Stock, p. xcii (extract).

5 March 1742

Your last letter, containing an account of the Queen of Hungary[1613] and her affairs, was all over agreeable. My wife and I are not a little pleased to find her situation so much better than we expected, and greatly applaud your zeal for

---

[1607] Frederick Lewis* (1707–51), Prince of Wales.
[1608] Sir Robert Walpole* (1676–1745) effectively resigned his post as prime minister on 2 February 1742.
[1609] Lionel Cranfield Sackville* (1688–1765), first Duke of Dorset. At this time Sackville was lord steward of the household.
[1610] Archibald Campbell (1682–1761), third Duke of Argyll.
[1611] John Russell (1710–71), fourth Duke of Bedford.
[1612] Richard Purcell* (c. 1690–?).
[1613] Maria Theresa (1717–80). She ascended to the Hapsburg throne in 1740 when her father Charles VI (1685–1740) died.

her interests, though we are divided upon the motive of it. She imagines you would be less zealous were the Queen old and ugly; and will have it that her beauty has set you on fire even at this distance. I, on the contrary, affirm, that you are not made of such combustible stuff; that you are affected only by the love of justice, and insensible to all other flames than those of patriotism. We hope soon for your presence at Cloyne to put an end to this controversy.

Your care in providing the Italian psalms set to music, the four-stringed bass violin, and the antique bass viol, require our repeated thanks. We have already a bass viol made in Southwark, A.D. 1730, and reputed the best in England. And through your means we are possessed of the best in France. So we have a fair chance for having the two best in Europe.

Your letter gives me hopes of a new and prosperous scene. We live in an age of revolutions so sudden and surprising in all parts of Europe, that I question whether the like has been ever known before. Hands are changed at home: it is well if measures are so too. If not, I shall be afraid of this change of hands; for hungry dogs bite deepest. But let those in power look to this. We behold these vicissitudes with an equal eye from the serene corner of Cloyne, where we hope soon to have the perusal of your budget of politics. Mean time accept our service and good wishes.

296 BERKELEY TO PERCIVAL (SON)[1614]

EP, BL Add. MS 47013B, fol. 14.

Cloyne, 26 March 1742

My good Lord,

It is with singular pleasure that I find your Lordship is blessed with a third son, and your Lady safe: two blessings natural and domestic, which may in some degree soften though not extinguish the sense of whatever you find amiss in this public jumble of affairs.[1615] The hopes of the future age depend on nothing so much as the education of the present. Early habits of hardiness and industry introduced into young children render their whole lives easy and happy to themselves, and useful to their country. And as your views extend to posterity, I doubt not you will be delighted to breed up a young race of patriots.

[1614] See Luce, "Some Unpublished Berkeley Letters with some New Berkeleiana," 149–51.

[1615] Viscount John Percival* (Perceval) (1711–70), son to John Percival* (1683–1748), the Earl of Egmont, married Catherine Cecil (1719–52), second daughter of James Cecil (1691–1728), fifth Earl of Salisbury, on 15 February 1737.

The letter you obliged me with (which was highly entertaining) should have been sooner acknowledged. But I imagined a letter from this corner to one at the fountain head, in the very centre of affairs, and at a juncture the most busy and critical that perhaps ever happened, must seem unseasonable, and only to be excused by the double motive of congratulating your happiness as well as acknowledging your favour.

Utopian schemes (I grant) are not suited to the present times, but a scheme the most perfect *in futuro* may take place in idea at present. The model or idea cannot be too perfect though perhaps it may never be perfectly attained in fact. Things though not adequate to a rule, will yet be less crooked for being, even clumsily, applied to it. And though no man hits the mark, they who come nearest merit applause.

As luxury seems the real original root of those evils under which we groan, avarice, ambition & corruption; must it not seem at the same time that agrarian and sumptuary laws are highly expedient if we would cut out the core of the national evil. To attempt or even mention such things now would be madness, but to have them in view is right: and to steer by that view may be useful. An excellent mathematician of the last age proposed to square the circle.[1616] He failed of his end, but by the way fell upon many useful discoveries. To grasp at more than we can hold is the way to lose all. But a man's aim may be immense though his grasp be but a span. And what cannot be seized at once may be grasped successively.

Though we live among dregs worse perhaps than the dregs of Romulus, yet Plato's republic may be kept in view, if not for a rule, yet for an incentive. There was something inhumanly rugged and austere in that iron virtue of the Spartans. We are in the other extreme. The more the bands of virtue and piety are loosed the coercive discipline of the laws should be so much the harder tied. The worst thing in a monarchy is that a court debauches the people: the best thing in a republic are sumptuary laws. And why we may not have them without change of government I do not see. They have them in France as well as in Venice or Genoa. And if we are wise they may be by little and little introduced to far better purpose at home.

It would be very impertinent to pretend to inform your Lordship, that without virtue liberty is precarious. There is now a noble field for bettering the manners of a people (the only way of mending their circumstances) opening itself to the young senators of virtue and resolution. A few such may do something, but old men are generally wanting in vigour as well as virtue. I should be

---

[1616] Thomas Hobbes (1588–1679). See Douglas Jesseph, *Squaring the Circle* (University of Chicago Press, 1999).

sorry to see Great Britain in labour and nothing brought forth but a mouse, a sorry scramble for employments.

The commoner your Lordship mentioned is a frugal prudent man, and such as are vulgarly esteemed prudent are often found to be under the influence of money. The Peer[1617] is too stately and too lazy for a premier minister. To find one man of virtue and capacity fit for a minister in these times is no easy matter. How difficult then must it be to furnish out a senate of such men? This is sufficient to show the madness of republican schemes. But whatever is amiss in our body politic may perhaps be remedied if not by a speedy purgation, yet by gentle alteratives.

I am sorry to find the Tories are quite excluded. I am not near enough to see the wisdom of this step. Certainly those Tories who are not Jacobites seem to me as good subjects and as deserving of favour as any other. Some men I suspect are for narrowing the public bottom that they may enlarge their private prospect. When I consider the wretched maxims that prevail both at home and abroad I am tempted to say with Cicero—*imbecillitate aliorum non nostra virtute valemus.*[1618] My good Lord you will pardon my day-dreams and believe me most sincerely

> your Lordship's most obedient and affectionate servant,
> George Cloyne

My wife and family were much honoured by your remembrance. We all join in service. I pray God preserve you and yours.

297 BERKELEY TO PERCIVAL (SON)

EP, BL Add. MS 47014A, fol. 40.

[Cloyne, early 1742?][1619]

My dear Lord

I was very much obliged by the letter you favoured me with amidst such a hurry of business. And I should have acknowledged the obligation sooner if I had not been shy of breaking in upon your busy moments. The scene of affairs on your

---

[1617] Luce reasonably speculates that the "Peer" is Spencer Compton* (*c.*1674–1743), Earl of Wilmington.

[1618] Cicero, *De Officiis*, II, 75. "We are strong because of the weakness of others, not [on account of] our own strength." Cicero has *valeamus* as the phrase occurs within an "ut" clause.

[1619] The date of this manuscript is uncertain. A later penciled note on the manuscript (twentieth century) says "*c.* 8 March 1744," but Rand dates it sometime in 1742 and Luce concurs with Rand (see *Works*, vol. VIII, p. 264). The content of the letter is consonant with topics discussed in other letters in 1742, thus I preserve that date.

side of the water is a very horrid one as your Lordship sketched it out; I doubt not your sketch is a very just one. Hard as it is to rid[e][1620] out such stormy weather, your Lordship is embarked and m[ust?] go through it with the utmost caution not to make a wron[g] step at this critical juncture. It is indeed very difficult not to make a censurable step on such tottering and unstable footing, especially wh[ilst] there are so many open and earnest eyes ready to remark. In a state [so?] unsettled and factious as that of England it must be owned, th[e] honestest and prudentest man alive may be often at a loss, ho[w] to act, with whom to act, or whether to act at all. This was the circumstance of Cicero in the Roman State, and his letters contain many useful hints and parallels to our present tim[e].

The modern patriots have to my thinking shown as little skill as honesty. Their dividing from their body puts them absolutely in the power [of] the late ministers, who have baited them with present advantages, and in all appearance will soon have them out again. For how is it possible they should long subsist without the favour either of prince or people? It seems therefore a clear case that the old ministry will bring in their old friends.

Much might be said for supporting the Queen of Hungary[1621] and demolishing the power of France. But whether this might not be better and cheaper done by supplies of money than troops is a question your Lordship can better decide than I. But I blame my self for pretending to speak of matters so much out of my sphere. This much however may be said in general, and it holds true at all times: that it is polit[ic] to stand by one's friends and honest to abide by principles: and that these two points of steadiness and honesty where they meet do constitute the surest basis for a great reputation, the most necessary of all engines for a man that would make a great and useful figure in public affairs. Pardon, my good Lord, this political stuff that I write for want of news.

This island is a region of dreams and trifles of so little consequence to the rest of the world that I am sure you expect no important news from it. But I could tell you a very ridiculous piece of news I lately heard from Dublin, which I am sure would make you laugh but as it would be at the expense of a prelate I must be excused from telling it. My best wishes and respects attend you and yours. I am my dear Lord your most obedient and faithful servant,

     G: Cloyne

[1620] The manuscript is damaged along the side and some parts of words cannot be made out. I have followed Luce's transcription when uncertain but noted the questionable words.
[1621] Maria Theresa (1717–80).

298 BERKELEY TO PERCIVAL (SON)[1622]

EP, BL Add. MS 47013B, fol. 62.

Cloyne, 2 July 1742

My Lord,

I was just now favoured with a letter of your Lordship by the hands of Mr. Brereton.[1623] You must not measure my inclination to serve you by my serving him this time, which I fear will not be in my power, though it always will be in my wishes to do what is agreeable to your Lordship.

It was no small mortification to find you had been within four miles of Cloyne, without my hearing any thing of it till you were gone. If I were in travelling circumstances, the distance of Cloyne from your castle should not hinder my waiting on your Lordship and Lady Percival. But for above three years together I have not gone three miles off, being nailed down to Cloyne by a cholic and pain in my side which is irritated by the motion of a horse or a coach.

My wife joins with me in best respects to Lady Percival and your Lordship, and we should reckon it a great good fortune, if you would both be pleased to make our house your inn while you wait for the going off of your ship, which may take you up within two miles of Cloyne. Be it days, so much the better: or be it hours, this is better than nothing. Deny us not this favour, and count on my being ever, my good Lord,

> your most affectionate and obedient servant,
> G: Cloyne

Cloyne, July 2, 1742

299 BERKELEY TO PERCIVAL (SON)

EP, BL Add. MS 47013B, fol. 65.

Cloyne, 9 July 1742

My Lord,

[1622] See Luce, "Some Unpublished Berkeley Letters with some New Berkeleiana," 151.

[1623] Robert Brereton (1705–64), one of the Breretons of Carrigslaney. He graduated from Trinity College, Dublin, in 1727 and was rector of Burton and Brahenny (1735–64). Brereton was seeking an additional benefice, which Berkeley initially declined to give. Later Berkeley did so, being "better than his word" by bestowing the vicarage of Kilbrun to Brereton in 1742. See Letter 300.

I happened to hear you have a carriage but no horses. Please to let me know by the bearer what horses and harness you would have, and on what day, and I shall not fail to send them, with my coachman and postilion who are very safe drivers and will I hope bring my Lady Percival and your Lordship safely to Cloyne, which honour is expected with great pleasure by

My Lord,

your Lordships most faithful & obedient servant,

G: Cloyne

My wife joins with me in compliments to her Ladyship.

Cloyne, July 9, 1742

300 BERKELEY TO PERCIVAL (SON)[1624]

EP, BL Add. MS 47013B, fol. 92–92v.

Cloyne, 17 November 1742

My Lord,

When you interested your self for Mr. Brereton I made, in answer to your letter, no promise choosing rather to be better than my word.[1625] I have now the pleasure to acquaint your Lordship that I have given him the vicarage of Kilbrin, being a benefice without cure, adjacent to that of Burton, and so lying most convenient for him. I am informed it let last year for fourscore pounds, and by increase of tillage is likely to grow more valuable. I need not tell your Lordship how much pleased I am with this opportunity of showing my attachment to your family as well as the ready inclination & sincere regard with which I am,

My Lord,

your Lordships most obedient and most faithful servant,

George Cloyne

Our respects and best wishes wait upon all your good family, including my Lord Egmont's.[1626]

[1624] See Luce, "Some Unpublished Berkeley Letters with some New Berkeleiana," 152.

[1625] Earlier the younger Percival asked Berkeley to provide another benefice to Robert Brereton (1705–64), one of the Breretons of Carrigslaney. See Letter 298.

[1626] John Percival* (1683–1748).

301 BENSON TO BERKELEY

BL Add. MS 39311, fols. 49–50.

Berry Street, Westminster, 23 April 1743

My Dear Lord,

I did not come up to attend the Session till it was half over, and it being now at an end, I am hastening to quit the town and return to my Diocese. Though I came up late, yet when I was here, I thought I was come up too soon, finding some points so doubtful that I did not know how to vote at all, and others so clear that I was grieved to be under a necessity of voting against the measures of men with whom I have had a good deal of acquaintance, and of whom when out of place I had a good opinion. But it was measures and not ministers I desired to see changed. And as I have now little hope of ever seeing the former, I have less concern about the latter. The taking the Hanover troops into English pay, if it was right in regard to our foreign affairs, was certainly very unpolitic in regard to our domestic ones; and there is nothing but the necessity which is pretended which can in any degree excuse an action, which it could not but be foreseen must occasion so much jealousy, and which it is too plainly seen has occasioned not only a dislike of Ministers, but some share of disloyalty even to the Throne itself. If this step were allowed to be in reality as necessary, as some have pleaded it to be, yet there cannot be the same plea of necessity for an action which much more wanted it, and that is the method of raising the sum to defray the expense of this measure. There was, I thought, an absolute necessity of doing something to prevent the drinking of that poison which is called gin, but, unhappily, the increasing of the vice was found to be a way to increase the revenue; and this is the fund chosen to borrow the millions wanted upon. It passed pretty quietly through the House of Commons, but the Lords opposed the Bill in every step of its progress, and the whole Bench of Bishops who were present not only voted, but most of them also protested against it.

As to the appointing of Rural Deans, your Lordship must know that all our Dioceses here are divided into Archdeaconries, and every Archdeaconry into so many Deaneries. In many Dioceses, Rural Deans are still nominally appointed, though in few they exercise any kind of jurisdiction. My Diocese consists but of one Archdeaconry, and the Archdeacon was, when I came into it, near 90 years old, so that if he were willing, he was incapable to do much duty; and while he was capable, I found he had scarcely ever done any. So that upon account both of his present infirmity and past neglect, there was great want in the Diocese of somebody to assist both him and me in relation to the duties which are reckoned more peculiarly incumbent upon the Archdeacon. One of these is to visit parochially all the churches, chapels, and houses of incumbents within his district. This afforded me a fair handle for appointing Deans Rural to perform this work, and I shall send you a copy of the commission I have given to them. This I thought could not be reckoned improper in this kingdom where this was the ancient and is still the regular form of government in each Diocese. But in Ireland, perhaps, it may be a thing quite new, and your beginning it may give offence both to the rest of the Bishops and to the Archdeacons, and also to the inferior clergy.

Your most faithful servant and affectionate brother,[1627]

302 BERKELEY TO GERVAIS

Stock, pp. xcii–xciii (extract).

6 September 1743

The book which you were so good as to procure for me (and which I shall not pay for till you come to receive the money in person) contains all that part of Dr. Pococke's[1628] travels for which I have any curiosity; so I shall, with my thanks for this, give you no further trouble about any other volume.

I find by the letter put into my hands by your son (who was so kind as to call here yesterday, but not kind enough to stay a night with us), that you are taken up with great matters, and, like other great men, in danger of overlooking your friends. Prepare, however, for a world of abuse, both as a courtier and an architect, if you do not find means to wedge in a visit to Cloyne between those two grand concerns. Courtiers you will find none here, and but such virtuosi as the country affords; I mean in the way of music, for that is at present the reigning passion at Cloyne. To be plain, we are musically mad. If you would know what that is, come and see.

[1627] Fraser adds the signature "M. Glocester," which no longer exists on the document.

[1628] Richard Pococke (1704–65). A traveler and later bishop of Ossory (1756), he traveled to the Near East (1737–40) and published a record of his travels in his *Description of the East*, appearing in two volumes (1743 and 1745).

303 BERKELEY TO GERVAIS

Stock, xciii (extract).

29 October 1743

A bird of the air has told me that your reverence is to be dean of Tuam.[1629] No nightingale could have sung a more pleasing song, not even my wife, who, I am told, is this day inferior to no singer in the kingdom. I promise you we are preparing no contemptible chorus to celebrate your preferment: and if you do not believe me, come this Christmas, and believe your own ears. In good earnest, none of your friends will be better pleased to see you with your broad seal in your pocket than your friends at Cloyne. I wish I were able to wish you joy at Dublin; but my health, though not a little mended, suffers me to make no excursions farther than a mile ot two.

What is this your favourite, the Queen of Hungary, has been doing by her emissaries at Petersburgh?[1630] France is again upon her legs. I foresee no good. I wish all this may be vapours and spleen: but I write in sun-shine.

304 BERKELEY TO PRIOR[1631]

BL 1406.d.32/1. Appended to Prior's Authentic Narrative *(London, 1746), pp. 212–39.*

A Letter from the Author of Siris, to Thomas Prior, Esq. Containing some farther Remarks on the Virtues of Tar-Water, and the Methods for Preparing it and Using it.

[1744]

[1629] Isaac Gervais* (1680–1756) would be formally made dean of Tuam in May 1744, but the matter was settled many months earlier.

[1630] Maria Theresa (1717–80). The reference to the queen's actions concerns an affair involving her envoy to St. Petersburg, Marquis Antoniotto de Botta-Adorno (1680–1774), who was accused of plotting to kill Elizabeth Petrovna (1709–62), tsarina of Russia. After an inquiry he was declared innocent, but relations between Austria and Russia were strained over the incident. See Letter 305.

[1631] First printed as a pamphlet, "A Letter to T—P—, Esq. from the Author of *Siris*" (Dublin: George Faulkner, 1744); BL 1406.d.32/1. It is also included in the 1746 edition of Thomas Prior's *Authentic Narrative*, pp. 212–39, which with the new London edition is the basis for the text here (being expanded over the original pamphlet). *An Authentic Narrative of the Success of Tar-water, in Curing a Great Number and Variety of Distempers, with Remarks and Occasional Papers Relative to the Subject* (Dublin: Innys, Hitch, Cooper & Davis; reprinted London, 1746, "A New Edition, complete"). A number of minor variations of the letter appear in the reprintings. Larger variations also exist, some of which blend the distinct letters to Prior concerning tar water into a single, shorter letter. See the letter to Prior appended to the front of a 1747 edition of the *Siris* ("A new edition, with additions and emendations") published by Innys, Hitch & Davis (Dublin; reprinted in London), catalogued in the BL as 1483.d.15.

Non sibi, sed toti[1632]

Nothing is more difficult and disagreeable than to argue men out of their prejudices; I shall not, therefore, enter into controversies on this subject, but, if men dispute and object, shall leave the decision to time and trial. Siris, § 68.

1. AMONG the great numbers who drink Tar-water in Dublin, your letter informs me, there are some that make or use it in an undue manner. To obviate those inconveniences, and render this water as generally useful as possible, you desire I would draw up some general rules and remarks in a small compass, which accordingly I here send you.

2. Pour a gallon of cold water on a quart of liquid tar, in a glazed earthen vessel; stir, mix, and work them thoroughly together, with a wooden ladle or flat stick for the space of five or six minutes. Then let the vessel stand close covered three days and nights, that the tar may have full time to subside. After which, having first carefully skimmed it without moving the vessel, pour off the clear water, and keep it in bottles, well corked, for use. This method will produce a liquor stronger than that first published in *Siris*,[1633] but not offensive if carefully skimmed. It is a good general rule, but, as stomachs and constitutions are various, it may admit of some latitude. Less water or more stirring makes it stronger, as more water or less stirring makes it weaker. It is to be noted that if several gallons are made at once in the same vessel, you must add five or six minutes stirring for every gallon. Thus two gallons of water and two quarts of tar require ten or twelve minutes' stirring.

3. The same tar will not do so well a second time, but may serve for other common uses: the putting off tar that hath been used for fresh tar would be a bad fraud. To prevent which, it is to be noted that tar already used is of a lighter brown than other tar. The only tar that I have used is that from our Northern Colonies in America, and that from Norway; the latter, being thinner, mixeth easier with water, and seems to have more spirit. If the former be made use of (as I have known it with good success), the tar-water will require longer stirring to make it.

4. Tar-water, when right, is not paler than French, nor deeper coloured than Spanish white wine, and full as clear; if there be not a spirit very sensibly perceived in drinking, you may conclude the tar-water is not good; if you would have it good, see it made yourself. Those who begin with it little and weak may by habit come to drink more and stronger. According to the season or

---

[1632] "Not for oneself, but for all."
[1633] See *Works*, vol. V, pp. 27–164.

the humour of the patient, it may be drank either cold or warm: in colics, I take it to be best warm. If it disgusts a patient warm, let him try it cold, and vice versa. If at first it creates, to some squeamish persons a little sickness at stomach, or nauseating, it may be reduced both in quality and quantity. In general, small inconveniences are either removed, or borne with small trouble; it lays under no restraint as to air, exercise, clothes, or diet, and may be taken at all times of the year.

5. As to the quantity in common chronical indispositions, one pint of tar-water a day may suffice, taken on an empty stomach, at two or four times, to wit, night and morning, and about two hours after dinner and breakfast; more may be taken by strong stomachs. Alteratives in general, taken in small doses, and often, mix best with the blood, how oft or how strong each stomach can bear, experience will shew. But those who labour under great and inveterate maladies must drink a greater quantity, at least one quart every twenty-four hours, taken at four, six, or eight glasses, as best suits the circumstances and case of the drinker. All of this class must have much patience and perseverance in the use of this as well as all other medicines, which, if sure and safe, must yet, from the nature of things, be slow in the cure of inveterate chronical disorders. In acute cases, fevers of all kinds, it must be drank in bed warm, and in great quantity (the fever still enabling the patient to drink), perhaps a pint every hour, which I have known to work surprising cures. But it works so quick, and gives such spirits, that the patients often think themselves cured before the fever hath quite left them. Such, therefore, should not be impatient to rise, or apply themselves too soon to business, or their usual diet.

6. To some, perhaps, it may seem that a slow alterative in chronical cases cannot be depended on in fevers and acute distempers, which demand immediate relief. But I affirm that this same medicine, which is a slow alterative in chronical cases, I have found to be also a most immediate remedy, when copiously taken, in acute and inflammatory cases. It might indeed be thought rash to have tried it in the most threatening fevers and pleurisies without bleeding, which in the common practice would have been held necessary. But for this I can say, that I have patients who would not be bled, and this obliged to make trials of tar-water without bleeding, which trials I never knew unsuccessful. The same tar-water I found a slow alterative, and a sudden febrifuge.[1634] If the reader is surprised, I own myself to be so too. But truth is truth, and from whatever hand it comes

---

[1634] A medicine that reduces fever.

should be candidly received. If physicians think they have a right to treat of religious matters, I think I have an equal right to treat of medicine.

7. Authority I have no pretence to; but reason is the common birthright of all. My reasons I have given in *Siris*: My motives every one will interpret from his own breast. But he must own himself a very bad man, who in my case (that is, after long experience, and under full conviction of the virtues and innocence of tar-water) would not have done as much. All men are, I will not say allowed, but obliged, to promote the common benefit; and for this end, what I could not in conscience conceal, that I do and shall publicly declare, maugre all the spleen and raillery of a world which cannot treat me worse than it hath done my betters.

8. As the morning's draught is most difficult to nice stomachs, such may lessen, or even omit it at the beginning, or rather postpone it till after breakfast, and take a larger dose at night: the distance from meal-time need not be more than one hour, for common stomachs, when the liquor is well clarified and skimmed. The oil that floats on the top and was skimmed off should be carefully laid by, and kept for outward sores. In the variety of cases and constitutions, it is not amiss that there should be different manners of preparing and taking tar-water: Trial will direct to the best. Whether there be any difference between old tar, or new tar, or which of all the various tars, produced from different trees, or in different parts of the world, is most medicinal, future trials must determine.

9. I have a second sort of tar-water to be used externally, as a wash or lotion, for the itch, scabs, ulcers, evil, leprosy, and all such foul cases, which I have tried with very good success, and recommend it to the trial of others. For inveterate cases of that kind, tar-water should be drank, a quart every twenty-four hours, at 4, 6, or 8 glasses: and, after this hath been done at least for a fortnight, the lotion is to be applied outwardly and warm, by bathing, fomenting, and steeping, and this several times in the twenty-four hours, to heal and dry up the sores, the drinking being still continued. This water, for external use, is made in the following manner: Pour two quarts of hot boiling water on a quart of tar; stir and work it strongly with a flat stick or ladle for a full quarter of an hour; let it stand six hours, then pour it off, and keep it close covered for use. It may be made weaker or stronger as there is occasion.

10. From what I have observed of the lotion, I am inclined to think it may be worth while, in obstinate and cutaneous ailments, leprosy, and weakness of limbs, to try a bath of tar-water; allowing a gallon of tar to every ten gallons of boiling-hot water; stirring the ingredients a full half–hour; suffering the vessel

to stand eight or ten hours, before the water is poured off, and using the bath a little more than milk-warm. This experiment may be made in different proportions of tar and water. In Dublin many cases occur for trial which are not to be met with in the country.

11. My experiments have been made in various cases, and on many persons; and I make no doubt its virtues will soon be more fully discovered, as tar-water is now growing into general use, though not without that opposition which usually attends upon novelty. The great objection I find made to this medicine is that it promises too much. What, say the objectors, do you pretend to a panacea, a thing strange, chimerical, and contrary to the opinion and experience of all mankind. Now, to speak out, and give this objection or question, a direct answer, I freely own that I suspect tar-water is a panacea. I may be mistaken, but it is worth trial: for the chance of so great and general a benefit, I am willing to stand the ridicule of proposing it. And as the old philosopher cried aloud from the house-tops to his fellow citizens, *Educate your children*, so, I confess, if I had a situation high enough, and a voice loud enough, I would cry out to all the valetudinarians upon earth *Drink tar-water*.

12. Having thus frankly owned the charge, I must explain to you, that by a panacea is not meant a medicine which cures all individuals (this consists not with mortality), but a medicine that cures or relieves all the different species of distempers. And if God hath given us so great a blessing, and made a medicine so cheap and plenty as tar, to be with all so universal in its effects, to ease the miseries of human life, shall men be ridiculed or bantered out of its use, especially when they run no risk in the trial? For I can truly affirm, that I never knew any harm attend it, more than sometimes a little nausea, which, if the liquor be well cleared, skimmed and bottled, need not, I think, be apprehended.

13. It must be owned I have not had opportunities of trying it myself in all cases; neither will I undertake to demonstrate *a priori* that tar-water is a panacea. But yet methinks I am not quite destitute of probable reasons, which, joined to what facts I have observed, induced me to entertain such a suspicion.

14. I knew tar was used to preserve cattle from contagion; and this may be supposed to have given rise to that practice of drinking tar-water for a preservative against the small-pox. But as the tar-water used for that purpose was made by mixing equal quantities of tar and water, it proved a most offensive potion: besides, as a fresh glass of water was put in for each glass that was taken out, and this for many days on the same tar, it followed that the water was not equally impregnated with the fine volatile spirit, though all alike strongly saturated with gross particles.

15. Having found this nauseous draught very useful against the small-pox to as many as could be prevailed on to take it, I began to consider the nature of tar. I reflected that tar is a balsam flowing from the trunks of aged evergreens; that it resists putrefaction; that it hath the virtues of turpentine, which in medicine are known to be very great and manifold; but I observed withal that turpentines or balsams are very offensive in the taking. I therefore considered distinctly the several constituent parts of balsams; which were those wherein the medicinal virtues resided, and which were to be regarded rather as a viscous matrix to receive, arrest, and retain the more volatile and active particles; and if these last could be so separated and disengaged from the grosser parts as to impregnate a clear and potable liquor, I concluded that such liquor must prove a medicine of great force and general use. I considered that nature was the best chemist and preparer of medicines, and that the fragrance and flavour of tar argued very active qualities and virtues.

16. I had of a long time entertained an opinion agreeable to the sentiments of many ancient philosophers, *That fire may be regarded as the animal spirit of this visible world*. And it seemed to me that the attracting and secreting of this fire in the various pores, tubes, and ducts of vegetables, did impart their specific virtues to each kind; that this same light or fire was the immediate instrumental or physical cause of sense and motion, and consequently of life and health to animals; that, on account of this solar light or fire, Phoebus was in the ancient mythology reputed the god of medicine. Which light, as it is leisurely intro-duced, and fixed in the viscid juice of old firs and pines, so the setting it free in part, that is, the changing its viscid for a volatile vehicle, which may mix with water, and convey it throughout the habit copiously and inoffensively, would be of infinite use in physic, extending to all cases whatsoever, inasmuch as all distempers are in effect a struggle between the *vis vitae*[1635] and the peculiar miasma or *fomes morbi*;[1636] and nothing strengthens nature, or lends such aid and vigour to life, as a cordial which doth not heat.

17. The solar light, in great quantity during the space of many successive years, being attracted and detained in the juice of ancient evergreens, doth form and lodge itself in an oil so fine and volatile as shall mix well with water, and lightly pass the *primae viae*,[1637] and penetrate every part and capillary of the organical system, when once exempt and freed from the grosser nauseous resin. It will not, therefore, seem unreasonable to whoever is acquainted with the

[1635] "force of life."
[1636] "the kindling of the ailment," i.e. that which produces disease or unhealthiness.
[1637] "first [prime] paths." A medical term for the major pathways in and around the body.

medicinal virtues of turpentine in so many different distempers, for which it hath been celebrated both by ancient and modern physicians, and withal reflects on the nausea or clog that prevents their full operation and effect on the human body; it will not, I say, seem unreasonable to such a one to suppose that, if this same clog were removed, numberless cures might be wrought in a great variety of cases.

18. The desideratum was, how to separate the active particles from the heavy viscid substance which served to attract and retain them; and so to order matters that the vehicle of the spirit should not on the one hand be volatile enough to escape, nor on the other gross enough to offend. For the performing of this, I have found a most easy, simple, and effectual method, which furnished a potable inoffensive liquor, clear and fine as the best white wine, cordial and stomachic, to be kept bottled, as being endued with a very sensible spirit, though not fermented.

19. I tried many experiments as to the quantity of water, and the time of stirring and standing, in order to impregnate and clarify it, and after all, fixed on the forementioned receipt, as the most generally useful for making this salutif-erous[1638] liquor well impregnated, and not offensive to common stomachs, and even drank with pleasure by many; in which the most medicinal and active particles, that is, the native salts and volatile oil of the balsam, being disen-tangled and separated from its gross oil and viscous resin, do, combined together, form a fine balsamic and vegetable soap, which not only can pass the stomach and *primae viae*, but also insinuate itself into the minutest capilla-ries, and freely pervade the whole animal system; and that in such full propor-tion and measure as suiteth every case and constitution.

20. The foregoing general considerations put me upon making experiments in many various and unlike cases, which otherwise I should never have thought of doing, and the success answered my hopes. Philosophical principles led me to make safe trials, and on those trials is founded my opinion of the salutary virtues of tar-water; which virtues are recommended from, and depend on, experi-ments and matters of fact, and neither stand nor fall with any theories or speculative principles whatever. Howbeit, those theories, as I said, enlarged my views of this medicine, led me to a greater variety of trials, and thereby engendered and nourished my suspicion, that it is a panacea. I have been the more prolix in these particulars, hoping that, to as many as shall candidly weigh and consider them, the high opinion I conceive of this medicine will not seem

---

[1638] Health bringing.

altogether an effect of vain prepossession, or blind empiric rashness, but rather the result of free thought and inquiry, and grounded on my best reason, judgment, and experience.

21. Those who have only the good of mankind at heart will give this medicine fair play; if there be any who act from other motives, the public will look sharp and beware. To do justice to tar-water, as well as to those who drink it, regard must be had to the particular strength and case of the patients. Grievous or inveterate maladies must not be treated as common cases. I cured a horrible case, a gangrene in the blood, which had broke out in several sores, and threatened speedy death, by obliging the person to drink nothing but this liquor for several weeks, as much and as often as his stomach would bear. Common sense will direct a proportionable conduct in the other cases. But this must be left to the conscience and discretion of the givers and takers.

22. After all that can be said, it is most certain that a panacea sounds odd, and conveys somewhat shocking to the ear and sense of most men, who are wont to rank the universal medicine with the philosopher's stone, and the squaring of the circle; whereof the chief if not sole reason I take to be, that it is thought incredible the same thing should produce contrary effects, as it must do if it cures opposite distempers. And yet this is no more than every day's experience verifies. Milk, for instance, makes some costive and others laxative. This regards the possibility of a panacea in general; as for tar-water in particular, I do not say it is a panacea, I only suspect it to be so; Time and trial will show.

23. But I am most sincerely persuaded, from what I have already seen and tried, that tar-water may be drank with great safety and success, for the cure or relief of most if not all diseases; of ulcers, itch, scald-heads, leprosy, King-evil,[1639] cancers, the foul disease, and all foul cases; scurvies of all kinds, disorders of the lungs, stomach, and bowels, in rheumatic, gouty and nephritic ailments, megrims, inveterate headaches, epilepsies, pleurisies, peripneumonies, erysipelas, small-pox, and all kinds of fevers, colics, hysteric and all nervous cases, obstructions, dropsies, decays, and other maladies. Note that for agues it should be drank warm, and often, in small glasses, both in and out of the fit, and continued for several days to prevent a relapse. Nor is it of use only in the cure of sickness; it is also useful to preserve health, and guard against infection; and in some measure even against old age, as it gives lasting spirits, and invigorates the blood. I am even induced, by the nature and analogy of things, and its wonderful success in fevers of all kinds, to

---

[1639] Also called scrofula; tuberculosis of the neck.

think that tar-water may be very useful against the plague, both as a preservative and a cure.

24. But I doubt no medicine can withstand that execrable plague of distilled spirits, which do all, without exception (there being a caustic and coagulating quality in all distilled spirits, whatever the subject or ingredients may be), operate as a slow poison, preying on the vitals, and wasting the health and strength of body and soul; which pest of human kind is, I am told, gaining ground in this country, already too thin of inhabitants.

I am, etc.

305 BERKELEY TO GERVAIS[1640]

HSP, Ferdinand Dreer Collection, English Clergy, vol. I, p. 16. Photostat at TCD ms 4309.

Cloyne, 8 January 1743/44

Revd. Sir,

You have obliged the ladies as well as my self by your candid judgment on the point submitted to your determination. I am glad this matter proved an amusement in your gout, by bringing you acquainted with several curious and select trials;[1641] which I should readily purchase, and accept your kind offer of procuring them, if I did not apprehend there might be some among them of too delicate a nature to be read by boys and girls, to whom my library, and particularly all French books, are open.

As to foreign affairs, we cannot descry or prognosticate any good event from this remote corner. The planets that seemed propitious are now retrograde: Russia, Sweden, and Prussia lost: and the Dutch a nominal ally at best. You may now admire the Queen of Hungary[1642] without a rival. Her conduct with respect to the Czarina[1643] and the Marquis de Botta[1644] hath, I fear, rendered cold the hearts of her friends, and their hands feeble. To be plain, from this time forward I doubt we shall languish and our enemies take heart. And while I am thus

---

[1640] Stock's version (pp. xciii–xcv) has minor errors.

[1641] The reference is probably to one of a series of books first published by François Gayot de Pitaval (1673–1743) entitled *Causes Célèbres*. The volumes chronicle famous French trials. Eighteen volumes were published between 1734 and 1741.

[1642] Maria Theresa (1717–80).

[1643] Elizabeth Petrovna (1709–62), tsarina of Russia (1741–62).

[1644] Marquis Antoniotto de Botta-Adorno (1680–1774), Maria Theresa's ambassador to St. Petersburg. He was accussed of plotting to kill the tsarina. See Letter 303.

perplexed about foreign affairs, my private economy (I mean the animal economy) is disordered by the sciatica; an evil which has attended me for some time past; and I apprehend will not leave me till the return of the sun.

Certainly the news that I want to hear at present is not from Rome, or Paris, or Vienna, but from Dublin; viz., when the Dean of Tuam is declared, and when he receives the congratulations of his friends. I constantly read the news from Dublin; but lest I should overlook this article, I take upon me to congratulate you at this moment; that as my good wishes were not, so my compliments may not be behind those of your other friends.

You have entertained me with so many curious things that I would fain send something in return worth reading. But, as this quarter affords nothing from itself, I must be obliged to transcribe a bit of an English letter that I received last week. It relates to what is now the subject of public attention, viz. the Hanover troops, and is as follows: 'General Campbell[1645] (a thorough courtier) being called upon in the House of Commons to give an account whether he had not observed some instances of partiality, replied, he could not say he had: but this he would say, that he thought the forces of the two nations could never draw together again. This, coming from the mouth of a courtier, was looked on as an ample confession: however, it was carried against the address by a large majority. Had the question been whether the Hanover troops should be continued, it would not have been a debate: but, it being well known that the contrary had been resolved upon before the meeting of Parliament, the moderate part of the opposition thought it was unnecessary, and might prove hurtful to address about it, and so voted with the court.'

You see how I am forced to lengthen out my letter by adding a borrowed scrap of news, which yet probably is no news to you. But, though I should show you nothing new, yet you must give me leave to show my inclination, at least, to acquit myself of the debts I owe you, and to declare myself,

Revd Sir,

your most faithful and obedient servant,

Geor: Cloyne

My wife and family join their compliments and sincere wishes to behold the Dean of Tuam at Cloyne.

[1645] Sir James Campbell of Lawers (*c.* 1680–1745). He was the commander of the English cavalry on the Continent and would die on 30 April 1745 in the battle of Fontenoy.

306 SMYTHE TO BERKELEY[1646]

BL Add. MS 39311, fol. 51.

Corke, 19 February 1744

My Lord,

Though I have not the honour of being known to your Lordship I hope you will excuse the liberty I now take of applying to you, in relation to Mr. Dallas, who solicits to be my curate, which I would readily grant, if he can obtain a good character from your Lordship, and that you will be so good to let me know in what manner he has behaved in your Diocese, that I may be enabled to give the Bishop of Corke[1647] such an account as may obtain his Lordship's approbation. I flatter myself your Lordship will honour me with a line, which will infinitely oblige

My Lord
your Lordship's
most humble
& most obedient
servant,
Strangford

307 BERKELEY TO GERVAIS

Stock, pp. xcv–xcvi (extract).

Cloyne, 16 March 1744

I think myself a piece of a prophet when I foretold that the Pretender's cardinal[1648] feigned to aim at your head, when he meant to strike you, like a skilful fencer, on the ribs. It is true, one would hardly think the French such bunglers: but this popish priest hath manifestly bungled so as to repair the breaches our own bunglers had made at home. This is the luckiest thing that could have happened, and will, I hope, confound all the measures of our enemies.

[1646] Philip Smythe* (1715–87), fourth Viscount Strangford.
[1647] Robert Clayton* (1695–1758).
[1648] Luce suggests the "Pretender's cardinal" is André-Hercule de Fleury (1653–1743). Fleury had died a year previous to this letter, in January 1743, but he did direct French foreign policy until his death.

I was much obliged and delighted with the good news you lately sent, which was yesterday confirmed by letters from Dublin. And though particulars are not yet known, I did not think fit to delay our public marks of joy, as a great bonfire before my gate, firing of guns, drinking of healths, etc. I was very glad of this opportunity to put a little spirit into our drooping Protestants of Cloyne, who have of late conceived no small fears on seeing themselves in such a defenceless condition among so great a number of Papists elated with the fame of these new enterprises in their favour. It is indeed terrible to reflect, that we have neither arms nor militia in a province where the Papists are eight to one, and have an earlier intelligence than we have of what passes: by what means I know not; but the fact is certainly true.

Good Mr. Dean[1649] (for Dean I will call you, resolving not to be behind your friends in Dublin), you must know that to us who live in this remote corner many things seem strange and unaccountable that may be solved by you who are near the fountain head. Why are draughts made from our forces when we most want them? Why are not the militia arrayed? How comes it to pass that arms are not put into the hands of Protestants, especially since they have been so long paid for? Did not our ministers know for a long time past that a squadron was forming at Brest? Why did they not then bruise the cockatrice in the egg? Would not the French works at Dunkirk have justified this step? Why was Sir John Norris[1650] called off from the chase when he had his enemies in full view, and was even at their heels with a superior force? As we have two hundred and forty men-of-war, whereof one hundred and twenty are of the line, how comes it that we did not appoint a squadron to watch and intercept the Spanish Admiral with his thirty millions of pieces of eight? In an age wherein articles of religious faith are canvassed with the utmost freedom, we think it lawful to propose these scruples in our political faith, which in many points wants to be enlightened and set right.[1651]

Your last was writ by the hand of a fair lady to whom both my wife and I send our compliments as well as to yourself: I wish you joy of being able to write yourself. My cholic is changed to gout and sciatica, the tar water having drove it into my limbs, and, as I hope, carrying it off by those ailments, which are nothing to the cholic.

[1649] Isaac Gervais* (1680–1756) was formally announced as dean of Tuam in May 1744, but the appointment had been decided months earlier.

[1650] Sir John Norris (1670/71–1749) was an admiral in the home fleet.

[1651] Berkeley's discussion of political tensions with France was prescient. War with France was declared in March 1744.

308 BERKELEY TO THE DUBLIN JOURNAL

Dublin Journal *1865 (8–12 May 1744): 2.*

8–12 May 1744

DUBLIN
Directions for the making and using Tar-Water
by the Author of *Siris*

To prevent mistakes in the making tar-water, the public is desired to take notice that Norway tar, which is liquid and of a brown colour, is fittest for this purpose. Four quarts of cold water having been poured on a quart of this tar, and strongly stirred together with a flat stick for three or four minutes, must, after it has stood eight and forty hours to settle, be poured off and kept for use, either in bottles or other vessels corked up. The same tar will not do well a second time, but may serve for other uses. Water drawn off the tar, the second or third time, if long stirred, may be as strong as the first water, but has not that spirit, and is more disagreeable to the stomach.

After various trials I fix on this as a good general rule, which may yet be varied as people have stronger or weaker stomachs: putting less water or stirring it more[1652] makes it weaker, as putting less water or stirring it longer gives it more strength. But it should never be made too strong for the stomach; weaker constitutions require milder medicines. For this everyone's experience is the best guide. It should not be lighter than French or deeper coloured than Spanish white wine. If a spirit be not sensibly perceived on drinking, either the tar was bad or already used, or the tar-water carelessly made. He that would have it good should see it made himself.

Alternatives in general, taken little and often, mix best with the blood. Of tar-water one pint a day may do in chronical cases, drunk on an empty stomach either at two or four doses, to wit, night and morning and two or three hours after dinner or breakfast; but to children it should be given in less quantity. It may be drunk cold or warm, as anyone likes best, but in acute cases, as fevers of all kinds and pleurisies, it should be drank warm and in bed, as much and as often as the patient can bear. For instance, half-a-pint or even a whole pint every hour, which will be made easy by the heat and thirst of the patient. I never knew it fail in the most threatening fevers. For outward fomentations or for beasts to drink, it may be made much stronger by infusion of warm water. I am persuaded tar-water may be drunk with great safety and success for the curing of most

---

[1652] Luce changes the line, switching "more" and "less," correcting an obvious error of Berkeley's.

diseases, particularly all foul cases, ulcers and eruptions, scurvies of all kinds, nervous disorders, inflammatory distempers, decays, etc.

309 BERKELEY TO GERVAIS [1653]

TCD MS 2167, fol. 5.

Cloyne, 30 May 1744

Revd Sir,

With my own I send you the sincere congratulations of all here on your promotion to the Deanery of Tuam, which agreeable news was brought us by the last pacquets and without compliment gave us more pleasure than all the victories of this war put together. From what I had heard of courts and ministers I began to suspect their dilatory proceedings in your affair. But it seems they have turned out honest at last. I conclude you are in motion between Tuam, Dublin and Lismore, so to direct a letter to you is the same thing as to shoot flying. I have therefore small hopes of this finding you, but could not dispense with doing my part on this occasion and assuring you that I am Revd Sir,

your most obedient & affectionate servant,

G: Cloyne

Our rocks and groves & stands as well as my wife & brother & all this neighbourhood long to wish you joy in person.

310 WARD TO BERKELEY [1654]

Newcastle Journal *291 (3 November 1744).*

8 June 1744 [1655]

I have been afflicted with an asthma upwards of twelve years, which, for the first five, was more moderate than it has been since. For, during the

[1653] The letter is printed in Luce, "Some Unpublished Berkeley Letters with some New Berkeleiana," 152–53.

[1654] Before the letter is printed "Agreeable to our promise, and the request of many of our readers, we now insert the following case of Mr. Ward, as some time ago sent to the Bishop of Cloyne." The letter (and Berkeley's reply) appear verbatim in *Scot's Magazine* (November 1744): 515. It is worth noting that *Scot's Magazine* excerpted and printed large bits of Berkeley's *Siris* and a letter to Prior about tar water in its June 1744 (pp. 279–84) and July 1744 (pp. 325–32) issues.

[1655] Date taken from Prior's* *Authentic Narrative*, sec. 33, where Prior excerpts a portion of it and lists the date of the letter addressed to Berkeley definitively as 8 June 1744.

last seven years, I have very rarely been able to lie a-bed once in a year, and then not above three or at most four hours altogether, when I flattered myself with being tolerably well. And at those times, upon waking out of my sleep, I always found the bed so hot, and my self under an appression, as if loaded with phlegm (though mine is a dry asthma) that I was obliged to rise immediately, and have recourse to a pipe of tobacco, which I always use when I am very ill. For I have not the least ease when I do not smoke; though I apprehend is must increase my heat, as I am of a thin habit, and therefore cannot afford to throw off much saliva: but I am compelled to this method for present relief.

My fit seldom leave me above three or four days before they return, and continue for about the same time; though those periods are not near equal, for the least change of weather bring on a fit. I am afraid this asthma will prove more inveterate, and be harder to cure, as I have some reason to doubt it is hereditary. For my grandmother died of this distemper, though in an advanced age, and my father now has it; though neither of them so constantly, or so violently afflicted with it, as my self.

I have had and followed the advice of many of the most eminent physicians; the methods I have been put into, and the medicines I have taken are innumerable; and all without benefit. Formerly I had issues on my shoulders, and at present I have one under each breast; though I cannot boast of any advantage from these. For a fortnight past I have been induced to try the virtues of *tar-water*: I drink it every night and morning, about one third of a pint at a time: I find it gently opens my body by stool; but my fits visit me as often and as violently as ever.

The Bishop's answer will be inserted in our next.

311 BERKELEY TO PRIOR

LR, pp. 283–85.

Cloyne, 19 June 1744

To drink or not to drink! that is the doubt,
With *pro* and *con* the learn'd would make it out.

Britons, drink on! the jolly prelate cries:
What the prelate persuades the doctor denies.
But why need the parties so learnedly fight,
Or choleric *Jurin* so fiercely indite?
Sure our senses can tell if the liquor be right.
What agrees with his stomach, and what with his head,
The drinker may feel, though he can't write or read.
Then authority's nothing: the doctors are men:
And *who drinks tar-water will drink it again.*

Dear Tom,

Last night being unable to sleep for the heat, I fell into a reverie on my pillow, which produced the foregoing lines; and it is all the answer I intend for Dr. Jurin's[1656] letter, for that I am told is the writer's name of a pamphlet addressed to me, and which was sent me from London. When you cause these lines to be printed in the public papers, you will take care to have them transcribed, that the verses may not be known to be mine. Because you desire remarks on the affidavits (things very obvious to make), I send them back to you, who will remark yourself. I send you at the same time a letter which I formerly wrote, before you sent the affidavits, as you will see by the date, but never sent, having changed my mind as to appearing myself in that affair, which can be better managed by a third hand. Let one of the letters, cut and stitched in marble paper, be sent to every body in Dublin to whom a book was given; and let one of the copies be sent Mr. Innys,[1657] to be printed in the same size in London; also for the magazine, where you talk of getting it inserted.

[1656] James Jurin (1684–1750). Jurin was a fellow (1717) and secretary of the Royal Society (1721–27). He was famous for his defense of the use of inoculation for combating small pox. He previously published works attacking Berkeley. His *Geometry no Friend to Infidelity* (1734) and *The Minute Mathematician* (1735) were critiques of Berkeley's *Analyst*. Luce reports that a letter dated 1744 in the library of the Royal College of Physicians (of which Jurin would later be president [in 1750]) entitled *A Letter to the Right Rev. the Bishop of Cloyne Occasioned by his Lordship's Treatise on the Virtues of Tar-water* was written by Jurin. See *Works*, vol. IX, p. 117.

[1657] William Innys (?–?) or John Innys (?–?), London booksellers and publishers.

I wish you to send the two volumes of *Universal History*,[1658] the six tomes of Wilkins's *Councils*,[1659] and the books from Innys, in a box together, to be left for me at Mr. Harper's in Cork. All here are yours. Adieu.

    yours affectionately,

    G. Cloyne

312 BERKELEY TO WARD[1660]

Newcastle Journal *292 (10 November 1744)*.

c. July 1744

In common asthmas *tar-water* hath been very successful; but so old, hereditary, and violent a case as yours, is extremely difficult to cure: And yet I am not without hopes of your being relieved by it, if the tar-water be regularly and constantly taken for a length of time.

Drink it copiously, little and often; for this will less offend your Stomach, and mix better with your blood. For a few weeks take a pint a day, at four glasses, and at such distance from your meals, as not to create a nauseating; and as soon as your stomach is reconciled to it, proceed to drink more, till you arrive at 8 glasses, or a quart, in 24 hours; which you must continue or lessen as your stomach can bear. See your tar-water made, cover it close till it is quite clear, keep it bottled and well cork'd for use. Take no other medicines along with it. Tobacco is an anodyne,[1661] I would not dissuade the use of it.

Be temperate in meats and drinks, both in quantity and quality. I believe you should beware of salt meats, or enflaming sauces or liquors. I apprehend, that food which warms, but not inflames, may be good, viz. onions, celery, and the like, dressed; particularly eat garlic, and season your meat with it. Beware of evening or night air. Go to bed bedtimes; and rise early. I imagine it may be worth your trial to get made a sloping or steep bedstead, from the head towards the foot, with a foot-board at the lower end; and also to provide a leathern matelas,[1662] stuffed with curled hair, to lie on, as being much cooler than a feather bed.

[1658] *An Universal History from the Earliest Account of Time to the Present*, 9 vols. (London: J. Batley et al., 1736–50).

[1659] David Wilkins, *Concilia Magnae Britanniae et Hiberniae a Synodo Verolamiensi A.D. 446 ad Londiniensem A.D. 1717* (London, 1737).

[1660] Printed in answer to Ward's letter (Letter 310). The letter (and Ward's preceeding letter) appear verbatim in *Scot's Magazine* (November 1744): 515–16.

[1661] Either a pain-killing medicine or something that is inoffensive.

[1662] In modern parlance, a mattress. See David Berman, "The Good Bishop: New Letters," in *Berkeley and Irish Philosophy* (London: Continuum, 2007), p. 217.

313 WARD TO BERKELEY[1663]

Thomas Prior, Authentic Narrative *(London, 1746), § 34–36 (extract).*

27 July 1744

[. . .] I now relate to you the success I have met with from the tar-water. The first month I took it, my fits were as violent and frequent as usual. The second month I had not one fit, but one night, which was very easy; and I believe I might have continued to have found a daily benefit, if I had not been obliged to attend at the assizes; where I have received a most violent cold, which has brought on both my asthma and a cough. So that at present I am very ill, but am taking all the care I can now to recover myself; for I found so much pleasure in that month's ease, that no temptation can induce me to swerve from rules. I can't so much as lie back in an easy chair; for I have a table set by the side of my chair, with pillows on it, so I lay my arm on them, and my head on my arm; and if I am very ill, can't even rest that way, so that no bed can be contrived for me to rest on yet; and though I say above, that I had not a fit for a month, yet if I lay back in my chair then, it made me uneasy in two minutes: I drank tar-water frequently in the day, but not a quarter of a pint at a time, for I find it agrees better with my stomach, than drinking a larger quantity; and in the day, I may take such a quantity five or six times, as agrees with me. I must beg to take notice of one very great effect it has had on me (which I hope is a good symptom).

Before I drank the tar-water, my feet were always as cold as ice, so that I had not the least perspiration in them; for if I had not washed them for a year, they were as clean and dry as the back of my hand: but now, in the last month, I was so easy, I found my feet sweat very copiously, and found, in wearing a pair of new stockings only a week, that all the soles were worn and mouldered away; and what was left was very red, as if I had burnt them.

I beg pardon for dwelling so long upon this particular, as it was so surprising; and my apothecary telling me, when I related it to him, that he was sure I should be cured by drinking the tar-water, as it had this effect; for it was what he and all my physicians had drove at, to make me have a perspiration in my feet, which was never in their power to get, not even by sitting with my feet in warm water.

[1663] That the letter is addressed to Berkeley is evidenced from the previous, 8 June 1744 letter (Letter 310) and Berkeley's reply. Berkeley apparently handed them over to Prior for publication in *Authentic Narrative.*

314 BERKELEY TO HANMER[1664]

MS *unknown. Printed in Sir Henry Bunbury,* The Correspondence of Sir Thomas Hanmer, *Bart. (London: Edward Moxon, 1838), pp. 230–32.*

Cloyne, 21 August 1744

Sir,

As I am with particular esteem and respect your humble servant, so I heartily wish your success in the use of tar-water may justify the kind things you say on that subject. But, since you are pleased to consult me about your taking it, I shall without further ceremony tell you what I think, how ill soever a physician's air may become one of my profession. Certainly, if I may conclude from parallel cases, there is room to entertain good hopes of yours: both giddiness and relaxed fibres having been, to my knowledge, much relieved by tar-water. The sooner you take it, so much the better. I could wish you saw it made yourself, and strongly stirred. While it stands to clarify, let it be close covered, and afterwards bottled and well corked. I find it agrees with most stomachs, when stirred even five or six minutes, provided it be skimmed before bottling. You may begin with a pint a day, and proceed to a pint and a half, or even a quart, as it shall agree with your stomach. And you may take this quantity either in half-pint or quarter-pint glasses, at proper intervals in the twenty-four hours. It may be drunk indifferently, at any season of the year. It lays under no restraint, nor obliges you to go out of your usual course of diet. Only, in general, I suppose light suppers, early hours, and gentle exercise (so as not to tire) good for all cases. With your tar-water I wish you may take no other medicines. I have had much experience of it, and can honestly say I never knew it do harm. The ill effects of drugs show themselves soonest on the weakest persons; such are children; and I assure you that my two youngest children (when they were one three, and the other not two years old) took it, as a preservative against the small-pox, constantly for six months together without any inconvenience. Upon the whole, I apprehend no harm and much benefit in your case, and shall be very glad to find my hopes confirmed by a line from yourself, which will always be received as a great favour by, Sir,

> your most obedient and most humble servant,
> George Cloyne

[1664] Thomas Hanmer* (1677–1746), fourth Baronet.

315 BERKELEY TO PRIOR

LR, *pp. 286–89.*

3 September 1744

ON SIRIS AND ITS ENEMIES. BY A DRINKER OF TAR-WATER.

How can devoted Siris stand
Such dire attacks? The licens'd band,
With upcast eyes and visage sad,
Proclaim, 'Alas! the world's run mad.
'The prelate's book has turn'd their brains;
'To set them right will cost us pains.
'His drug too makes our patients sick;
'And this doth vex us to the quick.
And, vex'd they must be, to be sure,
To find tar-water cannot cure,
But makes men sicker still and sicker,
And fees come thicker still and thicker.
   Bursting with pity for mankind,
But to their own advantage blind,
Many a wight, with face of fun'ral,
From mortar, still, and urinal,
Hastes to throw in his scurvy mite
Of spleen, of dullness, and of spite,
To furnish the revolving moons
With pamphlets, epigrams, lampoons,
Against tar water. You'd know why?
Think who they are: you'll soon descry
What means each angry doleful ditty,
Whether themselves or us they pity.

Dear Tom,

   The doctors, it seems, are grown very abusive. To silence them, I send you the above scrap of poetry, which I would by no means have known or suspected for mine. You will therefore burn the original, and send a copy to be printed in a newspaper, or the *Gentleman's Magazine*.[1665] I must desire you to get some bookseller in Dublin to procure me the *History of the Learned*,[1666] and the *Gentleman's Magazine*, two pamphlets that come out monthly. For the time past I would have the *History* or *Memoirs of the Learned* for the months of May, June, and July past, and the *Magazine* for last July. For the future, I would be supplied with them every month.

It is to be noted, that tar-water is best made in glazed earthen vessels. I would have the foregoing sentence inserted in the English edition, and next Irish edition of the *Letter*, at the end of the section that recites the manner of making tar-water. It is very lately I made this remark, that it is finer and clearer when so made than if in unglazed crocks.

Pray send the numbers of our tickets in this lottery. My sister[1667] wrote to Mrs. Hamilton, but has got no answer. Perhaps her niece might have been cured of her sore eye since she left Dublin. I am, dear Tom,

> your affectionate humble servant,
> George Cloyne

Sept. 5, 1744[1668]

P.S.: When you send the other books I desire you to put up with them two dissertations of Whiston's,[1669] upon our Saviour's miracles, and upon the Eternity of Hell Torments, if this can be got in town; also half a guinea's worth (i.e. 25) *Gifts to Maid-Servants*,[1670] printed by Falkner.

September 3, 1744

[1665] The poem appeared in the October 1744 issue of *Gentleman's Magazine*.

[1666] Luce reports (*Works*, vol. IX, p. 118) that *The History of the Works of the Learned* started in 1737, but in fact the first issue appeared in January 1699. The first series ran for twelve years. In 1737 a periodical of the same name revived and continued until 1743, when it was replaced by *A Literary Journal* (1744–49), published in Dublin. The periodical attempted to give an overview of the state of European learning and was subtitled *Or an Impartial Account of Books Lately Printed in all Parts of Europe*.

[1667] Luce reports that Berkeley did have a sister (c. 1690–?) who married a MacCarthy of Blarney Castle, but little is known about her. See *Works*, vol. IX, p. 119.

[1668] LR has 5 September. Luce corrects to 3 September.

[1669] William Whiston* (1667–1752). The second work mentioned is his *The Eternity of Hell Torments Considered* (London, 1740). The first is unclear, but might be either *Account of the Demoniaks both in the New Testament, and in the First Four Centuries* (London, 1737) or an older work entitled *Mr. Whiston's Account of the Exact Time when Miraculous Gifts Ceas'd in the Church* (London, 1728).

[1670] Eliza Fowler Haywood (1693–1756), *A Present for a Servant-Maid. Or, the Sure Means of Gaining Love and Esteem* (1743). The book was advertised in Faulkner's *Dublin Journal* in 1744.

316 WARD TO BERKELEY[1671]

Thomas Prior, Authentic Narrative *(London, 1746), § 37 (excerpt).*

18 September 1744

[. . .] As to my present state of health, I have the pleasure to tell you, I was in bed the 10th, 11th, 12th and 15th instant at night; I went to bed about 8 o'clock, and lay until 7 the next morning, as well as ever I was in my life: and found, when I awaked, I was lying on my back; and am quite another man.

317 LINDEN TO BERKELEY[1672]

MS *unknown. Printed in D. W. Linden,* Siris: Grundliche Historische Nachricht vom Theer-Wasser *(Amsterdam and Leipzig: Peter Mortier, 1745), pp. 7–10.*

30 November 1744

Hochwuerdiger, in Gott Andaechtiger Vater [usw?]

Ew[iger] Hochwuerdiger Gnaden bitte ganz gehorsamst, um Vergebung, dass ich mich abermahlen unterstehte beschwerlich zu fallen, welches Sie aber zu vergeben, ich gewisser Hoffnung lebe. Ich habe vor ungefaehr zwei Monaten bei meiner letzten Anwesenheit zu Amsterdam das Vergnuegen gehabt zu sehen, dass Ew[iger] Hochwuerd[iger] Gnaden Dissertation, unter dem Titel Siris, vom Theer-Wasser, ins Franzoesische und Hollaendische uebersetzt wird: und ich bin ersucht worden, eine gleiches ins Hochdeutsche damit zu unternehmen, welches denn auch in soweit uebernommen, dass einen Auszug in einer so viel mir moeglichen, ob zwar nicht gar zu angenehm doch begreiflichen Schreibart daraus liefern wolle. Weilen aber gerne dieses Endzwecks wegen wissen moechte, ob der erste Gebrauch des Theer-Wassers von denen Indianern, oder einer anderen Nation, unternommen sei, wie viele Jahre es bei denselben im Gebrauch gewesen, und auf was Art Ew[iger] Hochwuerd[iger] Gnaden zuerste Kundschaft von dieser Medizin erhalten, dessgleichen wenn dieselbe noch einige andere zu dieser Sachen gehoerige Nachricht besitzen, so will gleichfalls ganz gehorsamst darum gebeten haben [usw?].
London, den 30 Nov. 1744

[1671] That this letter is addressed to Berkeley is evidenced from the previous, 8 June 1744 letter and Berkeley's reply. Berkeley apparently handed them over to Prior for publication in *Authentic Narrative.*
[1672] D. W. Linden (?–after 1768). See *Works*, vol. IX, p. 119.

Honourable, God devoted father [etc.][1673]

Your honourable Grace, I most obediently beg your pardon that I, once again, dare to trouble you, but which, I certainly hope, you will forgive me. About two months ago, during my last visit to Amsterdam, I had the pleasure to see that Your revered Grace's treatise on tar-water is going to be translated into French and Dutch: And I have been asked to do the same into High German; which I then took upon myself in so far that I intend to render an excerpt of this [written] in as understandable a language [style] as I am able, though it might not be really too pleasing. But exactly for this purpose I would like to know whether tar-water was first used by Indians or by some other Nation, how many years these people used it, and by what means Your honourable Grace first learned about this medicine; at the same time, if you know about some other news concerning this matter, I would also most obediently beg you to pass it on [etc.?]

318 BERKELEY TO LINDEN[1674]

MS *unknown. Printed as an appendix to* Siris. Recherches sur les Vertus de l'eau de Goudron, ou l'on a Joint des Réfléxions Philosophiques sur Divers Autres Sujets
(Amsterdam: Pierre Mortier, 1745).

3 Décembre 1744

En réponse aux questions que vous me faites touchant l'eau de goudron, voici ce que j'ai à vous dire.

Je n'ai jamais sçû qu'on en fit usage dans aucune des parties de l'Amérique où j'ai été, mais j'ai appris qu'on la prenoit en Caroline comme un préservatif contre la petite vérole; c'est ce qui me fit résoudre, lorsque cette maladie régnoit dans mon diocèse, d'en tenter l'expérience. Le succès fut admirable; non seulement en qualité de préservatif, mais en qualité de remède. Ce qui m'engagea à tirer de là plusieurs conséquences, à faire divers raisonnemens et divers [diverses] expériences, concernant l'usage de l'eau de goudron, dans

---

[1673] The Jessop translation (see *Works*, IX, p. 119) is a bit freer. I have endeavored to provide a more literal translation since the original language is present.

[1674] This letter appears in a French translation of Berkeley's *Siris*. Linden includes a German translation of the letter in his *Siris: Grundliche Historische Nachricht vom Theer-Wasser*, pp. 7–10. See *Works*, vol. VIII, pp. 274–75 and vol. IX, p. 119. Changes to make the French more readable are made in square brackets.

l'autres [d'autres] maladies, aussi bien que dans la petite vérole, pour laquelle seule j'avois ouï dire qu'on s'en servît en Amérique. Mais au lieu que l'eau dont on use en Caroline est épaisse et dégoutante, je trouvai les moyens, après des essais réitérés, d'en faire d'une autre sorte, qui est claire et nullement désagréable. J'ai trouvé par quantité d'expériences que ses vertus sont d'une grande efficace dans la plupart des maladies, si ce n'est même dans toutes. Mais tout cela est exposé plus au long dans la seconde édition du [de la?] *Siris* faite à Dublin, et spécialement dans une lettre à Mr. T. P. qu'on ajoute à cette édition, que j'ai donné ordre de vous envoyer de Dublin, à cause qu'elle contient divers changemens qui rendront votre traduction plus récommandable [recommandable]. Quant à ce que vous demandez si ce sont les Indiens ou les Blancs, qui se sont avisés les premiers de l'usage de l'eau de goudron, je ne puis rien en dire avec certitude, mais je crois que ce sont les Indiens.

Pour votre autre question, sçavoir, comment je suis parvenu à découvrir la grande étendue de la vertu de cette eau, et ses différentes propriétés, je ne puis que répéter que j'ai déjà touché ci-dessus, sçavoir, que ç'a été en raisonnant, en faisant des observations et des expériences. C'est ce qui est déduit plus amplement dans la lettre que j'ai déjà citée. Je finis en priant Dieu de bénir votre entreprise, afin qu'elle tourne à votre satisfaction et à l'avantage du genre humain. Je suis, Monsieur, votre, etc.

De Cloyne le 3 Décembre 1744

In response to the questions you asked regarding tar-water, here is what I have to tell you.

I never knew a use of it has been made in any parts of America where I have been, but I heard it was taken in Carolina as a protection against smallpox; that was what made me decide, when that disease was reigning in my diocese, to try it. The success was admirable; not only in terms of its value as a protection [against smallpox], but also as a remedy. What engaged me to draw many conclusions from that, to make diverse deductions and diverse experiments regarding the use of tar-water, in other diseases, as well as with smallpox, for which alone I have heard it was used in America. But as the water used in Carolina is thick and disgusting, I found ways, after repeated trials, to make another kind, which is clear and not at all disagreeable. I have found by a lot of experiments that its virtues are greatly efficacious in most diseases, if not in all of them. But all of this is explained at greater length in the second edition of the *Siris* made in Dublin, and especially in a letter to Mr. T. P.[1675] which is added to this edition, that I ordered sent to you from Dublin because it contains diverse changes which will make your translation more commendable. Regarding what you are asking, whether it is the Indians or the Whites, who first became aware of the use of tar-water I cannot state with certitude, but I believe it was the Indians.

Regarding your other question, that is, how I came to discover the wide range of the powers of this water's virtues, and its different properties, I can only repeat what I have already mentioned above, that is, that it happened while reasoning, making observations and [conducting] experiments. This is what is concluded more fully in the letter I have already cited. I finish by praying for God to bless your enterprise, in order to bring it to a satisfactory completion and to the advantage of all human kind. I am, Sir, your, etc.

319 WARD TO BERKELEY[1676]

Thomas Prior, Authentic Narrative (London, 1746), § 38 (extract).

16 January 1744/45

[. . .] I find the least cold does me harm, and therefore keep close to my house, which is no inconveniency to me, since I am all air and vivacity, which before was a mere state of hebetude. I was obliged to go on *November* 4 last into *Northumberland*, when it was very cold with snow; and as the roads would not admit of wheels, I was compelled to go on horseback; and when I had rode a mile easily (for it is only since I took tar-water I could ride above a mile on horseback) I found I was able to go faster, and put on so fast, that I observed by my watch, that I rode at the rate of six miles an hour. My journey was thirty-six miles, which I completed between the hours of ten in the morning, and four in the afternoon, without drawing bridle; I rested one day, and came home on *November* 6 in the same time.

This I declare upon my honour to be fact, and which was as great a surprize to myself as others.

[1675] Thomas Prior* (1681–1751).

[1676] That the letter is addressed to Berkeley is evidenced from the previous, 8 June 1744 letter (Letter 310) and Berkeley's reply (Letter 312). Berkeley apparently handed them over to Prior for publication in *Authentic Narrative*.

320 PHILANTHROPOS TO BERKELEY[1677]

Daily Gazetteer 5001 (5 April 1745).

5 April 1745

To the Right Reverend the Bishop of Cloyne

My Lord,

Upon the Foundation of some hints I took from the 29th and 49th sections of your *Siris*, I resolved to attempt a solution of myrrh, by a low, aqueous menstruum; and considering the affinity, and similar properties that are in tar, and in myrrh, I was led to think, that as all homogeneous bodies attract more strongly than those of different classes, so possibly, the native vegetable salt, or acid spirit of tar, when gently fermented, might invite the like principle from myrrh. Accordingly I put a drachm of coarse myrrh, without any delicacy of choice, into half a pint of tar-water, and set it in a pint bottle, in a degree of heat of my fire, equal to that of a hot sun: in two or three days I obtained so perfect a solution, that, upon filtering, I found no other residuum, than such as is apt to stick to gummy bodies.

Of this infusion, I mix about half an ounce in each half-pint of tar-water, which I daily drink; and take them so mixed, with good success. It makes the tar-water much more pleasant, giving it an agreeable sub-acid-bitter taste.

The second process I used, after having spent my first preparation, was very inaccurate; for I threw in an indeterminate quantity (but as near as I can guess) four drachms of fine picked myrrh to a pint of tar-water. Upon filtering off this infusion, I had cause to think the tar-water was more than saturated with myrrh, because, among the residuum, I found a kind of stacte, or fine, transparent, liquid myrrh, of the consistency of the best turpentine; which, however, might perhaps have yielded to a longer infusion.

To you, my Lord, we owe the tar-water; and to you, how nearly had we owed the solution of myrrh? Since you furnished the only aqueous menstruum that will dissolve and render it fit for internal use. As your Lordship suggested the first hint, so I know no person so capable of improving, and so willing to apply this discovery (if it be one) to the good of mankind as your Lordship. To you, therefore, I address it, with all its virtues, all its honours. For my part, I have not skill enough in any branch of medical knowledge, to assure me whether there be any thing new or valuable in this experiment of mine, only I conjecture, that at least it must be a good vulnerary water. But, were the secret as rich as the treasures of *Loretto*, both my fortune and my love

---

[1677] This letter is reprinted in Thomas Prior,* *Authentic Narrative* (London, 1746), §§ 58–60.

to mankind, forbid me to make any private advantage of it; therefore I freely give it to the publick under your Lordship's patronage. I am, with great duty and esteem,

> your Lordship's most obedient humble servant,
> Philanthropos

321 BERKELEY TO GERVAIS

Stock, pp. xcvii–xcviii (extract).

3 June 1745

I congratulate with you on the success of your late dose of physic. The gout, as Dr. Sydenham[1678] styles it, is *amarissimum naturae pharmacum.*[1679] It throws off a sharp excrement from the blood to the limbs and extremities of the body, and is not less useful than painful. I think, Mr. Dean, you have paid for the gay excursion you made last winter to the metropolis and the Court. And yet, such is the condition of mortals, I foresee you will forget the pain next winter, and return to the same course of life which brought it on.

As to our warlike achievements, if I were to rate our successes by our merits, I could forebode little good.[1680] But if we are sinners, our enemies are no saints. It is my opinion we shall heartily maul one another, without any signal advantage on either side. How the sullen English squires who pay the piper will like this dance, I cannot tell. For my own part, I cannot help thinking that land expeditions are but ill suited either to the force or interest of England; and that our friends would do more if we did less on the continent.

Were I to send my son from home, I assure you there is no one to whose prudent care and good nature I would sooner trust him than yours.[1681] But, as I am his physician, I think myself obliged to keep him with me. Besides, as after so long an illness his constitution is very delicate, I imagine this warm vale of Cloyne is better suited to it than your lofty and exposed situation of Lismore.

[1678] Thomas Sydenham (1624–89), a physician who published *Tractatus de Podagra et Hydrope* (*Treatise on Gout and Dropsy*) in 1683.

[1679] "nature's most bitter drug."

[1680] England is at war with France and Spain.

[1681] Likely a reference to Berkeley's eldest son, Henry* (1729–after 1756). Berkeley previously refers to him as having a delicate constitution.

Nevertheless, my wife and I are extremely obliged by your kind offer, and concur in our hearty thanks for it.

322 BERKELEY TO WILMOT[1682]

Yale, Osborn Files "B," folder 1184.

28 June 1745

Sir,

The letter you honoured me with is just come to my hands. I acknowledge with all respect and thankfulness his Excellency's favour, in offering me an income at least double to that of Cloyne, though my circumstances and views will not permit me to accept it. Quiet and content have nailed me down to this corner, to which I am also invested by an indisposition that ill consists with moving from place to place. This hath kept me these eight years past from seeing Dublin and if it should deprive me of the pleasure of presenting my thanks in person, yet nothing shall ever make me lose the sense of his Excellency's most generous and unmerited favour, to whom I entreat you to present my humblest returns of duty and gratitude for the honour he has done me. Though nothing could flatter a man's vanity more than the being known to have been distinguished by the Earl of Chesterfield,[1683] yet I shall sacrifice that to the secrecy the present case requires.

The goodness expressed in your obliging letter, and in recollecting one who has lived so long out of the world demands my best thanks. At the same time, I beg leave to congratulate your coming into this kingdom with our Lord Lieutenant, in such an honourable post, which that it may be attended with all happiness and prosperity is the hearty wish of

Sir

your most obedient humble servant,

George Cloyne

Cloyne June 28, 1745

[1682] The letter is not addressed, but notes in the file at Yale indicate the recipient to be Sir Robert Wilmot (?-?) in the service of the lord lieutenant of Ireland, William Cavendish (1698–1755), third Duke of Devonshire. A note (apparently in the hand of Wilmot) on the back of the letter reads "1745 Bishop of Cloyne, 28th of June, refusing the Bishopric of Clogher, offered him by my Lord Lieutenant." See David Berman, "Mrs. Berkeley's Annotations in her Interleaved Copy of *An Account of the Life of George Berkeley (1776),*" *Hermathena* 122 (1977): esp. 24.
[1683] Philip Dormer Stanhope* (1694–1773), fourth Earl of Chesterfield.

323 BERKELEY TO HIS CLERGY[1684]

Dublin Journal 1942 (15–19 October 1745).

15–19 October 1745

My Reverend Brethren,

You are, I doubt not, sufficiently apprised of the calamities that must attend our being governed by a popish prince, as well as of the steps that are now taken to bring this about. If there be in some other part of His Majesty's[1685] dominions any Protestant subjects so infatuated to flatter themselves with hopes of enjoying their religious and civil rights under such a head, I dare say there are none such to be found among the Protestants of this kingdom, and least of all among the clergy, whose sure ruin is involved in that of the established Church, which, whatever quarter she may hope for elsewhere, can most assuredly, hope for none in Ireland.

To confirm this (could it be supposed to want confirmation) I can assure you from [a] very credible and unsuspected authority that upon an invasion in the late reign, when those who drew up the Pretender's manifesto had inserted a clause for securing the Churches of England and Ireland, as by law established, the Church of Ireland was struck out by his own hand. I say not this as if I suspected your loyalty, for whatever some prejudiced enemies to your order may suggest, no candid person will suppose you to be wicked without temptation.

I am persuaded no part of His Majesty's subjects are more loyal than our brethren of the established Church in this kingdom, and they have every motive spiritual and temporal to make them peculiarly so. It may not, nevertheless, be improper to stir up your apprehensions at the present critical juncture for yourselves and your flocks, who on this southern coast are most exposed to an invasion and (as our enemies too well know) least prepared against it. You will not therefore be wanting, to excite the people under your care to make proper remonstrances where they may be likeliest to take effect, and to concert measures for their common safety.

The worse we are provided with others, the better should we provide ourselves with spiritual weapons—humiliation, repentance, prayer, and trust in God. For be assured we never had, humanly speaking, so bad a chance for our religious liberties as at this time, if we should be so unhappy as to see the present

---

[1684] This and the next letter were published as "Two Letters on the occasion of the Jacobite Rebellion 1745" (*Works*, vol. VI, pp. 223–30). It was published in George Faulkner's *Dublin Journal* on the front page. The letter was reprinted in the 1752 *Miscellany*. This is an open letter prompted by the Jacobite rebellion and the landing in Scotland of the Young Pretender, Prince Charles Edward Stuart* (1720–88), in July 1745.

[1685] George II* (1683–1760).

enterprise succeed and a popish prince, nursed and brought up in the very bosom of spiritual blindness and superstition, placed on the throne.

The reign of the late King James[1686] produced few converts to his religion. But the great number of infidels which have since sprung up, how clamorous and vehement soever they may seem against Popery, may yet be presumed ready for a temporal interest to embrace it. Nor is it uncharitable to suppose that those who are inwardly of none will be outwardly of the court religion. From this quarter, as I know our adversaries conceive the greatest hopes, so I apprehend we have most to fear.

It behoveth us, therefore, my brethren, in this critical and dangerous con-juncture, not to behave (in the prophet's phrase)[1687] like dumb dogs, but to be earnest and instant in calling on our people to exert themselves with prudence and fortitude, and in putting up our prayers to Almighty God that He would avert the evils which threaten us, and that He would not deal with us according to our merits but His mercies, nor suffer the glorious light and liberty of the Reformation to be quenched or withdrawn for the sins of those who, by abusing them, have showed themselves unworthy of such inestimable blessings. I am,

> your faithful and affectionate brother,
> G. Cloyne

324 BERKELEY TO THE ROMAN CATHOLICS OF THE DIOCESE OF CLOYNE[1688]

Dublin Journal 1942 (15–19 October 1745).

15–19 October 1745

My Countrymen and Fellow Subjects,

Notwithstanding the differences of our religious opinions, I should be sorry to be wanting in any instance of humanity or good neighbourhood to any of you. For which reason I find myself strongly inclined, at this critical juncture, to put you in mind that you have been treated with a truly Christian lenity under the present government; that your persons have been protected and your properties secured

---

[1686] James II (James VII) (1633–1701).

[1687] Isaiah 56:10.

[1688] This letter is published in George Faulkner's *Dublin Journal* on the front page, not far after the letter to his clergy (Letter 323). The following week's *Journal* (19–22 October 1745) reprints the letter, noting "There having been a great demand for the following letter, it is again reprinted at the earnest request of several Protestants, as well as Roman Catholics." It was reprinted in the 1752 *Miscellany*. This is an open letter prompted by the Jacobite rebellion and the landing in Scotland of the Young Pretender, Prince Charles Edward Stuart* (1720–88), in July 1745.

by equal laws; and that it would be highly imprudent as well as ungrateful to forfeit these advantages by making yourselves tools to the ambition of foreign princes, who fancy it expedient to raise disturbances among us at present, but as soon as their own ends are served, will not fail to abandon you, as they have always done.

Is it not evident that your true interest consists in lying still and waiting the event, since Ireland must necessarily follow the fate of England; and that therefore prudence and policy prescribe quiet to the Roman Catholics of this kingdom, who, in case a change of hands should not succeed, after your attempting to bring it about, must then expect to be on a worse foot than ever?

But we will suppose it succeeds to your wish. What then? Would not this undermine even your own interests and fortunes, which are often interwoven with those of your neighbours? Would not all those who have debts or money or other effects in the hands of Protestants be fellow sufferers with them? Would not all those who hold under the Acts of Settlement be as liable as Protestants themselves to be dispossessed by the old proprietors? Or can even those who are styled proprietors flatter themselves with hopes of possessing the estates which they claim, which, in all likelihood, would be given to favourites (perhaps to foreigners) who are near the person, or who fought the battles, of their master.

Under Protestant governments those of your communion have formerly enjoyed a greater share of the lands of this kingdom, and more ample privileges. You bore your part in the magistracy and the legislature, and could complain of no hardships on the score of your religion. If these advantages have been since impaired or lost, was it not by the wrong measures yourselves took to enlarge them, in several successive attempts, each of which left you weaker and in a worse condition than you were before? And this notwithstanding the vaunted succours of France and Spain, whose vain efforts in conjunction with yours constantly recoiled on your own heads, even when your numbers and circumstances were far more considerable than they now are.

You all know these things to be true. I appeal to your own breasts. Dearbought experience hath taught you, and past times instruct the present. But perhaps you follow conscience rather than interest. Will any men amongst you pretend to plead conscience against being quiet, or against paying allegiance and peaceable submission to a Protestant prince, which the first Christians paid even to heathen, and which those of your communion at this day pay to Mahometan and to idolatrous princes in Turkey and China, and which you yourselves have so often professed to pay to our present gracious Sovereign? Conscience is quite out of the case. And what man in his senses would engage in a dangerous course to which neither interest doth invite nor conscience oblige him?

I heartily wish that this advice may be as well taken, as it is meant, and that you may maturely consider your true interest rather than rashly repeat the same errors which you have so often repented of. So, recommending you to the merciful guidance of Almighty God, I subscribe myself,

your real well-wisher,

George Cloyne

325 BERKELEY TO GERVAIS

NLI MS 2979. Stock, pp. xcviii–xcix.

24 November 1745

Revd sir,

You are in for life. Not all the philosophers have been saying these three thousand years on the vanity of riches, the cares of greatness, and the brevity of human life, will be able to reclaim you. However, as it is observed that most men have patience enough to bear the misfortunes of others, I am resolved not to break my heart for my old friend, if you should prove so unfortunate as to be made a bishop. The reception you met with from Lord Chesterfield[1689] was perfectly agreeable to his Excellency's character, who being so clairvoyant in everything else could not be supposed blind to your merit.

Your friends the Dutch have showed themselves, what I always took them to be, selfish and ungenerous. To crown all, we are now told the forces they sent us have private orders not to fight. I hope we shall not want them.

By the letter you favoured me with, I find the regents of our university have shown their loyalty at the expense of their wit. The poor dead Dean,[1690] though no idolater of the Whigs, was no more a Jacobite than Dr. Baldwin.[1691] And had he been even a Papist, what then? Wit is of no party.

[1689] Philip Dormer Stanhope* (1694–1773), fourth Earl of Chesterfield.

[1690] Jonathan Swift* (1667–1745) died 19 October. Stock recounts the occasion for Berkeley's remark in a note (1784, p. xcviii): "Immediately after Swift's death, the class of Senior Sophisters in the college of Dublin determined to apply a sum of money raised among themselves, and usually expended on an entertainment, to the purpose of honouring the memory of that great man by a bust to be set up in the college library. Provost Baldwin, being a staunch Whig, and having once smarted by an epigram of the Dean's, it was confidently thought, would have refused his consent to this measure, and the talk of the town about this time was, that the board of Senior Fellows would enter implicitly into the same sentiments. But the event soon proved the falsehood of such an unworthy report: the bust was admitted without the least opposition, and is now in the library."

[1691] Richard Baldwin (1666–1758), provost of Trinity College, Dublin. He would be provost for forty-one years (1717–58).

We have been alarmed with a report that a great body of rapparees[1692] is up in the county of Kilkenny: these are looked on by some as the forerunners of an insurrection. In opposition to this, our militia have been arrayed, that is, sworn: but alas! we want not oaths, we want muskets. I have bought up all I could get, and provided horses and arms for four-and-twenty of the Protestants of Cloyne, which, with a few more that can furnish themselves, make up a troop of thirty horse. This seemed necessary to keep off rogues in these doubtful times.

May we hope to gain a sight of you in the recess? Were I as able to go to town, how readily should I wait on my Lord Lieutenant and the Dean of Tuam![1693] My wife adds her compliments to mine, and we both desire the favor of you, to tender our service and best respects to Colonel Bryan and his Lady. I congratulate them both on their fine daughter's having escaped a very splendid and unfortunate match as I think it must have proved considering the conduct and behaviour of the party.

Your letters are so much tissue of gold and silver: in return I am forced to send you from this corner a patch-work of tailors' shreds, for which I entreat your compassion, and that you will believe me with great sincerity, Revd Sir,

> your most faithful and obedient servant,
> George Cloyne

Cloyne 9ber 24, 1745

326 BERKELEY TO PRIOR

LR, pp. 291–92. Stock, p. lxxvii.

Before 17 December 1745[?][1694]

Dear Tom,

The above letter contains a piece of advice which seems to me not unseasonable or useless. You may make use of Faulkner[1695] for conveying it to the public, without any intimation of the author.[1696] [I send you this inclosed bill on Swift & Co.,* which you will tender to them, and see that I have credit for it in their

---

[1692] From the Irish *ropairí*, meaning "pikemen." The term was a synonym at the time for Irish guerrillas.

[1693] Stock and Luce both omit the rest of the paragraph (from "My wife" to "the party.").

[1694] LR does not record a date, and Stock's dating of the letter in February 1746 must be wrong as the piece to be published (referred to in the letter) appeared in Faulkner's *Dublin Journal*, 17/21 December of 1745 (see Letter 327).

[1695] George Faulkner* (1703?–75).

[1696] The next sentence is omitted by Stock but is present in the LR version. It is oddly placed, and might well be an error in the LR.

books.] There is handed about a lampoon against our troop, which hath caused great indignation in the warriors of Cloyne.

I am informed that Dean Gervais[1697] had been looking for the *Querist*, and could not find one in the shops, for my Lord Lieutenant[1698] at his desire. I wish you could get one handsomely bound for his Excellency; or at least the last published relating to the bank, which consisted of excerpts out of the three parts of the *Querist*. I wrote to you before to procure two copies of this for his Excellency and Mr. Liddel. Adieu, dear Tom.

       your faithful humble servant,

       G. Cloyne

327 EUBULUS (BERKELEY) TO THE DUBLIN JOURNAL[1699]

Dublin Journal 1959 (17–21 December 1745).

17–21 December 1745

As several in this dangerous conjuncture have undertaken to advise the public, I am encouraged to hope that a hint concerning the dress of our soldiers may not be thought impertinent.

Whatever unnecessarily spends the force or strength of a man lessens its effect where it is necessary. The same force that carries one pound a hundred yards will carry two pounds but fifty yards; and so in proportion. The body of a man is an engine. Its force should be managed to produce its full effect where it is most wanted, and ought not, therefore, in time of action, to be dissipated on useless ornaments. There is a weight on our soldiers neither offensive nor defensive, but serving only for parade. This I would have removed; and the loss will not be much, if the man's vigour grows as his pomp lessens, *spectemur agendo*[1700] being the proper motto and ambition of warriors.

Sleeves, facings, caps, flaps, tall caps, double breasts, laces, frogs, cockades, plaited shirts, shoulder-knots, belts, and buttons more than enough are so many drawbacks or obstacles to a soldier's exerting his strength in the proper way, in

---

[1697] Isaac Gervais* (1680–1756).

[1698] Philip Dormer Stanhope* (1694–1773), fourth Earl of Chesterfield.

[1699] That the author is Berkeley is supported by the fact that this letter appears in *Literary Relics* (pp. 289–91) attached to an undated letter from Berkeley to Prior (see Letter 326). Luce makes additional observations that corroborate attributing the letter to Berkeley. See *Works*, vol. IX, p. 122 and Luce, "More Unpublished Berkeley Letters and New Berkeleiana," 45–50.

[1700] "let us be judged by what we do."

marching, fighting, and pursuing. Suppose two armies engage equal in strength, courage, and numbers, one clad in judges robes, the other in sailor's jackets; I need not ask on which side the advantage lies. The same holds proportionably in other cases, where the difference is less notorious.

Our sailors seem the best dressed of all our forces; and what is sufficient for a sailor may serve for a soldier. Their dress, therefore, I would recommend to the landmen, or if any other can be contrived yet more succinct and tight; that so our men may march and fight with the least incumbrance, their strength being employed upon their arms and enemies.

Soldiers thus clad will be more light, clever, and alert; and, when the eye hath been a little used to them, will look much better than in more cumbersome apparel. I may add too, that something will be saved to the men in the article of clothing.

I am, Sir, your humble servant,

Eubulus

328 EUBULUS (BERKELEY) TO THE DUBLIN JOURNAL[1701]

Dublin Journal 1964 (4–7 January 1745/46).

4–7 January 1746

Sir,

To a Greek or Roman eye what was apt or fit seemed decent. Their military dress, though far more succinct and tight than the civil, was not thought the less becoming; but our rude and Gothic eyes are taken with a great show. This false taste extends even to the men, who are chosen rather by measure than by fitness.

A soldier's end is fighting. This is best performed by strength and activity, neither of those can be rated by a man's stature. Many a tall body is heavy and ill made; and many a little compact fellow, though he may not fetch so weighty a stroke, or so large a stride, may yet make amends by fetching two strokes, or two steps for one. The make of a man is more to be considered than his bulk in the estimation of strength and agility.

The Roman standard reduced to our measure was but five feet four inches, and the Roman sword had a broad, strong pointed blade, not above fourteen or fifteen inches long; such were the men and such was the sword, that conquered the world.

But the modern discipline delighteth much in parade. This is a clog upon our levies and recruits, depriving the publick of the service of many a stout active

---

[1701] For evidence concerning the attribution of the letter, see note to Letter 327.

fellow, who falls short of the present standard. And yet such a one hath his advantages. At a distance he is a less mark, and in close fight less embarrassed, more nimble either to avoid or give a blow, he is fitter for dispatch in marches and pursuits, in passing through bad roads, in clambering over rocks and mountains, and scaling of walls, he is a less burthen on a horse or carriage.

Regiments of little active men may be fit for many peculiar services, where large-bodied men might not do so well; and those little men being formed into a distinct corps, the uniform appearance would be still preserved, and the eye pleased in a review.

And if such men are not so fit to fight with long swords or sabres, or clubbed muskets, yet they may succeed very well at other weapons. Long heavy sabres are not so easily managed as those short Roman swords—*habiles brevibus mucronibus enses.*[1702] It is more easy to ward off a stroke of the former, than a stroke or thrust of the latter, which being quickly redoubled, might be sped two or three for one.

A battalion of low, squat, well-set men, armed with Morrisons, targets, Roman swords, and blunderbusses, having made one fire, at a small distance, full in the face of the enemy, and instantly rushing on with their targets and short swords, would, if I mistake not, be found a match for any tall battalion.

I am, Sir, your humble Servant,

Eubulus

329 BERKELEY TO GERVAIS

Stock, p. xcvi (extract).

6 January 1746

Two days ago I was favoured with a very agreeable visit from Baron Mountnay[1703] and Mr. Bristow.[1704] I hear they have taken Lismore in their way to Dublin. We want a little of your foreign fire to raise our Irish spirits in this heavy season. This makes your purpose of coming very agreeable news. We will chop politics together, sing *Io Paean* to the Duke,[1705] revile the Dutch, admire the

---

[1702] Literally "manageable swords with short blades," but, more loosely, "nimble short-bladed swords."

[1703] Richard Mountenay (1707–68). He was baron of the Irish Exchequer and editor of *Demosthenes*, a collection of the orator's speeches (London: R. Griffiths, 1748).

[1704] Probably Peter Bristow (?–1769), vicar-choral of Cork and author of the comedy *The Harlequins* (London, 1753).

[1705] William Augustus (1721–65), Duke of Cumberland, third son of King George II* (1683–1760). The duke commanded the English forces at Culloden, where the Jacobite rebels were defeated on 16 April 1746.

King of Sardinia, and applaud the Earl of Chesterfield,[1706] whose name is sacred all over this island except Lismore; and what should put your citizens of Lismore out of humour with his Excellency I cannot comprehend. But the discussion of these points must be deferred to your wished-for arrival.

330 EUBULUS (BERKELEY) TO THE DUBLIN JOURNAL[1707]

Dublin Journal 1973 (4–8 February 1745/46).

4–8 February 1746

Sir,

Pro aris et focis[1708] hath been always esteemed the strongest motive to fighting. Foreigners want this motive, and therefore should not be depended on. Its own proper militia and soldiers raised at home, are the natural defence of a country. Great evils have ensued from calling in foreigners; history is full of such examples. Hence all wise nations have provided a domestic strength, by training up their youth to arms. The young Romans were betimes accustomed to military exercise; therefore, their levies were not made from raw men. Among the Greeks, gymnastic sports were accounted a necessary part of education. Both the Roman and Grecian games were calculated to promote strength and activity, and to fit men for war.

Public games are necessary to keep up the spirits and good humour of a people; and if games, why not martial games? To fence, race, wrestle, shoot at a mark, or go through military exercise would not be less diverting because useful. In former times, warlike sports, particularly shooting at buts, were the prevailing humour, encouraged also, and provided for by authority. The British youth were thus bred to arms. England was once a kingdom of warriors, and France felt the effects of it. We used indeed—but that spirit is gone. Witness the late inroad of our Highland neighbours, who have taught us a lesson never to be forgot.

They have showed us what a change hath been wrought by the disuse of arms, and that albeit we breathe the same air we are not the same men, which under our Edwards and Henrys followed their landlords into France. Notwithstanding the conduct and bravery of our leaders, it was impossible the regular troops could fly to every part. But a well-trained militia would have been ready in all places to oppose those invaders, and save the nation's honour, from being

---

[1706] Philip Dormer Stanhope* (1694–1773), fourth Earl of Chesterfield.
[1707] For evidence concerning the attribution of the letter, see note to Letter 327.
[1708] "Before the altars and hearths."

insulted by a handful of rebels. Would Swiss or Swedish peasants and burghers have tamely looked on such bold intruders?

Some are apt to undervalue a militia. But in effect what difference is there, after a long peace, between regular troops and militia? Did England ever make a greater figure than it hath done in former times by its militia? In our own times have not the militia of Sweden shown themselves an overmatch for a disciplined army of Danes? and nearer home, have not the northern rebels played their part at Sheriffmuir[1709] and Preston Pans[1710] as well as regular troops? and was not this solely owing to their having been accustomed to arms? It is not the name, the apparel, or the ornaments that make a soldier, but the familiar use of arms, a body hardened by toil, an intrepid heart and a resolute mind; talents to be found in labouring peasants, miners or tradesmen, if duly trained and exercised; and nowhere more likely to be found than in Englishmen. The military art like all others is attained by practice, strength and courage grow by repeated acts. Novelty startles but frequency lessens surprize. The use of his own arms may be terrible as well as awkward to a novice. These are truths not unknown but overlooked; if men asleep may be said to overlook.

I will not, nevertheless, presume to impute this neglect of cultivating the military virtue of these nations to the ignorance or indolence of our patriots, rather than to a fatality in the course of things, which hath changed the manners of our people. But whatever be the cause, it is plain we are no more the same men, nor delighted with the same amusements. There is no danger that tilts and tournaments should come again in play; on the other hand, it is to be hoped, (whatever the report may be) that our gentlemen will not choose this juncture for introducing masquerades among us.

Non hoc ista sibi tempus spectacula poscit.[1711] Manly and military exercises befit the times, which may be performed on holidays or summer evenings, without neglect of business, and without expense of uniforms and treats, merely as a pastime; which the genius of our people would readily take to, if encouraged by small premiums, or countenanced by the leading men of a parish.

I am, Sir, your humble Servant,

Eubulus

[1709] Battle where John Campbell*(1680–1743), second Duke of Argyll, defeated the rebel John Erskine* (1675–1732), Earl of Mar, on 13 November 1715.

[1710] Battle where the Young Pretender, Charles Edward Stuart* (1720–88), defeated Sir John Cope (1690–1760) on 21 September 1745.

[1711] Virgil, *Aeneid*, VI, 37. Literally: "At this point, time does not require those sights for itself." The passage occurs in the text where Aeneas is looking at Daedalus' door carvings on Sibyl's temple before he enters the underworld. A freer translation would thus be: "Now is not the time for gazing at those images."

331 BERKELEY TO GERVAIS

Stock, p. xcvii (extract).

6 February 1746

You say you carried away regret from Cloyne. I assure you that you did not carry it all away: there was a good share of it left with us: which was on the following news-day increased upon hearing the fate of your niece. My wife could not read this piece of news without tears, though her knowledge of that amiable young lady was no more than one day's acquaintance. Her mournful widower is beset with many temporal blessings: but the loss of such a wife must be long felt through them all. Complete happiness is not to be hoped for on this side Gascony. All those who are not Gascons must have a corner of woe to creep out at, and to comfort themselves with at parting from this world. Certainly if we had nothing to make us uneasy here, heaven itself would be less wished for. But I should remember I am writing to a philosopher and divine; so shall turn my thoughts to politics, concluding with this sad reflection, that, happen what will, I see the Dutch are still to be favourites, though I much apprehend the hearts of some warm friends may be lost at home, by endeavouring to gain the affection of those lukewarm neighbours.

332 BERKELEY TO GERVAIS

Stock, pp. xcix–c (extract).

24 February 1746

I am heartily sensible of your loss,[1712] which yet admits of alleviation, not only from the common motives which have been repeated every day for upwards of five thousand years, but also from your own peculiar knowledge of the world and the variety of distresses which occur in all ranks from the highest to the lowest: I may add, too, from the peculiar times in which we live, which seem to threaten still more wretched and unhappy times to come.

Aetas parentum, pejor avis, tulit
Nos nequiores, mox daturos
Progeniem vitiosiorem.[1713]

[1712] Presumably this is a reference to the death of his niece, mentioned in an earlier letter. See Letter 331.
[1713] Horace, *Odes*, III, 6. "The generation of our parents, worse than our grandparents', produced us – We, unequal to them [our parents], and soon to produce our own degenerate line." The

Nor is it a small advantage that you have a peculiar resource against distress from the gaiety of your own temper. Such is the hypochondriac melancholy complexion of us islanders, that we seem made of butter, every accident makes such a deep impression upon us; but those elastic spirits, which are your birth-right, cause the strokes of fortune to rebound without leaving a trace behind them; though, for a time, there is and will be a gloom, which, I agree with your friends, is best dispelled at the court and metropolis, amidst a variety of faces and amusements.

I wish I was able to go with you, and pay my duty to the Lord Lieutenant:[1714] but, alas! the disorder I had this winter, and my long retreat, have disabled me for the road, and disqualified me for a court. But if I see you not in Dublin, which I wish I may be able to do, I shall hope to see you at Cloyne when you can be spared from better company. These sudden changings and tossings from side to side betoken a fever in the state. But whatever ails the body politic, take care of your own bodily health, and let no anxious cares break in upon it.

333 BERKELEY TO CLARKE[1715]

Lambeth MS 1719, p. 67.

24 March 1745/46

Revd Sir,

It is now several weeks since I received a letter from you which supposed my going to Dublin. I had indeed for some time past projected such a journey. But an illness gotten by cold had left me so tender that I could not venture my self on the road. The same cause still renders my journey doubtful. But I would not

---

sense is clear: considering four generations, each succeeding generation is worse than the last.

[1714] Philip Dormer Stanhope* (1694–1773), fourth Earl of Chesterfield.

[1715] Addressed "To the Revd Doctor Clarke, Vice Provost of Trinity College, Dublin." This letter is reproduced in part with minor alterations in *Peplographia Dublinensis: Memorial Discourses Preached in the Chapel of Trinity College, Dublin 1895–1902* (London: Macmillan & Co., 1902), p. 77n. The sermon referenced in the title was preached in 1897 by John Henry Bernard, D.D., fellow of Trinity College, Dublin, and Archbishop King's lecturer in divinity. In the note Bernard relates that it was in the possession of the bishop of Ripon and verifies that it was written by Berkeley to Dr. Clarke. The addressee is Dr. Henry Clarke* (?–1764), who was vice-provost of Trinity College, Dublin (1744–47).

suppose your affairs are at all the worse for my not being in town; for, to speak the truth, I could have been of no use with my Lord Lieutenant,[1716] unless he had given me a decent opportunity of speaking to the point, by consulting or advising with me about it: a thing which I had no right to expect. I have been told his Excellency expressed a particular esteem for you publicly at the castle, on occasion of the compliment you made him on his first arrival. This personal prepossession in your favour, grounded on his own sense of your merit, is in my opinion worth twenty recommendations, even of those great men in power who alone have a right to make them. To conclude I wish you all success in your undertakings being with sincere regard,

> Revd Sir,
> your faithful &
> obedient servant,
> George Cloyne

334 BERKELEY TO PRIOR[1717]

Printed in Thomas Prior, Authentic Narrative *(Dublin, 1746), pp. 227–39.*

May 1746

A Second Letter from the Author of Siris to Thomas Prior, Esq.

1. YOUR attention to whatever promotes the public good of your country, or the common benefit of mankind, having engaged you in a particular inquiry concerning the virtues and effects of tar-water, you are entitled to know what farther discoveries, observations, and reflections I have made on that subject.

2. Tar-water, in the several editions of *Siris*, hath been directed to be made by stirring 3, 4, 5, or 6 minutes, for a gallon of water and a quart of tar. But, although it seem best made for general use, within those limits, yet the stomach of the patient is the best rule whereby to direct the strength of the water; with a little more stirring, six quarts of good tar-water may be made from one of tar;

[1716] Philip Dormer Stanhope* (1694–1773), fourth Earl of Chesterfield, who was appointed lord lieutenant of Ireland in January 1745, but did not actually arrive in Dublin until August. He replaced William Cavendish (1698–1755), third Duke of Devonshire.

[1717] Thomas Prior* (1681–1751) writes in the last paragraph of the main text that this letter was "lately sent" to him, but I see no other reason to date the letter, as Luce does, specifically in May, although 1746 seems accurate given the publication date. See *Works*, vol. V, p. 168.

and with eight minutes stirring I have known a gallon of tar-water produced from second-hand tar, which proved a good remedy in a very bad fever, when better tar could not be had. For the use of travellers, a tar-water may be made very strong, for instance, with one quart of water and a quart of tar, stirred together for the space of twenty minutes. A bottle of this may serve long on a road, a little being put to each glass of common water, more or less, as you would have it stronger or weaker.[1718] [Near ten years ago, a quart of about this strength was given to an old woman, to be taken at one draught by direction of a young lady, who had consulted one in my family, about the method of preparing and giving tar-water, which yet she happened to mistake. But even thus, it did service in the main, though it wrought the patient violently all manner of ways. Which shows that errors and excesses in tar-water are not so dangerous as in other medicines.]

3. The best tar I take to be that which is most liquid, or first running from the billets of fir or pine which grew on the mountains: It hath a greater share of those antiscorbutic vegetable juices, which are contained not only in the leaves and tender tops, but in all parts of the wood; and these, together with the salts of wood-soot, being in the composition of tar super-added to turpentine, render tar-water a medicine, if I am not mistaken, much more extensive and efficacious than any that can be obtained from turpentine alone.

4. The virtues of the wood-juices show themselves in spruce-beer, made of molasses, and the black spruce-fir in the northern parts of America; and the young shoots of our common spruce-fir have been put to malt liquor in my own family, and make a very wholesome drink.

5. Tar-water seldom fails to cure, or relieve, when rightly made of good tar, and duly taken. I say, of good tar, because the vile practice of adulterating tar, or of selling the dregs of tar, or used tar for fresh, is grown frequent, to the great wrong of those who take it. Whoever hath been used to good tar-water can readily discern the bad by its flat taste, void of that warm cordial quality found in the former; it may also be expedient, for knowing fresh tar, to observe whether a fat oily scum floats on the top of the water, which is found to be much less, if any at all, on the second making of tar-water. This scum was directed to be taken off, not from its being apt to do harm when drunk,[1719] but to render the tar-water more palatable to nice stomachs. Great quantities of tar are produced in Germany, Italy, and other parts of the world. The different qualities or virtues

---

[1718] What follows is included in the "new" edition (London reprint, 1746), but is not present in the original 1746 Dublin printing.

[1719] Luce repairs to "drank."

of these it may be worth while to try, and I wish the trial were made principally by observing, which giveth most sense of a lively cordial spirit upon drinking the water.

6. This medicine of tar-water worketh various ways, by urine, by perspiration, as a sudorific, carminative, cardiac, astringent, detergent, restorative, alterative, and sometimes as a gentle purgative or emetic, according to the case or constitution of the patient, or to the quantity that is taken; and its operation should not be disturbed. I knew two brothers ill of a fever about the same time; it wrought on the one by copious sweating, on the other altogether by urine; and I have known it to act at different times differently, even on the same person, and in the same disorder; one while as a diaphoretic, or sudorific, another as a diuretic. Its general character is diuretic, which shows that it cleanseth the urinary passages, preventing thereby both stone and gravel, against which it hath been found very useful, and much safer than mineral waters, by reason of its balsamic healing quality.

7. Tar-water doth recover and impart vital heat, but imparts no inflaming heat. I have seen a wonderful cure wrought on a child about eight years old, and past all hopes, by pouring several spoonfuls of tar-water down his throat, as he lay quite subdued by a most violent fever, without any appearance of sense or motion, the nostrils drawn back, the eyes fixed, the complexion deadly wan. And yet tar-water, forced down by spoonfuls, seemed to kindle up life anew; and this after sage-tea, saffron, milk-water, Venice treacle, etc., had been used without any success.

8. This is of itself a sufficient cordial, friendly and congenial to the vital heat and spirits of a man. If, therefore, strong liquors are in the accustomed quantity superadded, the blood being already, by tar-water, sufficiently warmed for vital heat, the strong liquors superadded will be apt to overheat it, which overheating is not to be imputed to the tar-water, since, taken alone, I could never observe it attended with that symptom.

9. And, though it may be no easy matter to persuade such as have long indulged themselves in the free use of strong fermented liquors and distilled spirits to forsake their pernicious habits, yet I am myself thoroughly persuaded that, in weakness or fatigue of body, or in low spirits, tar-water alone doth far surpass all those vulgarly esteemed cordials, which heat and intoxicate, and which coagulate the fluids, and, by their caustic force, dry up, stiffen, and destroy the fine vessels and fibres of the unhappy drinkers, obstructing the secretions, impairing the animal functions, producing various disorders, and bringing on the untimely symptoms of old age. Nothing doth so much obstruct

the good effects of tar-water as the abuse of strong liquors. Where this is avoided, it seems no chronical malady can keep its ground or stand before tar-water, constantly and regularly taken, not even hereditary distempers, as the most inveterate king's evil,[1720] nor even the most confirmed gout; provided it be drank a quart a day, at six or eight glasses, and at all seasons, both in and out of the fit, and that for a great length of time, the longer the better. It is to be noted that in fits of the gout, colic, or fever, it should be always drank warm; on other occasions, warm or cold, as the patient likes.

10. The inference I make is, that those who expect health from tar-water have less need of any other cordial, and would do well to sacrifice some part of their pleasure to their health. At the same time, I will venture to affirm that a fever produced either from hard drinking, or any other cause, is most effectually and speedily subdued by abstaining from all other cordials, and plentifully drinking of tar-water, for it warms the cold, and cools the hot. Simple water may cool, but this, at the same time that it cools, gives life and spirit. It is, in truth, a specific for all kinds of fevers; [the same medicine, which is a leisurely alterative in chronical disorders, being taken in larger quantities is a speedy cure in acute ones.][1721]

11. Those who, without knowledge or experience of tar-water, have been so active and earnest to discredit its virtues, have much to answer for, especially with regard to acute inflammatory distempers, in which it doth wonders. It is in those disorders, so fatal and frequent, that I have had most opportunies of observing its virtues; nor can the world ever know the just value of this medicine, but by trying it in the like cases.

12. When patients are given over, and all known methods fail, it is allowed to try new remedies. If tar-water was tried in such cases, I do verily believe, that many patients might thereby be rescued from the jaws of death: particularly, I would recommend the trial of it in the most malignant and desperate fevers, or small-pox, attended with purple, livid, or black spots. It is my sincere opinion that warm tar-water, drank copiously, may often prove salutary, even in those deplorable cases.

13. My opinion is grounded on its singular virtues in correcting, sweetening, and invigorating the blood, and in curing cancers and gangrenes, or beginning mortifications, such as those spots do indicate. I have lately known it drunk with good success in a very painful and unpromising wound; and am persuaded that if it were drank plentifully, during the dressing of all sorts of dangerous wounds,

---

[1720] Also called scrofula; tuberculosis of the neck.
[1721] Not in the original 1746 Dublin version; added in the 1746 "new edition" printed in London.

it might assuage the anguish, and forward the cure; as it abates feverish symptoms, and, by rendering the blood balsamic and disposing the parts to heal, prevents a gangrene.

14. Tar itself is an excellent medicine, being spread on a cloth, and applied warm to an ulcer or wound. I have known the same applied to a very large and painful tumour, caused by a sprain or bruise, speedily assuage the pain, and reduce the swelling. I may add that tar (mixed with honey to make it less offensive, and) taken inwardly, is an admirable balsam for the lungs; and a little of this, taken together with tar-water, hastens its effect in curing the most obstinate and wasting coughs; and an egg-shell full of tar, swallowed and washed down with a quart of tar-water, night and morning, hath been found very useful for the same disorder in horses.

15. Sitting over the vapour of the heated lotion, described in my former letter, is excellent in the case of piles or fistula; especially if fomenting with the said lotion be added, as also anointing with the oil scummed from the top of tar-water. Tar-water hath been snuffed up the nostrils, with good success, for a great heaviness of the head and drowsiness. It is a very useful wash for weak, dry, or itching eyes; an excellent preservative for the teeth and gums; also a good drink and gargle for a sore throat. I may add that I have known it succeed in cases where it has been tried without hopes of success, particularly in [stammering and][1722] deafness. I have known life sustained many days together only by drinking of tar-water, without any other nourishment, and without any remarkable diminution of strength or spirits; it may therefore be of singular use, and save many lives in the distress of famine at sea, or in sieges, and in seasons of great scarcity. The virtue of tar-water, flowing like the Nile[1723] from a secret and occult source, brancheth into innumerable channels, conveying health and relief, wherever it is applied; [nor is it more easy and various in its use than copious in quantity. How great havoc, nevertheless, is made by the small-pox, raging like a plague in New England, and other parts of America, which yet abound with tar! And how many thousand sailors, in all parts of the world, are rotting by the scurvy with their remedy at hand!][1724]

16. Many in this town of Cloyne have, by the copious drinking of tar-water alone, been recovered of the most violent fevers, attended with the most

---

[1722] The words "stammering and" are present in original 1746 Dublin edition but were removed from the "new edition" of 1746.

[1723] Berkeley adds a footnote here: "The Nile was by the ancient Aegyptians called *Siris*, which word also signifies in Greek, a chain, though not so commonly used as *Sira*."

[1724] Not in the original 1746 Dublin edition, added in London 1746 "new edition."

threatening symptoms, and much heightened by relapses from mismanagement. It would be tedious to enumerate all the cases of this kind which have happened at Cloyne and in my own family; where many fevers, pleuritic as well as others, [attended with violent stitches, difficulty of breathing, and spitting of blood,]¹⁷²⁵ have been cured by tar-water: and this I can with truth affirm, that I never knew it regularly tried, in any inflammatory case, without success. But then it must be given in bed, warm and very copiously, with all due caution against cold, noise, and improper diet.

17. [It gives such spirits, that I have known persons in a fever, pass several days without any other ailment, and yet all the while, in such a flow of spirits, as hardly to be kept in bed. And]¹⁷²⁶ I have often observed, when a patient, on the first attack of a fever, hath betaken himself to his bed, and drank tar-water regularly and constantly, that he hath had such favourable symptoms, so good appetite, and so sound sleep, that the fever passed almost as nothing; nor was to be distinguished otherwise than by a quickness of pulse, a little feverish heat, and thirst. The more that patients in a fever drink, the better they find themselves; and their liking to tar-water grows with their want of it, by a certain instinct or dictate of nature; insomuch that I have known children in very high fevers, who, at other times, could hardly be prevailed on to drink a single glass, drink six or eight in an hour.

18. I can truly affirm that, for the cases within my own observation, inflammatory acute distempers cured by tar-water have been at least ten times the number of any other. These indeed oftenest occur, as causing the chief destruction and general ravage of mankind: who are consequently debarred from the principal use and benefit of this medicine, so long as they give ear to the suggestions of those who, without any experience thereof, would persuade them it is of a heating or inflaming nature; which suggestion, as I am convinced myself, by long and manifold experience, that it is absolutely false, so may all others also be sufficiently convinced of its falsehood by the wonderful fact, attested by a solemn affidavit of Captain Drape at Liverpool;¹⁷²⁷ whereby it appears that of 170 negroes seized at once by the small-pox on the coast of Guinea one only died, who refused to drink tar-water; and the remaining 169 all recovered, by drinking it, without any other medicine, notwithstanding the heat of the climate, and the incommodities of the vessel. A fact so well vouched

---

¹⁷²⁵ Not in the original 1746 Dublin edition, added in London 1746 "new edition."

¹⁷²⁶ Omitted from the 1746 "new edition," but present in the original 1746 edition.

¹⁷²⁷ Captain Drape's affidavit is reproduced by Prior on page 24 of the 1746 edition of *Authentic Narrative*, sections 43 and 44 in the new edition.

must, with all unbiased men, outweigh the positive assertions of those who have declared themselves adversaries of tar-water, on the score of its pretended heating or inflaming quality.

19. The skill and learning of those gentlemen in their profession, I shall not dispute; but yet it seems strange that they should, without experience, pronounce at once concerning the virtues of tar-water, and ascribe to it pernicious qualities, which I, who had watched its workings and effects for years together, could never discover. These [two][1728] three last years I have taken it myself without one day's intermission; others in my family have taken it near the same time, and those of different ages and sexes; several in the neighbourhood have done as much, all without any injury, and much benefit.

20. It is to be noted, the skin and the belly are antagonists; that is, the more passeth by perspiration, the less will pass another way. Medicines, therefore, which cause the patient to perspire will be apt to make him costive. Therefore, when tar-water worketh much by perspiration, the body may chance to be bound. But such symptom, though it should be attended with a little more than ordinary warmth, need not be dreaded by the patient; it being only a sign that his cure is carried on by driving the peccant matter through the skin; which is one of the ways whereby tar-water worketh its effect. And when this effect or cure is wrought, the body of itself returneth to its former natural state; and if some have been bound in their bodies, I have known others affected in a contrary manner upon drinking tar-water, as it hath happened to operate either in the shape of a diaphoretic, or of a gentle opening medicine. I have even known a costive habit more than once removed by it, and that when the case was inveterate, and other methods had failed.

21. I mentioned the foregoing article, upon calling to mind, that two or three patients had, for a time, complained of a binding quality in tar-water. I likewise remember that one in a high degree of the scurvy was discouraged from the use of tar-water, by its having caused an uneasy itching all over his body. But this was a good symptom, which showed the peccant humours to be put in motion, and in a fair way of being discharged through the skin.

22. A humour or flatus put in motion, and dislodged from one part often produceth new pains in some other part; and an efficacious medicine, as it produceth a change in the economy, may be attended with some uneasiness,

[1728] "two" in the 1746 Dublin edition, emended to "three" in the "new edition."

which yet is not to be accounted a distemper, but only an effect or symptom of the cure.

23. The salts of tar-water have nothing of the fiery and corrosive nature of lixivial salts produced by the incineration of the subject; they not being fixed salts, made by the extreme force of fire, but volatile salts, such as pre-existed in the vegetable, and would have ascended in smoke, if not prevented by the sods or covering of the billet piles. This, though already hinted in *Siris*, and plain from the manner of making tar, I have thought fit to repeat and inculcate, because, if duly attended to, it may obviate suspicions about tar-water, proceeding only from an ignorance of its nature.

24. Every step that I advanced in discovering the virtues of tar-water, my own wonder and surprise increased, as much as theirs to whom I mentioned them. Nor could I, without great variety and evidence of facts, ever have been induced to suspect, that, in all sorts of ailments whatsoever it might relieve or cure, which at first sight may seem incredible and unaccountable, but, on maturer thought, will perhaps appear to agree with, and follow from, the nature of things. For it is to be noted that the general notion of a disease seemeth to consist in this: that what is taken in is not duly assimilated by the force of the animal economy; therefore it should seem whatever assists the *vis vitae* may be of general use in all diseases, enabling nature either to assimilate or discharge all unsubdued humours or particles whatsoever. But the light or aether detained in the volatile oil which impregnates tar-water, being of the same nature with the animal spirit, is an accession of so much strength to the constitution, which it assists to assimilate or expel whatever is alien or noxious.

Finis

335 BERKELEY TO PRIOR[1729]

Philosophical Transactions 481 (October–December 1746): 325–28.

Cloyne, 20 May 1746

Dear Sir,

I here send you back the curious dissertation of Mr. Simon, which I have perused with pleasure; and though variety of avocations gives me little time for

[1729] Annexed to a communication from Mr. James Simon (?–after 1756) on the petrifactions of Lough Neagh, read before the Royal Society in February 1747. Luce entitles the letter "Berkeley to Prior on Petrifications" and publishes it separately from the correspondence in *Works*, vol. IV, pp. 251–53.

remarks on a subject so much out of my way, I shall nevertheless venture to give my thoughts briefly upon it, especially since the author hath been pleased to invite me to it by a letter.

The author seems to put it out of doubt, that there is a petrifying quality both in the lake and adjacent earth. What he remarks on the unfrozen spots in the lake is curious, and furnisheth a sufficient answer to those who would deny any petrifying virtue to be in the water, from experiments not succeeding in some parts of it; since nothing but chance could have directed to the proper places, which, probably, were those unfrozen parts.

Stones have been thought by some to be organised vegetables, and to be produced from seed. To me it seems that stones are vegetables unorganised. Other vegetables are nourished and grow by a solution of salt attracted into their tubes or vessels. And stones grow by the accretion of salts, which often shoot into angular and regular figures. This appears in the formation of crystals on the Alps: and that stones are formed by the simple attraction and accretion of salts, appears in the tartar on the inside of a claret-vessel, and especially in the formation of a stone in the human body.

The air is in many places impregnated with such salts. I have seen at Agrigentum in Sicily the pillars of stone in an ancient temple corroded and consumed by the air, while the shells which entered into the composition of the stone remained intire and untouched.

I have elsewhere observed marble to be consumed in the same manner; and it is common to see softer kinds of stone moulder and dissolve merely by the air acting as a *menstruum*.[1730] Therefore the air may be presumed to contain many such salts, or stony particles.

Air, acting as a *menstruum* in the cavities of the earth, may become saturated (in like manner as above-ground) with such salts as, ascending in vapours or exhalations, may petrify wood, whether lying in the ground adjacent, or in the bottom of the lake. This is confirmed by the author's own remark on the bath called the Green Pillars in Hungary. The insinuating of such salts into the wood seems also confirmed by the author's having observed minute hexagonal crystals in the woody part of the petrifactions of Lough-Neagh.

A petrifying quality or virtue shews itself in all parts of this terraqueous globe, in water, earth, and sand; in Tartary, for instance, and Afric[a], in the

---

[1730] A solvent, typically for extracting medicinal compounds from plants.

bodies of most sorts of animals: it is even known that a child hath been petrified in the mother's womb. *Osteocolla*[1731] grows in the land, and coral in the sea. Grottoes, springs, lakes, and rivers are in many parts remarkable for this same quality. No man therefore can question the possibility of such a thing as petrified wood; though perhaps the petrifying quality might not be originally in the earth or water, but in the vapour or steam impregnated with saline or stony particles.

Perhaps the petrifaction of wood may receive some light from considering amber, which is dug up in the King of Prussia's dominions.

I have written these hasty lines in no small hurry; and send them to you not from an opinion that they contain anything worth imparting, but merely in compliance with your and Mr. Simon's request.

[Added from a letter to Dr. J. Fothergill,[1732] dated Dublin, 8 August 1746.]

And yet before I have done I must needs add another remark, which may be useful for the better understanding of the nature of stone. In the vulgar definition, it is said to be a fossil incapable of fusion. I have nevertheless known stone to be melted, and when cold to become stone again. Such is that stuff, by the natives called *Sciara*, which runs down in liquid burning torrents from the craters of Mount Aetna, and which, when cold and hard, I have seen hewed and employed at Catania and other places adjacent. It probably contains mineral and metallic particles; being a ponderous, hard, grey stone, used for the most part in the basements and coinage of buildings.

Hence it should seem not impossible for stone to be cast or run into the shape of columns, vases, statues, or relievos; which experiment may perhaps some time or other be attempted by the curious; who, following where nature has shown the way, may (possibly by the aid of certain salts and minerals) arrive at a method for melting and running stone, both to their own profit, and that of the public. I am,

> Dear Sir,
>
> your most humble servant,
>
> G. Cloyne

[1731] A carbonate of lime, a fossil formed by incrustation on the stem of a plant.
[1732] John Fothergill (1712–80) was a London physician and scientist interested in botannical gardening.

336 BERKELEY TO PRIOR

LR, pp. 304–05. Stock, p. lxxxiii.

23 June 1746

Dear Tom,

I perceive the Earl of Chesterfield[1733] is, whether absent or present, a friend to Ireland; and there could not have happened a luckier incident to this poor island than the friendship of such a man, when there are so few of her own great men who either care or know how to befriend her. As my own wishes and endeavours (howsoever weak and ineffectual) have had the same tendency, I flatter myself that on this score he honours me with his regard, which is an ample recompence for more public merit than I can pretend to. As you transcribed a line from his letter relating to me; so, in return, I send you a line transcribed from a letter of the Bishop of Gloucester's[1734] relating to you. I formerly told you I had mentioned you to the Bishop when I sent your scheme. These are his words: 'I have had a great deal of discourse with your Lord Lieutenant. He expressed his good esteem of Mr. Prior and his character, and commended him as one who had no view in life but to do the utmost good he is capable of. As he has seen the scheme, he may have opportunity of mentioning it to as many of the cabinet as he pleases. But it will not be a fashionable doctrine at this time.'—So far the Bishop. You are doubtless in the right, on all proper occasions, to cultivate a correspondence with Lord Chesterfield. When you write, you will perhaps let him know in the properest manner the thorough sense I have of the honour he does me in his remembrance, and my concern at not having been able to wait on him. Adieu, dear Tom,

  G. Cloyne

June 23, 1746

May we hope to see you this summer.

[1733] Philip Dormer Stanhope* (1694–1773), fourth Earl of Chesterfield.
[1734] Martin Benson* (1689–1752).

337 BERKELEY TO PRIOR

Stock, pp. lxxxiii–lxxxiv (extract).

Cloyne, 3 July 1746

Dear Tom,

I send you back my *Letter*,[1735] with the new paragraph to be added at the end, where you see the ^.

Lord Chesterfield's[1736] letter does great honour both to you and to his Excellency. The nation should not lose the opportunity of profiting by such a viceroy, which indeed is a rarity not to be met with every season, which grows not on every tree. I hope your society will find means of encouraging particularly the two points he recommends, glass and paper. For the former you would do well to get your workmen from Holland rather than from Bristol. You have heard of the trick the glassmen of Bristol were said to have played Dr. Helsham[1737] and Company.

My wife with her compliments sends you a present[1738] by the Cork carrier who set out yesterday. It is an offering of the first fruits of her painting. She began to draw in last November, and did not stick to it closely, but by way of amusement only at leisure hours. For my part, I think she shows a most uncommon genius; but others may be supposed to judge more impartially than I. My two younger children are beginning to employ themselves the same way. In short, here are two or three families in Imokilly[1739] bent upon painting; and I wish it was more general among the ladies and idle people as a thing that may divert the spleen, improve the manufactures, and increase the wealth of the nation. We will endeavour to profit by your Lord Lieutenant's advice, and kindle up new arts with a spark of his public spirit.

Mr. Simon has wrote to me, desiring that I would become a member of the Historico-Physical Society.[1740] I wish them well, but do not care to list myself

---

[1735] See Letter 344, Berkeley to Prior [1747]. Prior would append this letter to his *Authentic Narrative*.

[1736] Philip Dormer Stanhope* (1694–1773), fourth Earl of Chesterfield.

[1737] Richard Helsham (1683–1738), physician and natural philosopher. In addition to being a professor of mathematics and natural philosophy at Trinity College, Dublin, he was Jonathan Swift's* personal physician.

[1738] Stock's note: "The bishop's portrait painted by Mrs. Berkeley, now in the possession of the Rev. Mr. Archdall of Bolton street, Dublin."

[1739] The Barony of Imokilly, in which Cloyne lies.

[1740] James Simon (?–after 1756). He was a member of the Dublin-based Physico-Historical Society, which had been formed in 1744. He was a wine merchant on Fleet Street and authored *An Essay Towards an Historical Account of Irish Coins* (Dublin: S. Powell, 1749). For an account of the Physico-Historical Society, see Eoin Magennis, "'A Land of Milk and Honey': The

among them: for in that case I should think myself obliged to do somewhat which might interrupt my other studies. I must therefore depend on you for getting me out of this scrape, and hinder Mr. Simon's proposing me, which he inclines to do, at the request, it seems, of the Bishop of Meath.[1741] And this, with my service, will be a sufficient answer to Mr. Simon's letter.

338 BERKELEY TO PERCIVAL[1742]

EP, BL Add. MS 46997, fol. 72.

Cloyne, 24 August 1746

My Lord,

This day I received your favour of the twelfth, and thank your Lordship for your kind care in having got in my money.[1743] If it was unlucky for me that it could not be got while the stocks were lower, I do not in the least impute that to your Lordship.

As there is no sending a deed of mortgage by post, and as I have not the opportunity of a private hand, I must beg the favour of you to remit the money to your bankers at Corke, and appoint your Lordship's agent to receive the deed of mortgage and pay the money thereupon, which I shall then remit back to purchase annuities in London by Mr. Henry Hoare[1744] & Co. This will take time and the stocks are daily rising. So your Lordship will be so good as to consider, that the sooner it is done my loss will be the less.

My wife and I present our respects to your Lordship, good Lady Egmont and all your family.

I am my Lord,

your Lordship's most obedient & most humble servant,

G: Cloyne

Cloyne August 24, 1746

Physico-Historical Society, Improvement and the Surveys of Mid-Eighteenth-Century Ireland," *Proceedings of the Royal Irish Academy* 102C (2002): 199–217.
[1741] Henry Maule (1676–1758) translated from Dromore to Meath in 1744.
[1742] Rand (but not Luce) has *fils*. The 23 September 1746 letter refers to this one, and that letter is clearly to the Earl of Egmont, thus *fils* here is an error. See Luce, "Some Unpublished Berkeley Letters with some New Berkeleiana," 153–54.
[1743] John Percival* (1683–1748) had borrowed money (£3,000) from Berkeley in 1733 and is now repaying that loan.
[1744] Henry Hoare* (1705–85).

339 BERKELEY TO PRIOR

LR, *pp. 306–07. Stock, p. lxxxv.*

Cloyne, 12 September 1746

Dear Tom,

I am just returned from a tour through my diocese of 130 miles, almost shaken to pieces.

What you write of Bishop Stone's[1745] preferment is highly probable. For myself, though his Excellency the Lord Lieutenant[1746] might have a better opinion of me than I deserved; yet it was not likely that he would make an Irishman Primate.

The truth is, I have a scheme of my own for this long time past, in which I propose more satisfaction and enjoyment of myself than I could in that high station, which I neither solicited, nor so much as wished for.

It is true, the Primacy or Archbishopric of Dublin, if offered, might have tempted me by a greater opportunity of doing good; but there is no other preferment in the kingdom to be desired upon any other account than a greater income, which would not tempt me to remove from Cloyne, and set aside my Oxford scheme; which, though delayed by the illness of my son, yet I am as intent upon it, and as much resolved as ever.

I am glad you have a prospect of disposing of my debentures soon. Adieu.

> your affectionate humble servant,
> G. Cloyne

340 BERKELEY TO PERCIVAL[1747]

EP, BL Add. MS 46997, fol. 77.

Cloyne, 23 September 1746

My Lord,

I have the honour of your Lordship's long after its date occasioned by a stop of the pacquets by contrary winds. As I am at a loss for an attorney to

---

[1745] George Stone (1708–64). He was dean of Ferns (1733) and of Derry (1734) before becoming bishop of Ferns (1740). He then translated to Kildare (1743). In 1745 he translated again and was bishop of Derry. He would be made archbishop of Armagh and primate of all Ireland in 1747.

[1746] Philip Dormer Stanhope* (1694–1773), fourth Earl of Chesterfield.

[1747] See Luce, "Some Unpublished Berkeley Letters with some New Berkeleiana," 154.

receive my money in London, I must repeat my request that you will please to order payment at Corke or, if you find it more convenient, at Dublin, the place mentioned in the bond.[1748]

What English money according to the exchange then current was paid by me to make up the sum of £3,000 Irish I do not now remember having no memorial thereof; nor is it material, since Irish money alone is the subject of the bond, the obligation whereof is to pay £3,000 Irish whatever may be the value thereof on the present foot of exchange; and this wheresoever the money is paid, whether in Ireland or in England. Your Lordship therefore will be no loser by ordering payment to be made here or in Dublin, from whence I can have it remitted to London at three days sight, all which will be evident to your Lordship upon perusing the enclosed copy of the bond. In which you will observe that the principal (£3,000) as well as the interest (£150) is expressly limited to be paid in Irish money, whatsoever the current value thereof may be at the time of payment.

If your Lordship has any doubt about this matter, it may be referred to your agent or any other person whom you shall please to appoint to peruse the original deed and bond, and send your Lordship his opinion thereupon. I pray God preserve your life and recover your health, which will be a most acceptable blessing to all your friends and particularly to

My Lord,

> your Lordship's most obedient humble servant,
> George Cloyne

P.S.: If the payment be made here, I doubt not Mr. Brereton[1749] and Mr. Purcel[1750] can easily attend and receive the deeds and see everything done that you direct. My wife and all here concur in best respects to your Lordship and good Lady Egmont.

Cloyne, 7ber 23 1746

[1748] Concerning Berkeley's loan to Percival; see Letter 338.

[1749] Brereton is one of the Breretons of Carrigslaney, an agent for Percival. At the behest of the Percivals Berkeley granted the favor of a vicarage without cure in his diocese to one Robert Brereton (1705–64). See Letter 300.

[1750] Richard Purcell* (*c.* 1690–?).

341 PERCIVAL TO BERKELEY

EP, BL Add. MS 46997, fol. 86.

London, 11 October 1746

My Lord,

I have enclosed this day to Mr. Purcell[1751] a bill of Knocks [Knox][1752] and Craghead on Richard and Thomas Dawson[1753] of Dublin for £3000 for your use, which I have ordered him to wait on you with and deliver to you. Your Lordship had better have made use of it while it was here for you will see by the days sight on the Bill and by the like when you return your money back to England that much time will be lost before you can command it for the purchase you intend besides the loss on the exchange of your money hither. But I have obeyed your directions and what my bond to you required which you will please to return to Mr. Purcell with the mortgage deed after you have made the assignment thereof to my niece Catherine Dering on the back and make your receipt for the money as paid you by my niece.

The late action in Flanders has turned out to our disadvantage, but the news that Admiral Lestock[1754] has destroyed the French East India Company ships and magazines at Port l'Orient is believed and occasions much joy.

> I am
> your Lordships
> most affectionate obedient servant[1755]

My wife and niece desire their humble services to you and to your Lady

342 BERKELEY TO GERVAIS

TCD MS 2167, fol. 6. Stock, p. c.

Cloyne, 8 November 1746

Reverend Sir,

Your letter, with news from the Castle, found me in bed confined by the gout. In answer to which news I can only say, that I neither expect nor wish for any

---

[1751] Richard Purcell* (*c.* 1690–?).

[1752] The text actually reads "Knocks" but in the succeeding letter in the letterbook (Percival to Purcell, 11 October 1746) Percival provides directives on Berkeley's loan and the text reads "Knox."

[1753] Richard Dawson (?–1766). Dawson was a wealthy merchant and banker, establishing his bank in 1740. He was an alderman for Dublin and MP from Kilkenny 1727–60. Thomas is presumably his brother and partner.

[1754] Richard Lestock (1679–1746). Lestock launched a raid against the French port city of Lorient in the summer of 1746.

[1755] This letter is transcribed from an unsigned copy in Percival's business letterbooks. In the margin is this note: "Dr. Berkeley Bp. of Cloyne I remit to him £3,000 to pay off my mortgage to him."

dignity higher than I am incumbered with at present. That which more nearly concerns me is my credit which I am glad to find so well supported by Admiral Lestock.[1756] I had promised you that before the first of November he would take King Lewis[1757] by the beard. Now Quimpercorrentin, Quimperlay, and Quimperen,[1758] being certain extreme parts or excrescencies of his kingdom, may not improperly be styled the beard of France. In proof of his having been there, he has plundered the wardrobes of the peasants, and imported a great number of old petticoats, waistcoats, wooden shoes, and one shirt, all which are actually sold at Cove: the shirt was bought by a man of this town for a groat. And if you won't believe me, come and believe your own eyes. In case you doubt either the facts or the reasonings, I am ready to make them good, being now well on my feet, and longing to triumph over you at Cloyne, which I hope will be soon. Meantime I conclude

> Revd Mr. Dean
> your faithful & obedient servant,
> G: Cloyne

Cloyne, 9ber 8, 1746

All here salute you.

343 BERKELEY TO PERCIVAL[1759]

EP, BL Add. MS 46997, fol. 108.

Cloyne, 23 December 1746

My Lord,

I received the favour of your Lordship's letter and am glad to find that all things are transacted to your liking. You will give me leave to observe that for Miss Dering's further security I believe it will be proper that Mr. Purcell[1760] should get her mortgage registered.

[1756] Richard Lestock (1679–1746).
[1757] King Louis XV (1710–74).
[1758] Towns in Brittany between Brest and Lorient. Quimpercorentin is now known simply as Quimper and Quimperlay is Quimperlé.
[1759] Rand has (*fils*) and Luce correctly does not. See Luce, "Some Unpublished Berkeley Letters with some New Berkeleiana," 155.
[1760] Richard Purcell* (c. 1690–?).

Certainly if my money was to remain in this kingdom, there is no person in whose hands I should place it so willingly as in your Lordship's.[1761] But considering the uncertain fate and exposed condition of this island I was desirous of securing a provision for my family upon the credit of a British parliament.

If the war continues it is to be apprehended that our late weak and unsuccessful enterprise on the French coast may provoke them to make reprisals on our defenceless coast. In which case if Providence should not interpose by winds and weather we must, humanly speaking, become an easy prey.

I am glad to hear Lady Egmont takes to the drinking of tarwater believing she may receive great benefit by it. I wish she would take it in small doses not exceeding ¼ of a pint, and of these 2 or 4 in the day, as her stomach can bear. For cholic or any inward complaints in the viscera she will do well to drink it warm.

I hope your Lordship's health is better. I pray God long preserve her Ladyship and your self to the comfort of your friends among whom you will always allow a place to My Lord

your Lordship's most obedient & obliged servant,

George Cloyne

My wife sends her best respects.

344 BERKELEY TO PRIOR[1762]

Printed in "A Letter from the Author of Siris *to Thomas Prior, Esq. Concerning the Usefulness of Tar-Water in the Plague" (Dublin: George Faulkner, 1747).*

1747

A Letter to Thomas Prior, Esq. Concerning the Usefulness of Tar-Water in the Plague, Wherin also it is Considered, Whether Tar-Water Prepared with the Distilled Acid of Tar Should be Prefesser, to that Made in the Common Way, by Mixing Tar with Water, and Stirring them Together

They provoked Him to anger with their own inventions, and the Plague brake in upon them. Ps. cvi. 29.

[1761] For more about Berkeley's loan to Percival, see Letter 338.

[1762] This letter also appeared republished as "Two Letters from the Right Reverend Dr. George Berkeley, Lord Bishop of Cloyne, The one to Thomas Prior, Esq. .... The other to the Rev. Dr. Hales, on the Benefit of Tar-water in Fevers, for Cattle as well as the Human Species" (Dublin; London reprint: Innys, Hitch, Cooper, & Davis, 1747). See BL catalogue T.677.(3).

You observe, in a late letter of yours, that I had formerly hinted tar-water might be useful in the plague,[1763] and desire to know the reasons whereon my opinion was grounded, and that I would communicate my thoughts at large on the subject. I am the more willing to satisfy you in this particular, as the plague now raging in Barbary hath in some measure alarmed the public, and I think it may not be amiss to contribute my mite of advice towards averting or lessening the present danger; and, as fear begets caution, to possess my countrymen with an apprehension of this, the greatest of all temporal calamities, sufficient to put them on their guard, and prepare them against the worst that can happen.

A learned physician of our own observes that the plague does not visit these Britannic islands oftener than once in thirty or forty years, and it is now above twice that time since we felt the hand of the destroying angel.

It is also the opinion of physicians that the infection cannot spread except there is a suitable disposition in the air to receive it; the signs of which are wet summers, leaves and fruits blasted, an unusual quantity of insects, epidemical distempers among the cattle, to which I presume may be added long easterly winds, all which signs seem to have discovered themselves pretty plainly in the course of this present year.

Beside these natural forerunners of a plague or pestilence in the air, it is worth observing that a prognostic may be also made from the moral and religious disposition of the inhabitants. Certainly that the *digitus dei* (the τὸ θεῖον of Hippocrates)[1764] doth manifest itself in the plague was not only the opinion of mankind in general, but also in particular of the most eminent physicians throughout all ages down to our own. How far we of these islands have reason to expect this messenger of divine vengeance will best appear if we take a view of the prevailing principles and practices of our times, which many think have long called aloud for punishment or amendment.

Analogy and probability prevail in medicine: these are the proper guides where experience hath not gone before. I knew that tar-water was useful to prevent catching the small-pox, and consequently that its nature was contrary to the taint or venom producing that distemper; and therefore I concluded that it might be usefully applied to cure the same, though I never heard nor knew that it had been applied to that purpose, and the success answered my hopes.

[1763] See Letter 304, section 23; and *Siris*, sect. 83, in *Works*, vol. V, p. 59.
[1764] *Digitus dei*: "the finger of god." τὸ θεῖον: "the divine being."

In like manner, having known the virtue of tar-water in preserving from epidemical infection, I conceive in general it may be useful for the cure of distempers caused by such infection. Besides, being very well assured that tar-water was sovereign in the cure of all sorts of fevers, I think it not unreasonable to infer that it may prove a successful medicine for the plague, although I have never known it used in that distemper, forasmuch as the plague with all its symptoms may be considered as a species of fever, and hath been actually considered as such both by Hippocrates[1765] and Sydenham,[1766] not to mention others.

Having observed surprising effects of tar-water in the most deplorable cases, for instance, pleurisies, small-pox, spotted and erysipelatous fevers, I am induced to entertain great hopes of its success in pestilential fevers or plagues; which are also confirmed by its operating as a powerful diaphoretic and sudorific, when given warm and in great quantities. Add to this, that it frequently throws out pustules and ulcers, is apt to terminate the worst of fevers by an eruption of boils in various parts of the body; that it raises the spirits, is a great alexipharmacum and cordial, and must therefore be of the greatest use in malignant cases.

In cachexy, scurvy, gout, as well as in the close of fevers, I have often known tar-water cause troublesome eruptions or boils (the very method taken by nature in casting forth the venom of the plague) to break out in the surface of the body, expelling the morbific humours, the cause and relics of the disease, to the signal benefit of the patients; except such who, being frightened at the symptoms, have supposed the tar-water to produce those humours which it only drives out, and, in consequence of such their groundless suspicion, laid it aside, or perhaps took other medicines to hinder its effect, and thereby deprived themselves of the benefit they might otherwise have received.

In the plague are observed headache, drowsiness, anxiety, vigils, sinking of spirits, and weakness, for all which tar-water hath been found an effectual remedy. Bloody urine and spitting blood, which are also dangerous symptoms observed in the plague, have been often removed by the same medicine, which from numberless experiments I have found to be peculiarly fitted for purifying and strengthening the blood, and for giving it a due consistence, as well as a proper motion.

[1765] Hippocrates (*c.* 460–370 BCE.). See *Epidemiae*, III, sect. iii.
[1766] Thomas Sydenham (1624–89). See *Observationes Medicae* (London, 1666), sect. II, *c.* 2.

In the plague, pleurisies are esteemed mortal symptoms, and in the cure of these I never knew tar-water fail, if given warm in bed, a pint or more an hour, though the patient was neither bled nor blistered. The carbuncles and spots which shew themselves in the plague are of a gangrenous nature, tending to mortification. And gangrenes I have known effectually cured by copious drinking of tar-water.

An erysipelas, which sheweth a degree of malignity nearest to the plague, is easily cured by plentiful drinking of tar-water. I knew a person who had been six weeks ill of an erysipelas under the care of a celebrated physician, during which time she struggled with many dangerous symptoms, and hardly escaped with life. This person was a year after seized again in the same manner, and recovered in a week, by the sole use of tar-water. Costiveness is reckoned a very hopeful prognostic in the plague; and it is also a symptom which often attends the drinking of tar-water, when it throws out the venom of a distemper through the skin.

Diseases of the same season generally bear some affinity to each other in their nature and their cure; and it may not be improper on this occasion to observe that the reigning distemper of the black cattle hath been often cured by tar-water, and would (I am persuaded) have done much less mischief if the practice had been general to have given each distempered beast three gallons the first, two the second, and one the third day, in warm doses (from a pint to a quart), and at equal intervals.

Diemerbroeck[1767] recommends in the first appearance of a plague the use of sudorifics, putting the patient to bed, and covering him warm, till a copious sweat be raised, the very method I constantly follow in the beginning of fevers, using no other medicine than tar-water, which, after numberless experiments, I take to be the best sudorific that is known, inasmuch as it throws out the morbific miasma, without either heating the patient or weakening him, the common effect of other sudorifics, whereas this, at the same time that it allays the feverish heat, proves a most salutary cordial, giving great and lasting spirits.

Upon the whole, I am sincerely persuaded that for the cure of the plague there cannot be a better method followed, more general for use, more easy in practice, and more sure in effect, than to cover the patient warm in bed, and to make him drink every hour one quart of warm tar-water, of such strength as his stomach is able to bear; a thing not so impracticable as it may seem at

---

[1767] Isbrand de Diemerbroeck (1609–74). A Dutch physician, he made a careful study of the plague in his work *De Peste* (1646).

first sight, since I have known much more drank in fevers, even by children, and that eagerly and by choice, the distemper calling for drink, and the ease it gave encouraging to go on. This for the cure; but I conceive that one quart per diem may suffice for prevention; especially if there be added an even temper of mind, and an exact regimen, which are both highly useful against the plague. For carbuncles and buboes I would recommend a liniment of the oil of tar, or a plaster of pitch mixed with tar, which last was used by the vulgar in the Dutch plague described by Diemerbroeck.

It has pleased divine Providence to visit us not long since, first with famine,[1768] then with the sword;[1769] and if it shall please the same good Providence yet further to visit us for our sins with the third and greatest of human woes, this, by God's blessing, is the course I mean to take for myself and family; and if generally practised, it would, I doubt not (under God), save the lives of many thousands; whereof being persuaded in my own mind, both from the many trials I have made of tar-water, and the best judgment and reasonings I could form thereupon, I think myself obliged to declare to the world what I am convinced of myself.

And I am the rather moved to this by the great uncertainty and disagreement among physicians, in their methods of treating the plague. Diemerbroeck, for instance, a physician of great experience in the Dutch plague that raged about eighty years ago, dissuades by all means from bleeding in that distemper. On the other hand, Sydenham recommends what the other disapproves. If we believe Dr. Sydenham, the free use of wine, as a preservative, hath thrown many into the plague who otherwise might have escaped. Dr. Willis,[1770] on the contrary, avers that he knew many who, being well fortified by wine, freely entered amongst the infected without catching the infection.

Bleeding cools, but at the same time weakens nature. Wine gives spirits, but heats withal. They are both, therefore, to be suspected; whereas tar-water cools without weakening, and gives spirit without heating, a sure indication of its sovereign virtue in all inflammatory and malignant cases; which is confirmed by such numbers of instances that matter of fact keeps pace (at least) with reason and argument in recommending this medicine.

Plagues as well as fevers are observed to be of different kinds: and it is observed of fevers that, as they change their genius in different seasons, so

---

[1768] Ireland suffered famine in 1740/41.

[1769] Most likely a reference to the Jacobite rebellion of 1745–46.

[1770] Thomas Willis (1621–75), physician. He allegedly penned *A Plain and Easie Method of Preserving those that are Well from the Plague* (London, 1691) after the plagues in England in 1666.

they must be treated differently, that very method that succeeded in one season often proving hurtful in another. Now it is very remarkable, that tar-water has been known to vary its working, and wonderfully adapt itself to the particular case of the patient, a thing I frequently have experienced.

Last spring two children, a boy and a girl, the former ten years old, the latter eight years old, were seized with fevers; the boy had an inflammation in his breast. In less than two hours they drank each about five quarts of warm tar--water, which wrought them very differently, the girl as an emetic, the boy as a gentle purge, but both alike immediately recovered, without the use of any other medicine: of this I was an eye-witness, and I have found by frequent experience that the best way is, to let this medicine take its own course, not hindered nor interrupted by any other medicines; and, this being observed, I never knew it to fail so much as once, in above a hundred trials in all sorts of fevers.

Nevertheless, there are not wanting those who would insinuate that tar-water made in the common way contains noxious oils or particles of tar, which render it dangerous to those who drink it, a thing contrary to all my experience. This was the old objection made by those who opposed it from the beginning. But I am convinced, by innumerable trials, that tar-water is so far from doing hurt by any caustic or fiery quality, that it is, on the contrary, a most potent medicine for the allaying of heat, and curing of all inflammatory distempers. The perpetual returning to the same objection makes it necessary to repeat the same answer.

And yet some who are not afraid to argue against experience would still persuade us that the common tar-water is a dangerous medicine, and that the acid freed from the volatile oil is much more safe and efficacious:[1771] but I am of opinion that, being robbed of its fine volatile oil (which neither sinks to the bottom, nor floats at the top, but is throughout and intimately united with it, and appears to the eye only in the colour of tar-water); being robbed, I say, of this oil, it is my opinion it can be no cordial; which opinion (not to mention the reason of the thing) I ground on my own experience, having observed that the most acid water is the least cordial, so far am I from imputing the whole virtue to the acid, as some seem to think.

It seems not very reasonable to suppose that the caustic quality of tar-water (if such there was) should be removed or lessened by distillation, or that a still should furnish a cooler and better medicine than that which is commonly prepared by the simple affusion and stirring of cold water. However the ends of chemists or distillers may be served thereby, yet it by no means seemeth

---

[1771] See Andrew Reid, *A Letter to the Rev. Dr. Hales, Concerning the Nature of Tar, and a Method of Obtaining its Medical Virtues from its Hurtful Oils* (London, 1747).

calculated for the benefit of mankind in general to attempt to make people suspect, and frighten them from the use of a medicine, so easily and so readily made, and everywhere at hand, of such approved and known safety, and, at the same time, recommended by cures the most extraordinary, on persons of all sexes and ages, in such variety of distempers, and in so many distant parts of Christendom.

By most men, I believe, it will be judged, at best, a needless undertaking, instead of an easy-tried medicine to introduce one more operose and expensive, unsupported by experiments, and recommended by wrong suppositions, that all the virtue is in the acid, and that the tar-water, being impregnated with volatile oil, is caustic, which are both notorious mistakes.

Though it be the character of resin not to dissolve and mix with water as salts do, yet these attract some fine particles of essential oil, which serves as a vehicle for such acid salts; and the colour of the tar-water showeth the fine oil, in which the vegetable salts are lodged, to be dissolved and mixed therein. The combination of two such different substances as oil and salt constitutes a very subtle and active medicine, fitted to mix with all humours, and resolve all obstructions, and which may properly be called an acid soap.

Tar-water operates more gently and safely, as the acid salts are sheathed in oil, and, thereby losing their acrimony, approach the nature of neutral salts, and so become more friendly to the animal system. By the help of a smooth insinuating oil, these acid salts are more easily and safely introduced into the fine capillaries. I may add, that the crasis[1772] of the blood is perfected by tar-water, being good against too great a solution and fluidity as a balsam, and against viscidity as a soap, all which entirely depends upon the mixture of oil with the acid, without which it could neither operate as a balsam nor a soap. Briefly, it was not mere acid or distilled water, or tincture of tar, but tar-water, as commonly made, by affusion and stirring of cold water upon tar, which hath wrought all those great cures and salutary effects which have recommended it as a medicine to the general esteem of the world.

The mixture of volatile oil, which is or contains the spirit, is so far from noxious that it is the very thing that makes tar-water a cordial; this gives it a grateful warmth, and raiseth the spirits of the hysteric and hypochondriacal; this also, rendering the blood balsamic, disposeth wounds of all sorts to an easy cure; this also it is that fortifies the vitals, and invigorates nature, driving the gout to the extremities, and shortening the fits, till it entirely subdues that

[1772] A medical term for the blending of physical qualities giving rise to health. The word comes from the Greek literally meaning "mixture."

obstinate and cruel enemy, as it hath been often known to do; but acid alone is so far from being able to do this, that on the contrary, the free use of acids is reckoned amongst the causes of the gout.

I never could find that the volatile oil drawn from tar by the affusion of cold water produced any inflammation, or was otherwise hurtful, not even though the water by longer stirring had imbibed far more of the oil than in the common manner, having been assured, that some of strong stomachs have drank it after twenty minutes' stirring, without any the least harm, and with very great benefit.

It hath been indeed insinuated that the oil was ordered to be skimmed off, because it is caustic and dangerous; but this is a mistake. I myself, among many others, drank the tar-water for two years together, with its oil upon it; which never proved hurtful, otherwise than, as being somewhat gross, and floating on the top, it rendered the water less palatable, for which reason alone it was ordered to be skimmed.

It hath also been hinted that making tar-water the second time of the same tar was cautioned against, for that it was apprehended such water would prove too heating; which is so far from being true that, when I could not get fresh tar, I used the second water without difficulty, by means whereof it pleased God to recover from the small-pox two children in my own family, who drank it very copiously, a sufficient proof that it is not of that fiery caustic nature which some would persuade us.

The truth is, my sole reason for advising the tar not to be used a second time was, because I did not think it would sufficiently impregnate the water, or render it strong enough, after so much of the fine volatile parts had been carried off by the former infusion. Truth obligeth me to affirm that there is no danger (for as much as I could ever observe) to be apprehended from tar-water, as commonly made; the fine volatile oil, on which I take its cordial quality to depend, is, in its own nature, so soft and gentle, and so tempered by the acid, and both so blended and diluted with so great a quantity of water, as to make a compound, cherishing and cordial, producing a genial kindly warmth without any inflaming heat, a thing I have often said, and still find it necessary to inculcate.

Some medicines indeed are so violent that the least excess is dangerous; these require an exactness in the dose, where a small error may produce a great mischief. But tar is, in truth, no such dangerous medicine, not even in substance; as I have more than once known it taken innocently, mixed with honey, for a speedy cure of a cold.

But, notwithstanding all that hath been said on that subject, it is still sometimes asked, What precise quantity or degree of strength is required? To which I answer (agreeably to what hath been formerly and frequently observed), the palate, the stomach, the particular case and constitution of the patient, the very climate or season of the year, will dispose and require him to drink more or less in quantity, stronger or weaker in degree; precisely to measure its strength, by a scrupulous exactness, is by no means necessary. Every one may settle that matter for himself, with the same safety that malt is proportioned to water in making beer, and by the same rule, to wit, the palate.

Only in general thus much may be said, that the proportions I formerly recommended will be found agreeable to most stomachs, and withal of sufficient strength, as many thousands have found, and daily find, by experience. I take this opportunity to observe, that I use tar-water made in stone ware or earthen very well glazed, earthen vessels unglazed being apt to communicate a nauseous sweetness to the water.

Tar-water is a diet-drink, in the making whereof there is great latitude, its perfection not consisting in a point, but varying with the constitution and palate of the patient, being, nevertheless, at times, taken by the same person, weaker or stronger, with much the same effect, provided it be proportionably in greater or lesser quantity. It may indeed be so very weak as to have little or no effect; and, on the other hand, so very strong as to offend the stomach; but its degree of strength is easily discerned by the colour, smell, and taste, which alone are the natural and proper guides whereby to judge thereof: which strength may be easily varied, in any proportion, by changing the quantity either of tar or water, or the time of stirring. As for setting tar-water to stand, this is not to make it stronger, but more clear and palatable.

I found myself obliged to assert the innocence and safety, as well as usefulness, of the tar-water as it is commonly made by the methods laid down in my former writings on this subject; and this was not only in regard to truth, but much more in charity to a multitude, which may otherwise perhaps be influenced by the authority of some who endeavour to put them out of conceit with a medicine so cheap, so efficacious, and so universal, by suggesting and propagating scruples about a caustic quality arising from the volatile oily particles of tar, or resin imbibed together with the acid in making tar-water; an apprehension so vain that the reverse thereof is true, for which I appeal to the experience of many thousands, who can answer for the innocence and safety, as well as efficacy, of this medicine, of which there are such ample and numerous certificates published to the world.

I shall finish my essay on the plague and its cure with observing that, in case God should with-hold His hand for the present, yet these reflections will not be altogether fruitless, if they dispose men to a proper temper of mind, and a cautious regimen, avoiding all extremes (which things are justly reckoned among the chief preservatives against infection) but especially if the apprehension of this destroyer shall beget serious thoughts on the frailty of human life, and, in consequence thereof, a reformation of manners; advantages that would sufficiently repay the trouble of writing and reading this letter, even though the trial of tar-water, as a remedy for the plague, should be postponed (as God grant it may) to some future and distant opportunity.

[Finis]

345 BERKELEY TO HALES [1773]

Gentleman's Magazine 17 (February 1747): 64–65.

17 January 1747

A Letter by the Author of Siris to the Reverend Dr. Hales on the Benefit of Tar-Water in Fevers, for Cattle as well as the Human Species

Published at his Lordship's Desire, on Occasion of the present Distemper among the Cattle, and for the general Good of Mankind.

To one gallon of fresh tar, pour six gallons of cold water; stir and work them strongly together, with a large flat stick, for the space of one full hour; let the whole stand six or eight hours, that the tar may subside; then scum it, and pour off the water, whereof three gallons warm are to be given the first day, two the second, and one the third day, at equal intervals, the dose not being less than a pint, not more than a quart; and the beast being all that time, and for two or three days after, kept warm and nourished, if it will not eat hay, with mash or gruel.

I believe this course will rarely fail of success, having often observed fevers in human kind to have been cured by a similar method. But as in fevers it often throws out pustules or ulcers on the surface of the body, so in beasts it may be

---

[1773] Stephen Hales* (1677–1761). The letter was republished in October 1747 in *Two Letters from the Right Reverend Dr. George Berkeley . . . to Thomas Prior . . . to the Rev. Dr. Hales* (London, 1747). Berkeley likely addressed this letter to Hales on account of the latter's *Account of some Experiments and Observations on Tar-Water* (1745; 2nd. edn, London, 1747), a paper read before the Royal Society.

presumed to do the like; which ulcers, being anointed with a little tar, will, I doubt not, in a short time dry up and disappear.

By this means the lives of infected cattle may be preserved at the expense of a gallon of tar for each. A thing which I repeat and inculcate, not only for the sake of the cattle and their owners, but also for the benefit of mankind in general, with regard to a fever; which terrible subduer and destroyer of our species, I have constantly found to be itself easily subdued by tar-water. Nevertheless, though in most other cases I find that the use of this medicine hath generally obtained, yet in this most dangerous and frequent case, where its aid is most wanted, and at the same time most sure, I do not find that the use thereof has equally obtained abroad in the world.

It grieves me to think that so many thousands of our species should daily perish by a distemper which may be easily cured by a remedy so ready at hand, so easy to take, and so cheap to purchase as tar-water, which I never knew to fail when copiously drank, in any sort of fever. All this I say after more than a hundred trials, in my own family and neighbourhood.

But, whatever backwardness people may have to try experiments on themselves or their friends, yet it is hoped they may venture to try them on their cattle, and that the success of such trials in fevers of brutes (for a fever it plainly is) may dispose them to probable hopes of the same success in their own species.

Experiments, I grant, ought to be made with caution, and yet they may be made, and actually are made every day on probable reasons and analogy. Thus, for instance, because I knew that tar-water was cordial and diaphoretic, and yet no inflamer, I ventured to give it in every stage of the small-pox, though I had never heard of its being given otherwise than as a preservative against that distemper; and the success answered my expectation.

If I can but introduce the general use of tar-water for this murrain,[1774] which is in truth a fever, I flatter myself this may pave the way for its general use in all fevers whatsoever.

A murrain among cattle hath been sometimes observed to be the forerunner of the plague among men. If that should prove the present case (which God forbid) I would earnestly recommend the copious drinking of warm tar-water,- from the very first appearance of the symptoms of such plague. I do also recommend it to be tried in like manner against the bite of a mad dog, when other approved medicines are not at hand.

[*Finis*]

[1774] A plague or pestilence.

346 BERKELEY TO PRIOR

Stock, p. lxxvii (extract).

24 January 1747

You asked me in your last letter, whether we had not provided a house in Cloyne for the reception and cure of sick persons. By your query it seems there is some such report: but what gave rise to it could be no more than this, viz. that we are used to lodge a few stroling sick with a poor tenant or two in Cloyne, and employ a poor woman or two to tend them, and supply them with a few necessaries from our house. This may be magnified (as things gather in the telling) into an hospital: but the truth is merely what I tell you. I wish you would send a political pamphlet now and then, with what news you hear. Is there any apprehension of an invasion upon Ireland?

347 BERKELEY TO PRIOR[1775]

LR, pp. 293–95. Stock, p. lxxviii (extract).

Cloyne, 6 February 1746/47

Dear Tom,

Your manner of accounting for the weather seems to have reason in it; and yet there still remains something unaccountable, viz. why there should be no rain in the regions mentioned. If the bulk, figure, situation, and motion of the earth are given, and the luminaries remain the same, should there not be a certain cycle of the seasons ever returning at certain periods? To me it seems, that the exhalations perpetually sent up from the bowels of the earth have no small share in the weather; that nitrous exhalations produce cold and frost; and that the same causes which produce earthquakes within the earth produce storms above it. Such are the variable causes of our weather; which, if it proceeded only from fixed and given causes, the changes thereof would be as regular as the vicissitudes of the days, or the return of eclipses. I have writ this extempore, *valeat quantum valere potest.*[1776]

[1775] Stock only reproduces the first paragraph.
[1776] Literally "may it be as strong as it is able [to be]." More freely: "it will have as much of an effect as it is able to have."

In my last I mentioned my cousin's death.[1777] My brothers and I are his heirs at law. I know nothing of his circumstances. He has been captain of a man of war for about twenty years, and must have left something. It is true he always commanded great ships, which have the fewest opportunities of getting, his very first having been a sixty gun ship: but still, as I said, there must be something probably worth looking after. I would therefore be advised by you what course to take. Would it not be right to employ your friend the solicitor, Mr. Levinge, to enquire at the late Captain George Berkeley's house in Lisle street, and see what is become of his effects? Also to examine whether he has left a will, and what it contains? If this be the right way, pray lose no time. Adieu, dear Tom.

> your affectionate humble servant,
> G. Cloyne

Cloyne, Feb. 6 1746-7

Dear Tom, Desire your friend Mr. Levinge, without delay, to enter a caveat, in my name, in Doctors' Commons,* against any one's taking out administration.

348 BERKELEY TO PRIOR[1778]

LR, pp. 295-97. Stock, p. lxxviii (extract).

Cloyne, 9 February 1746/47

Dear Tom,

You ask me if I had no hints from England about the primacy. I can only say, that last week I had a letter from a person of no mean rank who seemed to wonder that he could not find I had entertained any thoughts of the primacy, while so many others of our bench were so earnestly contending for it. He added, that he hoped I would not take it ill if my friends wished me in that station. My answer was, that I am so far from soliciting, that I do not

---

[1777] George Berkeley (?-1746), a captain in the Royal Navy. He was commissioned captain in 1728. Captain Berkeley in his will left money to "my cousin Captain William Berkeley*," Berkeley's younger brother. Not much is known about William, except that he held a command in Fife in 1745.

[1778] Stock only reproduces the first paragraph.

even wish for it; that I do not think myself the fittest man for that high post; and that therefore I neither have, nor ever will, ask it.

I hear it reported that my cousin died worth about eighteen thousand pounds.[1779] He had spent the summer at the Earl of Berkeley's[1780] hunting-seat in Wiltshire. He came to town in an ill state of health, which he hoped Dr. Mead[1781] would have set right, but was mistaken. Had I known his illness, perhaps it might have been better for him. The Earl of Berkeley's agent, one Mr. Young, who was also my cousin's agent, pretends to be executor, with another gentleman, one Mr. Brome. By all means take the readiest method that some person whom you know at London gets a sight of the original Will; and you will do a good service to, dear Tom,

> your faithful servant,
> G. Cloyne

I am unknowing in these matters; but think that the best advice how to proceed.

349 BERKELEY TO PRIOR[1782]

LR, pp. 297-98. Stock, pp. lxxviii-lxxix (extract).

Cloyne, 10 February 1746/47

Dear Tom,

In my other letter that comes to you this post, I forgot to say what I now think very necessary, viz. that you must be so good as to get your friend by all means to send a copy of the will, written in a close hand, by post, without loss of time.[1783]

In a letter from England, which I told you came a week ago, it was said that several of our Irish bishops were earnestly contending for the primacy. Pray who are they? I thought Bishop Stone[1784] was only talked of at present. I ask

---

[1779] George Berkeley (?-1746), a captain in the Royal Navy. See Letter 347.
[1780] Augustus Berkeley (1716-55), fourth Earl of Berkeley.
[1781] Richard Mead (1673-1754), physician and book collector. He authored *Short Discourse Concerning Pestilential Contagion and the Methods to be used to Prevent It* (1720) and *De Variolis et Morbillis Liber* (*Discourse on the Small-Pox and Measles*, 1747).
[1782] Stock includes only the second paragraph, without the closing.
[1783] A reference to the will of Berkeley's cousin, George Berkeley (?-1746), who was a captain in the Royal Navy. See Letter 347.
[1784] George Stone (1708-64). He was dean of Ferns (1733) and of Derry (1734) before becoming bishop of Ferns (1740). He then translated to Kildare (1743). In 1745 he translated again

this question merely out of curiosity, and not from any interest, I assure you; for I am no man's rival or competitor in this matter. I am not in love with feasts, and crowds, and visits, and late hours, and strange faces, and a hurry of affairs often insignificant. For my own private satisfaction, I had rather be master of my time than wear a diadem. I repeat these things to you that I may not seem to have declined all steps to the primacy out of singularity, or pride, or stupidity, but from solid motives. As for the argument from the opportunity of doing good, I observe that duty obliges men in high stations not to decline occasions of doing good; but duty doth not oblige men to solicit such high stations. Adieu.

    yours,

    G. Cloyne

350 BERKELEY TO PRIOR[1785]

LR, pp. 299–300. Stock, p. lxxix (extract).

Cloyne, 19 February 1746/47

Dear Tom,

It was very agreeable to hear you had taken proper measures to procure a copy of my cousin's will, and to enter the caveat.[1786]

The ballad you sent has mirth in it, with a political sting in the tail; but the speech of Van Haaren is excellent. I believe it Lord Chesterfield's.[1787]

We have at present, and for these two days past had, frost and some snow. Our military-men are at length sailed from Cork harbour. We hear they are designed for Flanders.

I must desire you to make, at leisure, the most exact and distinct inquiry you can into the characters of the senior fellows, as to their behaviour, temper, piety, parts, and learning; also to make a list of them, with each

---

and was bishop of Derry. He would be made archbishop of Armagh and primate of all Ireland in 1747.

[1785] Stock omits the first paragraph and closing.

[1786] A reference to the will of Berkeley's cousin, George Berkeley (?–1746), who was a captain in the Royal Navy. See Letter 347.

[1787] Philip Dormer Stanhope* (1694–1773), fourth Earl of Chesterfield.

man's character annexed to his name. I think it of so great consequence to the public to have a good provost that I would willingly look before hand, and stir a little, to prepare an interest, or at least to contribute my mite, where I properly may, in favour of a worthy man, to fill that post when it shall become vacant.

Dr. Hales,[1788] in a letter to me, has made very honourable mention of you. It would not be amiss if you should correspond with him, especially for the sake of granaries and prisons. Adieu.

 yours,

 George Cloyne

351 BERKELEY TO PRIOR[1789]

LR, pp. 300–02. Stock, pp. lxxix–lxxx (extract).

Cloyne, 20 February 1746/47

Dear Tom,

 Though the situation of the earth with respect to the sun changes, yet the changes are fixed and regular: if therefore this were the cause of the variation of winds, the variation of the winds must be regular, i.e. regularly returning in a cycle. To me it seems that the variable cause of the variable winds are the subterraneous fires, which, constantly burning, but altering their operation according to the various quantity or kind of combustible materials they happen to meet with, send up exhalations more or less of this or that species; which, diversely fermenting in the atmosphere, produce uncertain variable winds and tempests. This, if I mistake not, is the true solution of that crux.

 As to the papers about petrifications which I sent to you and Mr. Simon,[1790] I do not well remember the contents. But be you so good as to look them over, and show them to some other of your society; and if, after this, you shall think them worth publishing in your collections, you may do as you please: otherwise I would not have things hastily and carelessly written thrust into public view.

[1788] Stephen Hales* (1677–1761).
[1789] Stock omits the final paragraph and closing.
[1790] James Simon (?–after 1756). See Letter 335.

As to your query, there were two mad women recovered, it seems, by a method we made use of, though not, as you have been told, by sweating. When you come, you shall know the particulars.

yours,

George Cloyne

352 BERKELEY TO PELHAM-HOLLES[1791]

BL Add. MS 32710, fol. 299.

Cloyne, 5 March 1746/47

My good Lord,

Your Lordship's letter with which I was favoured last post needed no apology. I wish it may have come time enough to be of use to the patient. Her distemper being of so long continuance arrived to so great a height, and nature spent and worn out by different courses of medicine, she cannot hope for a perfect recovery without length of time and a more attentive care than people commonly have of their health. I have nevertheless reason to hope she will find in a few months great relief from a constant drinking of tar water joined with a prudent regimen and abstinence from all other medicines.

I would advise that at first her tar water be made by stirring a gallon of water in a quart of tar strongly with a flat stick for the space only of two minutes; and that she take of this daily a pint and a half in six glasses, a quarter of a pint in each glass. She may drink it cold or warm as she best likes upon trial. But she may drink it first cold, and if this agrees with her, continue it so. It should be drunk night and morning and at an hour's distance at least from her meals. I verily think this course and a proper regimen of early hours, light nourishing food, and gentle exercise in good air will by the blessing of God give her great relief.

Her disorder is nervous in the highest degree, and nervous cases are slowest and most difficult to cure. However I do not think this case hopeless

---

[1791] Thomas Pelham-Holles* (1693–1768), Duke of Newcastle upon Tyne and first Duke of Newcastle under Lyme. This letter was first published in Luce, "More Unpublished Berkeley Letters and New Berkeleiana," 51–53.

having known those symptoms of pain and stiffeness in the head and neck, terrours and agonies of mind, trembling and giddiness, and indeed all sorts of hysterical disorders to have been removed by tar water. I have also known that weakening wasting disorder peculiar to the female sex, which is often the cause and often the effect of low spirits to have been cured by the same medicine, which both supplies spirits and strengthens the tone of the vessels.

I cannot indeed say that I have known all the above named symptoms together in so high a degree in one and the same person. But I have known very high hypocondriac disorders that would yield to no other medicine removed by tar water. Some cures of this kind your Lordship may find in Mr. Prior's *Narrative*,[1792] particularly if you give yourself the trouble of looking into the case of John Ussher[1793] Esquire of Lismore. I observe the patient is about that time of life wherein the monthly discharges of women are wont to cease, which period is often attended with dangerous disorders against which I take tar water to be a medicine of singular efficacy.[1794]

After her stomach is by custom reconciled a little to the tar water she will be able to take it a little stronger (made so by a minute or two longer stirring) and in greater quantity, perhaps so far as one quart per diem, which need not be exceeded. If her stomach could bear it at first as strong as four minutes stirring would make it, it would be so much the better. I shall be glad to know what success the patient finds when she has continued this course for a month or six weeks. And on any occasion where your Lordship thinks I may be of use, you may freely command him who is with all respect

> My Lord,
> your Lordship's affectionate brother & obedient servant,
> George Cloyne

P.S.: Drams are often known to produce the most desperate & incurable hysterics, which (if this should happen to be the patient's case) ought by all means to be laid aside, though not altogether at once, but gradually; as soon as possible with safety. This may be whispered to her friend.

[1792] Thomas Prior* (1681–1751) published his *Authentic Narrative* in Dublin (1746).

[1793] John Usher (Ussher) (1703–48). He was MP in Ireland for Dungarvon, County Waterford. See *Burke's Irish Family Records*, American edn (New York: Arco, 1976), 1156. For Usher's letters, see sections 111–16 in the second edition of Prior's *Authentic Narrative*.

[1794] This sentence is excluded by Luce, presumably on account of the nature of its content. I here reproduce the letter in its entirety.

353 BERKELEY TO PERCIVAL[1795]

EP, BL Add. MS 47000, fol. 120.

Cloyne, 14 March 1746/47

My Lord,

Nothing but the necessity I am under could tempt me to give your Lordship this trouble of employing you in so small a matter and so much beneath you, but to me and my family of no small concern. Last summer I wrote to Naples, and we have since ransacked all the music shops in Ireland, without being able to get one good string for the violincello: this is one bad effect of the present war which interrupts our commerce with Italy. The strings we get break as fast as they are put on, so that for several months past it has been impossible for my children to practice, and without practice they will be in danger of losing an art which has cost them much pains, and me a great deal of money. It will therefore be a very seasonable and obliging benefaction if your Lordship will be so good as to send me by post one dozen of first and one dozen of second strings for the four stringed bass or violincello, enclosed in four covers, six in each. I depend upon your Lordship's so often experienced goodness, that you will pardon the freedom of this address from

My Lord,

your most obedient & obliged humble servant,

G: Cloyne

P.S.: Being unwilling the Princess Caroline[1796] should suffer or tar water lose its credit I took the liberty in my last to desire your Lordship to give some hints to Mr. Schutz[1797] for the right way of using it to which I must now add that as her stomach may happen to be squeamish, it will not be amiss to begin with tar water made by only two minute's stirring, and when she is accustomed it may be given stronger i.e. made by stirring it 3 or 4 minutes.

354 BERKELEY TO PRIOR[1798]

LR, pp. 302–03. Stock, pp. lxxxii–lxxxiii (extract).

Cloyne, 22 March 1746/47

Dear Tom,

[1795] See Luce, "Some Unpublished Berkeley Letters with some New Berkeleiana," 155–56.
[1796] Likely a reference to Elizabeth Caroline (1713–57), the fourth child of King George II.*
[1797] Augustus Schutz (c. 1693–1757), keeper of the privy purse and master of robes to King George II.*
[1798] Stock omits the first paragraph and the closing.

There is another query which arises on the will, viz. whether a mortgage be not a freehold, and whether it can be bequeathed without three witnesses?[1799] This, and the two other queries of the residue, etc., I would have stated to Mr. Kelly my wife's cousin. He is a very sensible man, and would consider the matter, as a friend, more attentively than those who, of greater name, might offer their first thoughts. Pray give him the usual fee for the best lawyer; and if he refuses to take it, tell him you cannot take his advice if he does not take his fee.

As to what you say, that the primacy would have been a glorious thing; for my part I do not see (all things considered) the glory of wearing the name of primate in these days, or of getting so much money; a thing every tradesman in London may get if he pleases. I should not choose to be primate in pity to my children; and for doing good to the world, I imagine I may upon the whole do as much in a lower station. Adieu, dear Tom.

> yours affectionately,
> G. Cloyne

355 BERKELEY TO BEARCROFT[1800]

SPG Ser. B, vol. 15, fol. 191.

[Before 10 April 1747][1801]

Revd Sir,

Two hundred pounds of the money contributed towards the college intended at Bermuda I have left many years lodged in the bank of Messrs. Hoare & Arnold[1802] in Fleet Street designing to return it (as I had already done by other

---

[1799] Most likely a reference to the will of Berkeley's cousin, George Berkeley (?–1746), who was a captain in the Royal Navy. See Letter 347.

[1800] The original has gone missing, at least as of my visit to the SPG archives at Rhodes House, Oxford University, in June 2010. A microfilm record of the letter is present, however (USPG microfilm of Ser. B, vol. 15, fol. 191). A synopsis of the letter with quoted excerpts is present in the summary catalog, USPG B15–17, North American and West Indian letters, 1746–50. Another microfilm copy is available at NLI no. 2889, p. 2510.

[1801] The letter is undated, but given subsequent correspondence, it must have been penned before 10 April 1747, when it had already been received by the SPG and discussed. See Rhodes House, Journal of the SPG, vol. 10, fol. 245, committee minutes for 10 April 1747.

[1802] Henry Hoare* (1705–85). Christopher Arnold (?–1759), a goldsmith, was made a partner in Hoare's Bank in 1725. See Victoria Hutchings, *Messrs Hoare, Bankers: A History of the Hoare Banking Dynasty* (London: Constable, 2005), esp. pp. 56–57.

sums) to the donors when known. But as these continue still unknown, and there is no likelyhood of my ever knowing them, I think the properest use that can be made of that sum is to place it in the hands of your Society for Popagating the Gospel, to be employed by them in the furtherance of their good work, in such manner as to them shall seem most useful.[1803] If the Society thinks fit, I believe fifty pounds of it might be usefully employed in purchasing the most approved writings of the divines of the Church of England, to which I would have added the Earl of Clarendon's *History of the Civil Wars*,[1804] and the whole sent as a benefaction to Harvard College at Cambridge near Boston, New England, as a proper means to inform their judgment and dispose them to think better of our church. I am Revd. Sir

> your faithful humble servant,
>
> G: Cloyne

356 BEARCROFT TO BERKELEY[1805]

SPG Ser. B, vol. 15, fol. 249.

Charterhouse [After April 1747][1806]

My Lord,

Messieur Hoare & Arnold[1807] very readily paid your draught on them for two hundred pounds to me for the use of the Society for the Propagation of the Gospel in Foreign Parts and I return your Lordship their most hearty thanks for it. Fifty pounds of this benefaction or more if you shall be pleased to direct, will be laid out in purchasing the most approved books of the divines of the Church

---

[1803] According to the benefactions journal of the SPG, the sum of £200 was received on 10 April 1747 from the Lord Bishop of Cloyne. SPG X787 Benefactions Book 1701–1750/51, p. 228.

[1804] Edward Hyde (1609–74), first Earl of Clarendon, author of the multivolume *History of the Rebellion and Civil Wars in England* (1702–04).

[1805] Another microfilm copy is available at NLI no. 2889, p. 2510.

[1806] There is some question as to the date of the letters to and from Bearcroft. This letter has two dates, 8 July 1748 and 18 April 1747. The latter is probably the time of its writing and the former is likely a reference date added afterwards. Other SPG entries record Berkeley's letter and gift in 1747 and it is unlikely the society would wait more than a year to respond to such a gift. Another entry records a letter dated 25 July 1748 to William Shirley (1694–1771) at Harvard announcing the gift of books from the Bishop of Cloyne, suggesting that the books were bought prior to July 1748. Another letter from the SPG archives (Ser. B, vol. 16, fol. 38) is from Edward Holyoke of Harvard College, acknowledging and giving thanks for the gift of the books from the SPG, dated 18 February 1748/49 – a reasonable time frame for the purchase and transportation of the books across the Atlantic. See note to Letter 357.

[1807] Henry Hoare* (1705–1785). Christopher Arnold (?–1759), a goldsmith, was made a partner in Hoare's Bank in 1725. See Hutchings, *Messrs Hoare, Bankers*, esp. pp. 56–57.

of England, together with Clarendon's *History of the Civil Wars*[1808] to be sent as a benefaction to Harvard College at Cambridge near Boston. But as it is somewhat doubtful what of these sort of writings will be received there, if your Lordship approves of it, I will write to Mr. Shirley[1809] the present governor of the province and President of Harvard College,[1810] a worthy member of the Church of England, to consult him about the matter as to what books are in his opinion most proper, and how far he will undertake for their being received, and placed to best advantage in the college. And if your Lordship would be pleased yourself to name any particular books, they shall make part of the number. And I shall be further obliged to your Lordship if you will let me know how the two hundred pounds should be entered on the books of the society, whether thus—'Two Hundred Pounds from the Right Revd. the Lord Bishop of Cloyne, sent in to his Lordship from Pensions to him unknown towards the Establishment of the College intended at Bermudas, but that design being now laid aside, his Lordship is pleased to think the most proper use to be made of that Sum is to place it in the hands of the Society for the Propagation of the Gospel in Foreign Parts, to help forward that good work': or if you approve not of this that you would be pleased to direct in what words you would have this considerable benefaction entered. I think I may say your Lordship's prescription of tar-water has cured me of an inveterate rheumatism and I most heartily thank you for it, and I am

My Lord your most
obedient etc.

P.S.: Mr. Hoare desired me to acquaint your Lordship that there are fourteen shillings yet remaining due your Lordship to balance that account.

357 BERKELEY TO BEARCROFT

SPG Ser. B, vol. 15, fol. 191a.

Cloyne [After April 1747][1811]

Revd Sir,

[1808] Edward Hyde, first Earl of Clarendon (1609–74), author of the multivolume *History of the Rebellion and Civil Wars in England* (1702–04).

[1809] William Shirley (1694–1771), governor of the colony of Massachusetts 1741–49 and 1753–56.

[1810] Edward Holyoke (1689–1769), ninth President of Harvard (1737–69).

[1811] There is some question as to the date of this letter. The date 18 April 1747 is present on the original letter and its envelope, but Bearcroft's reply to Berkeley's previous letter (Letter 354) and to which this letter is a reply is itself dated 8 July 1748. The latter letter is a copy, but given the distances

I begin to apprehend as you do that a present coming from your Society[1812] may be regarded with some jealousy or distrust. But if the books come as a benefaction procured by me for the use of Harvard College I doubt not they will meet with a good reception having formerly made that college a present of some books of my own when I was in those parts, and since my return having sent them others as a benefaction procured from my friends all which were very thankfully received. The books given from my self were ancient Greek authors which I found they wanted. Those sent afterwards were Latin books of literature. These make way for another benefaction which they seemed to hope and wish for upon receiving the last. And I have reason to think the books undernamed (if the Society approve thereof) may not improperly be admitted in such benefaction. I do not therefore think it necessary to trouble Governour Shirley[1813] or to take any other steps in this matter. As to the method of entering the benefaction in the books of the Society I leave that to you having no objection to what you offer on that head. I sincerely congratulate with you on the recovery of your health and wish you the continuance of it being very truly Revd Sir

your most faithful and obedient servant,

G: Cloyne

P.S.: As you intimated a desire that I should name some more books I have ventured to set down the following, with due submission nevertheless to the judgment of the venerable Society. Hooker,[1814] Chillingworth,[1815] the Sermons of Barrow,[1816] Tillotson[1817] Sharp[1818] & Clarke,[1819] Scot's Christian

---

involved (Berkeley is in Cloyne while Bearcroft is in London) it would seem likely that at least one of the letters is misdated, but there is a small mystery here. Luce speculates that the date is 8 July 1747, which is consistent with the index to the SPG letters that lists Berkeley's letter as having been received in 1747. Thus Bearcroft's reply (dated 8 July 1748) should be 1747, and this letter would have been written sometime after that. See *Works*, vol. IX, p. 131. The journal for the SPG (i.e. its committee minutes) for 15 January 1747/48 (Journal of the SPG, vol. 10, fol. 328) mentions that Bearcroft laid before the committee a list of books totaling £50 to be sent to Harvard College pursuant to the request of the Bishop of Cloyne. A total of £200 is listed as a gift to the SPG.

[1812] Society for the Propagation of the Gospel in Foreign Parts.

[1813] William Shirley (1694–1771), governor of the colony of Massachusetts (1741–49 and 1753–56).

[1814] Richard Hooker (1554?–1600), theologian, author of *Of the Laws of Ecclesiastical Politie* (1593).

[1815] William Chillingworth (1602–44), theologian, most famous for *The Religion of Protestants* (1638).

[1816] Isaac Barrow (1630–77), mathematician and theologian, master of Trinity College, Cambridge.

[1817] John Tillotson (1630–94), archbishop of Canterbury.

[1818] Most likely Thomas Sharp (1693–1758), Church of England clergyman. He published many influential sermons, including *The Necessary Knowledge of the Lord's Supper* (1727), to which it is likely Berkeley is referring here.

[1819] The reference here is probably to Richard Clerke's (Clarke) (?–1634) *Sermons Preached by that Reverend and Learned Divine Richard Clerke* (1637).

life,[1820] Pearson on the Creed,[1821] Burnet on the 39 Articles, Burnet's history of the Reformation,[1822] A. B. Spotswood's history of the church of Scotland,[1823] Clarendon's history,[1824] Prideaux's connection,[1825] Cave's historia literaria eccles:[1826] Hammond's annotations,[1827] Pool's Synopsis Critic.,[1828] the Patres Apostolici published by Le Clerc with the dissertations of Pearson etc. in the epistles of S. Ignatius.[1829] These I guess will amount to about thirty pounds; if approved of, the Society will be pleased to add as many more as will make up the fifty pounds, or otherwise they will be pleased to name them all.

358 PERCIVAL TO BERKELEY[1830]

EP, BL Add. MS 46998, fol. 75.

25 May 1747

My Lord,

The lawyer into whose hands I put your Lordship's assignment of my mortgage to my niece Dering in order for him to make a memorial thereof to be sent to the Register Office in Ireland.[1831] Upon perusing the assignment

---

[1820] John Scott (1638/39–95), rector at St. Peter-le-Poer, London. The reference is to *The Christian Life from its Beginning to its Consummation in Glory: Together with the Several Means and Instruments of Christianity Conducing Thereunto, with Directions for Private Devotion and Forms of Prayer, Fitted to the Several States of Christians* (1681; expanded 2nd edn., 1683–87, two volumes each published in two parts).

[1821] John Pearson (1613–86), bishop of Chester. The work is *An Exposition of the Creed* (1659), which underwent numerous reprintings well into the eighteenth century.

[1822] Gilbert Burnet (1643–1715), bishop of Salisbury and historian. He authored *History of the Reformation of the Church of England*, 3 vols. (London: Chiswell, 1679, 1681, 1714) and *An Exposition of the Thirty-nine Articles of the Church of England*, 3rd edn. (London: Chiswell, 1705).

[1823] John Spotswood (Spottiswoode) (1565–1639), archbishop of St. Andrews, author of *History of the Church and State of Scotland from the Year of Our Lord 203 to the End of the Reign of King James VI, 1625* (London, 1655).

[1824] Edward Hyde (1609–74), first Earl of Clarendon, author of the multivolume *History of the Rebellion and Civil Wars in England* (1702–04).

[1825] Humphrey Prideaux (1648–1724), dean of Norwich, author of *Connection* (1716–18).

[1826] William Cave (1637–1713), author of *Scriptorum Ecclesiasticorum Historia Literaria a Christo Nato Usque ad Saeculum XIV* (London, 1688).

[1827] Henry Hammond (1605–60), Church of England clergyman, author of *A Paraphrase and Annotations on All the Books of the New Testament* (1653).

[1828] Matthew Poole (Pool) (1624–79), author of *Synopsis Criticorum* (London, 1669).

[1829] Jean le Clerc* (1657–1736). The edition to which Berkeley is referring is, I believe, *Patres Apostolici* (Amsterdam, 1724) edited by Le Clerc. It contains the *Vindiciae Epistolarum S. Ignatii* (1672) of John Pearson (1613–86), bishop of Chester.

[1830] A loose letter in Percival's papers, and an unsigned copy. The back reads "London 25 May 1747 to the Bishop of Cloyne."

[1831] Concerning Berkeley's loan to Percival and its repayment, see Letter 338.

says that that which your Lordship made was not rightly drawn which he has explained on the [?] leaf of the enclosed paper, which brings you the proper form, for your perusal, which when you have approved and returned he will copy out the same on the mortgage deed for your Lordship to sign. It was unlucky that this was not thought of before, and that the lawyer to whom you left it to draw up your assignment, did not peruse the mortgage which, had he done, he would have found it was made for a term of 500 years only and not as a mortgage in fee. There are forms of [some?] which I understand not, but I hope the reason of this fresh trouble we are at, is sufficiently clearly explained to your Lordship.

I hope your Lordship and family are well and wish you joy of Admiral Anson's[1832] lucky success against the French. I am

your Lordships

most affectionate humble servant

359 BERKELEY TO JOHN BOYLE[1833]

Harvard, Orrery Papers MS *Eng. 218.2, vol. 5, pp. 56–58.*

Cloyne, 11 July 1747

My Lord,

A letter should be natural and easy, and yet I must confess I write with no small concern, since your Lordship is pleased to say you expect improvement from my letters,[1834] that same improvement which in good earnest I should myself have hoped for from corresponding with a person so conversant in the classics as well as the *grand monde*,[1835] did not my years, and the nature of my studies, stand in the way.

[1832] George Anson (1697–1762), Baron Anson, admiral of the Royal Navy. On 3 May 1747 Anson's fleet successfully intercepted two combined French convoys, taking most of them.

[1833] John Boyle* (1707–62), fifth Earl of Cork and fifth Earl of Orrery. According to the preface of the letterbook from which this letter is transcribed, the Earl of Orrery was in Ireland from 1746 until June 1749, returning to Ireland from England on 30 October 1749. Two-thirds of the letter is printed in *The Orrery Papers*, 2 vols. (London: Duckworth, 1903), vol. II, pp. 4–5.

[1834] This line suggests there is more to the correspondence, but no trace of additional letters has been found. We know that Boyle (Lord Orrery) used tar water and apparently advocated its use to his neighbors, which might have been what started the exchange of letters. See the letter of 7 July 1744 from Boyle to William P., Esq. (Orrery Papers MS Eng. 218.2, vol. 5, no pagination at the end of volume) where he discusses first using tar water.

[1835] Literally "great world." The phrase connotes fashionable society.

Your Lordship's lot is fallen in a pleasant land. For my part, I admire the *belles let[t]res*[1836] without possessing them (A truth I need not mention), my studies having been of the dry and crabbed kind, which give a certain gouty stiffness to the style.[1837]

Give me leave to say, your Lordship is a little unreasonable, who, not content with the management of an ample fortune, and a share in the great councils of both Kingdoms, must needs invade the provinces of private men, and be at once, the best husbandman, and the politest scholar, in the nation.

In hopes your children will take after you, I do most sincerely congratulate your Lordship on their recovery, from a distemper so often fatal, and, that hangs like a general doom, over all that come into the world.

I have just now read over Mr. West's book,[1838] a performance worthy your Lordship's recommendation, and in the reading thereof I have been much edified, instructed and entertained. To me it seems extremely well wrote, and if it had been worse wrote, it could not yet have failed of doing good among many who do not consider what is said so much as who it is that say it. Certainly, men of the world, courtiers and fine gentlemen, are more easily wrought on by those of their own sort, than by recluse and professed divines.

The Christian religion, since its first planting in these islands, hath been never so openly and profanely insulted, as in these our days, which call loudly for information or for punishment.[1839] But it is to be hoped the public, by a timely and serious reflexion (whereof I take this gentleman's attempt to be a noble specimen and leading step), will recover their lost sense of duty, so far as to avert that vengeance which the posture of our affairs abroad and the plague hovering round our coasts, do threaten. But, come what will, that your Lordship and family may safely ride out the storm is the sincere wish of my Lord, your Lordship's most obedient and most etc.,

George Cloyne

[1836] Literally "fine letters." The phrase is used to refer to stylish or literary letters.

[1837] The following two paragraphs were apparently omitted from the 1903 edition of the Orrery Papers.

[1838] Likely Gilbert West (1703–56), who published *Observations on the History and Evidence of the Resurrection of Jesus Christ* (1747).

[1839] The preceding sentence is omitted from the 1903 edition.

360 BERKELEY TO PERCIVAL[1840]

EP, BL Add. MS 46998, fol. 14.

Cloyne, 3 December 1747

My Lord,

Ever since I was favoured with your Lordship's letter I have expected to see Mr. Purcell[1841] with the draught of the new conveyance such as I agreed to sign, which I was ready to do when called on, but he has not yet been with me.[1842]

I was much obliged for the hints your Lordship gave me of the present state of our affairs, which indeed are in a bad situation, but I doubt in no worse than we deserve, but as our enemies do not seem to be better than we are, it is to be hoped providence will not suffer them to trample upon us, and our late successes at sea[1843] are I think a proof of this. It should seem we are designed mutually to punish each other.

It would give me great pleasure to hear of your and Lady Egmont's improvement in health. But as this season is very severe, I beg leave to observe that your Lordship cannot be too careful to guard against the cold, which is very apt to increase nervous disorders.

I cannot conclude my letter without returning my thanks for the account you were pleased to send me of Mr. West.[1844] Since I read his excellent book, I have met with another very well writ treatise of Mr. Lyttleton's,[1845] who (I understand) is one of the lords of the treasury. As these gentlemen cannot be supposed to write out of interest, they are so much the fitter to draw their pens in defence of Christianity, as they have done to very good purpose. Our best respects wait on your Lordship and good Lady Egmont.

I am your Lordship's most obedient servant,

G: Cloyne

[1840] See Luce, "Some Unpublished Berkeley Letters with some New Berkeleiana," 156–57.
[1841] Richard Purcell* (c. 1690 –?).
[1842] See Letter 358.
[1843] The British won major naval victories over the French at sea on 3 May and 14 October 1747.
[1844] Likely Gilbert West (1703–56), who published *Observations on the History and Evidence of the Resurrection of Jesus Christ* (1747).
[1845] George Lyttelton (1709–73), first Baron Lyttelton. He was made a lord of the treasury in December 1744. In 1747 he anonymously published *A Letter to the Tories* and argued as a non-Jacobite Tory for a rapprochement with the ministerial Whigs, but his authorship was quickly well known.

361 BERKELEY TO PERCIVAL (SON)

EP, BL Add. MS 47014A, fol. 120.

Cloyne,14 May 1748

My dear Lord,

I think my self obliged to condole with your Lordship on the death of a father[1846] who honoured me with his friendship for about forty years, and whose life adorned every part of that private path he chose to walk in. At the same time I console myself with the share I hope I have in the good graces of the son, and congratulate your Lordship on coming to an honour and estate that may enable you to make a more conspicuous figure in that active scene of life to which your genius leads with so remarkable success. The late Earl your father was a right honest man and a good Christian. Your Lordship by adding these qualities to those of a courtier and politician will create a new character, that will render you beloved by God and man, which that you, your Lady and family may always be is most sincerely wished by

My Lord,

your Lordship's most faithful and most obedient servant,

George Cloyne

P.S.: I must beg your Lordship to present my best respects and complements of condolance to the good Lady Dowager your mother

Cloyne, May 14, 1748

362 BERKELEY TO PRIOR

Stock, pp. lxxxv–lxxxvi (extract).

Cloyne, 2 February 1749

Three days ago we received the box of pictures. The two men's heads with ruffs are well done; the third is a copy, and ill coloured: they are all Flemish: so is the woman, which is also very well painted, though it hath not the beauty and freedom of an Italian pencil. The two Dutch pictures, containing animals, are well done as to the animals: but the human figures and sky are ill done. The two pictures of ruins are very well done, and are Italian. My son William[1847]

[1846] John Percival* (1683–1748), first Earl of Egmont, died on 1 May 1748 in London.
[1847] William Berkeley (1736–51).

had already copied two other pictures of the same kind, and by the same hand. He and his sister[1848] are both employed in copying pictures at present; which shall be dispatched as soon as possible; after which they will set about some of yours. Their stint, on account of health, is an hour and half a day for painting. So I doubt two months will not suffice for copying: but no time shall be lost, and great care taken of your pictures, for which we hold ourselves much obliged.[1849]

Our round tower stands where it did; but a little stone arched vault on the top was cracked, and must be repaired: the bell also was thrown down, and broke its way through three boarded stories, but remains entire. The door was shivered into many small pieces, and dispersed; and there was a stone forced out of the wall. The whole damage, it is thought, will not amount to twenty pounds. The thunder-clap was by far the greatest that I ever heard in Ireland.

363 BERKELEY TO JOHNSON[1850]

CU, Spec. MS Coll. Samuel Johnson, vol. I, p. 116.

Cloyne, 23 August 1749

Reverend Sir,

I am obliged for the account you have sent me of the prosperous estate of learning in your college of Newhaven.[1851] I approve of the regulations made there, and am particularly pleased to find your sons have made such a progress as appears from their elegant address to me in the Latin tongue. It must indeed give me a very sensible satisfaction to hear that my weak endeavours have been of some use and service to that part of the world.

I have two letters of yours at once on my hands to answer, for which business of various kinds must be my apology. As to the first, wherein you enclosed a small pamphlet relating to tar water, I can only say in behalf of those points in which the ingenious author seems to differ from me, that I advance nothing which is not grounded on experience, as may be seen at large in Mr. Prior's

---

[1848] Julia Berkeley (1738–after 1756), Berkeley's only daughter that survived him.

[1849] Concerning the return of the pictures, see Letter 382.

[1850] Also printed in Herbert and Carol Schneider, eds, *Samuel Johnson, President of King's College: His Career and Writings*, 4 vols (New York: Columbia University Press, 1929), I: pp. 134–35 and E. Edwards Beardsley, *Life and Correspondence of Samuel Johnson* (New York: Hurd and Houghton, 1874), pp. 154–55. The volume is catalogued at CU as BK 811 J36 06.

[1851] Yale.

narrative of the effects of tar-water,[1852] printed three or four years ago, and which may be supposed to have reached America.

For the rest, I am glad to find a spirit towards learning prevail in those parts, particularly New York where you say a college is projected which has my best wishes.[1853] At the same time I am sorry that the condition of Ireland containing such numbers of poor, uneducated people, for whose sake charity schools are erecting throughout the kingdom, obligeth us to draw charities from England so far are we from being able to extend our bounty to New York a country in proportion much richer than our own. But as you are pleased to desire my advice upon this undertaking, I send the following hints to be enlarged and improved by your own judgment.

I would not advise the applying to England for charters or statutes (which might cause great trouble expense and delay), but to do the business quietly within themselves.

I believe it may suffice to begin with a president and two fellows. If they can procure but three fit persons, I doubt not the college from the smallest beginnings would soon grow considerable. I should conceive good hopes were you at the head of it.

Let them by all means supply themselves out of the seminarys in New England. For I am very apprehensive none can be got in Old England (who are willing to go) worth sending.

Let the Greek and Latin classics be well taught. Be this the first care as to learning. But the principal care must be good life and morals to which (as well as to study) early hours and temperate meals will much conduce.

If the terms for degrees are the same as in Oxford & Cambridge, this would give credit to the college, and pave the way for admitting their graduates *ad eundem*[1854] in the English Universities.

Small premiums in books, or distinctions in habit may prove useful encouragements to the students.

I would advise that the building be regular, plain and cheap, and that each student have a small room (about ten feet square) to himself.

I recommended this nascent seminary to an English bishop to try what might be done there. But by his answer it seems the colony is judged rich enough to educate its own youth.

[1852] Thomas Prior* (1681–1751) published his *Authentic Narrative* in Dublin in 1746.
[1853] King's College (later Columbia University) would be founded in 1754. Johnson would be its first president.
[1854] "with equivalent status."

Colleges from small beginnings grow great by subsequent bequests and benefactions. A small matter will suffice to set one a going. And when this is once well done, there is no doubt it will go on and thrive. The chief concern must be to set out in a good method, and introduce from the very first a good taste into the Society. For this end its principal expense should be in making a handsome provision for the President and Fellows.

I have thrown together these few crude thoughts for you to ruminate upon and digest in your own judgment, and propose from yourself, as you see convenient.

My correspondence with patients who drink tar-water obliges me to be less punctual in corresponding with my friends. But I shall be always glad to hear from you. My sincere good wishes and prayers attend you in all your laudable undertakings.

I am, your faithful, humble servant,

G. Cloyne

364 BERKELEY TO THE ROMAN CATHOLIC CLERGY[1855]

A Word to the Wise: or an Exhortation to the Roman Catholic Clergy of Ireland. By a Member of the Established Church *(Dublin: Faulkner, 1749). Announced in* Dublin Journal *2357 (10–14 October 1749).*

[October 1749]

A Word to the Wise or an Exhortation to the Roman Catholic Clergy of Ireland

Homo sum, nihil a me alienum puto[1856]

Be not startled, Reverend Sirs, to find yourselves addressed to by one of a different communion. We are indeed (to our shame be it spoken) more inclined to hate for those articles wherein we differ, than to love one another for those wherein we agree. But if we cannot extinguish, let us at least suspend our animosities, and,

---

[1855] Although an address published as a pamphlet in 1749, this has the form of a letter and was responded to by the Catholic clergy in a letter (Letter 365), and is thus included in the present volume. Subsequent publications of the pamphlet list the author explicitly as the Bishop of Cloyne. The piece also appears as *A Word to the Wise; or, the Bishop of Cloyne's Exhortation to the Roman Catholic Clergy of Ireland*, 4th edn. (Boston: S. Kneeland, 1750); in the 1752 *Miscellany*, pp. 89–108; in the *Querist* (London, 1750); and in the second edition of the same (London, 1751).

[1856] Berkeley is modifying (or perhaps misremembering) Terence, *Heautontimorumenos* ("The Self-Tormentor"), line 25. The original reads *Homo sum, humani nihil a me alienum puto:* "I am a man; I think nothing human alien to me." Berkeley's version translates as "I am a man; I think nothing alien to me."

forgetting our religious feuds, consider ourselves in the amiable light of country-men and neighbours. Let us for once turn our eyes on those things in which we have one common interest. Why should disputes about faith interrupt the duties of civil life, or the different roads we take to heaven prevent our taking the same steps on earth? Do we not inhabit the same spot of ground, breathe the same air, and live under the same government? Why, then, should we not conspire in one and the same design, to promote the common good of our country?

We are all agreed about the usefulness of meat, drink, and clothes, and, without doubt, we all sincerely wish our poor neighbours were better supplied with them. Providence and nature have done their part; no country is better qualified to furnish the necessaries of life, and yet no people are worse provided. In vain is the earth fertile, and the climate benign, if human labour be wanting. Nature supplies the materials, which art and industry improve to the use of man, and it is the want of this industry that occasions all our other wants.

The public hath endeavoured to excite and encourage this useful virtue. Much hath been done; but whether it be from the heaviness of the climate, or from the Spanish or Scythian blood that runs in their veins, or whatever else may be the cause, there still remains in the natives of this island a remarkable antipathy to labour. You, gentlemen, can alone conquer their innate hereditary sloth. Do you then, as you love your country, exert yourselves.

You are known to have great influence on the minds of your people; be so good as to use this influence for their benefit. Since other methods fail, try what you can do. 'Be instant in season, out of season; reprove, rebuke, exhort' (2 Tim., iv. 2). Make them thoroughly sensible of the sin and folly of sloth. Show your charity in clothing the naked and feeding the hungry, which you may do by the mere breath of your mouths. Give me leave to tell you that no set of men upon earth have it in their power to do good on easier terms, with more advantage to others, and less pains or loss to themselves. Your flocks are of all others most disposed to follow directions, and of all others want them most; and indeed what do they not want?

The house of an Irish peasant is the cave of poverty; within, you see a pot and a little straw; without, a heap of children tumbling on the dunghill. Their fields and gardens are a lively counterpart of Solomon's description in the Proverbs: 'I went (saith that wise king) by the field of the slothful, and by the vineyard of the man void of understanding; and, lo, it was all grown over with thorns, and nettles had covered the face thereof, and the stone wall thereof was broken down' (Prov., xxiv. 30, 31). In every road the ragged ensigns of poverty are displayed; you often meet caravans of poor, whole families in a drove, without clothes to cover or bread to feed them, both which might be easily procured by moderate labour. They are encouraged in this vagabond life by the miserable hospitality they meet with in every cottage, whose inhabitants expect the same kind reception in their turn when they become beggars themselves; beggary being the last refuge of these improvident creatures.

If I seem to go out of my province, or to prescribe to those who must be supposed to know their own business, or to paint the lower inhabitants of this land in no very pleasing colours, you will candidly forgive a well-meant zeal, which obligeth me to say things rather useful than agreeable, and to lay open the sore in order to heal it.

But whatever is said must be so taken as not to reflect on persons of rank and education, who are no way inferior to their neighbours; nor yet to include all even of the lowest sort, though it may well extend to the generality of those especially in the western and southern parts of the kingdom, where the British manners have less prevailed. We take our notions from what we see, mine are a faithful transcript from originals about me.

The Scythians were noted for wandering, and the Spaniards for sloth and pride; our Irish are behind neither of these nations from which they descend, in their respective characteristics. 'Better is he that laboureth and aboundeth in all things, than he that boasteth himself and wanteth bread,' saith the son of Sirach (x. 27);[1857] but so saith not the Irishman. In my own family a kitchen-wench refused to carry out cinders, because she was descended from an old Irish stock. Never was there a more monstrous conjunction than that of pride with beggary; and yet this prodigy is seen every day in almost every part of this kingdom. At the same time these proud people are more destitute than savages, and more abject than negroes. The negroes in our plantations have a saying, 'If negro was not negro, Irishman would be negro.' And it may be affirmed with truth that the very savages of America are better clad and better lodged than the Irish cottagers throughout the fine fertile counties of Limerick and Tipperary.

Having long observed and bewailed this wretched state of my countrymen, and the insufficiency of several methods set on foot to reclaim them, I have recourse to your Reverences as the *dernier ressort*.[1858] Make them to understand that you have their interest at heart, that you persuade them to work for their own sakes, and that God hath ordered matters so as that they who will not work for themselves must work for others. The terrors of debt, slavery, and famine should, one would think, drive the most slothful to labour. Make them sensible of these things, and that the ends of Providence and order of the world require industry in human creatures. 'Man goeth forth to his work and to his labour until the evening,' saith the Psalmist (Ps. civ. 23), when he is describing the

---

[1857] i.e. Ecclesiasticus or Siracides, in the Apocrypha.
[1858] "last resort."

beauty, order, and perfection of the works of God. But what saith the slothful person? 'Yet a little sleep, a little slumber, a little folding of the hands to sleep' (Prov., vi. 10). But what saith the wise man? 'So shall thy poverty come as one that travelleth, and thy want as an armed man' (Prov., vi. 11).

All nature will furnish you with arguments and examples against sloth: 'Go to the ant, thou sluggard,' cries Solomon. The ant, the bee, the beetle, and every insect but the drone, reads a lesson of industry to man. But the shortest and most effectual lesson is that of St. Paul: 'If any man will not work, neither should he eat' (2 Thess., iii. 10). This command was enjoined the Thessalonians, and equally respects all Christians, and indeed all mankind; it being evident by the light of nature that the whole creation works together for good, and that no part was designed to be useless. As therefore the idle man is of no use, it follows that he hath no right to a subsistence. 'Let them work (saith the apostle), and eat their own bread' (2 Thess., iii. 12); not bread got by begging, not bread earned by the sweat of other men, but their own bread, that which is got by their own labour. 'Then shalt thou eat the labour of thine hands,' saith the Psalmist; to which he adds, 'Happy shalt thou be, and it shall be well with thee' (Ps. cxxxviii. 2), intimating that to work and enjoy the fruits thereof is a great blessing.

A slothful man's imagination is apt to dress up labour in a horrible mask; but, horrible as it is, idleness is more to be dreaded, and a life of poverty (its necessary consequence) is far more painful. It was the advice of Pythagoras, *to choose the best kind of life*; for that use would render it agreeable, reconciling men even to the roughest exercise. By practice, pains become at first easy, and in the progress pleasant; and this is so true, that whoever examines things will find there can be no such thing as a happy life without labour, and that whoever doth not labour with his hands must, in his own defence, labour with his brains.

Certainly, planting and tilling the earth is an exercise not less pleasing than useful; it takes the peasant from his smoky cabin into the fresh air and the open field, rendering his lot far more desirable than that of the sluggard, who lies in the straw, or sits whole days by the fire.

Convince your people that not only pleasure invites but necessity also drives them to labour. If you have any compassion for these poor creatures, put them in mind how many of them perished in a late memorable distress,[1859] through want of that provident care against a hard season, observable not only in all other men, but even in irrational animals. Set before their eyes, in lively colours, their own indigent and sordid lives, compared with those of other people, whose industry hath procured them hearty food, warm clothes, and decent dwellings.

[1859] A famine started in 1739 in Ireland; it was at its worst in 1740–41.

Make them sensible what a reproach it is that a nation which makes so great pretensions to antiquity, and is said to have flourished many ages ago in arts and learning, should in these our days turn out a lazy, destitute, and degenerate race.

Raise your voices, Reverend Sirs, exert your influence, show your authority over the multitude, by engaging them to the practice of an honest industry, a duty necessary to all, and required in all, whether Protestants, or Roman Catholics, whether Christians, Jews, or pagans. Be so good, among other points, to find room for this, than which none is of more concern to the souls and bodies of your hearers, nor consequently deserves to be more amply or frequently insisted on.

Many and obvious are the motives that recommend this duty. Upon a subject so copious you can never be at a loss for something to say. And while, by these means, you rescue your countrymen from want and misery, you will have the satisfaction to behold your country itself improved. What pleasure must it give you to see these waste and wild scenes, these naked ditches and miserable hovels, exchanged for fine plantations, rich meadows, well-tilled fields, and neat dwellings; to see people well fed, and well clad, instead of famished, ragged scarecrows; and those very persons tilling the fields that used to beg in the streets.

Neither ought the difficulty of the enterprise to frighten you from attempting it. It must be confessed, a habit of industry is not at once introduced; neighbour, nevertheless, will emulate neighbour, and the contagion of good example will spread as surely as of bad, though perhaps not so speedily. It may be hoped there are many that would be allured by a plentiful and decent manner of life to take pains, especially when they observe it to be attained by the industry of their neighbours, in no sort better qualified than themselves.

If the same gentle spirit of sloth did not soothe our squires as well as peasants, one would imagine there should be no idle hands among us. Alas! how many incentives to industry offer themselves in this island, crying aloud to the inhabitants for work? Roads to be repaired, rivers made navigable, fisheries on the coasts, mines to be wrought, plantations to be raised, manufactures improved, and, above all, lands to be tilled, and sowed with all sorts of grain.

When so many circumstances provoke and animate your people to labour; when their private wants, and the necessities of the public; when the laws, the magistrates, and the very country calls upon them; you cannot think it becomes you alone to be silent, or hindmost in every project for promoting the public good. Why should you, whose influence is greatest, be least active? Why should you, whose words are most likely to prevail, say least in the common cause?

Perhaps it will be said, the discouragements attending those of your communion are a bar against all endeavours for exciting them to a laudable industry. Men are stirred up to labour by the prospect of bettering their fortunes, by getting estates, or employments; but those who are limited in the purchase of estates, and excluded from all civil employments, are deprived of those spurs to industry.

To this it may be answered, that, admitting these considerations do, in some measure, damp industry and ambition in persons of a certain rank, yet they can be no let to the industry of poor people, or supply an argument against endeavouring to procure meat, drink, and clothes. It is not proposed that you should persuade the better sort to acquire estates, or qualify themselves for becoming magistrates; but only that you should set the lowest of the people at work, to provide themselves with necessaries, and supply the wants of nature.

It will be alleged in excuse of their idleness, that the country people want encouragement to labour, as not having a property in the lands. There is small encouragement, say you, for them to build or plant upon another's land, wherein they have only a temporary interest. To which I answer that life itself is but temporary; that all tenures are not of the same kind; that the case of our English and the original Irish is equal in this respect; and that the true aborigines, or natural Irish, are noted for want of industry in improving even on their own lands, whereof they have both possession and property.

How many industrious persons are there in all civilized countries, without any properties in lands, or any prospect of estates, or employments? Industry never fails to reward her votaries. There is no one but can earn a little, and little added to little makes a heap. In this fertile and plentiful island, none can perish for want but the idle and improvident. None who have industry, frugality, and foresight but may get into tolerable, if not wealthy, circumstances. Are not all trades and manufactures open to those of your communion? Have you not the same free use, and may you not make the same advantage, of fairs and markets as other men? Do you pay higher duties, or are you liable to greater impositions, than your fellow subjects? And are not the public premiums and encouragements given indifferently to artists of all communions? Have not, in fact, those of your communion a very great share of the commerce of this kingdom in their hands? And is not more to be got by this than by purchasing estates, or possessing civil employments, whose incomes are often attended with large expenses?

A tight house, warm apparel, and wholesome food, are sufficient motives to labour. If all had them, we should be a flourishing nation. And if those who take pains may have them, those who will not take pains are not to be pitied; they are to be looked on and treated as drones, the pest and disgrace of society.

It will be said, the hardness of the landlord cramps the industry of the tenant. But if rent be high, and the landlord rigorous, there is more need of industry in the tenant. It is well known that in Holland taxes are much higher, and rent both of land and houses far dearer, than in Ireland. But this is no objection or impediment to the industry of the people, who are rather animated and spurred on to earn a livelihood by labour, that is not to be got without it.

You will say, it is an easy matter to make a plausible discourse on industry, and its advantages; but what can be expected from poor creatures who are destitute of all conveniences for exerting their industry, who have nothing to improve upon, nothing to begin the world with? I answer, they have their four quarters, and five senses. Is it nothing to possess the bodily organs sound and entire? That wonderful machine, the hand, was it formed to be idle?

Was there but will to work, there are not wanting in this island either opportunities or encouragements. Spinning alone might employ all idle hands (children as well as parents), being soon learned, easily performed, and never failing of a market, requiring neither wit nor strength, but suited to all ages and capacities. The public provides utensils, and persons for teaching the use of them; but the public cannot provide a heart and will to be industrious. These, I will not deny, may be found in several persons in some other parts of the kingdom, and wherever they are found the comfortable effects show themselves. But seldom, very seldom, are they found in these southern people, whose indolence figureth a lion in the way, and is proof against all encouragement.

But you will insist, how can a poor man, whose daily labour goes for the payment of his rent, be able to provide present necessaries for his family, much less to lay up a store for the future? It must be owned, a considerable share of the poor man's time and labour goes towards paying his rent. But how are his wife and children employed, or how doth he employ himself the rest of his time? The same work tires, but different works relieve. Where there is a true spirit of industry, there will never be wanting something to do, without doors or within, by candlelight if not by day-light. *Labor ipse voluptas*,[1860] saith the poet, and this is verified in fact.

In England, when the labour of the field is over, it is usual for men to betake themselves to some other labour of a different kind. In the northern parts of that industrious land, the inhabitants meet, a jolly crew, at one another's houses, where they merrily and frugally pass the long and dark winter evenings; several families, by the same light and the same fire, working at their different manufactures of wool, flax, or hemp; company, meanwhile, mutually cheering and provoking to labour. In certain other[1861] parts you may see, on a summer's evening, the common labourers sitting along the street of a town or village,

[1860] "Work itself is the pleasure."
[1861] The *Miscellany* (1752) has the following footnote: "E.g. Newport-Pagnel in Buckinghamshire."

each at his own door, with a cushion before him making bonelace and earning more in an evening's pastime than an Irish family would in a whole day. Those people, instead of closing the day with a game on greasy cards, or lying stretched before the fire, pass their time much more cheerfully in some useful employment, which custom hath rendered light and agreeable.

But admitting, for the various reasons above alleged, that it is impossible for our cottagers to be rich, yet it is certain they may be clean. Now, bring them to be cleanly, and your work is half done. A little washing, scrubbing, and rubbing, bestowed on their persons and houses, would introduce a sort of industry; and industry in any one kind is apt to beget it in another.

Indolence in dirt is a terrible symptom, which shows itself in our lower Irish more, perhaps, than in any people on this side the Cape of Good Hope. I will venture to add that, look throughout the kingdom, and you shall not find a clean house inhabited by clean people, and yet wanting necessaries; the same spirit of industry that keeps folk clean being sufficient to keep them also in food and raiment.

But alas! our poor Irish are wedded to dirt upon principle. It is with some of them a maxim that the way to make children thrive is to keep them dirty. And I do verily believe that the familiarity with dirt, contracted and nourished from their infancy, is one great cause of that sloth which attends them in every stage of life. Were children but brought up in an abhorrence of dirt, and obliged to keep themselves clean, they would have something to do, whereas now they do nothing.

It is past all doubt that those who are educated in a supine neglect of all things, either profitable or decent, must needs contract a sleepiness and indolence, which doth necessarily lead to poverty, and every other distress that attends it. 'Love not sleep (cries Solomon), lest thou come to poverty; open thine eyes and thou shalt be satisfied with bread' (Prov., xx. 13). It is therefore greatly to be wished, that you would persuade parents to inure their children betimes to a habit of industry, as the surest way to shun the miseries that must otherwise befall them.

An early habit, whether of sloth or diligence, will not fail to show itself throughout the whole course of a man's life. 'Train up a child (saith the wise man) in the way he should go, and when he is old he will not depart from it' (Prov., xxii. 6). The first tincture often leaves so deep a stain as no afterthought or endeavour can wash out. Hence sloth in some minds is proof against all arguments and examples whatsoever, all motives of interest and duty, all impressions even of cold and hunger. This habit, rooted in the child, grows up and adheres to the man, producing a general listlessness, and aversion from labour. This I take to be our great calamity.

For, admitting that some of our squires and landlords are vultures with iron bowels, and that their hardness and severity is a great discouragement to the tenant, who will naturally prefer want and ease before want and toil; it must at the same time be admitted that neither is the landlord, generally speaking, so hard, nor the climate so severe, nor the soil so ungrateful, as not to answer the husbandman's labour, where there is a spirit of industry, the want of which is the true cause of our national distress. Of this there are many evident proofs.

I have myself known a man, from the lowest condition of life, without friends or education, not knowing so much as to write or read, bred to no trade or calling, by pure dint of day-labour, frugality, and foresight, to have grown wealthy, even in this island, and under all the above-mentioned disadvantages. And what is done by one, is possible to another.

In Holland a child five years old is maintained by its own labour; in Ireland many children of twice that age do nothing but steal, or encumber the hearth and dunghill. This shameful neglect of education shows itself through the whole course of their lives, in a matchless sloth bred in the very bone, and not to be accounted for by any outward hardship or discouragement whatever. It is the native colour, if we may so speak, and complexion of the people. Dutch, English, French, or Flemish cannot match them.

Mark an Irishman at work in the field; if a coach or horseman go by, he is sure to suspend his labour, and stand staring until they are out of sight. A neighbour of mine made it his remark in a journey from London to Bristol, that all the labourers of whom he inquired the road constantly answered without looking up, or interrupting their work, except one who stood staring and leaning on his spade, and him he found to be an Irishman.

It is a shameful thing, and peculiar to this nation, to see lusty vagabonds strolling about the country, and begging without any pretence to beg. Ask them why they do not labour to earn their own livelihood, they will tell you, they want employment; offer to employ them, and they shall refuse your offer; or, if you get them to work one day, you may be sure not to see them the next. I have known them decline even the lightest labour, that of haymaking, having at the same time neither clothes for their backs nor food for their bellies.

A sore leg is an estate to such a fellow; and this may be easily got, and continued with small trouble. Such is their laziness, that rather than work they will cherish a distemper. This I know to be true, having seen more than one instance wherein the second nature so far prevailed over the first, that sloth was preferred to health. To these beggars, who make much of their sores and prolong their diseases, you cannot do a more thankless office than cure them, except it be to shave their beards, which conciliate a sort of reverence to that order of men.

It is indeed a difficult task to reclaim such fellows from their slothful and brutal manner of life, to which they seem wedded with an attachment that no temporal motives can conquer; nor is there, humanly speaking, any hopes they will mend, except their respect for your lessons and fear of something beyond the grave be able to work a change in them.

Certainly, if I may advise, you should, in return for the lenity and indulgence of the government, endeavour to make yourselves useful to the public; and this will best be performed by rousing your poor countrymen from their beloved sloth. I shall not now dispute the truth or importance of other points, but will venture to say that you may still find time to inculcate this doctrine of an honest industry; and that this would by no means be time thrown away, if promoting your country's interest, and rescuing so many unhappy wretches of your communion from beggary or the gallows, be thought worth your pains.

It should seem you cannot in your sermons do better than inveigh against idleness, that extensive parent of many miseries and many sins; idleness, the mother of hunger and sister of theft: 'idleness which,' the son of Sirach assures us, 'teacheth many vices.' [Ecclesiasticus, xxxiii. 27.]

The same doctrine is often preached from the gallows. And indeed the poverty, nakedness, and famine which idleness entaileth on her votaries, do make men so wretched that they may well think it better to die than to live such lives. Hence a courage for all villainous undertakings, which bringing men to a shameful death, do then open their eyes when they are going to be closed for ever.

If you have any regard (as it is not to be doubted) either for the souls or bodies of your people, or even for your own interest and credit, you cannot fail to inveigh against this crying sin of your country. Seeing you are obnoxious to the laws, should you not in prudence try to reconcile yourselves to the favour of the public; and can you do this more effectually than by co-operating with the public spirit of the legislature, and men in power?

Were this but done heartily, would you but 'be instant in season, and out of season, reprove, rebuke, exhort' (2 Tim., iv. 2), such is the ascendant you have gained over the people that we might soon expect to see the good effects thereof. We might hope 'that our garners would be soon full, affording all manner of store, that our sheep would bring forth thousands, that our oxen would be strong to labour, that there would be no breaking in, nor going out (no robbery, nor migration for bread), and that there would be no complaining in our streets' (Ps. cxliv. 13, 14).

It stands upon you to act with vigour in this cause, and shake off the shackles of sloth from your countrymen, the rather because there be some who surmise that yourselves have put them on. Right or wrong, men will be apt to judge of your doctrines by their fruits. It will reflect small honour on their teachers if, instead of honesty and industry, those of your communion are peculiarly distinguished by the contrary qualities, or if the nation converted by the great and glorious St. Patrick should, above all other nations, be stigmatized and marked out as good for nothing.

I can never suppose you so much your own enemies as to be friends to this odious sloth. But were this once abolished, and a laudable industry introduced in its stead, it may perhaps be asked, who are to be gainers? I answer, your Reverences are like to be great gainers; for every penny you now gain you will gain a shilling: you would gain also in your credit; and your lives would be more comfortable.

You need not be told how hard it is to rake from rags and penury a tolerable subsistence; or how offensive to perform the duties of your function amidst stench and nastiness; or how much things would change for the better in proportion to the industry and wealth of your flocks. Duty as well as interest calls upon you to clothe the naked, and feed the hungry, by persuading them to 'eat (in the apostle's phrase) their own bread'; or, as the Psalmist expresseth it, 'the labour of their own hands'. By inspiring your flocks with a love of industry, you will at once strike at the root of many vices, and dispose them to practise many virtues. This therefore is the readiest way to improve them.

Consult your superiors. They shall tell you the doctrine here delivered is a sound Catholic doctrine, not limited to Protestants but extending to all, and admitted by all, whether Protestants or Roman Catholics, Christians or Mahometans, Jews or Gentiles. And as it is of the greatest extent, so it is also of the highest importance. St. Paul expressly saith that 'if any provide not for his own, and especially for those of his own house, he hath denied the faith, and is worse than an infidel' (1 Tim., v. 8).

In vain, then, do you endeavour to make men orthodox in points of faith if at the same time, in the eyes of Christ and His apostles, you suffer them to be worse than infidels, than those who have no faith at all. There is something it seems worse than even infidelity; and to incite and stimulate you to put away that cursed thing from among you is the design and aim of this address. The doctrine we recommend is an evident branch of the Law of Nature; it was taught by prophets, inculcated by apostles, encouraged and enforced by philosophers, legislators, and all wise States, in all ages and in all parts of the world. Let me therefore entreat you to exert yourselves, *to be instant in season, and out of season, rebuke, reprove, exhort.* Take all opportunities to drive the lion out of the way; raise your voices, omit no occasion, public or private, of awakening your wretched countrymen from their sweet dream of sloth.

Many suspect your religion to be the cause of that notorious idleness which prevails so generally among the natives of this island, as if the Roman Catholic faith was inconsistent with an honest diligence in a man's calling. But whoever considers the great spirit of industry that reigns in Flanders and France, and even beyond the Alps, must acknowledge this to be a groundless suspicion. In Piedmont and Genoa, in the Milanese and the Venetian state, and indeed throughout all Lombardy, how well is the soil cultivated, and what manufactures of silk, velvet, paper and other commodities, flourish? The King of Sardinia will suffer no idle hands in his territories, no beggar to live by the sweat of another's brow; it has even been made penal at Turin to relieve a strolling beggar. To which I might add that the person whose authority will be of the greatest weight with you, even the Pope himself, is at this day endeavouring to put new life into the trade and manufactures of his country.

Though I am in no secret of the Court of Rome, yet I will venture to affirm, that neither Pope nor cardinals will be pleased to hear that those of their communion are distinguished above all others by sloth, dirt, and beggary; or be displeased at your endeavouring to rescue them from the reproach of such an infamous distinction.

The case is as clear as the sun; what we urge is enforced by every motive that can work on a reasonable mind. The good of your country, your own private interest, the duty of your function, the cries and distresses of the poor, do with one voice call for your assistance. And if it is on all hands allowed to be right and just, if agreeable both to reason and religion, if coincident with the views both of your temporal and spiritual superiors, it is to be hoped this address may find a favourable reception, and that a zeal for disputed points will not hinder your concurring to propagate so plain and useful a doctrine, wherein we are all agreed.

When a leak is to be stopped, or a fire extinguished, do not all hands co-operate-without distinction of sect or party? Or if I am fallen into a ditch, shall I not suffer a man to help me out, until I have first examined his creed? Or when I am sick, shall I refuse the physic, because my physician doth or doth not believe the Pope's supremacy?

Fas est et ab hoste doceri.[1862] But, in truth, I am no enemy to your persons, whatever I may think of your tenets. On the contrary, I am your sincere

---

[1862] Ovid, *Metamorphoses*, IV, 28. "It is right to be taught even by the enemy."

well-wisher. I consider you as my countrymen, as fellow subjects, as professing belief in the same Christ. And I do most sincerely wish there was no other contest between us but who shall most completely practise the precepts of Him by whose name we are called, and whose disciples we all profess to be.

365 ROMAN CATHOLIC CLERGYMEN TO THE DUBLIN JOURNAL[1863]

Dublin Journal 2365 (14–18 November 1749).

14–18 November 1749

You will very much oblige many of your constant readers, if you acquaint the public that the address you lately published, entitled, *A Word to the Wise; or an Exhortation to the Roman Catholic Clergy of Ireland*, was received by the Roman Catholic clergy of Dublin with the highest sense of gratitude; and they take the liberty, in this public manner, to return their sincere and hearty thanks to the worthy author, assuring him that they are determined to comply with every particular recommended in it, to the utmost of their power. In every page it contains a proof of the author's extensive charity. His views are only towards the public good. The means he prescribeth are easily complied with, and his manner of treating persons in their circumstances so very singular that they plainly show the good man, the polite gentleman, and the true patriot. All this hath so great an effect upon them, that they have already directed circular letters to the parish priests of this diocese, recommending in the most earnest manner the perusal and zealous execution of what is contained in the said address; and it is hoped that by publishing this in your journal, the Roman Catholic clergy of the other parts of this kingdom will be induced to follow their example, which must promote the laudable views of that great and good man. At the same time, he may

---

[1863] The letter appears in Faulkner's *Dublin Journal* on 18 November 1749. An introduction to the letter reads: "There having been a very great demand for a pamphlet, entitled, *A Word to the Wise, or the Bishop of Cloyne's Exhortation to the Roman Catholic Clergy of Ireland*, the same is now reprinted in a neat Elziver letter, at the price of a penny, for the benefit of the poor Protestants, as well as Roman Catholics of this nation. N.B. Numbers of these pamphlets have been bought by many worthy noblemen and gentlemen, who wish well to their country, and the community in general, and who give these pamphlets away to their tenants and labourers, to spirit them up to cleanliness, industry, honesty, and riches. There being an extraordinary demand for the following letter, it is again printed, at the earnest request of the public." This letter is also printed in the 1752 *Miscellany*, pp. 108–09. In the *Miscellany* the letter is printed with the following preface: "Soon after the preceding Address was published [i.e. Letter 364], the printer hereof received the following 'Letter from the Roman Catholic Clergy of the Diocese of Dublin,' desiring it to be inserted in the Dublin Journal of November 18, 1749."

be assured that the Roman Catholic clergy of this city have frequently taken considerable pains to recommend to their respective flocks, industry and a due application to their different trades and callings, as an indispensable duty, and the means of avoiding the many vices and bad consequences which generally attend criminal poverty and want. But the more effectually to prevent these evils and remove all excuses for sloth and idleness, they have, several months ago, pursuant to the example of many bishoprics in Lombardy, Spain, Naples, etc., taken the steps most proper and expedient, in their opinion, to lessen considerably the number of holidays in this kingdom; and they make no doubt but their expectations will, in a short time, be fully answered, to the great advantage of the public.

We are, etc.

366 BERKELEY TO DOROTHY BOYLE[1864]

Devonshire MSS, Chatsworth, First Series, 364.0. By permission of the Duke of Devonshire and the Chatsworth House Trust.

Cloyne, 2 April 1750

Madam,

Permit me to thank your Ladyship for a present[1865] very valuable in it self, and much more so on account of the giver, who is so good as to remember an humble servant in this remote corner; where, to my sorrow, I am haunted with a taste for good company and fine arts which I got at Burlington house, the worst preparative in the world for a retreat at Cloyne. But, wherever I am, your Ladyship and my good Lord Burlington[1866] may always count upon the best respects and most sincere good wishes of

Madam

your most obedient

and most obliged

servant,

G. Cloyne

Cloyne, April 2, 1750

[1864] Dorothy (*née* Savile) Boyle* (1699–1758), Countess of Burlington.

[1865] John Stephens, in his article "Berkeley and Lady Burlington: A Footnote," *Berkeley Newsletter* 12 (1991–92): 17, identifies the gift as a book entitled *Character of King Charles the Second* authored by the second Marquis of Halifax – the father of Countess Burlington. The evidence is an inscription from Lady Burlington to Berkeley in the text.

[1866] Richard Boyle* (1694–1753), third Earl of Burlington and fourth Earl of Cork. He married Dorothy Savile (1699–1758) 21 March 1721.

367 BERKELEY TO THE DUBLIN JOURNAL[1867]

Dublin Journal 2409 (10–14 April 1750). Stock, pp. lxxx–lxxxii.

April 1750

Observations by a Rt. Rev. Prelate in Ireland
Concerning Earthquakes

Having observed that it hath been offered as a reason to persuade the public that the late shocks felt in and about London were not caused by an earthquake, because the motion was lateral, which it is asserted the motion of an earthquake never is, I take upon me to affirm the contrary. I have myself felt an earthquake at Messina in the year 1718, when the motion was horizontal or lateral. It did no harm in that city, but threw down several houses about a day's journey from thence.

We are not to think the late shocks merely an air-quake (as they call it), on account of signs and changes in the air, such being usually observed to attend earthquakes. There is a correspondence between the subterraneous air and our atmosphere. It is probable that storms or great concussions of the air do often, if not always, owe their origin to vapours or exhalations issuing from below.

I remember to have heard Count Tezzani[1868] at Catanea say, that some hours before the memorable earthquake of 1692, which overturned the whole city, he observed a line in the air (proceeding, as he judged, from exhalations poised and suspended in the atmosphere); also that he heard a hollow frightful murmur about a minute before the shock. Of 25,000 inhabitants 18,000 absolutely perished, not to mention others who were miserably bruised and wounded. There did not escape so much as one single house. The streets were narrow and the buildings high, so there was no safety in running into the streets; but on the first tremor (which happened a small space, perhaps a few minutes, before the downfall), they found it the safest way to stand under a doorcase, or at the corners of the house.

The Count was dug out of the ruins of his own house, which had over-whelmed above twenty persons, only seven whereof were got out alive.

[1867] The letter is addressed "To the Author of the Dublin Journal," i.e. George Faulkner.* The letter also appears in *Gentleman's Magazine* 20 (April 1750): 166–67, and in the *Literary Relics*, with only minor spelling variations, pp. 310–14.

[1868] Perhaps Nicholas Tezzano (?–?), a physician and professor at the University of Catania, who survived the earthquake of 1692 and reported upon it.

Though he rebuilt his house with stone, yet he ever after lay in a small adjoining apartment made of reeds plastered over. Catanea was rebuilt more regular and beautiful than ever. The houses indeed are lower, and the streets broader than before, for security against future shocks. By their account, the first shock seldom or never doth the mischief, but the *repliches* (as they term them) are most to be dreaded. The earth, I was told, moved up and down like the boiling of a pot, *terra bollente di sotto in sopra*,[1869] to use their own expression. This sort of subsultive motion is ever accounted the most dangerous.

Pliny in the second book of his natural history, observes that all earthquakes are attended with a great stillness of the air. The same was observed at Catanea. Pliny further observes, that a murmuring noise precedes the earthquake. He also remarks, that there is *signum in coelo, praeceditque motu futuro, aut interdiu, aut paulo post occasum sereno, ceu tenuis linea nubis in longum porrectae spatium;*[1870] which agrees with what was observed by Count Tezzani and others at Catania. And all these things plainly show the mistake of those who surmise that noises and signs in the air do not belong to or betoken an earthquake, but only an air-quake.

The naturalist above cited, speaking of the earth, saith, that *varie quatitur*,[1871] up and down sometimes, at others from side to side. He adds, that the effects are very various: cities, one while demolished, another swallowed up; sometimes overwhelmed by water, at other times consumed by fire bursting from the earth. One while the gulph remains open and yawning; another the sides close, not leaving the least trace or sign of the city swallowed up.

Britain is an island; (*maritima autem maxime quatiuntur*, saith Pliny)[1872] and in this island are many mineral and sulphureous waters. I see nothing in the natural constitution of London, or the parts adjacent, that should render an earthquake impossible or improbable. Whether there be any thing in the moral state thereof that should exempt it from that fear, I leave others to judge. I am,

> your humble servant,
>
> A. B.[1873]

[1869] Literally "boiling earth upwards from below."

[1870] Pliny, *Natural History*, II, 84. "[There is] a sign in the sky that precedes a future earthquake [literally "a future motion," but the context is clear that it is the motion of the earth], either during the day, or a little after sunset on a clear night: a slender thread of cloud stretched out a long ways."

[1871] "it is shaken in various ways."

[1872] Pliny, *Natural History*, II, 83. "Maritime places, morever, are especially shaken."

[1873] The heading of the article refers the reader to a previous article (in the same issue) that names Berkeley explicitly, a reprint of the account of the eruption of Vesuvius.

368 LLOYD TO BERKELEY[1874]

MS *unknown. Printed in L. Tyerman,* The Life and Times of the Rev. John Wesley, M.A., *3 vols.*
(London: Hodder & Stoughton, 1880), vol. II, p. 79 (extract).

4 July 1750

[...] I confess that Mr. Wesley[1875] has preached (though seldomer than has been wished) in my church.[1876] And I thought, that a fellow of Lincoln College, Oxford, who is admitted to preach before the university there, and has preached in many churches in London, and other parts of England, as also in Dublin, might be permitted to preach here also [...]

The mobs at Cork, and some other places in this kingdom, have obliged the Methodists to seek the protection of government, which undoubtedly they will have. Several of them, of good fortunes, to escape the persecution, are preparing to settle in England; and, because the clergy are supposed to have encouraged it, numbers of others resolve to quit our church. At this rate, we may, in a short time, have only the refuse left. Religion, my Lord, is now at a very low ebb in the world; and we can scarce see the outward form of it remaining. But corrupt as the world is, it is thought better that the devil should reign, than that Mr. Wesley should preach, especially in a church [...]

369 BERKELEY TO LLOYD

MS *unknown. Printed in L. Tyerman,* The Life and Times of the Rev. John Wesley, M.A., *3 vols.*
(London: Hodder & Stoughton, 1880), vol. II, pp. 79–80 (extract).

Cloyne, 4 July 1750

Reverend Sir,

I have that opinion of your prudence, that I doubt not you will be cautious whom you admit into your pulpit; and that you will avoid doing or

---

[1874] The Revd. Tyerman notes that the letter is "long," but only reproduces a small portion of it and provides no hint as to where the original letter might be found.

[1875] John Wesley (1703–91), Church of England clergyman and a founder of Methodism.

[1876] Richard Lloyd* (1699–1775) was the clergyman at Rathcormuck (1742–75) who had, the previous year, met and allowed John Welsey to preach from his pulpit. Upon Wesley's return in 1750, Lloyd did so again. Apparently the neighboring clergy complained to their bishop – Berkeley – who in turn ordered via Mr. Davies, the archdeacon, to deliver a command to Lloyd that he must not "suffer any person to preach in his church who was not a licensed preacher of that or the neighboring diocese." This letter is a response to that order, and is followed by a letter from Bishop Berkeley dated the same day (Letter 369).

countenancing anything that may offend your brethren of the clergy, or give occasion to mobs and riots.[1877]

I am reverend Sir, your faithful brother and humble servant,

G. Cloyne

370 BERKELEY TO JOHNSON[1878]

MS unknown. Printed in Schneider, vol. I, p. 137.

Cloyne, 17 July 1750

Rev. Sir,

A few months ago I had an opportunity of writing to you and Mr. Honyman[1879] by an inhabitant of Rhode Island government. I would not nevertheless omit the present occasion of saluting you, and letting you know that it gave me great pleasure to hear from Mr. Bourk, a passenger from those parts, that a late sermon of yours at New Haven hath had a very good effect in reconciling several to the Church. I find also by a letter from Mr. Clap[1880] that learning continues to make notable advances in your college. This gives me great satisfaction. And that God may bless your worthy endeavours, and crown them with success, is the sincere prayer of, Rev. Sir,

your faithful brother and humble servant,

G. Cloyne

P.S.: I hope your ingenious sons are still an ornament to Yale College, and tread in their father's steps.[1881]

[1877] According to Tyerman (vol. II) John Wesley (1703–91) left Rathcormuck for Cork on 19 May 1750. After preaching once in the morning, a mob formed and harrassed Wesley, forcing him to leave. One mob allegedly burnt Wesley in effigy. The mayor of Cork was not well disposed to Wesley, and allowed the mobs to form and do mischief. There is no evidence that Wesley met with Berkeley or had any concern with him. See Letter 368.

[1878] This letter also appears in Beardsley, pp. 169–70. Schneider makes no mention of the original manuscript.

[1879] James Honeyman* (Honyman) (c. 1675–1750).

[1880] Thomas Clap* (1703–67), rector and subsequently president of Yale.

[1881] Beardsley and Schneider have "footsteps" for "steps."

371 BERKELEY TO CLAP [1882]

Yale, MS Vault File Berkeley.

17 July 1750

Revd. Sir,

Mr. Bourk, a passenger from New Haven, hath lately put into my hands the letter you favoured me with, and at the same time the agreeable specimens of learning which it enclosed, for which you have my sincere thanks. By them I find a considerable progress made in astronomy and other academical studies in your college,[1883] in the welfare and prosperity whereof I sincerely interest myself, and recommending you to God's good providence I conclude with my prayers and best wishes for your Society,

> Revd. Sir,
>
> your faithful, humble Servant,
>
> G: Cloyne

Cloyne July 17, 1750

372 JOHNSON TO BERKELEY [1884]

MS *Unknown. Printed in Schneider, vol. I, pp. 135–37.*

10 September 1750

May it please your Lordship: —

I am most humbly thankful to your Lordship for your very kind letter of August 23, 1749, which did not arrive here before last June, and this is the first opportunity that has offered since from these parts, which I beg may be my apology for answering no sooner.

[1882] Thomas Clap* (1703–67), rector and subsequently president of Yale. First published in *Yale University Library Gazette* 8.1 (July 1933): 27–28.

[1883] An unknown scholar adds to the original manuscript a separate typed note: "The specimens of learning here mentioned, as evincing 'a considerable progress made in astronomy' are supposed to be certain calculations by Berkeleian scholars, which Rector Clap sent to the Bishop: 'one, of the comet at the time of the flood, which appeared 1680, having a periodical revolution of 575 1/2 years, which Mr. Whiston* supposes to have been the cause of the deluge; and another, of the remarkable eclipse of the sun in the 10th year of Jehoiakim, mentioned in Herodotus, Lib. 1, cap. 74, and in Usher's Annals.'" Fraser reports the note (*LL*, p. 324n) as does Luce (*Works*, vol. IX, p. 134).

[1884] According to a comment in one of Berkeley's later letters (Letter 377), it appears Berkeley never received this letter, which the Schneiders likely got from a copy made by Johnson. The whereabouts of this copy (as well as the original) is now a mystery; Schneider makes no mention of the location of either.

As to our College,[1885] the want of taste, or indeed any notion of classical learning with which it set out, it is extreme[ly] difficult to retrieve; it is therefore a great satisfaction that your Lordship's donations have done so much towards it though it be but in comparatively a few instances in which it attains the desired end, and that it is gaining ground from year to year though not so fast as were to be wished.[1886]

The wise and excellent things your Lordship suggests I hope may be good use to our college, and I shall make them as useful as I can to others, but soon after I wrote there arose an unhappy controversy between the Governor and Assembly at New York which ran very high and has subsisted to this day, though there are said to be some hopes of its being healed. This controversy put an entire stop to their college, as it did to all other public interests in that province, and nothing has been done since. But as they have raised a considerable sum which lies in bank I hope it will not be long before they go on with their design, when I shall make your Lordship's hints as useful to them as I can.

Meantime as they are vigorously engaged at Philadelphia in founding an academy there, and I have a correspondence with some of the founders (who have indeed solicited my removal thither), I have made use of your Lordship's name and suggestions towards laying a good foundation for learning there. I am extremely obliged to your Lordship for the kind opinion you are pleased to express of me, that you should conceive good hopes if I were to preside in their college at New York.[1887] It was the design of the gentlemen there if they had gone on that I should be [concerned?], but as I am but poorly qualified for such business, and it will be difficult for me to leave this colony without much detriment to the Church here, and it looks as if they should be so long before they proceed that I shall be too far advanced in life to think of such an undertaking, it will scarce do for me to think of any such thing.

I know not how I expressed myself but I would beg your Lordship to understand that I had no thoughts of asking the trouble of you to promote any collection for this intended college. The utmost that I had in my thoughts was that as I had heard your Lordship was collecting some books for a present to the library of Cambridge College,[1888] I apprehended if you knew of an Episcopal

---

[1885] Yale.

[1886] Berkeley donated both his land in Rhode Island and a large number of books to the college. See Letters 216 and 223.

[1887] King's College (later Columbia University) would be founded in 1754. Johnson would be its first president.

[1888] Berkeley donated books to Harvard College in 1733 and 1747. See Letter 223 and Letters 355–57.

college going forward in these parts, you would perhaps rather turn such a benevolent design towards founding a library for that.

Mr. Prior's narrative has of late been published at Boston and given fresh life to the use of tar-water which is everywhere much practised and with good success in many cases, and in some instances very remarkable.[1889]

Our good friend Mr. Honyman has lately departed this life,[1890] and I have been urged by his people to succeed him, but the reasons above mentioned have prevailed with me to continue in my present station.

I humbly thank your Lordship for your prayers and good wishes and beg the continuance of them and I earnestly pray God preserve your Lordship's life and health which is of so great importance to mankind, and (with my humblest duty to your lady), remain

etc.,

S. J.

373 JOHNSON TO BERKELEY[1891]

MS unknown. Printed in Schneider, vol. I, p. 138.

17 December 1750

My Lord:—

I yesterday received your Lordship's kind letter of July 17, from New Haven, and as there is a vessel soon going from New York, I take the opportunity of making my most humble acknowledgments to your Lordship, though I lately wrote by the way of New York, my humble thanks for your kind letter before received which came not to hand till last summer. In that letter I informed you of the death of good Mr. Honyman,[1892] and of the controversy between the Governor of New York and their Assembly, which hath hindered their College from going forward—since which, things have been so far accommodated that they have nominated the trustees, and I hope they will proceed.[1893] They are very thankful for the notice you so kindly took of what I had mentioned to you in

---

[1889] Thomas Prior* (1681–1751) published his *Authentic Narrative* in Dublin in 1746. An American edition was published in Boston in 1749. See Geoffrey Keynes, *A Bibliography of George Berkeley* (Oxford: Clarendon Press, 1976), p. 188.

[1890] James Honeyman* (Honyman) (c. 1675–1750).

[1891] The letter also appears in Beardsley, pp. 170–71. Schneider makes no mention of the location of the original.

[1892] James Honeyman* (Honyman) (c. 1675–1750).

[1893] A reference to the founding of King's College (later Columbia University), of which Johnson would be the first president.

their behalf, and will form their college upon the model you suggested to me. I intended to have written by Mr. Bourk, but he was just going when I saw him, and I had not time, nor had I then received your Lordship's last kind letter.

We should soon have a flourishing church at New Haven, if we could get a minister—but the Secretary of the Society[1894] writes very discouragingly about expecting any more ministers for these parts. Here is one of your Lordship's scholars, one Colton,[1895] that is a worthy candidate, and another equally deserving, one Camp,[1896] but we cannot yet have leave for their going home for orders.[1897] No endeavours of mine shall be wanting, my Lord, while I live, to promote sound learning and religion in these parts, and particularly your Lordship's excellent system, in order to which I am preparing a short draught for the use of pupils, but it will much want your Lordship's correction.

I thank God my sons yet give me good hopes, and there is scarce anything I want to hear of more than of Mr. Harry's welfare,[1898] and of your Lordship's family, for whom I most ardently pray. I heartily thank your Lordship for your prayers and good wishes for me and mine, and beg the continuance of them, and remain, my Lord, your Lordship's etc.

S. J.

374 BERKELEY TO BRACKSTONE[1899]

TCD MS 2167, fol. 7.

Cloyne, 5 January 1750/51

Sir,

In my opinion the acid extracted from tar hath no more virtue than any other common acid. The acid of tar being mixed with it is fine volatile oil doth form a soap of a most subtle and penetrating nature fitted to remove obstructions and scour the smallest capillaries; but being separated from the oil, and left by it self

---

[1894] Society for the Propagation of the Gospel in Foreign Parts.

[1895] Jonathan Colton (1726–52). He was afterwards admitted to holy orders, but died of small pox on the return trip to the colony.

[1896] Ichabod Camp (1725–86), a graduate of Yale College in 1743, who was ordained at the same time as Colton.

[1897] It was the policy of England at the time to preclude the establishment of bishoprics in the American colonies in order to keep them dependent. As a result, ministers in the colonies had to return to England to be ordained, an expensive and often difficult journey.

[1898] Henry Berkeley* (1729–after 1756) was Berkeley's eldest child, born in Newport. He was plagued with infirmities throughout his life.

[1899] James Brackstone (Blackstone)* (?–1753?).

it no longer retains its saponaceous medicinal nature. If tar-water be nauseous it is less so than most other medicines; moreover by use it becomes easy to take, and even agreeable to many. For your fuller satisfaction concerning the acid of tar I refer you to Doctor Linden's treatise on Selter water p. 302.[1900]

Tar water taken copiously and constantly (i.e. a pint, or pint and half, or a quart per diem) is I am persuaded the best medicine in the world against the gout. I am Sir,

> your most humble servant,
> G: Cloyne

375 BERKELEY TO BENSON

MS *unknown. Printed in Eliza Berkeley,* Poems by the late George Monck Berkeley *(London: J. Nichols, 1797), pp. ccccxxxvii–ccccxxxix.*

Cloyne, 8 March 1751

My dear Lord,

I was a man retired from the amusement of politics, visits, and what the world calls pleasure. I had a little friend, educated always under mine own eye, whose painting delighted me, whose music ravished me, and whose lively, gay spirit was a continual feast. It has pleased God to take him hence.[1901] God, I say, in mercy, hath deprived me of this pretty, gay plaything. His parts and person, his innocence and piety, his particularly uncommon affection for me, had gained too much upon me. Not content to be fond of him, I was *vain* of him. I had set my heart too much upon him, more perhaps than I ought to have done upon anything in this world.

Thus much suffer me to say in the overflowings of my soul, to say to your Lordship, who, though distant in place, are much nearer my heart than any of my neighbours.

Adieu, my dear Lord, and believe me, with the utmost esteem and affection,

> your faithful, humble servant,
> G. Cloyne

Cloyne, 8 March 1750[1902]

[1900] D. W. Linden* (?–after 1768), *A Treatise on the Origin, Nature, and Virtues of Chalybeat Waters and Natural Hot Baths* ... (London, 1748).

[1901] Berkeley's son William* (1736–51) died 3 March 1751.

[1902] An old style date. See General Introduction above.

376 BERKELEY TO PRIOR

Stock, p. lxxxvi (extract).

Cloyne, 30 March 1751

[. . .] They are going to print at Glasgow two editions at once, in quarto and in folio, of all Plato's works, in most magnificent types. This work should be encouraged. It would be right to mention it as you have opportunity [. . .][1903]

377 BERKELEY TO JOHNSON[1904]

HSP, Simon Gratz Collection, British Authors, Case 10, Box 26. Photostat at TCD MS 4309.

Cloyne, 25 July 1751

Revd. Sir,

I would not let Mr. Hall depart without a line from me in acknowledgment of your letter which he put into my hands.

As for Mr. Hutchinson's writings,[1905] I am not acquainted with them. I live in a remote corner, where many modern things escape me. Only this I can say, that I have observed that author to be mentioned as an enthusiast, which gave me no prepossession in his favour.

I am glad to find by Mr. Clap's[1906] letter, and the specimens of literature enclosed in his pacquet, that learning continues to make a progress in Yale College; and hope that virtue and Christian charity keep pace with it.

The letters which you and Mr. Clap say you had written, in answer to my last, never came into my hands. I am glad to hear, by Mr. Hall, of the good health and condition of yourself and family. I pray God to bless you and yours, and prosper your good endeavours. I am, Revd. Sir,

> your faithful friend and humble servant,
> George Cloyne

[1903] Stock's note: "Mr. Prior died the 21st of October following, aged 71. Foulis, Glasgow printer, made an offer in 1746 to publish by subscription an edition of Plato's works. The offer was repeated in 1751, but never came to fruition." See *Works*, vol. IX, p. 135 and *LL*, p. 327n.

[1904] The letter is also printed in Schneider, vol. I, p. 139 and in Beardsley, p. 171.

[1905] John Hutchinson (1674–1737), naturalist and theologian. He published *Moses's Principia* (1724, 1727) and his *Works* were published posthumously in twelve volumes in 1748.

[1906] Thomas Clap* (1703–67).

378 BERKELEY TO CLAP[1907]

Yale, MS Vault File Berkeley.

Cloyne, 25 July 1751

Reverend Sir,

The daily increase of learning and religion in your seminary of Yale College give me very sensible pleasure and an ample recompense for my poor endeavours to further those good ends.

May God's Providence continue to prosper and cherish the rudiments of good education which have hitherto taken root and thrive so well under your auspicious care and government.

I snatch this opportunity given me by Mr. Hall to acknowledge the receipt of your letter which he put into my hands together with the learned specimens that accompanied it, and to assure you that I am very sincerely

Revd. Sir,

your faithful well wisher and humble servant,

G. Cloyne

P.S.: The letter which you mention as written two months before your last never came to my hands.

379 BERKELEY TO PRIOR

BL Add. MS 39311, fol. 59.

Cloyne, 6 August 1751

Dear Tom,

Brother Will:[1908] in a few days proposes being in Dublin. He brings with him two debentures of mine drawn some time ago, I think in 1749. I must desire you to receive their value at the treasury. He also carries with him a note of mine for fifteen pounds upon Gleadowe,[1909] which you will put into his bank to my credit. The enclosed sum of 846 pds. 15 shill. you may leave in Alderman

---

[1907] First published in *Yale University Library Gazette* vol. 8.1 (July 1933): 28–29.

[1908] William Berkeley* (?–?).

[1909] Formerly Swift & Company,* a Dublin bank. When its owner, James Swift, died in 1745 the business was taken over by Thomas Gleadowe and the name changed to Gleadowe & Co.

Dawson's bank,[1910] as likewise the value of my two debentures, sending me his note for the whole, and seeing it placed in his books to my credit.

My intention was to have purchased ten debentures with this sum, but am at a loss in what banker's hands to leave them. Do you know any safe bank that would be at the trouble to keep my debentures and receive their produce letting the whole lie in their hands till such time as I may hereafter have occasion to draw for it?[1911] Perhaps if you know Mr. Clements[1912] of the treasury you may get him to let my debentures lie in his bank and give his receipt for them; in which case I would have them all ensured. Alderman Dawson, I doubt, is too wealthy to take such trouble on him. But if nothing of all this can be done, you will be so good as to place them in Gleadowe's bank, taking his receipt and directing him to receive the interest. It is the bank I have dealt with above thirty years, and if you think it as secure as another [I] should not desire to change it. There hath been some talk as if the late change in our cash (being mostly Spanish) might cause a run on some of our banks. If there be any likelihood of this, you'll be so good as to act accordingly. Instead of the books I returned pray send the book called *L'Esprit des loix* by the Baron Montesquieu.[1913] Adieu dear Tom.

 your affectionate humble servant,

 G. Cloyne

380 BERKELEY TO ARCHDALE[1914]

MS *unknown. Stock. pp. lxxxvii–lxxxviii (likely an extract).*

[*c.* 1 November 1751]

For the particulars of your last favour I give you thanks. I send the above bill to clear what you have expended on my account, and also ten guineas beside;

[1910] Richard Dawson (?–1766). Dawson was a wealthy merchant and banker, establishing his bank in 1740. He was an alderman for Dublin and MP for Kilkenny from 1727 to 1760.

[1911] A number of Dublin banks had failed since the 1730s (e.g. Burton's bank) and only a few of them were stable. A crisis in 1754–55 would see only three survive. See Hall, *History of the Bank of Ireland*.

[1912] Nathaniel Clements (1705–77). He was a teller of the Irish Exchequer and held a large number of other offices. He also served as a private banker for influential members of the nobility, including the lord lieutenants of Ireland.

[1913] Berkeley intends *L'Esprit des Lois* (*The Spirit of the Laws*, 1748) by Charles Montesquieu (1689–1755).

[1914] Stock does not date the letter, but I concur with Luce that, given the evidence of the following correspondence with Archdale, around 1 November 1751 is probable.

which is my contribution towards the monument which I understand is intended for our deceased friend.[1915] Yesterday, though ill of the cholic, yet I could not forbear sketching out the inclosed. I wish it did justice to his character. Such as it is, I submit it to you and your friends.

Enclosed:[1916]

Memoriae facrum
Thomae Prior
Viri, si quis unquam alius, de patria
optime meriti:
Qui, cum prodesse mallet quam conspici
nec in senatum cooptatus
nec consiliorum aulae particeps
nec ullo publico munere insignitus
rem tamen publicam
mirifice auxit et ornavit
auspiciis, consiliis, labore indefesso:
Vir innocuus, probus, pius
partium studiis minime addictus
de re familiari parum solicitus
cum civium commoda unice spectaret
Quicquid vel ad inopiae levamen
vel ad vitae elegantiam facit
quicquid ad desidiam populi vincendam
aut ad bonas artes excitandas pertinet
id omne pro virili excoluit
Societatis Dubleniensis
auctor, institutor, curator:
Quae fecerit
pluribus dicere haud refert:
quorsum narraret marmor
illa quae omnes norunt
illae quae civium animis insculpta
nulla dies delebit?

Sacred to the memory of Thomas Prior, a man most deserving of merit, if any ever was, from the fatherland:

Who, because he preferred to be useful to being admired, even though un-elected to the senate, a non-participant in court counsels, and undecorated by any public office, nevertheless mar-vellously increased and adorned the state by his guidance, counsel, and tireless labouring.

A man innocent, honest, conscien-tious, least bound to the desires of fac-tions, nor particularly anxious about his estate when each time he observed the good fortunes of citizens;

Whatever makes for an alleviation of poverty or a refinement of life, what-ever is suited to conquering the peo-ple's slothfulness or the awakening of good skills, he cultivated it all to the best of his ability.

Author, founder, curator of the Dublin Society:

The things he did, few bother to say: To what end does marble relate those things which everyone knows, those things sculpted onto the citizens' souls and which no day will destroy?

[1915] Thomas Prior* (1681–1751) died 21 October 1751.
[1916] There are multiple drafts of the memorial to Prior. The first draft omits reference to the Dublin Society. I here reprint the later corrected draft. See Letter 381.

381 BERKELEY TO ARCHDALE[1917]

BL Add. MS 39311, fol. 61.

Cloyne, 3 November 1751

Revd Sir,

In the hurry in which I wrote the inscription sent in my last I forgot to mention the Dublin Society, which I have done in that I now enclose, and have added two or three punctums to distinguish the periods.

I am your faithful servant,

G. Cloyne

I have chosen to do this in Latin as the universal and most lasting tongue.

382 BERKELEY TO ARCHDALE

LR, pp. 307–09.

Cloyne, 22 November 1751

Reverend Sir,

You will see by the inclosed paragraph, from *Faulkner's Journal* for Saturday, November the 16th, that the late Bishop of Clogher[1918] had left gold medals for encouraging the study of Greek in the college. Now I desire you will do me the favour to inquire what the value of those medals was, and in whose custody they were left, and let me know. Certainly if I had been informed of this, I should not have annually, for eighteen years past, have given two gold medals for the same purpose, through the hands of our friend Mr. Prior,[1919] who did constantly distribute them, and charge them to my account. I must entreat you to get the dye for those medals, which I left in Mr. Prior's hands, and secure it for me.

There is also an account between Mr. Prior and me, of which I must desire you to get a copy from the executor, and send it enclosed to myself,

I must further trouble you to secure for me two small books which I lent Mr. Prior, and cannot be had. One of them is a French translation of *Siris*; the other was a small tract relative to the same subject, printed in America. There are, I doubt not, many letters and memoirs relating to cures done by

---

[1917] See Luce, "Some Unpublished Berkeley Letters with some New Berkeleiana," 158–59.

[1918] The *Dublin Journal* in fact misprinted *Clogher* for *Cloyne*. As a result of the confusion that followed Berkeley elected to permanently endow the awards for the study of Greek. See *Works*, vol. IX, pp. 137–38.

[1919] Thomas Prior* (1681–1751).

tar-water among Mr. Prior's papers, which I hope you will take care shall not be lost. What trouble you are at in these matters will oblige,

> Reverend Sir,
>
> your faithful humble servant,
>
> G. Cloyne

P.S.: All here send their compliments. The pictures borrowed from Mr. Prior are this day boxed up, and shall be sent on Monday to Corke, to the Dublin carrier.[1920]

383 BERKELEY TO ARCHDALE

LR, pp. 309–10. Stock, p. lxxxvi.

Cloyne, 8 December 1751

Rev. Sir,

This is to desire you may publish the inscription I sent you in Faulkner's paper. But say nothing of the author.

I must desire you to cause the letters G. B., being the initial letters of my name, to be engraved on the dye of the gold medal, at the bottom beneath the race-horse; whereby mine will be distinguished from medals given by others.

> I am, Reverend Sir,
>
> your faithful humble servant,
>
> G. Cloyne

384 JOHNSON TO BERKELEY[1921]

HSP, British Authors Case 10, Box 26.

9 December 1751

My Lord,

I have lately received your Lordship's very kind letter by Mr. Hall which he sent being not yet returned himself. As to Mr. Hutchinson[1922] I cannot say but he is somewhat enthusiastical and [?] in many things [?] and is [sore?] bitter against the

---

[1920] Concerning the pictures, see Letter 362.
[1921] This is a draft of a letter, written on the back of Letter 377. The letter is hastily written and the text is difficult to make out. The draft is dated, but there is no indication of whether the letter was sent or received.
[1922] John Hutchinson (1674–1737). In his works he consistently attacked Newton and his theories, and he was known for his facility with the Hebrew language.

late Sir Isaac[1923] and Dr. Clark,[1924] and has I believe a great many [?] criticisms in [Hebrew?] which he seems to have established this, which I take to be a matter of great importance is 'That the Gospel, the Trinity, Incarnation, and [salvation?] were much more clearly revealed [to ?]. I am assert/[after?] [the?] Fall and [?] [?] [?] the ancient patriarchs than had before been commonly apprehended. But if your lordship should light on a little piece called [Thought] on Rel. a – [?] Mr. [-erby?] late Lord Judiciary of Scotland you would thence judge whether you would think it worth your while to peruse Hutchinson's works which I find considerably obtain with some [?] Gent. at hand who do not seem to know any teachers of enthusiasm.

As your Lordship did not receive my last letter of Dec. 17 1750 and it seemed to be a pleasure to you to receive some account of the [greek: Ἐ῎ιο?] of [K.l. and L?] in these parts of the world I presume to give you some account of it which was to the following effort[1925]

385 BERKELEY TO ARCHDALE

Stock, pp. lxxxvi–lxxxvii (extract).

Cloyne, 22 December 1751

I thank you for the care you have taken in publishing the inscription so correctly, as likewise for your trouble in getting G. B. engraved on the plain at the bottom of the medal. When that is done, you may order two medals to be made, and given as usual. I would have only two made by my dye: the multiplying of premiums lessens their value.

If my inscription is to take place, let me know before it is engraved; I may perhaps make some trifling alteration.

386 BERKELEY TO ARCHDALE

Stock, p. lxxxviii (likely an extract).

Cloyne, 7 January 1752

I here send you enclosed the inscription, with my last amendments. In the printed copy *si quis* was one word; it had better be two, divided, as in this. There

---

[1923] Sir Isaac Newton (1642–1727).
[1924] Samuel Clarke (1675–1729).
[1925] Draft ends here, incomplete.

are some other small changes which you will observe. The Bishop of Meath[1926] was for having somewhat in English: accordingly, I subjoin an English addition, to be engraved in a different character and in continued lines (as it is written) beneath the Latin. The Bishop writes that contributions come in slowly, but that near one hundred guineas are got. Now, it should seem that if the first plan, rated at two hundred guineas, was reduced or altered, there might be a plain, neat, monument erected for one hundred guineas, and so (as the proverb directs) the coat be cut according to the cloth.

387 BENSON TO BERKELEY

BL Add. MS 39311, fols. 65–66.

Berry Street, Westminster, 18 February 1752

My dear Lord,

I am very glad to hear in this that the symptoms you complained of in your former letter are ceased. But very sorry to find that in another complaint still more sensibly affecting you there is after so long time so little change made, and that the wound is still opening and bleeding afresh.[1927] Your Lordship inquires in your letter after Lord Pomfret.[1928] He is lately gone to the Bath in a very bad state of body. But he has suffered much more in his mind from the irregular and undutiful behaviour of his son, now the only son left.[1929] He is as happy in his daughters, as he is unhappy in him. He has lately married a fourth to Mr. Penn, the proprietor of Pensylvania, a gentleman of good character as well as great fortune and a constant Churchman. Your Lordship will reflect how much sadder a cause he has for his than you for your grief. He has lost a son living, you one dead, and one you can reflect upon with great satisfaction as well as concern. He has no view of anything but sorrow ever from his.

Your Lordship speaks of the loss of friends. It is what I have been so long experiencing, that I begin to comfort myself that my own age will not allow me to lose many more. The mortality alone which I see upon the Bench on which I am sitting must be very sufficient to put me in mind of my own. In 17 years' time I have but four seniors upon it, and many juniors besides I have lost. Are not things so durable as these well worth the striving for? One symptom of old age, if I feel not, others I doubt will think very strong upon me, which is to be

[1926] Henry Maule (1676–1758), translated from Dromore to Meath in 1744.
[1927] An allusion to the death of Berkeley's son, William Berkeley (1736–51), who died 3 March 1751.
[1928] Thomas Fermor (1698–1753), the first Earl of Pomfret.
[1929] The wayward son is George Fermor (1722–85), later the second Earl of Pomfret.

querulous; and if not *laudator temporis acti*,[1930] yet a censurer of the present times. Which latter I am sure I have the greatest reason for, and greater still likely every day to have. Your Lordship calls this the freest country in Europe. There is indeed freedom of one kind in it, more it is to be hoped than in any other, a most unbounded licentiousness of all sorts, a disregard to all authority, sacred and civil, a regard to nothing but diversion and vicious pleasures. There is not only no safety of living in this town, but scarcely in the country now: robbery and murther are grown so frequent. Our people are now become, what they never before were, cruel and inhumane. Those accursed spirituous liquors which, to the shame of our Government, are so easily to be had and in such quantities drunk, have changed the very nature of our people. And they will, if continued to be drank, destroy the very race of the people themselves.

The corruption of manners, profusion of expense, the bad condition in which we and all our affairs are, and the good one into which the French are putting themselves, their navy, their finances, and everything else, are common and constant topics in Parliament and public, as well as in conversation and private. But it is only matter of talk, and nothing is done to prevent the evils which are coming upon us.

I have discoursed the Bishop of Bristol[1931] about a tutor for your son, and the person your letter mentions is the very person whom he designed to recommend to you. I hope the comfort you will have in him will be a balance for the sorrow you have had for the amiable son you have lost. Mrs. Berkeley has always my sincerest respects, and with the truest regard I ever am, my dear Lord,

> your most faithful servant and affectionate brother,
> M. Glocester

My Lord Berkeley[1932] desired me, when I wrote, to present his compliments to you.

388 BERKELEY TO GERVAIS[1933]

Redwood Library, Roderick Terry Jr. Autograph Collection, "Berkeley." Photostat at TCD MS 4309.

6 April 1752

Good Mr. Dean,

Your letter by last post was very agreeable, but the trembling hand with which it was written is a drawback from the satisfaction I should otherwise have had in

---

[1930] "the praiser of a time gone by."
[1931] John Conybeare (1692–1755) was bishop of Bristol (1750–55).
[1932] Augustus Berkeley (1716–55), fourth Earl of Berkeley.
[1933] The letter is addressed: "To the Reverend Dean Gervais at Mr. Duggan's next door to Archdeacon Pococke's at the upper end of Stephen's Green, Dublin."

hearing from you. If my advice had been taken, you would have escaped so many miserable months in the gout, and the bad air of Dublin. But advice against inclination is seldom successful. Mine was very sincere, though I must own a little interested: for we often wanted your enlivening company to dissipate the gloom of Cloyne. This I look on as enjoying France at second hand. I wish any thing but the gout could fix you among us. But bustle and intrigue and great affairs have and will, as long as you exist on this globe, fix your attention. For my own part, I submit to years and infirmities. My views in this world are mean and narrow: it is a thing in which I have small share, and which ought to give me small concern. I abhor business, and especially to have to do with great persons and great affairs, which I leave to such as you who delight in them and are fit for them.

The evening of life I choose to pass in a quiet retreat. Ambitious projects, intrigues and quarrels of statesmen, are things I have formerly been amused with; but they now seem to me a vain, fugitive dream. If you thought as I do, we should have more of your company, and you less of the gout. We have not those transports of you Castle-hunters; but our lives are more calm and serene. We do, however, long to see you open your budget of politics by our fireside. My wife and all here salute you, and send you, instead of compliments, their best sincere wishes for your health and safe return. The part you take in my son's recovery is very obliging to us all, and particularly to your reverence's

> most faithful brother and obedient servant,
> G: Cloyne

Cloyne April 6, 1752

389 JOHNSON TO BERKELEY[1934]

CU Spec. MS Coll. Samuel Johnson, vol. I, p. 135, fols. 6v–7.

12 August 1752

My Lord:

This will go by [Miles?]. I must begin with most humbly begging your Lordship's candor and pardon for the liberty I am now presuming to take in handing you the poor performance here inclosed which I assure your Lordship does not proceed from the least imagination that there is anything worth your notice or that might otherwise dare to venture under your eye, but from an

---

[1934] The letter is also printed in Schneider, vol. II, p. 328. The volume is cataloged at CU as BK 811 J63 06.

earnest desire that I might if possible be some way instrumental in promoting the interest of learning in this uncultivated country, which I have long thought could not be better done so far as these studies are concerned than by endeavouring as much as I could to gain their attention to your Lordship's most excellent writings, and I have thought this would best be done by publishing some small manual for young students exhibiting a short sketch of them with references, which I have here attempted, adding in their places some of the best things I could find in others.[1935] Indeed I first drew these pieces up for the use of my sons in assisting and methodizing their thoughts on these subjects and had then no thoughts of printing, but they thereby coming to be known, I was put upon revising and printing them by one Mr. Franklin,[1936] an ingenius public-spirited gentleman of Philadelphia, a zealous promoter, and one of the founders of their college, for the use of that and with some view also at our own and at the college at New York when that should go on (which by the way as yet through their uneasiness proceeds very heavily).[1937] Now as they have actually begun to lecture upon these pieces at Philadelphia and by that means the frequent call for this impression may in time occasion another, since I could not consult your Lordship before printing this, I thought I would humbly ask the favour of your remarks that wheresoever I have made any mistakes or misrepresented your sense or injected any wrong notions of others, you would do us the favour to take notice of them to me if you do not find them so many as would make it too troublesome, that I may correct them against any future impression. This favour I would by no means ask but that the public utility is concerned in it here on which account I the rather hope for your Lordship's pardon, whose zeal and labours for the good of mankind, however distant as well as near you, are so great, so [excellent?], and so conspicuous. But it would be infinitely better if this should be the occasion of inducing your Lordship to condescend to draw up something of your own of this kind fitted for the use of such as are young beginners in these kind of studies. I must also beg your Lordship's pardon for

---

[1935] In 1743 Johnson published his *Introduction to Philosophy*, the aim of which was to give students an overview of what they should learn and the relationship of the branches of knowledge to one another. In 1752 he released a revised and enlarged edition that suggested at what age students should study particular subjects.

[1936] Benjamin Franklin (1706–90). Franklin was instrumental in the founding of the University of Pennsylvania, to which reference is made here. One of Johnson's sons, William Samuel Johnson (1727–1819), would later play a prominent role in the American Revolution, helping to frame the Constitution of the United States.

[1937] In 1731 Johnson published his *Elementa Philosophica* and in 1746 he published *Ethica*. In 1752 Benjamin Franklin printed both texts in a single volume. A third edition appeared in 1754 with corrections by Johnson. The volumes include references to Berkeley's system, of which Johnson was an advocate.

presuming to prefix your name to this slender feeble attempt, which I should not have ventured to do but that it was thought it might contribute something towards my aim above-mentioned, viz. gaining the attention of our youth to your admirable writings. This my Lord is the best apology I am able to make for the trouble I now give you, and with my humblest duty to your Lady, begging your blessing, I remain,

My Lord,

Etc.,

S. J.

P.S. I hear Mr. Hall is just returned with a high sense of your Lordship's favour to him.

390 BROWNE TO BERKELEY

BL Add. MS 39311, fols. 67–68.

Corke, 28 September 1752

My good Lord,

Had not honest George[1938] given me first an account of your voyage, journey, and good health, I might truely have said I never received a letter that gave me more pleasure than the one you favoured me with—though it was long coming, I suppose owing to the want of 3 or 4 pacquets.

I do most sincerely congratulate you on your having made your voyage and journey so easy, and on the good health you enjoy, and that Mrs. Berkeley,[1939] Mrs. Juliana,[1940] and George are well and all happy together and where you would be. I never doubted the change of air and gentle exercise and a new scene would be of use to you—and if you are provided with a convenient habitation I am sure you will meet with every[thing] at Oxford that may make it agreeable to you; though I must allow the loss of such a friend as the Bishop of Gloucester[1941] is scarce to be repaired—he is indeed a loss to the Church also. It is, however, I hope for your comfort that the worthy Bishop of Bristol[1942] is so near you, but as I have not the pleasure of being known to him I can only judge of him from his writings and character, which raise him high in my esteem, and as a Christian Bishop I rejoiced at his promotion; he has highly honoured me by his favourable mention

[1938] Berkeley's son George Berkeley (1733–95).
[1939] Anne (*née* Forster) Berkeley* (?–1786).
[1940] Julia Berkeley* (1738–after 1756).
[1941] Martin Benson* (1689–1752) died on 30 August 1752.
[1942] John Conybeare (1692–1755), bishop of Bristol (1750–55).

of me to you, and I should be oblidged to your Lordship if you would present my best respects to him and assure him of my regard for him. I also pray you to present my compliments to Dr. Fanshaw, if he is so happy as to be known to you.

I have scarce stirred from home but to my Visitation at Ross since I saw you, and am not furnished with any news for you or the Ladies. I suppose it is none that Lady Dorothy and Count Dubois[1943] were married lately in Shandon Church on a Sunday, and that they went off directly to the County of Wexford.

I shall be ready to set out to confirm in the Diocese of Cloyne, as soon as Dr. Berkeley[1944] has fixed the most convenient time and places; the weather has been so bad until now that the roads were very deep, etc. I must again repeat it, that I pray you may not spare to employ me in any duty in your Diocese that you may wish to have done, as I should cheerful contribute all in my power to prevent your absence being attended with the least[1945] inconvenience to you. If you have looked into a late performance of Dr. Hodges,[1946] addressed to Dr. Conybeare, or hear a good account of it, I should be glad to know it, and would send for it; from his treatise on Job I am inclined to think well of any performance of his. I am sorry to be able to assure[1947] you that the Bishop of Cr[1948] pushed to be our Metropolitan, for I fear he would not have attempted it had he not had some powerful support.

My family thanks to God are all tolerably well except the chil[dren? . . . additional text damaged] and most sincerely wish you and yours well. I look well and am growing fat, but I sensibly feel that I am growing feeble. Should I ever come to debate about a jaunt to Bath or [Spa?]—my friends at Oxford would, I believe, determine me for going—for really I long to see you all. I pray you to present my sincere good wishes to Mrs. Berkeley, Miss Berkeley, and honest George, and be assured, my good Lord, that I am

    Your Lordship's

      most affectionate brother and faithful servant,

      Jemmett Corke and Ross.

I had thought of enclosing this to B. of Bristoll but I cannot get a fk.

[1943] Dorothea (*née* Annesley) Dubois* (1728–74). In 1752 she married a French musician, M. du Bois (?–?), about whom little is known.

[1944] Robert Berkeley* (*c.* 1699–1787), rector of Middleton.

[1945] Fraser has "with any" instead of "with the least."

[1946] Walter Hodges (1695–1757), provost of Oriel College (1727–51). He authored *Elihu; or, an Inquiry into the Principal Scope and Design of the Book of Job* (London, 1750) and the work referred to here: *The Christian Plan Exhibited in the Interpretation of Elohim* (London, 1752).

[1947] Fraser has "inform" for "assure."

[1948] Robert Clayton (1695–1758), bishop of Clogher (1745–58). A millenarian and Arian, he had connections at court, but his heterodox views eventually barred his further advancement.

391 DUBOIS (ANNESLEY) TO BERKELEY[1949]

NLI MS 987.

[1752]

My Lord,

My mean abilities are very incapable of writing in a style proportioned to the great veneration I have for that exalted understanding and unparalleled good-ness so conspicuous in your Lordship. The first awes me into a silence, and bids me tremble at the bold attempt of exposing my demerits before so excellent a judge. But the latter encourages me to endeavour to express some part of that gratitude which actuates my soul. The sense I have of my own imperfections shall not prevent my paying a tribute of those acknowledgments so justly due from me to your Lordship.

Mr. Dubois tells me he has acquainted your Lordship with the sacred engage-ments we are under; and I hope my conduct will show I am no stranger to the duties I am really entered into.[1950]

The stability of my resolution can brave the frowns of fortune, and view the [? text obscured] fortunes here but as preparations to more durable blessings than any to be found in this world. My notions would be ridiculed by the polite part of it, who for the generality make a little paltry wealth and grandeur the ultimate end of their wishes; but I am in search of happiness of a different nature and build my hopes on a more solid basis.

Now my Lord I must enter on a subject that has given me more joy than I am well able to express: my husband is a Protestant! Wheres! wheres should I find words suitable to my obligations? And how thanks the kind author (under God) of his conversion? It is to you my Lord I owe this happy change and to you great part of my acknowledgments are due. Some blessing more than ordinary attends it. Or why are my spirits so elated? And why my soul filled with more transport than that even you experienced. Indeed my Lord it is not in my power to account for the surprising alteration I find in my breast.

I readily accept of the pleasing task of perusing the Bible, as your Lordship directs, nor shall my poor labours want an interpretator [*sic*] (as far as my little judgment reaches) while heaven spares me to him; but I must entreat your Lordship to give the dear convert a true light into that faith, whose greatest ornament is yourself. The obligations we are under to the best of men shall be

---

[1949] The letter is a copy, apparently not in Dubois' hand, and lists the date as 1752.

[1950] In 1752 Dorothea married a French musician, M. du Bois (?–?), about whom little is known.

stored in our breasts, and as your Lordship was the means of uniting our prayers, you and yours shall be gratefully remembered in them.

I wish it were practicable that we might be married pursuant to the laws of the land. My interest requires that it should be kept secret from my father (the Earl of Anglesy),[1951] but notwithstanding this considerations I will gladly do what even your Lordship pleases. I should esteem it the highest honour would you favour me with your advice, which I will carefully follow in every particular, and am with the profoundest respect,

My Lord,
Your Lordship's most obliged
dutiful, and obedient servant,
Dorothy Dubois

392 BERKELEY TO DUBOIS (ANNESLEY)[1952]

NLI MS 987.

[1752]

Madam,

The letter your Ladyship hath been pleased to honour me with engages me in a difficult task, that of writing to a lady of so much taste as must make her a critic in spite of good nature. For my part I have just wit enough to know I am no match for your Ladyship. This should make me decline writing; but I recollect that if I cannot say polite and witty things yet I may say some things that are true and agreeable.

The person on whom you have placed your affection is in my opinion much above the common level of those amongst whom fortunes had placed him. Had I known your Ladyship I should never have advised the taking this step; but since it is taken, I advise by all means to make the best of it.

A lady of your quality and pretentions hath done the greatest honour and at the same time laid the greatest obligation possible on Mr. Dubois,[1953] who is fortunate enough to know his happiness, and while I doubt not endeavour to become it. He hath lived on a familiar foot in my family for some years, which gave me an opportunity of knowing him to be a sober, civil, well bred, and well natured man, and free from those gross vices that are too common amongst

---

[1951] Richard Annesley (1693–1761), sixth Earl of Anglesey.
[1952] There is no date given on the copy of the letter. Given that it is a reply to Letter 391 I have used that as a guide.
[1953] In 1752 Dorothea married a French musician, M. du Bois (?–?), about whom little is known.

persons of his age and character. Whatever was done in relation to the sacred engagements you mention, was done in a private illegal manner. The next step must be to satisfy the law by a public legal marriage: the omission of this necessary step would be (as I apprehend) attended with far greater inconveniences than seemed for a good while to sit loose towards popery. He attended our family prayers, went sometimes to church, and heard the Scriptures, and other useful books often read in the family; by these means his prejudices have gradually worn away, and he is become a professed Protestant. I have given him the best reasons I could, and your Ladyship gave him [what?] I take him at present to be a sincere [commitment?]. It is attachment to our holy religion and all things laudable will grow with his interest in your Ladyship, and in proportion to the opportunity of knowing your merit and accomplishments, which will be to him a school of virtue and a guide to happiness. And that it may prove so I recommend you both to the good providence of Almighty God and remain,

> Madam
>
> your most obedient and most humble servant,
>
> G: Cloyne

393 BERKELEY TO FAULKNER[1954]

Gentleman's Magazine 24 (September 1754): 434.

[1752]

There is, at present, while I am writing, a most remarkable case here at Cloyne of a poor soldier in a dropsy, whose belly was swollen to a most immoderate size. He said he had been five months in a hospital at Dublin, and having tried other methods in vain, left it to avoid being tapped. It is a fortnight since he came to Cloyne, during which time he hath drank two quarts of tar-water every day. His belly is now quite reduced; his appetite and sleep, which were gone, are restored; he gathered strength every moment; and he who was despaired of, seems to be quite out of danger, both to himself and to all who see him. It is remarkable that upon drinking the tar-water, he voided several worms of a very extraordinary size. This medicine which is observed to make some persons costive is but one of several instances, wherein the dropsy hath been cured by tar-water, which I never knew to fail in any species of that malady.

[1954] Printed in *Gentleman's Magazine* under "Historical Chronicle" with the following: "Dublin, August 31. The late bishop of Cloyne, a little before his death, sent Mr. Faulkner, the printer, the following case:"

BIOGRAPHICAL AND PLACE REGISTER

All the fully named correspondents of Berkeley have entries in this register. Names and places that appear frequently in the correspondence also have entries and have been marked with an asterisk in the text in order to reduce the size and repetitiveness of the footnotes. Common alternate spellings for surnames are placed in parentheses after the names. The entries are designed to give a brief general background with an emphasis on any relevance to Berkeley. Readers are urged to consult the *Oxford Dictionary of National Biography* and other sources for more in-depth discussions.

Joseph Addison (1672–1719). Born on 1 May 1672, Joseph Addison spent his youth at Lichfield, where his father, Lancelot Addison (1632–1703), was dean in the cathedral. His father would gain some recognition as an author of theological works and no doubt instilled an appreciation for the established church in his son. Joseph attended Queen's College, Oxford, and later Magdalen College, demonstrating considerable skill in Classics and especially in Latin composition. He graduated with his bachelors in 1691, took his masters in 1693, and had a good lifelong relationship with the university.

An ardent Whig, Addison married his political fortunes to several key Whig politicians, most notably Charles Montagu (1661–1715), Earl of Halifax, and Thomas Wharton (1648–1715), first Marquess of Wharton, first Marquess of Malmesbury, and first Marquess of Catherlough. He published the unabashedly pro-Whig poem *The Campaign, a Poem, to His Grace the Duke of Marlborough. By Mr. Addison* (London, 1704), which cemented his fame and the patronage of prominent Whigs. In 1709, when Wharton was appointed lord lieutenant of Ireland, Addison went with him to Dublin as his secretary. It is likely that both Berkeley and Jonathan Swift* first met Addison at that time.

Upon returning to London, Addison maintained both his literary and political activities. He was a friend of Richard Steele,* whom he met at the age of 13, and he promptly renewed that friendship. He worked with Steele on the *Tatler*, a periodical that appeared thrice weekly between 1709 and 1711, authoring over fifty independent articles that appeared in the magazine and collaborating on many more. With the close of the *Tatler* Addison and Steele jointly edited *The Spectator*, a periodical that appeared six days a week and achieved considerable success.

He contributed to Steele's periodical *The Guardian*. Addison also penned a play, *Cato*, which opened in London on 14 April 1713. Berkeley attended its premiere and effused about the play (see Letters 42 and 43).

As he aged, Addison engaged in some brief personal battles with his friends. In 1714 he caused a dispute with his friend Alexander Pope.* Pope was working on a translation of the *Iliad* when Addison's protégé, Mr. Thomas Tickell (1685-1740), embarked on a rival translation, which Addison publicly supported over Pope's (see Letter 69). Pope never forgave the insult and parodied Addison. Tickell never actually completed his own translation. Addison also had a brief public dispute with Steele over a minor political matter in 1719, which ended with Addison's death on 17 June 1719.

Queen Anne (Anne Stuart) (1665-1714). Born 6 February 1665, Anne was the fourth child and second daughter of James, Duke of York (1633-1701), subsequently king of England, Scotland, and Ireland, and his first wife, Anne, Duchess of York (1637-1671). Her sister Mary would become Queen of England (Mary II) as the wife of William of Orange. By their uncle's express command both sisters were brought up as members of the Church of England. Lady Anne's governess was the Protestant Lady Frances Villiers, wife of Colonel Edward Villiers, and her preceptor was Henry Compton, bishop of London. Despite her father's absolutist Catholicism, she became and remained a staunch defender of the established church.

She married Prince George (1653-1708) of Denmark on 28 July 1683. In 1685 Charles II died, making her father, James II, King of England. Relations were not good between father and daughter, and Anne and her husband supported William when he arrived in England in 1688. The Convention Parliament, which met in January 1689, ultimately declared that James II, by fleeing abroad, had voluntarily abdicated the crown, which was vested jointly in William and Mary; the succession was accorded to any children of theirs, then to Princess Anne and her offspring, and finally to any children of William III by a second marriage. When William III was thrown from a horse and died, Anne became Queen of England and was crowned on 23 April 1702.

Berkeley became friends with her personal physician, John Arbuthnot,* and lodged at her palace at least once (see Letter 43). Jonathan Swift* presented Berkeley to Queen Anne on one occasion, but there is no evidence that he had a special or direct relationship with her. Never in excellent health, she ruled as a virtual invalid after the death of her husband. She died on 1 August 1714.

Dorothea Annesley. See **Dorothea Dubois**.

John Arbuthnot (1667-1735). A Scotsman, Arbuthnot became celebrated both for his medical knowledge and his satirical wit. Likely educated at Marischal College in Aberdeen, he went to London in 1691 and supported himself by teaching mathematics. He published *Of the Laws of Chance* (1692), partly translated from Huygens's treatise *De Ratiociniis in Ludo Aleae* (*On the Theory of the Game of Dice*, 1654). It applies probability theory to games, including whist, a personal interest of Arbuthnot's. While tutoring the son of a wealthy London merchant and Member of Parliament, Arbuthnot studied medicine privately at Oxford. In order to practice medicine creditably he needed an MD, which he secured in 1696 from the University of St. Andrews by enrolling for a single day and immediately defending seven theses (published as *De Secretione Animalium*, 1696).

According to tradition, Anne's* husband George, the prince of Denmark, was taken ill at Epsom and Arbuthnot, who was standing by, successfully treated him. We know he was officially George's personal physician by at least June 1703. By 1705 he was Queen Anne's physician as well. He flourished during the queen's reign. He was elected fellow of the Royal Society on 16 April 1705. He worked with Sir Isaac Newton. Politically, he predictably aligned himself with his patron, supporting the Act of Union in print. Just after the treaty was signed, on 12 December 1707, Arbuthnot was elected honorary fellow of the Royal College of Physicians in Edinburgh. In November 1709 he was appointed fourth physician-in-ordinary, one of the permanent royal household. He was admitted fellow of the Royal College of Physicians in London on 27 April 1710.

When Jonathan Swift* moved to London, in 1710, he and Arbuthnot quickly became close friends and collaborators. Arbuthnot was a vital member of the Scriblerus and Brothers' clubs and frequently published or assisted publishing a variety of political and satirical tracts. He did not, however, place any emphasis on being recognized for his efforts and as a result left a less clear record of his own literary exploits. Like his famous friend, he was a voluminous letter writer and maintained his place in a circle of literary giants.

Berkeley claims Arbuthnot as a convert to immaterialism, writing in 1713: "This Dr. Arbuthnot is the first proselyte I have made by the Treatise I came over to print, which will be soon published" (Letter 43; see also Letter 52). Berkeley used Arbuthnot as his entree into scientific circles (his description of the eruption of Mount Vesuvius is addressed to Arbuthnot; see Letter 89), and although there is no extant personal correspondence between them, we have some evidence that Berkeley and Arbuthnot continued to correspond for some time (see, for example, Letter 98).

With the death of the queen, in 1714, Arbuthnot lost his place of privilege at court, but lived well as a physician. His first serious medical work, *An Essay Concerning the Nature of Ailments, and the Choice of Them, According to the Different Constitutions of Human Bodies* (1731) was well received. He died a well-respected man on 27 February 1735.

Mervyn Archdale (Archdall) (1723–91). Graduating from Trinity College, Dublin, with a BA in 1744 and a MA in 1747, Archdale served as a clergyman in Berkeley's diocese in Cloyne. He was a younger relative of some sort of Thomas Prior,* and after Prior's death in 1751 he attended to some of Berkeley's business in Dublin, as Prior had done before. Apparently Archdale developed a taste for antiquities and literary research while at Trinity and Berkeley relied upon him for a variety of purposes, some of which drew on his literary and classical talents.

Later in life Archdale achieved some recognition for his *Monasticum Hibericum; or, An History of the Abbies, Priories and other Religious Houses of Ireland* (1786) and he served as rector of Attanagh. Apparently he secured the letters written to Berkeley by Thomas Prior,* as he and Isaac Gervais* are thanked for providing letters in the advertisement for the 1784 edition of Berkeley's works by Joseph Stock. He also at one point had possession of a portrait of Berkeley painted by Berkeley's wife Anne (see Letter 337), perhaps inherited from Prior. He continued to be involved with Berkeley's family after the latter's death, lending letters to his grandson George Monck Berkeley in the 1780s.

Duke of Argyll. See John Campbell.

St. George Ashe (1658–1718). Born at Castle Strange, in the county of Roscommon, on 3 March 1658, St. George was the second of the three sons of Thomas Ashe, who belonged to a Wiltshire family that had settled in Ireland. As the family estates were inherited by the eldest son, St. George opted for an academic and clerical career. He was educated at Trinity College, Dublin, and graduated BA in 1676 and MA in 1679. In the latter year his college elected him fellow and tutor, and in 1685 appointed him Donegal lecturer and professor of mathematics. By this time Ashe had become involved in the "New Science," not only assisting William Molyneux in founding the Dublin Philosophical Society and succeeding his friend as secretary, but also becoming one of its most active members. He was made a member of the Royal Society in 1686.

In addition to his scientific pursuits, St. George managed a career in the church. He served as the provost of Trinity College, Dublin, until 1695, which he resigned upon being named bishop of Cloyne. Consecrated in Feburary 1696, he translated to Clogher in 1697 and then again to Derry in 1717.

As he was Jonathan Swift's teacher at Trinity College. They became close friends and, in what is most likely an apocryphal account, Ashe is alleged to have married Swift and Stella in 1716.[1955] Berkeley was well known to his elder; it was he who, as Bishop of Clogher, ordained Berkeley a deacon in 1710, inadvertently incurring the wrath of Archbishop King* (see Letter 13). Berkeley was sufficiently impressive in learning to incline Ashe to ask Berkeley to serve as a tutor to Ashe's son, also named St. George. Berkeley accompanied the young man on a tour of France and Italy starting in the autumn of 1716.

Ashe died in Dublin on 27 February 1718 while Berkeley and the younger St. George were still traveling on the Continent.

[1955] See Hone and Rossi, *Bishop Berkeley*, pp. 124–25.

St. George Ashe (1698–1721). The son of Bishop St. George Ashe.* Not much is known about him, except that he had a delicate constitution and was something of an invalid. Berkeley was appointed St. George's tutor and traveling companion in the fall of 1716 and he accompanied Ashe on a tour of France and Italy. Berkeley reports him to be amiable and appropriately modest (see Letter 82). Ashe's father died in February of 1718, but the young man remained in Italy on his tours. Berkeley reports that he and St. George were going to Venice "in our way home-wards" (Letter 95) in November 1718, but they both remained abroad until late 1720. The younger St. George died shortly thereafter, in 1721, in Brussels (see Letter 103).

Richard Aspinwall. See **Wogan** and **Richard Aspinwall**.

Francis Atterbury (1663–1732). Born 6 March 1663, Francis was the younger son of Lewis Atterbury, then rector of Milton Keynes. Educated at Westminster School and Christ Church, Oxford, Atterbury displayed wit and literary talent at an early age. He graduated BA in 1684. He won early admiration for his *Answer to some Considerations on the Spirit of Martin Luther* (1687), a tract that defended the character of Martin Luther without actually endorsing anything particular to Lutheran doctrine.

Ordained in 1687, he took his MA that same year. In 1691 he was appointed lecturer in the vestry of St. Bride's. His oratorical prowess became widely known and he preached before Queen Mary II, becoming chaplain-in-ordinary to the royals in 1693. In addition to preaching, he achieved widespread recognition for his written work, especially his *Letter to a Convocation Man* (1696). The piece argued for the right of the convocation of the Church of England to meet alongside Parliament, which spurred efforts for ecclesiastical reform and launched the so-called "convocation controversy." Although it and some other pieces in the controversy were initially published anonymously, his authorship was widely known and he became the acknowledged champion of high-churchmanship.

Atterbury's political and church machinations brought him into the circle of a group of young Tories, including the Speaker of the House of Commons, Robert Harley. Promoted to dean of Carlisle in 1704, Atterbury continued to play a prominent role in national politics, pushing a high-church program. He likely helped Dr. Henry Sacheverell* (a fellow high-churchman and controversialist) prepare his defense speech made to the House of Lords. In September 1711 he was appointed dean of Christ Church, and was made bishop of Rochester in 1713. The bishopric came with the lucrative and prestigious deanery of Westminster and secured him a seat in the House of Lords.

His Tory and high-church politics were not tempered by his new status. He proved an able leader of the Tories in the House of Lords. He was not involved in the Jacobite conspiracy leading up to the rebellion in 1715, but charges of

Jacobitism were not entirely unfounded. Increasingly convinced that the new monarchy was irrevocably Whig and would undermine the power of the church, he involved himself with a Jacobite plot led by the Swedish ambassador Count Gyllenborg to remove the Hanoverian line. He raised funds for the conspirators and sought to co-opt others, but in the end decided that the plan would come to nothing. When some letters fell into the hands of the government, he ceased all contact with the conspirators. The pattern was set, however, and Atterbury again entered into a conspiracy in 1720. Believing that military invasion from abroad was a prerequisite for a successful coup, in November 1721 he agreed to proposals presented by agents of the Pretender* for an armed landing in England. Owing to the lethargy and ineffectiveness of his fellow conspirators and the illness of his wife, Atterbury removed himself from the intrigues in 1722.

John Erskine,* Earl of Mar, betrayed Atterbury to a government agent, leading to his arrest on 24 August 1722. Confined to the Tower of London, Robert Walpole* eventually secured the passage of a bill stripping Atterbury of his preferment and exiling him from England. Atterbury traveled to the court of the Old Pretender and served in effect as his secretary of state, but the Catholicism of the court was distasteful to him. He left the service of the Pretender in 1728 and died in Paris on 22 February 1732.

There is evidence that Atterbury and Berkeley were at least reasonably well acquainted, as Alexander Pope* remarks in a letter to Berkeley on the distress of Atterbury at missing an opportunity to converse with him (see Letter 97). Although we have no reason to believe they were intimates, Berkeley apparently made quite the impression. The editor of *The Correspondence of John Hughes, Esq.* adds the following in a footnote: "Atterbury, who, having heard much of Mr. Berkeley, wished to see him. Accordingly he was one day introduced to the bishop by the Earl of Berkeley. After some time, Mr. B. quitted the room: on which lord B. said to the bishop, 'Does my cousin answer your Lordship's expectations?' The bishop, lifting up his hands in astonishment, replied, 'So much understanding, so much knowledge, so much innocence, and such humility, I did not think had been the portion of any but angels, till I saw this gentleman.'"[1956]

Philip Bearcroft (1695–1761). An antiquarian and clergyman, Bearcroft was ordained in 1718 and first served as a deacon at Bristol before becoming a priest at Gloucester in 1719. He was appointed preacher to the Charterhouse in 1724 and chaplain to the king in 1738, having received his DD in 1730.

In 1739 he took the position of secretary to the Society for the Propagation of the Gospel in Foreign Parts, a role which led him to exchange some letters with Berkeley. He was by all accounts an able secretary. Bearcroft would likely have been known previously to Berkeley, as the former was a tutor to John Percival's* children.

[1956] *Correspondence of John Hughes*, vol. I, pp. 53–54n.

Bearcroft was well respected, but his literary achievements did not match his ambitions. He published *An Historical Account of Thomas Sutton, Esquire, and of his Foundation in Charter-House* (1737) and a number of discourses on moral and religious subjects, although many of them were published posthumously. In 1753 he was elected master of the Charterhouse. He was allegedly promised a bishopric late in his life, but died in October 1761 before any preferment was conferred.

Jonathan Belcher (1682–1757). A merchant and colonial governor, Belcher was born on 8 January 1682 in Cambridge, Massachusetts. He graduated from Harvard with a BA and an MA and then spent four years in Europe establishing connections and cultivating patrons for the family business, which relied on lucrative government contracts to supply provincial and British forces, especially during the War of Spanish Succession. Berkeley made use of his business to secure books and other items shipped from England and Ireland.

Belcher used the influence of his patrons in Europe and his business connections to win the governorship of both Massachusetts and New Hampshire. He served as governor for eleven years, finally being replaced by William Shirley in 1741. In 1743 he was appointed governor of New Jersey. Although his tenure as governor of New Jersey was fraught with difficulties, he did found Princeton University and sourced the resources to support evangelical reform in the colony. He died on 31 August 1757.

Martin Benson (1689–1752). A clerical colleague of Berkeley's, Martin Benson was born on 23 April 1689. After attending Christ Church, Oxford, and taking a BA and MA, he was ordained a priest in March 1715. Benson accompanied Thomas Fermor* on a tour of the Continent, during which he met Berkeley in Italy and Thomas Secker* in France. These meetings started lifelong friendships with both men.

Benson advanced quickly inside the Church of England. He was made prebend of Salisbury in 1720, archdeacon of Berkshire in 1721, and prebend of Durham in 1724. In 1727 he was presented to the rectory of Bletchley and on the accession of George II* he was made a royal chaplain. In 1734 he was offered the bishopric of Gloucester, being consecrated in January 1735.

Berkeley and Benson shared similar views about many things, including the licentiousness of the times. Benson referred to himself as "a censurer of the present times," complaining of "a most unbounded licentiousness of all sorts" (Letter 387). In fact, his concern about the corruption of manners and disregard for things sacred was long-standing, and in particular he feared that the very nature of the English people was being changed by the consumption of alcohol. In the House of Lords Benson was an active advocate for the interests of the Church (see, for instance, Letters 251 and 260), but he was also an active diocesan bishop. He championed the cause of American bishoprics, reopening the issue in 1740 in a sermon delivered to the Society for the Propagation of the Gospel. The sermon emphasized the problems in the American colonies resulting from the lack of a resident episcopate.

The extant correspondence between Benson and Berkeley suggests a close relationship. Benson supported the Bermuda scheme, and when Robert Clayton* was made a bishop, Benson took over as Berkeley's lieutenant in England (see Letter 204). Benson died on 30 August 1752.

Anne Berkeley (*née* Forster) (?–1786). Anne Forster was the eldest daughter of John Forster (1668–1720), a prominent Irish politician who had been Speaker of the Irish House of Commons (1707–9) and chief justice of the Irish Common Pleas (1714–20). Anne was well educated and studied in France long enough to become competent in the French language.

She married Berkeley on 1 August 1728, probably in England, right before debarking with him for the American colonies. Berkeley apparently chose his spouse well: she was an able woman, with both domestic and intellectual skills worthy of a prominent philosopher and bishop. She managed the farm in Rhode Island, the glebe in Cloyne, coordinated significant relief efforts in Ireland, and reared several children. She gave birth to seven, three of whom survived into adulthood. There is evidence that her intellectual leanings were mystical[1957] and she is said to have been a follower of Fénelon and Madame de Guyon. After Berkeley's death, in 1753, she guarded his reputation as best she could. She died on 27 May 1786.

Ralph Berkeley (?–?). Brother to George Berkeley, he was the third eldest of the Berkeley siblings. He married Anne Hobson, but little else is known about him.

Robert Berkeley (*c.* 1699–1787). George Berkeley's younger brother, to whom Berkeley frequently refers as "Robin." He entered Trinity College in 1717, doing well and earning a scholarship en-route to his BA in 1721. Robert became a distinguished churchman. Berkeley gave him the living of Middleton in the Cloyne diocese, but he was independently respected. He was the treasurer for the chapter of Cloyne and later made vicar-general of the diocese.

He married Anne Elizabeth Dawson of Castle Dawson, with whom he had eight children. Robert provided Joseph Stock the materials for his early account of Berkeley's life and from the letters we have cause to think that their filial relationship was a good one. In his letters Berkeley frequently makes financial provisions for Robert, and late in his life arranges to have Robert hold visitations for him while he is away in Oxford.

William Berkeley (brother) (?–?). One of Berkeley's younger brothers, although aside from his being a military officer not much is known about him (see Letter 141, where he is mentioned as "Cornet William Berkeley" stationed in Sligo). Eliza

---

[1957] See Luce, *Life*, p. 111.

Berkeley later speaks of him as "a most excellent officer" that held a command in Fife in 1745.[1958]

Gabriel Bernon (1644–1736). Born in 1644 in La Rochelle, France, Bernon was a Huguenot who fled France in 1686 to avoid religious persecution after the revocation of the Edict of Nantes. He came from a prominent and wealthy merchant family. He initially settled in Oxford, Massachusetts, but the settlement was abandoned twice as a result of Indian attacks. Bernon left Massachusetts after the first abandonment, settling in Rhode Island in 1697. He stayed in Newport until roughly 1706 and thereafter lived in Kingston and Providence. He was a successful merchant, working mainly in the shipbuilding business providing items required for ship manufacture.

He is most celebrated, however, for his religious zeal for the Church of England in the colonies. He served as a resident minister, starting in 1723, and agitated along with many others for the establishment of American bishoprics. The arrival of Berkeley in Rhode Island coincided with some of these efforts and Bernon sought Berkeley's aid, which the latter was judicious enough to politely sidestep (see Letters 178 and 183), referring Bernon to the Bishop of London.[1959] Bernon died in 1736 at the age of 92.

John Bligh (Blithe, Blith) (1687–1728). John Bligh was the son of the Thomas Blithe (*c.* 1654–1710), whose family had an estate in County Meath. Berkeley tutored John and was on sufficiently good terms with the family to spend time at the family estate (see Letter 22) and socialize with him in London (see Letter 39). Bligh was created Baron Clifton of Rathmore in 1721, Viscount Darnley in 1723, and Earl of Darnley in June 1725. He married Theodosia Hide (Hyde) (1695–1722) on 24 August 1713, an event about which Berkeley makes mention (Letter 53).

Lord Bolingbroke. See Henry St. John.

Dorothy Boyle (*née* Savile) (1699–1758). Born in London on 13 September 1699, Dorothy Savile was the eldest daughter of William Savile (1665–1700), second Marquess of Halifax, and Lady Mary Finch (1677–1718). At the age of 18 Dorothy and her sister Mary inherited the Halifax estates. Her standing and wealth made her an attractive marriage partner, and Dorothy married Richard Boyle* (1694–1753), third Earl of Burlington, on 21 March 1721, making her Countess Burlington.

Lady Burlington was a patron of the arts and a painter herself (mostly portraits), although she is mostly remembered for some of her caricatures. She and her husband enjoyed music, theatre and had a special passion for design and

---

[1958] See Luce, *Life*, p. 27.

[1959] For some suggestive details about the issue Bernon might have brought to Berkeley, see Updike, *History of the Episcopal Church in Narrangansett Rhode Island*, esp. pp. 41–60.

architecture. She moved in literary circles as well, befriending Alexander Pope.*
Lord Burlington died in 1753, leaving everything to the countess for her lifetime.
Berkeley knew Dorothy through her husband, whom he apparently met in London
via Pope. She gifted Berkeley a book (see Letter 366) in 1750. She died on 21
September 1758.

John Boyle, fifth Earl of Cork and fifth Earl of Orrery (1707-62). The only son of
Charles Boyle (1674-1731), fourth Earl of Orrery, John was born in London on 2
January 1707. Tutored at home as a child, he matriculated at Christ Church,
Oxford, in 1723, but never completed a degree there. Upon his father's death in
1731, the new earl moved to Ireland in 1732. His wife died shortly thereafter,
leaving him with three young children. On 30 June 1738 Orrery married Margaret
Hamilton (1710-58) of Caledon, County Tyrone.

He took his seat in the House of Lords in 1735, and, although avoiding public
affairs, he nonetheless was active politically. He started out as a Tory Jacobite,
associating with Bolingbroke* and opposing the Whig ministry. He communicated
with the Pretender's* court and joined others in appealing to Louis XV of France to
send ten thousand troops to support the uprising of 1745. He was betrayed by a
prisoner in 1746 but was not prosecuted. Over time he drifted into the circle of
opposition centered around Frederick, the Prince of Wales. In 1749 he was listed as
a potential office holder on Frederick's accession. However, after the death of
Frederick, in 1751, Boyle essentially removed himself from politics to tend to his
estates.

Berkeley's acquaintance with Boyle was no doubt facilitated by the latter's
intimate friendship with Alexander Pope.* Although not a literary giant, Orrery
did publish. The most famous (and controversial) of his works was *Remarks on the
Life and Writings of Dr. Jonathan Swift* (1751). He also translated two of Horace's odes
(1741) and Pliny's letters (1751). Today he is best known for his voluminous letter
writing, most of which is available at the Houghton Library at Harvard University.
He was in Ireland from 1746 until June 1749, returning to Ireland from England on
30 October 1749, during which time he corresponded with Berkeley and was
apparently an advocate of the use of tar water (see Letter 359). He died on 16
November 1762.

Richard Boyle, third Earl of Burlington and fourth Earl of Cork (1694-1753).
Richard Boyle was born in London on 25 April 1694, the only son of Charles
Boyle (?-1704), second Earl of Burlington and third Earl of Cork, and Juliana
(1672-1750), daughter and heir to Henry Noel, second son of the fourth Viscount
Campden. He was educated at home, and upon his father's death, on 9 February
1704, he succeeded to his titles and estates as third Earl of Burlington and fourth
Earl of Cork.

In 1715 Boyle was made lord treasurer of Ireland, governor of County Cork, and
was sworn into the Irish Privy Council. He held other offices in England (including

service on the Privy Council there) and was elected a fellow of the Royal Society in November 1722.

On 21 March 1721 he married Dorothy Savile* (1699–1758), with whom he had three daughters. Although his vast estate in Ireland (more than forty thousand acres in County Cork and Waterford) provided most of his income, Boyle never visited Ireland.

Famous as a patron of the arts, Boyle also pursued architecture as an avocation and designed a large number of town and country houses. He acquired a modest but quality collection of fine art, emphasizing architectural scenes from Italy and classical sculpture. Musically, he patronized composers and musicians and held musical performances at his various estates. As an example, George Handel was given an apartment at Burlington House, where he wrote *Amadigi di Gaula* (1715), dedicating its libretto to Boyle. He did not neglect the literary arts, either, serving as a patron to many writers. At least thirty-nine publications were dedicated to him, a testament to his generous support. He often subscribed to multiple copies of the same publications. His favorite, however, was undoubtedly Alexander Pope,* who was a member of Burlington's inner circle of intimates. It was Pope who introduced Berkeley to Boyle (see *Works*, vol. IX, p. 47). Although not much is known about the relationship between Berkeley and Boyle, they were sufficiently friendly that Berkeley considered appealing to him for help in the Dromore affair (see Letters 98 and 114) and was later invited to take deer from Burlington's Irish estates (see Letter 266). Boyle died on 3 December 1753.

James Brackstone (Blackstone) (?–1753?). Brackstone was a London bookseller and publisher. Given the one extant letter we have, he was apparently interested in tar water (see Letter 374). Little else is known about him. He appears in Henry Plomer's list of printers and booksellers in the British Isles.[1960]

Jemmett Browne (*c.* 1703–82). A relation of Peter Browne,* Jemmett was born in County Cork, descended from English settlers who came to Ireland around 1660. His father, Edward Browne (1676–?), was mayor of Cork (1714). Jemmett had a meteoric rise in the church. Educated at Westminster School, he was ordained in 1723. He was treasurer of Ross (1723), vicar-choral of Cork (1724), precentor of Cork (1725), and prebendary of Cork (1732), before serving as the Dean of Ross (1733–43). In 1743 he was made bishop of Killaloe and translated to Dromore for three months in 1745 before settling in as bishop of Cork for the better part of three decades (1745–72). In 1772 he translated again to Elphin and finished his career as the archbishop of Tuam (1775–82).

Browne and his family were apparently friends of the Berkeleys; Browne was at least an amiable neigboring divine.[1961] Berkeley refers to "Dean Browne" (Browne

[1960] See Plomer et al., eds., *Dictionary of the Printers and Booksellers from 1726 to 1775*, p. 27.
[1961] See Luce, *Life*, p. 184, which says that the Browne family was "on the best of terms" with the Berkeleys.

was dean of Ross at the time) with respect to finding strings for his musical instruments (Letter 292), and when Berkeley was making arrangements to follow his son to Oxford, Browne (then Bishop of Cork) accepted the responsibility of the Cloyne confirmations in Berkeley's absence (see Letter 390).

Peter Browne (?–1735). An author and clergyman, Browne graduated with a BA from Trinity College, Dublin, in 1686 and was ordained in London in 1689. Returning to Dublin, he received his MA in 1691 and his BD and DD from Trinity College in 1699. Browne's ecclesiastical career started in earnest in 1697 when he was made rector of the parish of St. Mary. He was well respected within the college community, being asking to refute Toland's *Christianity not Mysterious*, which he did in his *A Letter in Answer to a Book Entitled Christianity not Mysterious* (1697). He was chosen as provost of Trinity College in 1699, where Berkeley was one of his students at the time. He was made bishop of Cork and Ross in 1710.

Doubts about his political reliability and suspected Jacobitism plagued him throughout his career. While bishop at Cork and Ross he was embroiled in an unpleasant dispute with his dean, Rowland Davies, over the ordination of two candidates. In 1722 he published objections to the practice of toasting the dead (toasts made to the memory of William III were particularly common), arguing that such a practice made a mockery of the Eucharist. Browne held that Protestant nonconformists were a greater threat to the church than Catholics.

Browne continued to engage in theological and philosophical disputes, authoring *The Procedure, Extent and Limits of the Human Understanding* (1728), where he argued that it is possible to understand God by analogy. Berkeley criticized the work in his *Alciphron* (see *Works*, vol. III, pp. 163 ff.), which prompted Browne to add nearly two hundred pages of rebuttal to the final chapter of his *Things Divine and Supernatural Conceived by Analogy* (1732). Berkeley did not think it necessary to respond a second time (see Letter 246). Browne died in Cork on 25 August 1735.

Earl of Burlington. See **Richard Boyle**.

James Butler, second Duke of Ormond (1665–1745). A notorious Jacobite conspirator, James Butler was born in Dublin on 29 April 1665. He was the eldest surviving son of Thomas Butler (1634–80), sixth Earl of Ossory, but his more famous title would come from his paternal grandfather, James Butler (1610–88), first Duke of Ormond.

On 21 July 1688 Butler succeeded his grandfather as Duke of Ormond in the Irish and English peerages. Despite reservations about the policies of James II, he voted against the motion to declare William and Mary king and queen and against the motion to declare that James had abdicated the throne. This effectively made Butler a Tory Jacobite, but his personal friendship with William gave him opportunities in the new regime. He was appointed a gentleman of the bedchamber and was named lord high constable of England for William's coronation. He fought as a military commander in Holland and with William in his Irish campaigns. In December 1690 he was sworn of the Irish Privy Council and in February 1691 he was named lord lieutenant of Somerset. After Anne* became queen he was named lord lieutenant of Ireland in 1703. Replaced by Thomas Herbert,* eighth Earl of Pembroke, in 1707, he returned to the lieutenancy of Ireland (1710–13). During this period Butler was a consistent Tory, voting, for instance, against the impeachment of Sacheverell* in 1710.

In October 1713 he began exchanging letters with the exiled Jacobite court, working with Francis Atterbury* and others in England to unite the Tories in advance of the elections of 1715. The Whig electoral victory led to an investigation of the previous Tory ministry, including Butler, who was impeached for "high treason and other high crimes and misdemeanours" by the House of Commons on 21 June 1715 (see Letter 72). He left at the end of July and arrived in Paris on 8 August. His removal disrupted plans for a Jacobite rising in the west of England, which was subsequently abandoned by the arrest of its putative leaders, such as George Granville.*

Once in France, Butler requested assistance from Louis XIV and attempted to reactivate the western rising, which was to coincide with the Scottish expedition under John Erskine,* Earl of Mar. He was duly appointed captain-general by the Pretender* in October 1715. However, this plan was aborted following the betrayal of the plans to the ministry in England. With the Pretender no longer welcome in France, in April 1716 Ormond accompanied the exiled court to the papal enclave at Avignon, where he was made Knight of the Thistle in April. Butler participated in other Jacobite plots, including the one that would lead to the arrest of Francis Atterbury,* but none of them came to fruition. Butler died on 16 November 1745.

Henry Caldwell (?–1726). Possibly the "Caldwell" Berkeley mentions a few times in the letters (see Letters 128, 133, 142, and 164), Henry Caldwell was the son of Sir James Caldwell (?–1717) "of Castle Caldwell." Not much of worth is known about Henry. He married, firstly, Catharine Hume, daughter of Sir John Hume, second Baronet, and Sidney Hamilton. He married, secondly, an unknown woman *circa* 14 July 1722. Caldwell held the office of sheriff of County Fermanagh in 1693, and worked as a merchant in Killigerge in County Donegal. He succeeded to the title of second Baronet of Wellsburrow, County Fermanagh, in February 1717. He died somewhere around 5 November 1726.

John Campbell, second Duke of Argyll (1680?–1743). The eldest son of Archibald Campbell, tenth Earl and first Duke of Argyll (d. 1703), Campbell was destined for a military career. He was commissioned as a colonel at the age of 14, leading a regiment for William III in 1689. He fought in Holland, eventually commanding his father's regiment of Scots horse guards after inheriting his title. As a result of wrangling over the succession to the throne of Scotland, Campbell managed to secure an English peerage (Duke of Greenwich) and later a promotion to general in exchange for helping Queen Anne in 1705 with the union with Scotland.*

He was appointed commander-in-chief in Scotland in 1712 and was deeply involved in the Hanoverian succession in 1714. He fought against the Jacobite rebellion in 1715, winning a narrow victory at Sheriffmuir. As peace descended on England, Argyll spent his political energies mostly in opposition to Walpole and the Whigs. He died on 4 October 1743.

John Carteret, second Earl Granville (1690–1763). The eldest son of George Carteret, first Baron Carteret (1667–95), and Lady Grace (*c.* 1667–1744), John Carteret was born on 22 April 1690. He, like his family, was solidly Tory. He inherited the baronetcy at the age of 5, taking his seat in the House of Lords in 1711.

After the death of Anne,* Carteret supported the Hannoverians and achieved rapid advancement. He was appointed a lord of the bedchamber and was made bailiff of Jersey. In 1715 he was sent down to Cornwall to root out potential traitors associated with the Jacobite rebellion, and in 1716 became lord lieutenant of Devon. At the relatively young age of 30 he was appointed secretary of the south and involved in the highest levels of domestic and foreign policy. In 1724 Carteret became lord lieutenant of Ireland, where for six years he served with distinction, earning the approbation of many Irish, including Jonathan Swift.* Berkeley, from the evidence available, was not an intimate of his, although John Percival,* as might be expected, had considerable dealings with the lord lieutenant.

After leaving his post as lord lieutenant, Carteret continued his political career in opposition to the Whig government, opposing Walpole and his ministry. Along with Chesterfield, Carteret shared the leadership of the Tories in the House of Lords for more than a decade, until Walpole was ousted in early 1742. Carteret then became secretary of state for the north, until he resigned in November 1744. He became Earl Granville in October of the same year, inheriting the title upon the death of his mother.

After 1744 Carteret moved to the role of an elder statesman, being named lord president in 1751, a position which gave him a role in the Cabinet without onerous duties. He retained this prestigious office until the end of his life, dying 2 January 1763.

Charlton. Charlton was John Percival's* house near Greenwich in England, just outside London. Berkeley was a frequent visitor there whenever he was in London.

John Churchill, first Duke of Marlborough (1650–1722). Born 26 May 1650, the second but first surviving son of Sir Winston Churchill (1620–88) and Elizabeth (*c.* 1622–98), Churchill quickly distinguished himself in military service as a young man, serving abroad in several campaigns. Having earned a reputation for skill in combat, he returned to England in 1674 to serve as a gentleman of the bedchamber for the Duke of York.

Churchill climbed the military and political ranks quickly. He was elected Member of Parliament in 1679 and served as the Duke of York's master of robes.

He obtained a number of prestigious positions in the court of James II, who also made him Baron Churchill of Sandridge in 1685. Until the revolution Churchill was a loyalist, but he defected to support William, who subsequently created him Earl of Marlborough in 1689.

Churchill then rose to become the most important figure in English military and diplomatic affairs through the reign of Queen Anne,* conducting the war in Holland and France as Anne's commander-in-chief. As a result of his service, he was elevated to Duke at the end of 1702. His military successes included the major victory over the French at Blenheim (1704) and securing the Netherlands against French threats for the duration of the war. Marlborough's wife Sarah was an intimate of the queen and involved in court politics, which complicated his political standing in England. Problems with his wife were compounded by the publication of *Conduct of the Allies* by Jonathan Swift,* who alleged that Marlborough was using the war to enrich himself at the expense of England. The queen dismissed Marlborough at the end of December 1711. Berkeley followed the events of his day, noting the rise and fall of Marlborough and his participation in national events (see, e.g., Letters 40, 46, and 75).

With the death of Anne and the arrival of the new king George I in 1714, Marlborough was restored to his high offices and participated in the suppression of the rebellion of 1715, but thereafter he suffered a stroke and ill health hampered his activities. He played no major role in the rest of the new administration, occasionally appearing in the House of Lords. He died on 16 June 1722.

Thomas Clap (1703–67). Rector and subsequent president of Yale, Clap was born on 26 June 1703 in Scituate, Massachusetts. A fourth-generation British-American, his ancestors were Puritans and Congregationalists. He entered Harvard College in 1718 and graduated in 1722, leaving to study for the ministry. He began his pastoral career in 1726 in rural Connecticut and established a reputation as a champion of orthodox religion.

In 1739 Clap was appointed rector of the collegiate school, subsequently called Yale, at New Haven, Connecticut. He was installed in that position on 2 April 1740 (Samuel Johnson* reports on the appointment; see Letters 275 and 283). Clap guided Yale for twenty-six years, instituting administrative order, expanding the physical facilities, and making the college one of the leading institutions of higher learning in the colonies. It was to Yale that Berkeley would donate the largest part of his library in America. He kept in touch with Clap, exchanging letters about the state of learning in the colonies and providing occasional support in the form of specimens and other equipment (see Letters 371 and 378).

Clap's administration and his contribution to the college would later be overshadowed by the religious strife of the 1750s and 1760s, exacerbated by his reputation as a stern and authoritarian religious conservative. He resigned as president of Yale in September 1766, dying a few months later on 7 January 1767.

Henry Clarke (?–1764). Henry Clarke attended Trinity College, Dublin, and was a fellow in 1724, but little is known about his origins. He would later serve as vice-provost of Trinity (1744–47). Berkeley corresponds with Clarke on business related to the college (see Letter 333).

Samuel Clarke (1675–1729). A well-respected theologian and philosopher, Clarke was born on 11 October 1675. He first made his mark in the area of natural philosophy as a young man by elucidating and defending the consequences of Newton's *Principia* in his bachelor's disputation in 1695. He became known as a prominent Newtonian and engaged in an important exchange of letters with Leibniz as an intermediary for Newton.

Clarke's first theological publication, *Three Practical Essays on Baptism, Confirmation, and Repentance: Containing Full Instructions to a Holy Life* (1699), was well received and uncontroversial. His delivery of the Boyle lectures in 1704 and 1705 elevated him to the role of a prominent and public defender of Anglicanism. His *Demonstration of the Being and Attributes of God* (1705) reflects his Newtonian mathematical training and his strong penchant for attempting to reconcile revealed and natural religion. He engaged in a controversy with Henry Dodwell and subsequently Anthony Collins, resisting in particular the claim of Dodwell's that thought could arise from matter.

Berkeley sought to gain attention for his philosophical endeavors by entreating Clarke to read and respond to his *Principles of Human Knowledge*. Percival* reports that Clarke "perused" the book but thought its principles were false (see Letter 20). Berkeley then spent much energy fruitlessly trying to elicit explicit criticisms from Clarke and others, but to no avail (see Letters 21, 23, and 24). Clarke died in London on 17 May 1729.

Robert Clayton (1695–1758). A Dubliner and fellow of Trinity College, Clayton was a religious controversialist who was also involved in Berkeley's plans for St. Paul's College. He was Berkeley's lieutenant (see, e.g., Letter 173), handling affairs for the scheme in England and Ireland until he was appointed bishop of Killala and Achonry in 1729–30. In 1735 he was translated to the diocese of Cork and Ross and in 1745 to the diocese of Clogher.

A millenarian and Arian, he likely authored *Essay of Spirit* (1751). Although he had connections at court, his heterodox views eventually barred his further advancement. He was being prosecuted by the government for advancing heretical views inconsistent with the Thirty-Nine Articles when he died, before his case was heard, on 26 February 1758.

Marmaduke Coghill (1673–1739). Elected first, in 1692, to sit in the Irish House of Commons for County Armagh, Coghill continued to sit in the Irish House from 1713 onwards as a member for Trinity College. In 1699 he succeeded his father as judge of the Irish prerogative court, an elevation that began his close involvement with the affairs of the established Church of Ireland (including the patronage of clergy; see Letter 244). In 1729 he was appointed commissioner of the revenue (which earned him a seat in the Privy Council) and in 1735 he would be promoted to chancellor of the Irish exchequer. Gravely ill from gout and attendant complications, Coghill resigned his judgeship in January 1739, dying on 9 March 1739.

Spencer Compton, Earl of Wilmington (*c.* 1674–1743). A prominent Whig politican, Compton had unusual roots, coming from a family of Church Tories (his father, Henry Compton, was bishop of London). Elected to the House of Commons, by the middle of Queen Anne's* reign he had established himself as a leading public figure. In March 1715 he was voted Speaker of the House and made treasurer to the Prince of Wales (later George II*). Although not a gifted speaker, his talent for rules and precedent made him an efficient Speaker; he held the post for twelve years.

A favorite of George II, Compton was created Baron Wilmington in 1728 and later elevated to earl. He briefly held the post of prime minister, but he fared so poorly that he was quickly removed. George II's continuing regard for Compton kept him in the ministry as paymaster, but he served from that point forward without special distinction. He died on 2 July 1743.

William Conolly (1662–1729). Born in Ballyshannon, County Donegal, Ireland, William Conolly was a prominent Irish politician and Speaker of the Irish House of Commons. In 1694 he married Katherine Conyngham, daughter of Sir Albert Conyngham. This marriage connected Conolly to the most important families in west Ulster. Conolly's career, however, was equally built on his considerable wealth. He used his wife's dowry of £2,300 to buy his first estates in County Meath, and made his fortune during the 1690s by buying and acting as agent for the sale of forfeited Jacobite estates. He served as the collector of the revenue for Londonderry (1697–1729) and sat as a Member of Parliament from 1703 until his death. Berkeley contributed some architectural ideas for a large house Conolly was constructing in the 1720s (see Letters 110 and 111), but there is no evidence of any additional connection between them.

Conolly rose to national prominence in the early 1700s as a leading figure in the Irish Whig Party. The Whig lord lieutenant, Thomas, Earl of Wharton, appointed him a revenue commissioner and an Irish privy councillor in 1709. After being briefly removed by the Tory Duke of Ormond, the return to power of the Whigs in Ireland saw him restored to the Privy Council. He was elected Speaker of the Irish House of Commons on 12 November 1715. Under the tenure of Grafton* as lord lieutenant, his influence was so marked that he was described as the "prime minister" of Ireland. He resigned as Speaker on 13 October 1729, dying shortly thereafter on 30 October 1729.

Thomas Corbett (?–1751). A sailor who rose to prominence through his service in the Navy under the patronage of Admiral George Byng, Thomas Corbett became secretary to the Admiralty board and remained in that capacity from 1741 until his death in 1751. He also served as a Member of Parliament (1734–50), representing Saltash in Cornwall. During his service Corbett was apparently in charge of mail packets before becoming secretary, as Berkeley makes use of him in the Admiralty office for relaying correspondence to him while in Rhode Island (see Letters 172 and 185).

Richard Dalton (*c.* 1695–1769). Relatively little is known about Dalton, other than that his family was from Lincolnshire. He and John James* were traveling companions and journeyed with Berkeley to the American colonies, where they took a house in Boston for some time. Dalton was thrice married and enough of a friend of Berkeley to merit a letter congratulating him on his third marriage (see Letter 286).

Charles Dering (?–?). The eldest son of John Percival's* uncle, Dering was first deputy auditor general and then auditor general of Ireland. He married Margaret Moore in October 1691. Berkeley makes occasional references to him as a friend of the family (see Letters 38, 87, and 88).

Daniel Dering (?–1730). Daniel Dering was the grandson of Edward Dering, second Baronet (1625–84), a politician. A cousin of John Percival's,* he is by all accounts a friend of Berkeley's and is often mentioned in the correspondence. Reference is made to an exchange of letters between them, but none survive. Dering married Mary Parker* in 1719 and died, probably of complications from kidney stones, on 4 December 1730 (see Letter 185).

Mary Dering (*née* Parker) (1692–1731). Sister to Catherine Parker,* Mary wed Daniel Dering* in 1719. She is often referred to as "Mrs. Parker" by Berkeley, as "Mrs." was not reserved for married women by convention until late in the eighteenth century. She died in early 1731 shortly after the death of her husband.

Doctors' Commons. Also called the College of Civilians, the Doctors' Commons was an association or college of ecclesiastical lawyers founded in 1511 and situated in Knightrider Street, London. It was dissolved following the Court of Probate Act in 1857. What records of the association that remain are housed in the library at Lambeth Palace, London.

Dorothea Dubois (*née* Annesley) (1728–74). A writer and poet, Dorothea was the eldest daughter of Richard Annesley, sixth Earl of Anglesey (1693–1761). The earl disowned her and her sisters, producing a long-lasting dispute that prompted much of her literary output. In 1752 she married a French musician, M. Dubois (?–?), about whom little is known. She wrote to Berkeley as bishop of Cloyne about her marriage (see Letters 391 and 392).

Henry Ecles (?–?). Ecles was a steward for the estates of Richard Boyle,* third Earl of Burlington and fourth Earl of Cork. Berkeley writes to Ecles to claim a buck Boyle promised him (see Letter 266). Nothing else is known about him.

Charles Edward (1720–88). Known as the "Young Pretender" and "Bonnie Prince Charlie," Charles Edward was the Jacobite claimant to the English, Scottish, and Irish thrones. He was born Charles Edward Louis John Casimir Silvester Severino Maria at the Palazzo Muti, Rome, on 31 December 1720, the eldest son of James Francis Edward (1688–1766) and Clementina, *née* Sobieska, princess of Poland (1702–35). He is best known as the instigator of the unsuccessful Jacobite uprising of 1745, where he led an insurrection which ended in defeat at the Battle of Culloden and effectively ended the Jacobite cause.

James Francis Edward (1688–1766). Styled the "Old Pretender" or "The Old Chevalier," he was the son of the deposed James II of England (James VII of Scotland). As such, he claimed the English, Scottish, and Irish thrones (as James III of England and Ireland and James VIII of Scotland) from the death of his father in 1701, when he was recognized as king by his cousin Louis XIV of France. He briefly landed in Scotland to support the rebellion of 1715, but quickly realized his prospects were dim and returned to France. He supported his eldest son, Charles Edward, in the 1745 rebellion, which also failed. Following his death, in 1766, he was succeeded by his son Charles Edward in the Jacobite succession.

John Erskine, twenty-second or sixth Earl of Mar and Jacobite Duke of Mar (1675–1732). A Scottish Jacobite army officer, politician, and architect, Erskine was the first of four surviving children of Charles Erskine, twenty-first or fifth Earl of Mar (1650–89), and his wife, Lady Mary Maule (1655–1710?). Erskine first took his seat in the Scottish parliament in September 1696 and quickly connected himself to the Duke of Queensberry, securing a powerful patron. He served on the Scottish commission that negotiated the Act of Union and was appointed secretary of state within Scotland in 1705. During the reign of Queen Anne* Mar flourished, even being sworn into the English Privy Council in May 1707.

Sometime, probably as early as 1710, Mar established contacts with the exiled Stuart court. After the death of Anne, in 1714, Mar became deeply embroiled in a Jacobite plot, although his early role is difficult to define. In any event, he became the only major Jacobite in England to take direct action, raising an army of nearly twenty thousand men in Scotland by October of 1715. Effectively losing the battle of Sheriffmuir to Argyll on 13 November, Mar retreated northwards, ceding initiative to the government forces. The cause being lost, he left to join the Stuart court in exile in France and Italy. He was involved in various internal intrigues in the Jacobite court, but died a marginal figure in May 1732.

Bryan Fairfax (1676–1749). An antiquary and scholar, Fairfax was born on 11 April 1676. Educated at Westminster School and Trinity College, Cambridge, he became employed as commissioner of the customs in 1723. He held the post until his death. He lived with his younger brother, Ferdinando, in London, where he collected a large library and gallery of pictures. Berkeley corresponded with Fairfax in his official capacity when he was shipping items back and forth across the Atlantic. Fairfax died, unmarried, on 7 January 1749.

George Faulkner (1703?–75). Faulkner was a Dublin printer and owner of the *Dublin Journal*. A political activist for the well-being of Ireland, he also served as an alderman of Dublin in 1770.

Around 1717 he was apprenticed to the printer and bookseller Thomas Hume, from whom he learned his trade. By 1724 he had set up his own shop in Dublin. Starting in the 1730s, Faulkner became Jonathan Swift's* only publisher and the two were friends and mutual patriots for the Irish cause. Swift would even write public letters defending Faulkner on several occasions, including once when accused of pirating English works for sale in Ireland. He printed several volumes for Berkeley, mostly late in Berkeley's life, including *The Querist* (multiple editions, including 1750), *A Miscellany* (1752), and *A Word to the Wise, or, An Exhortation to the Roman Catholic Clergy of Ireland* (1749, 1752). By 1748 Faulkner listed more than a thousand titles in stock and was arguably the most successful printer in Dublin. He died in Dublin on 30 August 1775.

Charles Fitzroy, second Duke of Grafton (1683–1757). The only child of Henry FitzRoy, first Duke of Grafton (1663–90), and his wife Isabella (1667/8–1723), Fitzroy was born on 25 October 1683. He came of age in 1704 and took his seat in the House of Lords as the second Duke of Grafton. He had Whiggish sympathies and served early in his career as lord lieutenant of Suffolk. He married Henrietta Somerset (1690–1726), the daughter of Charles Somerset, Marquess of Worcester, in 1713.

In 1715 Grafton was appointed to join the commission of lords justices nominated to deputize at Dublin Castle, and accordingly was sworn into the Irish Privy Council on 31 August. During this time Berkeley asks Percival to make introductions (see Letter 81) and presumably makes his first acquaintance with Grafton during this time. In 1720 Grafton was appointed lord lieutenant of Ireland. Berkeley was apparently on good terms with Grafton and the duchess. When the deanery of Dromore became vacant, in 1721, Berkeley applied for the position. Apparently Grafton had previously made promises to Berkeley about preferment (see Letter 98). Berkeley was indeed appointed by Grafton to the post, but the bishop of the diocese (Ralph Lambert*) installed his own nominee, Henry Lesley, embroiling Berkeley in an unsuccessful lawsuit that lasted years. Grafton did make good on his promise, however, appointing Berkeley to the deanery of Derry in 1724.

As lord justice in Ireland, Grafton had excellent connections, especially with William Conolly,* who was then Speaker of the Irish House of Commons. Yet his tenure as lord lieutenant was generally difficult. In the wake of the Wood's halfpence debacle, Grafton was politically isolated, defending an unpopular government policy. He was removed from his post in 1724 but named lord chamberlain, a position he retained for the remainder of his life. He died on 6 May 1757.

Henrietta Fitzroy (*née* Somerset), Duchess of Grafton (1690–1726). The wife of Charles Fitzroy, the second Duke of Grafton (1683–1757), whom she married in 1713. While her husband was lord lieutenant of Ireland, she became acquainted with Berkeley through the Percivals and apparently knew Catherine Percival* well enough to take advice from her. Berkeley remarks upon the favorable influence that Lady Percival had with respect to his preferments (see Letters 98 and 104).

Anne Forster (?–1786). See **Anne Berkeley**, (*née* Forster).

Nicholas Forster (1672–1743). Not much is known about Forster, other than that he was the bishop of Killaoe (1714–16) and Bishop of Rapho (1716–43). He was the uncle of Berkeley's wife Anne Forster.*

George I (1660–1727). The king of Great Britain and Ireland and elector of Hanover was born Georg Ludwig (George Lewis) in Hanover on 28 May 1660. He was the first of the seven surviving children of Ernst August (1629–98) of Brunswick-Lüneburg and Sophia (1630–1714), who was the grandchild of James I of England.

Immediately upon the death of Anne* (1 August 1714) the procedures set out in the Act of Regency of 1706 were set into motion. That same day George I was proclaimed king, although he did not arrive in England until 18 September. Berkeley was, from the start, a clear and loyal Tory supporter of the Hanoverian line. George I would, shortly before his death, approve the warrant for the grant for Berkeley's scheme to locate a college in Bermuda (see Letter 166), but the king died before the process was completed, in the early hours of 12 June 1727.

George II (1683–1760). The son of Georg Ludwig, George I* of England, was born George Augustus. George accompanied his father to England in 1714 upon his accession to the English throne, and a few days later became the Prince of Wales. He had a troubled relationship with his father and the rivalry was public enough that Benson* comments upon some of it in a letter to Berkeley (see Letter 262). He ascended to the throne in June 1727. George II rapidly and surprisingly reapproved the patent for Berkeley's college in Bermuda. He died at Kensington Palace on 25 October 1760.

Isaac Gervais (1680–1756). Born in Montpellier, France, Gervais was brought to Ireland as a child after the revocation of the Edict of Nantes. A French Huguenot, he was vicar-choral at Lismore in 1708, prebendary of Lismore in 1713, and dean of Tuam from 1744 until his death in 1756. He was an advocate of Berkeley's tar water, giving testimony in Thomas Prior's* *Authentic Narrative*. He was, judging by the correspondence, a close friend of Berkeley.

Edmund Gibson (1669–1748). The influential bishop of Lincoln and then bishop of London during the period when Berkeley was seeking preferment and support for his scheme to locate a college in Bermuda, Gibson was a quality scholar and divine. He was widely perceived as a low-churchman Whig, but this did not prevent his advancement. He was appointed to the archdeanery of Surrey in 1710, where he established the pattern of being a vigorous clergyman, increasing pastoral oversight and implementing a more rigorous policy of visitation.

In 1713 he published his two-volume *Codex Juris Ecclesiastici Anglicani*, a careful collection and commentary on the statutes, canons, and articles of the Church of England. The work, which was still in use in the twentieth century, provides a sense of Gibson's accomplishments as a church scholar. He published a variety of other tracts during his lifetime, and was particularly interested in publishing pieces that were accessible to ordinary Christians. He wrote a series of pastoral letters designed to combat the profaneness and impiety of the age.

In 1715 he was made bishop of Lincoln, translating to London in 1723. Upon his translation he became aware of the needs of the colonial church and started advocating for the creation of an American episcopate. As Berkeley was a churchman trying to establish a college in the colonies that included religious education, he kept Gibson informed of his actions (see Letter 173). Around 1725 Gibson laid before the Privy Council a plan to appoint two suffragan bishops for the mainland colonies and two more for the island colonies. Nothing came of his efforts, however, as the plan was viewed as a prelude to reducing the general dependency of the colonies on England. Gibson died on 6 September 1748.

Duchess of Grafton. See Henrietta Fitzroy.

Duke of Grafton. See Charles Fitzroy.

George Granville, Baron Lansdowne and Jacobite Duke of Albemarle (1666–1735). Famous for his literary talents in his own lifetime, Granville was a major Tory and Jacobite politician. Born on 9 March 1666, he became financially secure on the death of his parents and an uncle, both of whom left him pensions. His family connections secured him a seat in Parliament and an entree into court society.

In 1710 he was appointed secretary at war and played the role of a political "whip" rousing support for Tories in elections. After the accession of George I* he lost his offices and started a more serious correspondence with members of the exiled Stuart court. Lansdowne supported the rebellion of 1715, but thought there was no hope for the Jacobites without French military intervention. He was arrested in September 1715 on charges of treason, but was never brought to trial. In 1720 he went with John Erskine* to France and became one of the key players in the Jacobite plot involving Atterbury.*

Granville later tried to reconcile with the Hanoverian government and was allowed to return to England in 1729, dedicating the 1732 edition of his works to Queen Caroline. He died on 3 February 1735.

Stephen Hales (1677–1761). A natural philosopher, inventor, and clergyman, Hales was born on 17 September 1677. He attended Corpus Christi College, Cambridge, earning a BA in 1700 and an MA in 1703.

Elected a fellow of the Royal Society in 1718, he pursued a lifelong interest in experimental science. His important scientific works include *Vegetable Statics* (1727) and *Statical Essays* (1733; referred to in *Siris*, section 196). Although keenly interested in science, a family connection secured Hales's presentation to the perpetual curacy of Teddington in Middlesex, a ministry that he held until his death. He was much involved in local affairs such as the rebuilding of the parish church and the provision of an adequate water supply for the village. His sermons were popular and two were published. He contributed anti-alcohol tracts and was, involved, with Oglethorpe,* in the foundation of the Georgia colony. He was created a DD by Oxford University in 1733 and in 1751 was named the chaplain of the dowager princess of Wales.

Hales worked with the Society for the Propagation of the Gospel in Foreign Parts, of which he had been an active member since 1722, and with the Bray Associates, a missionary and educational foundation. We know Berkeley corresponded with Hales, although only one letter intended for publication concerning tar water remains (see Letter 345). Hales died on 4 January 1761 at the age of 83.

Thomas Hanmer, fourth Baronet (1677–1746). A committed high-church Tory politician, Hanmer was born on 24 September 1677, the only son of William Hanmer (?–1695) and grandson of Sir Thomas Hanmer, second Baronet. He was an elegant orator and found success in Parliament as leader of a group of Hanoverian Tories. He was Speaker of the House (1714–15) and influential for many years through the Prince of Wales (later George II*), until they had a falling-out.

We have no evidence of any close connection between Hanmer and Berkeley, although apparently Hanmer did use tar water for his family and consulted Berkeley about its use (see Letter 314). Hanmer died on 7 May 1746 without issue and the baronetcy became extinct.

Robert Harley, first Earl of Oxford (1661–1724). Harley was born on 5 December 1661, the eldest son of Sir Edward Harley (1624–1700). During the revolution of 1688 Harley and his father raised troops for William and in 1689 the young Harley first entered the House of Commons representing Tregony. There he displayed a talent for politics and procedure.

Elected Speaker in 1701, the accession of Anne* to the throne brought Harley to the pinnacle of power. He played a large part in the union with Scotland and was an intimate of Godolphin and Marlborough, although a disagreement with them forced him from office in February 1708. With the sensational trial of Sacheverell* in 1710, Harley returned to the limelight and Anne made him lord treasurer in 1711, a position which effectively made him first minister (although the post of prime minister was not effectively established until Robert Walpole). At this point Harley was at the height of his power, helped by a failed assassination attempt against him on 8 March. He was made Earl of Oxford and Mortimer on 23 May 1711.

Despite the centrality of his person during the reign of Anne, upon the accession of George I* Harley found himself marginalized. He was associated with the Treaty of Utrecht that the new king viewed as a betrayal of the allies (including Hanover). In 1715 Harley was impeached by a Whig-dominated parliament, mostly concerning charges related to the Utrecht treaty and alleged Jacobitism. Despite rumors to the contrary, there is no real evidence that Harley was attracted to the cause of the Pretender.* The articles of impeachment were never pressed, and in June 1717 the charges were dropped. From this point forward he continued to participate in the House of Lords, but his political dominance was gone. He died in London on 21 May 1724.

Thomas Herbert, eighth Earl of Pembroke and fifth Earl of Montgomery (1656/7– 1733). A moderate Tory, Herbert briefly served in Parliament before claiming his titles in 1683. He was named lord lieutenant of Wiltshire in that year, serving in that post almost uninterruptedly until his death. Although he offered his services to King James upon the landing of William in 1688, he nonetheless corresponded with the Prince of Orange during the revolution, leaving him in a position to retain favor despite voting against declaring William and Mary king and queen. Herbert thus began a surprisingly distinguished career in service to William III, being named ambassador to the Dutch states and serving on the Privy Council and as lord of trade and plantations. In 1690 he became first lord of the Admiralty, in 1692 was lord of the Privy Seal, and in 1699 was lord president of the council.

Under Queen Anne* Pembroke remained a reliable court Tory. She appointed him lord lieutenant of Ireland in 1707 and, after the death of Prince George, renamed him to the post of lord high admiral. By 1714 Pembroke was effectively retired from active public service, but was well respected for his political contributions.

Pembroke also had a reputation as a patron of the arts and sciences. He was elected a fellow of the Royal Society in 1685, and served as the president of the society (1689–90). He supported John Locke, who dedicated his *Essay Concerning Human Understanding* to him. This was no doubt an incentive to Berkeley, who later dedicated his own *Principles of Human Knowledge* to Lord Pembroke as well. Percival reports in December of 1710 that Pembroke found the book smart but unconvincing (see *Works*, vol. II, p. 4). It is possible that Berkeley met Pembroke during the latter's tenure as lord lieutenant of Ireland, but Berkeley consistently appeals to Percival* as an intermediary, removing any hint of a closer relationship. Pembroke died in London on 22 January 1733.

John Hoadly (1678–1746). A Church of Ireland archbishop of Armagh, Hoadly was born on 27 September 1678 and educated at Catharine's College, Cambridge. He became chaplain to Bishop Gilbert Burnet, who between 1706 and 1713 helped him with preferment to several posts in his diocese. In 1717 he was appointed chaplain-in-ordinary to George II.*

Hoadly was consecrated bishop of Ferns and Leighlin in September 1727 and translated to Dublin in January 1730. When Hugh Boulter died, in 1742, Hoadly was appointed primate and archbishop of Armagh on 7 October. Not a deep or prolific writer, he published only a few items, mostly sermons and a pastoral letter about the Jacobite uprising of 1745. He was more involved, however, in political matters, serving on the Irish Privy Council and in the House of Lords. He was primate when Berkeley was made bishop of Cloyne, and their relationship appears to have been only professional in nature. Hoadly died on 16 July 1746.

Benjamin Hoare (1693–1749/50). A member of a prominent banking family, Benjamin's father, Sir Richard Hoare (1648–1719), was the founder of Hoare's Bank. Benjamin was partners with his nephew Henry Hoare.* Both Percival and Berkeley made use of Hoare's Bank in conducting business matters.[1962]

Henry Hoare (1705–85). The eldest son of Henry Hoare (1677–1725), his grandfather, Sir Richard Hoare (1648–1719), was the founder of Hoare's Bank. Starting in 1726 he was partners with his uncle, Benjamin Hoare,* who handled much of the business of Percival and Berkeley. Henry was well known as a patron of the arts and for his art collection. He died on 8 September 1785.[1963]

James Honeyman (Honyman), (*c.* 1675–1750). James Honeyman was the rector of Trinity Church in Newport, Rhode Island, from 1704 until the end of his life in 1750. At the time, Honeyman was the only episcopal churchman on the island and Berkeley thought well of him (see Letter 177). Honeyman was appointed by the Society for the Propagation of the Gospel in Foreign Parts to be their missionary in the area and at various times had the charge of a number of congregations. By 1709 he complains of a need for an American episcopate. In 1732 he petitions for an increase in salary, which Berkeley endorses in January 1733 (see Letter 217). Berkeley and his new wife stayed with the Honeyman's for several weeks when

---

[1962] See Hutchings, *History of the Hoare Banking Dynasty*.
[1963] See Hutchings, *History of the Hoare Banking Dynasty*.

they first arrived in Rhode Island until they secured Whitehall. James Honeyman died on 2 July 1750.

David Humphreys (1690–1740). Humphreys was a Church of England clergyman. Born 20 January 1690, the son of a London leather seller, he was educated at Trinity College, Cambridge, receiving his BA in 1711, his MA in 1715, his BD in 1715, and his DD by royal mandate in 1728.

In 1716 Humphreys was appointed secretary of the Society for the Propagation of the Gospel in Foreign Parts, and he held this appointment until his death. He wrote the first book about the society, *An Historical Account of the Incorporated Society for the Propagation of the Gospel in Foreign Parts* (1730). Humphreys was ordained a deacon on 25 April 1722 and a priest on 29 April. He became vicar of Ware in Hertfordshire on 6 January 1730, and of nearby Thundridge on 30 June 1732. As the secretary for the society, he handled the correspondence with Berkeley concerning some of the society's business in the American colonies (see Letters 193 and 217). He died in 1740.

John James (?–1741). Later created Sir John James of Bury St. Edmunds in 1736, James was a gentleman of means traveling to America for pleasure along with Richard Dalton.* He took a house for some time in Boston and traveled to the colonies with Berkeley. He would later contemplate joining the Roman Church, which prompted a long letter from Berkeley (see Letter 282). Not much is otherwise known about him.

Joseph Jekyll (1662–1738). Master of the Rolls in England from 1717 to 1738, Jekyll also served as a parliamentary leader for the Society for Promoting Christian Knowledge, the Society for the Propagation of the Gospel, and the Georgia Society. Jekyll Island in Georgia now bears his name.

In 1687 he was called to the bar and through his work cultivated the patronage of Lord Chancellor Somers. In 1697 Jekyll married Somers's second sister and had the active support of his new family. In June of that year he was appointed chief justice of Chester and knighted in December. From that point his legal career flourished and he was ultimately made prime serjeant by George I* in 1714. He frequently tried cases before the House of Lords and as Master of the Rolls he defended the Chancery. In 1710 he drafted the articles and managed the impeachment of Sacheverell.*

Jekyll served as a Member of Parliament starting in 1713, representing at different times Eye and Lymington. His parliamentary activity centered around moral and anticlerical issues. He supported or drafted legislation to ban duelling, to censor the stage, to reform the poor law, and to build hospitals, workhouses, and houses of correction. He was most famous for his drafting and sponsorship of the Gin Act in 1736, which sought to regulate retailers of spirits in order to limit drunkenness.

Berkeley was active enough in his pursuit of the Bermuda scheme in Parliament to know Jekyll at least professionally (see Letter 242). There is no hint that their relationship extended any further. Jekyll died in August 1738 and was buried on 1 September.

Samuel Johnson (1696-1772). Samuel Johnson was a philosopher, Church of England clergyman, and educator in America. He was born on 14 October 1696 in Guilford, Connecticut, the second child of Samuel Johnson (?-*c.* 1728), a farmer and proprietor of a fulling mill. Johnson demonstrated academic ability from a young age and graduated from the collegiate school in New Haven that later became Yale, eventually securing an MA there in 1717.

He was ordained in 1720 and installed as the minister of the church in West Haven. While there he came to doubt the validity of his ordination. In 1722, despite opposition from his Congregationalist colleagues, Johnson and several others traveled to England where they were ordained by the bishop of Norwich as priests in the Church of England. As a result Johnson became a missionary for the Society for the Propagation of the Gospel and was assigned to Stratford, Connecticut, at the end of 1724.

When Berkeley arrived in Rhode Island, Johnson became a convert to his philosophical system and the two exchanged a series of letters that are the most philosophically illuminating of the extant correspondence (see Letters 190, 194, 197, 199, 205, and 231). The friendship between the men was founded on their common philosophical interests and their passion for both religious and secular education. As a partial result of the influence of Berkeley, Johnson published *Introduction to Philosophy* (1743; revised and enlarged in 1752), a work designed to give students an overview of what they should learn and the relationships amongst the branches of knowledge. Johnson solicits comments from Berkeley on the revised edition (see Letter 389). As the work espoused immaterialism it was not popular, but his publications earned him an honorary doctorate from Oxford in 1744.

In 1750 Benjamin Franklin invited him to lead the new College of Philadelphia (later the University of Pennsylvania). Johnson declined, citing poor health, but he was involved in the formation of King's College in New York. In 1754 he became president of the college, which was renamed Columbia University after the American War of Independence. Johnson wrote to Berkeley for advice about the foundation of the college (see Letters 360, 370, 372, and 373). Johnson died in Stratford on 6 January 1772.

William King (1650-1729). Theologian and Church of Ireland archbishop of Dublin, King was born on 1 May 1650. Educated at Trinity College, Dublin, he was appointed chaplain to the lord deputy in 1683 and as chaplain to the lord lieutenant of Ireland, the Duke of Ormond, in 1684. During the revolution of 1688 and its aftermath, King labored to maintain church discipline and to protect

Protestants. He was imprisoned in Dublin Castle and held until the city was occupied by Williamite forces following the battle of the Boyne.

In December 1690 he was appointed bishop of Derry. While there King worked to improve pastoral standards in his diocese and sought to reform the church in Ireland. In particular, he was sensitive to the issue of ecclesiastical appointments. Berkeley would inadvertently run afoul of King's concerns here with his own ordination in 1710 (see Letter 13).

In 1702 King published his most important philosophical work, *De Origine Male* (*The Origin of Evil*), which argued that we can gain a form of knowledge of God by analogy from His works in the world. The book prompted responses from Bayle and Leibniz as well as Berkeley. King later published *Divine Predestination and Foreknowledge, Consistent with the Freedom of Man's Will* (1709), which also sought to reconcile divine omniscience with human freedom by invoking the limits of our merely analogical knowledge of the divine.

On 11 March 1703 King was appointed archbishop of Dublin. He was by this time the leading spokesman for the established church in Ireland and remained so until his death on 8 May 1729.

Ralph Lambert (1666–1732). Not much is known about the details of Lambert's life. He was the vicar of Dundalk in 1706 and the dean of Down some years later. Lambert was made bishop of Dromore in 1717. He was the bishop who proposed and installed his own candidate for the deanery of Dromore in 1722 after the Duke of Grafton* selected Berkeley for the post. A lawsuit ensued over who had the right to fill the position, which Berkeley eventually let drop as he achieved another preferment (see Letter 104). Lambert was translated to Meath in 1727. He published several works, most notably *Partiality Detected* (1705).

Jean Le Clerc (1657–1736). A theologian and philosopher, Le Clerc was born on 29 March 1657 in Geneva, the second son of Étienne Le Clerc (1599–1676), professor at the *académie* in Geneva. Le Clerc was an accomplished scholar, but is mostly known for his work on scholarly journals, in which he reviewed and summarized many English works. These included his *Bibliothèque Universelle et Historique* (1686–93), *Bibliothèque Choisie* (1703–13), and *Bibliothèque Ancienne et Moderne* (1714–27). His linguistic competences enabled him to discuss a wider range of books than many of his rivals. After receiving his education, Le Clerc lived primarily in Holland, but he sought to gain an appointment in England, using the support of friends like John Locke and Joseph Addison.*

Berkeley had his *Essay Towards a New Theory of Vision* reviewed in *Bibliothèque Choisie* and wrote to Le Clerc to make corrections and also to seek a wider scholarly audience for his *Principles of Human Knowledge* (see Letters 27–28 and 32–33), although there is no record that Le Clerc ever responded. Le Clerc died in Amsterdam on 8 January 1736.

Pierre François le Courayer (1681–1776). A Roman Catholic priest who authored a dissertation (*Dissertation sur la Validité des Ordinations des Anglais et sur la Succession des Évêques de l'Eglise Anglicane, avec les Preuves Justificatives des Faits Avancés* [Brussels, 1723]) attempting to establish that there was no break in the line of ordination from the apostles to the present Anglican Church, thus defending the validity of Anglican orders. An English version appeared in 1725. Courayer was excommunicated and retired to England, where he was graciously received, especially by John Percival* and William Wake.*

Born on 17 November 1681 in Rouen, France, Courayer was educated at Vernon and Paris. He became a canon regular in 1706, sublibrarian in 1711, and librarian in 1714. By the age of 40 he had become respected as a scholar. His study on the Anglican ordinations, however, provoked a storm of controversy. The most important of these attacks were made by the Jesuit Jean Hardouin in 1724 and by the Dominican Michel le Quien in the following year. Courayer replied to his critics in *Défense de la Dissertation* (1726), but his thesis was condemned by a commission of French bishops. Faced with a possible trial for heresy, he fled to England in January 1728. He remained a Roman Catholic throughout his life, and published other works critical of various Catholic doctrines. He died in London on 17 October 1776.

Frederick Lewis Prince of Wales (1707–51). Born at the Leine Palace, Hanover, on 20 January 1707, Frederick was the first child of George Augustus (later George II*). He arrived in London in December 1728 and was made Prince of Wales on 8 January 1729.

Frederick, like his father before him, had a strained relationship with his father, the king, as he attempted in various ways to assert his independence. He married Princess Augusta of Saxe-Gotha (1719–72) on 25 April 1736, and shortly thereafter his allowance was raised to £50,000. After the election of 1741 provided Frederick with a substantial parliamentary following, he helped assist with the removal of Walpole from office 1742. He used his success to negotiate an increase in his allowance from George II to £100,000 per annum. The king was not pleased, but reluctantly agreed and the new sum passed the Commons in May 1742. The entire affair was big news, and it appears in Berkeley's correspondence (see Letter 262). Frederick died unexpectedly after a short illness on 20 March 1751.

D[iederick] W[essel] Linden (?–after 1768). A Westphalian doctor who moved to Flintshire in 1747, Linden is most famous for his study of spa water: *A Treatise on the Three Medicinal Waters at Llandrindod* (London, 1756). He approached Berkeley asking for clarifications about his work on tar water when preparing a German-language version of *Siris* (see Letters 317 and 318).

Richard Lloyd (1699–1775). Richard Lloyd was a clergyman at Rathcormuck (1742–75) in the diocese of Cloyne when Berkeley was bishop. Lloyd had, in 1749, met and allowed John Wesley to preach from his pulpit. Upon Wesley's return, the following year, Lloyd had him preach again in Rathcormuck. Wesley was a controversial figure and his presence incited riots, so the neighboring clergy complained to Berkeley, who in turn ordered Lloyd not to allow unlicensed preachers access to the pulpit (see Letters 368 and 369). Little else is known about Lloyd.

Earl of Mar. See **John Erskine**.

Duke of Marlborough. See **John Churchill**.

Robert Marshall (*c.* 1690–1772). An attorney from Clonmel, Marshall was later in life a justice of common pleas in Ireland. He was named as coexecutor, with Berkeley, for the will of Hester Van Homrigh.* Berkeley complains incessantly in his correspondence with Thomas Prior* about Marshall's obstructionism with respect to the disposing of her estate. Not much of detail is known about Marshall.[1964]

Robert McCausland (*c.* 1685–1734?). A landowner and colonel who resided in County Derry, McCausland had business dealings with Berkeley concerning his deanery in Derry. McCausland married Hannah Moore in 1709 and reputedly inherited lands through her uncle, William Conolly*. Little else is known about him, but he is often mentioned in Berkeley's correspondence with Thomas Prior* (see Letters 139, 142, 144, 150, and 155–57).

McManus (?–?). A Derry solicitor, McManus was Berkeley's agent concerned with the farming of the deanery benefice at Derry. Virtually nothing is known about him, including his first name (see *Works*, vol. IX, p. 57 and Letters 130–31, 150, 152, 154–57, 160–61, 169, 174, and 198).

Samuel Molyneux (1689–1728). Born on 18 July 1689, Samuel was the third but only surviving child of the experimental philosopher William Molyneux (1656–98). When his father died, he was reared by his uncle, Dr. Thomas Molyneux (1661–1733). He attended Trinity College, Dublin, where he befriended Berkeley (see Letters 3, 7, and 9–10), who dedicated his *Miscellanea Mathematica* (1707) to him. Molyneux graduated in 1708 with a BA and in 1710 with an MA.

In 1714, while traveling in England and on the Continent, he met the Duke and Duchess of Marlborough, who dispatched him on a political mission to the Hanoverian court. He made a good impression there and returned with the court to England after the death of Anne* as the secretary to the Prince of Wales, a post he held until the prince became George II.* In addition to his court post, he was a Member of Parliament representing several different constituencies, including Trinity College, Dublin, in 1727.

[1964] For a brief discussion see Burke, *History of Clonmel*, pp. 487–89.

Like his father, Molyneux studied astronomy and optics, and he contributed to the manufacture of reflecting telescopes. He was elected a fellow of the Royal Society in 1712. After the ascension of George II, he was appointed Lord of the Admiralty, a post that curtailed his scientific work. After a fit suffered in the House of Commons, Molyneux died on 13 April 1728.

Charles Mordaunt third Earl of Peterborough and first Earl of Monmouth (1658?–1735). An army officer and diplomat, Mordaunt was born into a noble family. On his father's death, in 1675, he became the second Viscount of Avalon and Baron of Ryegate. He was allegedly the first noble to suggest that the Prince of Orange should succeed to the English throne, and William rewarded him after the revolution of 1688. Mordaunt was made privy councillor, gentleman of the bedchamber, lord lieutenant of Northamptonshire, and first commissioner of the Treasury, all in 1689. On 9 April of that same year he was created Earl of Monmouth, and upon the death of his uncle, in 1697, he also became the third Earl of Peterborough.

With the ascension of Anne* to the throne, in 1702, he again found favor, being appointed governor of Jamaica. In 1705 he was appointed commander-in-chief of the troops of the fleet. He served in a variety of ambassadorial posts, including the appointment in 1713 as the ambassador to the duke of Savoy, who was soon to be crowned king of Sicily. As he embarked for Sicily to represent England at the coronation, he took Berkeley along as his chaplain. Berkeley had been introduced to him by Jonathan Swift.*

Peterborough was also a significant patron of the arts. He supported John Locke and was an intimate of both Alexander Pope* and Swift. He died on 21 October 1735.

Henry Newman (1670–1743). Henry Newman was born in Massachusetts, the son of a Congregational minister. He attended Harvard and served as librarian there until 1693, leaving to pursue a career in business, primarily in the fishing industry in Newfoundland.

In 1703 he settled in England and became a corresponding member of the Society for Promoting Christian Knowledge (SPCK), which was founded by Dr. Thomas Bray. In 1708 he was appointed its secretary. By all accounts he was well suited to this role and helped to broaden the influence of the society. His primary task was to handle the correspondence, which brought him into contact with Berkeley during the latter's stay in Rhode Island (see Letters 175, 182, 188, 191, 193, 196, 201, 208, 214–15, 227, 229–30, and 236). Newman worked for the SPCK until his death, from asthma, on 15 June 1743.

James Edward Oglethorpe (1696–1785). An army officer and founder of the colony of Georgia, Oglethorpe was born in London on 22 December 1696, the son of Sir Theophilus Oglethorpe (1650–1702), a politician and army officer. As a young man he saw military action in the war between Austria and the Turks in 1716–17 and again in Sicily in 1718, where he distinguished himself and was promoted to lieutenant-colonel. In 1719 he returned to England and joined Parliament.

In 1728, after a friend of his who had fallen into debt died in Fleet prison, Oglethorpe persuaded the House of Commons to investigate prison conditions in England. John Percival* served with him on the committee (see Letter 185). In 1730 Oglethorpe advanced the ambitious plan of founding a colony of debtors in what would become the Georgia colony. He writes to Berkeley in 1731, attempting to drum up support for his cause (see Letter 211). In October 1732 Oglethorpe set out with the first settlers and led the fledgling colony, helping it to succeed. In 1739, when war with Spain broke out, Oglethorpe was ordered to harrass the Spanish in Florida. After an ill-conceived attack on St. Augustine failed, he successfully repelled the Spanish in May 1740 at the battle of the Bloody Marsh, securing the English colonies. In recognition of his service, he was promoted to brigadier-general.

He returned to England in 1743 and fought against the Jacobites in the rebellion of 1745. Accused of being dilatory in the prosecution of his military duties, he was court-martialed. Although he was acquitted, his military career was ended. He served in Parliament for nine years before losing his seat. He died on 1 July 1785.

Duke of Orleans. See **Charles Philippe**.

Duke of Ormond. See **James Butler**, second Duke of Ormond.

Earl of Orrery. See **John Boyle**.

Pall Mall. Pall Mall is a street in the City of Westminster borough in London. The name apparently derives from the name of a game ("pall mall") played in front of St. James's Palace in that area in the seventeenth century.

Catherine Parker. See **Catherine Percival** (*née* Parker).

Mary Parker. See **Mary Dering** (*née* Parker).

Philip Parker (1682–1741). Philip Parker was the brother of Lady Catherine (*née* Parker) Percival. Relatively little is known about him, except that he was ennobled and made Sir Philip Parker-a-Morley-Long, third Baronet. He served as Member of Parliament for Harwich (1715–34).

Peter Partinton (?–?). Partinton was the executor for the estate of the father and brother of Hester Van Homrigh.* Prior to her death, Van Homrigh had brought a lawsuit against Partinton in order to resolve the family estate. When she died and Berkeley was named a coexecutor of her will, he was also forced to engage with Partinton to resolve the increasingly complicated estate of the Van Homrigh family. Many of Berkeley's letters to Thomas Prior* are preoccupied with wrangling over the Van Homrigh estate and with Partinton's role in particular. No other details about Partinton are known.

Philip Pearson (?–?). An alderman in Dublin, Pearson was Jonathan Swift's* tenant and the coexecutor of Lord Mayor Van Homrigh's will, along with Peter Partinton.* Little other information about Pearson is known to us.[1965]

Thomas Pelham-Holles, Duke of Newcastle-upon-Tyne and first Duke of Newcastle-under-Lyme (1693–1768). A politician and eventual prime minister of England, Pelham-Holles was born on 21 July 1693. He became wealthy while young through two inheritances. The first came in July 1711, when his mother's brother, John Holles, duke of Newcastle-upon-Tyne, died, bequeathing Thomas a vast estate. The heir's only obligation was to append "Holles" to his name, which he did. The second inheritance came in February 1712 upon the death of his father. Thomas succeeded both to the title of Baron Pelham of Laughton and to the Pelham estates in Sussex. His land and wealth gave him significant influence over a dozen Members of Parliament elected from areas where he held estates.

A committed Whig politically, he found royal favor as well. In 1714 George I* appointed him lord lieutenant of Middlesex and Nottinghamshire and raised him in the peerage, making him Viscount Houghton and Earl of Clare, titles formerly held by his uncle. During the Jacobite rebellion of 1714 he raised a troop and defended the monarchy. After marrying Henrietta Godolphin in 1717 and tying himself politically to Sunderland, Pelham-Holles was rewarded with the office of lord chamberlain. In the House of Lords he continued to support the government and aligned himself with Walpole. In 1724 he was installed as secretary for the south, giving him influence over England's foreign policy.

Pelham-Holles continued to be influential in the government after the ascension of George II,* collecting a variety of offices and expanding his political influence. Focused primarily on English affairs, he opposed attempts to create new episcopates in the American colonies. His offices included first lord of the Treasury and prime minister (1754–56). In 1762 he was forced out of government. After a failed attempt to return to the political stage in 1768, he died on 17 November of the same year.

Earl of Pembroke. See **Thomas Herbert**.

Catherine Percival (*née* Parker) (1687/8–1749). The daughter of Sir Philip Parker, second Baronet (*c.* 1650–*c.* 1698), she married John Percival* on 10 June 1710. She and Percival had seven children, three of whom survived into adulthood.

[1965] See *Correspondence of Jonathan Swift*, ed. Williams, Swift to Rev. John Worrall, 12 September 1727.

She presented through her husband a clever objection concerning the Mosaic account of creation and its compatibility with Berkeley's immaterialist principles (see Letters 17–18). She and Berkeley apparently got along well; Lady Percival used her friendship with the Duchess of Grafton to intervene on Berkeley's behalf concerning preferment, and Berkeley often asks after her in his letters to her husband. Ill for much of her later life, she survived her husband by a year, dying on 22 August 1749.

John Percival (Perceval),[1966] first Earl of Egmont (1683–1748). Percival was born at Burton, County Cork, on 12 July 1683, the second son of Sir John Perceval, third Baronet (?–1686), and his wife, Catherine (?–1692), the fourth daughter of Sir Edward Dering, second Baronet, of Surrenden Dering, Kent. When their father died, in 1686, John and his brothers Edward and Philip were reared by their great-uncle, Robert Southwell, in England.

On the death of his elder brother Edward in 1691, Percival became fifth Baronet. Educated at Magdalen College, Oxford, he left without a taking a degree in 1701, but was nonetheless elected a fellow of the Royal Society in 1702. Apparently Percival first met Berkeley on a visit to Ireland in 1708, although the exact details of their meeting are unknown. On 10 June 1710 Percival married Catherine Parker,* siring seven children, of whom only three survived to adulthood.

In 1704 he inherited large estates in Cork and Tipperary, securing his finances. In that same year he also started his political career, serving in the Irish House of Commons for County Cork. In 1713 he was made Baron of Burton and took his seat in the Irish House of Lords. In 1723 he was made Viscount of Kanturk. These, however, were Irish titles and Percival desired an English one. He spent much of his time in England, and in 1727 secured a seat in Parliament representing Harwich. In 1729 Percival served on the committee chaired by James Oglethorpe* reviewing the state of English prisons (see Letter 185) and assisted Oglethorpe in founding and maintaining the Georgia colony. On 6 November 1733 he was created Earl of Egmont, an Irish peerage.

Percival's relationship with Berkeley was that of an intimate friend. Much of their correspondence survives and Berkeley dedicated his *New Theory of Vision* (1709) to Percival. He and his wife exerted some influence on Berkeley's behalf and they borrowed money from one another. Several of the letters fondly reflect on time spent together discussing matters political and philosophical. Percival died on 1 May 1748 in London, prompting a heartfelt letter of condolence from Berkeley to Percival's eldest son John* (see Letter 361).

John Percival (Perceval), second Earl of Egmont (1711–70). The eldest son of John and Catherine Percival,* the younger John was born on 24 February 1711 in London. Following his father's political ambitions, Percival represented Dingle

---

[1966] There are several variants in the spelling of his surname, including most commonly "Perceval" and "Percivale" in addition to "Percival."

in the Irish parliament at the age of 20. In 1734 his father stood down from his parliamentary seat at Harwich in his favor, but he lost the election. Not long after, he married Catherine Cecil, the second daughter of James Cecil, Earl of Salisbury, on 15 February 1737 (he would later marry again, in 1756, Catherine Compton). Percival tried on two other occasions to gain a seat in the House of Commons before finally succeeding in 1741, when he represented Westminster. He would thereafter be returned to Parliament from various different constituencies.

On 1 May 1748 Perceval succeeded his father as second Earl of Egmont in the Irish peerage. He aligned himself politically with Frederick Lewis,* the Prince of Wales, and became a prominent opposition figure in Parliament. The prince died in 1751, however, putting his political situation adrift. Percival spent his remaining years seeking an English title, which was finally granted him on 7 May 1762 when he was created Baron Lovel and Holland of Enmore, Somerset. He then aligned himself more closely with the crown, being rewarded on 10 September 1763 when appointed first lord of the Admiralty, where he served until 1766.

He died at his home in Pall Mall, London, on 4 December 1770.

Earl of Peterborough. See Charles Mordaunt.

Charles Philippe (1674-1723). A member of the royal family of France, Philippe served as regent of the Kingdom from 1715 to 1723. He was known from birth as the Duke of Chartres; his father was Louis XIV's younger brother Philippe I, Duke of Orléans. Named regent of France for Louis XV until Louis attained the age of majority in 1723, the era of Philippe's rule was known as the Regency (1715-23). He died at Versailles in 1723.

Constantine Phipps (*c.* 1656-1723). Politician and lord chancellor of Ireland, Phipps started his career as a lawyer, appearing as junior counsel for the crown in political cases. He married Catherine Sawyer (*c.* 1667-1728), the niece of the attorney general Sir Robert Sawyer, whose patronage quickly advanced Phipps's career.

His most famous appearance came in 1710 when he served as one of the defending counsels during Sacheverell's* impeachment. His performance at the trial was sufficient for him to be considered for office, but his Tory leanings precluded most posts. Instead, he was appointed lord chancellor of Ireland in December 1710. Knighted in advance of leaving England for the post, Phipps served as a partisan Tory, becoming embroiled in several partisan disputes as lord lieutenant. The most important of these concerned the election of the lord mayor of Dublin. Phipps led a Tory majority and refused to sanction the choice of the mostly Whiggish Dublin City Council, instead proposing a slate of candidates that included Phipps himself. The outrage that ensued drew the attention of Berkeley (see Letter 55).

With the death of Anne* in 1714, Phipps returned to England and practiced law. He was suspected by many of having Jacobite sympathies and was closely associated with the Duke of Ormond.* His name figures prominently in Jacobite correspondence after 1715 and he was consulted by the Stuart court in exile on a legal matter in 1718. He channeled funds to conspirators in the Atterbury* plot of 1723 and defended the bishop after his arrest. Nothing came of his intrigues, however, as he died on 9 October 1723.

Alexander Pope (1688–1744). An acquaintance and correspondent of Berkeley as well as many prominent persons of influence, Alexander Pope was one of the foremost literary figures of the eighteenth century. He was born on 21 May 1688, the son of Alexander Pope (1646–1717), a linen merchant in London.

Pope became acquainted with Richard Steele* and Joseph Addison,* and wrote for their magazines. He also wrote the prologue to Addison's play *Cato*. Pope was openly a Catholic but associated indiscriminately, drawing ire from friends and opponents alike. He is the author of *Essay on Criticism* (1711), *Rape of the Lock* (1712), and *Windsor Forest* (1713), among others. Berkeley writes from Italy to compliment Pope on *Rape of the Lock* (see Letter 65) and there is some evidence that Berkeley stayed at Pope's residence on at least one occasion, but little to suggest they were close friends. For Berkeleyphiles, Pope is best remembered for the following lines penned in *Epilogue to the Satires* (Dialogue II, 170):

Ev'n in a bishop I can spy desert

Secker is decent, Rundel has a heart;

Manners with candour are to Benson giv'n,

To Berkeley ev'ry virtue under heaven.

Pope died on 30 May 1744.

Old Pretender. See **James Francis Edward**.

Young Pretender. See **Charles Edward**.

Prince of Wales. See **Frederick Lewis**.

Thomas Prior (1681–1751). Author, founder of the Dublin Society, and close personal friend of Berkeley, Thomas Prior was born at Garriston, near Rathdowney, in Ireland. He was educated at the public school at Kilkenny between 1697 and 1699. It was here that he met Berkeley and the two formed a lifelong friendship. He graduated from Trinity College, Dublin, with a BA in 1703.

His family settled in Ireland in 1636, giving Prior claim to be a genuine Irishman, and he devoted much of his life to its welfare, especially by promoting trade and industry among the Protestant population. In 1729 he published *List of the Absentees of Ireland*, which contained details of estates and incomes from rents. He claimed that upwards of £600,000 went overseas in remitted rents (the figure is now disputed), an implicit indictment against said absentees. Berkeley was listed in one edition (he was in Rhode Island while holding the deanery of Derry), a fact that did not diminish their friendship. In 1731 Prior and twelve others established the Dublin Society for the Promotion of Agriculture, Manufactures, Arts and Sciences. In 1749 it received a grant of £500 per annum from Parliament and subsequently became the Royal Dublin Society.

Prior acted as an agent for Berkeley in Ireland, most notably by assisting with the resolution of the Van Homrigh* estate. He was also an advocate for Berkeley's tar water, publishing *Authentic Narrative of the Success of Tar-Water in Curing a Great Number and Variety of Distempers* in 1746. Prior died on 21 October 1751, after a long illness. Berkeley wrote the inscription on a monument erected to his memory in Christ Church, Dublin (see Letter 380).

Richard Purcell (*c.* 1690–?). Richard Purcell of Ballygraddy was a land agent for John Percival* in southern Ireland. Generations of Purcells had served as land agents for the Percivals, including Purcell's father and grandfather. Little else of detail is known about this particular Purcell.

John Rawdon third Baronet of Moira (1690–1723). John Rawdon was the grandson of the first baronet, Sir George Rawdon (1604–84), army officer and Irish MP for Belfast (1640) and later Carlingford (1661).[1967] His son, also John Rawdon,* would marry John Percival's* daughter Helena in 1741.

John Rawdon fourth Baronet of Moira (1720–93). The son of John Rawdon,* third Baronet of Moira, the younger Rawdon married Helena Percival on 10 November 1741. After her death, in 1746, he married, secondly, Anne Hill in December of that year and, thirdly, Elizabeth Hastings, sixteenth Baroness Botreaux, on 26 February 1752. He was created Earl of Moira in 1762. He is occasionally mentioned in the correspondence as a friend of both Berkeley and John Percival.*

Robert Roberts (?–?). Robert Roberts was apparently an agent of the creditors for the bill against the heirs of Burton's bank that failed in Ireland. Little else is known about him (see Letter 244).

Thomas Rundle (1687/8–1743). A Church of Ireland clergyman and bishop of Derry, Rundle was the son of Thomas Rundle, an Exeter clergyman. In 1712 Rundle met William Whiston* and worked with him to promote the Society for Promoting Primitive Christianity. In December 1733 Rundle was nominated to the see of Gloucester by the lord chancellor, Charles Talbot.* Edmund Gibson,* the bishop of London, blocked the appointment for political reasons, although accusations of deism were levelled against Rundle during the affair. An impressive array of dignitaries came to Rundle's defense, including John Conybeare and William

---

[1967] Luce mistakenly reports (*Works*, vol. IX, p. 30) John Rawdon as the son of the first Baronet.

Whiston.* A compromise was reached and Rundle was appointed bishop of Derry in 1735.

Berkeley was apparently on good terms with Rundle and there is evidence that they corresponded (see Letter 179), but no letters have survived. Rundle died, unmarried, on 15 April 1743.

Henry Sacheverell (1674–1724). A religious controversialist and Church of England clergyman, Sacheverell graduated from Magdalen College, Oxford; with a BA in 1693 and an MA in 1695. He was ordained a deacon in Oxford, but in 1697 the bishop of Lichfield refused to ordain him a priest on the grounds that his command of Latin was inadequate. Sacheverell denied the allegation and eventually won his ordination, being assigned to Cannock in Staffordshire. He returned to Oxford in 1701 and was granted a DD in 1708.

Sacheverell proved to be a popular preacher with a bent for passionate high-church rhetoric. He routinely attacked dissenters and nonconformists in his sermons. He published a tract in 1702, *The Character of a Low-Church-Man*, which was an attack on the bishop of Worcester, who had allegedly himself attacked the Tory Sir John Pakington. Pakington then supported Sacheverell in his bid to become the chaplain for the Speaker of the House of Commons, an offer Speaker Harley* politely declined.

On 5 November 1709 Sacheverell delivered a sermon to the lord mayor and aldermen of London in St. Paul's Church. The sermon was a rant against nonconformists and contained a number of incendiary claims. Despite some hesitance from the city elders, the sermon was published and became an instant sensation, with multiple editions appearing. Whigs were offended by the sermon, which contained personal attacks on prominent Whig figures, including an unflattering reference to the lord treasurer, Godolphin. Some immediately clamored to have Sacheverell tried for seditious libel, but the actual text of the sermon was somewhat tortuous, making it difficult to prove any ill intent. The decision was made to impeach Sacheverell before the House of Lords. On 13 December the House of Commons censured his pamphlets and impeached him for high crimes and misdemeanors.

The articles of impeachment were not drawn up until 9 January 1710. The most important article was the first, which charged Sacheverell with suggesting that there had been no resistance in the revolution of 1688, thus making the means used to bring about the revolution unjustified. On 12 January the articles were presented to the Lords. Sacheverell responded to the charges with yet more inflammatory remarks, defending passive obedience (and hence implicitly attacking the legitimacy of the Williamite line). His response was, in general, so uncompromising that several members of his defense team resigned. He was left with Sir Simon Harcourt, one of the ablest Tory lawyers in England, and Constantine Phipps.*

Upon his impeachment there was a groundswell of support for Sacheverell, and numerous pamphlets were published defending his cause. The affair became a public drama, and the trial was moved to Westminster Hall to accommodate the entire House of Commons. It opened on 27 February 1710. Sacheverell delivered his own summation in a carefully contrived speech probably written by Francis Atterbury.* On 20 March the members of the House of Lords found the doctor guilty by sixty-nine votes to fifty-two. The sentence, however, was lenient: he was prevented from preaching for three years. The Tories celebrated the trial as a victory.

After his trial, Sacheverell gained the rectory of St. Andrew's in Holborn, but never achieved a prestigious preferment. When his ban was lifted, three years later, he caused a brief sensation again and preached to the House of Commons, but caused little stir afterwards. Following the death of Anne* in 1714, he, like many Tories, seemed sympathetic to Jacobitism, but there is no evidence of him actively conspiring with other Jacobites.

The sensational nature of the trial and of the person of Sacheverell is well reflected in Berkeley's letters, and he even tells an interesting anecdote relating to some of Sacheverell's supporters (see Letter 18). Sacheverell died on 5 June 1724.

Lionel Cranfield Sackville, first Duke of Dorset (1688–1765). Born on 18 January 1688, Lionel was the only son of Charles Sackville, sixth Earl of Dorset (1643–1706), and his second wife, Lady Mary (1668–91). An outspoken champion of the Hanoverian line since the end of the reign of Anne,* Sackville served the court in a variety of offices. He was created duke of Dorset on 17 June 1720 and appointed lord steward of the household on 30 May 1725.

On 23 June 1730 he was appointed lord lieutenant of Ireland and would serve in that role until 1737. Apparently he was keen for the position and kept regular tabs on the state of affairs in Ireland, even when he was out of office. There is nothing to suggest Berkeley knew the duke well beyond his indirect connections through John Percival* and other friends in Dublin, although he does remark that Sackville endorsed his candidacy for Bishop of Cloyne (see Letter 233). Replaced by William Cavendish, third Duke of Devonshire, in March 1737, Sackville was reappointed lord steward of the household. Nonetheless, he pressed the government to return him to Ireland, and his persistence paid off in April 1750, when he was appointed lord lieutenant of Ireland for a second time. Sackville was dismissed in early February 1755 and replaced by William Cavendish, Marquess of Hartington. In England he was appointed master of the horse on 29 March 1755 and held that post until July 1757, when he was reinstalled as constable of Dover Castle and lord warden of the Cinque Ports for life. He died on 9 October 1765.

John Scrope (Scroop) (*c.* 1662–1752). The only son of Thomas Scrope (?–1704), a merchant in Bristol, John Scrope became a barrister and was influential in the Godolphin ministry. He is often referred to as "Scroop," a popular variant of his name. In May 1708 he was appointed one of the five barons of the new court of exchequer in Scotland. In the years following the union with Scotland, Scrope became one of the most influential figures in the Scottish administration, serving as an advisor to Harley concerning Scottish affairs. He retained office at the Hanoverian accession in 1714, and in 1722 was elected to Parliament for Ripon. On the death of William Lowndes, in January 1724, Scrope was appointed secretary to the Treasury. He was in charge of collecting and disbursing the funds from the sale of the lands on St. Christopher* Island related to Berkeley's scheme to found a college in Bermuda. Scrope served as a Member of Parliament representing several districts, but retained his high office until his death on 9 April 1752.

Thomas Secker (1693–1768). Secker, later archbishop of Canterbury, was born on 21 September 1693, the son of a butcher. As a young man he contemplated a life in the church, but was uncertain about conforming to the Church of England and thus elected first to spend time studying medicine. In 1718 he traveled to Paris and studied anatomy, although he continued to read theology as well. He met Berkeley in France, starting a lifelong friendship. In 1721 he took an MD from Leiden and then returned to England.

On 6 July 1722, having satisfied the residency requirements at Oxford, Secker received his BA and moved to London. He spent much of the time socializing with William Talbot,* who, upon being translated to the bishopric of Durham, ordained Secker as deacon in St. James's, Piccadilly, on 23 December 1722. Exactly when he stopped dissenting from the established church is unclear, but over his career he slowly shifted to being a firm defender of the orthodox church. He was ordained a priest on 10 March 1723 and followed Talbot to Durham as joint chaplain with Thomas Rundle.*

Secker married Catherine Benson, sister to Martin Benson,* on 28 October 1725. Though married, his wife did not wish to leave the household of Talbot on account of his widowed daughter-in-law, who had a small child. Thus the two families lived together in London. In 1733 Secker was made rector of St. James's, Piccadilly, in part owing to the patronage of Edmund Gibson,* bishop of London. In 1734 he was unexpectedly made bishop of Bristol, being consecrated on 19 January 1735. In 1737 he was offered the bishopric of Oxford. He initially declined the offer on financial grounds, but eventually accepted the post. As a bishop he was politically active. He regularly attended sessions of the House of Lords and was active on some measures, especially the Quaker Tithe Bill of 1736, where he joined other bishops in opposing the measure (see Letter 260, about the bill). In general, however, Secker was a pro-Hanoverian supporter of the government.

In 1750 he was promoted to the deanery of St. Paul's, and upon the death of Matthew Hutton, in 1758, he was appointed archbishop of Canterbury, being confirmed on 21 April. As archbishop, Secker fought to establish a resident bishop in the American colonies, but was unsuccessful. He died at Lambeth Palace on 3 August 1768.

Hans Sloane (1660–1753). A physician and leading member of the Royal Society, Sloane was born at Killyleagh in County Down on 16 April 1660. As a young man he studied natural philosophy, especially chemistry and botany. In 1683 he took the degree of doctor of physic. His academic and medical skills were quickly recognized and he was elected to the Royal Society in 1685 and admitted a fellow of the Royal College of Physicians in 1687. After serving as the duke of Albemarle's personal physician, with whom he traveled to Jamaica, he returned to London and established his own sucessful practice. On 11 May 1695 he married Elizabeth Langley (?–1724), and through her inherited a sizable estate. His travels and comfortable living enabled him to publish his observations on the West Indies as well as to amass a considerable collection of specimens, texts, and rare manuscripts. Along with the Harleian and Cotton collections, Sloane's materials constituted the founding collection of the British Museum in 1753.

Although notable for his contributions to medicine, Sloane acquired his greatest reputation for his administrative work in the Royal Society. In 1693 he was elected second secretary of the society and in 1695 was made first secretary. As first secretary he was responsible (among other things) for the publication of the society's journal, *Philosophical Transactions*. In this capacity Berkeley writes to Sloane as a young man (see Letter 2), seeking the publication of some of his critical thoughts in natural philosophy. Sloane would later become the president of the society in 1727 after the death of Newton. He remained in that post for fourteen years. Despite some health issues Sloane lived to an advanced age, dying on 11 January 1753.

George Smalridge (1662–1719). Smalridge was born on 18 May 1662, the son of Thomas Smalridge, a dyer of Lichfield. He attended Christ Church, Oxford, taking his BA in 1686 and his MA in 1689. Ordained in 1689 after taking his degree, he became prebendary of Flixton in Lichfield Cathedral, where he remained until 1714. In 1713 he was appointed dean of Christ Church. After John Robinson was translated to London, in 1714, Smalridge was appointed bishop of Bristol.

A Tory throughout his life, he defended Robert Harley* during the impeachment proceedings of 1715 and refused to sign the declaration against the Pretender* the following year. Berkeley knew Smalridge and thought well of him personally and as a conversationalist, but the relationship does not appear to be intimate (see Letters 48 and 51). Smalridge died suddenly on 27 September 1719.

John Smibert (1688–1751). Born in Edinburgh on 24 March 1688, Smibert was the youngest of the six children of a wool dyer. In 1719 he went to Italy, where he remained until 1722, studying works of art while painting and developing his skills as a painter. He apparently met Berkeley in Italy; they were well enough acquainted for Berkeley to persuade Smibert to join him on his mission to establish a college in Bermuda. Smibert's masterpiece, *The Bermuda Group* (c. 1729–31; Yale University Art Gallery, New Haven, Connecticut), commemorates the principals who traveled to the American colonies in 1728. With his health failing, he ceased painting in 1746 and died in Boston on 2 April 1751.

Philip Smythe, fourth Viscount Strangford (1715–87). The son of Endymion Smythe, third Viscount Strangford (?–1724), not much is known about him other than the fact that he was landed gentry in Ireland. He married Mary Jephson, daughter of Anthony Jephson, in 1741. Smythe applies to Berkeley for a reference about a person applying to be his curate (see Letter 306). He died on 29 April 1787.

South Sea. The South Sea Company was a British joint-stock company founded in 1711 by lord treasurer Robert Harley.* Based on the example of the Mississippi Company set up by John Law in France, the company was founded in part as a scheme to buy the national debt of England. It was granted a monopoly to trade in Spain's South American colonies as a part of the treaty following the War of Spanish Succession. Speculation in the stock resulted in an economic bubble (the "South Sea Bubble") in 1720–21, causing widespread financial ruin. The company was restructured and continued to operate for another century after the bubble; Berkeley owned shares after the bubble. The headquarters of the company was on Threadneedle Street in London.[1968]

Edward Southwell (1671–1730). Cousin to John Percival,* Edward Southwell was born on 4 September 1671, the only surviving son of Sir Robert Southwell (1635–1702), diplomat and government official. Edward entered Merton College, Oxford, but was recalled home in 1688 out of fear over the policies of King James. Edward was nonetheless quite capable and impressive enough to be elected to the Royal Society in 1692. That same year he was elected to the Irish parliament. He then held a succession of posts, including clerk of the Privy Council and chief secretary to the Duke of Ormond* when the latter was lord lieutenant of Ireland (he served during both of Ormond's terms, 1703–07 and 1710–13).

Southwell was an advocate of the Society for the Propagation of the Gospel in Foreign Parts and generally respected for his piety and administrative competence. As a relative of Percival,* he naturally became acquainted with Berkeley, and they appear to have been on friendly terms. Berkeley was introduced to Lord Pembroke* via Southwell (see Letter 38) and Berkeley follows events in Southwell's family (see, e.g., Letter 185). Southwell died on 4 December 1730.

St. Christopher Island. Certain portions of the island of St. Christopher (now named St. Kitts) were ceded to England by France under the Treaty of Utrecht. Those lands were to be sold for public use, and Berkeley proposed that some of the revenue from the sale be earmarked for use by his proposed college in Bermuda. The king approved. The money was raised and Berkeley's charter for the college was granted, but the funds from the sale of the lands were never released.

[1968] For accounts of the financial scheme and disaster, see Carswell, *South Sea Bubble*; Dale, *First Crash*; and Balen, *The King, The Crook, and The Gambler*.

Henry St. John, first Viscount Bolingbroke (1678–1751). A politician, diplomat, and author, Henry was the son of Henry St. John, Viscount St. John (1652–1742) and born on 16 September 1678. By all accounts an intelligent and talented individual, St. John also acquired the reputation of being a flagrant libertine, even as he excelled in public affairs.

A committed Tory, he first entered Parliament in February 1701. A defender of the established church, he was vital in advancing bills against the practice of occasional conformity (where nonconformists would qualify for offices by taking communion occasionally in the Church of England), even though those bills were defeated in the House of Lords. In 1704 he was appointed secretary at war and moderated his formerly extreme Tory position. In September 1710 he was made secretary of the north and created Viscount Bolingbroke in 1712.

With the death of Anne,* Bolingbroke found his fortunes reversed. Although he took the oath of allegiance to George I,* he was not a favorite at court and lost his offices. As the Whigs gained the upper hand in the government after 1715, investigations were launched into the conduct of the Tory administration during the war, including his own role as secretary at war. Bolingbroke, fearing for his life, fled to France on 27 March 1715, escaping arrest. His flight was popularly seen as an admission of guilt and evidence of Jacobitism. He denied that he had betrayed or planned to betray the Hanoverian line, but he accepted an earldom from the Pretender* in July 1715 and agreed to serve as the Stuart secretary of state.

After the failure of the 1715 rebellion, the Jacobites made Bolingbroke the scapegoat, and he proceeded to try and secure a pardon in exchange for information about the Stuart court in exile. In 1717 he circulated a letter from himself to Sir William Windham, defending his actions since 1710 and aimed at weaning Tories from the Jacobite cause. While in exile, Bolingbroke increasingly devoted himself to the study of philosophy and theology. Luce reports that Bolingbroke had read Berkeley's *Alciphron* by July 1732.[1969] We know they were acquainted in some fashion; in 1725 Bolingbroke writes to Swift that Ford brought Berkeley to him but he was away.[1970] It is unclear, however, whether the two ever met.

Bolingbroke was finally pardoned on 25 May 1723, but he was not released from all the penalties and forfeitures incurred as a result of his flight in 1715. Eventually he was allowed to own and inherit land in England again and he returned in 1725. Once back, he re-entered politics, opposing Walpole and writing a large slate of political essays. He died on 12 December 1751.

Philip Dormer Stanhope, fourth Earl of Chesterfield (1694–1773). The son of Philip Stanhope, third Earl of Chesterfield (1673–1726), Philip Dormer Stanhope was born on 22 September 1694. Coming from an established noble family, Stanhope began his career early, serving as gentleman of the bedchamber to

[1969] See Luce, *Life*, p. 154.
[1970] Luce, *Life*, pp 106 and 232.

George, Prince of Wales and as Member of Parliament in 1715, under age in the case of his seat in the House.

In January 1726 his father died, making him the fourth Earl of Chesterfield, and he took his place in the House of Lords. He had some talent for languages and was appointed by George II* after his accession as ambassador to The Hague in 1727. Although typically in opposition to the government, in 1744 he was appointed lord lieutenant of Ireland. He arrived in August 1745 in the midst of the Jacobite rebellion. Prince Charles Edward* had recently landed in Scotland and it was Stanhope's task to make sure that Ireland did not rise up in sympathy. He took immediate action, raising new regiments of troops among the Protestants, and generally kept a lid on dissent in Ireland by refusing to take punitive actions against Catholics or Catholic churches.

Stanhope resigned his post as lord lieutenant in October 1746, becoming secretary of state of the north. He served in that post only sixteen months. He stayed on in the House of Lords, contributing most notably by passing the calendar reform of 1751. He died on 24 March 1773.

William Stanhope, Earl of Harrington (1683?–1756). Diplomat and military officer, William Stanhope was a committed Whig, both in the House of Commons and once elevated to the peerage. In 1703 he became a captain in the army, rising in rank to full colonel by 1711. In 1715 he was elected Member of Parliament for Derby. Although he did not see active military service again, he was promoted to the rank of general in 1747. Most of his career, however, was spent as a diplomat. He served in a variety of diplomatic posts related to Spain between 1717 and 1720. On 6 January 1730 he was made Baron Harrington and appointed secretary of state of the north later that same year. Made Earl of Harrington in February 1742, he later served as lord lieutenant of Ireland (1747–50). Afterwards he spent his remaining years out of politics. He died on 8 December 1756.

John Stearne (Sterne) (1660–1745). Church of Ireland bishop of Clogher, Stearne was born in Dublin. He attended Trinity College, Dublin, graduating with a BA in 1678, an MA in 1681, and a DD in 1693. Ordained a deacon in 1682, in 1688 he was made vicar of Trim. On 11 September 1702 he was made chancellor of St. Patrick's Cathedral, Dublin. A friend and colleague of Jonathan Swift,* they assisted one another in their careers; Swift helped Stearne obtain the deanery of St. Patrick's and later the bishopric of Dromore in 1713. While dean of St. Patrick's, Stearne reported on the events surrounding the irregular ordination of several young clergymen, including Berkeley, which roused the ire of Archbishop King (see Letter 13). Stearne was translated to Clogher in March 1717.

In 1721 Stearne was appointed vice-chancellor of Trinity College, Dublin. In 1726 he gave a bequest to found the university printing house, which was formally established in 1734. He engaged in numerous acts of charity, supporting several hospitals and building projects for churches and providing books for Marsh's Library in Dublin. He died, unmarried, on 6 June 1745.

Richard Steele (1672–1729). Writer and Whig politician, Richard Steele was born in Dublin on 12 March 1672, the second child and only son of Richard Steele, an attorney. His grandfather, also Richard Steele, was an explorer in Persia and India who had been awarded a pension and land by Charles I for his services. Steele was thus born into Protestant gentry in Ireland. He attended Oxford briefly, but left without obtaining a degree. After serving in a military regiment that saw combat in 1692 and 1694 in Flanders, Steele turned to literature and politics, authoring plays and editing periodicals.

Already publishing as early as 1695, his first major publications appeared in 1701. *The Christian Hero* was a philosophical tract and *The Funeral* a stage comedy that was a considerable success. In April of 1709 Steele launched *The Tatler*, a magazine that appeared three times a week. Part of its success may be attributed to Steele's collaborators; both Jonathan Swift* and Joseph Addison* were contributors. In 1711 he and Addison launched another magazine, *The Spectator*, designed to be politically neutral yet witty and entertaining. Steele initiated yet another essay periodical, *The Guardian*, on 12 March 1713, with an editorial persona named Nestor Ironside. Here again the success of the paper was due in part to its contributors, which included Alexander Pope and Berkeley.

In 1713 he shifted to pursue a career in politics and was elected a Member of Parliament from Stockbridge in Hampshire. He turned *The Guardian* over to Addison and turned his attention full time to politics and propaganda. In late 1713 he published *The Crisis*, a piece of Whig political propaganda concerning the royal succession, which was so successful that it prompted a reply from Swift, who argued that the succession was in no danger and branded Steele's doubts as sedition. As a result charges were leveled against Steele and he was expelled from the House of Commons on 18 March 1714.

After the death of Anne* he returned to Parliament in 1715, representing Boroughbridge in Yorkshire. With the rise of Whig influence under George I,* Steele's fortunes also rose and he was knighted on 9 April. In 1716 he was appointed to the commission that would administer the sale of the lands of noblemen involved in the 1715 Jacobite rebellion. He suffered what was likely a stroke the following year, which effectively ended his active political career. He died on 1 September 1729.

Swift & Company. Owned by James Swift (?–1745), Swift & Company was a Dublin bank. Berkeley did much of his Irish business with this particular bank. When James Swift died, in 1745, the business was taken over by Thomas Gleadowe and the name changed to Gleadowe & Co.[1971]

Jonathan Swift (1667–1745). Literary giant and dean of St. Patrick's Cathedral, Dublin, Jonathan Swift was born on 30 November 1667. He entered Trinity College, Dublin, in the spring of 1682. He was tutored by St. George Ashe* the

---

[1971] See Hall, *History of the Bank of Ireland*, p. 12.

elder, later bishop of Clogher. Not a spectacular student, he nonetheless earned his BA, leaving Trinity to serve ten years (with interruptions) with Sir William Temple as his sectretary. In the Temple household Swift first met Esther Johnson (the famous Stella of his correspondence and writings), the daughter of Temple's housekeeper. His employment settled, he was ordained a deacon in October 1694 and a priest on 13 January 1695. In February of that year he was appointed prebend of Kilroot in the cathedral of Connor. On 22 October 1696 Swift was given the more important post of prebend of Dunlavin in the cathedral of St. Patrick.

Swift attended the Earl of Pembroke, then the lord lieutenant of Ireland, in London, from November 1707 to June 1709. At some point during this time he met Hester Van Homrigh,* a woman two decades younger than him. During this time he also met and impressed influential people in London, including Joseph Addison,* with his wit and literary abilities. After a brief return to Dublin, Swift again traveled to London in September 1710 to represent Archbishop King and plead the cause of the Irish clergy. His mission brought him into contact with important government officials, including Robert Harley,* and other literary figures such as Alexander Pope.* In 1713 Swift was appointed dean of St. Patrick's, but initially spent most of his time in London.

While in London he began contributing to periodicals, mostly essays written from a Tory standpoint. Berkeley claims to have first met Swift on 5 March 1713 (see Letter 40), and they both contributed essays to *The Guardian* during this time. At Windsor in early October, Swift composed *Cadenus and Vanessa*, a lengthy poem about his relationship with Hester Van Homrigh. During this time he also engaged in Tory political propaganda, writing a reply to Richard Steele's *The Crisis* entitled *The Publick Spirit of the Whigs*. In February 1714 Swift was elected a governor of Bethlem Hospital and had his license for absence from Ireland renewed. He thus continued his career as a literary figure and political propagandist for roughly two more years in London.

Returning to Ireland, a persistent rumor alleges that Swift secretly married Stella sometime during the summer of 1716. Although possible, the marriage is unlikely and the evidence is inconclusive. Once back in Ireland, however, he resumed writing and entered Irish politics, writing a series of scathing pieces about Wood's half-pence in 1722. As a result, Swift became openly associated with the Irish national cause. In early June 1723 Hester Van Homrigh died, naming Berkeley as one of the executors of her estate despite the fact that she did not know him well. Although no correspondence between Swift and Berkeley survives, we know that the event did nothing to dampen the friendship between them, for on 3 September 1724 Swift wrote an enthusiastic endorsement of Berkeley and his Bermuda scheme to Lord Carteret (then lord lieutenant of Ireland).

Swift finished his career engaged in his writing, Irish politics, and the care of his deanery. His most famous piece, *Gulliver's Travels*, was completed in 1725. He died on 19 October 1745.

Edward Synge (1659–1741). Church of Ireland archbishop of Tuam, Edward Synge was born on 5 April 1659 in County Cork, the second son of Edward Synge (1614–78), bishop of Cork, Cloyne, and Ross. His family connections were of use to him, and he was appointed bishop of Raphoe in 1714. In 1715 he was considered for translation to the bishopric of Meath, but George I* nominated the bishop of Bangor. The intervention caused an uproar amongst the Irish clergy, leading to Synge's compensatory appointment as archbishop of Tuam in June 1716.

Synge was thereafter active in the Irish House of Lords, defending the Irish cause in the 1719 case *Annesley* vs. *Sherlock*, a case concerning the supremacy of the English House of Lords as a final court of appeal for Ireland. Along with Archbishop King, he also opposed the Toleration Bill. He published prolificly, authoring nearly sixty pieces, mostly sermons and other religious tracts. He also cultivated the ecclesiastical career of his eldest son, Edward Synge* (1691–1762), who would later become an Irish bishop as well. Synge died in Tuam on 24 July 1741.

Edward Synge (1691–1762). Born in Cork on 18 October 1691, Edward Synge was the eldest son of Edward Synge* (1659–1741), then vicar of Christ Church, Cork, but later archbishop of Tuam. He came from a family filled with prominent Irish clergy and his younger brother, Nicholas Synge, would later become bishop of Killaloe. He entered Trinity College, Dublin in 1706, receiving his BA in 1709. In 1710 he became a fellow of the college, and in the same year junior dean. He was a near contemporary of Berkeley's at Trinity and apparently attended some of Berkeley's lectures. His father was made archbishop of Tuam in 1716; the younger Synge was therefore well placed for advancement.

In 1719 he was given the living of St. Audoen's, Dublin, which carried with it a prebendal stall in St. Patrick's Cathedral. He advanced quickly. He was appointed provost of Tuam in 1726, bishop of Clonfert in 1730, and in 1731 was translated to Cloyne. In 1733 he was again translated, to Ferns and Leighlin (Berkeley succeeded him as bishop of Cloyne), and in 1740 he went to Elphin, where he remained until his death, on 27 January 1762.

Charles Talbot, first Baron Talbot of Hensol (1685–1737). Born in December 1685, Charles Talbot was the eldest son of William Talbot,* a Church of England clergyman, later bishop successively of Oxford, Salisbury, and Durham. Charles elected to pursue the practice of law, being called to the bar in 1711. On 26 April 1714 he obtained the degree of LLB from the archbishop of Canterbury in order to qualify for the post (appointed by his father) of chancellor of the diocese of Oxford. In May 1717 he was appointed solicitor general to the Prince of Wales, later George II.*

On 19 November 1733, lord chancellor King was forced to retire following a stroke, and in a political deal involving Philip York,* Talbot was soon appointed lord chancellor and raised to the peerage as Baron Hensol. Talbot's three-year tenure as lord chancellor was by all accounts successful. In May 1736 he joined with the bishops to kill the 1736 Quaker Tithe Bill. He died suddenly in London on 14 February 1737.

William Talbot (1659–1730). William Talbot attended Oriel College, Oxford, and, through the influence of his kinsman, Charles Talbot, twelfth Earl of Shrewsbury, obtained the deanery of Worcester on 23 April 1691. On 8 June of the same year he received a Lambeth DD from the archbishop of Canterbury.

Well respected for his oratorical abilities, he preached on several occasions for the court and was appointed bishop of Oxford on 24 September 1699. In the House of Lords he supported the union with Scotland in 1707 and was one of only four bishops who recommended the condemnation of Sacheverell* in his trial in 1710. He was translated to Salisbury on 23 April 1715 and again to Durham on 7 November 1721. Berkeley was indirectly acquainted with Talbot via Martin Benson* and Thomas Secker,* the latter of whom married Catherine Benson and resided in the Talbot home (see Letter 249). Talbot died on 10 October 1730.

Charles Townshend, second Viscount Townshend (1674–1738). Born on 18 April 1674, Charles Townshend was a Whig politician who came from a noble Tory family. In 1701 he was appointed high steward of King's Lynn and of Norwich Cathedral. He also served as lord lieutenant of Norfolk (1701–13 and 1714–30), a position that gave him considerable political influence.

In 1706 he was elected a member of the Royal Society and in 1709 Queen Anne* appointed him ambassador to The Hague. Townshend was recalled in 1711 after the Tories returned to power. He was then caught up in the politics of recrimination against Whig officials and censured by the House of Commons for exceeding his instructions while in Holland, and was finally condemned as a public enemy. It was during this time that he briefly lost his lord lieutenancy of Norfolk. Townshend remained in politics in opposition to the government.

With the ascension of George I,* Townshend was restored to his post as lord lieutenant and was made secretary of state for the north. He helped suppress the Jacobite rebellion of 1715 and on 1 October 1716 he was sworn into the Privy Council. On 24 February 1717 he was appointed lord lieutenant of Ireland, although he never actually traveled there. In 1720 he was appointed president of the council and in 1721 he was re-appointed secretary of state for the north. Although a consistent Whig, Townshend quarreled constantly with Walpole,* and eventually retired from politics in May 1730. He died on 21 June 1738.

Van Homrigh, Hester (Esther) (1688–1723). A correspondent and lover of Jonathan Swift,* Van Homrigh was the elder daughter of a leading and wealthy Dublin citizen, Bartholomew Van Homrigh (?–1703), and Esther, *née* Stone (?–1714). In 1707 the family moved to London, where their social circle brought them into contact with Jonathan Swift.

By 1711 the Van Homrighs had set aside a room in their London home for Swift's use; he apparently used it with regularity. Twenty-eight of Swift's letters to Vanessa (his code name for Hester; a contraction of "van" and "hessy") and seventeen drafts of her letters to Swift survive. Hester demanded a passionate relationship, one which Swift was less willing to provide. Swift's long poem *Cadenus and Vanessa* about their relationship was written in 1712. In 1714, after Swift was installed as dean of St. Patrick's, in Dublin, Hester followed him, living nearby in Celbridge, about eleven miles distant.

Hester died in early June 1723. Despite barely knowing either of them, she named Berkeley and Robert Marshall* as executors of her will (see Letter 118). She had previously been involved in a lawsuit with Peter Partinton* over the resolution of the estate of her mother, who had predeceased her. Although Berkeley did receive perhaps as much as £3,000 from the bequest, he was drawn into a long and difficult affair while trying to settle the estate, a process that took several years and occupies much of his correspondence with Thomas Prior* in the 1720s.

Benjamin Wadsworth (1670–1737). Born in the Massachusetts colony, Benjamin Wadsworth was educated at Harvard College. After his graduation, in 1690, he studied theology and earned an MA in 1693. He was licensed to preach, became an assistant teacher in the First Church in Boston in November 1693, and on 8 September 1696 was made its pastor. At the time, the post was one of the most prestigious and influential in New England. Wadsworth was considered religiously moderate and his sermons were popular with his congregation. He remained pastor at the First Church for over thirty years. He published numerous essays and sermons, including *An Artillery Election Sermon* (1700) and *Five Sermons* (1711). On 7 July 1725 he was inaugurated as the eighth president of Harvard College, holding the post until his death in 1737. In 1733 Berkeley donated a box of books to Harvard (see Letter 225), which Wadsworth received.

John Wainwright (?–1741). Baron of the Exchequer of Ireland starting in 1732, Wainwright was apparently a good friend of Berkeley. He defended Berkeley both against attacks on his philosophy and those leveled at the Bermuda scheme, although little else is known about their relationship. In a letter to the Viscountess Sundon, Wainwright wrote: "Forget Bermuda, and he will shine among the clergy, and do honour to the church by his virtue and learning."[1972]

William Wake (1657–1737). William Wake was born on 26 January 1657, the son of Colonel William Wake (1628–1705), a royalist army officer, and his wife Amie, the daughter of Edward Cutler. Ordained in 1681, Wake was appointed chaplain to

---

[1972] Wainright to Charlotte Clayton, 31 December 1731. See *Memoirs of Viscountess Sundon, Mistress of the Robes to Queen Caroline, Consort of George II, Including Letters from the Most Celebrated Persons of her Time*, 2 vols., 2nd edn. (London: Henry Colburn, 1848).

Richard Graham, Viscount Preston, during his embassy to France (1682–85). While in France, Wake was exposed to both Catholic and Huguenot influences, and authored his first major publication, *An Exposition of the Doctrine of the Church of England*. The piece engaged work by Bishop Bossuet and won Wake applause as it defended Church of England doctrine on those points where it differed from Roman Catholic dogma. He continued to write on the same subject for the next few years, producing polemical tracts about the differences between the Church of England and Rome.

In 1695 he was appointed rector of St. James's in Westminster and he was shortly drawn into another controversy, this time with Francis Atterbury.* Wake published *Authority of Christian Princes* (1697) as a refutation of Atterbury's case for restoring a sitting convocation. He contributed to the convocation controversy once more with a piece in 1698, and his role made him a champion of the Whig clergy. As a result, preferment came quickly and he was offered the bishopric of Bristol in April 1700. He declined the offer and instead accepted the deanery of Exeter in 1701. In 1705 he accepted the bishopric of Oxford, but elected to take the bishopric of Lincoln instead when it was offered one week later.

On 16 January 1716 Wake was confirmed as archbishop of Canterbury. Quickly after assuming his post, he became embroiled in the debate surrounding the repeal of the Test Act, which he, like most Whig bishops, opposed. While archbishop, he kept up many of his contacts in France and supported le Courayer* in his work defending the legitimacy of the Church of England ordination. He welcomed le Courayer to England when the latter was excommunicated, and helped arrange a government pension for him.

Berkeley wrote to Wake, keeping him informed of his actions while pursuing his scheme to found St. Paul's College in Bermuda (see Letter 132). There is no evidence of other correspondence between the two. Wake died at Lambeth on 24 January 1737.

Robert Walpole, first Earl of Orford (1676–1745). One of the most important political figures of the first half of the eighteenth century in England, Robert Walpole was born on 26 August 1676, the fifth of seventeen children of Robert Walpole (1650–1700), landowner and Member of Parliament. Walpole began his political career as a young man, entering the House of Commons for Castle Rising in 1701. He would be returned to Parliament thereafter representing King's Lynn until his elevation to the House of Lords in 1742.

Once in the House, he was active immediately, earning enough influence to be appointed to the Admiralty board in June 1705. After the fall of the Harley ministry, Walpole was appointed secretary of war on 25 February 1708. There he distinguished himself with his administrative competence and made valuable contacts, especially with the Duke of Marlborough. In January 1710 Walpole was made treasurer of the Navy while retaining his post as secretary of war until September of the same year.

With the fall of the Whig ministry, Walpole was imprisoned in 1712 on charges of financial irregularities. While in the Tower, he stood his ground and became a Whig martyr, eventually winning his case and being released in July. By 1715 he had emerged as the clear leader of the ministry in the Commons. In October 1715 he was appointed first lord of the Treasury and chancellor of the exchequer, two appointments that in part helped bring about a dramatic increase in his wealth.

He spent 1720–21 managing the South Sea* crisis and then expended considerable energy afterwards obstructing the investigation of the bubble to protect the political interests of the crown and his own party. He was largely successful, however, and by 1723 the Townshend*–Walpole ministry was firmly established. Although the Prince of Wales was not fond of Walpole, his ascension in 1727 as George II* did not see Walpole removed from power. His political dominance from the 1720s through the early 1740s earned him the title of "prime minister."

Berkeley did not know Walpole intimately, but the latter was instrumental in blocking Berkeley's plan to found St. Paul's College in Bermuda. Although the king had granted the warrant for the scheme and allocated funds for it out of the sale of the lands on St. Christopher Island,* Walpole controlled the treasury and refused to actually release the funds. The precise reasons for this refusal are not clear, but Walpole was aligned with Townshend, who was vocally opposed to any provision that might weaken the dependence of the colonies on England. Townshend opposed Berkeley's college on such grounds and it is likely that he and others in the administration were the reasons the payment was blocked (see Letters 206 and 209).

By 1742 Walpole's power was waning and on 11 February he resigned the seals of his office. The previous week, on 6 February, he had been created Earl of Orford. He died on 18 March 1745.

Peter Ward (?–?). Dr. Peter Ward was the subdean of Derry Cathedral and prebendary of Moville during the time that Berkeley was dean of Derry. Ward ran the day-to-day church business of Berkeley's deanery while Berkeley was away. Little else is known about him.

William Whiston (1667–1752). Born on 9 December 1667, William Whiston was the fourth of nine children of Josiah Whiston (1622–85), rector at Norton. As a young man he came into contact with Newton's natural philosophy and rapidly became a convert. His first publication, *A New Theory of the Earth* (1696), applied Newtonian principles to cosmogony and attempted to show how the new philosophy was consistent with scriptural accounts, including the flood. As a result of this work Whiston became a minor celebrity.

In 1698 Whiston was given the living of Lowestoft-cum-Kessingland in Suffolk and there he delivered sermons and attended to his parishioners. In 1701 Newton called Whiston to Cambridge to lecture as his deputy with a full income. When Newton retired, at the end of that year, he ensured that Whiston replaced him as the Lucasian professor of mathematics. His contact with Newton's circle led Whiston to embrace heterodox theological views along the lines of Arianism. Unlike others in the circle, however, Whiston was bold about his challenges to orthodoxy. In 1709, against the advice of his friends, he published *Sermons and Essays*, a work which led to his expulsion from the university for heresy.

John Percival* reports that Whiston and Samuel Clarke* had read Berkeley's recently published *Principles of Human Knowledge* in 1710 (see Letter 20). Despite Berkeley's best efforts, however, he was unable to elicit any actual careful criticisms from either Whiston or Clarke. We do not actually know whether Whiston carefully read the work or not.

After his expulsion, Whiston published *Primitive Christianity Revived* (1711–12), a series of commentaries on early Christian writings designed to support his religious views. In 1715 he founded the Society for Promoting Primitive Christianity. Although heresy proceedings against him were dropped on the death of Queen Anne* in 1714, he and his work attracted a stream of critical opposition. All told, Whiston published well over one hundred pieces, from books to pamphlets in fields ranging from natural philosophy to astrology to theology. He is still considered important for popularizing Newtonianism. Whiston died on 22 August 1752.

Elisha Williams (1694–1755). Elisha Williams was rector and then president of Yale College (1726–39). He assumed the position in a period of dissension when there had effectively been no rector for four years. Williams helped establish a firm foundation for the institution, which included the vital acquisition of a large gift of books from Berkeley.

Williams was born on 24 August 1694, the son of the Reverend William Williams, minister at Hatfield, Massachusetts. In 1708 Williams entered Harvard and was graduated in 1711 with honors at the age of 17. The following year he took charge of the grammar school at Hadley, but he soon returned to Hatfield to study theology with his father. For reasons not exactly clear, Williams settled in Wethersfield and acquired a farm there. Failing to find a good parish, he began the study of law, and in 1717 he was chosen to represent Wethersfield in the Connecticut General Assembly. For the next four years he was elected clerk of the lower house and the auditor of public accounts for a fifth. After an illness in 1719, William resolved to enter the ministry. In 1720 he became pastor of Newington Parish in western Wethersfield and was ordained there on 17 October 1722. He remained in that post until 1726, when he became rector of Yale College, having been elected to that post on 29 September 1725. While rector, he not only governed the institution, but taught classes and delivered sermons. Under his tenure the college grew and prospered.

As Berkeley made preparations to return to Ireland after the failure of his Bermuda scheme, he arranged for a donation to Yale. He gifted the young college over nine hundred books – reputed to constitute the best library in the Americas at the time – as well as his Whitehall estate in Rhode Island. Berkeley also endowed several scholarships at the college, which was known to Berkeley as the "College in New Haven" (see Letters 223 and 226).

Williams resigned on 31 October 1739 and retired to his farm, where he entered politics and was elected a deputy to the General Assembly. He was also appointed an associate judge of the superior court. In 1744 he served as the chaplain of the Connecticut troops who fought in the War of the Austrian Succession and later was colonel in another regiment but did not see action. He traveled to England in 1749 to secure pay for his troops and won half of his claim. Upon his return, he helped to establish the College of New Jersey (later Princeton University). He died on 24 July 1755.

Wogan (?-?) and Richard Aspinwall (1684?-?). Richard Aspinwall and his partner Wogan (his first name is unknown) were agents who conducted legal and banking business in London. Both Berkeley and John Percival* used them to conduct some of their business affairs. They most likely served as agents for Swift & Company,* the Dublin bank Berkeley used.[1973]

Philip York (Yorke), first Earl of Hardwicke (1690–1764). Philip York was born on 1 December 1690, the only surviving son of Philip Yorke (1651–1721), an attorney of Dover. Following in his father's footsteps, Philip was called to the bar on 6 May 1715. His talent and notable political connections helped his career.

York's ability attracted the attention of the Duke of Newcastle, who was similar in age. They forged a friendship and Newcastle brought York into Parliament at a by-election on 21 April 1719 for the borough of Lewes. At the general election of 1722 York transferred to another of Newcastle's boroughs, Seaford. York quickly became Newcastle's chief confidant. In March 1720 York's connections secured him the post of solicitor general, an astonishing achievement since he was not yet 30 years of age. He was knighted on 11 June 1720 and promoted to attorney general on 31 January 1724. Berkeley remarks on how York helped advance his Bermuda scheme by facilitating his acquisition of the patents (see Letter 179).

In 1733 York sagely waived precedence to allow Charles Talbot* to leap-frog him to the post of lord chancellor. York became lord chief justice instead. Just four years later when Talbot died, the political arrangement worked to his advantage and York became lord chancellor. He remained in this post for nineteen years. He died on 6 March 1764.

[1973] See Cullen, *Anglo-Irish Trade* p. 189n. Cullen asserts that Wogan and Aspinwall were agents of Swift & Co. on the strength of a comment in Percival's letterbooks: EP, BL Add. MS 46990, fol. 109.

BIBLIOGRAPHY OF WORKS CITED

This bibliography only contains works cited in the text and editorial material. It is not intended to be a bibliography of Berkeley scholarship.

Allen, W. O. B. and McClure, Edmund. *History of the Society for Promoting Christian Knowledge: 1698–1898*. New York: Burt Franklin, 1898.

Arbuthnot, John [uncertain authorship]. *Art of Political Lying*. London, 1712.

   Law is a Bottomless Pit, or the History of John Bull. 1712; reprinted, Gale ECCO, 2010.

Balen, Malcolm. *The King, the Crook, and the Gambler*. London: HarperCollins, 2003.

Baxter, Andrew. *An Enquiry into the Nature of the Human Soul*. 1733; reprinted in 2 vols., Charleston, SC: Nabu Press, 2011.

Beardsley, E. Edwards. *The History of the Episcopal Church in Connecticut*. Boston, MA: Houghton, Mifflin & Co., 1883.

   Life and Correspondence of Samuel Johnson. New York: Hurd & Houghton, 1874.

Bellemare, Peter and Raynor, David. "Berkeley's Letters to Le Clerc (1711)." *Hermathena* 146 (1989): 7–23.

Benton, A. Wood, ed. *The English Reports, House of Lords*. Vol. III. London: Stevens & Sons, 1901.

Berkeley, Eliza, ed. *Poems by the Late George Monck Berkeley*. London: J. Nichols, 1797.

Berkeley, George. *Advice to the Tories who have Taken the Oaths*. London, 1715.

   Alciphron, or, the Minute Philosopher. London, 1732.

   The Analyst. Dublin, 1734.

   Arithmetica with *Miscellanea Mathematica*. London, 1707.

   De Motu. London, 1721.

   A Discourse Addressed to Magistrates. Dublin, 1738.

   Essay Towards a New Theory of Vision. Dublin, 1709.

   An Essay Towards Preventing the Ruin of Great Britain. London, 1721.

   "A Letter to the Roman Catholics" in *An Impartial History of James II*. Dublin, 1746.

   A Letter to T. P. Esq. Dublin, 1744.

   A Miscellany. Dublin, 1752.

   Passive Obedience. Dublin, 1712.

   Proposal for the Better Supplying of Churches in our Foreign Plantations, and for Converting the Savage Americans to Christianity. London, 1724.

Queries relating to a National Bank, extracted from the Querist. Dublin: George Faulkner, 1737.

The Querist. Published in three parts. Dublin, 1725, 1736, 1737.

Siris: A Chain of Philosophical Reflexions and Inquiries Concerning the Virtues of Tar Water. Dublin, 1744.

Siris. Recherches sur les Vertus de l'eau de Goudron, ou l'on a Joint des Réfléxions Philosophiques sur Divers Autres Sujets. Amsterdam: Pierre Mortier, 1745.

Theory of Vision . . . Vindicated and Explained. London, 1733.

Three Dialogues Between Hylas and Philonous. London, 1713.

Treatise Concerning the Principles of Human Knowledge. Dublin, 1710.

A Word to the Wise. Dublin, 1749.

The Works of George Berkeley. Edited by Alexander Campbell Fraser. 4 vols. Oxford: Clarendon Press, 1871.

The Works of George Berkeley. Edited by A. A. Luce, and T. E. Jessop. 9 vols. London: Nelson, 1948–57.

The Works of George Berkeley. Edited by G. N. Wright. 2 vols. London: Thomas Tegg, 1843.

"Berkeley [George]" in *Biographia Britannica*. Vol. IV, part 2. London: J. Walthoe et al., 1766.

Berman, David. "Berkeley's Departure for America: A New Letter." *Berkeley Newsletter* 4 (December 1980): 14.

"The Good Bishop: New Letters" in *Berkeley and Irish Philosophy*. London: Continuum, 2007: 215–25.

"Mrs. Berkeley's Annotations in her Interleaved Copy of *An Account of the Life of George Berkeley (1776)*." *Hermathena* 122 (1977): 15–28.

Beveridge, William. *Exposition of the XXXIX Articles*. 1710.

The Book of Trinity College Dublin. Belfast: Marcus Ward & Co., 1892.

Borelli, Giovanni Alfonso. *Historia et Meteorologia Incendii Aetnaei Anni 1669*. Reggio di Calabria: Domenico Ferro, 1670.

Bouillet, Jean. *Sur la Manière de Traiter la Petite Vérole*. 1733.

Brady, W. M. *Clerical and Parochial Records of Cork, Cloyne, and Ross*. London: Longman et al., 1864.

Brewer, Cobham. *The Reader's Handbook of Allusions, References, Plots and Stories*. Philadelphia, PA: J. B. Lippincott & Co., 1889.

Bristow, Peter. *The Harlequins*. 1753.

Browne, Peter. *The Procedure, Extent and Limits of the Human Understanding*. 1728.

Things Divine and Supernatural Conceived by Analogy. 1733.

Bulkeley, Richard. *An Answer to Several Treatises Lately Publish'd on the Subject of the Prophets*. 1708.

Bunbury, Sir Henry, ed. *The Correspondence of Sir Thomas Hanmer, Bart*. London: Edward Moxon, 1838.

Burke, William P. *History of Clonmel*. Waterford: N. Harvey & Co., 1907.

Burke's Irish Family Records. American edn. New York: Arco, 1976.

Burnet, Gilbert. *An Exposition of the Thirty-Nine Articles of the Church of England.* 3rd edn. London: Chiswell, 1705.

    History of the Reformation of the Church of England. 3 vols. London: Chiswell, 1679, 1681, 1714.

Burnet, Thomas, *Sacred Theory of the Earth.* London, 1684.

Butler, Joseph. *The Analogy of Religion.* 1736.

Carswell, John. *The South Sea Bubble.* Stanford University Press, 1960; revised editions available.

Cary, Lucius. *Of the Infallibilities of the Church of Rome.* 1645.

Cary, Seth Cooley. *John Cary, the Plymouth Pilgrim.* Boston, 1911.

Cave, William. *Scriptorum Ecclesiasticorum Historia Literaria a Christo Nato Usque ad Saeculum XIV.* London, 1688.

Chandler, Thomas Bradbury. *The Life of Samuel Johnson, D.D. the First President of King's College, in New York.* New York: T. & J. Swords, 1824.

Chillingworth, William. *The Religion of Protestants.* 1638.

Chubb, Thomas. *The Previous Question with Regard to Religion.* 1725.

    The Supremacy of the Father Asserted ... Eight Arguments from Scripture. 1715.

Clarke, Samuel. *A Demonstration of the Being and Attributes of God: More Particularly in Answer to Mr. Hobbes, Spinoza and their Followers, Wherein the Notion of Liberty is Stated, and the Possibility and Certainty of it Proved, in Opposition to Necessity and Fate.* London, 1704.

Clerke, Richard. *Sermons Preached by that Reverend and Learned Divine Richard Clerke.* 1637.

Colby, Colonel. *Ordnance Survey of the County of Londonderry.* Dublin: Hodges & Smith, 1837.

Collins, Anthony. *Discourse of Free-thinking.* London, 1713.

The Correspondence of John Hughes, Esq. 2 vols. Dublin: Thomas Ewing, 1773.

Cullen, L. M. *Anglo-Irish Trade: 1660–1800.* Manchester University Press, 1968.

Dacier, André. *The Works of Plato, Abridged.* 2 vols. London: A. Bell, 1701.

Dale, Richard. *The First Crash.* Princeton University Press, 2004.

Daniel, G. *Voyage du Monde de Descartes.* Paris, 1690.

    Voyage to the World of Cartesius. 1692.

De Vita Solitaria. 1130–1200? Attributed to St. Victor Bernard in the fourteenth century, probably authored by William of St. Thierry.

Descartes, René. *Meditations on First Philosophy.* 1641.

Dexter, Franklin B. *Biographical Sketches of the Graduates of Yale College.* New York: Holt & Co., 1885.

Diemerbroeck, Isbrand de. *De Peste.* 1646; translated into English, 1722.

Dixon, W. Macneile. *Trinity College, Dublin.* London: Robinson & Co., 1902.

Doody, Margaret Anne. "Swift and Women" in *The Cambridge Companion to Jonathan Swift*, ed. Christopher Fox. Cambridge University Press, 2003: 87–111.

Drake, Michael. *The Irish Demographic Crisis of 1740–41.* Historical Studies 6, ed. T. W. Moody. London: Routledge & Kegan Paul, 1968.

Durandus of Saint-Pourçain. *In Petri Lombardi Sententias Theologicas Commentarium.* Venice, 1571.

Eagle, F. K., and Younge, E. *A Collection of the Reports of Cases, the Statutes, and Ecclesiastical Laws, Relating to Tithes.* London, 1826.

Erasmus, Desiderius. *Colloquies.* 1518.

Fraser, Alexander Campbell. *Life and Letters of George Berkeley.* Oxford: Clarendon Press, 1871.

Gaustad, Edwin. *George Berkeley in America.* New Haven, CT: Yale University Press, 1979.

Giannone, Pietro. *Storia Civile del Regno di Napoli.* 1723.

Gibson, Edmund. *A Preservative Against Popery.* 3 vols. 1738.

Hales, Stephen. *Account of some Experiments and Observations on Tar-Water.* London, 1745; 2nd edn., London, 1747.

Hall, F. G. *History of the Bank of Ireland.* Dublin: Hodges, Figgis & Co., 1949.

Hammond, Henry. *A Paraphrase and Annotations on all the Books of the New Testament.* 1653.

   Practical Catechism. 1644.

Haywood, Eliza Fowler. *A Present for a Servant-Maid. Or, the Sure Means of Gaining Love and Esteem.* 1743.

Higden, William. *A View of the English Constitution.* London, 1709.

Historical Manuscripts Commission. *Report on the Manuscripts of the Mrs. Stopford-Sackville of Drayton House, Northamptonshire.* Vol. I. London: Mackie & Co., 1904.

Hodges, Walter. *The Christian Plan Exhibited in the Interpretation of Elohim.* London, 1752.

   Elihu; or, an Inquiry into the Principal Scope and Design of the Book of Job. London, 1750.

Hone, J. M., and Rossi, M. M. *Bishop Berkeley.* London: Faber & Faber, 1931.

Hooker, Richard. *Of the Laws of Ecclesiastical Politie.* 1593.

Howell, T. B., comp. *A Complete Collection of State Trials and Proceedings for High Treason and Other Crimes and Misdemeanours.* Vol. XIV. London: Hansard, 1816.

Hutchings, Victoria. *Messrs Hoare, Bankers: A History of the Hoare Banking Dynasty.* London: Constable, 2005.

Hutchinson, John. *Moses's Principia.* 1724, 1727.

   Works. 12 vols. 1748.

Hyde, Edward. *The History of the Rebellion and Civil Wars in England.* 1702–04.

Jesseph, Douglas. *Squaring the Circle.* University of Chicago Press, 1999.

Jewel, John. *Apologia pro Ecclesia Anglicana.* 1562.

Johnson, Samuel. *Elementa Philosophica.* 1731.

   Ethica. 1746.

   Introduction to Philosophy. 1743; revised 1752.

Johnston, Swift. "Supposed Autograph Letter of Bishop Berkeley in the Library of the Royal Irish Academy." *Proceedings of the Royal Irish Academy* 6.2 (1901): 272–78.

Journal of the Cork Historical and Archeological Society 3, (1894).

Jurin, James. *Geometry no Friend to Infidelity*. 1734.

    The Minute Mathematician. 1735.

Kennett, Basil. *The Antiquities of Rome*. 1696.

Keynes, Geoffrey. *A Bibliography of George Berkeley*. Oxford: Clarendon Press, 1976.

Lambert, Ralph. *Partiality Detected; or, A Reply to a Late Pamphlet, Entituled, Some Proceedings in the Convocation, A.D. 1705. Faithfully Represented, etc.* London: A. & J. Churchill, 1708.

Law is a Bottomless Pit; or, the History of John Bull. 1712. (Published anonymously but attributed to John Arbuthnot.)

Le Clerc, Jean. *Bibliothèque Choisie*. 1703–13.

    Patres Apostolici. Amsterdam, 1724.

Le Courayer, Pierre-François. *Dissertation sur la Validité des Ordinations des Anglais et sur la Succession des Évéques de l'Eglise Anglicane, avec les Preuves Justificatives des Faits Avancés*. Brussels, 1723.

Le Quien, Michel. *La Nullité des Ordinations Anglicanes*. 2 vols. Paris, 1725.

    La Nullité des Ordinationes Anglicanes Démontrée de Nouveau. 2 vols. Paris, 1730.

Lecky, William Edward Hartpole. *History of Ireland in the Eighteenth Century*. Vol. V. London: Longmans, Green & Co., 1913.

Letters, by Several Eminent Persons Deceased, Including the Correspondence of John Hughes Esq. 3 vols. London: J. Johnson, 1772.

Lettres Édifiantes et Curieuses Écrites des Missions Étrangères. 1703–76.

Linden, D. W. *Siris: Grundliche Historische Nachricht vom Theer-Wasser*. Amsterdam and Leipzig: Peter Mortier, 1745.

    A Treatise on the Origin, Nature, and Virtues of Chalybeat Waters and Natural Hot Baths. London, 1748.

Literary Relics, ed. George Monck Berkeley. London, 1789.

Locke, John. *On Education*. 1693.

    An Essay Concerning Human Understanding. 4th edn., London, 1700; reprinted Oxford: Clarendon Press, 1991.

    Two Treatises of Government. 3rd edn., London, 1698.

Lucas, Richard. *Enquiry after Happiness*. 1685.

Luce, A. A. "Berkeley's Bermuda Project and his Benefactions to American Universities, with Unpublished Letters and Extracts from the Egmont Papers." *Proceedings of the Royal Irish Academy* 42 (1933): 97–120.

    "Berkeley's *Description of the Cave of Dunmore*." *Hermathena* 46 (1931): 149–61.

    The Life of George Berkeley. London: Nelson & Sons, 1949; reprinted London: Routledge/Thoemmes Press, 1992.

    "More Unpublished Berkeley Letters and New Berkeleiana." *Hermathena* 23 (1933): 25–53.

    "A New Berkeley Letter and the Endorsement." *Proceedings of the Royal Irish Academy* 51, section C (1945/46): 83–87.

    "The Purpose and the Date of Berkeley's *Commonplace Book*." *Proceedings of the Royal Irish Academy* 48 (1942/43): 273–89.

"Some Unpublished Berkeley Letters with some New Berkeleiana." *Proceedings of the Royal Irish Academy* 41 (1932): 141–61.

Lyttelton, George. *A Letter to the Tories*. 1747.

Madden, Samuel. *Themistocles, the Lover of his Country: A Tragedy in Five Acts and in Verse*. 1729.

Magennis, Eoin. "'A Land of Milk and Honey': The Physico-Historical Society, Improvement and the Surveys of Mid-Eighteenth-Century Ireland." *Proceedings of the Royal Irish Academy* 1.102C (2002): 199–217.

Malebranche, Nicolas. *The Search After Truth*, ed. Thomas Lennon, and Paul Olscamp. Cambridge University Press, 1997.

Martin, Martin. *Description of the Western Islands of Scotland*. 1703.

The Late Voyage to St. Kilda. 1698.

Maxwell, Henry. *Reasons Offer'd for Erecting a Bank in Ireland; In a Letter to Hercules Rowley, Esq.* Dublin, 1721.

McDowell, R. B., and Webb, D. A. *Trinity College Dublin 1592–1952: An Academic History*. Cambridge University Press, 1982.

Mead, Richard. *De Imperio Solis ac Lunae in Corpora Humana, et Moribus inde Oriundis*. London, 1704.

De Variolis et Morbillis Liber. 1747.

Short Discourse Concerning Pestilential Contagion and the Methods to be used to Prevent it. 1720.

The Memoires of Cardinal de Retz. 1717.

Memoirs of Viscountess Sundon, Mistress of the Robes to Queen Caroline, Consort of George II, Including Letters from the Most Celebrated Persons of her Time. 2 vols. 2nd edn. London: Henry Colburn, 1848.

Memorial of the Whittelsey Family in the United States. n.p.: Case, Tiffany & Co., 1855.

Montesquieu, Charles. *L'Esprit des Lois*. 1748.

Morgan, Thomas. *Physico-Theology*. 1741.

Nelson, Robert. *Companion for the Festivals and the Fasts of the Church of England*. 1704.

A New History of Ireland, ed. T. W. Moody, and W. E. Vaughan. 9 vols. Oxford University Press, 2009.

Newton, Isaac. *Philosophiae Naturalis Principia Mathematica*. London, 1687.

The Orrery Papers. 2 vols. London: Duckworth, 1903.

Papers Relating to the Quakers Tythe Bill. 3rd edn. 1736.

Parnell, Thomas (published anonymously). *Essay on the Different Stiles of Poetry*. 1713.

Pearson, John. *An Exposition of the Creed*. 1659.

Vindiciae Epistolarum S. Ignatii. 1672.

Peplographia Dublinensis: Memorial Discourses Preached in the Chapel of Trinity College, Dublin 1895–1902. London: Macmillan & Co., 1902.

Perault, Pierre. *De l'Origine des Fontaines*. Paris, 1678.

Pitaval, François Gayot de. *Causes Célèbres*. 18 vols. 1734–41.

Plomer, Henry. et al., eds. *A Dictionary of the Printers and Booksellers who were at Work in England, Scotland, and Ireland from 1726 to 1775*. Oxford University Press, 1932.

Pococke, Richard. *Description of the East.* 2 vols. 1743 and 1745.

Poole, Matthew. *Synopsis Criticorum.* London, 1669.

Pope, Alexander. *The Correspondence of Alexander Pope,* ed. George Sherburn. 4 vols. Oxford: Clarendon Press, 1956.

   Mr. Pope's Literary Correspondence: For Thirty Years, from 1704 to 1734. London: E. Curll, 1735.

   Rape of the Lock. 1712.

   The Works of Alexander Pope, ed. John Wilson Croker. 10 vols. New York: Gordian Press, 1967.

Prideaux, Humphrey. *Connection.* 1716–18.

Prior, Thomas. *An Authentic Narrative of the Success of Tar-Water, in Curing a Great Number and Variety of Distempers, with Remarks and Occasional Papers Relative to the Subject.* Dublin: Innys, Hitch, Cooper & Davis, 1746; reprinted London, 1746 ("A New Edition, complete").

   List of the Absentees of Ireland. Dublin, 1729.

Rand, Benjamin. *Berkeley and Percival.* Cambridge University Press, 1914.

Raphson, Joseph. *De Spatio Reali* in *Analysis Aequationum Universalis.* 2nd edn. 1697.

Reid, Andrew. *A Letter to the Rev. Dr. Hales, Concerning the Nature of Tar, and a Method of Obtaining its Medical Virtues from its Hurtful Oils.* London, 1747.

Roberts, Robert. *A State of the Case of the Creditors of Burton's Bank.* Dublin, 1751.

Rowley, Hercules. *An Answer to a Book, Intitl'd, Reasons Offer'd for Erecting a Bank in Ireland, in a Letter to Henry Maxwell, Esq.* Dublin, 1721.

Salmon, George. *The Infallibility of the Church.* London: John Murray, 1888.

Sanderson, Robert. *Sermons by the Right Reverend Robert Sanderson, Late Lord Bishop of Lincoln.* 2 vols. London: Ball, Arnold & Co., 1841.

Schneider, Herbert and Carol, eds. *Samuel Johnson, President of King's College: His Career and Writings.* 4 vols. New York: Columbia University Press, 1929.

Scott, John. *The Christian Life from its Beginning to its Consummation in Glory: Together with the Several Means and Instruments of Christianity Conducing Thereunto, with Directions for Private Devotion and Forms of Prayer, Fitted to the Several States of Christians.* 2 vols. 1681; Expanded 2nd edn., 1683–87.

Sharp, Thomas. *The Necessary Knowledge of the Lord's Supper.* 1727.

Sherburn, George, ed. *The Correspondence of Alexander Pope.* 4 vols. Oxford: Clarendon Press, 1956.

Simon, James. *An Essay Towards an Historical Account of Irish Coins.* Dublin: S. Powell, 1749.

   "A Letter from Mr. James Simon, of Dublin, to Martin Folkes, Esq. Pr. R.S. Concerning the Petrifactions of Lough-Neagh in Ireland: To Which is Annexed a Letter from the Right Rev. Dr. George Berkeley Lord Bishop of Cloyne to Tho. Prior, Esq." *Philosophical Transactions* 44 (1746–47): 305–28.

Smalbroke, Richard. *A Vindication of the Miracles of our Blessed Saviour.* 2 vols. 1729 and 1731.

Spotswood, John. *History of the Church and State of Scotland from the Year of Our Lord 203 to the End of the Reign of King James VI, 1625.* 4th edn. London: R. Royston, 1677.

Stanhope, George. *Paraphrase and Comment upon the Epistles and Gospels.* 4 vols. 1705–08.

Stark, James Henry. *The Loyalists of Massachusetts and the other side of the American Revolution.* Salem Press, 1910.

Stephens, John. "Berkeley and Lady Burlington: A Footnote." *Berkeley Newsletter* 12 (1991–92): 17.

Stock, Joseph. *Life of Berkeley.* London, 1776. Additional editions: 2nd, Dublin, 1777; 3rd (misleadingly called 2nd), London, 1784.

   Memoirs of George Berkeley: Late Bishop of Cloyne in Ireland. 2nd edn. London: John Murray, 1784.

Stock, Joseph, ed. *The Works of George Berkeley.* 2 vols. Dublin and London, 1784.

Swift, Jonathan. *Letter to the Shopkeepers Tradesmen Farmers and Common People of Ireland by M. B. Drapier.* John Harding, 1724.

Sydenham, Thomas. *Observationes Medicae.* London, 1666.

   Tractatus de Podagra et Hydrope. 1683.

Taylor, Jeremy. *Holy Dying.* 1651.

   The Rule and Exercise of Holy Living. 1650.

Tenison, C. M. "Cork MP's [*sic*] 1559–1800." *Journal of the Cork Historical and Archaeological Society* 1, 2nd series (1895): 425.

The Tribune 21. London: T. Warner, 1729: 149–55.

Tyerman, L. *The Life and Times of the Rev. John Wesley, M.A.* 3 vols. London: Hodder & Stoughton, 1880.

An Universal History from the Earliest Account of Time to the Present. 9 vols. London: J. Batley et al., 1736–50.

Updike, Wilkins. *A History of the Episcopal Church in Narrangansett Rhode Island.* 2nd edn, revised and enlarged by Daniel Goodwin. Boston: Merymount Press, 1907.

Wake, William. *Authority of Christian Princes.* 1697.

   An Exposition of the Doctrine of the Church of England. 1687.

West, Gilbert. *Observations on the History and Evidence of the Resurrection of Jesus Christ.* 1747.

Whiston, William. *Account of the Demoniaks both in the New Testament and in the First Four Centuries.* London, 1737.

   The Eternity of Hell Torments Considered. London, 1740.

   Mr. Whiston's Account of the Exact Time when Miraculous Gifts Ceas'd in the Church. London, 1728.

   A New Theory of the Earth. 1696.

   Primitive Christianity Revived. 1711–12.

   Sermons and Essays. 1709.

Whole Duty of Man. (Author uncertain.) 1658.

Wilkins, David. *Concilia Magnae Britanniae et Hiberniae a Synodo Verolamiensi A.D. 446 ad Londiniensem A.D. 1717.* London, 1737.

Williams, Harold, ed. *The Correspondence of Jonathan Swift*. 5 vols. Oxford University Press, 1963.

Willis, Thomas. *A Plain and Easie Method of Preserving those that are Well from the Plague*. London, 1691.

Woodward, John. *An Essay Toward a Natural History of the Earth. With an Account of the Universal Deluge and of the Effects that it had upon the Earth*. 1695; 2nd edn. 1702.

Yale University Library Gazette 8.1 (July 1933): 26–27.

Young, Amy Isabel. *Three Hundred Years in Innishowen*. Belfast: McCaw, Stevenson & Orr, 1929.

INDEX OF CORRESPONDENTS

References here in italics are to numbered letters and not page numbers.

GENERAL INDEX

Page numbers in **bold** refer to footnotes on the indicated page. The index includes references to Berkeley's works and to other works mentioned in the letters.

Printed in the United States
By Bookmasters